# THE CONSTITUTION

AND WHAT IT MEANS TODAY

Edward S. Corwin's

# THE
# CONSTITUTION

## AND WHAT IT MEANS
## TODAY

Revised by Harold W. Chase

and Craig R. Ducat

1973 EDITION

PRINCETON UNIVERSITY PRESS

Copyright © 1920, 1924, 1930, 1946, 1947, 1954, 1958, 1973
by Princeton University Press
ALL RIGHTS RESERVED
L.C. No.: 72-7800
ISBN: 0-691-09228-1 (cloth edition)
ISBN: 0-691-02754-4 (paperback edition)

Published 1920
Second Edition, 1921
Third Edition, 1924
*Second Printing*, 1926
*Third Printing*, 1927
Fourth Edition, 1930
Fifth Edition, 1937
Sixth Edition, 1938
Seventh Edition, 1941
Eighth Edition, 1946
Ninth Edition, 1947
Tenth Edition, 1948
*Second Printing*, 1951
Eleventh Edition, 1954
Twelfth Edition, 1958
*Second Printing*, 1961
*Third Printing*, 1965
*Fourth Printing*, 1966
*Fifth Printing*, 1971
Thirteenth Edition, 1973

Printed in the United States of America
by Princeton University Press, Princeton, New Jersey

*To:* Alpheus T. Mason

*The third in a line of extraordinary
teacher-scholars who have served as
McCormick Professors of Jurisprudence,
Princeton University:*

Woodrow Wilson 1898-1910

Edward S. Corwin 1918-1946

Alpheus T. Mason 1947-1968

# PREFACE TO EDITION XIII

We who have had the responsibility for revising this classic work of Edward S. Corwin wish to acknowledge what a great and rare privilege it has been. Working with a classic is not easy; for it carries with it the heavy responsibility of attempting to maintain the quality of the work. Even so, for us who have long admired the work of Professor Corwin and, particularly for the one for whom Professor Corwin was a remarkable, lovable, and inspiring teacher, it was truly a labor of love.

As we worked on the manuscript, two initial impressions were reinforced day by day. The first was the enormous change in the meaning of the Constitution over the last fifteen years. One does not fully appreciate the full impact of that change until he goes over the Constitution provision by provision. The second impression was how very good the work of Corwin had been in earlier editions both as to substance and style. He had a very special skill for being pithy. Words were used sparingly, and every word carried meaning. His summaries of historical development, his evaluations and judgments were remarkably good as measured by hindsight. Consequently, even in the face of great change, we endeavored to preserve as much of the original Corwin as was possible. Where we added to his work we tried to emulate his style and the quality of his work. Nothing would make us more proud than acceptance of this edition as a worthy successor to the twelve that preceded it.

Corwin's words in a Preface to an earlier edition serve as the best explication of his approach: "Although *The Constitution and What It Means Today* utilizes now and then other materials, decisions of the Supreme Court contribute its principal substance. . . . I have endeavored, especially in connection with such important subjects as judicial review, the commerce clause, executive power, freedom of speech, press and religion, etc., to accompany explanation of currently prevailing doctrine and practice with a brief summation of the historical development thereof. The serviceability of history to make the present more understandable has been remarked upon by writers from Aristotle to the late Samuel Butler, famed author of *Erewhon and The Way of All Flesh*; and the idea is particularly pertinent to legal ideas and institutions."

We owe some special thanks to those who helped in their own ways to make this edition a reality, Herbert Bailey and Carol Orr of the Princeton University Press; Bernice M. Chase, whose varied editorial skills were put to good use; Vera M. Fadden: and to O. James Werner (and to his predecessor, Leland C. Stanford) and his staff at the most accommodating library we have ever worked in, the San Diego County Law Library. We owe particular thanks to William B. Rohan of that library, who served us well as a first and on-going critic as well as devil's advocate and to Gail Filion, an editor of extraordinary skill and understanding.

H.W.C.
C.R.D.

*Publisher's Note*: Each year the scope of this volume will be extended by means of a supplement that will cover the current session of the Supreme Court. Supplements will be included in the paperback edition as they appear.

# CONTENTS

# CONTENTS

# CONTENTS

# CONTENTS

# Some Judicial Diversities

"IN *the Constitution of the United States—the most wonderful instrument ever drawn by the hand of man—there is a comprehension and precision that is unparalleled; and I can truly say that after spending my life in studying it, I still daily find in it some new excellence.*"—JUSTICE JOHNSON. In Elkinson v. Deliesseline, 8 Federal Cases 593 (1823)

---

"THE *subject is the execution of those great powers on which the welfare of a nation essentially depends. . . . This provision is made in a Constitution intended to endure for ages to come and, consequently, to be adapted to the various crises of human affairs.*"—CHIEF JUSTICE MARSHALL. In McCulloch v. Maryland, 4 Wheaton 316 (1819)

---

"IT *[the Constitution] speaks not only in the same words, but with the same meaning and intent with which it spoke when it came from the hands of its framers, and was voted on and adopted by the people of the United States. Any other rule of construction would abrogate the judicial character of this Court and make it the mere reflex of the popular opinion or passion of the day.*"—CHIEF JUSTICE TANEY. In the Dred Scott Case, 19 Howard 393 (1857)

---

"WE *read its [the Constitution's] words, not as we read legislative codes which are subject to continuous revision with the changing course of events, but as the revelation of the great purposes which were intended to be achieved by the Constitution as a continuing instrument of government.*"—CHIEF JUSTICE STONE. In United States v. Classic, 313 U.S. 299 (1941)

---

"JUDICIAL *power, as contradistinguished from the power of the laws, has no existence. Courts are the mere instruments of the law, and can will nothing.*"—CHIEF JUSTICE MARSHALL. In Osborn v. U.S. Bank, 9 Wheaton 738 (1824)

---

"WE *are under a Constitution, but the Constitution is what the judges say it is . . .*"—FORMER CHIEF JUSTICE HUGHES when Governor of New York

---

"WHEN *an act of Congress is appropriately challenged in the courts as not conforming to the constitutional mandate the judicial branch of the Government has only one duty,—to lay the article of the Constitution which is invoked beside the statute which is challenged and to decide whether the latter squares with the former.*"—JUSTICE ROBERTS. In United States v. Butler, 297 U.S. 1 (1936)

XV

## SOME JUDICIAL DIVERSITIES

"WHILE *unconstitutional exercise of power by the executive and legislative branches of the Government is subject to judicial restraint, the only check on our own exercise of power is our own sense of self-restraint.*"—JUSTICE STONE (dissenting), *ibid.*

---

"THE *glory and ornament of our system which distinguishes it from every other government on the face of the earth is that there is a great and mighty power hovering over the Constitution of the land to which has been delegated the awful responsibility of restraining all the coordinate departments of government within the walls of the governmental fabric which our fathers built for our protection and immunity.*"—CHIEF JUSTICE EDWARD DOUGLASS WHITE when Senator from Louisiana. In 23 *Cong. Rec.* 6516 (1892)

---

"JUDICIAL *review, itself a limitation on popular government, is a fundamental part of our constitutional scheme. But to the legislature no less than to courts is committed the guardianship of deeply cherished constitutional rights.*"—JUSTICE FRANKFURTER. In Minersville School Dist. *v.* Gobitis, 310 U.S. 586 (1940)

---

"CASE-BY-CASE *adjudication gives to the judicial process the impact of actuality and thereby saves it from the hazards of generalizations insufficiently nourished by experience. There is, however, an attendant weakness to a system that purports to pass merely on what are deemed to be the particular circumstances of a case. Consciously or unconsciously the pronouncements in an opinion too often exceed the justification of the circumstances on which they are based, or, contrariwise, judicial preoccupation with the claims of the immediate leads to a succession of ad hoc determinations making for eventual confusion and conflict. There comes a time when the general considerations underlying each specific situation must be exposed in order to bring the too unruly instances into more fruitful harmony. The case before us presents one of those problems for the rational solution of which it becomes necessary, as a matter of judicial self-respect, to take soundings in order to know where we are and wither we are going.*"—JUSTICE FRANKFURTER (dissenting). In Larson *v.* Domestic & Foreign Corp., 337 U.S. 682, 705 (1949).

---

"ORDINARILY *it is sound policy to adhere to prior decisions but this practice has quite properly never been a blind, inflexible rule. Courts are not omniscient. Like every other human agency, they too can profit from trial and error, from experience and reflection. As others have demonstrated, the principle commonly referred to as* stare decisis *has never been thought to extend so far as to prevent the courts from correcting their own errors. Accordingly, this Court has time and time again from the very beginning reconsidered the merits of its earlier decisions even though they claimed great longevity and repeated reaffirmation. . . . Indeed, the Court has a special responsibility where questions of constitutional law are involved to review its decisions*

*from time to time and where compelling reasons present them-
selves to refuse to follow erroneous precedents; otherwise its
mistakes in interpreting the Constitution are extremely difficult
to alleviate and needlessly so."*—JUSTICE BLACK (dissenting). In
Green v. U.S., 356 U.S. 165, 195 (1958).

---

"To *give blind adherence to a rule or policy that no decision
of this Court is to be overruled would be itself to overrule many
decisions of the Court which do not accept that view. But the
rule of* stare decisis *embodies a wise policy because it is often
more important that a rule of law be settled than that it be
settled right."*—CHIEF JUSTICE STONE (dissenting). In U.S. v.
Underwriters Assn., 322 U.S. 533, 579 (1944).

---

"A MILITARY *order, however unconstitutional, is not apt to last
longer than the military emergency. Even during that period a
succeeding commander may revoke it all. But once a judicial
opinion rationalizes such an order to show that it conforms to
the Constitution, or rather rationalizes the Constitution to show
that the Constitution sanctions such an order, the Court for all
time has validated the principle of racial discrimination in criminal procedure and of transplanting American citizens. The
principle then lies about like a loaded weapon ready for the
hand of any authority that can bring forward a plausible claim
of an urgent need. Every repetition imbeds that principle more
deeply in our law and thinking and expands it to new purposes.
All who observe the work of courts are familiar with what Judge
Cardozo described as 'the tendency of a principle to expand itself
to the limit of its logic.' A military commander may overstep
the bounds of constitutionality, and it is an incident. But if we
review and approve, that passing incident becomes the doctrine
of the Constitution. There it has a generative power of its own,
and all that it creates will be in its own image."*—JUSTICE JACKSON
(dissenting). In Korematsu v. U.S., 323 U.S. 214, 246 (1944).

---

"ONE *who belongs to the most vilified and persecuted minority
in history is not likely to be insensible to the freedoms guaranteed by our Constitution. Were my purely personal attitude
relevant I should wholeheartedly associate myself with the general libertarian views in the Court's opinion, representing as
they do the thought and action of a lifetime. But as judges we
are neither Jew nor Gentile, neither Catholic nor agnostic. We
owe equal attachment to the Constitution and are equally
bound by our judicial obligations whether we derive our citizenship from the earliest or the latest immigrants to these shores.
As a member of this Court I am not justified in writing my
private notions of policy into the Constitution, no matter how
deeply I may cherish them or how mischievous I may deem their
disregard. The duty of a judge who must decide which of two
claims before the Court shall prevail, that of a State to enact
and enforce laws within its general competence or that of an
individual to refuse obedience because of the demands of his
conscience, is not that of the ordinary person. It can never be*

xvii

*emphasized too much that one's own opinion about the wisdom or evil of a law should be excluded altogether when one is doing one's duty on the bench."*—JUSTICE FRANKFURTER (dissenting). In Board of Education *v.* Barnette, 319 U.S. 624, 646-647 (1943).

---

"THE *case confronts us again with the duty our system places on this Court to say where the individual's freedom ends and the State's power begins. Choice on that border, now as always delicate, is perhaps more so where the usual presumption supporting legislation is balanced by the preferred place given in our scheme to the great, the indispensable democratic freedoms secured by the First Amendment. . . . That priority gives these liberties a sanctity and a sanction not permitting dubious intrusions. And it is the character of the right, not of the limitation, which determines what standard governs the choice."*
—JUSTICE RUTLEDGE. In Thomas *v.* Collins, 323 U.S. 516, 529-530 (1945).

# THE PREAMBLE

WE, THE PEOPLE OF THE UNITED STATES, IN ORDER TO FORM A MORE PERFECT UNION, ESTABLISH JUSTICE, INSURE DOMESTIC TRANQUILLITY, PROVIDE FOR THE COMMON DEFENSE, PROMOTE THE GENERAL WELFARE, AND SECURE THE BLESSINGS OF LIBERTY TO OURSELVES AND OUR POSTERITY, DO ORDAIN AND ESTABLISH THIS CONSTITUTION FOR THE UNITED STATES OF AMERICA

THE Preamble, strictly speaking, is not a part of the Constitution, but "walks before" it. By itself alone it can afford no basis for a claim either of governmental power or of private right.[1] It serves, nevertheless, two very important ends: first, it indicates the source from which the Constitution comes, from which it derives its claim to obedience, namely, the people of the United States; second, it states the great objects which the Constitution and the Government established by it are expected to promote: national unity, justice, peace at home and abroad, liberty, and the general welfare.[2]

"We, the people of the United States," in other words, We, the citizens of the United States, whether voters or non-voters.[3] In theory the former represent and speak for the latter; actually from the very beginning of our national history, the constant tendency has been to extend the voting privilege more and more widely: Woman's suffrage was established by the addition of the Nineteenth Amendment. More recently the right to vote in national elections has been extended to residents of the District of Columbia by the Twenty-Third Amendment, and in 1971 the Twenty-Sixth Amendment was

"We, the People"

[1] Jacobson v. Mass. 197 U.S. 11 (1905).

[2] "Its true office," says Story "is to expound the nature and extent and application of the powers actually conferred by the Constitution, and not substantively to create them." Joseph Story, *Commentaries on the Constitution* (Cambridge, Mass.: 1833), 462.

[3] "The words 'people of the United States' and 'citizens' are synonymous terms. . . . They both describe the political body who, according to our republican institutions, form the sovereignty, and who hold the power and conduct the government through their representative. They are what we familiarly call the 'sovereign people,' and every citizen is one of this people, and a constituent member of this sovereignty." Chief Justice Taney, in Dred Scott v. Sanford, 19 How. 393, 404 (1857). On the relationship between citizenship and voting, *see* Chief Justice Chase in Minor v. Happerset, 21 Wall 162 (1874).

1

passed insuring that citizens eighteen years of age or older shall not be denied the right to vote "by the United States or by any state on account of age." More vigorous implementation of the Fifteenth Amendment and passage of the Twenty-Fourth Amendment have enabled an ever-increasing percentage of Black citizens to vote. Consequently, the terms "voter" and "citizen" are becoming practically interchangeable as applied to the adult American.

"Do ordain and establish," not *did* ordain and establish. As a *document* the Constitution came from the generation of 1787; as a *law* it derives its force and effect from the present generation of American citizens, and hence should be interpreted in the light of present conditions and with a view to meeting present problems.[4]

The term "United States" is used in the Constitution in various senses (*see e.g.* Article III, Section III). In the Preamble it signifies, as was just implied, the States which compose the Union, and whose voting citizens directly or indirectly choose the government at Washington and participate in amending the Constitution.[5]

The Frame-work of Government
Articles I, II, and III set up the framework of the National Government in accordance with the doctrine of the Separation of Powers of "the celebrated Montesquieu," which teaches that there are three, and only three, functions of government, the "legislative," the "executive," and the "judicial," and that these three functions should be exercised by distinct bodies of men in order to prevent an undue concentration of power. The importance of this doctrine as a working principle of government under the Constitution has been much diminished by Presidential actions in foreign affairs particularly with respect to employing United States forces abroad, by the growth of Presidential leadership in legislation, by the increasing resort by Congress to the practice of delegating what amounts to legislative power to the President and other administrative agencies, and by the mergence in the latter of all three powers of government according to earlier definitions.[6]

Recently, Congress has shown signs of becoming restive,

[4] *See* the words of Chief Justice Marshall in 4 Wheat. 316, 421 (1819).

[5] The most comprehensive discussion of this subject is that by counsel and the Court in Downes *v.* Bidwell, the chief of the famous Insular Cases of 1901. *See* 182 U.S. 244 (1901).

[6] So broad a principle as the doctrine of the Separation of Powers has naturally received at times rather conflicting interpretations, occasionally

largely because of dissatisfaction with Presidential actions with respect to Southeast Asia. It is presently exploring a variety of approaches to restore vitality to the doctrine of Separation of Powers.[7]

---

from the same judges. *Cf.* in this connection Chief Justice Taft's opinion for the Court in *ex parte* Grossman 267 U.S. 87, 119-120 (1925) with the same Justice's opinion in Myers *v.* U.S., 272 U.S. 52, 116 (1926); also Justice Black, for the Court, in Youngstown Sheet and Tube Co., 343 U.S. 579, 585-589, with Chief Justice Vinson, for the minority, *ibid.*, 683-700 (1952).

[7] *See* pp. 83-85. Also, on the homefront, some Congressmen were deeply disturbed by President Nixon's directive giving the Subversive Activities Control Board new functions without apparent legislative authority. For the President's Order see 36 *Fed. Reg.* 1283 (1971); for report of Congressional concern, *see Cong. Quart. Weekly Report* (1971), 1549-1552. For report of Senate's retribution (voting to cut off funds for SACB), *see* 1972 *Cong. Quart. Weekly Report* 1553. *See* 118 *Cong. Rec.* No. 175, S17968ff. (1972).

# ARTICLE I

Article I defines the legislative powers of the United States, which it vests in Congress.

## SECTION I

¶ All legislative powers herein granted shall be vested in a Congress of the United States, which shall consist of a Senate and House of Representatives.

This seems to mean that no other branch of the Government except Congress may make laws; but as a matter of fact, by Article VI, ¶2, treaties which are made "under the authority of the United States" have for some purposes the force of laws, and the same has on a few occasions been held to be true of "executive agreements" entered into by the President by virtue of his diplomatic powers.[1] Also, of course, judicial decisions make law since later decisions may be, by the principle of *stare decisis*, based upon them. Indeed, the Supreme Court, by its decisions interpreting the Constitution, constantly alters the practical effect and application thereof. As Woodrow Wilson aptly put it, the Supreme Court is "a kind of Constitutional Convention in continuous session." Likewise, regulations laid down by the President, heads of departments, or administrative bodies, such as the Interstate Commerce Commission, the Securities and Exchange Commission, and so on, are laws and will be treated by the courts as such when they are made in the exercise of authority validly "delegated" by Congress. — "Law" in the Constitution

From this section, in particular, is derived the doctrine that the National Government is one of "enumerated powers," a doctrine which was given classic expression by Chief Justice Marshall in 1819 in the following words: "This government is acknowledged by all, to be one of enumerated powers. The principle, that it can exercise only the powers granted to it, would seem too apparent, to have required to be enforced by all those arguments, which its enlightened friends, while it was depending before the people, found it necessary to urge; that principle is now universally admitted."[2] The doctrine is today — "A Government of Enumerated Powers"

[1] B. Altman & Co. v. U.S. 224 U.S. 583 (1912); United States v. Belmont, 301 U.S. 324 (1937); United States v. Pink, 315 U.S. 203 (1942). *Cf.* Tucker v. Alexandroff, 183 U.S. 424, both opinions (1902).
[2] McCulloch v. Md., 4 Wheat. 316, 405 (1819).

5

subject to many exceptions. In particular, "the executive power" and "the judicial power" have not been confined to "enumerated powers" (*see* p. 111 and p. 161). Indeed, in 1828 Marshall himself held that "the Constitution confers absolutely on the government of the Union, the powers of making war, and of making treaties; consequently, that government possesses the power of acquiring territory, either by conquest or by treaty."[3] And from the power to acquire territory, he continued, arose as "the inevitable consequence" the right to govern it.[4] Subsequently powers have been repeatedly ascribed to the National Government by the Court on grounds which ill accord with the doctrine of enumerated powers: the power to legislate in effectuation of the "rights expressly given, and duties expressly enjoined" by the Constitution,[5] the power to impart to the paper currency of the Government the quality of legal tender in the payment of debts;[6] the power to acquire territory by discovery;[7] the power to legislate for the protection of the Indian tribes wherever situated in the United States;[8] the power to exclude and deport aliens;[9] and to require that those who are admitted be registered and fingerprinted;[10] and finally the complete powers of sovereignty, both those of war and peace, in the conduct of foreign relations.[11]

For the most part, the great expansion of the power of the National Government has not come about by breaching the *doctrine* of enumerated powers as it pertains to Congress, but rather by broad interpretation of those specific powers, notably the commerce clause, and by a liberal interpretation of the "necessary and proper" clause. Nonetheless, the Supreme Court has, in the main, limited Congress to its enumerated powers.

---

[3] 1 Pet. 511, 542 (1828).　　　　[4] *Ibid.*, 543.

[5] Prigg *v.* Pa., 16 Pet. 539, 616, 618-619 (1842).

[6] Juilliard *v.* Greenman, 110 U.S. 421, 449-450 (1884). *See also* Justice Bradley concurring opinion in Knox *v.* Lee, 12 Wall. 457, 565 (1871).

[7] United States *v.* Jones, 109 U.S. 513 (1883).

[8] United States *v.* Kagama, 118 U.S. 375 (1886); Mescalero Apache Tribe *v.* Jones, 489 P. 2d. 666, 668 (1971).

[9] Fong Yue Ting *v.* U.S., 149 U.S. 698 (1893).

[10] Hines *v.* Davidowitz *et al.*, 312 U.S. 52 (1941).

[11] United States *v.* Curtiss-Wright Export Corp., 299 U.S. 304, 315, 316-318 *passim* (1936). For anticipations of this conception of the powers of the National Government in the field of foreign relations, *see* Penhallow *v.* Doane, 3 Dall. 54, 80, 81 (1795); *also ibid.*, 74 and 76 (argument of counsel); *also* Chief Justice Taney's opinion in Holmes *v.* Jennison, 14 Pet. 540, 575-576 (1840).

Also ascribable to Section I is the doctrine that "the legislature" (*i.e.* Congress) "may not delegate its powers," which was once expounded by Chief Justice Taft as follows: "The well-known maxim '*Delegata potestas non potest delegari*,' applicable to the law of agency in the general and common law, is well understood and has had wider application in the construction of our Federal and State Constitutions than it has in private law. The Federal Constitution and State Constitutions of this country divide the governmental power into three branches . . . in carrying out that constitutional division . . . it is a breach of the National fundamental law if Congress gives up its legislative power and transfers it to the President, or to the Judicial branch, or if by law it attempts to invest itself or its members with either executive power or judicial power. This is not to say that the three branches are not co-ordinate parts of one government and that each in the field of its duties may not invoke the action of the two other branches in so far as the action invoked shall not be an assumption of the constitutional field of action of another branch. In determining what it may do in seeking assistance from another branch, the extent and character of that assistance must be fixed according to common sense and the inherent necessities of the governmental coordination."[12]

As above indicated, this doctrine, too, considered as a judicially enforcible constitutional limitation, has suffered enfeeblement, especially within recent years. This results, in the first place, from the vast expansion of the national legislative power over private enterprise and industrial relations, through the independent regulatory agencies, such as the I.C.C., the F.T.C., the S.E.C., the N.L.R.B., etc. From the nature of the case a good deal of latitude must be accorded such bodies in the discharge of their duties. In the second place, war has eroded the doctrine. Legislation conferring upon the President and his subordinates powers to deal with a fluid war situation must necessarily be couched in fluid terms. The subject is illustrated in later pages.[13]

Although the Supreme Court has insisted that Congress

---

[12] Hampton Jr. & Co. *v.* U.S., 276 U.S. 394, 405, 406 (1928). *See also* the excellent article by P. W. Duff and Horace E. Whiteside, "Delegata Potestas non Potest Delegari," in Douglas B. Maggs (ed.), *Selected Essays on Constitutional Law*, IV (Chicago, 1938), 291-316.

[13] *See infra* pp. 83-85 and 120-125.

must set an "intelligible standard"[14] in delegating power, it has not been loathe to accept such general terms as "public interest" and "public convenience," "interest" or "necessity" as meeting constitutional requirements.[15]

Lastly, the term "legislative powers" connotes certain powers of the individual houses of Congress which are essential to their satisfactory performance of their legislative role. Some of these are conferred upon them in specific terms in the following sections, some are "inherent," or more strictly speaking are *inherited*. The subject is treated below.

## SECTION II

The House of Representatives

¶1. The House of Representatives shall be composed of members chosen every second year by the people of the several States, and the electors in each State shall have the qualifications requisite for electors of the most numerous branch of the State legislature.

"Electors" are voters. The right here conferred is extended by Amendment XVII to the choice of Senators. While the enjoyment of this right is confined by these provisions to persons who are able to meet the requirements prescribed by the States for voting, provided these do not transgress the Constitution (*e.g.* Amendments XV, XIX, and XXIV), yet the right itself comes, not from the States, but from the Constitution, and so is a "privilege and immunity" of national citizenship, about the exercise of which Congress may throw the protection of its legislation and which, under Section I of the Fourteenth Amendment, no State may "abridge."[1]

In 1964, in the landmark case Wesberry *v.* Sanders, the Supreme Court further enhanced the meaning of this provision by its decision that "we hold that, construed in its historical

---

[14] Sunshine Coal Co. *v.* Adkins, 310 U.S. 381, 398 (1940); U.S. *v.* Rock Royal Co-op, 307 U.S. 533, 577 (1939).
[15] N.Y. Central Securities Co. *v.* U.S. 287 U.S. 12, 24 (1932); Radio Com'n *v.* Nelson Bros. Co. 289 U.S. 266, 285 (1933); Nat. Broadcasting Co. *v.* U.S., 319 U.S. 190, 225 (1943); Federal Com'n *v.* Broadcasting Co., 309 U.S. 134, 138 (1940); U.S. *ex. rel.* Knauff *v.* Shaughnessy, 338 U.S. 537 (1950). *But see* Panama Refining Co. *v.* Ryan, 293 U.S. 388 (1935); Schechter Corp. *v.* U.S., 295 U.S. 495 (1935); Kent *v.* Dulles, 357 U.S. 116 (1958); Justice Brennan's separate opinion in Robel *v.* U.S. 389 U.S. 258, 274 (1967) and dissenters' rejoinder at 288, note 2.

[1] *Ex parte* Yarbrough, 110 U.S. 651 (1884); United States *v.* Classic, 313 U.S. 299 (1941); United States *v.* Saylor, 322 U.S. 385 (1944).

context, the command of Art. I§2, that representatives be chosen 'by the people of the several states' means that as nearly as practicable one man's vote in a congressional election is to be worth as much as another's.''[2]

¶2. No person shall be a Representative who shall not have attained the age of twenty-five years, and been seven years a citizen of the United States, and who shall not, when elected, be an inhabitant of that State in which he shall be chosen.

It was early established in the case of Henry Clay, who was elected to the Senate before he was thirty years of age, that it is sufficient if a Senator possesses the qualifications of that office when he takes his seat; and the corresponding rule has always been applied to Representatives as well.[3]

An "inhabitant" is a resident. Custom alone has established the rule that a Representative must be a resident of the *district* from which he is chosen.[4]

¶3. Representatives and direct taxes shall be apportioned among the several States which may be included within this Union, according to their respective numbers, which shall be determined by adding to the whole number of free persons, including those bound to service for a term of years, and excluding Indians not taxed, three-fifths of all other persons. The actual enumeration shall be made within three years after the first meeting of the Congress of the United States, and within every subsequent term of ten years, in such manner as they shall by law direct. The number of Representatives shall not exceed one for every thirty thousand, but each State shall have at least one Representative; and until such enumeration shall be made, the State of *New Hampshire* shall be entitled to choose three, *Massachusetts* eight, *Rhode Island and Providence Plantations* one, *Connecticut* five, *New York* six, *New Jersey* four, *Pennsylvania* eight, *Delaware* one, *Maryland* six, *Virginia* ten, *North Carolina* five, *South Carolina* five, and *Georgia* three.

[2] 376 U.S. 1 (1964).
[3] U.S., 74th Congress, 1st Sess. Senate Report 904 (1935); 79 *Cong. Rec.* 9651-9653 (1935).
[4] Asher C. Hinds, *Precedents of the House of Representatives*, I (Washington, 1907-1908), §414.

This paragraph embodies one of the famous compromises of the Constitution. The term "three-fifths of all other persons" meant three-fifths of all slaves. Amendment XIII has rendered this clause obsolete and Amendment XIV, Section II, has superseded it.

The basis of representation following the census of 1910 was one Representative for substantially 212,000 inhabitants. Following the census of 1920 Congress ignored its constitutional duty to make a reapportionment, but reapportionment on the basis of the census of 1930 was provided for beforehand, by the Act of June 18, 1929. Under this act, the size of the House **The Basis** was restricted to 435 members, who were allotted among the **of Appor-** States by the same method as was employed in the apportion- **tionment** ment of 1911, the so-called "method of major fractions." The problem—obviously one for the statistical expert—was to find a number, or "electoral quotient," to divide into the population of each State which would give the predetermined total of Representatives—435—when, for each remainder in a State which was in excess of one-half of such number or "electoral quotient," an additional representative was allotted. By an act passed in 1941, however, this cumbersome method is replaced by the original "method of equal proportions," which is made possible by permitting Congress to depart from the number 435 within moderate limits.[5]

The duty of Congress created by this paragraph to provide for an "enumeration" of population every ten years has grown into a vast, indefinite power to gratify official curiosity respecting the belongings and activities of the people. Thus in the decennial survey of 1940 a near revolt was provoked in up- **The Census** state New York by the rumor that 232 questions would be put by the enumerators. But popular irritation was allayed when it turned out that only (!) sixty-four questions would have to be answered and after the President had issued a proclamation warning people of the legal penalties they would incur if they failed to cooperate.[6]

A different kind of complaint emerged from the census of

[5] For a detailed description and analysis of the various modes of apportionment, *see* the document prepared for the Senate in 1940 by a Harvard mathematician, Edward V. Huntington, 76th Congress, 3rd Sess., Senate Document 304 (1940).

[6] *New York Times*, Feb. 11, 1940. The source of the penalties referred to by the President in his proclamation was the Act of June 18, 1929, 46 *Stat.* 21 (1929).

1970. In hearings before the House Census and Statistics Subcommittee of the Post Office and Civil Service Committee, it was charged that there was an "undercount" of 15% in the ghettos.[7]

¶4. When vacancies happen in the representation from any State, the executive authority thereof shall issue writs of election to fill such vacancies.

*A.* A governor does not have the discretion to refrain from filling a vacancy.[8] (Compare this provision with provision for vacancies in Senate, which confers certain powers on State legislatures. *See* Amendment XVII, ¶ 2.)

¶5. The House of Representatives shall choose their Speaker and other officers, and shall have the sole power of impeachment.

The powers of the Speaker have varied greatly at different times. They depend altogether upon the rules of the House.

The subject of impeachment is dealt with at the end of the next section.

## SECTION III

¶1. The Senate of the United States shall be composed of two Senators from each State, chosen by the legislature thereof, for six years; and each Senator shall have one vote.

The Senate, a Continuing Body

This paragraph has been superseded by Amendment XVII.

¶2. Immediately after they shall be assembled in consequence of the first election, they shall be divided as equally as may be into three classes. The seats of the Senators of the first class shall be vacated at the expiration of the second year, of the second class, at the expiration of the fourth year, and of the third class, at the expiration of the sixth year, so that one-third may be chosen every second year; and if vacancies happen by resignation or otherwise dur-

---

[7] 1970 *Cong. Quart. Almanac* 527.
[8] Jackson *v.* Ogilvie, 426 F. 2d. 1333 (1970). The Massachusetts Supreme Judicial Court recently held that in filling a vacancy the applicable boundaries of the district would be those in effect at the last regular election if these boundaries had been changed in an intervening reapportionment statute. Opinion of Justices, 282 N.E. 2d. 629 (1972).

ing the recess of the legislature of any State, the executive thereof may make temporary appointments until the next meeting of the legislature, which shall then fill such vacancies.

This paragraph explains how it came about that one-third of the Senators retire every two years, as well as why the Senate is a continuing body.[1] While there have been 92 Congresses to date, there has been only one Senate, and this will apparently be the case till the crack of doom.

The final clause of this paragraph also has been superseded by Amendment XVII.

¶3. No person shall be a Senator who shall not have attained to the age of thirty years, and been nine years a citizen of the United States, and who shall not, when elected, be an inhabitant of that State for which he shall be chosen.

Following the precedent set in the case of Henry Clay, mentioned above, it is not necessary for a person to possess these qualifications when he is chosen Senator; it is sufficient if he has them when he takes the oath of office and enters upon his official duties.[2]

¶4. The Vice-President of the United States shall be President of the Senate, but shall have no vote, unless they be equally divided.

The "Casting Vote" of the Vice President
This is the source of the "casting vote" of the Vice-President, which has been decisive on more than one critical occasion. Indeed, John Adams, our first Vice-President, thus turned the scales in the Senate some twenty times, one of them being the occasion when the President was first conceded the power to remove important executive officers of the United States without consulting the Senate, with whose "advice and consent" they are appointed.[3] All other powers of the Vice-President as presiding officer depend upon the rules of the Senate, or his own initiative. In early days they were considerably broader than today.

[1] McGrain v. Daugherty, 273 U.S. 135, 181-182 (1927).
[2] See 79 Cong. Rec. 5915-5917, 9650-9657, 9749-9778, 9824-9842 (1935). Senator Biden, Jr., of Delaware was elected at age 29 but turned 30 prior to taking office.
[3] Charles Francis Adams (ed.), Life and Works of John Adams, I (Boston, 1856), 448-450.

¶5. The Senate shall choose their other officers, and also a President *pro tempore* in the absence of the Vice-President, or when he shall exercise the office of President of the United States.

(*See* Amendment XXV.)

¶6. The Senate shall have the sole power to try all impeachments. When sitting for that purpose, they shall be on oath or affirmation. When the President of the United States is tried, the Chief Justice shall preside: and no person shall be convicted without the concurrence of two-thirds of the members present.

The Impeachment Power

Impeachments are charges of misconduct in office, and are comparable to presentments or indictments by grand jury. They are voted by the House of Representatives by a majority vote, that is, a majority of a quorum (*see* Section V, ¶1).

The persons subject to impeachment are "civil officers of the United States" (*see* Article II, Section IV), which term does not include members of the House or the Senate (*see* Article I, Section VI, ¶2), who, however, are subject to discipline and expulsion by their respective houses (*see* Section V, ¶2).

The charge of misconduct must amount to a charge of "treason, bribery, or other high crimes and misdemeanors" (*see* Article II, Section IV); but the term "high crimes and misdemeanors" is used in a broad sense, being equivalent presumably to lack of that "good behavior" which is specifically required of judges (*see* Article III, Section I). It is for the House of Representatives to judge in the first instance and for the Senate to judge finally whether alleged misconduct on the part of a civil officer of the United States falls within the terms "high crimes and misdemeanors," and from this decision there is no appeal.

In 1803 District Judge Pickering was removed from office by the process of impeachment on account of drunkenness and other unseemly conduct on the bench. The defense of insanity was urged in his behalf, but unsuccessfully. One hundred and ten years later Judge Archbald of the Commerce Court was similarly removed for soliciting for himself and friends valuable favors from railroad companies, some of which were at the time litigants in his court; and in 1936 Judge Ritter of the Florida District Court was removed for conduct in connection

13

with a receivership case which raised serious question of his integrity, although on the specific charges against him he was acquitted.[4]

When trying an impeachment the Senate sits as a court, but has full power in determining its procedure and is not required to disqualify its members for alleged prejudice or interest. However, "when the President of the United States is tried, the Chief Justice shall preside," the idea being no doubt to obviate the possibility of bias and unfairness on the part of the Vice-President, who would succeed to the President's powers if the latter was removed.

"Two-thirds of the members present" logically implies two-thirds of a quorum at least (see Section V, ¶1).

¶7. Judgment in cases of impeachment shall not extend further than to removal from office, and disqualification to hold and enjoy any office of honor, trust, or profit under the United States; but the party convicted shall, nevertheless, be liable and subject to indictment, trial, judgment, and punishment, according to law.

The House has impeached twelve civil officers of the United States, of whom the Senate convicted four. The two most famous cases of impeachment were those of Supreme Court Justice Samuel Chase (1802) and of President Andrew Johnson (1868), both of which failed. All of those who have been convicted were judges of inferior Federal courts. In several instances, however, Federal officers have resigned to escape impeachment or trial.[5]

Since conviction upon impeachment does not constitute "jeopardy of life or limb" (see Amendment V), a person ousted from office by process of impeachment may still be reached by the ordinary penalties of the law for his offense if it was of a penal character.[6]

---

[4] W. S. Carpenter, *Judicial Tenure in the United States* (New Haven, 1918), 145-152; 80 *Cong. Rec.* 5602-5608 (1936).

[5] John D. Feerick, "Impeaching Federal Judges: A Study of the Constitutional Provisions," 39 *Fordham Law Review* 1, 25 (1970).

[6] Roger Foster, *Commentaries on the Constitution*, I (Boston, 1895), 505 ff. This work, of which only the first volume was ever published, contains a valuable, although considerably out-of-date, discussion of the entire subject of impeachment under the Constitution. *See also* remarks of Senator Joseph D. Tydings in 89th Congress, 2d Sess., Senate Committee on the Judiciary, *Hearings*, "Judicial Fitness," February 15, 1966, pp. 3-4.

On account of the cumbersomeness of the impeachment proceeding and the amount of time it is apt to consume, it has
been proposed that a special court should be created to try
cases of alleged misbehavior in office, especially of inferior
judges of the United States. There can be little doubt that
Congress has power to establish such a court and to authorize
such proceedings.[7]

## SECTION IV

¶ 1. The times, places, and manner of holding elections for
Senators and Representatives shall be prescribed in each
State by the legislature thereof; but the Congress may at
any time by law make or alter such regulations, except as
to the places of choosing Senators.

Congres-
sional Reg-
ulation of
Elections

This is one of the few clauses of the Constitution to delegate
power to the States. "Legislature" here means the State legislature acting in its *law making* capacity and consequently subject to the governor's veto, where this exists under the State
constitution,[1] as it does today in all the States except North
Carolina. Until 1842 State regulations of Congressional elections went unaltered by Congress, and Representatives were
frequently chosen on State-wide tickets. By an act passed that
year Congress imposed the district system on the States, and
by one passed in 1911 added further requirements: Representatives must "be elected by districts composed of a compact
and contiguous territory and containing as nearly as practicable an equal number of inhabitants." These provisions were
omitted from the Act of June 18, 1929 (*see* p. 10).[2] As a result
remarkable disparities in population existed at times even as
between districts in the same State. The seventh Illinois district, for example, at one time contained over 900,000 inhabitants as against only 112,000 in the fifth Illinois district. Thus a
single vote in the latter district counted more than eight votes
did in the former in the choice of a Representative. Ultimately

---

For difficulties in impeaching even corrupt judges, *see* Joseph Borkin, *The
Corrupt Judge* (New York, 1962), pp. 189-204.
[7] Burke Shartel, "Federal Judges," 28 *Michigan Law Review*, 870-907
(1930); speech of Senator Wm. G. McAdoo, 80 *Cong. Rec.* 5933-5940 (1936).
*See also* Raoul Berger, "Impeachment of Judges and 'Good Behavior'
Tenure," 79 *Yale Law Journal* 1475, 1530 (1970).

[1] Smiley *v.* Holm, 285 U.S. 355 (1932).
[2] 46 *Stat.* 20, 26 (1929); Wood *v.* Brown, 287 U.S. 1 (1932).

the Supreme Court decided that such disparity was unconstitutional on the grounds that Article I, Section II, required that as nearly as practicable "one man's vote in a congressional election is to be worth as much as another's."[3]

Under earlier legislation which the Act of 1929 leaves unimpaired, unless the State constitution specifies some other date —no State constitution does so now—elections for members of the House take place on the Tuesday following the first Monday of November of the even years; and votes must be by written or printed ballot, or by voting machine where this method is authorized by State law.[4]

Party Primaries as "Elections"

May Congress, by way of regulating "the manner of holding elections," limit the expenditures of candidates for nomination or election to Congress? In the Newberry case,[5] which concerned a candidate for the Senate, four members of the Supreme Court took the view that the above quoted words referred only to the last formal act whereby the voter registers his choice, and so answered this question, "no"; but a fifth Justice, who with these constituted the majority of the Court on this occasion, expressly confined his opinion to the state of Congress's power before the adoption of the Seventeenth Amendment, when the election of Senators, being by the State legislatures, was much more evidently separable from the preliminary stages of candidacy than it is today. In United States *v.* Classic[6] the Court ruled in 1941 that certain Louisiana election officials who were charged with tampering with ballots cast in a primary election for Representative had been properly indicted under the United States Criminal Code for conspiring to deprive citizens of the United States of a right secured to them by the Constitution, namely, the right to participate in the choice of Representatives in Congress. This was held to include not only the right of the elector "to cast a ballot and to have it counted at the general election whether for the successful candidate or not," but also his right to have his vote counted in the primary in cases where the State law has made the primary "an integral part of the procedure of choice," or where "the primary effectively controls the choice." Three Justices dissented on a question of statutory interpretation, but took pains to voice their belief that Congress may regulate pri-

[3] Wesberry *v.* Sanders, 376 U.S. 1 (1964).
[4] 2 U.S.C. 1 and 9.
[5] Newberry *v.* U.S., 256 U.S. 232 (1921).
[6] 313 U.S. 299.

maries at which candidates for the Senate and House are selected, a position which is further bolstered by later holdings that the Fifteenth Amendment protects the right to vote in party primaries.[7] Years earlier, moreover, the Court had asserted that the National Government must, simply by virtue of its republican character, possess "power to protect the elections on which its existence depends from violence and corruption," a sentiment which it reiterated and emphasized in 1934 with the *Newberry* case before it.[8]

In recent years Congress has endeavored to protect voters in Federal elections from intimidation, interference, and more subtle forms of voting discrimination in provisions of the Civil Rights Acts of 1957, 1960, 1964, and 1968 and the Voting Rights Acts of 1965 and 1970.[9] The 1957 act was based primarily on Congress's power under Section IV, but the later provisions aimed at vindication of voting rights were based on Congress's power under Amendment XV.[10]

When U.S. Senate candidate Richard L. Roudebush sought a recount of the vote in his close 1970 race with Senator R. Vance Hartke of Indiana, it served as the occasion for the Supreme Court to address the question of the relationship between Article I, Section IV, and Article I, Section V. In 1972, the Court held that: "Unless Congress acts, Art. I, § 4, empowers the States to regulate the conduct of senatorial elections. . . . A recount is an integral part of the Indiana electoral process and is within the ambit of the broad powers delegated to the States by Art. I, § 4. . . . It is true that a state's verification of the accuracy of election results pursuant to its Art. I, § 4 powers, is not totally separable from the Senate's power to judge elections and returns. But a recount can be said to 'usurp' the Senate's function only if it frustrates the Senate's ability to make an independent final judgment. A recount does not prevent the Senate from independently evaluating the

---

[7] Smith *v.* Allwright, 321 U.S. 649 (1944); Terry *v.* Adams, 345 U.S. 461 (1953).

[8] *Ex parte* Yarbrough, 110 U.S. 651 (1884); Burroughs *v.* U.S., 290 U.S. 534 (1934). The right to have a vote counted means the right to have it counted honestly. United States *v.* Mosley, 238 U.S. 383 (1915); United States *v.* Saylor, 322 U.S. 385 (1944).

[9] 71 *Stat.* 634 (1957); 74 *Stat.* 86 (1960); 78 *Stat.* 241 (1964); 79 *Stat.* 437 (1965); 82 *Stat.* 73 (1968); 84 *Stat.* 314 (1970).

[10] U.S., 85th Congress, 1st Sess., House Report 291 (1957); 2 *U.S. Cong. & Adm. News* 1925, 1936 (1960); South Carolina *v.* Katzenbach, 383 U.S. 301 (1966); 2 *U.S. Cong. & Adm. News* 3278 (1970).

17

election any more than the initial count does. The Senate is free to accept or reject the apparent winner in either count, and, if it chooses, to conduct its own recount."[11]

¶2. The Congress shall assemble at least once in every year, and such meeting shall be on the first Monday in December, unless they shall by law appoint a different day.

This provision has been superseded by Amendment XX—the so-called Norris "Lame Duck" Amendment.

## SECTION V

Powers of the Houses over Members

¶1. Each house shall be the judge of the elections, returns, and qualifications of its own members, and a majority of each shall constitute a quorum to do business; but a smaller number may adjourn from day to day, and may be authorized to compel the attendance of absent members, in such manner, and under such penalties, as each house may provide.

The power conferred by this paragraph carries with it authority to take all necessary steps to secure information which may form the basis of intelligent action, including the right to summon witnesses and compel them to answer;[1] as well as the right to delegate such powers to a committee. And whenever either house doubts the qualifications of one claiming membership it may, during investigation, suspend him or even refuse to swear him in.

For a good many years the "qualifications" here referred to did not consist solely of the qualifications prescribed in Sections II and III above for Representatives and Senators, respectively. "Congress," it was said, "may impose disqualifications for reasons that appeal to the common judgment of mankind." In 1900 the House of Representatives excluded a Representative from Utah as "a notorious, demoralizing and audacious violator of State and Federal laws relating to polygamy and its attendant crimes";[2] while in 1928 the Senate refused to seat a Senator-elect from Illinois on the ground that his acceptance of certain sums in promotion of his candidacy

---

[11] Roudebush *v.* Hartke, 405 U.S. 15 (1972).

[1] Barry *v.* U.S., 279 U.S. 597 (1929).
[2] J. A. Woodburn, *The American Republic and Its Government* (New York, 1903), 247.

had been "contrary to sound policy, harmful to the dignity of the Senate, dangerous to the perpetuity of free government," and had tainted his credentials "with fraud and corruption."[3] But when Adam Clayton Powell was elected to the House for the 90th Congress and was not permitted to take his seat on the grounds that he "had asserted an unwarranted privilege and immunity from the processes of the courts of New York; that he had wrongfully diverted House funds for the use of others and himself; and that he had made false reports on expenditures of foreign currency to the Committee on House Administration," the Supreme Court decided that "our examination of the relevant historical materials leads us to the conclusion . . . that the Constitution leaves the House without authority to *exclude* any person, duly elected by his constituents, who meets all the requirements for membership expressly prescribed in" Article I, Section II.[4]

The circumstance that refusal by the Senate to seat one claiming membership must cause a State to lose its equality of representation in that body for a time is a fact of no importance constitutionally, equality of representation being guaranteed merely as against the power to amend the Constitution.[5]

For the relationship between this provision and Article I, Section IV, *see* p. 16 above.

¶2. Each house may determine the rules of its proceedings, punish its members for disorderly behavior, and with the concurrence of two-thirds, expel a member.

It is by virtue of its power to "determine the rules of its proceedings" that the Senate has been able to develop that most peculiar institution, the "filibuster." The core of the filibuster is the right of any Senator who can secure recognition from the Chair to talk on any subject that may enter his head, however remote it may be from the business underway, for as long as his legs will hold him up. For a time this unique institution

---

[3] 69 *Cong. Rec.* 1581-1597, 1665-1672, 1703-1718 (1928). On the privileges and procedure of the House generally, and supporting precedents, *see* Asher C. Hinds, *Precedents of the House of Representatives* (Washington, 1907-1908), 8 vols.

[4] Powell *v.* McCormack, 395 U.S. 486, 522 (1969). Also instructive on this point is the decision on an exclusion by a State legislature, Bond *v.* Floyd, 385 U.S. 116 (1966).

[5] Barry *v.* U.S., 279 U.S. 597 (1929).

seemed to be losing ground. Indeed, in 1917 the Senate for the first time in its history adopted a mitigated cloture rule. However, in 1948 Senator Vandenberg ruled in his capacity as President *pro tem*, that a motion to change the Senate's rules required the affirmative vote of two-thirds of the entire Senate membership, and this ruling was adopted by the Senate as "Rule 22." Asked for a clarification of this rule in 1957, Vice President Nixon expressed the opinion that it was "unconstitutional," inasmuch as it "denied the membership of the Senate the power to make its own rules." He acknowledged, however, that only the Senate could decide the issue.[6] Efforts to change the rule in recent years have been interesting but unsuccessful.[7] However, the Senate in 1959 agreed that only two-thirds of those present would be enough to invoke cloture even on proposals for rules changes. Paradoxically, by virtue of its power to make its own rules, the Senate has adopted a practice that limits this power.

The Power of Each House over its Proceedings    In the exercise of their constitutional power to determine their rules of proceedings, the Houses of Congress may not "ignore constitutional restraints or violate fundamental rights, and there should be a reasonable relation between the mode or method of proceeding established by the rule and the result which is sought to be attained. But within these limitations all matters of method are open to the determination of the House. . . . The power to make rules is not one which once exercised is exhausted. It is a continuous power, always subject to be exercised by the House, and within the limitations suggested, absolute and beyond the challenge of any other body or tribunal."[8] But when a rule affects private rights, the construction thereof may become a judicial question. In Christoffel *v.* United States[9] a sharply divided Court upset a conviction for perjury in the district courts of one who had denied under oath before a House Committee any affiliation with Communism. The reversal was based on the ground that, inasmuch as a quorum of the committee, while present at the outset, was not present at the time of the alleged perjury, testimony before

---

[6] 103 *Cong. Rec.* 178 (1957).
[7] For a brief and illuminating history of the cloture rule, *see* U.S., 92d Congress, 1st Sess., Senate Committee on Rules and Administration, *Senate Cloture Rule.*
[8] U.S. *v.* Ballin, 144 U.S. 1, 5 (1892).
[9] 338 U.S. 84 (1949).

it was not before a "competent tribunal" within the sense of the District of Columbia Code.

In recent years the Supreme Court ruled that Congressional committees conducting investigations must abide by their own rules.[10]

The Legislative Reorganization Act of 1946 stems in part from the powers here conferred on the houses individually.[11] So far as it purports to limit such powers, the measure would, seemingly, amount to a sort of gentleman's agreement rather than a true law.[12]

¶3. Each house shall keep a journal of its proceedings, and from time to time publish the same, excepting such parts as may in their judgment require secrecy, and the ayes and nays of the members of either house on any question shall, at the desire of one-fifth of those present, be entered on the journal.

The obvious purpose of this paragraph is to make it possible for the people to watch the official conduct of their Representatives and Senators. It may be, and frequently is, circumvented by the "house" resolving itself into "committee of the whole," to whose proceedings the provision is not regarded as applying.[13]

¶4. Neither house, during the session of Congress, shall, without the consent of the other, adjourn for more than three days, nor to any other place than that in which the two houses shall be sitting.

\* \* \*

In addition to the powers enumerated above, each house also possesses certain "inherent" powers which are implied in the fact that it is a deliberative body or which were inherited, *via*   Legislative Contempts

10 Yellin *v.* U.S., 374 U.S. 109 (1963) and Gojack *v.* U.S., 384 U.S. 702 (1966).

11 60 *Stat.* 812 (1946).

12 Some of the provisions of 53 *Stat.* 561 (1939) raised similar questions. 83 *Cong. Rec.* 3457-3484 (1938).

13 On the availability of the Journal as evidence concerning the presence of a quorum, the passage of an act, and collaterial questions, *see* United States *v.* Ballin, 144 U.S. 1, 4 (1892). Field *v.* Clark, 143 U.S. 649 (1892); and Flint *v.* Stone Tracy Co., 220 U.S. 107, 143 (1911).

the early State legislatures, from the Parliament of Great Britain. Each house may pass resolutions, either separately or "concurrently" with the other house, with a view to expressing its opinion on any subject whatsoever, and may create committees to deal with the matters which come before it. Also, each house has certain powers of a judicial character over outsiders. If a stranger rudely interrupts or physically obstructs the proceedings of one of the houses, he may be arrested and brought before the bar of the house involved and punished by the vote of its members "for contempt";[14] but if the punishment takes the form of imprisonment it terminates with the session of the house imposing it. Also, each house has full power to authorize investigations by committees looking to possible action within the scope of its powers or of those of Congress as a whole, which committees have the right to examine witnesses and take testimony; and if such witnesses prove recalcitrant, they too may be punished "for contempt," though in this case the punishment is nowadays imposed, under an act of Congress passed in 1857, by the District Court of the District of Columbia, for "misdemeanor."[15] But it is not within the power of either house to pry into the purely personal affairs of private individuals, or to investigate them for the purpose of "exposing" them, or to deprive them of freedom of speech, press, and association; and whether in a particular investigation a committee of Congress has attempted to do any of these things rests with the Supreme Court to say.[16] Indeed, in Watkins *v.* U.S. the Court went so far as to suggest that it is entitled to rule whether a question put to a person under investigation by a Congressional committee was "relevant."[17]

The Investigatory Power

[14] In the noteworthy case, involving Father Groppi's disruption of the Wisconsin legislature, the Court held in 1972 that: "The past decisions of this Court expressly recognizing the power of the Houses of Congress to punish contemptuous conduct leave little question that the Constitution imposes no general barriers to the legislative exercise of such power. . . . We are therefore concerned only with the procedures which the Due Process Clause of the Federal Constitution requires a state legislature to meet in imposing punishment for contemptuous conduct committed in its presence." Groppi *v.* Leslie, 404 U.S. 496 (1972).

[15] 11 *Stat.* 155 (1857); for revised version of law, *see* 2 U.S.C. 192.

[16] On this topic of Anderson *v.* Dunn, 6 Wheat. 204 (1821); Kilbourn *v.* Thompson 103 U.S. 168 (1880); *in re* Chapman, 166 U.S. 661 (1897); Marshall *v.* Gordon, 243 U.S. 521 (1917); McGrain *v.* Daugherty, 273 U.S. 135 (1927); Jurney *v.* McCracken, 294 U.S. 125 (1935); 2 U.S.C. 192; United States *v.* Bryan, 339 U.S. 323 (1950); Watkins *v.* United States, 354 U.S. 178 (1957); Barenblatt *v.* U.S., 360 U.S. 109 (1959).

[17] 354 U.S. 178 (1957); *see also* Barenblatt *v.* U.S., 360 U.S. 109 (1959);

## SECTION VI

¶1. The Senators and Representatives shall receive a compen- Privileges
sation for their services, to be ascertained by law and paid and Immu-
out of the Treasury of the United States. They shall, in all nities of
cases except treason, felony, and breach of the peace, be Members
privileged from arrest, during their attendance at the session of their respective houses, and in going to and returning from the same; and for any speech or debate in either
house they shall not be questioned in any other place.

Since "treason, felony, and breach of the peace" cover violations of State as well as national laws, the immunity from arrest here conferred applies only to civil suits; it does not include immunity from service of summons in a civil suit; nor,
by reasoning and authority, from being required to testify before a Congressional committee.[1] To illustrate, failure to obey
a subpoena in a civil case resulted in a thirty-day jail sentence
for Congressman Adam Clayton Powell. When appealed, the
State appeals court's uneasiness about upholding the decision
was manifested in *dicta* and the staying of the sentence to give
Powell time to comply. But, nonetheless, the appeals court
agreed with the lower court that Section VI was not a bar to
sentencing Powell to jail for failure to obey the subpoena.[2]

In practice, since the abolition of imprisonment for debt,
this particular clause has lost most of its importance.

The provision concerning "speech or debate" not only re-
moves every restriction upon freedom of utterance on the floor
of the houses by members thereof except that supplied by
their own rules of order, but applies also to reports and resolutions which, though in writing, may be reproduced in speech;
and, "in short, to things generally done in a session of the
House by one of its members in relation to the business before it."[3] Nor will the claim of an unworthy purpose suffice to

---

Wilkinson *v.* U.S., 365 U.S. 399 (1961); Braden *v.* U.S., 365 U.S. 431 (1961);
Deutch *v.* U.S., 367 U.S. 456 (1961).

---

[1] *See* Long *v.* Ansell, 293 U.S. 76 (1934), and cases there cited.
[2] James *v.* Powell, 274 N.Y.S. 2d. 192, 195 (1966), *affirmed*, 18 N.Y. 2d.
931 (1966) and 19 N.Y. 2d. 813 (1967).
[3] Kilbourn *v.* Thompson, 103 U.S. 168, 203-204 (1880), citing and quoting
from Chief Justice Parsons' famous opinion in Coffin *v.* Coffin, 4 Mass. 1
(1808); Powell *v.* McCormack, 395 U.S. 486 (1969).

destroy the privilege. "One must not expect uncommon courage even in legislators."[4]

A covey of recent highly publicized cases have buttressed broad claims for the immunity privilege as it relates to the "speech or debate" provision.[5] As Chief Justice Warren put it in the *Powell* case: "Although the clause sprang from a fear of seditious libel actions instituted by the Crown to punish unfavorable speeches made in Parliament, we have held that it would be a 'narrow view' to confine the protection of the Speech and Debate Clause to words spoken in debate. Committee reports, resolutions, and the act of voting are equally covered as are 'things generally done in a session of the House by one of its members in relation to the business before it.' "[6] The Court had a short time before explained that the purpose of the clause is "to prevent intimidation [of legislators] by the executive and accountability before a possibly hostile judiciary."[7] But it should be borne in mind that Congressmen can still be held accountable for acts and utterances which cannot be construed as part of their *legitimate* legislative duties. Thomas F. Johnson was ultimately convicted for violations of a conflict of interest statute while he was a Congressman. He was found guilty of accepting payment for attempting to have the Justice Department dismiss a mail fraud indictment against the officers of a savings and loan association.[8] The first time around, the Supreme Court had upheld the court of appeals which had overturned Johnson's original conviction on the grounds that a speech he had given in the House and the preparation for it were part of the evidence used against him.[9] In June 1972, the Supreme Court overturned a district court ruling that former Senator Daniel B. Brewster could not be indicted for alleged bribery to perform a legislative act. Chief Justice Burger speaking for the Court insisted that: "Taking

[4] Justice Frankfurter, for the Court in Tenney v. Brandhove, 341 U.S. 367, 377 (1951).

[5] U.S. v. Johnson, 383 U.S. 169 (1966); U.S. v. Johnson, 419 F. 2d. 56 (1969); *cert. denied*, 397 U.S. 1010 (1970); Powell v. McCormack, 395 U.S. 486 (1969); U.S. v. Brewster 408, U.S. 501 (1972); U.S. v. Doe, 332 F. Supp. 930 (1971), 455 F. 2d. 753 (1972) and 408 U.S. 606 (1972) (cited as Gravel v. U.S.); Stamler v. Willis, 287 F. Supp. 734 (1968).

[6] Powell v. McCormack, 395 U.S. 486, 502 (1969).

[7] U.S. v. Johnson, 383 U.S. 169, 181 (1966).

[8] U.S. v. Johnson, 419 F. 2d. 56 (1969); *cert. denied*, 397 U.S. 1010 (1970).

[9] U.S. v. Johnson, 383 U.S. 169 (1966).

a bribe is, obviously, no part of the legislative process or function; it is not a legislative act. It is not, by any conceivable interpretation, an act performed as part of or even incidental to the role of a legislator. . . . When a bribe is taken, it does not matter whether the promise for which the bribe was given was for the performance of a legislative act as here or, as in Johnson, for use of a Congressman's influence with the Executive Branch. And an inquiry into the purpose of a bribe 'does not draw into question the legislative acts of the defendant member of Congress or his motives for performing them.' "[10]

More recently, U.S. District Judge W. Arthur Garrity, Jr., concluded that, although Senator Mike Gravel could with impunity read the Pentagon Papers to his subcommittee and hence into the public record even while publication of the papers was temporarily barred pending a Supreme Court decision, *"Senator Gravel's arranging for private publication of the Pentagon Papers by Beacon Press stands on a different footing and, in the court's opinion, is not embraced by the Speech or Debate Clause. The test is not the public benefit or the political value of such private publication but whether it is a legislative act"*[11] (emphasis supplied). Subsequently, the Supreme Court buttressed this decision. It held that "We have no doubt that Senator Gravel may not be made to answer—either in terms of questions or in defending himself from prosecution—for the events that occurred at the subcommittee meeting. Our decision is made easier by the fact that the United States appears to have abandoned whatever position it took to the contrary in the lower courts."[12] The Court went on "We are convinced also that the Court of Appeals correctly determined that Senator Gravel's alleged arrangement with Beacon Press to publish the Pentagon Papers was not protected speech or debate."

Significantly, Justice Harlan speaking for the Court in *Johnson* suggested an interesting possibility for limiting immunity in the future: "Without intimating any view thereon we expressly leave open for consideration, when the case arises, a prosecution which though possibly entailing inquiry into legislative acts or motivations, is founded upon a narrowly drawn

10 U.S. *v.* Brewster, 408 U.S. 501 (1972). Subsequently, Brewster was convicted in district court.

11 U.S. *v.* Doe, 332 F. Supp. 930 (1971).

12 Gravel *v.* U.S., 408 U.S. 606, 616 (1972).

statute passed by Congress in the exercise of its legislative power to regulate the conduct of its members."[13] Congress has not yet accepted Harlan's invitation to pass such a statute.

Another interesting question which arose in the Gravel case was the question of the immunity of Congressmen's staffs. The Supreme Court resolved that issue by holding that "We agree with the Court of Appeals that for the purpose of construing the privilege a Member and his aide are to be 'treated as one.' "[14] But the Court was also quick to conclude that "Neither do we perceive any constitutional or other privilege that shields Rodberg [the Senator's aide], any more than any other witness, from grand jury questions relevant to tracing the source of obviously highly classified documents that came into the Senator's possession and are the basic subject matter of inquiry in this case, as long as no legislative act is implicated by the questions." The Court then provided specific guidelines and remanded the case to the court of appeals. Consequently, the way was opened for the Government to seek indictments for the alleged arrangement with Beacon Press to publish the Pentagon Papers.

Disabilities of Members

¶2. No Senator or Representative shall, during the time for which he was elected, be appointed to any civil office under the authority of the United States, which shall have been created, or the emoluments whereof shall have been increased during such time; and no person holding any office under the United States shall be a member of either house during his continuance in office.

Despite this paragraph Presidents have frequently appointed members of the houses as commissioners to act in a diplomatic capacity; but as such posts, whether created by act of Congress or not, carried no emoluments and were only temporary, they were not, it would seem, "offices" in the sense of the Constitution.[15]

The first clause became a subject of discussion in 1937, when Justice Black was appointed to the Supreme Court in face of

[13] 383 U.S. 169, 185 (1966).
[14] Gravel v. U.S., 408 U.S. 606, 616 (1972). *But see* Powell v. McCormack 395 U.S. 486, 504-505 (1969).
[15] United States v. Hartwell, 6 Wall. 385, 393 (1867). *Cf.* W. W. Willoughby, *The Constitutional Law of the United States*, I (New York, 1929), 605-607.

the fact that Congress had recently improved the financial position of Justices retiring at seventy and the term for which
Mr. Black had been elected to the Senate from Alabama in
1932 had still some time to run. The appointment was defended by the argument that inasmuch as Mr. Black was only
fifty-one years old at the time and so would be ineligible for
the "increased emolument" for nineteen years, it was not *as to
him* an increased emolument. Similarly, when in 1909 Senator
Knox of Pennsylvania wished to become Secretary of State in
President Taft's Cabinet, the salary of which office had been
recently increased, Congress accommodatingly repealed the
increase for the period which still remained of Mr. Knox's Senatorial term. In other words, a Senator or Representative—
and especially a Senator—may, "during the time for which he
was elected, be appointed to any civil office under the authority of the United States, . . . the emoluments whereof shall
have been increased during such time," *provided only* that the
increase in emolument is not available to the appointee "during such time."

Another question concerning the first clause arose when the
91st Congress passed the Federal Salary Act of 1967, which
authorized the President to include in his budget message for
fiscal 1970 recommendations for an increase for Federal officials including the Secretary of Defense. President-elect Nixon
announced his intention to appoint Melvin R. Laird, a Representative in the 91st Congress, to the post of Secretary of Defense. Laird asked the Attorney General of the United States
for an official opinion as to whether or not the Constitution
precluded him from accepting the post. The Attorney General,
Ramsey Clark, wrote Laird that: "Assuming that you are, in
the normal practice at the beginning of a new administration,
nominated, confirmed, and appointed as Secretary of Defense
within a few days following the inauguration, *i.e.*, during the
period in which it remains uncertain whether Congress may
disapprove the Presidential salary recommendations, I believe
your appointment will not be precluded by this constitutional
clause."[16]

The second clause derives from an act of Parliament passed "Cabinet"
in 1701, which sought to reduce the royal influence by exclud- versus
ing all "placemen" from the House of Commons. The act, how- "Presiden-
ever, so cut the Commons off from direct knowledge of the tial" system

[16] 42 *Op. Atty. Gen.*, Jan. 3, 1969.

business of government that it was largely repealed within a few years; and so the way was paved for the British "Cabinet System," wherein the executive power of the realm is placed in the hands of the leaders of the controlling party in the House of Commons. Conversely, the revival of the provision in the Constitution, in conformity with the doctrine of the Separation of Powers, lies at the basis of the American "Presidential System," in which the business of legislation and that of administration proceed largely in *formal*, though not *actual*, independence of each other. (*See*, however, Article II, Section II, ¶1, and Section III.)

In 1970, a committee of anti-war armed forces reservists filed suit in the United States District Court for the District of Columbia to force the expulsion of nine Senators and fifty Representatives from commissioned status as Reserve and National Guard officers on the grounds that such service by Congressmen violated this provision of the Constitution. The District Court of the District of Columbia held that the Constitution did, indeed, render "a member of Congress ineligible to hold a commission in the Armed Forces Reserve during his continuance in office." However, the court did not insist on compliance: "In the absence of an urgent necessity, and none is shown, the Court is loathe to take injunctive action which might prejudice the rights of Congressmen now seated who in some cases have been members of the Reserve for many years and may leave Congress at the end of their present terms. . . . In any event, if the issue of incompatibility is finally determined on appeal consistent with this decision, there is no reason to believe that Congress and the Executive will be unable to accommodate themselves voluntarily. . . ."[17]

## SECTION VII

¶1. All bills for raising revenue shall originate in the House of Representatives; but the Senate may propose or concur with amendments as on other bills.

The House has frequently contended that this provision covers appropriation as well as taxation measures, and also bills for

[17] Reservists Committee to Stop War *v.* Laird, 323 F. Supp. 833 (1971). Rep. McCloskey, Jr., resigned as a Colonel, U.S.M.C. Reserve, following an appeals court decision upholding the lower court. *N.Y. Times*, Dec. 10, 1972. *See also* 40 *George Washington Law Review*, 542, and 50 *Texas Law Review*, 509 (1972).

repealing revenue acts.[1] Although in practice most appropriation, as well as *all* taxation, measures do originate in the House the provision is otherwise negligble, inasmuch as the Senate may "amend" any bill from the House by substituting an entirely new measure under the enacting clause.

¶2. Every bill which shall have passed the House of Representatives and the Senate shall, before it become a law, be presented to the President of the United States; if he approve he shall sign it, but if not he shall return it, with his objections, to that house in which it shall have originated, who shall enter the objections at large on their journal and proceed to reconsider it. If after such reconsideration two-thirds of that house shall agree to pass the bill, it shall be sent, together with the objections, to the other house, by which it shall likewise be reconsidered, and if approved by two-thirds of that house it shall become a law. But in all such cases the votes of both houses shall be determined by yeas and nays, and the names of the persons voting for and against the bill shall be entered on the journal of each house respectively. If any bills shall not be returned by the President within ten days (Sundays excepted) after it shall have been presented to him, the same shall be a law in like manner as if he had signed it, unless the Congress by their adjournment prevent its return, in which case it shall not be a law.

*The Veto Power*

A bill which has been duly passed by the two houses may become law in any one of three ways: first, with the approval of the President, which it has been generally assumed must be given within ten calendar days, Sundays excepted, after the *presentation* of the bill to him—not after its passage; secondly, without the President's approval, if he does not return it with his signature within ten calendar days, Sundays excepted, after such presentation; thirdly, despite his disapproval, if it is repassed by "two-thirds of each house," that is, two-thirds of a quorum of each house[2] (*see* Section V, ¶1).

Bills which have been passed within ten days of the end of a session may be kept from becoming law by a "pocket veto,"

---

[1] Richard F. Fenno, Jr., *The Power of the Purse* (Boston, 1966), 97-98 and 616-678.
[2] Missouri Pac. Ry. Co. *v.* Kan., 248 U.S. 276 (1919).

that is, by the President's failing to return them till an adjournment of Congress has intervened; nor does it make any difference that the adjournment was not a final one for the Congress which passed the bill, but a merely *ad interim* one between sessions.[3] Likewise, the President may effectively sign a bill at any time within ten calendar days of its presentation to him, Sundays excepted, even though Congress has adjourned in the meantime, whether finally or for the session;[4] and, on the other hand, he may return a bill with his objections to the house of its origin, *via* an appropriate officer thereof, while it is in recess in accordance with ¶4 of Section V above.[5]

The fact that the President has ten days from their *presentation* rather than their *passage* within which to sign bills became a matter of great importance when President Wilson went abroad in 1919 to participate in the making of the Treaty of Versailles. Indeed, by a curious combination of circumstances plus a little contriving, the late President Roosevelt was enabled on one occasion to sign a bill no less than twenty-three days after the adjournment of Congress.[6] And in 1964 the Court of Claims held that where President Eisenhower during a trip abroad had determined with congressional acquiescence, that bills from Congress were to be received at the White House only for presentation to him upon his return, the President's veto of a bill more than ten days after delivery to the White House, but less than ten days from his return to the country, was timely.[7]

Before President Jackson's time, it was generally held that the President ought to reserve his veto power for measures which he deemed to be unconstitutional. Today the President exercises this power for any reason that seems good to him.[8] But in no case may a President by executive action repeal a congressional enactment. As the Supreme Court has said: "No

[3] Okanogan Indians *v.* U.S., 279 U.S. 655 (1929). Senator Kennedy has initiated a new test in the Federal courts of the President's pocket veto powers. *New York Times*, Aug. 10, 1972. *See Cong. Rec. Weekly Report*, 3039-3041.
[4] Edwards *v.* U.S., 286 U.S. 482 (1932).
[5] Wright *v.* U.S., 302 U.S. 583 (1938).
[6] *See* L. F. Schmeckebier, "Approval of Bills After Adjournment of Congress," 33 *American Political Science Review*, 52-54 (1939).
[7] Eber Bros., *v.* U.S., 337 F. 2d. 624 (1964); *cert. denied*, 380 U.S. 950 (1965).
[8] For further details concerning the President's veto, *see* Edward S. Corwin, *The President, Office and Powers* (New York, 1957), 277-283.

Power was ever vested in the President to repeal an act of Congress."[9]

As to the question of when a statute takes effect, the Supreme Court has held: "There is no statute fixing the time when acts of Congress shall take effect, but it is settled that where no other time is prescribed, they take effect from their date."[10]

¶3. Every order, resolution or vote to which the concurrence of the Senate and House of Representatives may be necessary (except on a question of adjournment) shall be presented to the President of the United States; and before the same shall take effect shall be approved by him, or being disapproved by him, shall be repassed by two-thirds of the Senate and House of Representatives, according to the rules and limitations prescribed in the case of a bill.

The "Concurrent Resolution"

"Necessary" here means necessary to give an "order," etc., the force of law.[11] Accordingly "votes" taken in either house preliminary to the final passage of legislation need not be submitted to the President, nor resolutions passed by either house separately or by both houses "concurrently" with a view simply to expressing an opinion or to devising a common program of parliamentary action or to directing the expenditure of money appropriated to the use of the two houses. However, the "concurrent resolution" has been shaped to a different and highly important use. It has been employed as a means of claiming for the houses the power to control or recover powers delegated by Congress to the President. Thus the Reorganization Act of 1939 delegated power to the President to regroup certain executive agencies and functions subject to the condition that his orders to that end might be vetoed within sixty days by a concurrent resolution. Similarly, the Lend-Lease Act of 1941, the First War Powers Act of 1941, the Emergency Price Control Act of 1942, the Stabilization Act of 1942, the War Labor Disputes Act of 1943, all rendered the powers which they delegated subject to repeal sooner or later by "concurrent resolution." Congress has gone a step further

[9] Confiscation Cases, 20 Wall. 92, 112, 113 (1874); Catano *v.* Local Board, 298 F. Supp. 1183 (1969).
[10] Lapeyre *v.* U.S., 17 Wall. 191, 198 (1872).
[11] U.S., 54th Congress, 2d. Sess., Senate Report 1335 (1897).

in recent Reorganization Acts by stipulating that a majority of *either* house is enough to veto a Presidential order.[12] That Congress may qualify in this way its delegations of powers which it might withhold altogether would seem to be obvious.[13]

Also, it has been settled by practice, which is generally considered, albeit without sufficient reason, to have been ratified by judicial decision, that resolutions of Congress proposing amendments to the Constitution do not have to be submitted to the President[14] (*see* Article V).

# SECTION VIII

The National Legislative Power

This is one of the most important sections of the Constitution since it describes, for the most part, the field within which Congress may exercise its legislative power, which is also the field to which the President and the National Courts are in great part confined.

Congress's legislative powers may be classified as follows: First, its "enumerated" powers, that is, those which are defined rather specifically in ¶s 1 to 17, following; second, certain other powers which also are specifically or impliedly delegated in other parts of the Constitution (*see* Section IV, above; also Articles II, III, IV, and V, *passim*, and Amendments XIII - XX, and XXIII - XXVI); third, its power conferred by ¶ 18, below, the so-called "coefficient clause" of the Constitution, to

12 William J. Keefe and Morris S. Ogul, *The American Legislative Process* (Englewood Cliffs, N.J., 1968), 442-443; Congressional Quarterly Service, *Congress and the Nation* (Washington, D.C., 1969), II, 658; *U.S. Cong. & Adm. News*, 3487 (1971).

13 On the "concurrent resolution" *see* Edward S. Corwin, *Total War and the Constitution* (New York, 1947), 45-47; U.S., 54th Congress, 2d. Sess., Senate Report 1335 (1897); Howard White, "The Concurrent Resolution in Congress," 35 *American Political Science Review*, 886 (1941). Justice Jackson of the Supreme Court, who was President F. D. Roosevelt's Attorney General at the time of the enactment of the Lend-Lease Act, brought to light a memorandum of Roosevelt's in which the latter contended that the provision of the act giving the Houses of Congress the right to cancel the measure by a simple concurrent resolution, rather than by legislation subject to Presidential veto, was unconstitutional, notwithstanding which, however, he signed the bill for "political reasons." It would appear that President Roosevelt's constitutional qualms were ill-based. Robert H. Jackson, "Presidential Legal Opinion," 66 *Harvard Law Review*, 1353 (1953).

14 Hollingsworth *v.* Va., 3 Dall. 378 (1798). The case arose under Amendment XI after it had been approved by the required number of State legislatures. In these circumstances the Court declined to interfere.

pass all laws "necessary and proper" to carry into execution any of the powers of the National Government, or of any department or officer thereof; fourth, certain "inherent" powers, that is, powers which belong to it simply because it is the national legislature, the outstanding instances of which were listed earlier (*see* p. 6 above).

In studying each of the first seventeen paragraphs of this section, one should always bear in mind ¶18, for this clause furnishes each of the "enumerated" powers of Congress with its second dimension, so to speak.

¶1. The Congress shall have power to lay and collect taxes, duties, imposts and excises, to pay the debts and provide for the common defense and general welfare of the United States; but all duties, imposts and excises shall be uniform throughout the United States.

The Taxing Power

Complete power of taxation is conferred upon Congress by this paragraph, as well as the largest measure of discretion in the selection of purposes for which the national revenues shall be expended. This complete power "to lay and collect taxes" is, however, later curtailed by the provision that no tax shall be levied on exports (*see* Section IX, ¶5) . Also, it was ruled by the Supreme Court, shortly after the Civil War, that on principle Congress could not tax the instrumentalities of State government, and that the salary of a State judge, though in his pocket, was to be regarded as such an instrumentality;[1] and the benefits of this doctrine were subsequently extended to the holders of State and municipal bonds,[2] who were thereby exempted to the extent that their income was derived from such securities from paying income taxes to the National Government. It was at first widely believed that the Sixteenth Amendment had removed the grounds of this discrimination, so far as income taxes were concerned,[3] but the Court eventually ruled otherwise.[4] Indeed, at one time it appeared to be

The Doctrine of Tax Exemption

---

[1] Collector v. Day, 11 Wall. 113 (1870).
[2] Pollock v. Farmers Loan and Trust Co., 157 U.S. 429 and 158 U.S. 601 (1895).
[3] *See* the evidence compiled in Edward S. Corwin, "Constitutional Tax Exemption," *Supplement to the National Municipal Review*, XIII, No. 1 (January 1924).
[4] Brushaber v. Un. Pac. R.R. Co., 240 U.S. 1 (1916); Evans v. Gore, 253 U.S. 245 (1920).

bent on seeing how far it could carry the principle of exemption, going to the length of holding that a manufacturer of motorcycles was not subject to the Federal excise tax on sales thereof with respect to sales to a municipality.[5] The Court has since abandoned this position completely. In Graves v. New York, decided early in 1939, Collector v. Day and New York v. Graves (decided early in 1937) were pronounced "overruled so far as they recognize an implied constitutional immunity from income taxation of the salaries of officers or employees of the national or a State government or their instrumentalities";[6] and it appears highly probable that the same rule would be applied, should Congress choose to invoke it, to the non-discriminatory taxation of income from State and municipal bonds. The power of Congress, however, to exempt national instrumentalities from State taxation, by virtue of the "necessary and proper" clause, still stands[7] (see pp. 225-228). Furthermore, when a State embarks upon an enterprise which if carried on by private concerns would be taxable, like selling liquor or mineral waters, or holding football exhibitions, such activities—once, but no longer, termed "non-governmental"—are subject to a non-discriminatory imposition of applicable national taxes.[8]

Again, Congress must levy its taxes in one of two ways: all "duties, imposts and excises" must be "uniform throughout the United States," that is, the rule of liability to the tax must take no account of geography;[9] while on the other hand, the burden of "direct taxes" must be imposed upon the States in proportion to population (see Section II, ¶3, and Section IX, ¶4).

"Duties" are customs duties. If a certain article imported from abroad is taxed five per cent at New York it must be taxed at the same rate at San Francisco, etc.

"Excises" are taxes upon the production, sale, or use of articles; also taxes upon certain privileges and procedures of a business nature. Congress has for years taxed the privilege of

---

[5] Indian Motorcycle Co. v. U.S., 283 U.S. 570 (1931).
[6] Graves v. N.Y., 306 U.S. 466 (1939).
[7] Pittman v. HOLC, 308 U.S. 21 (1939); United States v. Stewart 311 U.S. 60 (1940). Indeed, the Supreme Court has held that national securities are intrinsically exempt from State taxation. Society for Savings v. Bowers, 349 U.S. 143 (1955).
[8] South Carolina v. U.S., 199 U.S. 437 (1905); Allen v. Regents, 30 U.S. 439 (1938); New York and Saratoga Springs Com'n v. U.S., 326 U.S. 572 (1946); Wilmette Park Dist. v. Campbell, 338 U.S. 411 (1949).
[9] Florida v. Mellon, 273 U.S. 12 (1927).

34

doing business as a corporation, and the Social Security Act of 1935 levies a tax on payrolls.[10]

"Imposts" is a general term comprehending both duties and excises.

From the time of the Carriage Tax case,[11] decided in 1796, to the Income Tax cases of 1895,[12] the Court proceeded on the theory that the "direct tax" clauses should be confined to land taxes and capitation taxes and should not be extended to taxes which were not easily apportionable on the basis of population. But in 1895, convinced by Mr. Joseph H. Choate that the country was about to go Socialistic, a narrowly divided Bench, one Justice—Justice Gray apparently—changing his mind at the last moment, ruled that a tax on incomes derived from property was a "direct tax" and one, therefore, that must be apportioned according to population; also, that incomes derived from State and municipal bonds might not be taxed at all by the National Government. This decision, which put most of the taxable wealth of the country out of the reach of the National Government, led in 1913 to the adoption of the Sixteenth Amendment.

"Direct" Taxes

Nor has the Court, since 1895, invoked its definition of "direct tax" except once in order to overturn a national tax measure, and that was in the Stock Dividend case of 1920[13] (see p. 437). At other times it has been satisfied to sustain challenged taxes on historical grounds as "excises," saying in this connection that "a page of history is worth a volume of logic."[14] Today inheritance taxes are so classified, as are also estate taxes and taxes on gifts, with the result that it is sufficient if they are "uniform throughout the United States" in the geographical sense.[15]

While the raising of revenue is the primary purpose of taxation it does not have to be its only purpose, as the history of the protective tariff suffices to demonstrate. And in the field of excise taxation, if Congress is entitled to regulate a matter, it

10 Flint v. Stone Tracy Co., 220 U.S. 107 (1911); Steward Mach. Co. v. Davis, 301 U.S. 548 (1937).

11 Hylton v. U.S., 3 Dall. 171 (1796).

12 Pollock v. Farmers Loan and Trust Co., 157 U.S. 429 and 158 U.S. 601 (1895).

13 Eisner v. Macomber, 252 U.S. 189 (1920). But for a subsequent view of the Court, see Helvering v. Griffiths, 318 U.S. 371, 404 (1943).

14 New York Trust Co. v. Eisner, 256 U.S. 345, 349 (1921).

15 Ibid.; Knowlton v. Moore, 178 U.S. 41 (1900); Bromley v. McCaughn, 280 U.S. 124 (1929).

Regulation by Taxation
may do so by taxing it.[16] Also, Congress may use its power to tax to require gamblers and marijuana sellers to identify themselves by purchasing tax stamps and/or paying a special occupational tax. But in so doing, Congress must be careful that the legislation does not permit violations of the privilege against self-incrimination for the Court has again and again in recent years held that "a timely and proper assertion of the privilege" is "a complete defense to prosecution" under such measures.[17] As the Court explained in *Marchetti*: "The Constitution of course obliges this Court to give full recognition to the taxing powers and to measures reasonably incidental to their exercise. But we are equally obliged to give full effect to the constitutional restrictions which attend the exercise of those powers.[18] (*See* discussion of self-incrimination clause pp. 318-321.) Furthermore, there are some businesses which Congress may tax so heavily as to drive them out of existence, one example being the production of white sulphur matches, another the sale of oleomargarine colored to look like butter, another the dealing of sawed-off shotguns.[19] On the other hand, the Court some years ago held void a special tax on the profits of concerns employing child labor, on the ground that the act was not a *bona fide* attempt to raise revenue, but represented an effort by Congress to bring within its control matters reserved to the States;[20] and later it set aside a special tax on liquor dealers conducting business in violation of State law, as being a "penalty" and "an invasion of the police power inherent in the States."[21] That such attempts to "psychoanalyze" Congress, as the late Justice Cardozo derisively characterized them,[22] would be repeated today, seems at least doubtful.[23]

[16] Veazie Bank *v.* Fenno, 8 Wall. 533 (1869); Mulford *v.* Smith, 307 U.S. 38 (1939).
[17] Leary *v.* U.S., 395 U.S. 6, 27 (1969). *See also* U.S. *v.* Covington, 395 U.S. 57 (1969); Marchetti *v.* U.S., 390 U.S. 39 (1968); Grosso *v.* U.S., 390 U.S. 62 (1968); U.S. *v.* Freed, 401, U.S. 601 (1971).
[18] Marchetti *v.* U.S., 390 U.S. 39, 58 (1968).
[19] McCray *v.* U.S., 195 U.S. 27 (1904); Sonzinsky *v.* U.S., 300 U.S. 506 (1937); United States *v.* Sanchez, 340 U.S. 42, 44 (1950).
[20] Bailey *v.* Drexel Furniture Co., 259 U.S. 20 (1922).
[21] United States *v.* Constantine, 296 U.S. 287 (1935). For other examples of earlier Supreme Court decisions finding that particular laws purported to be so were not really revenue laws, *see* U.S. *v.* Norton 91 U.S. 566 (1875) and Twin City Bank *v.* Nebeker, 167 U.S. 196 (1897).
[22] United States *v.* Constantine, 296 U.S. 287 (1936).
[23] *See especially* Mulford *v.* Smith, 307 U.S. 38 (1939) and United States *v.* Darby, 312 U.S. 100 (1941). *But see* Marchetti *v.* U.S., 390 U.S. 39, 58-59 (1968) and Leary *v.* U.S., 395 U.S. 6, 21-25 (1969).

The money which it raises by taxation Congress may expend "to pay the debts and provide for the common defense and general welfare of the United States." The important term here is "general welfare of the United States." Madison contended that Congress was empowered by it to tax and spend only to the extent necessary to carry into execution the *other* powers granted by the Constitution to the United States. Hamilton contended that the phrase should be read literally, and that the taxing-spending power was *in addition* to the other powers.[24] Time has vindicated Hamilton. Not only has Congress from the first frequently acted on his view, but the Court has gone out of its way to endorse it. This occurred in the case of United States *v.* Butler,[25] in which, nevertheless, the Court overturned the AAA on the ground that in requiring agriculturists to sign contracts agreeing to curtail production as a condition to their receiving certain payments under it, the act "coerced" said agriculturists in an attempt to "regulate" a matter, namely production, which was reserved to the States. Three Justices dissented on the ground that Congress was entitled when spending the national revenues for "the general welfare" to see to it that the country got its money's worth of "general welfare," and that the condemned contracts were "necessary and proper" to that end. Later cases, moreover, uphold the power of the National Government to spend money in support of unemployment insurance, to provide old-age pensions, to loan money to municipalities to enable them to erect their own electric plants; and, generally, to subsidize by so-called "grants-in-aid" all sorts of welfare programs carried on by the States.[26]

The view has been advanced at times that the clause "provide for the . . . general welfare of the United States" is much more than a mere grant of power to tax and spend for the general welfare, and authorizes Congress to legislate generally for that purpose.[27] This view, however, which would render

*The Spending Power*

*Social Security*

---

[24] On the general subject *see* Edward S. Corwin, "The Spending Power of Congress," 36 *Harvard Law Review*, 548-582 (1923). *Also* Charles Warren, *Congress as Santa Claus* (Charlottesville, Va., 1932).

[25] United States *v.* Butler, 297 U.S. 1 (1936).

[26] Steward Mach. Co. *v.* Davis, 301 U.S. 548 (1937); Helvering *v.* Davis, 301 U.S. 619 (1937); Alabama Power Co. *v.* Ickes, 302 U.S. 464 (1938). On Federal Grants-in-Aid, *see* pp. 108-109 below.

[27] Corwin, "The Spending Power of Congress," *Harvard Law Review*, 548, 550-552; J. F. Lawson, *The General Welfare Clause* (Washington, D.C. 1926).

the succeeding enumeration of powers largely tautological, has never so far been directly countenanced by the Court.

In a novel attempt to have the Vietnam conflict declared unconstitutional, Professor Lawrence B. Velvel filed suit contending among other things that, in taxing and spending for the war, Congress was exceeding its power in that the effort in Vietnam could not be construed as paying the debts or providing for the common defense and general welfare of the United States. The United States Court of Appeals deciding the case on appeal held: "Since congressional appropriations for the war are made under authority of the powers 'to raise and support Armies' and 'to provide and maintain a Navy' such expenditures are not exercises of the power to spend for the general welfare, but rather represent exercises of power under later enumerated powers, powers which are separate and distinct from the grant of authority to tax and spend for the general welfare."[28]

**The Borrowing Power**

¶2. To borrow money on the credit of the United States:

Logically this power would seem to be limited to borrowing money to provide for "the common defense and general welfare of the United States." In practice it is limited only by "the credit of the United States," which today appears to be without limits, inasmuch as the Gross National Debt now tops 450 billions of dollars, a sum more than ten times the size of the debt in 1940. But Congress may not, by any of its powers, alter the terms of outstanding obligations of the United States without providing for compensation to the holders of such obligations for "actual loss";[29] but this, unfortunately, does not signify that, by pursuing inflationary fiscal policies, it may not render such obligations practically worthless without being required to compensate the holders thereof for their loss, which is held to be "incidental" or "consequential" merely, and not a "taking" of property in the sense of Amendment V.[30] May Congress authorize "forced loans" under this clause? Not if history counts for anything. Such a "loan" would not be a loan at all, the element of negotiation being absent from the trans-

[28] Velvel v. Nixon, 415 F. 2d. 236 (1969); cert. denied, 396 U.S. 1042 (1970).

[29] Perry v. U.S., 294 U.S. 330 (1935). See also Lynch v. U.S., 292 U.S. 571 (1934).

[30] Knox v. Lee, 12 Wall. 457 (1871); Norman v. Balt. & O. R.R. Co., 294 U.S. 240 (1935). See also Omnia Com'l Co. v. U.S. 261 U.S. 502 (1923).

action; it would be either a supplementary income tax, or if it took more than "income," would be a capital levy which, to be constitutional, would have to be apportioned among the States.

The above clauses and clauses 5 and 6 following comprise what may be called the fiscal powers of the National Government. By virtue of these, taken along with the necessary and proper clause, Congress has the power to charter national banks, to put their functions beyond the reach of the taxing power of the States, to alter the metal content and value of the coinage of the United States, to issue paper money and confer upon it the quality of legal tender for debts, to invalidate private contracts of debt which call for payment in something other than legal tender, to tax the notes of issue of State banks out of existence, to confer on national banks the powers of trust companies, to establish a "Federal Reserve System," a "Farm Loan Bank," etc.[31] (*See also* ¶5 of this Section.) *Other Fiscal Powers*

¶3. To regulate commerce with foreign nations, and among the several States, and with the Indian tribes: *The Commerce Clause*

"Commerce" is *traffic*, that is, the buying and selling of commodities, and includes as an important incident the *transportation* of such commodities from seller to buyer. But the term has also been defined much more broadly. In the famous case of Gibbons *v.* Ogden,[32] which was decided in 1824, Chief Justice Marshall said: "Commerce undoubtedly is traffic, but it is something more—it is intercourse"; and on the basis of this definition the Supreme Court has held that the mere passage of people from one State to another, as well as the sending of intelligence by telegraph—stock quotations, for instance—from one State to another, is "commerce among the States." Likewise radio broadcasting is "commerce" within this definition, and hence subject to regulation by Congress; as are also the activities of a holding company and its subsidiaries in control and direction of gas and electric companies which are scattered through several States and make continuous use of

---

[31] McCulloch *v.* Md., 4 Wheat. 316 (1819); Knox *v.* Lee, 12 Wall. 457 (1871); Veazie Bank *v.* Fenno, 8 Wall. 533 (1869); Smith *v.* Kansas City T. and T. Co., 255 U.S. 180 (1921); Norman *v.* Balt. & O. R.R. Co., 294 U.S. 240 (1935); Holyoke Water Co. *v.* Am. Writing Paper Co., 300 U.S. 324 (1937); Smyth *v.* U.S., 302 U.S. 329 (1937).
[32] 9 Wheat. 1 (1824).

the mails and the instrumentalities of interstate commerce; also, transactions in insurance which involve two or more States; as well as the gathering of news by a press association and its transmission to client newspapers.[33]

Despite contentions that Congress's power to regulate with respect to foreign commerce differed to some degree from its power with respect to interstate commerce,[34] Chief Justice Taney stated the view which has prevailed: "The power to regulate commerce among the several States is granted to Congress in the same clause, and by the same words, as the power to regulate commerce with foreign nations and is co-extensive with it."[35]

"Among the States," that is, to employ Chief Justice Marshall's words, "that commerce which concerns more States than one," and not "the exclusively internal commerce of a State"; or to use more modern phraseology, *interstate,* in contrast to *intrastate* or *local* commerce.[36]

The power "to regulate" is the power to govern, that is, the power to restrain, to prohibit, to protect, to encourage, to promote, in the furtherance of any public purpose whatsoever, *provided* the constitutional rights of persons be not transgressed. The restrictive aspects of this power have, nevertheless, within recent times been subject, so far as *interstate* commerce is concerned, to an indefinite veto power of the Court, but one which appears today to be in abeyance.

Justice Black, speaking for the Court in 1944, concisely summarized the foregoing: "The power granted Congress is a positive power. It is the power to legislate concerning transactions which, reaching across state boundaries, affect the people of more states than one;—to govern affairs which the individual states, with their limited territorial jurisdictions, are not fully capable of governing."[37] It is within this broad frame-

---

[33] Pensacola Tel. Co. v. Western Un. Tel. Co., 96 U.S. 1 (1877); Western Un. Tel. Co. v. Pendleton, 122 U.S. 347 (1887); Covington Bridge Co. v. Ky., 154 U.S. 204 (1894); International Text Book Co. v. Pigg, 217 U.S. 91 (1910); Western Un. Tel. Co. v. Foster, 247 U.S. 105 (1918); Federal Radio Com'n v. Nelson Bros., 289 U.S. 266 (1933); Electric Bond and Share Co. v. SEC, 303 U.S. 419 (1938); United States v. South-Eastern Underwriters Assoc., 322 U.S. 533 (1944); Associated Press v. U.S., 326 U.S. 1 (1945).
[34] Lottery Case, 188 U.S. 321, 373-374 (1903).
[35] License Cases, 5 How. 504, 578 (1847).
[36] Cf. however, Bob-Lo Excursion Co. v. Michigan, 333 U.S. 28 (1947).
[37] U.S. v. South-Eastern Underwriters Assoc., 322 U.S. 533, 552 (1944).

work that the Supreme Court has been able to uphold efforts to eliminate discrimination through the commerce clause in recent years. The Court upheld the public accommodations provisions of the Civil Rights Act of 1964 as applied against a motel and a family-owned restaurant, businesses which surely would have been regarded in earlier years as local businesses not subject to Congressional regulation under the commerce clause.[38]

Some additional striking assertions as to what can be legitimately encompassed by the commerce clause have currency. In 1968 Congress passed a law making it a crime for anyone "who travels in interstate or foreign commerce . . . to organize, promote, encourage, participate in, or carry on a riot. . . ."[39] The test case on the matter, which involves the Chicago Seven, has yet to make its way through the Supreme Court. It is significant, however that the U.S. Court of Appeals, by a 2-1 vote, held the act constitutional (41 *LW* 2283, 1972).

A United States District Court has held that Congress had a rational basis for finding that air pollution affected commerce.[40] That decision recalls a startling proposition conjured up a few years ago by the Chief of the Environmental Health Branch of HEW. In discussing pollution control, he wrote: "The validity of the exercise of such power by Congress must therefore hinge on the determination that the movement of such pollution is *itself* commerce."[41] But the Supreme Court has relied on other concepts to uphold Congressional efforts to rid the nation of pollution. One, the idea that Congress has the power to outlaw "obstructions" (broadly interpreted) in interstate or navigable waters.[42] Two, the idea that "It is a fair and reasonable demand on the part of the sovereign that the air over its territory should not be polluted on a great scale. . . ."[43]

<sup></sup>*Pollution*

*Commerce as Transportation*

Historically, until the early Thirties, Congress had exercised its powers over interstate commerce, for the most part, only

---

[38] Heart of Atlanta Motel, Inc. *v.* U.S., 379 U.S. 241 (1964); Katzenbach *v.* McClung, 379 U.S. 294 (1964).
[39] 18 U.S.C. 2101.
[40] U.S. *v.* Bishop Processing Co., 287 F. Supp. 624 (1968).
[41] Sidney Edelman, "Federal Air and Water Control. . . ." *George Washington Law Review*, 1067, 1071-1072 (1965).
[42] U.S. *v.* Standard Oil Co., 384 U.S. 224 (1966); Illinois *v.* City of Milwaukee, 406 U.S. 91 (1972).
[43] Illinois *v.* City of Milwaukee, 406 U.S. 91, 104 (1972).

over interstate *transportation*, and especially transportation by rail. Since the power to regulate is the power to promote, it was determined early that Congress could build railways and bridges, or charter corporations and authorize them to build railways and bridges; and it could vest such corporations with the power of eminent domain and render their franchises immune from State taxation.[44] For the like reason the Court, in the Adamson Act case of 1916,[45] recognized that Congress had very wide discretion in dealing with an emergency which threatened to stop interstate transportation. When, however, Congress sought in 1933 to invoke the same principle in behalf of the commerce in the sense of *traffic*, in the enactment of the NIRA, the Court declined to give any weight to the emergency justification.[46] Later decisions eliminated this difference between Congress's power over "commerce" in the sense of *transportation* and commerce in the sense of *traffic*.

Requisites of Rate Regulation
Again, Congress may regulate the rates of transportation from one State to another, or authorize an agent like the Interstate Commerce Commission, to do so.[47] But the rates set must yield a "fair return" to the carrier on the "value" of its property, the theory being that since this property is being used in the service of the public, to compel its public use without just compensation would amount to confiscation.[48] (*See* the "private property" clause of Amendment V.)

But just how is such "value" to be ascertained? For many years two formulas competed for the Court's favor. One, "reproduction less depreciation," implied that "fair value" should be deemed the equivalent of what it would cost to reproduce the road at current prices, minus an allowance for the road's depreciation. The other, the "historical cost" or "original prudent investment" formula, suggested that the company was entitled to get a fair return on what it had actually put into the road in dollars and cents, less again allowance for deteriora-

---

[44] California v. Cent. Pac. R.R. Co., 127 U.S. 1 (1888); Luxton v. No. River B. Co., 153 U.S. 525 (1894).

[45] Wilson v. New, 243 U.S. 332 (1917).

[46] Schechter Bros. Corp. v. U.S., 295 U.S. 495 (1935).

[47] For a remarkable argument against the power of Congress to regulate rates, based on extreme *laissez-faire* principles, *see* the speech of Senator William M. Evarts of New York in the course of the debate on the bill to establish the Interstate Commerce Commission. 18 *Cong. Rec.*, 603-604 (1887).

[48] Smyth v. Ames, 169 U.S. 466 (1898).

tion. The former theory, which until the 1940's was favored by the Court, was considerate of the casual investor's interest in an era of rising prices, but by the same token supplied to shifting a basis for rate-making as to be administratively impracticable.[49] The latter theory escaped this disadvantage, and was also a logical corollary of the legal doctrine upon which rate regulation originally rested, namely, that the property of a common carrier, or other public utility, was "impressed with a public use" and its business "affected with a public interest" *from the very outset*, and that investors were forewarned of this fact. However, the Court has since the 1940's been disposed to leave the whole business to the regulatory authority, *provided* it affords a fair opportunity to be heard to the interests affected.[50] It had become clear to the Court by that time that the determination of "fair value" was a more complicated matter than it had thought in earlier times. Actually there were more than just the two aforementioned theories being pressed on the Court.[51] Where the Court had found in 1890 that "The question of reasonableness of a rate . . . is eminently a question for *judicial* investigation, requiring due process of law for its determination"[52] (emphasis supplied), the Court conceded in 1944: "It is not theory but the impact of the rate order which counts. If the total effect of the rate order cannot be said to be unjust and unreasonable, judicial inquiry under the Act is at an end. The fact that the method employed to reach that result may contain infirmities is not then important. Moreover, the Commission's order does not become suspect by reason of the fact that it is challenged. It is the product of expert judgment which carries a presumption of validity. And he who would upset the rate order under the Act carries the heavy burden of making a convincing showing that it is invalid because it is unjust and unreasonable in its consequences."[53]

[49] *See* briefs and opinions in St. Louis and O'Fallon R. Co. *v.* U.S., 279 U.S. 461 (1929), and cases there cited.

[50] *See* Driscoll *v.* Edison Light and P. Co., 307 U.S. 104 (1939); Federal Power Com'n *v.* Natural Gas Pipeline Co., 315 U.S. 575 (1942); Federal Power Com'n *v.* Hope Natural Gas Co., 320 U.S. 591 (1944); Colorado Interstate Gas Co. *v.* FPC, 324 U.S. 581 (1945).

[51] For a concise description of theories available *see* U.S., 88th Cong., 1st Sess., Senate Document 39 (1964) pp. 1117-1120.

[52] Chicago, Milwaukee and St. Paul Railway Co. *v.* Minnesota, 134 U.S. 418, 458 (1890).

[53] Federal Power Com'n *v.* Hope Natural Gas Co., 320 U.S. 591, 602 (1944).

National
Supremacy

In the Shreveport case,[54] decided in 1914, the Court ruled that "wherever the interstate and intrastate transactions of carriers are so related that the government of the one involves the control of the other," Congress is entitled to regulate both classes of transactions. In other words, whenever circumstances make it "necessary and proper" for Congress to regulate *local* transportation in order to make its control of *interstate* transportation really effective, it may do so—a principle to which the Transportation Act of 1920 gave new application and extension.[55] Similarly, Congress, in protecting interstate telephone messages, may prohibit the disclosure of intercepted intrastate messages;[56] and in sustaining the Fair Labor Standards Act of 1938[57] the Court reached even more striking results. (*See* pp. 51-52 below.)

Instruments
and Agents
of Trans-
portation

Furthermore, Congress may regulate the *instruments* and *agents* of interstate transportation; and hence may protect them from injury from any source, whether *interstate* or *local* in character. Thus, when cars engaged in local transportation are hauled as part of a train along with cars which are engaged in interstate transportation, the former as well as the latter must be provided with the safety appliances which are required by the Federal Safety Appliance Act, otherwise they might impede or endanger the interstate transportation.[58] And it is on an extension of this principle that the Federal Employers' Liability Act of 1908 rests, which modified the rules of the common law of the States for determining the liability of railways engaged in interstate commerce to those of their employees who are injured while employed in connection with such commerce.[59]

When, however, Congress, in 1934, passed an act requiring railway carriers to contribute to a pension fund for superannuated employees, the Court, five Justices to four, held the act void both as violative of the "due process" clause of the Fifth

[54] 234 U.S. 342.
[55] 49 U.S.C. 13 (4); Wisconsin *v.* C.B. & A. R.R. Co., 257 U.S. 563 (1922). But a determination of the I.C.C. superseding a local rate set by a State commission may be set aside by the Supreme Court as being in excess of the I.C.C.'s power under the Act of 1920, Illinois Com. Com'n *v.* Thomson, 318 U.S. 675 (1943); Alabama *v.* U.S., 325 U.S. 535 (1945).
[56] Weiss *v.* U.S., 308 U.S. 321 (1939).
[57] 29 U.S.C. 201-219.
[58] Southern Ry. Co. *v.* U.S., 222 U.S. 20 (1911). For a parallel case, involving bills of lading considered as instruments of interstate commerce, *see* United States *v.* Ferger, 250 U.S. 199 (1919).
[59] 45 U.S.C. ch. 2; Second Employers' Liability Cases, 223 U.S. 1 (1912).

Amendment and as not falling within the power to regulate interstate commerce.[60] The measure, Justice Roberts said, had "no relation to the promotion of efficiency . . . by separating the unfit from the industry." Chief Justice Hughes, on the other hand, speaking for the minority, denied that Congress's power to regulate commerce and to "make all laws which shall be necessary and proper" to that end was limited merely to securing efficiency. "The fundamental consideration which supports this type of legislation," said he "is that industry should take care of its human wastage, whether that is due to accident or age";[61] and it followed that Congress could require interstate carriers to live up to this obligation. Subsequently, when Congress passed legislation very similar to that rejected by the Court in 1935, its constitutionality was not seriously questioned.[62]

The fact that in an earlier time Congressional regulation of interstate transportation focused on railroads was not of legal consequence. It was just that other modes of transportation were developed later. It was established early that other modes and instrumentalities of interstate transportation like trucking, airlines, and pipelines were as subject to regulation by Congress as railroads.[63] But it was not until New Deal days that Congress moved to regulate comprehensively in these other areas of transportation (Federal Communications Act of 1934; Federal Motor Carrier Act of 1935; Civil Aeronautics Act of 1938).

Navigation, too, is a branch of transportation and so of commerce, and the power to regulate it includes the power to protect navigable streams from obstruction and to improve their navigability, as by the erection of dams.[64] Furthermore, as was held in 1940, in the case of United States v. Appalachian Electric Power Co., this power does not stop with the needs of *navigation*, but embraces also flood control, watershed development, and the production of electric power by the erection of dams in "navigable streams." Nor is the term "naviga-

*Navigation and Super-Power*

---

[60] Railroad Retirement Bd. v. Alton R.R. Co., 295 U.S. 330 (1935).
[61] *Ibid.*, at 384.
[62] 45 U.S.C. 228, 261-273; 351-367; *see* Railroad Board v. Duquesne Co., 326 U.S. 446 (1946); and Mandeville Farms v. Sugar Co., 334 U.S. 219, 230 (1948).
[63] The Pipeline Cases, 234 U.S. 548 (1914); Buck v. Kukendall, 267 U.S. 307 (1925).
[64] United States v. Chandler-Dunbar Co., 229 U.S. 53 (1913); and cases there reviewed.

ble streams" any longer confined by the Court, as once it was, to streams which are "navigable in their natural condition," but also includes, under the holding just mentioned, those which may be rendered navigable by "reasonable improvements."[65] And any electrical power developed at such a dam is "property belonging to the United States" (see Article IV, Section III, ¶2), in disposing of which, it was held in the TVA case,[66] the United States may, in order to reach a distant market, purchase transmission lines from a private company. Indeed, the Court will not intervene to prevent the Government from attempting to create a market for its electrical power by staking potential customers, as by authorizing loans to municipalities to enable them to go into the business of furnishing their residents power which they would purchase from the United States.[67] However convincing the argument may be for allowing the sale of electrical power developed as a consequence of building dams, the argument that Congress can authorize TVA to build steam plants (which obviously do not come as a result of damming) to generate electricity for sale under its power to regulate commerce is less convincing. Yet two Federal courts had no difficulty finding that TVA's "Paradise Steam Plant and the transmission lines connecting it with the TVA system are parts of an integrated system of multipurpose dams, steam plants, and transmission lines, which together improve navigation, help control floods, produce power, and serve generally to develop the Tennessee River watershed and are authorized by the commerce clause of the Constitution...."[68]

Commerce as Traffic   But, as was indicated above, the primitive subject-matter of Congress's power of regulation is *traffic*, that is, the purchase and sale of commodities among the States. This is indicated by the etymology of the word: L. *cum merce*, "with merchandise." The first important piece of legislation to govern inter-

---

[65] United States v. Appalachian Elec. P. Co., 311 U.S. 377 (1940); Oklahoma *ex rel* Phillips v. Atkinson Co., 313 U.S. 508, 523-534 *passim* (1941). For the earlier view, cf. *The Daniel Ball*, 10 Wall. 557 (1870).

[66] Ashwander v. TVA, 297 U.S. 288 (1935).

[67] Alabama Power Co. v. Ickes, 302 U.S. 464 (1938).

[68] U.S. v. An Easement and Right-of-Way, 246 F. Supp. 263, 270 (1965); *affirmed* 375 F. 2d. 120 (1967). In answer to our query in January 1972, the General Counsel of TVA wrote: "Based on our current docket we do not expect the question of TVA's constitutional and statutory authority to build and operate steam plants to be before the Supreme Court in the foreseeable future."

state commerce in this sense was the Sherman Anti-Trust Act of 1890,[69] the opening section of which declares "illegal" "every contract, combination in the form of trust or otherwise, or conspiracy in restraint of trade or commerce among the several States, or with foreign nations." The main purpose of the act was to check the development of industrial trusts; but in the first important case to arise under it, the Sugar Trust case of 1895,[70] the Court held that its provisions could not be constitutionally applied to a combination which was admitted to manufacture ninety-eight per cent of the refined sugar used in the United States, inasmuch as manufacture and commerce were distinct and the control of the former belonged solely to the States. Any effect of a contract with respect to manufacturing or production upon commerce among the States, the Court asserted, "would be an indirect result, however inevitable and whatever its extent," and hence would be beyond the power of Congress. Only the States, therefore, could deal with industrial monopolies.

*The Sherman Act and later Acts Regulating Traffic*

The effect of this holding was to put the Anti-Trust Act to sleep for a decade, during which period most of the great industrial trusts of today got their start. But in the Swift case,[71] ten years later, the Court largely abandoned this mode of approach for the view that where the facts show "an established course of business" which involves "a current of commerce" among the States in a certain commodity, Congress is entitled to govern the local incidents of such current. Thus the Anti-Trust Act was formally held to reach labor combinations interruptive of commerce among the States,[72] and while the Court later largely retracted this construction of the act, it did not do so on constitutional grounds.[73] And meantime, in sustaining

[69] 15 U.S.C. ch. 1.

[70] United States *v.* E. C. Knight Co., 156 U.S. 1 (1895). As Justice Harlan contended, in his notable dissenting opinion, the doctrine of the case boiled down to the proposition that commerce was transportation simply. Actually, however, he pointed out, "both the Court and counsel recognized buying and selling or barter as *included in commerce.*" His conclusion was that "whatever a State may do to protect its completely interior traffic or trade against unlawful restraints, the general government is empowered to do for the protection of the people of all the states." *Ibid.* 22-42 *passim.*

[71] Swift and Co. *v.* U.S., 196 U.S. 375 (1905).

[72] Bedford Cut Stone Co. *v.* Journeymen, 274 U.S. 37 (1927), and cases there reviewed.

[73] *See* especially Apex Hosiery Co. *v.* Leader, 310 U.S. 469 (1940); and United States *v.* Hutcheson 312 U.S. 219 (1941).

in 1922 the Packers and Stockyards Act[74] of the previous year the Court, speaking by Chief Justice Taft, had asserted broadly: "Whatever amounts to a more or less constant practice, and threatens to obstruct or unduly to burden the freedom of interstate commerce is within the regulatory power of Congress under the commerce clause, and it is primarily for Congress to consider and decide the fact of the danger and meet it. This Court will certainly not substitute its judgment for that of Congress in such a matter unless the relation of the subject to interstate commerce and its effects upon it are clearly nonexistent."[75]

To return for a moment to the Sherman Act—a decision in 1944, supported however by only a bare majority of the seven Justices participating in it, held that it applied to fire insurance transactions carried on across State lines, although when the act was passed, and for long afterwards, it was the doctrine of the Court that the business of insurance was not "commerce" in the sense of the Constitution.[76] And later the act was projected into the amusement field—to football; to the promotion of boxing on a multiple scale, coupled with sale of television, broadcast and film rights; to the business of booking and presenting theatrical attractions (plays, musicals and operettas).[77]

The "New Deal" Constitutional Revolution  In June 1933, Congress enacted that nine-day wonder, the National Industrial Recovery Act ("NIRA"), which, among other things, attempted to govern hours of labor and wages in productive industry, on the theory, in part, that in the circum-

[74] 7 U.S.C. ch. 9.

[75] Stafford *v.* Wallace, 258 U.S. 495 at 521 (1922). The statement is repeated in Board of Trade *v.* Olsen, 262 U.S. 137 (1923). *See also* 259 U.S. at 408.

[76] United States *v.* South-Eastern Underwriters Assoc., 322 U.S. 533 (1944). The earlier cases holding the business of insurance not to be "commerce" are reviewed in Justice Black's opinion. They are headed by Paul *v.* Va., 8 Wall. 168 (1868).

[77] Radovich *v.* National Football League, 352 U.S. 445 (1957); United States *v.* Boxing Club of New York, 348 U.S. 236 (1955); United States *v.* Shubert, 348 U.S. 222 (1955). Baseball continues to be treated as an exception. In 1972 the Supreme Court held that although "Professional baseball is a business and it is engaged in interstate commerce." . . . We continue to be loathe, fifty years after *Federal Baseball* and almost two decades after *Toolson*, to overturn those cases judicially when Congress, by its positive inaction has allowed those decisions to stand for so long and, far beyond mere inference and implication, has clearly evinced a desire not to disapprove them legislatively." Flood *v.* Kuhn, 407 U.S. 258, 283 (1972).

stances of the then existing emergency they affected commerce among the States. The act, however, was set aside by the Court in the *Poultry* ("*Sick Chicken*") case, largely on the basis of the doctrine of the old *Sugar Trust* case; and in the spring of 1936 the same doctrine was reiterated by the Court in setting aside the Guffey Coal Conservation Act of 1935, although the trial court had found that as a matter of fact interstate commerce in soft coal had been repeatedly interrupted for long periods by disputes between owners and workers on questions of hours of labor and of wages.[78]

This extremely artificial view of the subject has since been abandoned. In the *Jones-Laughlin* case and attendant cases,[79] decided on April 12, 1937, a five-to-four Court, speaking by Chief Justice Hughes, declined longer "to deal with the question of direct and indirect effects in an intellectual vacuum," and held that the question whether incidents of the employer-employee relationship in productive industries affected interstate commerce was one of fact and degree; and on this ground held that the Wagner Labor Relations Act of 1935, which requires employers to permit their employees freely to organize and to bargain with them collectively, was constitutionally applicable to certain manufacturing companies seeking an interstate market for their products. But the doctrine of the case applies also to "natural" products, to coal mined, to stone quarried, to fruit and vegetables grown;[80] nor is it restricted "by the smallness of the volume of the commerce affected in any particular case."[81]

Also Congress—subject no doubt to the due process clause of Amendment V—may regulate the prices of commodities sold in interstate commerce, and even the local prices of commodities which affect the interstate prices thereof.[82] Indeed, the power to regulate rates of transportation sometimes carries with it the power to regulate the price of the commodity transported, as in the case of gas and electric power.[83]

---

[78] Schechter Bros. *v.* U.S., 295 U.S. 495 (1935); Carter *v.* Carter Coal Co., 298 U.S. 238 (1936).
[79] National Labor Relations Bd. *v.* Jones & L. Steel Corp., 301 U.S. 1 (1937).
[80] Santa Cruz Fruit Packing Co. *v.* NLRB, 303 U.S. 453 (1938).
[81] National Labor Relations Bd. *v.* Fainblatt, 306 U.S. 601 (1939).
[82] United States *v.* Rock Royal Co-op, 307 U.S. 533 (1939).
[83] *See* Public Utilities Com'n *v.* Attleboro Steam and Elec. Co., 273 U.S. 83 (1927); Sunshine Anthracite Coal Co. *v.* Adkins, 310 U.S. 381 (1940); Federal Power Com'n *v.* Natural Gas Pipeline Co., 315 U.S. 575 (1942);

Prohibitions of Commerce

It was assumed by the Framers of the Constitution that the power to regulate commerce included the power to prohibit it at the will of the regulatory body. Proof of this is afforded by the provision of Article I, Section IX, which forbade Congress to put a stop to the slave trade until 1808; and one of the constitutional amendments which were suggested early in 1861 for the purpose of settling the slavery question would have forbidden Congress to prohibit the interstate slave trade. As to commerce with foreign nations, moreover, this doctrine has been frequently illustrated from an early date, as in the case of tariff and embargo legislation.[84] As to commerce among the States, on the other hand, the doctrine had come to be established after 1900 that Congress was not ordinarily entitled to prohibit such commerce if its doing so would enable it to control matters which were in the past regulated by the States when they were regulated at all.[85]

Yet, even during the period just referred to, the Court repeatedly recognized that the welfare of interstate commerce as a whole might require that certain portions of it be prohibited, as, for instance, the shipment of high explosives, except under stringent regulations. Indeed it presently went much farther, and laid down this doctrine: "Congress can certainly regulate interstate commerce to the extent of forbidding and punishing the use of such commerce as an agency to promote immorality, dishonesty, or the spread of any evil or harm to the people of other States from the State of origin. In doing this, it is merely exercising the police power, for the benefit of the public, within the field of interstate commerce."[86] And proceeding on this basis, Congress has prohibited the knowing transportation of lottery tickets from one

"Cooperative Federalism"

State to another; of impure or falsely branded foods; of "filled" milk; of women for immoral purposes; of liquor; of stolen automobiles; of stolen goods in general; while by the so-called

Federal Power Com'n v. Hope Natural Gas Co., 320 U.S. 591 (1944); Colorado Interstate Gas Co. v. F.P.C., 324 U.S. 581 (1945); Federal Power Com'n v. East Ohio Gas Co., 338 U.S. 464 (1950).

[84] Hampton, Jr. & Co. v. U.S. 276 U.S. 394 (1928); University of Illinois v. U.S., 289 U.S. 48 (1933); United States v. Curtiss-Wright Export Corp., 299 U.S. 304 (1936).

[85] See Edward S. Corwin, The Commerce Power versus States Rights (Princeton, 1936) chs. II and III; and "The Power of Congress to Prohibit Commerce," Douglas B. Maggs (ed.), Selected Essays on Constitutional Law, III (Chicago, 1938), 103-129.

[86] Brooks v. U.S., 267 U.S. 432, 436 (1925).

"Lindbergh Law" of 1932 it has made kidnapping, when the victim is taken across State lines, a crime against the United States; and all these measures have been duly sustained by the Court, or their validity has not been challenged before it.[87] Whether or not the First Amendment will be held a bar to the exercise of this police power to forbid people to move in interstate commerce for the purpose of rioting remains to be seen as indicated earlier (p. 41).

Nevertheless, when in 1916 Congress endeavored to break up a widespread traffic in child-made goods, by forbidding the transportation of such goods outside the State where produced, it was informed, in the case of Hammer *v.* Dagenhart,[88] by a closely divided Court, that it was not regulating commerce among the States but was invading "the reserved powers of the States," meaning thereby the power of the States over the employer-employee relationship in productive industry. But as Justice Holmes pointed out in his celebrated dissenting opinion, while a State is free to permit production for its own local market to take place under any conditions whatever, so far as national power is concerned, when it seeks a market outside its boundaries for its products it is no longer within its rights, but enters a field where before the Constitution was adopted it could have been met by the prohibitions of sister States, and where under the Constitution Congress is entitled to govern.[89] What is more, as the decisions stood at that date, *both* Congress and the States were forbidden to prohibit the free flow of the products of child labor from one State to another—the former on the ground that it would be usurping power reserved to the States; the latter on the ground that they would be usurping Congress's power to regulate commerce![90]

This gap in governmental authority in this country was soon closed. In the notable case of United States *v.* Darby[91] the Court gave a clean bill-of-health to the Fair Labor Standards

*The "New Deal" Constitutional Revolution Completed*

[87] 18 U.S.C., 1201; Champion *v.* Ames, 188 U.S. 321 (1903); Hipolite Egg Co. *v.* U.S., 220 U.S. 45 (1911); Hoke *v.* U.S., 227 U.S. 308 (1913); Clark Distilling Co. *v.* W. Md. Ry., 242 U.S. 311 (1917); Brooks *v.* U.S., 267 U.S. 432 (1925); Gooch *v.* U.S., 297 U.S. 124 (1936); United States *v.* Carolene Products Co., 304 U.S. 144 (1938). But *see* U.S. *v.* Bass, 404 U.S. 336 (1971).

[88] 247 U.S. 251 (1918). [89] *Ibid.*, 277-281.

[90] *See* Edward S. Corwin, *The Twilight of the Supreme Court* (New Haven, 1934), 26-37.

[91] 312 U.S. 100 (1941).

51

Act of 1938, which not only prohibits interstate transportation of goods produced by labor whose hours of work and wages do not conform to the standards imposed under the act, but even interdicts the production of such goods "for commerce." The decision, which explicitly overrules Hammer v. Dagenhart, invokes both the commerce clause and the necessary and proper clause. Subsequently the Court has held that the caretakers of a 22-story building in New York City were covered by the act, heat being essential to warm the fingers of the seamstresses employed by a clothing manufacturer who rented space in the building and who sold goods across State lines,[92] likewise, the maintenance employees of the central office building of a manufacturing corporation engaging in interstate commerce in a product coming from plants located elsewhere;[93] also the employees of a window-cleaning company, the greater part of whose work was done on the windows of industrial plants producing goods for interstate commerce;[94] etc., etc. In the second of the above cases Chief Justice Stone and Justice Roberts had indeed protested, albeit unavailingly, against the "house-that-Jack-built chain of causation" whereby "the sweep of the statute" was extended to "the ultimate *causa causarum* which result in the production of goods for commerce."[95] Quite justifiably Justice Roberts remarked in his Holmes Lectures for 1951, that the Fair Labor Standards Act today places "the whole matter of wages and hours of persons employed in the United States, with slight exceptions, under a single federal regulatory scheme and in this way . . . supersedes state exercise of the police power in this field."[96]

And in Wickard v. Filburn, decided some months after the *Darby* case, a still deeper penetration by Congress into the field of production was sustained. As amended by the act of 1941, the Agricultural Adjustment Act of 1938,[97] regulates production even when not intended for commerce but wholly for consumption on the producer's farm. Sustaining this extension of the act, the Court pointed out that the effect of the statute

[92] Kirschbaum v. Walling, 316 U.S. 517 (1942).
[93] Borden Co. v. Borella, 325 U.S. 679 (1945).
[94] Martino v. Mich. Window Cleaning Co., 327 U.S. 173 (1946).
[95] 325 U.S. 679, 685.
[96] Owen J. Roberts, *The Court and the Constitution* (Cambridge, Mass. 1951) 56. *See* Mitchell v. H. B. Zachry Co., 362 U.S. 310 (1960).
[97] 52 *Stat.* 31.

was to support the market. It said: "It can hardly be denied that a factor of such volume and variability as home-consumed wheat would have a substantial influence on price and market conditions. This may arise because being in marketable condition such wheat overhangs the market and, if induced by rising prices, tends to flow into the market and check price increases. But if we assume that it is never marketed, it supplies a need of the man who grew it which would otherwise be reflected by purchases in the open market. Home-grown wheat in this sense competes with wheat in commerce. The stimulation of commerce is a use of the regulatory function quite as definitely as prohibitions or restrictions thereon. This record leaves us in no doubt that Congress may properly have considered that wheat consumed on the farm where grown, if wholly outside the scheme of regulation, would have a substantial effect in defeating and obstructing its purpose to stimulate trade therein at increased prices." And it elsewhere stated: "Questions of the power of Congress are not to be decided by reference to any formula which would give controlling force to nomenclature such as 'production' and 'indirect' and foreclose consideration of the actual effects of the activity in question upon interstate commerce. . . . The Court's recognition of the relevance of the economic effects in the application of the Commerce Clause, . . . has made the mechanical application of legal formulas no longer feasible."[98]

It was also in reliance on its power to prohibit interstate commerce and to exert like power over the mails that Congress enacted the Securities Exchange Act of 1934 and the Public Utility Holding Company Act ("Wheeler-Rayburn Act") of 1935.[99] The former authorized the Securities and Exchange Commission, which it created, to lay down regulations designed to keep dealing in securities honest and above-board and closed the channels of interstate commerce and the mails to dealers refusing to register under the act. The latter required, by sections 4 (a) and 5, the companies which are governed by it to register with the Securities and Exchange Commission and to inform it concerning their business, organization and financial structure, all on pain of being prohibited use of the facilities of interstate commerce and the mails; while by section 11, the so-called "death sentence" clause, the

[98] Wickard v. Filburn, 317 U.S. 111, 128-129 (1942).
[99] 48 Stat. 881 (1934); 49 Stat. 803 (1935).

same act closed after a certain date the channels of interstate communication to certain types of public utility companies whose operations, Congress found, were calculated chiefly to exploit the investing and consuming public. All of the above provisions were sustained.[100]

**The Commerce Clause as a Restraint on the States**

The commerce clause comprises, however, not only the direct source of the most important peace-time powers of the National Government; it is also, except for the Due Process of Law Clause of Amendment XIV, the most important basis for judicial review in limitation of State power. The latter, or restrictive, operation of the clause was, in fact, long the more important one from the point of view of Constitutional Law. Of the approximately 1400 cases which reached the Supreme Court under the clause prior to 1900, the overwhelming proportion stemmed from State legislation.[101] It resulted that, except for the great case of Gibbons v. Ogden, which was dealt with above, the guiding lines in construction of the clause were initially laid down by the Court from the point of view of its operation as a curb on State power, rather than of its operation as a source of national power; and the consequence of this was that the word "commerce," as designating the thing to be protected against State interference, long came to dominate the clause, while the potential word "regulate" remained in the background. The correction of this bias was the very essence of "the Constitutional Revolution" which culminated in United States v. Darby.

Unquestionably, one of the great advantages anticipated from the grant to Congress of power over commerce was that State interferences with trade, which had become a source of sharp discontent under the Articles of Confederation, would be thereby brought to an end. As Webster stated in his argument for appellant in Gibbons v. Ogden: "The prevailing motive was to regulate commerce; to rescue it from the embarrassing and destructive consequences, resulting from the legislation of so many different States, and to place it under the protection of a uniform law." In other words, the constitutional grant was itself a regulation of commerce in the interest of

---

[100] Electric Bond and Share Co. v. S.E.C., 303 U.S. 419 (1938); North American Co. v. S.E.C., 327 U.S. 686 (1946); American Power and Light Co., v. S.E.C., 329 U.S. 90 (1946).

[101] E. Parmalee Prentice and John G. Egan, *The Commerce Clause and the Federal Constitution* (Chicago, 1898), 14. The balance began to be adjusted with the enactment of the Interstate Commerce Act in 1887.

uniformity. Justice Johnson's testimony in his concurring opinion in the same case is to like effect: "There was not a State in the Union, in which there did not, at that time, exist a variety of commercial regulations; . . . By common consent, those laws dropped lifeless from their statute books, for want of sustaining power that had been relinquished to Congress";[102] and Madison's assertion, late in life, that power had been granted Congress over interstate commerce mainly as "a negative and preventive provision against injustice among the States,"[103] carries a like implication.

The first case in which the clause was treated by the Court as a *limitation* on State power was Brown *v.* Maryland,[104] decided in 1827. Here Marshall laid down the double rule that a State may not tax goods imported *from abroad* so long as they remained in the "original package" *in the hands of the importer*; and that the right to import includes the right to sell. This doctrine still remains the basic law on the subject, a unique instance of longevity in this general field, which may be described as a graveyard of discarded concepts. (But *see* p. 105.)

State Taxation Affecting Commerce

Practically, foreign commerce is one thing, interstate commerce, a quite different thing. The latter is conducted in the interior of the country by persons and corporations that are ordinarily engaged also in local business; its usual incidents are acts which, if unconnected with commerce among the States, would fall within the State's powers of police and taxation; while the things it deals in and the instruments by which it is carried on comprise the most ordinary subject matter of State power. In this field the Court has, consequently, been unable to rely upon sweeping solutions. To the contrary, its judgments have often been fluctuating and tentative, even contradictory; and this is particularly the case as respects the infringement of the State taxing power on interstate commerce. In the words of Justice Frankfurter: "The power of the States to tax and the limitations upon that power imposed by the Commerce Clause have necessitated a long, continuous process of judicial adjustment. The need for such adjustment

The Court's Problem Today

[102] 9 Wheat. 1, 226 (1824).

[103] James Madison, *Letters and Other Writings*, IV (Philadelphia, 1865), 14-15.

[104] 12 Wheat. 419 (1827). The benefits of this holding were extended as recently as 1945 to certain imports from the Philippine Islands. Hooven and Allison Co. *v.* Evatt, 324 U.S. 652 (1945).

is inherent in a Federal Government like ours, where the same transaction has aspects that may concern the interests and involve the authority of both the central government and the constituent States. The history of this problem is spread over hundreds of volumes of our Reports. To attempt to harmonize all that has been said in the past would neither clarify what has gone before nor guide the future. Suffice it to say that especially in this field opinions must be read in the setting of the particular cases and as the product of preoccupation with their special facts."[105]

The "Police Power" vis-à-vis Commerce
But while Justice Frankfurter was speaking primarily with the State's taxing power in mind, his words apply also to the Court's work in endeavoring to draw the line between the commercial interest and the State's police power. In this field the great leading case prior to the Civil War, one which is still invoked by the Court was Cooley v. Board of Wardens of the Port of Philadelphia,[106] decided in 1851. The question at issue was the validity of a Pennsylvania pilotage act so far as it applied to vessels engaged in foreign commerce and the coastwise trade. The Court, speaking through Justice Curtis, sustained the act on the basis of a distinction, which was earlier advanced by Webster in Gibbons v. Ogden, between those subjects of commerce which "imperatively demand a single uniform rule" operating throughout the country and those which "as imperatively" demand "that diversity which alone can meet the local necessities of navigation," that is to say, of commerce. As to the former, the Court held Congress's power to be "exclusive"; as to the latter it held that the States enjoyed a power of "concurrent legislation." These general propositions are still good law.[107] But they were (and are) too general to resolve all the complicated cases which arose when States exercised their "concurrent" power. Consequently, following the Civil War, other formulas emerged from the judicial smithy, several of which were brought together into something like a doctrinal system, in Justice Hughes's comprehensive opinion for the Court in the Minnesota Rate cases[108] decided in 1913. "Direct" regulation of foreign or interstate commerce

[105] Freeman v. Hewit, 329 U.S. 249, 251 (1946).
[106] 12 How. 299 (1851).
[107] Florida Avocado Growers v. Paul, 373 U.S. 132, 143 (1963); Colorado Com'n v. Continental, 372 U.S. 714, 718 (1963); Toye Bros. Yellow Cab Co. v. Irby, 437, F. 2d. 806, 809 (1971).
[108] Simpson v. Shepard, 230 U.S. 352, 402 (1913).

by a State was held to be out of the question. At the same time, it was held that the States have their police and taxing powers and may use them as their own views of sound public policy may dictate, even though interstate commerce may be "incidentally" or "indirectly" regulated, it being understood that such "incidental" or "indirect" effects are always subject to Congressional disallowance. "Our system of government," Justice Hughes reflects, "is a practical adjustment by which the National authority as conferred by the Constitution is maintained in its full scope without unnecessary loss of local efficiency."

In more concrete terms, the varied formulas which characterize this branch of our Constitutional Law have been devised by the Court from time to time in an endeavor to effect "a practical adjustment" between two great interests, the maintenance of freedom of commerce *except so far as Congress may choose to restrain it,* and the maintenance in the States of efficient local governments. Thus, while formulas may serve to steady and guide its judgment, the Court's real function in this area of judicial review is essentially that of an arbitral or quasi-legislative body. As the Court speaking through Justice Black summed it up in 1944: ". . . there is a wide range of business and other activities which, though subject to federal regulation, are so intimately related to local welfare that, in the absence of Congressional action, they may be regulated or taxed by the states. In marking out these activities the primary test applied by the Court is not a mechanical one of whether the particular activity affected by the state regulation is part of interstate commerce, but rather whether, in each case, the competing demands of the state and national interests involved can be accommodated."[109]

The following situations and the results reached by the

The Court's
Arbitral
Role

[109] U.S. *v.* South-Eastern Underwriters Assoc., 322 U.S. 533, 548-549 (1944); F.D.G. Ribble's *State and National Power Over Commerce* (Columbia University Press, 1937) is an excellent study both of the Court's formulas and of the arbitral character of its task in this field of Constitutional Law. On the latter point, *see especially* chs. X and XII. *See also* Noel Dowling, "Interstate Commerce and State Power," 27 *Virginia Law Review,* 1 (1940). Chief Justice Stone took repeated occasion to stress the "balancing" and "adjusting" role of the Court when applying the commerce clause in relation to State power. *See* his words in South Carolina State Highway Dept. *v.* Barnwell Bros., 303 U.S. 177, 184-192 (1938); California *v.* Thompson, 313 U.S. 109, 113-116 (1941); Parker *v.* Brown, 317 U.S. 341, 362-363 (1943); and Southern Pacific Co. *v.* Ariz., 325 U.S. 761, 766-770 (1945).

Holdings *in re* State Taxation Affecting Commerce — Court in treating them are illustrative of its work in the field of State taxation affecting interstate commerce. While the "original package" doctrine does not protect goods imported from sister States from non-discriminatory taxation,[110] goods in transit from one State to another are removed from the taxable wealth of the State of origin from the beginning of their journey,[111] and are not taxable by the State of destination until "they have come to rest there for final sale or disposal."[112] Local sales of goods brought from another State are, however, subject to non-discriminatory taxation.[113] At one time the negotiation of sales to be filled by importations from another State was regarded as "interstate commerce" which could not be taxed. This doctrine, which was first laid down in 1887, in the famous case of Robbins *v.* Shelby Taxing District,[114] was for a time extended to cover deliveries of goods attended by many "local incidents";[115] but later, due primarily to the Depression, this attitude of concession to the commercial interest was considerably curtailed. It was held early in 1937 that States which have sales taxes—at that time the principal defense against bankruptcy in many States—might levy "compensating taxes" upon the use within their territory of articles brought in from other States.[116]

Later, the Court decided that out-of-state corporations could be required to *collect* the use tax if there was a "nexus," that is "some definite link, some minimum connection, between a state and the person, property or transaction it seeks to tax."[117]

[110] Woodruff *v.* Parham, 8 Wall. 123 (1868); Sonneborn Bros. *v.* Cureton, 262 U.S. 506 (1923); Ingels *v.* Morf, 300 U.S. 290 (1937).
[111] State Freight Tax Case, 15 Wall. 232 (1873); Coe *v.* Errol, 116 U.S. 517 (1886).
[112] Brown *v.* Houston, 114 U.S. 622 (1885); Youngstown Co. *v.* Bowers, 358 U.S. 534 (1959).
[113] Emert *v.* Mo., 156 U.S. 296 (1895); Wagner *v.* Covington, 251 U.S. 95 (1919); Eastern Air Transport, Inc. *v.* S.C. Tax Com'n, 285 U.S. 147 (1932); *Cf.* Welton *v.* 91 U.S. 275 (1875), where a tax discriminating against goods from other States was overturned.
[114] 120 U.S. 489 (1887).
[115] *See* Caldwell *v.* N.C., 187 U.S. 622 (1903); Norfolk W. R. Co. *v.* Sims, 191 U.S. 441 (1903); Rearick *v.* Pa., 203 U.S. 507 (1906); Dozier *v.* Ala., 218 U.S. 124 (1910).
[116] Henneford *v.* Silas Mason Co., 300 U.S. 577 (1937). In a case decided in 1969, the Supreme Court held that servicemen who were stationed in Connecticut who were residents or domiciliaries of other States were not exempted from use taxes imposed by Connecticut. Sullivan *v.* U.S., 395 U.S. 169 (1969).
[117] Miller Bros. Co. *v.* Maryland, 347 U.S. 340, 344-345 (1954); Scripto *v.*

A sale of goods intended for shipment to another State may not be taxed,[118] though their production may be,[119] and the line is not always an easy one to plot.[120]

The decision in Robbins v. Shelby Taxing District retained its precedential vitality longest with respect to "license" and "occupation" taxes. As late as 1946 on the authority of that decision, the Court struck down a municipal ordinance which among other things imposed an annual license tax on solicitors from out of state.[121] However, more recently, the Supreme Court did not find a privilege tax imposed by the State of Washington upon the privilege of engaging in business activities within the State and as applied against an out-of-state corporation, "constitutionally impermissible."[122] The Court reasoned: "Although mere entry into a State does not take from a corporation the right to continue to do an interstate business with tax immunity, it does not follow that the corporation can channel its operations through such a maze of local connections as does General Motors, and take advantage of its gain on domesticity, and still maintain that same degree of immunity." When in 1965 the Supreme Court dismissed an appeal (for want of a substantial Federal question) of a lower court decision upholding a licensing tax, Justice Douglas complained: "Our decisions have heretofore precluded a State from exacting a license of a firm doing an exclusively interstate business as a condition of entry into the State" but to no avail.[123]

A State may, however, tax the property that is within its borders (and presumably receiving its protection) of a company which engaged in interstate commerce. "The State must be allowed to tax the property and to tax it at its actual

---

Carson, 362 U.S. 207, 210-211 (1960). *Cf.* National Bellas Hess v. Dept. of Revenue, 386 U.S. 753 (1967). *Cf.* Halliburton Oil Well Co. v. Retly, 373 U.S. 64 (1963).

[118] Dahnke-Walker Milling Co. v. Bondurant, 257 U.S. 282 (1921). *Cf.* however, Minnesota v. Blasius. 290 U.S. 1 (1933).

[119] Oliver Iron Co. v. Lord 262 U.S. 172 (1923), and cases there cited. *See also* Alaska v. Arctic Maid, 366 U.S. 199 (1961).

[120] Eureka Pipe Line Co. v. Hallanan, 257 U.S. 265 (1921); Utah Power and Light Co. v. Pfost 286 U.S. 165 (1932); Toomer v. Witsell, 334 U.S. 385 (1948).

[121] Nippert v. Richmond, 327 U.S. 416 (1946).

[122] General Motors v. Washington, 377 U.S. 436, 448 (1964).

[123] Fairfax Family Fund v. California, 382 U.S. 1, 2 (1965). *See also* Rabren v. Pullman Co., 254 So. 2d. 324 (1971); United Air Lines, Inc. v. Porterfield, 276 N.E. 2d. 629 (1971).

value as a going concern."[124] Further, such taxes may take into account the "augmentation of value from the commerce in which it is engaged. . . . So it has been held that a tax on the property and business of a railroad operated within the State might be estimated *prima facie* by gross income, computed by adding to the income derived from business within the State the proportion of interstate business equal to the proportion between the road over which the business was carried within the State to the total length of the road over which it was carried."[125] This is the concept of an "apportioned" tax, or the "unit of use" rule, the Court's main reliance till 1938 in this area of Constitutional Law. Cases cited below illustrate its application.[126] Likewise, taxation by a State of the gross receipts of companies engaged in interstate commerce within its borders must be "fairly apportioned," at least ordinarily.[127] By an earlier rule a State was entitled also to levy indefinite so-called "franchise taxes" upon companies chartered by it, but this label appears nowadays to possess little or no specific saving quality of its own.[128] In 1938 Justice Stone, speaking for the Court, advanced what has been called the "multiple taxation" test. The question it poses is, what would happen to the interstate commerce affected by it if everybody—that is, every "State which the commerce touches"—did the same?[129] Some of the Justices hastily concluded that the new rubric might safely replace the "apportionment" rule, with all its difficulties and uncertainties, but later holdings dashed this hope.[130]

---

[124] Justice Holmes's language in Galveston, Harrisburg, & S.A. R.R. Co. *v.* Texas, 210 U.S. 217, 225, 227 (1908). *See also* Cudahy Packing Co. *v.* Minn., 246 U.S. 450 (1918); Pullman Co. *v.* Richardson, 261 U.S. 330 (1923); and Virginia *v.* Imperial Coal Sales Co., 293 U.S. 15 (1934).

[125] *Ibid.*

[126] The foundations of the rule were laid in Western Un. Tel. Co. *v.* Mass., 125 U.S. 530 (1888); Pullman's Palace Car Co. *v.* Pa., 141 U.S. 18 (1891); *and* Adams Express Co. *v.* Ohio, 165 U.S. 194 and 166 U.S. 185 (1897). *See also* Ott *v.* Miss. Barge Line Co., 336 U.S. 169 (1949).

[127] *See* Freeman *v.* Hewit, 329 U.S. 249, 265-266, note 13 (1946), citing cases. *Cf.* Evco Designs *v.* Jones, 41 *LW* 4037 (1972).

[128] Maine *v.* Grand Trunk R. Co., 142 U.S. 217 (1891), was the leading case. *Cf.* Galveston, Harrisburgh & San Antonio R. Co. *v.* Tex., 210 U.S. 217 (1908). *See also* Interstate Pipe Line Co. *v.* Stone, 337 U.S. 662 (1949), for an extensive review of the cases.

[129] Western Live Stock *v.* Bureau of Revenue, 303 U.S. 250, 255-256 (1938).

[130] *See* Joseph *v.* Carter and Weekes Stevedoring Co., 330 U.S. 422, 433 (1947); Braniff Airways *v.* Nebraska Board, 347 U.S. 590 (1954); Northwestern Cement Co. *v.* Minn., 358 U.S. 450 (1959).

As the Court summed it up in 1964: "A careful analysis of the cases in this field teaches that the validity of a tax rests upon whether the State is exacting a constitutionally fair demand for that aspect of interstate commerce to which it bears a special relation. For our purposes the decisive issue turns on the operating incidence of the tax. In other words, the question is whether the State has exerted its power in proper proportion to appellant's consequent enjoyment of opportunities and protections which the State has afforded."[131] This summary was further validated in 1972, when the Supreme Court upheld the constitutionality of State and municipal charges of "$1 per commercial airline passenger to help defray the costs of airport construction and maintenance."[132]

As was said before, the States have also their so-called "police power"; that is, the power "to promote the health, safety, morals and general welfare." Laws passed in exercise of this power may often affect commerce incidentally, but if the resultant burden is found by the Court to be on the whole justified by the local interest involved, such laws will be sustained. In other words, the Court's function in the handling of this type of case is, even more emphatically than in the taxation field, that of an arbitral, rather than of a strictly judicial, body. Thus in 1943 it held that a State is entitled to authorize, in the interest of maintaining producers' prices, a scheme imposing restrictions on the sale within the State of a crop ninety-five per cent of which eventually enters interstate and foreign commerce, there being no act of Congress with which the State act was found to conflict.[133] But this holding does not necessarily disturb an earlier one that a State has no right to promote its own "economic welfare" at the expense of the rest of the country, by prohibiting the entrance within its borders or the exit from them of "legitimate articles of commerce," the Constitution having been "framed upon the theory that the

*Holdings in re the "Police Power"*

---

[131] General Motors v. Washington, 377 U.S. 436, 440-441 (1964).

[132] Evansville-Vanderburgh A.A. Dist. v. Delta Airlines, Inc., 405 U.S. 707 (1972). The Supreme Court of Hawaii recently decided that application of a general excise tax to commissions received by travel agents "From solicitation and sale of interstate and foreign transportation, hotel accommodations, and sight-seeing tours does not contravene the Commerce Clause. . . ." Ramsay Travel, Inc. v. Kondo, 495 P. 2d. 1172 (1972). See also Kennecott Copper Corp. v. State Tax Com'n, 493 P. 2d. 632 (1972) and Sinclair Refining Co. v. Department of Revenue, 277 N.E. 2d. 858 (1972).

[133] Parker v. Brown, 317 U.S. 341 (1943).

people of the several States must sink or swim together, and that in the long run prosperity and salvation are in union and not division."[134]

Similarly, a State may require all engineers operating within its borders, even those driving through trains, to be tested for color-blindness; but it may not limit the length of trains, nor apply a Jim Crow law to interstate bus passengers.[135] Nor may a State regulate rates of transportation in the case of goods being brought from or carried to points outside the State; and while it may regulate rates for goods bound simply from one point to another within its own borders, yet even such rates are subject to be set aside by national authority if they discriminate against or burden interstate commerce.[136]

In recent years, the Court has seemed more willing than previously to allow for the exercise of the State police power. For example, the Court upheld as constitutional the application of a Detroit Smoke Abatement Code, forbidding ships to blow their stacks in the harbor, against ships operating in interstate commerce and in accordance with a comprehensive system of regulation devised by Congress.[137] And the Court also held that a Colorado commission's order requiring that an airline refrain from racial discrimination in its hiring of pilots did not unduly burden interstate commerce.[138] Justice Stewart provided the present posture of the Court in these matters this way: "Although the criteria for determining the validity of state statutes affecting interstate commerce have been variously stated, the general rule that emerges can be phrased as follows: Where the statute regulates evenhandedly to effectuate a legitimate local public interest, and its effects on interstate commerce are only incidental, it will be upheld unless the burden imposed on such commerce is clearly exces-

134 Baldwin v. Seelig, 294 U.S. 511, 523 (1935).
135 Smith v. Ala., 124 U.S. 465 (1888); Southern Pacific Co. v. Ariz. 325 U.S. 761 (1945); Morgan v. Va., 328 U.S. 373 (1946). The survey of such cases in Justice Hughes' opinion for the Court in the Minnesota Rate Cases, 230 U.S. at pp. 402-412 (1913) and that by Chief Justice Stone in the just cited Arizona case are very informative. The latter opinion is also a model of hard-hitting factual criticism.
136 Wabash Ry. Co. v. Ill., 118 U.S. 557 (1886); the Shreveport Case, 234 U.S. 342 (1914). State-imposed rates, no less than nationally imposed rates, must yield the carrier a "fair return" on the "value" of its property. Smyth v. Ames, 169 U.S. 466 (1898).
137 Portland Huron Cement Co. v. Detroit, 362 U.S. 440 (1960).
138 Colorado Com'n v. Continental Airlines, 372 U.S. 714 (1963); Cf. Pike v. Bruce Church, Inc., 397 U.S. 137 (1970).

sive in relation to the putative local benefits. If a legitimate local purpose is found, then the question becomes one of degree. And the extent of the burden that will be tolerated will of course depend on the nature of the local interest involved, and on whether it could be promoted as well with a lesser impact on interstate activities."[139]

Nor is the Court's *quasi*-arbitral function confined to the question whether State legislation has unconstitutionally invaded the field of power which the commerce clause is thought to reserve to Congress exclusively. It is also brought into requisition, and with the extension of national power into the industrial field more and more so, in determining whether certain State legislation conflicts with a certain act or acts of Congress. If such is the case, then of course the State legislation must be treated as void so long as the conflicting national legislation remains on the statute books, *provided* it is constitutional; and the Court will not ordinarily be keen to discover such a conflict.[140] For example, the Court sustained the Federal Motor Carriers Act, which precludes a State from suspending the right of an interstate carrier to use the State's highways for interstate goods because of repeated violation of certain state regulations. The State's remedy, the Court said, lay in an appeal to the Interstate Commerce Commission.[141]

When<br>National<br>and State<br>Laws<br>Overlap

Nor, in fact, does Congress always *subtract* from the powers of the States affecting commerce—sometimes it *adds* to them. Thus, the serious confusion that would otherwise have resulted from the Court's decision in 1944 in the South-Eastern Underwriters case (*see* p. 48) was obviated by the passage early in 1945 of the McCarran Act, which provides that the insurance business shall continue to be subject to the laws of the several States except as Congress may specifically decree otherwise,[142] and years ago Congress, by the Webb-Kenyon Act of 1916, subjected interstate shipments of intoxicants to regulation by the State of destination, thereby in effect delegating power over such interstate commerce to the States. And

---

[139] *Ibid.* at 142. *But see* the unusual decision of a New Jersey court, State *v.* Comfort Cab, Inc., 286 A. 2d. 742 (1972) and the novel contention in West *v.* Broderick & Bascom Rope Co. 197 N.W. 202, 214 (1972).

[140] Parker *v.* Brown, 317 U.S. 341, 351 (1943). *See also* Allen-Bradley Local No. 1111 *et al. v.* Wisconsin Employment Rels. Bd., 315 U.S. 740 (1912); Penn Dairies *v.* Milk Control Com'n, 318 U.S. 261 (1943); Hill *v.* Fla., 325 U.S. 538 (1945).

[141] Castle *v.* Hayes Freight Lines, Inc., 348 U.S. 61 (1954).

[142] 59 *Stat.* 33 (1945).

in both these instances Congress was sustained by the Court.[143]

A parsing of the cases in which the Court has performed in its arbitral role invites the observation that this is a very difficult role for the Court to play well and suggests that Justices Black, Frankfurter, and Douglas may have had a valid point when, in a dissent some years ago, they wrote: "Judicial control of national commerce—unlike legislative regulations—must from inherent limitations of the judicial process treat the subject by the hit-and-miss method of deciding single local controversies upon evidence and information limited by the narrow rules of litigation. Spasmodic and unrelated instances of litigation cannot afford an adequate basis for the creation of integrated national rules which alone can afford that full protection for interstate commerce intended by the Constitution."[144]

¶4. To establish an uniform rule of naturalization, and uniform laws on the subject of bankruptcies throughout the United States;

There seems to be no good reason why two such entirely different subjects should be dealt with in the same clause other than that legislation regarding each has to be "uniform."

Naturalization and Citizenship     Some are born citizens; some achieve citizenship, some have citizenship thrust upon them. The first category fall into two groups. First, those who are born in the United States, "subject to the jurisdiction thereof," are pronounced "citizens of the United States and of the State wherein they reside" by the opening clause of Amendment XIV, which derives from the principle of *jus soli* ("the law of the soil") of the English common law, and further back still from the feudal law. As rather improvidently interpreted by the Court in the Wong Kim Ark

---

[143] *See* Prudential Ins. Co. *v.* Benjamin, 328 U.S. 408 (1946); and Clark Distilling Co. *v.* W. Md. Ry., 242 U.S. 311 (1917). The Supreme Court has never forgotten the lesson administered to it by the act of Congress of August 31, 1852, which pronounced the Wheeling Bridge "a lawful structure," thereby setting aside the Court's determination to the contrary earlier the same year. *See* Pennsylvania *v.* Wheeling and Belmont Bridge, 13 How. 518 (1852); 18 How. 421 (1856). This lesson, stated in the Court's own language thirty years later, was, "It is Congress, and not the Judicial Department, to which the Constitution has given the power to regulate commerce. . . ." Transportation Co. *v.* Parkersburg, 107 U.S. 691, 701 (1883).

[144] McCarroll *v.* Dixie Lines, 309 U.S. 176, 188-189 (1940).

case,[145] this clause endows with American citizenship even the children of temporary residents in the United States, provided they do not have diplomatic status. The second group of "citizens at birth" owe their citizenship to Congressional legislation which applies the *jus sanguinis* ("the law of blood relationship") of the Roman civil law, and embraces with certain qualifications persons born outside the United States and its outlying possessions to parents one or both of whom are citizens of the United States.[146]

Those who achieve citizenship are persons who were born aliens but who have become "naturalized" in conformance with the laws of Congress. Formerly this privilege was confined to "white persons and persons of African nativity or descent," but was extended by the Act of December 17, 1943, to "descendants of races indigenous to the Western Hemisphere and Chinese persons or persons of Chinese descent."[147] And in 1952 the law was amended to read: "The right of a person to become a naturalized citizen . . . shall not be denied or abridged because of race or sex or because such person is married."[148] But naturalization is by no means a favor for the asking by those who are qualified. No person may be naturalized who advocates or belongs to a group which advocates "opposition to all organized government" or who "believes in" or belongs to a group which "believes in," "the overthrow by force or violence of the Government of the United States or of all forms of law,"[149] and any person petitioning for naturalization must "before being admitted to citizenship, take an oath in open court . . . to renounce and abjure absolutely . . . all allegiance and fidelity to any foreign prince" or state "of whom or which the petitioner was before a subject or citizen"; "to support and defend the Constitution and laws of the United States against all enemies, foreign and domestic"; and "to bear

Some Acts of Congress

---

[145] United States *v*. Wong Kim Ark, 169 U.S. 649 (1898).
[146] 8 U.S.C. 1401.     [147] 57 *Stat.* 600 (1943).
[148] 8 U.S.C. 1422.

[149] 8 U.S.C. 1424. These restrictive provisions are, moreover, by the Act of June 27, 1952, "applicable to any applicant for naturalization who at any time within a period of ten years immediately preceding the filing of the petition for naturalization or after such filing and before taking the final oath of citizenship is, or has been found to be within any of the classes enumerated within this section, notwithstanding that at the time the petition is filed he may not be included within such classes." 8 U.S.C. 1424C.

full faith and allegiance to the same."[150] Prior to a Supreme Court decision in 1946, these provisions were interpreted as requiring a petitioner to swear a willingness to bear arms for the United States. As a consequence of that decision, the law on the matter, drawn up in 1952, specifically permits the petitioner the options of promising to bear arms or to performing "non-combatant service in the Armed Forces" or "work of national importance under civilian direction" when it is required by law.[151] In view of recent lower court decisions, it is doubtful that a conscientious objector can be denied naturalization solely for refusing to promise to accept any of the options.[152] But any naturalized person who takes this oath with mental reservations or conceals beliefs and affiliations which under the statute disqualify one for naturalization, is subject, upon these facts being conclusively shown in a proper proceeding, to have his certificate of naturalization cancelled for "fraud." However, as the Court has admonished: "The Government carries a heavy burden of proof in a proceeding to divest a naturalized citizen of his citizenship."[153] In all other respects, however, the naturalized citizen stands "under the Constitution . . . on an equal footing with the native citizen" save as regards eligibility to the Presidency.[154] He enjoys, therefore, the same freedom of speech and publication, the same right to criticize public men and measures, whether informedly or foolishly, the same right to assemble to petition the government, in short, the same civil rights as do citizens from birth. Nevertheless, the naturalized citizen's vulnerability to charges of having obtained citizenship through fraud does raise a question about "equal footing," in spite of Justice Douglas's admonition years ago: "To hold otherwise would be an anomaly. It would mean in effect that where a person . . . perpetrated a fraud on the naturalization court, the United States would be remediless to correct the wrong."[155]

Illustrative of persons who have had citizenship thrust upon them are members of an Indian "or other aboriginal

150 U.S. *v.* Schwimmer, 279 U.S. 644 (1929); U.S. *v.* Macintosh, 283 U.S. 605 (1931); Girouard *v.* U.S., 328 U.S. 61 (1946).
151 8 U.S.C. 1448.
152 *In re* Weitzman, 426 F. 2d. 439 (1970); *In re* Pisciattano, 308 F. Supp. 818 (1970).
153 Costello *v.* U.S., 365 U.S. 265, 269 (1961); 8 U.S.C. 1451.
154 Osborn *v.* Bk. of U.S., 9 Wheat. 738 at 827 (1824); Luria *v.* U.S., 231 U.S. 9 (1913); Knauer *v.* U.S., 328 U.S. 654 (1946).
155 Knauer *v.* U.S., 328 U.S. 654, 673-674 (1946).

tribe" who, by the Act of 1887 and succeeding legislation, are declared "to be citizens of the United States" if they were born within the United States;[156] and by the Act of June 27, 1952, certain categories of persons born in the Canal Zone, Panama, Puerto Rico, Alaska, Hawaii, the Virgin Islands, and Guam, on or after certain stated dates.[157]

The interesting question arises whether Congress, when it extends American citizenship to certain categories "at birth," does so by virtue of the constitutional clause here under discussion or by virtue of an "inherent" power ascribable to it in its quality as the national legislature. While the point has never been adjudicated, the dictionary definition of "naturalize" "*to adopt, as a foreigner, into a nation or state,*"[158] tends to confirm the latter theory, as does also the fact that in the pioneer Act of 1855, dealing with the matter, Congress "declared" children born abroad of American citizens to be citizens. Even more clearly does Congress's power to deal with the subject of expatriation seem to require some such explanation. At the common law the *jus soli* was accompanied by the principle of "indelible allegiance," out of which stemmed, for instance, Great Britain's claim of right in early days to impress naturalized American seamen of British birth; and even as far down as 1868 American courts often implicitly accepted this principle. Our Secretaries of State, on the other hand, usually asserted the doctrine of expatriation in their negotiations with other governments respecting the rights abroad of American citizens by naturalization, and on July 27, 1868, Congress passed an act declaring the latter doctrine to be a fundamental principle of this Government, one not to be questioned by any of its officers in any of their opinions, orders, decisions.[159] Then by an act passed in 1907, although since repealed in this respect, Congress enacted that any woman marrying a foreigner should take the nationality of her husband. To the contention that this provision deprived American citizens of their constitutional right to that status, the Court replied that the maintenance of "the ancient principle of the identity of hus-

*Marginal note:* Congress's Inherent Power over Citizenship and Expatriation

---

156 8 U.S.C. 1401.

157 8 U.S.C. 1402-1407. *See also*, on Collective Naturalization, Boyd *v.* Neb., 143 U.S. 135, 162 (1892).

158 *See also* Chief Justice Taney's *dictum* in the Dred Scott case that the naturalization clause applies only to "persons born in a foreign country, under a foreign government." 19 How. 393, 417, 419 (1857).

159 15 *Stat.* 223-224; and *see* generally John Bassett Moore, *Digest of International Law*, III (Washington, 1906).

band and wife" was a reasonable requirement of international policy, a field in which the National Government was "invested with all the attributes of sovereignty." While Congress, said the Court, may not "arbitrarily impose a renunciation of citizenship," yet marriage with a foreigner was "tantamount to voluntary expatriation."[160] And for like reasons Congress may provide that naturalized citizens shall lose their acquired status under certain conditions by protracted residence abroad, although their minor children born in the United States, not sharing the parent's intention in the eyes of the law, do not share his fate.[161]

Law presently on the statute books spells out ten ways in which "a national of the United States whether by birth or naturalization, shall lose his nationality." These range from "obtaining naturalization in a foreign state upon his own application" to "departing from or remaining outside the jurisdiction of the United States in time of war or . . . national emergency for the purpose of evading . . . service. . . ."[162] In recent years the Supreme Court has been deeply perplexed and divided on the problem of whether or not these provisions are constitutional.[163] In a sweeping decision, albeit by a five-four majority, the Court in 1967, speaking through Justice Black, held that a citizen had "a constitutional right to remain a citizen in a free country unless he voluntarily relinquishes that citizenship."[164] And apparently voluntariness must not be implied, for the Court said: "To uphold Congress' power to take away

---

[160] Mackenzie v. Hare, 239 U.S. 299, 311-312 (1915); cf. United States v. Wong Kim Ark, 169 U.S. 649, 703 (1898).

[161] Perkins v. Elg, 307 U.S. 325 (1939); Rogers v. Bellei, 401 U.S. 815 (1971). Congress's power over naturalization is an exclusive power. A State cannot denationalize a foreign subject who has not complied with Federal naturalization law and constitute him a citizen of the United States, or of the State, so as to deprive the Federal courts of jurisdiction over a controversy between him and a citizen of a State. Chirac v. Chirac, 2 Wheat. 259, 269 (1817). But power to naturalize aliens may be, and early was, devolved by Congress upon State courts having a common law jurisdiction. Holmgren v. U.S., 217 U.S. 509 (1910), where it is also held that Congress may provide for the punishment of false swearing in such proceedings. Ibid. 520. Also, States may confer the right of suffrage upon resident aliens who have declared their intention to become citizens, and have frequently done so. Spragius v. Houghton, 3 Ill. 377 (1840); Stewart v. Foster, 2 Binney (Pa.) 110 (1800).

[162] 8 U.S.C. 1481.

[163] Perez v. Brownell, 356 U.S. 44 (1958); Nishikawa v. Dulles, 356 U.S. 129 (1958); Trop v. Dulles, 356 U.S. 86 (1958); Kennedy v. Mendoza-Martinez, 372 U.S. 144 (1963); Afroyim v. Rusk, 387 U.S. 253 (1967).

[164] Afroyim v. Rusk, 387 U.S. 253, 268 (1967).

a man's citizenship because he voted in a foreign election in violation of . . . [law] would be equivalent to holding that Congress has the power to . . . 'take . . . away' citizenship. Because the Fourteenth Amendment prevents Congress from doing any of these things, we agree with the Chief Justice's dissent in the *Perez* case that the Government is without power to rob a citizen of his citizenship. . . ."[165] Since only two members of that majority remain on the Court, it does not seem too hazardous to predict that the current Court might narrow or reverse that decision, given the occasion.[166]

Merging with its delegated power over the subject of naturalization is the inherent power of Congress to exclude aliens from the United States. This is absolute. In the words of the Court: "That the government of the United States, through the action of the legislative department, can exclude aliens from its territory is a proposition which we do not think open to controversy. Jurisdiction over its own territory to that extent is an incident of every independent nation. It is a part of its independence. If it could not exclude aliens, it would be to that extent subject to the control of another power. . . . The United States, in their relation to foreign countries and their subjects or citizens are one nation, invested with powers which belong to independent nations, the exercise of which can be invoked for the maintenance of its absolute independence and security throughout its entire territory."[167] The Immigration and Nationality Act of June 27, 1952, excludes some thirty-one categories of aliens from the United States, including "aliens who are, or at any time have been, members . . . of or affiliated with any organization that advocates or teaches . . . the overthrow by force, violence, or other unconstitutional means of the Government of the United States. . . ."[168]

With the power of exclusion goes, moreover, the power to assert a considerable degree of control over aliens after their admission to the country. By the Alien Registration Act

*Congress's Inherent Power to Exclude Aliens*

[165] *Ibid.* at 267.
[166] Rogers *v.* Bellei, 401 U.S. 815 (1971).
[167] Chinese Exclusion case, 130 U.S. 581, 603, 604 (1889); *see also* Fong Yue Ting *v.* U.S., 149 U.S. 698, 705 (1893); Japanese Immigrant case, 189 U.S. 86 (1903); Turner *v.* Williams 194 U.S. 279 (1904); Bugajewitz *v.* Adams, 228 U.S. 585 (1913); Hines *v.* Davidowitz, 312 U.S. 52 (1941); Hsieh *v.* Civil Service Commission of City of Seattle, 488 P. 2d. 515, 519 (1971).
[168] 66 *Stat.* 163, tit. 2 § 212 (1952).

69

of 1940[169] it was provided that all aliens in the United States, fourteen years of age and over, should submit to registration and finger printing, and willful failure to do so was made a criminal offense against the United States. The Act of June 27, 1952, repeats these requirements, and Supreme Court decisions, which ascribe to the Executive certain inherent powers in the same field, enlarge them.[170] In theory, however, they are all reasonable concomitants of the exclusion power, and do not embrace the right to lay down a special code of conduct for alien residents of the United States to govern private relations with them.[171]

For a good part of our history, deportation of aliens has been a vexing issue. The issue was stated succinctly by Justice Frankfurter some years ago: "The power of Congress over the admission of aliens and their right to remain is necessarily very broad, touching as it does basic aspects of national sovereignty, more particularly our foreign relations and the national security. Nevertheless, considering what it means to deport an alien who legally became part of the American community, and the extent to which, since he is a 'person,' an alien has the same protection for his life, liberty and property under the Due Process Clause as is afforded to a citizen, deportation without permitting the alien to prove that he was unaware of the Communist Party's advocacy of violence strikes one with a sense of harsh incongruity. If due process bars Congress from enactments that shock the sense of fair play—which is the essence of due process—one is entitled to ask whether it is not beyond the power of Congress to deport an alien who was duped into joining the Communist Party, particularly when his conduct antedated the enactment of the legislation under which his deportation is sought. And this because deportation may . . . deprive a man of all that makes life worth living; and deportation is a drastic measure and at times the equivalent of banishment or exile."[172] He went on to say, however: "In light of the expansion of the concept of substantive

---

[169] 54 *Stat.* 670; sustained in Hines *v.* Davidowitz, 312 U.S. 52, 69-70 (1941).

[170] Knauff *v.* Shaughnessy, 338 U.S. 537 (1950); Carlson *v.* Landon, 342 U.S. 524 (1952); Harisiades *v.* Shaughnessy, 342 U.S. 580, 587 (1952); United States *v.* Specter, 343 U.S. 169 (1952).

[171] Keller *v.* U.S., 213 U.S. 138 (1909).

[172] Galvan *v.* Press, 347 U.S. 522, 530 (1954).

due process as a limitation upon all powers of Congress, even the war power, . . . much could be said for the view, were we writing on a clean slate, that the Due Process Clause qualifies the scope of political discretion heretofore recognized as belonging to Congress in regulating the entry and deportation of aliens. And since the intrinsic consequences of deportation are so close to punishment for crime, it might fairly be said also that the *ex post facto* Clause, even though applicable only to punitive legislation, should be applied to deportation."[173] However, he then concluded: "But the slate is not clean. As to the extent of the power of Congress under review, there is not merely a page of history, . . . but a whole volume. Policies pertaining to the entry of aliens and their right to remain here are peculiarly concerned with the political conduct of government. In the enforcement of these policies, the Executive Branch of the Government must respect the procedural safeguards of due process. But that the formulation of these policies is entrusted exclusively to Congress has become about as firmly imbedded in the legislative and judicial tissues of our body politic as any aspect of our government. And whatever might have been said at an earlier date for applying the *ex post facto* Clause, it has been the unbroken rule of this Court that it has no application to deportation."[174] Subsequently, the Court endeavored to soften the impact of this decision by statutory interpretation, but it left unchallenged Frankfurter's description of Congressional power.[175]

In 1972, the Supreme Court upheld the action of the Attorney General in refusing to allow an alien scholar, a self-acknowledged "revolutionary Marxist" to enter the country to attend academic meetings, stating that he "as an unadmitted and nonresident alien, had no constitutional right of entry to this country as a nonimmigrant or otherwise." To the contention that refusal to admit the scholar trenched on the First Amendment rights of those who desired to hear what he had to say, the Supreme Court gave short shrift: "We hold that when the Executive exercises this power [congressional delegation of power] negatively on the basis of a facially legitimate and bona fide reason, the courts will neither look behind the

---

173 *Ibid.* at 530-531.     174 *Ibid.* at 531.
175 Rowoldt *v.* Perfetto, 355 U.S. 115 (1957); Gastelum-Quinones *v.* Kennedy, 374 U.S. 469 (1963).

The<br>Bankruptcy<br>Power

exercise of that discretion, nor test it by balancing its justification against the First Amendment interests of those who seek personal communication with the applicant."[176]

Congress's power in the field of bankruptcy legislation has been a steadily growing power. In the words of Justice Cardozo, summarizing Mr. Warren's volume on the subject: "The history is one of an expanding concept," but of "an expanding concept that has had to fight its way. Almost every change has been hotly denounced in its beginning as a usurpation of power. Only time or judicial decision has had capacity to silence opposition. At the adoption of the Constitution the English and Colonial bankruptcy laws were limited to traders and to involuntary proceedings. An act of Congress passed in 1800 added bankers, brokers, factors, and underwriters. Doubt was expressed as to the validity of the extension, which established itself, however, with the passing of the years. Other classes were brought in later, through the Bankruptcy Act of 1841 and its successors, until now practically all classes of persons and corporations are included."[177] And where bankruptcy legislation was originally framed solely from the point of view of the immediate reimbursement of creditors, it is today designed also as a relief to debtors and as a mode of putting them back on their feet ("voluntary bankruptcy"). Yet the creditor's interest has not been lost sight of, since it is usually better secured, especially in times of financial depression, by conservation of the debtor's resources than by their sale and distribution.

To be sure, a closely divided Court held in 1936 that Congress could not extend the benefits of voluntary bankruptcy proceedings to municipalities and other political subdivisions of the States, since to do so would be to invade the rights of the States even though the act required that they first give their consent to such proceedings; but this decision was speedily superseded by one to the contrary effect, which is now law of the land.[178]

While Congress is not forbidden to impair "the obligation of contracts" (*see* Article I, Section X, ¶1), in legislating re-

[176] Kleindienst v. Mandel, 408 U.S. 753, 770 (1972).

[177] Ashton v. Cameron County, 298 U.S. 513, 535-536 (1936); Charles Warren, *Bankruptcy in United States History* (Boston, 1935), 9.

[178] The case just cited; and United States v. Bekins, 304 U.S. 27 (1938).

garding bankruptcies it may not, under the Fifth Amendment, unduly invade the property rights of creditors, which, however, is just what, in the opinion of a unanimous Court, it attempted to do by the Frazier-Lemke Farm Moratorium Act of 1933. A revised act, designed to meet the Court's objections, was in due course challenged and sustained.[179]

Unlike the situation with respect to the commerce clause, it was settled early that States could legislate with respect to bankruptcies if Congress had not acted. In 1819, the Supreme Court held: "The omission of Congress to legislate, amounts to a declaration, that they do not think a *uniform* system is necessary; and they, therefore, leave the States to legislate upon the subject, whenever they think it proper and expedient to do so."[180] When Congress does act, however, it preempts or supersedes State law, but only if there is "a clear collision."[181]

¶5. To coin money, regulate the value thereof, and of foreign coin, and fix the standard of weights and measures;

The framers of the Constitution apparently assumed a bimetallic currency, and the power to regulate "the value thereof" was probably thought of chiefly as the power to regulate the value of lesser coins in relation to the dollar and the metallic content of the two kinds of dollars with a view to keeping both gold and silver in circulation. As a result of Civil War legislation, however, Congress established its power to authorize paper money with the quality of legal tender in the payment of debts, both past and future; while by the Gold Clause cases of 1934 it is recognized as possessing the power to lower the metal content of the dollar in order to stimulate prices. In short, "the value thereof" comes to mean "value" in the sense of *purchasing power*. Nor may private parties, by resort to the "gold clause" device, contract themselves out of the reach of Congress's power thus to lower the purchasing power of the dollar.[182] (*See also* ¶2, above.)

*The Currency Power*

---

[179] Louisville Joint Stock Land Bank *v.* Radford, 295 U.S. 555 (1935); Wright *v.* Vinton Branch, 300 U.S. 440 (1937).
[180] Sturges *v.* Crowningshield, 17 U.S. 122, 176 (1819).
[181] Kesler *v.* Department of Public Safety, 369 U.S. 153 (1962).
[182] Phanor J. Eder, "The Gold Clause Cases in the Light of History," 23 *Georgetown Law Journal*, 359-388 and 722-760 (1935). *Cf.* Perry *v.* U.S., 294 U.S. 330 (1935).

¶6. To provide for the punishment of counterfeiting the securities and current coin of the United States;

This clause of the Constitution is superfluous. Congress would have had this power without it, under the "co-efficient clause."[183] (See ¶18, below.)

¶7. To establish post-offices and post-roads;

The Postal Clause In earlier times narrow constructionists advanced the theory that these words did not confer upon Congress the right to *build* post-offices and post-roads, but only the power to *designate* from existing places and routes those which should serve as post-offices and post-routes.[184] The debate on the subject was terminated in 1876 by the decision in Kohl v. United States[185] sustaining a proceeding by the United States to appropriate a parcel of land in Cincinnati as a site for a post-office and courthouse.

It is from this clause also that Congress derives its power to carry the mails, which power comprehends the power to protect them and assure their quick and efficient distribution;[186] also the power to prevent the postal facilities from being abused for purposes of fraud and exploitation, or for the distribution of legitimately forbidden matter.[187] Indeed, it may close the mails to induce conformity with regulations within its power to enact.[188] But all restraints on the use of the mails are in general subject to judicial review because of the close connection between the subject and First Amendment freedoms. In 1965, the Supreme Court held that an act which required the Postmaster General to detain and deliver only upon request of the addressee unsealed foreign mailings of "communist political propaganda" as construed and applied in that case was unconstitutional "because it requires an official act (*viz.*, returning the reply card) as a limitation on the unfettered exercise of the addressee's First Amendment rights."[189]

---

[183] *See e.g.* United States v. Marigold, 9 How. 560, 568 (1850); Fox v. Ohio, 5 How. 410 (1847); Baender v. Barnett, 255 U.S. 224 (1921).
[184] United States v. Railroad Bridge Co., Fed. Cas. No. 16, 114 (1855).
[185] 91 U.S. 367 (1875).   [186] *In re* Debs, 158 U.S. 564 (1895).
[187] *In re* Rapier, 143 U.S. 110 (1892); Public Clearing House v. Coyne, 194 U.S. 497 (1904); Lewis Pub. Co. v. Morgan, 229 U.S. 288 (1913); Hennegan v. Esquire, Inc., 327 U.S. 146 (1946); Donaldson v. Read Magazine, 333 U.S. 178 (1948).
[188] Electric Bond and Share Co. v. S.E.C., 303 U.S. 419 (1938).
[189] Lamont v. Postmaster General, 381 U.S. 301, 305 (1965).

¶8. To promote the progress of science and useful arts by securing for limited times to authors and inventors the exclusive right to their respective writings and discoveries;

Congress may exercise the power conferred by this clause by
either general or special acts, but the provision has reference
only to writings and discoveries which are the result of intellectual labor and exhibit novelty[190] and which "add to the sum
of useful knowledge."[191] Nor is Congress authorized by the
clause to grant monopolies in the guise of patents or copyrights, and the rights which the present statutes confer are
subject to the Anti-Trust Act.[192] Also, patented articles are
subject to the police power and the taxing power of the States,
but must not be discriminated against as such,[193] and a State
may tax royalties from patents or copyrights as so much income, a decision to the contrary effect in 1928 having been
later overruled.[194] But as the Court has cautioned: "Just as a
State cannot encroach upon federal patent laws directly, it
cannot, under some other law, such as that forbidding unfair
competition, give protection of a kind that clashes with the objectives of the federal patent laws."[195] The term "writings" has
been given an expanded meaning, and covers photographs and
photographic films.[196] On the other hand, it was held in the
*Trade-Mark* cases[197] that a trade-mark is neither a "writing"
nor "discovery" within the sense of the clause, with the result

Patents and
Copyrights

[190] Higgins *v.* Keuffel, 140 U.S. 428 (1891); Cuno Engineering Corp. *v.*
Automatic Devices Corp., 314 U.S. 84 (1941); E. Burke Inlow, *The Patent
Grant* (Baltimore, 1950), ch. VI. For discussion of difference in require-
ments for copyrights as distinguished from patents, *see* Imperial Homes
Corp. *v.* Lamont, 458 F. 2d. 895 (1972).

[191] "Innovation, advancement, and things which add to the sum of useful knowledge are inherent requisites in a patent system which by constitutional command must 'promote the Progress of . . . useful Arts,'" Graham
*v.* John Deere Co., 383 U.S. 1, 6 (1966); Anderson's-Black Rock *v.* Pave-
ment Co., 396 U.S. 57 (1969). Re computer programs, *see* Gottschalk *v.*
Benson, 41 *LW* 4015 (1972).

[192] *See* Motion Picture Patents Co. *v.* Universal Film Mfg. Co., 243 U.S.
502 (1917); Morton Salt Co. *v.* G. S. Suppiger Co., 314 U.S. 488 (1942);
United States *v.* Masonite Corp., 316 U.S. 265 (1942); United States *v.* New
Wrinkle, Inc., 342 U.S. 371 (1952); Inlow, *Patent Grant*, ch. V.

[193] Patterson *v.* Ky., 97 U.S. 501 (1878); Webber *v.* Va., 103 U.S. 344
(1880). *See also* Watson *v.* Buck, 313 U.S. 387 (1941).

[194] The cases referred to are Long *v.* Rockwood, 277 U.S. 142 (1928); and
Fox Film Co. *v.* Doyal, 286 U.S. 123 (1932).

[195] Sears, Roebuck & Co., *v.* Stiffel Co., 376 U.S. 225, 231 (1964).

[196] Burrows-Giles Lithographic Co. *v.* Sarony, 111 U.S. 53 (1884). *See
also* Mazer *v.* Stein, 347 U.S. 201 (1954); CBS *v.* DeCosta, 377 F. 2d. 315
(1967); *cert. denied*, 389 U.S. 1007 (1967).     [197] 100 U.S. 82 (1879).

that Congress could validly legislate for their protection only as they were instruments of foreign or interstate commerce and at that time the Court had a very restrictive view of Congress's power to regulate commerce.[198] Not improbably, however, recently established views of Congress's protective power over commerce and its instruments would today vindicate the kind of act which was overturned in 1879. As the Court held most recently, "the direction of Art. I is that *Congress* shall have the power to promote the progress of science and the useful arts. When, as here, the constitution is permissive, the sign of how far Congress has chosen to go can come only from Congress."[199] The international agreements on the subject of patents and copyrights to which the United States is party where entered into under authority conferred by Congress under this clause.

It is worth noting in passing that courts have found litigation in patent cases inordinately difficult. As Justice White recently observed: "We are also aware that some courts have frankly stated that patent litigation can present issues so complex that legal minds, without appropriate grounding in science and technology, may have difficulty in reaching decision."[200]

¶9. To constitute tribunals inferior to the Supreme Court (*See* Article III, Section I.)

¶10. To define and punish piracies and felonies committed on the high seas and offenses against the law of nations;

Congress
and
International
Law
In Chancellor Kent's words: "When the United States ceased to be a part of the British empire, and assumed the character of an independent nation, they became subject to that system of rules which reason, morality, and custom had established among civilized nations of Europe, as their public law. . . . The faithful observance of this law is essential to na-

---

[198] ". . . there still remains a very large amount of commerce, perhaps the largest, which being trade or traffic between citizens of the same State, is beyond the control of Congress." *Ibid.*, at 96.
[199] Deepsouth Packing Co. *v.* Laitram Corp., 406 U.S. 518, 530 (1972). In this case, the Supreme Court held that *the statute* which proscribed the making of any patented invention within the United States, did not preclude a manufacturer from exporting abroad the parts of someone else's patented item.
[200] Blonder-Tongue Lab. Inc., *v.* University of Illinois Found. 402 U.S. 313 (1971); *see* note 32 therein. Gottschalk *v.* Benson, 41 *LW* 4015 (1972).

tional character, . . ."[201] The power here conferred has been broadly construed. Thus, taking the position that the Law of Nations casts upon every government the duty to prevent a wrong being done within its own dominion to another nation with which it is at peace, or to the people thereof, the Court sustained Congress in making the counterfeiting within the United States of notes, bonds and other securities of a foreign government an offense against the United States.[202]

It is under this provision that the Supreme Court has held that Congress may set up a military commission "as it had previously existed in United States Army practice, as an appropriate tribunal for the trial and punishment of offenses against the law of war."[203]

¶11. To declare war, grant letters of marque and reprisal, and make rules concerning captures on land and water;

This paragraph, together with paragraphs 12, 13, 14, 15, 16 and 18 following, and paragraph 1 of Section II of Article II, comprise the "War Power" of the United States, but are not, necessarily, the whole of it. Three different views of the source and scope of the power found expression in the early years of the Constitution and have continued to vie for supremacy for more than a century and a half. In *The Federalist*, Hamilton advanced the theory that the power is an aggregate of particular powers—those listed above.[204] In 1795 the theory was elaborated, on the basis of the fact that even before the Constitution was adopted the American people had asserted their right to wage war as a unit, and to act in regard to all their foreign relations as a unit, that these powers were an attribute of sovereignty; and hence not dependent upon the affirmative grants of the Constitution.[205] A third view was adumbrated by Chief Justice Marshall, who in McCulloch *v.* Maryland listed the power "to declare *and conduct* a war" as one of the "enumerated powers" from which the power of the National Government to charter the Bank of the United States was deduci-

*The War Power; Theories of Its Source*

---

[201] *See* James Kent, *Commentaries on American Law*, I (Boston, 1826), 1-2.

[202] United States *v.* Arjona, 120 U.S. 479 (1887).

[203] *In re* Yamashita, 327 U.S. 1, 7 (1946); *Ex parte* Quirin, 317 U.S. 1 (1942).

[204] *The Federalist*, No. 23.

[205] Penhallow *v.* Doane, 3 Dall. 54 (1795).

ble.[206] During the Civil War the two latter theories were both given countenance by the Supreme Court.[207] Then, following World War I, the Court, speaking by Justice Sutherland, plumped squarely for the "attribute of sovereignty" theory. Said he: "The power to declare and wage war, to conclude peace, to make treaties, to maintain diplomatic relations with other sovereignties, if they had never been mentioned in the Constitution, would have vested in the Federal Government as necessary concomitants of nationality";[208] and although the Court, in 1948, lent its sanction, perhaps somewhat casually, to the "enumerated powers" theory,[209] there can be no doubt that the attribute of "sovereignty theory" does fullest justice to the actual holdings of the Court, and especially to those rendered in the course of, or in consequence of, World War II.

"When we are at war, we are not in revolution," the late Chief Justice Hughes once declared.[210] The fact is, none the less, that certain major characteristics of the Constitution as it operates in peacetime recede into the background in wartime. Under the doctrine of "enumerated powers," silence on the part of the Constitution is a *denial* of power to Congress; in wartime it is an *affirmance* of power.[211] Nor is the principle of Dual Sovereignty an ingredient of the War Power. As against it there are no States Rights; to the contrary, an active duty rests on the States to cooperate with the National Government in the prosecution of the war on the home front.[212]

[206] 4 Wheat. 316, 407 (1819) (emphasis supplied).

[207] *Ex parte* Milligan, 4 Wall. 2,139 (1866) (dissenting opinion); Hamilton *v.* Dillin, 21 Wall. 73, 86 (1875). *See also* 58 *Cong. Globe*, app. 1 (1861); Miller *v.* U.S. 11 Wall. 268, 305 (1871); and United States *v.* Macintosh, 283 U.S. 605, 622 (1931).

[208] United States *v.* Curtiss-Wright Export Corp., 299 U.S. 304, 316, 318 (1936). *See also* the same Justice's sweeping opinion for the Court on the scope of the War Power in relation to private rights, in United States *v.* Macintosh, 283 U.S. 605, 622 (1931).

[209] Lichter *v.* U.S., 334 U.S. 742, 755, 757-758 (1948).

[210] Address before the American Bar Association at Saratoga, September 1917. Merlo Pusey, *Charles Evans Hughes*, I (N.Y., 1951) 369. In his opinion for the Court in 1934, in the Minnesota Moratorium case, Chief Justice Hughes said: "The war power of the Federal Government is a power to wage war successfully, and thus permits the harnessing of the entire energies of the people in a supreme cooperative effort to preserve the Nation." 290 U.S. 398, 426. Fourteen years earlier, with the facts of World War I before him, Mr. Hughes raised the question "whether constitutional government as hitherto maintained in this Republic could survive another great war, even victoriously waged." *New York Times*, June 22, 1920.

[211] This is a generalization from the cases reviewed below.

[212] *See* note 210 above; *also* University of Illinois *v.* U.S., 289 U.S. 48 (1933); Gilbert *v.* Minn., 254 U.S. 325 (1920). In World War II the Office of

Likewise, in wartime the constitutional ban on the delegation by Congress of its powers to the President is in almost complete abeyance. What are termed the "cognate powers" of the two departments may be merged by Congress substantially at will.[213]

Probably the thing that Mr. Hughes had foremost in mind were the restraints which are imposed by the Bill of Rights in behalf of private rights, and especially the due process clause of Amendment V: "nor shall any person be deprived of life, liberty, or property without due process of law"—that is, without what the Supreme Court finds to be justifying circumstances (*see* pp. 326-330). But Total War is itself a highly justifying, not to say compulsive circumstance, in the presence of which judicial review is apt to be properly self-distrustful, and proportionately ineffective. Witness, for example, the vast powers which by authorization of Congress the War Production Board (WPB) exercised in control of the distribution of materials and facilities, and of industrial production and output during World War II, and the almost equally great powers which the Office of Price Administration (OPA) exercised in rationing supplies and controlling prices, rents, and wages, without any restraint by the courts—almost, in fact, without their exercise of power being challenged in court.[214]

*The War Power and the Bill of Rights*

And what Total War can do to personal rights despite the due process clause, and despite its chosen instrument judicial review, is shown by the measures which the National Government adopted early in World War II respecting Japanese residents on the West Coast. What, in brief, these measures ac-

*The Impact of Total War on Private Rights: the West Coast Japanese*

Civilian Defense (OCD) was dependent entirely on the local authorities for the enforcement of its "directives" whenever the patriotic impulses of the public proved an insufficient reliance. Mr. Byrnes's curfew "request" of February 28, 1945, issued in his capacity as Director of War Mobilization, was similarly circumstanced, with the result of producing a sharp controversy between Mr. Byrnes and Mayor LaGuardia over the question of closing-time for New York City's restaurants. See Mr. Byrnes's statement in the *New York Times*, March 20, 1945.

213 *See* opinion cited in note 208 above at pp. 320-329; *also* Lichter *v.* U.S., 334 U.S. 742, 778-779, 782-783 (1948).

214 As to WPB's powers, *see* 56 *Stat.* 351 (1942). Steuart & Bro., Inc. *v.* Bowles, 322 U.S. 398 (1944); John Lord O'Brian and Manly Fleischmann, "The War Production Board, Administrative Policies and Procedures," 13 *George Washington Law Review* (1944). On OPA's powers, *see* 56 *Stat.* 23 (1942); Yakus *v.* U.S., 321 U.S. 414 (1944); Bowles *v.* Willingham, 321 U.S. 503 (1944); Case *v.* Bowles, 327 U.S. 92 (1946). Against enemies of the United States, the War Power is constitutionally unlimited. Brown *v.* U.S., 8 Cr. 110 (1814); Miller *v.* U.S. 11 Wall. 268 (1870).

complished was the removal of 112,000 Japanese, two-thirds of them citizens of the United States by birth, from their homes and properties, and their temporary segregation in "assembly centers," later in "relocation centers." No such wholesale or drastic invasion of the rights of citizens of the United States by their own Government had ever before occurred in the history of the country. Nevertheless, taking judicial notice of what they perceived as the facts of the dubious state of our defenses on the West Coast and of the reasonable apprehension of invasion following the attack on Pearl Harbor, of the manifest sympathy of many Japanese residents for Japan and the consequent danger of "Fifth Column" activities, and of certain other more or less speculative possibilities, and asserting the broad scope of the blended powers of Congress and the President in war time, the Court said, "We cannot say that these facts and circumstances, considered in the particular war setting, could afford no ground for differentiating citizens of Japanese ancestry from other groups in the United States." The measures in question were therefore pronounced valid, but with the later stipulation by the Court that they must be construed and applied strictly as anti-espionage and anti-sabotage measures, not as concessions to community hostility toward the Japanese. A Japanese citizen, accordingly, whose loyalty the Government did not challenge was held to be entitled at any time to unconditional release from a relocation center. At the same time it was clearly implied that the privilege of the writ of *habeas corpus* was always available in like cases unless suspended for reasons deemed by the Constitution to be sufficient.[215]

Perhaps chastened by the recognition of the injustice done

---

[215] Hirabayashi *v.* U.S., 320 U.S. 81 (1943); Korematsu *v.* U.S., 323 U.S. 214 (1944); *ex parte* Endo, 323 U.S. 283 (1944). Hindsight makes it clear that there was no necessity for the Japanese segregation measures. Certainly, chronology supports such skepticism. The Japanese attack on Pearl Harbor occurred December 7, 1941. Yet it was not until February 19 that this policy was inaugurated by the President's order, nor until March 21 that Congress acted, and the Civilian Exclusion Order did not come till May 3—five months after Pearl Harbor! What was the real cause, then, of the segregation measures—increased danger of Japanese invasion, to be aided by sabotage in the United States, or increased pressure from interested and/or hysterical groups of West Coast citizens? Had the authorities stopped short with a curfew order, enforcible by the police, they would have taken ample precaution. *Not one single Japanese, citizen or otherwise, either in continental United States or in Hawaii, was found guilty of one single effort at sabotage or espionage.* Harold W. Chase, *Security and Liberty* (New York, 1954), 20-23.

to Americans of Japanese ancestry under the War Power, the Supreme Court took the occasion in 1967 in striking down a statute aimed at keeping communists from working in defense facilities to say: "The Government seeks to defend the statute on the ground that it was passed pursuant to Congress' war power. . . . However, the phrase 'war power' cannot be invoked as a talismanic incantation to support any exercise of congressional power which can be brought within its ambit. Even the war power does not remove constitutional limitations safeguarding essential liberties."[216] Despite this recent decision rendered during a time of less than all-out war, the question arises whether, the *habeas corpus* privilege aside, the Constitution permits the possibility of its own suspension in any other respect in time of war or other serious crisis. In the Milligan case, which was decided shortly after the Civil War, a majority of the Court took pains to stigmatize any such idea in the strongest terms. "No doctrine," said Justice Davis, "involving more pernicious consequences, was ever invented by the wit of man than that any of its [the Constitution's] provisions can be suspended during any of the great exigencies of government."[217] Unfortunately, this strongly worded assertion is contradicted by the very decision in justification of which it was pronounced, for this held Milligan to have been deprived of his constitutional rights, and his was but one of many such cases, President Lincoln's policy as to which, based on the theory that the entire country was a theater of military operations, may have been a material factor in the war's outcome.

Can the Constitution Be Suspended in Wartime?

Far different was the outlook of President Roosevelt's message to Congress of September 7, 1942, in which he proclaimed his intention and his constitutional right to disregard certain provisions of the Emergency Price Control Act unless Congress repealed them by the following October 1. "The American people," said he, "can be sure that I will use my powers with a full sense of my responsibility to the Constitution and to my country. . . . When the war is won, the powers under which I act will automatically revert to the people—to whom they belong." While the situation which the President foreshadowed did not materialize, thanks to Congress's compliance with his demand, albeit a day late, yet any candid person must admit the possibility of conditions arising in which

[216] U.S. *v.* Robel, 389 U.S. 258, 263-264 (1967).
[217] 4 Wall. 2, 121 (1866).

81

the safety of the republic would require the waiving of constitutional methods. When Mr. Hughes uttered his dictum the
atomic bomb had not been invented, or used against civilian
populations. The circumstances of nuclear warfare would, not
improbably, bring about the total supplantation for an indefinite period of the forms of constitutional government by the
drastic procedures of military government.

The Power to Prepare for War: the Atomic Energy Act   To some indeterminate extent the power to wage war includes the power to prevent it. It was on this ground in part
that, following World War I, the Court sustained TVA as a
legitimate governmental enterprise.[218] But the outstanding example of legislation adopted at a time when no actual "shooting war" was in progress, with the object of providing for the
national defense, is the Atomic Energy Act of 1946. That law
establishes an Atomic Energy Commission of five members
which is empowered to conduct through its own facilities, or
by contracts with or loans to private persons, research and developmental activities relating to nuclear processes, the theory
and production of atomic energy, and the utilization of fissionable and radioactive materials for medical, industrial, and
other purposes. The act further provides that the Commission
shall be the exclusive owner of all facilities (with minor exceptions) for the production of fissionable materials; that all
fissionable material produced shall become its property; that
it shall allocate such materials for research and developmental
activities, and shall license all transfers of source materials.
The Commission is charged with the duty of producing atomic
bombs, bomb parts, and other atomic military weapons at the
direction of the President. Patents relating to fissionable materials must be filed with the Commission, the "just compensation" payable to the owners to be determined by a Patent
Compensation Board designated by the Commission from
among its employees.[219]

Again, the War Power "is not limited to victories in the field.
It carries with it inherently the power to guard against the
immediate renewal of the conflict, and to remedy the evils
which have arisen from its rise and progress."[220] So spoke the
Court in Reconstruction days. Yet this power cannot be without metes and bounds. For, as the Court has recognized, "if

[218] Ashwander *v.* TVA, 297 U.S. 288, 327-328 (1936).
[219] 60 *Stat.* 755 (1948).
[220] Stewart *v.* Kahn, 11 Wall. 493, 507 (1871).

the war power can be used in days of peace to treat all the wounds which war inflicts on our society, it may not only swallow up all other powers of Congress but largely obliterate the Ninth and Tenth Amendments."[221] The issue thus adumbrated is not susceptible to cut-and-dried solutions.[222]

Despite their apparent simplicity and clarity, the words "The Congress shall have power . . . to declare war" have been a source of consternation throughout our history. (*See* pp. 153-154 for brief historical development.) As we have come to learn, war comes in many shapes and a variety of ways. The Marquis of Queensberry rules do not apply. We have learned that we can be attacked without warning, and that we can slowly move one small step after another into a genuine shooting war before we fully realize what has happened. It is not always possible for a prudent President to wait for a Congressional declaration before he acts. As the Supreme Court pointed out in the Prize cases in 1863: "This greatest of civil wars was not gradually developed by popular commotion, tumultuous assemblies, or local unorganized insurrections. However long may have been its previous conception, it nevertheless sprung forth suddenly from the parent brain, a Minerva in the full panoply of *war*. The President was bound to meet it in the shape it presented itself, without waiting for Congress to baptize it with a name; and no name given it by him or them could change the fact."[223]

In contrast to the situation the Court described, there have been situations where Presidential initiatives toward involving the nation in warfare seemed unwarranted because there was time for the President to seek a Congressional declaration of war and he chose not to. Certainly, there are many who would contend that that was the case with respect to hostilities in Korea and Vietnam. However, when opportunities arose for the Supreme Court to review a challenge of the constitutionality of the Vietnam war, it refused to do so.[224] But Justices

*The Power to Declare War*

221 Woods *v.* Miller, 333 U.S. 138, 144 (1948).
222 *Cf.* Chastleton *v.* Sinclair, 264 U.S. 543 (1924); Ludecke *v.* Watkins, 335 U.S. 160, 170 (1948).
223 Prize Cases, 67 U.S. 635, 688-689 (1863).
224 Mora *v.* McNamara, 389 U.S. 934 (1967); Orlando *v.* Laird, 443 F. 2d. 1039 (1971); *cert. denied,* 404 U.S. 869 (1971); Massachusetts *v.* Laird, 400 U.S. 886 (1970), but *see* Justice Douglas's dissent. *See also* Da Costa *v.* Laird, 448 F. 2d. 1368 (1971); *cert. denied,* 405 U.S. 979 (1972). *See also* 40 *LW* 2803 (1972).

Stewart and Douglas wrote pithy dissents in one case worthy of close study. They thought that "the Court should squarely face" the questions: "I. Is the present United States military activity in Vietnam a 'war' within the meaning of Article I, Section 8, Clause 11 of the Constitution? II. If so, may the Executive constitutionally order the petitioners to participate in that military activity, when no war has been declared by the Congress?"

Frustrated, and unhappy with the war in Vietnam, some Congressmen have been seeking ways to reassert what they regard as their constitutional duty. The Senate bill which passed April 13, 1972, by a vote of 68-16 seems to take into account the realities suggested by the Court in the Prize cases, that sometimes hostilities break out before thoughtful deliberation is possible. Basically, but with some qualifications, this bill would permit the President to commit the Armed Forces to "hostilities, or in situations where imminent involvement in hostilities is clearly indicated by the circumstances" in specified emergencies for a period of only thirty days without specific authorization from Congress to continue. And Congress would have the power to terminate the action earlier by "an Act or joint resolution," if it saw fit to do so before the thirty days were up.[225]

Clearly such legislation would not require a constitutional amendment, since it only spells out how a power already granted to Congress is to be exercised. Conceivably, a President could assert that such a law would be an unconstitutional limitation on his powers as chief executive and Commander-in-Chief. Of course he can veto such a bill, but then Congress could override the veto. What the Supreme Court would do in such a case is conjectural, of course, but on the basis of the precedent of the *Steel Seizure* case[226] discussed below (pp. 155-157) it is probable that the Court would uphold the act of Congress.

In evaluating any proposal to reassert Congress's power to declare war, a consideration suggested by former President Lyndon B. Johnson in his memoirs is worth some thought: If it is in the national interest to conduct a limited war, would it

[225] 1972 *Cong. Quart. Weekly Report*, 405-407, 658-663, 766, 811-812, 830, 918-919, 1008.
[226] Youngstown Co. *v.* Sawyer, 343 U.S. 579 (1952).

be possible to keep a declared war from becoming an all-out war?[227]

"Letters of marque and reprisal" were formerly issued to privateers, sometimes for the purpose of enabling their grantees to wage a species of private war upon some state against which they had a grievance. Because of the ban which International Law has put upon privateering increasingly since the Declaration of Paris of 1856, this power of Congress must today be deemed obsolete. Letters of Marque and Reprisal

¶12. To raise and support armies, but no appropriation of money to that use shall be for a longer term than two years;

¶13. To provide and maintain a navy;

The office of these clauses is to assign the powers which they define and which are part of the War Power, to *Congress*, since otherwise they might have been claimed, by analogy to the British constitution, for the President.[228] When Congress, by the National Security Act of 1947, set up the Air Force as a separate service not mentioned in the Constitution, its constitutional power to do so was conceded.[229] The Air Force

The only type of standing army known to the Framers was a mercenary, volunteer force, and the only compulsory type of military service known to them was service in the militia, which was confined to local and limited purposes, as it had been in medieval England, and as it still is in clause 15 below. Conscription was first employed to raise an army for service abroad in World War I,[230] and the first peacetime conscription Development of Conscription

[227] Mr. Johnson explained that the reason he did not go to Congress and ask for great sums of money, call up the reserves, and go on a war footing was that he deliberately wanted to keep the war a limited one. Lyndon B. Johnson, *Vantage Point* (New York, 1971), p. 149.

[228] Story, *Commentaries*, § 1187.

[229] A California member of the House introduced a resolution looking to a constitutional amendment authorizing the establishment of an air force (H. J. Res. 298, 80th Cong., 2nd Sess.), but nothing happened to it.

[230] The act was sustained in the Selective Draft cases, 245 U.S. 366 (1918). The same Act of June 15, 1917, gave the President sweeping powers to commandeer shipbuilding plants and facilities. Commenting on this feature of the act in United States v. Bethlehem Steel Corp., 315 U.S. 289 (1942), the Court said: "Under the Constitutional authority to raise and support armies, to provide and maintain a navy, and to make all laws

was that authorized by the Selective Training and Service Act of September 16, 1940, which as enacted forbade the sending of selectees outside the Western Hemisphere except to possessions of the United States and the Philippine Islands.[231] Following Pearl Harbor this restriction was quickly suspended for the duration.[232] Conscription for recruitment of the Navy rests on a more ancient precedent, namely, impressment into the British Navy, which, although confined to seamen, antedated 1789.

From the first time the compulsory draft was employed after the enactment of the Thirteenth Amendment, it was a natural for those who were opposed to being drafted to see it as "involuntary servitude" of a type forbidden by that amendment. But from the first, the Supreme Court has not seen it that way.[233]

A more compelling argument can be made against forced military service for those who can claim that such service runs against their religious scruples and, consequently, denies them the religious freedom safeguarded by the First Amendment. But such an argument is rendered academic by the fact that Congress has long provided exemptions from military service for conscientious objectors.[234] Significantly, courts have upheld Congress's power to require alternative types of service for conscientious objectors and have not regarded them as "involuntary servitude" or invasions of religious freedom.[235]

The plethora of interesting draft cases reaching the Supreme Court in recent years have all turned on the question of who may truly claim to be a conscientious objector under the statute. The Court gave us a good capsule description of where it now stands in the attention-getting case involving the former heavyweight boxing champion Muhammad Ali: "In order to qualify for classification as a conscientious objector,

---

necessary and proper to carry these powers into execution, the power of Congress to draft business organizations is not less than its power to draft men for battle service." *Ibid.* 305.

[231] 54 *Stat.* 885, 886 (1940).        [232] 55 *Stat.* 799 (1941).

[233] Butler *v.* Perry, 240 U.S. 328 (1916); Selective Draft Law cases, 245 U.S. 316 (1918). As late as 1968, the Supreme Court cited the Selective Draft cases with approval. U.S. *v.* O'Brien, 391 U.S. 367, 376 (1968).

[234] The current law, The Military Service Act of 1967, provides exemption from military service for any person "who, by reason of religious training and belief, is conscientiously opposed to participation in war in any form." 50 App. U.S.C. 456 (j).

[235] Roodenko *v.* U.S. 147 F. 2d. 752 (1945); *cert. denied*, 324 U.S. 860 (1945); Heflin *v.* Sanford, 142 F. 2d. 798 (1944).

a registrant must satisfy three basic tests. He must show that he is conscientiously opposed to war in any form. He must show that this opposition is based upon religious training and belief, as the term has been construed in our decisions. And he must show that this objection is sincere."[236] But the issue is not as cut and dried as the Court suggests. As Justice Douglas pointed out in another recent case, the Court's decisions in this matter "leave considerable latitude for administrative findings."[237]

Limitation of appropriations for the Army to two years reflects the American fear of standing armies. For the Navy and Air Force, on the other hand, building programs may be laid down to run over several years.[238]

The power to create an Army, Navy, and Air Force involves, naturally, the power to adopt measures designed to safeguard the health and welfare of their personnel, and such measures are enforcible within the States. Thus, for example, Congress may authorize the suppression of houses of ill-fame in the vicinity of places where military personnel are stationed.[239]

¶ 14. To make rules for the government and regulation of the land and naval forces;

It is by virtue of this paragraph that Congress has enacted the Code of Military Justice, which constitutes the basis of discipline in the Armed Forces.

In view of the sweep of the two clauses preceding, this clause is superfluous except for the purpose of vesting Congress with a power which might be otherwise claimed exclusively for the Commander-in-Chief.

Until the 1950's Congress exercised this power extensively without a serious challenge by the Supreme Court. In 1858 the Court held that: "Congress has the power to provide for the trial of military and naval offenses in the manner then and now practiced by civilized nations; and that the power to do so is

---

[236] Clay v. U.S., 403 U.S. 698, 700 (1971). To support these points, the Court cited the following cases: Gillette v. U.S., 401 U.S. 437 (1971); U.S. v. Seeger, 380 U.S. 163 (1965); Welsh v. U.S., 398 U.S. 333 (1970); Witmer v. U.S., 348 U.S. 375 (1955). For a summary of more recent draft cases, see Fein v. Selective Service, 405 U.S. 365 (1972) and cases cited therein.

[237] Ehlert v. U.S., 402 U.S. 99, 112 (1971).

[238] 40 Op. Atty. Gen. 555 (1948).

[239] McKinley v. U.S., 249 U.S. 397 (1919). See also Wissner v. Wissner, 338 U.S. 655, 660 (1950).

given without any connection between it and the 3rd article of the Constitution defining the judicial power of the United States."[240] Nor in an earlier day did the Court find the Bill of Rights a limiting factor at least with reference to those attached to "the army, or navy, or militia in actual service." As the Court explained in 1866: "The sixth amendment affirms that 'in all criminal prosecutions the accused shall enjoy the right to a speedy and public trial by an impartial jury,' language broad enough to embrace all persons and cases; but the fifth, recognizing the necessity of an indictment, or presentment, before any one can be held to answer for high crime, '*excepts* cases arising in the land, or naval forces, or in the militia, when in actual service, in time of war or public danger'; and the framers of the Constitution, doubtless, meant to limit the right of trial by jury, in the sixth amendment, to those persons who were subject to indictment or presentment in the fifth."[241]

It is not surprising that Justices deeply committed to civil liberties in the 1950's found the Congressional grant of jurisdiction to military courts over certain civilians unconstitutional.[242] And, as Justice Douglas described it, the Court "held in a series of decisions that court-martial jurisdiction cannot be extended to reach any person not a member of the Armed Forces at the times of both the offense and the trial. Thus, discharged soldiers cannot be court-martialed for offenses committed while in service. Similarly, neither civilian employees of the Armed Forces overseas, nor civilian dependents of military personnel accompanying them overseas, may be tried by court-martial."[243]

The matter was not allowed to rest there. Even though Congress has over the years made great efforts to provide men in the service with a better brand of justice, the Court operating under the premise that "Determining the scope of the constitutional power of Congress to authorize trial by court-martial presents another instance calling for limitation to '*the least*

<hr/>

240 Dynes *v.* Hoover, 20 How. 65, 75 (1858).
241 *Ex parte* Milligan, 4 Wall. 2, 123 (1866). *See also* opinion of the Chief Justice, *ibid.* at 138-139.
242 Toth *v.* Quarles, 350 U.S. 11, 17-18 (1955).
243 O'Callahan *v.* Parker, 395 U.S. 258, 267 (1969). The cases cited by Justice Douglas were: Toth *v.* Quarles, 350 U.S. 11 (1955); McElroy *v.* Guagliardo, 361 U.S. 281 (1960); Grisham *v.* Hagen, 361 U.S. 278 (1960); Kinsella *v.* Singleton, 361 U.S. 234 (1960). Reid *v.* Covert, 354 U.S. 1 (1957).

*possible power adequate to the end proposed,' "*[244] has decided that a "crime to be under military jurisdiction must be service connected."[245] Thus a serviceman committing a crime in the civilian community off the base must be tried in a civilian court.

Apparently, encouraged by the direction the Court has taken with respect to their rights, servicemen have recently taken to challenging service regulations and actions on First Amendment grounds. A group of army bandsmen who were ordered transferred because they arranged or sanctioned an incident in which a fiancée and wives attempted to march with the band in a public parade while carrying signs protesting the Vietnam war contended that the transfers had a chilling effect on their First Amendment rights. The District Court upheld them but was reversed by the Court of Appeals, which said: "We do not say that a case would never arise where a transfer order could be invalidated by a civilian court on such a basis. But any such judicial intrusion into the area broadly confided by the Constitution to the President as Commander-in-Chief and his authorized subordinates must await a stronger case than this one."[246] Airmen objecting to enforcement of an Air Force regulation prohibiting them from wearing uniforms at a public anti-war meeting were told that they must first exhaust the available military remedies before seeking relief in civilian courts.[247] And a Marine Reserve who objected to Marine Corps haircut regulations for reservists attending drills was found by a Court of Appeals to be subject to courts-martial jurisdiction: "it is fair to say that the inactive duty reservist, at least when on active duty, is a soldier rather than a civilian."[248] Despite these decisions, it is a good prospect that in keeping with the times there will be continuing efforts to obtain for men and women in the service the full sweep of First Amendment protections. But the decisions just men-

[244] O'Callahan v. Parker, 395 U.S. 258, 265 (1969).
[245] *Ibid.*, at 272. For a detailed listing of commentaries on the O'Callahan case, *see* Relford v. U.S. Disciplinary Commandant 401 U.S. 355 (1971).
[246] Cortright v. Resor, 447 F. 2d. 245, 246 (1971). For the District Court decision *see* 325 F. Supp. 797 (1971).
[247] Locks v. Laird, 441 F. 2d. 479 (1971); *cert. denied*, 404 U.S. 986 (1971)—cited as Bright *et al. v.* Laird.
[248] Wallace v. Chafee, 451 F. 2d. 1374, 1380 (1971); *also*, 323 F. Supp. 902 (1971). But, in 1972, when Federal district court rejected a Harvard Law School student's petition to wear a short-haired wig over his long hair at National Guard drills, it was reversed by the 1st Circuit Court of Appeals.

tioned do not hold promise that these efforts will be successful in the courts.[249]

National Purposes of the Militia ¶15. To provide for calling forth the militia to execute the laws of the Union, suppress insurrections, and repel invasions;

Congress passed such an act in 1795, which basically still remains on the statute books. It leaves with the President the right to decide whether an insurrection exists or an invasion threatens.[250]

¶16. To provide for organizing, arming and disciplining the militia, and for governing such part of them as may be employed in the service of the United States, reserving to the States respectively the appointment of the officers, and the authority of training the militia according to the discipline prescribed by Congress;

Who Constitute the Militia The militia was long regarded as a purely State affair, but in the National Defense Act of June 3, 1916, "the militia of the United States" was defined as consisting "of all able-bodied male citizens of the United States" and all similar declarants between the ages of 18 and 45. The same act also provided for the nationalization of the National Guard, which was recognized as constituting a part of the militia of the United States, and provided for its being drafted into the military service of the United States in certain contingencies.[251] The act rested on the principle that the right of the States to maintain a militia is always subordinate to the power of Congress "to raise and support armies," a doctrine which has received the sanction of the Supreme Court.[252] Subsequent legislation has reinforced these provisions and lowered the age for inclusion in the militia to 17.[253] (*See also* Section X, ¶3.)

¶17. To exercise exclusive legislation in all cases whatsoever over such district (not exceeding ten miles square) as may, by cession of particular States and the acceptance

[249] *But see* Friedberg *v.* Resor, 453 F. 2d. 935 (1971).
[250] Martin *v.* Mott, 12 Wheat. 19 (1827); 10 U.S.C. 3500 and 8500.
[251] 39 *Stat.* 166 (1916).
[252] Selective Draft cases, 245 U.S. 366 (1918); Cox *v.* Wood, 247 U.S. 3 (1918).
[253] 10 U.S.C. 311, 3500-3501; 32 U.S.C. 302, 303, 307, 313.

of Congress, become the seat of the Government of the United States, and to exercise like authority over all places purchased by the consent of the legislature of the State in which the same shall be, for the erection of forts, magazines, arsenals, dockyards, and other needful buildings; and

This paragraph is, of course, the source of Congress's power to govern the District of Columbia. Congress itself, however, is not required to exercise this power, but may at any time create a government for the District and vest in it the same range of law-making power as it has always customarily vested in territories of the United States. In 1871 it did, in fact, do so; and while this government was later (1874) abolished and the commission form of government was instituted, certain of its legislative acts forbidding discrimination by restaurants against Negroes remained in force.[254] The system set up in 1874 provided for an executive board of three commissioners with limited governmental powers, with Congress retaining the power to legislate for the District. This system was extensively overhauled in 1967 in a Reorganization Plan intended, in President Johnson's words: "to bring Twentieth Century government to the Capital of this Nation." But, he added, the plan would not "in any way detract from the powers which the Congress exercises with respect to the District." He conceded that the reorganization "is in no way a substitute for home rule."[255]

Challenges to Congress's power to legislate for the District have been singularly unsuccessful in the courts.[256]

At an early time it was thought that a State's consent to surrender of jurisdiction under this paragraph had to be substantially unqualified; but later decisions held that a State may concede and Congress accept a qualified jurisdiction. Nor is the power of a State to concede and of the United States to receive and exercise jurisdiction, over places purchased by the latter within the boundaries of the former, limited by this paragraph. In fact, the paragraph is today largely superfluous.[257]

*The District of Columbia*

*Places Purchased from State*

[254] District of Columbia v. Thompson Co., 346 U.S. 100 (1953).
[255] 5 App. U.S.C. 401-442.
[256] *See* Hobson v. Tobriner, 255 F. Supp. 295 (1966) and cases cited therein; Palmore v. U.S., 290 A. 2d. 573 (1972).
[257] James v. Dravo Contracting Co., 302 U.S. 134 (1937); Collins v. Yosemite Park & Curry Co., 304 U.S. 518 (1938); Stewart & Co. v. Sandrakula, 309 U.S. 94 (1940); S.R.A., Inc. v. Minnesota, 327 U.S. 558 (1946).

¶18. To make all laws which shall be necessary and proper for carrying into execution the foregoing powers, and all other powers vested by this Constitution in the Government of the United States, or in any department or officer thereof.

"The Co-
efficient
Clause"

What is a "necessary and proper" law under this paragraph? This question arose in 1819, in the great case of McCulloch *v.* Maryland, and was answered by Chief Justice Marshall thus: "Let the end be legitimate, let it be within the scope of the Constitution, and all means which are appropriate, which are plainly adapted to that end, which are not prohibited, but consist with the letter and spirit of the Constitution, are constitutional."[258]

The basis of this declaration was furnished by three ideas: First, that the Constitution was ordained by the people and so was intended for their benefit; secondly, that it was "intended to endure for ages to come and, consequently, to be adapted to the various crises of human affairs"; and thirdly, that while the National Government is one of enumerated powers—a proposition which is today unqualifiedly applicable only to its internal powers—it is sovereign as to those powers. Marshall's view was opposed by the theory that the Constitution was a compact of sovereign States and so should be strictly construed, in the interest of safeguarding the powers of said States. From this point of view the necessary and proper clause was urged to be a limitation on Congress's powers, and was interpreted as meaning, in substance, that Congress could pass no laws except those which were "absolutely necessary" to carry into effect the powers of the General Government.

Broadly speaking, Marshall's doctrine has prevailed with the Court since the Civil War. It is true that certain of its decisions touching the New Deal legislation narrowed Congress's discretion in the choice of measures for the effective exercise of national power by subordinating it to certain powers of the States; but subsequent decisions indicate that this trend was only temporary. In the *Darby* case,[259] referred to earlier, Justice Stone, speaking for the Court, asserted that Congress's

[258] 4 Wheat. 316, 421. *See also ibid.*, 415.
[259] 312 U.S. 100 (1941); followed in Fernandez *v.* Wiener, 326 U.S. 340 (1945); and Case *v.* Bowles, 327 U.S. 92 (1946).

powers under the necessary and proper clause are no more limited by the reserved powers of the States than are its more specific powers. (*Cf.* Article VI, ¶2, and Amendment X.)

The "coefficient clause" is further important because of the control which it gives Congress over the powers of the other departments of government, but in this connection the doctrines of the Supreme Court at times confront the clause with certain "inherent" executive and judicial powers, of which the Court itself is the final determinator.[260]

On an earlier page were listed certain "inherent" powers of the National Government, claimed for it as "concomitants of nationality," as "inherent in sovereignty," or simply from the necessity of the case.[261] In the words of the Court, "it is not lightly to be assumed that in matters requiring national action, a power which must belong to and somewhere reside in every civilized government is not to be found."[262] Moreover, "even constitutional power may be established by usage," both in the case of Congress and in that of the President.[263]

*(margin note: Inherent Powers of the National Government)*

The foregoing may have created the impression that today there is precious little that Congress cannot do under the Constitution as it has been interpreted by the Supreme Court. This would be a false impression. For legislation to pass muster in the Supreme Court, there must still be a reasonable basis in the Constitution for the exercise of power and, above all, the exercise must not arbitrarily abridge constitutionally protected rights such as First Amendment rights. Despite the enormity of the power which Congress has exercised with the acquiescence of the Court, the Court still finds occasion to declare acts of Congress unconstitutional. The fact that there have been relatively few in recent years may as well be evidence of prudence on the part of Congress as evidence of permissiveness by the Court or Congressional fears of having its actions upset by the Court.[264]

---

[260] *Cf. ex parte* Grossman, 267 U.S. 87 (1925); and Myers *v.* U.S. 272 U.S. 52 (1926).

[261] *See* p. 6 above.

[262] Missouri *v.* Holland, 252 U.S. 416, 433 (1920), quoting Andrews *v.* Andrews, 188 U.S. 14, 33 (1903).

[263] Inland Waterways Corp. *v.* Young, 309 U.S. 517 (1940); United States *v.* Midwest Oil Co., 236 U.S. 459 (1915).

[264] For a listing of acts held unconstitutional *see* U.S., 88 Cong., 1st Sess., Senate, Document 39 (1964), 1387-1402.

## SECTION IX

The purpose of this section is to impose certain limitations on the powers of Congress.

¶1. The migration or importation of such persons as any of the States now existing shall think proper to admit shall not be prohibited by the Congress prior to the year one thousand eight hundred and eight, but a tax or duty may be imposed on such importation, not exceeding ten dollars for each person.

This paragraph referred to the African slave trade and is, of course, now obsolete. It is still interesting, nevertheless, for the evidence it affords of the belief of the Framers of the Constitution that, "under the power to regulate commerce, Congress would be authorized to abridge it in favor of the great principles of humanity and justice"[1] and of the belief of the Framers that "such persons" were not "citizens" in a constitutional sense.[2]

¶2. The privilege of the writ of *habeas corpus* shall not be suspended, unless when in cases of rebellion or invasion the Public safety may require it.

The Writ of *Habeas Corpus* The writ of *habeas corpus* is the most important single safeguard of personal liberty known to Anglo-American law. Often traced to Magna Carta itself, it dates from, at latest, the seventeenth century, and it is interesting to note that the Constitution simply assumes that, of course, it will be a part of the law of the land. The importance of the writ is that it enables anybody who has been put under personal restraint to secure immediate inquiry by a court into the cause of his detention and, if he is not detained for good cause, his liberty.[3] While the writ may not be used as a substitute for appeal, it provides a remedy for jurisdictional and constitutional errors without limit as to time, and may be used to correct such errors by military as well as by civil courts.[4]

[1] United States *v. The William*, 28 Fed. Cas. No. 16700 (1808).
[2] Scott *v.* Sandford, 19 How. 393, 411 (1857).
[3] Edward Jenks, *Short History of English Law* (Boston, 1913), 333-335; David Hutchinson, *Foundations of the Constitution* (New York, 1928), 137-139; Zechariah Chafee, "The Most Important Human Right in the Constitution," 32 *Boston Univ. Law Review*, 143 (1947).
[4] United States *v.* Smith, 331 U.S. 469, 475 (1947); Gusik *v.* Schiller, 340 U.S. 128 (1950).

Early in the Civil War, President Lincoln, without authorization by Congress, temporarily suspended the privilege of the writ for the line of transit for troops en route to Washington, thereby giving rise to the famous case of *ex parte* Merryman,[5] in which Chief Justice Taney, after vainly attempting to serve the writ, filed an opinion denouncing the President's course as violative of the Constitution. Whether the President or the Chief Justice was in the right seems to depend on whether the district for which the writ was suspended was properly to be regarded as within the field of military operations at this time, for, if it was, the President's power as Commander-in-Chief had full sway. Subsequently Congress passed an act declaring the President "authorized" to suspend the writ "whenever, in his judgment, the public safety may require it," though whether "authorized" by the act or by the Constitution itself was not made clear.[6]

In recent years, the writ has been invoked most conspicuously to protect in Federal courts those who were apparently incarcerated unjustly in State jurisdictions. The basis for doing so was laid back in 1867 when, according to Justice Brennan, Congress anticipating resistance to its Reconstruction measures had passed legislation which provided that a State prisoner should not have to "abide state court determination of his constitutional defense—the necessary predicate of direct review by this Court—before resorting to federal *habeas corpus*. Rather, a remedy almost in the nature of *removal* from the state to the federal courts of prisoners' constitutional contentions seems to have been envisaged."[7] A 1948 law currently on the books states that an application for a writ in Federal courts "in behalf of a person in custody pursuant to the judgment of a State court shall not be granted unless it appears that the applicant has exhausted the remedies available in the courts of the State, or that there is either an absence of available State corrective process or *the existence of circumstances rendering such process ineffective to protect the rights of the prisoner*"[8] (emphasis supplied).

The Supreme Court held in 1962 that "The language of Congress, the history of the writ, the decisions of this Court, all make clear that the power of inquiry on federal *habeas corpus*

---

[5] 17 Fed. Cas. 145 (1861).
[6] Edward S. Corwin, *The President, Office and Powers* (New York, 1957), 144-145.
[7] Fay *v.* Noia, 372 U.S. 391, 416 (1963).
[8] 28 U.S.C. 2254.

is plenary. Therefore, where an applicant for a writ of *habeas corpus* alleges facts which, if proved, would entitle him to relief, the federal court to which the application is made has the power to receive evidence and try the facts."[9] In view of the above, it is not surprising that the Federal courts' *habeas corpus* business has increased,[10] particularly since the Court has also determined that one who believes he is about to be inducted into the Armed Forces unjustly may also avail himself of the writ in Federal Court.[11] (*See* pp. 191-192 for further discussion.)

¶3. No bill of attainder or *ex post facto* law shall be passed.

By this clause Congress is forbidden to pass bills of attainder and *ex post facto* laws. In the following section a similar prohibition is laid upon the States. It will be convenient to proceed as if both clauses were before us at this point.

"Bills of Attainder"    In English history, a "bill of attainder" was an act of Parliament charging somebody with treason and pronouncing upon him the penalty of death and the confiscation of his estates; but following our Civil War a divided Court held in the famous *Test Oath* cases[12] that the clause ruled out any legislative act "which inflicts punishment without a judicial trial"; and on this ground set aside certain statutes which, by requiring persons who followed certain callings to take an oath declaring they had never borne arms against the United States, excluded former members of the Confederate forces from the pursuit of their chosen professions. And in 1946 the Court, in reliance on these precedents, held void under this same clause a "rider" to a Congressional appropriation act which forbade the payment after a certain date of any compensation to three *named* persons then holding office by executive appointment, unless prior to that date they had been reappointed by the President with the advice and consent of the Senate. The

9 Townsend *v.* Sain, 372 U.S. 293, 312 (1963).

10 Key decisions include Fay *v.* Noia, 372 U.S. 391 (1963); Townsend *v.* Sain, 373 U.S. 293 (1963); Harris *v.* Nelson, 394 U.S. 286 (1969); Kaufman *v.* U.S., 394 U.S. 217 (1969).

11 Oestereich *v.* Selective Service Bd., 393 U.S. 233 (1968); Parisi *v.* Davidson, 405 U.S. 34 (1972). For use of *habeas corpus* by a Reservist who was held in service beyond his contract time *see* Scaggs *v.* Larson, 396 U.S. 1206 (1969).

12 *Ex parte* Garland, 4 Wall. 333 (1867). *See also* Cummings *v.* Mo., 4 Wall. 277.

Court took notice of the fact, which does not appear in the rider itself, that the three persons had been found by a House sub-committee to have engaged in "subversive activities," as the sub-committee defined this term; it also construed the rider as intended to bar its victims from government service.[13]

So, from being a protection of life against legislative wrath, the "bills of attainder" clause has become a protection of livelihood, and even a protection of livelihood at public expense. That the rider in the above case might have been held void as an attempt by Congress to usurp the executive power of removal seems obvious, the fact being notorious that—"dollar-a-year" men aside—people do not often serve government gratuitously. A general provision aimed at officials advocating certain doctrines presents a different question, as indicated by the Supreme Court's decision that the provision of the Subversive Activities Control Act of 1950 requiring "Communist-action" organizations to register was not a bill of attainder.[14] However, the Court later held that a statute which made it a crime for a member of the Communist Party to serve as an officer of a labor union was a bill of attainder, hence unconstitutional.[15]

Although it was undoubtedly the belief of many of the Framers of the Constitution that the ban here placed on *ex post facto* laws and its counterpart in Section X would henceforth rule out all retroactive legislation, and particularly all special acts interfering with "vested rights,"[16] the Court in the early case of Calder *v.* Bull[17] confined the prohibition to retroactive *penal* legislation. An "*ex post facto* law" today is a law which imposes penalties retroactively, that is, upon acts already done, or which increases the penalty for such acts; but laws which might seem at first glance to do these things have been frequently sustained as within State legislative power. Thus a New York statute which forbade physicians who had

*"Ex Post Facto* Laws"

---

[13] United States *v.* Lovett, 328 U.S. (1946). On June 13, 1940, the House passed a bill, later dropped, ordering the Secretary of Labor to deport Harry Bridges to Australia, his own country.

[14] Communist Party *v.* Subversive Activities Control Board, 367 U.S. 1 (1961).

[15] U.S. *v.* Brown, 381 U.S. 437 (1965). The opinion provides a good historical summary and a review of pertinent cases on the subject. Significantly, it was a five-four decision with a forceful dissenting opinion.

[16] Story, *Commentaries*, § 1345; note appended to Justice Johnson's opinion in Satterlee *v.* Matthewson, 2 Pet. 380, 681 ff. (1829).

[17] 3 Dall. 386 (1798).

been convicted of certain offenses to continue in the practice of the medical profession was held not to be an *"ex post facto law"* as to one who prior to the passage of the act had been convicted of such an offense. The Court held that since the statute merely laid down a thoroughly justifiable test of fitness for the practice of medicine, and was entirely devoid of any punitive intention, it was well within the State's police power.[18] Likewise, laws which impose heavier penalties on old than on first offenders for the same offense are not considered to add an additional penalty to the old offender's previous crimes, but merely to punish more suitably and effectively his latest crime.[19] And it is now well settled that statutory changes in the mode of trial or the rules of evidence, which do not deprive the accused of a defense and which operate only in a limited and unsubstantial manner to his disadvantage, are not prohibited by the *ex post facto* clause . . . and this includes statutes which change the 'rules of evidence . . . so as to render admissible against the accused evidence previously held inadmissible.' "[20]

Curiously, the Supreme Court has held that neither deportation nor termination of old age benefits constitutes punishment in a legal sense; consequently, it has upheld legislation which permitted both for Communist affiliation prior to enactment of the legislation.[21] But a three-judge District Court in 1972 struck down as an *ex post facto* law, the Hiss Act, which forbids Government pension payments to those who before enactment of the act concealed material facts concerning affiliation or support of the Communist Party in a Federal employment application or who were convicted of perjury under a Federal statute in connection with a matter involving national security.[22]

[18] Hawker *v.* N.Y., 170 U.S. 189 (1898); *ex parte* Scott, 471 S.W. 2d. 54 (1971); Schmidt *v.* Masters, 490 P. 2d. 1029 (1971).

[19] Graham *v.* W. Va., 224 U.S. 616 (1912).

[20] Dixon *v.* U.S., 287a. 2d. 89 (1972) citing Thompson *v.* Missouri, 299 U.S. 167, 170-171 (1925). *See also* Todd *v.* State, 187 S.E. 2d. 835 (1972).

[21] Galvan *v.* Press, 347 U.S. 522 (1954); Flemming *v.* Nestor, 363 U.S. 603 (1960). *See also* Keefer *v.* Al Johnson Construction Co., 193 N.W. 2d. 305 (1971).

[22] Hiss *v.* Hampton, 338 F. Supp. 1141 (1972). The Court held: "We think disabilities imposed upon the plaintiffs by the Hiss Act are punitive and not regulatory. Neither Hiss nor Strasburger was a federal employee at the time the Act was passed and we do not understand how the conduct of federal employees could be regulated or their moral standards elevated by imposing a financial penalty for their prior conduct upon

While Congress may not pass *ex post facto* laws, the President is not thus hampered in his capacity as Commander-in-Chief in wartime of our forces in the field. Otherwise, Presidents Roosevelt and Truman would be chargeable with violating the Constitution in agreeing at Yalta and Potsdam to the creation of the Nuremberg Court for the trial of leading Nazis on the charge of plotting war, a crime not previously punishable under either International Law or any other law.[23]

¶4. No capitation or other direct tax shall be laid, unless in proportion to the census or enumeration hereinbefore directed to be taken.

A "capitation tax" is a poll tax. The requirement that such taxes should be apportioned grew, in part at least, out of the fear that otherwise Congress might endeavor by a heavy tax on negro slaves *per* poll, to drive "the peculiar institution" out of existence.[24] In other words, the Framers were of the opinion, later voiced by Marshall, that "the power to tax involves the power to destroy," and may be used for that purpose.

"Direct tax" was defined under Section VIII, ¶1. (*See* p. 35 above.)

¶5. No tax or duty shall be laid on articles exported from any State.

"Exported" means exported to a foreign country.[25] This provision has been held applicable even to general imposts with respect to goods in process of being sold for exportation.[26] Although the conditions in light of which this provision was framed have long since disappeared, it is good to be informed

---

men who were not federal employees or likely ever again to become federal employees. Retroactive punishment of former employees for their past misdoings has no reasonable bearing upon regulation of the conduct of those presently employed. The proper function of regulation is to guide and control present and future conduct, not to penalize former employees for acts done long ago."

[23] *Cf. in re* Yamashita, 327 U.S. 1, 26 (1946), for Justice Murphy's dissenting opinion; and Hirota *v.* MacArthur, 338 U.S. 197, 198 (1948), for concurring opinion of Justice Douglas. *See also* the article by Leo Gross on "The Criminality of Aggressive War," 41 *American Political Science Review*, 205 (1947).

[24] Ware *v.* Hylton, 3 Dall. 171 (1796).

[25] Woodruff *v.* Parham, 8 Wall. 123 (1868).

[26] Spalding and Bros. *v.* Edwards, 262 U.S. 66 (1923). *Cf.* Peck & Co. *v.* Lowe, 247 U.S. 165 (1918).

that there is still something which Congress cannot clamp a tax on.

¶6. No preference shall be given by any regulation of commerce or revenue to the ports of one State over those of another; nor shall vessels bound to or from one State be obliged to enter, clear or pay duties in another.

The Supreme Court summarized the meaning of this provision in 1931: "The specified limitations on the power of Congress were set to prevent preference as between States in respect of their ports or the entry and clearance of vessels. It does not forbid . . . discriminations as between ports. Congress, acting under the commerce clause, causes many things to be done that greatly benefit particular ports in the same or neighboring states. The establishing of ports of entry, erection and operation of lighthouses, improvement of rivers and harbors and the providing of structures for the convenient and economical handling of traffic are examples."[27]

Appropriations and Expenditures

¶7. No money shall be drawn from the Treasury but in consequence of appropriations made by laws; and a regular statement and account of the receipts and expenditures of all public money shall be published from time to time.

This paragraph is obviously addressed to the Executive, whose power is thus assumed to embrace that of expenditure. Throughout our history Congress has had occasion to make large lump-sum grants for such things as public works and relief, not to mention the sweeping terms in which appropriations are made in war time for the use of the Armed Services. It seems clear that such grants to an executive agency do not violate the maxim against delegation of legislative power, first, because the function of expenditure is historically an executive function; second, because appropriation acts are not "laws" in the true sense of the term, inasmuch as they do not lay down general rules of action for society at large. Rather, they are administrative regulations, and may go into detail or not, as the appropriating body—Congress—may choose.[28]

[27] Commission *v.* Texas & N.O.R. Co., 284 U.S. 125, 131 (1931); Alabama G.S.R. Co. *v.* U.S., 340 U.S. 216 (1951).
[28] Edward S. Corwin, "Constitutional Aspects of Federal Housing," 84 *University of Pennsylvania Law Review*, 131-156 (1935); *also* Cincinnati Soap *v.* U.S., 301 U.S. 308, 321 (1937).

The above clause was once violated by none other than Abraham Lincoln, who early in the Civil War paid out two millions of dollars from unappropriated funds in the Treasury to persons unauthorized to receive them, for confidential services deemed by him to be of the utmost necessity at the time.[29] But this exception does not dispose of the fact that the clause is the most important single curb in the Constitution on Presidential power. The President can always veto Congressional measures intended to curb him directly, and his veto will be effective nine times out of ten. But a President cannot do much very long without funds, and these Congress can withhold from him simply by inaction.[30]

The question has sometimes arisen whether Congress by attaching provisos or "riders" to its appropriations is constitutionally entitled to lay down conditions by which the President becomes bound if he accepts the appropriation, even though otherwise Congress could not have controlled his discretion, as for example, in deploying the Army and Navy. A logically conclusive argument can be made on either side of this question which, being of a "political" nature, appears to have been left to be determined by the tussle of political forces. *The Legislative "Rider"*

Congressmen in recent years have been perturbed when the President has refused to spend funds which Congress has appropriated. For example, in 1967, when President Johnson impounded several billions of Federal-aid highway funds which had been apportioned to the States, his lawyer, the Attorney General, said he had the power, at least in that particular fact situation.[31] And, more recently, Senators McGovern and Humphrey "assailed . . . the Nixon Administration for withholding $202-million in spending for the food stamp program."[32] What can Congress do under these circumstances? Aggrieved parties have not gone to the courts, indicating a prevailing belief that they would uphold the President's exercise of power. And impeachment hardly seems an appropriate remedy. All that

[29] James D. Richardson, *Messages and Papers of the President,* VI (Washington, 1909), 77-79.
[30] Of course, the major problems involving government spending are complex, but not constitutional issues. *See* Aaron Wildavsky, *The Politics of the Budgetary Process* (Boston, 1964); Charles L. Schultze, *The Politics and Economics of Public Spending* (Washington, D.C., 1968); David J. Ott and Attiat F. Ott, *Federal Budget Policy* (Washington, D.C., 1969).
[31] 42 *Op. Atty. Gen.,* Feb. 25, 1967.
[32] *New York Times,* Jan. 13, 1972. The struggle goes on, *see* Sen. Humphrey's remarks, 118 *Cong. Rec.* No. 165, S18039ff. (1972).

remains is a resort to the tugging and hauling of political forces.

¶8. No title of nobility shall be granted by the United States; and no person holding any office of profit or trust under them shall, without the consent of the Congress, accept of any present, emolument, office or title of any kind whatever from any king, prince or foreign State.

This provision has almost never served as the basis for litigation. A New York court not so long ago held that an American-born citizen was not entitled under this provision to add "von" to his surname.[33] And the Comptroller General has advised that certain retired enlisted servicemen could not take posts with foreign governments and still claim retired pay.[34]

Aware of the penchant of foreign officials to give presents and decorations, Congress has passed legislation "consenting" to employees' (defined to include all officials and, specifically, the President) accepting and retaining gifts of "minimal value tendered . . . as a souvenir or mark of courtesy" and accepting gifts of "more than minimal value when it appears that to refuse the gift would be likely to cause offense or embarrassment. . . . However, a gift of more than minimal value is deemed to have been accepted on behalf of the United States and shall be deposited by the donee for use and disposal as property of the United States."[35] The President is delegated the power under the Act of 1967 to prescribe regulations to carry out its purposes. President Johnson delegated that power to the Secretary of State by Executive Order.[36] Undoubtedly, not every gift of more than "minimal value" is turned over to the Government. Clearly, that requirement is most difficult to police.

## SECTION X

Restraints on the States

¶1. No State shall enter into any treaty, alliance or confederation; grant letters of marque and reprisal; coin money, emit bills of credit; make anything but gold and silver coin a tender in payment of debts; pass any bill of attain-

[33] Application of Jama, 272 N.Y.S. 2d. 677 (1966).
[34] 44 *Comp. Gen.* 130, 227 (1964).
[35] 5 U.S.C. 7342.  [36] *Ibid.*

der, *ex post facto* law or law impairing the obligation of contracts, or grant any title of nobility.

Because of the restrictions imposed on them by this paragraph and ¶3 below, as well as those which result from the powers of the National Government, the States of the Union retain only a very limited capacity at International Law and may exercise that only by allowance of Congress.[1]

In an earlier day, the Supreme Court found that on the basis of this provision, the Confederation cannot "be regarded in this Court as having any legal existence."[2]

As the context shows, the kind of "treaty" here referred to is one whose purpose is the setting up of an arrangement of a distinctly political nature. (*See* ¶3, below.)

"Bills of credit" are bills based on the credit of the State. Banks chartered by a State may issue notes of small denomination despite this provision, although, of course, they cannot be given the quality of legal tender; and since 1866 such notes have been subject to such a heavy tax by the United States as to render them unprofitable.[3] (*See* Article I, Section VIII, ¶2.)

In a recent case, a Texas court rejected the appellant's argument that credit restrictions in a private club set by the Texas Liquor Control Board which did not permit guests to pay in cash put the State of Texas "in a position of prohibiting a club from accepting legal tender in contravention of [this provision of the Constitution and the Federal Code]."[4]

A "law impairing the obligation of contracts" is a law materially weakening the commitments of one of the parties thereto, or making its enforcement unduly difficult, as by the repeal of essential supporting legislation.[5]

"The Obligation of Contracts" Clause

The clause was framed primarily for the purpose of preventing the States from passing laws to relieve debtors of their legal obligation to pay their debts, the power to afford such

[1] Zschernig *v.* Miller, 389 U.S. 429 (1968); Chief Justice Taney's opinion in Holmes *v.* Jennison, 14 Pet. 540 (1841); Skiriotes *v.* Fla., 313 U.S. 69 (1941); United States *v.* Calif., 332 U.S. 19 (1947).

[2] Williams *v.* Bruffy, 96 U.S. 176, 182 (1878).

[3] Briscoe *v.* Bank of Ky., 11 Pet. 257 (1837); Veazie Bank *v.* Fenno, 8 Wall. 533 (1869).

[4] Attic Club Inc. *v.* Texas Liquor Control Board, 450 S.W. 2d. 149, 153 (1970).

[5] Home Building and Loan Asso. *v.* Blaisdell, 290 U.S. 398, 431, 435 (1934); Von Hoffman *v.* Quincy, 4 Wall. 535, 552 (1867).

relief having been transferred to the National Government[6] (*see* Section VIII, ¶4). Later, the Supreme Court under Chief Justice Marshall, in an effort to offset the narrow construction given the ban on *ex post facto* legislation in Calder *v.* Bull (*see* p. 97 above), extended the protection of the clause first to public grants of land; then to exemptions from taxation; then, in the celebrated *Dartmouth College* case, to charters of corporations.[7]

Yet even with this extension the clause nowadays no longer interferes seriously with the power of the States to protect the public health, safety, and morals, or even that larger interest which is called the "general welfare," for the simple reason that a State has no right to bargain away this power.[8] Moreover, "nothing passes by implication in public grants," which are accordingly construed in favor of the State whenever possible.[9] Thus the mere fact that a corporation has a charter enabling it to manufacture intoxicating beverages will not protect it from the operation of a prohibition enactment.[10] Similarly, a contract between two persons by which they agree to buy and sell intoxicating beverages would be immediately cancelled by a prohibition law going into effect.[11] And in modern times the Court has relaxed its standards in cases affecting private contracts. In the *Minnesota Moratorium* case, the Court held that a State could, in the midst of an industrial depression, enable debtors to postpone meeting their obligations for a "reasonable" period.[12]

The "Police Power"  Generally speaking, the protection afforded by this clause does not today go much, if at all, beyond that afforded by Section I of the Fourteenth Amendment. In the words of the Court: "It is settled that neither the 'contract' clause nor the 'due process' clause has the effect of overriding the power of the State to establish all regulations that are reasonably necessary to secure the health, safety, good order, comfort, or gen-

---

[6] Sturges *v.* Crowninshield, 4 Wheat. 122 (1819).

[7] Fletcher *v.* Peck, 6 Cranch 87 (1810); New Jersey *v.* Wilson, 7 Cranch 164 (1812); Dartmouth College *v.* Woodward, 4 Wheat. 518 (1819).

[8] Stone *v.* Miss., 101 U.S. 814 (1879); Levine *v.* L.I.R.R. Co., 331 N.Y.S. 2d. 451 (1972). *But see* People *v.* Northwestern U., 281 N.E. 2d. 334 (1972).

[9] Charles River Bridge Co. *v.* Warren Bridge Co., 11 Pet. 420, 545-554 (1837); Blair *v.* Chicago, 201 U.S. 400 (1906).

[10] Boston Beer Co. *v.* Mass., 97 U.S. 25 (1877).

[11] Manigault *v.* Springs, 199 U.S. 473 (1905).

[12] 290 U.S. 398 (1934). *Cf.* Bronson *v.* Kinzie, 1 How. 311 (1843); McCracken *v.* Hayward, 2 How. 608 (1844).

eral welfare of the community"[13]—in short, its police power. And what *is* "reasonably necessary" for these purposes is today a question ultimately for the Supreme Court; and the present disposition of the Court is to put the burden of proof upon any person who challenges State action as *not* "reasonably necessary."[14]

Until after the Civil War, the "obligation of contracts" clause was the principal source of cases challenging the validity of State legislation. Today the clause is of negligible importance, and might well be stricken from the Constitution. For most practical purposes, in fact, it has been.[15]

¶2. No State shall, without the consent of Congress, lay any imposts or duties on imports or exports, except what may be absolutely necessary for executing its inspection laws; and the net produce of all duties and imposts, laid by any State on imports or exports, shall be for the use of the Treasury of the United States; and all such laws shall be subject to the revision and control of the Congress.

"Imports" and "exports" refer only to goods brought from or destined to foreign countries.[16] For a long time in our history, all taxes on imports still in the original package and in the hands of the importer were prohibited by this clause.[17] But in 1959 the Court upheld particular State *ad valorem* taxes, on imported ores and bundles of veneers in their "original

---

[13] Atlantic Coast Line Co. *v.* Goldsboro, 232 U.S. 548 (1914); Totten *v.* Saionz, 327 N.Y.S. 2d. 55 (1971); Schmidt *v.* Masters, 490 P. 2d. 1029 (1971). *But see* Opinion of the Justices, 283 A. 2d. 832 (1971).

[14] El Paso *v.* Simmons, 379 U.S. 497, 508 (1965); Thorpe *v.* Housing Authority, 393 U.S. 268, 280 (1969). *See also* Helvering *v.* Northwest Steel Rolling Mills, 311 U.S. 46 (1940); and Gelfert *v.* National City Bk., 313 U.S. 221 (1941). In Higginbotham *v.* Baton Rouge, 306 U.S. 535 (1939), it was held that the "obligation of contracts" clause does not protect a right to office. The same result had been reached nearly a century earlier in Butler *v.* Pa., 10 How. 402 (1851). For a statistical survey of the rise and decline of the obligation clause as a restraint on State power, *see* Benjamin F. Wright's *Contract Clause of the Constitution* (Cambridge, Mass. 1938), ch. IV.

[15] Recent decisions by lower courts make the issuance of the clause's death certificate premature. *See* People *v.* Northwestern U., 281 N.E. 2d. 334 (1972) and Opinion of the Justices, 283 A. 2d. 832 (1971).

[16] Woodruff *v.* Parham, 8 Wall. 123 (1868); Sonneborn Bros. *v.* Cureton, 262 U. S. 506 (1923). *Cf.* however, Baldwin *v.* Seelig, 294 U.S. 511 (1935), where a different view was advanced, but quite unnecessarily for the decision of the case, and probably inadvertently.

[17] Brown *v.* Md., 12 Wheat. 419 (1827). Hooven & Allison Co. *v.* Evatt, 324 U.S. 652 (1945).

packages" because, the Court said, "Breaking the original package is only one of the ways by which packaged goods that have been imported for use in manufacturing may lose their distinctive character as imports. Another way is by putting them 'to the use for which they were imported.' "[18]

¶3. No State shall, without the consent of Congress, lay any duty of tonnage, keep troops or ships of war in time of peace, enter into any agreement or compact with another State or with a foreign power, or engage in war, unless actually invaded or in such imminent danger as will not admit of delay.

The full possibilities of securing cooperation among States by means of "agreement or compact" sanctioned by Congress have only begun to be realized within the last forty years.[19] In 1834 New York and New Jersey entered into such a compact "for fixing and determining the rights and obligations of the two States in and about the waters" between them; and in 1921, by a further agreement, they created the "Port of New York District" and established the "Port of New York Authority," which is "a body both corporate and politic," for the comprehensive development of the port. Two years later Congress was asked to sanction an agreement among seven western States which had for its purpose the reclamation of a vast stretch of arid land in the great Colorado River basin. Then in May, 1934, seven northeastern States signed a compact looking to the establishment within their respective jurisdictions of minimum wages for women and minors; while by an act passed June 6 of the same year, Congress gave its consent in general terms "to any two or more States to enter into agreements or compacts for cooperative effort and mutual assistance in the prevention of crime and in the enforcement of

18 Youngstown v. Bowers, 358 U.S. 534, 549 (1959); American Smelting & Refin. Co. v. County of Contra Costa, 77 Cal. Rptr. 570 (1969); *appeal dismissed* 396 U.S. 273 (1970); Nestle Co. v. Porterfield, 277 N.E. 2d. 222 (1971); Halo Sales Corp. v. City and County of San Francisco, 98 Cal. Rptr. 473 (1971); Detroit v. Klockener, 173 N.W. 2d. 214 (1970); Thyssen Steel Corp. v. Mich. Tax Com'n, 196 N.W. 2d. 325 (1972); Volkswagen Pacific Inc. v. Los Angeles, 496 P. 2d. 1237 (1972); *in re* Asheville Citizen-Times Pub. Co., 188 S.E. 2d. 310 (1972); Citroen Cars Corp. v. City of N.Y., 283 N.E. 2d. 758 (1972).
19 Richard H. Leach and Redding S. Sugg, Jr., *The Administration of Interstate Compacts* (Baton Rouge, 1959); W. Brooke Graves, *American Intergovernmental Relations* (New York, 1964), ch. XVII.

their criminal laws and policies."[20] Subsequently Congress authorized, on varying conditions, compacts touching the production of tobacco, the conservation of natural gas, the regulation of fishing in inland waters, the furtherance of flood and pollution control, and other matters.[21] Moreover, since 1935 all the states, beginning with New Jersey, have set up permanent commissions for interstate cooperation, which have led to the formation of a Council of State Governments ("Cosgo" for short), the creation of special commissions for the study of the crime problem, the problem of highway safety, the trailer problem, problems created by social security legislation, etc., and the framing of uniform State legislation for dealing with some of these.

One of a series of such statutes drawn up in 1935 gives State officers in "fresh pursuit" of a criminal the right to ignore State lines; another expedites the process of interstate extradition (*see* Article IV, Section II, ¶2); while a third provides for the extradition of material witnesses. Many States have already adopted all these measures. The interstate compact device, supplemented by commissions on interstate cooperation and by uniform legislation, is today producing cooperation among the States on a grand scale even if it has not fulfilled all of its promise.[22]

The question arises whether the assent of Congress is constitutionally essential to any and all agreements among two or more States. Apparently Chief Justice Taney thought so in 1840;[23] but a half century later the Court indicated the opinion that such assent was not required to agreements having no tendency to increase the political powers of the States or to encroach on the just supremacy of the National Government.[24]

As to what form and to what timing Congress must adhere, the Supreme Court has been most permissive: "Congress may give its approval after the fact or permit the States wide discretion in implementing details, and its approval may even be inferred by circumstance."[25] This permissiveness is indicated

[20] 48 *Stat.* 909 (1934).
[21] 7 U.S.C. 515; 15 U.S.C. 717j; 16 U.S.C. 552 and 667a; 33 U.S.C. 11 and 567-567b.
[22] Leach and Sugg, *Interstate Compacts.*
[23] *See* his opinion in Holmes *v.* Jennison, 14 Pet. 540, 570-572 (1840).
[24] Virginia *v.* Tenn., 148 U.S. 503, 518 (1893).
[25] Virginia *v.* Tenn., 148 U.S. 503 (1893); Virginia *v.* West Virginia, 11 Wall. 39 (1871); Wharton *v.* Wise, 153 U.S. 155 (1894); Deveau *v.* Braisted, 363 U.S. 144 (1960).

in the observation of two highly regarded experts in the field that "Congress plays a merely formal role with regard to most compacts, however, simply granting its consent to compacts already drawn and agreed to by the party states. As as matter of fact, some compacts have gone into effect without benefit of consent legislation passed by Congress."[26]

Federal Grants-in-Aid: Social Security From a comparatively early date the National Government has systematically entered into compacts with newly admitted States whereby, in return for a grant of lands for educational purposes, and other concessions, such States have pledged themselves to refrain from taxing for a term of years lands sold by the National Government to settlers.[27] And since 1911, through so-called "Federal Grants-in-Aid," a quasi-contractual relationship between the National Government and the States has developed on a much more extensive scale. Thus Congress has voted money to subsidize forest-protection, education in agricultural and industrial subjects and in home economics, vocational rehabilitation and education, the maintenance of nautical schools, experimentation in reforestation, highway construction, etc., in the States; in return for which cooperating States have appropriated equal sums for the same purposes, and have brought their further powers to the support thereof along lines laid down by Congress.[28] The Social Security Act of August 14, 1935, is illustrative of this type of National-State cooperation. It brought the national taxing-spending power to the support of such States as desired to cooperate in the maintenance of old-age pensions, unemployment insurance, maternal welfare work, vocational rehabilitation, and public health work, and in financial assistance to the impoverished aged, dependent children, and the blind. Such legislation is, as we have seen, within the national taxing-spending power (see p. 37) but what of the objection that it "coerces" complying States into "abdicating" their powers? Speaking to this point in the Social Security Act cases, the Court said: "The . . . contention confuses motive with coercion. . . . To hold that motive or temptation is equivalent to coercion is to plunge the law in endless difficulties." And again: "The United States and the state of Alabama are not alien governments. They coexist

26 Leach and Sugg, *Interstate Compacts*, pp. 15-16.
27 Stearns *v.* Minn., 179 U.S. 223 (1900).
28 U.S., Advisory Commission on Intergovernmental Relations, *Fiscal Balance in the American Federal System* (Washington, D.C., 1967), ch. V.

within the same territory. Unemployment is their common concern. Together the two statutes before us [the Act of Congress and the Alabama Act] embody a cooperative legislative effort by State and National Governments, for carrying out a public purpose common to both, which neither could fully achieve without the cooperation of the other. The Constitution does not prohibit such cooperation."[29]

In short, expansion of national power within recent years has been matched by *increased* governmental activity on the part of the States also, sometimes in cooperation with each other, sometimes in cooperation with the National Government, sometimes in cooperation with both.

In entering upon a compact to which Congress has given its consent a State accepts obligations of a legal character which the Court and/or Congress possess ample powers to enforce.[30] Nor will it avail a State to endeavor to read itself out of its obligations by pleading that it had no constitutional power to enter upon such an arrangement and has none to fulfill its duties thereunder.[31]

[29] Steward Mach. Co. *v.* Davis, 301 U.S. 548 (1937); Carmichael *v.* So. Coal and Coke Co., 301 U.S. 495, 526 (1937).
[30] Virginia *v.* West Virginia, 246 U.S. 565 (1918).
[31] West Virginia *v.* Sims, 341 U.S. 22 (1951).

# ARTICLE II

This article makes provision for the executive power of the United States, which it vests in a single individual, the President.

## SECTION I

¶1. The executive power shall be vested in a President of the United States of America. He shall hold his office during the term of four years, and together with the Vice-President, chosen for the same term, be elected as follows:

What, precisely, does the opening clause of this paragraph do? Does it confer on the President his power, or merely his title? If the former, then the remaining provisions of this article exist only to emphasize or to qualify "the executive power," as, for instance, where they provide for the participation of the Senate in the appointing and treaty-making powers. If the latter, then the President has only such powers as are conferred on him in more specific terms by these same remaining provisions.

"Executive Power"

The question is one which has been debated from the adoption of the Constitution. The first occasion was in 1789, when Congress, in the absence of a specific constitutional provision regarding the power of removal, conceded the power in the case of the heads of the executive departments to the President alone.[1] Then in 1793 Hamilton and Madison renewed the debate with reference to Washington's Neutrality Proclamation of that year. No provision either of the Constitution or of an act of Congress gave the President the power to issue such a proclamation, but Hamilton defended it, nevertheless, as within the "executive power"; while Madison, reversing his position in the debate of four years earlier, urged the opposed view.[2]

Today the honors of war rest distinctly with the "power" theory of the clause. Especially is this so when one consults the views and practices of some incumbents of the Presidency. The first Roosevelt classified all Presidents as of either the Buchanan or the Lincoln type. Mr. Taft was a Buchanan Pres-

[1] Edward S. Corwin, *The President's Removal Power* (New York, 1927), 10-23.
[2] Corwin, *The President, Office and Powers*, 179-181.

111

ident, sticking as close as bark to a tree to the letter of the Constitution and the statutes in interpreting his powers. T. R., on the other hand, was the Lincoln type, taking the position that the President was a "steward of the people," and as such entrusted with the duty of doing "anything that the needs of the Nation demanded unless such action was forbidden by the Constitution and the laws."[3] Although in his book on the Presidency *Professor* Taft denounced this view as making the President "a universal Providence,"[4] *Chief Justice* Taft in his opinion for the Court in the Oregon Postmaster case supplied the constitutional basis for it when he invoked the opening clause of Article II.[5] For the second Roosevelt's conception of his powers one turns not to the "stewardship theory," but the Stuart theory, which is summed up by John Locke in his second *Treatise on Civil Government* in his description of "Prerogative" as "the power to act according to discretion for the public good, without the prescription of the law and sometimes even against it." Mr. Roosevelt's incumbency was marked by a succession of emergencies, and in meeting them he did not always keep to the path of constitutional or legal prescription. In handing over to Great Britain in the late summer of 1940 fifty reconditioned naval craft the President violated several statutes and appropriated to himself temporarily Congress's power to "dispose of property of the United States" (*see* Article IV, Section III).[6] Yet that this was done with the general approval of the American people there can be no reasonable doubt—thus confirming Locke's further remark that "the people are very seldom or never scrupulous or nice in the point of questioning the prerogative whilst it is in any tolerable degree employed for the use it was meant—that is, the good of the people and not manifestly against it." It is true that the Court's decision in the *Steel Seizure* case has been interpreted by some as marking a definite setback for strong theories of Presidential power, but this diagnosis hardly survives examination of the opinions of the Justices accompanying the case. (*See* pp. 155-157 below).

The President's Term     The President's term of four years, prior to the adoption of the Twentieth, Norris "Lame Duck," Amendment, began on

[3] Theodore Roosevelt, *Autobiography* (New York, 1913), 388-389.
[4] William H. Taft, *Our Chief Magistrate and His Powers* (New York, 1916), 114.
[5] Myers *v.* U.S., 272 U.S. 52 (1926).
[6] See Edward S. Corwin, *New York Times*, Oct. 13, 1940.

March 4 of the year following each leap-year. This happened for two reasons. In the first place, the old Congress of the Confederation set the first Wednesday in March 1789, which chanced to be March 4, as the date on which the Constitution should go into effect. Actually Washington did not take the oath of office until April 30 of that year. Nevertheless, disregarding this fact, the first Congress, by an act which Washington himself approved on March 1, 1792, provided that "the term of four years for which a President and Vice-President shall be elected, shall, in all cases, commence on the fourth day of March next succeeding the day on which the votes of the election shall have been given." Thus Washington's first term was in effect, if not technically, shortened by act of Congress nearly two months; while that of the late President Roosevelt was similarly curtailed by the going into effect of the Twentieth Amendment.

Although the original Constitution made no provision regarding the re-election of a President, there can be no doubt that the prevailing sentiment of the Philadelphia Convention favored his indefinite reeligibility. It was Jefferson (who was not at the Convention) who raised the objection that indefinite eligibility would in fact be for life and degenerate into an inheritance. Prior to 1940 the idea that no President should hold for more than two terms was generally thought to be a fixed tradition, although some quibbles had been raised as to the meaning of the word "term." President Roosevelt's violation of the tradition led to the proposal by Congress on March 24, 1947, of an amendment to the Constitution to rescue the tradition by embodying it in the Constitutional Document. The proposal became a part of the Constitution on February 27, 1951, in consequence of its adoption by the necessary thirty-sixth State, which was Minnesota.[7]

¶2. Each State shall appoint, in such manner as the legislature thereof may direct, a number of electors, equal to the whole number of Senators and Representatives to which the State may be entitled in the Congress; but no Senator or Representative, or person holding an office of trust or profit under the United States, shall be appointed an elector.

The "Electoral College"

---

[7] On the anti-third term tradition, *see* Corwin, *The President, Office and Powers,* 34-38, 331-334.

This and the following paragraph provide for the so-called "Electoral College," or Colleges. It was supposed that the members of these bodies would exercise their individual judgments in their choice of a President and Vice-President, but since 1796 the Electors have been no more than party dummies.

The word "appoint" in this section is used, the Court has said, "as conveying the broadest power of determination." Electors have consequently been chosen, first and last, in the most diverse ways: "by the legislature itself on joint ballot; by the legislature through a concurrent vote of the two houses; by vote of the people for a general ticket; by vote of the people in districts; by choice partly by the people in districts and partly by the legislature; by choice by the legislature from candidates voted for by the people; and in other ways. . . ."[8]

Although Madison testified that the district system was the one contemplated by the Framers, Electors are today universally chosen by popular vote on State-wide tickets. The result is that the successful candidate may have considerably less than a majority, or even than a plurality, of the popular vote cast. Thus, suppose that New York and Pennsylvania were the only two States in the Union, and that New York with forty-one electoral votes went Democratic by a narrow margin, while Pennsylvania with twenty-seven electoral votes and with a somewhat smaller population than New York went overwhelmingly Republican. The Democratic candidate would be elected, although the Republican candidate would have the larger popular vote.

"Minority Presidents" In fact, both Lincoln in 1860 and Wilson in 1912, while carrying much less than a majority of the popular vote in the country at large, had sweeping majorities in the "Electoral College." This was because the defeated party was split in those particular elections. Should, however, a strong third party arise which drew about equally from the two old-line parties, the probable result would be to throw successive elections into the House of Representatives, where the constitutional method of choice would give Nevada equal weight with New York in choosing from the persons, "not exceeding three," having the highest votes in the College. (*See* Amendment XII, p. 378 below.) For this reason, and some others, Senator Norris urged an amendment to the Constitution abolishing the

[8] McPherson *v.* Blacker, 146 U.S. 1, 27, 29 (1892).

College and requiring that the electoral vote of each State be divided among its principal parties in proportion to their strength at the polls; and early in 1949 the Senate adopted such a proposal, which, however, was rejected by the House.[9]

The elections of 1948, 1960, and 1968 have served to feed the fears of a Presidential election being decided by the House. In those elections Presidents Truman, Kennedy, and Nixon failed to receive a majority of the votes cast even though they ended up with substantial majorities in the Electoral College. In 1969 the House passed a resolution for a proposed constitutional amendment to abolish the Electoral College. After a great deal of fireworks, the proposal died a victim of filibusters by Southern and small-State Senators.[10]

Although the Court has characterized Electors as "State officers,"[11] the truth of the matter is that they are not "officers" at all, by the usual tests of office.[12] They have neither tenure nor salary and, having performed their single function, they cease to exist as Electors. This function is, moreover, "a federal function,"[13] their capacity to perform which results from no power which was originally resident in the States, but springs directly from the Constitution of the United States.[14] In the face, therefore, of the proposition that Electors are State officers, the Court has upheld the power of Congress to protect the right of all citizens who are entitled to vote to lend aid and support in any legal manner to the election of any legally qualified person as a Presidential Elector;[15] and its power to protect the choice of Electors from fraud or corruption. "If this government," said the Court, "is anything more than a mere aggregation of delegated agents of other States and governments, each of which is superior to the general government,

---

9 S. J. Res. 2, 81st Cong., 1st Sess., was introduced by Senator Lodge and others, legislative day January 4, 1949, and passed February 1 (same legislative day); reported to the House, March 29, 1950; rejected July 17, 1950. *See* Lucius Wilmerding, Jr. on "Reforming the Electoral System," 64 *Political Science Quarterly*, 1 (1949), for well-documented criticism of the proposal; *also* 32 *Congressional Digest*, Nos. 8-9 (1953).

10 1969 *Cong. Quart. Almanac* 895-901; 1970 *Cong. Quart. Almanac* 840-845.

11 *In re* Green, 134 U.S. 377, 379-380 (1890).

12 United States *v.* Hartwell, 6 Wall. 385, 393 (1868).

13 Hawke *v.* Smith, 253 U.S. 221 (1920).

14 Burroughs *v.* U.S., 290 U.S. 534, 545 (1934).

15 *Ex Parte* Yarbrough, 110 U.S. 651 (1884). *See* the interesting decision of the Alabama Supreme Court, Opinion of the Justices, 217 So. 2d. 53 (1968).

it must have the power to protect the elections on which its existence depends from violence and corruption. If it has not this power it is left helpless before the two great natural and historical enemies of all republics, open violence and insidious corruption."[16] The conception of Electors as State officers is still, nevertheless, of some importance, as was shown in the case of Ray *v.* Blair,[17] which is dealt with in connection with Amendment XII.

To recent predictable challenges that the Electoral College was a "variation" from the "one man-one vote" criterion, the courts have not been sympathetic. As one District Court put it: "Obviously, it cannot be questioned constitutionally since the Electoral College is established in the Constitution." The Court went on to liken the situation constitutionally to that of the Senate where each state "has two senators irrespective of population."[18]

¶3. The electors shall meet in their respective States and vote by ballot for two persons, of whom one at least shall not be an inhabitant of the same State with themselves. And they shall make a list of all the persons voted for, and of the number of votes for each; which list they shall sign and certify, and transmit sealed to the seat of government of the United States, directed to the President of the Senate. The President of the Senate shall, in the presence of

[16] Burroughs *v.* U.S., 290 U.S. 534, 546 (1934).

[17] 343 U.S. 214 (1952). During World War II Congress laid claim in the Act of September 16, 1942, to the power "in time of war" to secure to every member of the armed forces the right to vote for Members of Congress and Presidential Electors, notwithstanding any provisions of State law relating to the registration of qualified voters or any poll tax requirement under, State law. The constitutional validity of this act at that time was open to serious question and by the Act of April 1, 1944, was abandoned. The latter act established a War Ballot Commission, which was directed to prepare an adequate number of official war ballots, whereby the servicemen would be enabled in certain contingencies to vote for Members of Congress and Presidential Electors; but the validity of such ballots was left to be determined by State election officials under State laws. 58 *Stat.* 140, 146 (1944). All of which is, perhaps, a point in favor of the "State officer" idea. In an act passed in 1956, a serviceman "notwithstanding any State law relating to the registration of voters," absent from his home in time of war was entitled to vote for Electors if he was eligible to register and vote except for his absence. He was in that situation exempted from any requirement to pay a poll tax, 70 A *Stat.* 82 (1956). Curiously, these provisions were repealed in 1958, 72 *Stat.* 1570.

[18] Irish *v.* Democratic-Farm-Labor Party of Minnesota, 287 F. Supp. 794 (1968); *affirmed* 399 F. 2d. 119 (1968); Williams *v.* Virginia State Board, 288 F. Supp. 622 (1968).

the Senate and House of Representatives, open all the certificates, and the votes shall then be counted. The person
having the greatest number of votes shall be the President, if such number be a majority of the whole number
of electors appointed; and if there be more than one who
have such majority, and have an equal number of votes,
then the House of Representatives shall immediately
choose by ballot one of them for President; and if no person have a majority, then from the five highest on the list
the said House shall in like manner choose the President.
But in choosing the President the votes shall be taken by
States, the representation from each State having one
vote; a quorum for this purpose shall consist of a member
or members from two-thirds of the States, and a majority
of all the States shall be necessary to a choice. In every
case, after the choice of the President, the person having
the greatest number of votes of the electors shall be the
Vice-President. But if there should remain two or more
who have equal votes, the Senate shall choose from them
by ballot the Vice-President.

This provision was early superseded by Amendment XII.

¶4. The Congress may determine the time of choosing the
electors and the day on which they shall give their votes,
which day shall be the same throughout the United States.

Under the Act of March 1, 1792, previously mentioned, the
Electors are chosen on the Tuesday following the first Monday
in November of every fourth year; while by the Act of June 5,
1934, enacted to give effect to the Twentieth Amendment, the
Electors of each State meet and give their votes on the first
Monday after the second Wednesday in December, following
the November election, and the two houses meet to count the
votes in the hall of the House of Representatives on the ensuing January 6, at 1 p.m.[19] (*See also* Article I, Section IV, ¶2.)
A question which has plagued us for some time is, what can
be done about an Elector who casts his ballot contrary to the
choice indicated by the voters? Apparently, under the present
arrangement of law and custom, there are no sanctions available other than possible public opprobrium.[20] The courts,

[19] 3 U.S.C. 7 and 15.
[20] State *v.* Albritton, 37 So. 2d. 640 (1948).

117

however, might well regard the matter differently, if a Presidential contest were decided by defecting Electors. That to date has never happened, although there were some fears that it might in 1968.

¶5. No person except a natural-born citizen, or citizen of the United States at the time of the adoption of this Constitution, shall be eligible to the office of President; neither shall any person be eligible to that office who shall not have attained to the age of thirty-five years, and been fourteen years a resident within the United States.

All Presidents since, and including Martin Van Buren, except his immediate successor, William Henry Harrison, having been born in the United States subsequently to the Declaration of Independence, have been "natural-born" citizens of the United States, the earlier ones having been born subjects of the King of Great Britain. The question, however, has been frequently mooted, whether a child born abroad of American parents is "a natural-born citizen" in the sense of this clause. Although the courts have never been called upon to decide the question, there is a substantial body of authoritative opinion supporting the position that they are.[21] It should be borne in mind that the term used is "natural-born" and not "native-born."

Does "fourteen years a resident within the United States" mean residence immediately preceding election to office? This question would seem to have been answered in the negative in the case of President Hoover.

¶6. In case of the removal of the President from office, or of his death, resignation, or inability to discharge the powers and duties of the said office, the same shall devolve on the Vice-President, and the Congress may by law provide for the case of removal, death, resignation, or inability, both of the President and Vice-President, declaring what officer shall then act as President, and such officer shall act accordingly until the disability be removed or a President shall be elected.

[21] Warren Freedman, "Presidential Timber: Foreign Born Children of American Parents," 35 *Cornell Law Quarterly*, 357 (1950). When George

This provision has been superseded by Amendment XXV ratified in 1967. Its historical significance is discussed below, pp. 454-456.

¶7. The President shall, at stated times, receive for his services a compensation, which shall neither be increased nor diminished during the period for which he shall have been elected, and he shall not receive within that period any other emolument from the United States or any of them.

Earlier decisions exempting federal judicial salaries from taxation under a general income tax having been overruled, doubtless the President's salary is subject to the same kind of exaction. A special tax on the President's salary would be void on the face of it.[22]

¶8. Before he enter on the execution of his office he shall take the following oath or affirmation:

"I do solemnly swear (or affirm) that I will faithfully execute the office of President of the United States, and will to the best of my ability preserve, protect and defend the Constitution of the United States." *The President's Oath of Office*

What is the time relationship between a President's assumption of office and his taking the oath? Apparently the former comes first. This answer seems to be required by the language of the clause itself, and is further supported by the fact that, while the act of March 1, 1792, assumes that Washington became President March 4, 1789, he did not take the oath till April 30. Also, in the parallel case of the coronation oath of the British monarch, its taking has been at times postponed for years after the heir's succession.

Why then did President Johnson within recent memory make such haste to take the oath? His answer: "Attorney General Kennedy said he would look into the matter and report to me on whether the oath should be administered immedi-

Romney announced his candidacy for the Presidency in 1967, he said the question had been studied by several law firms and there was no question that as the son of Americans he was a "natural born" American even though born in Mexico. *New York Times*, Nov. 19, 1967.

[22] *See* O'Mally *v.* Woodrough, 307 U.S. 277 (1939), overruling Evans *v.* Gore, 253 U.S. 245 (1920), and Miles *v.* Graham, 268 U.S. 501 (1925).

ately or after we returned to Washington. . . . He said [later] that the oath of office should be administered immediately."[23]

The fact that the President takes an oath "to preserve and protect" the Constitution does not authorize him to exceed his own powers under the Constitution on the pretext of preserving and protecting it. The President may veto a bill on the ground that in his opinion it violates the Constitution, but if the bill is passed over his veto, he must, by the great weight of authority, ordinarily regard it as law until it is set aside by judicial decision, since the power of interpreting the law, except as it is delegated by the law itself, is not an attribute of "executive power."[24]

It may be, nevertheless, that in an extreme case the President would be morally justified in defying an act of Congress which he regarded as depriving him of his constitutional powers, until there could be an appeal to the courts or to the people, and in point of fact such defiances have in a few instances occurred.[25]

## SECTION II

¶ 1. The President shall be Commander-in-Chief of the Army and Navy of the United States, and of the militia of the several States when called into the actual service of the United States; he may require the opinion, in writing, of the principal officer in each of the executive departments, upon any subject relating to the duties of their respective offices, and he shall have power to grant reprieves and pardons for offenses against the United States, except in cases of impeachment.

The purely military aspects of the Commander-in-Chiefship were those which were originally stressed. Hamilton said the office "would amount to nothing more than the supreme com-

---

[23] Johnson, *Vantage Point*, p. 13.

[24] For an illustration of Presidential interpretation of the Constitution that did not "come off," *see* the final draft of Jefferson's message to Congress of December 8, 1801. A. J. Beveridge, *Life of John Marshall*, III (Boston, 1919), 605-606. The supposition that Jackson "asserted a right not to carry out a court decision when acting in an executive capacity" is denied by Mr. Charles Warren in his *Supreme Court in United States History*, II (Boston, 1926), 222-224; *see also ibid.* 205 ff.

[25] *See* the speeches of Curtis, Groesbeck and Stanbery in President Johnson's behalf, U.S. Congress, *Trial of Andrew Johnson* (Washington, 1868) I, 377; II, 189 and 359; also Corwin, *The President, Office and Powers*, 62-66.

mand and direction of the military and naval forces, as first general and admiral of the confederacy."[1] Story wrote to the same effect in his *Commentaries*;[2] and in 1850 the Court, speaking by Chief Justice Taney, asserted: "His [the President's] duty and power are purely military."[3]

The modern expanded conception of "the power of Commander-in-Chief in wartime," stems in the first instance from Lincoln, who brought the clause to the support of his duty "to take care that the laws be faithfully executed" in proceeding against an insurrection which be treated as public war. Claiming on these premises "the War Power," he declared, following the attack on Fort Sumter in April, 1861, a blockade of Southern ports, raised a large force of volunteers, increased the Army and Navy, took over the railroad between Washington and Baltimore, and declared a suspension of the writ of *habeas corpus* along the line, eventually as far as Boston. In 1862 he established a temporary draft and suspended the writ of *habeas corpus* in the case of persons suspected of "disloyal practices." At the outset of 1863 he issued the Emancipation Proclamation.[4]

*"Commander-in-Chief in Wartime": Lincoln and F.D.R.*

In the *Prize* cases[5] the Supreme Court, by a narrow majority, ratified his conception of "the greatest civil war in history" as "public war," and hence as vesting the President with the full powers of a supreme military commander against the persons and property of the enemy. Substantially all his acts were, on his suggestion, sooner or later ratified by Congress, or were replaced with legislation designed to accomplish the same ends.[6] Early in 1866, in the famous *Milligan* case,[7] certain military trials ordered or sanctioned by him were overruled, but four of the Justices held that Congress could have authorized

---

[1] *The Federalist*, No. 69.    [2] § 1492.
[3] Fleming *v.* Page, 9 How. 603, 615, 618 (1850).
[4] On Lincoln's view of his powers as Commander-in-Chief in wartime *see* J. G. Randall, *Constitutional Problems Under Lincoln* (New York, 1926). Randall deals with the legal basis of the Emancipation Proclamation at pp. 372-385. *See also* Lincoln's famous message to Congress of July 4, 1861. Richardson, *Messages and Papers*, VI, 20 ff.
[5] 2 Black 635 (1863). *See also* Martin *v.* Mott, 12 Wheat. 19, 32-33 (1827), asserting the finality of the President's judgment of the existence of a state of facts requiring his exercise of the powers conferred by the early acts of Congress authorizing the calling forth of the militia and the employment of the Army and Navy in repressing unruly combinations. 1 *Stat.* 424 (1795); 2 *Stat.* 443 (1807).
[6] *See* 12 *Stat.* 326 (1861).
[7] *Ex parte* Milligan, 4 Wall. 2 (1866).

them, had it deemed such action necessary for the successful prosecution of the war or for the safety of the armed forces.

Presidential
Legislation:
"Indirect
Sanctions"

In World War II Mr. Roosevelt quite frankly avowed the belief that as "Commander-in-Chief in wartime" he possessed powers *other* than those of military command, powers which, if claimable at all by the National Government in peacetime, would have first to be put in operation by Congressional legislation, and then enforced through the usual peacetime agencies in conformity with such legislation. Thus, to take the most conspicuous exemplification of the President's theory, industrial relations were governed in the main throughout the war under an agreement between the President and certain representatives of employers and employees which was entered into shortly after Pearl Harbor. By this agreement labor was pledged not to strike for the duration and ownership was pledged not to resort to the lock out; and all disputes between employers and employees were referred to the War Labor Board, a body which was without legal status and whose decisions were only "advisory." Suppose, however, its advice was not accepted by one of the parties to a dispute; what then? At this point the President stepped in, and brought to bear upon the recalcitrants such "indirect sanctions" as were available from various acts of Congress, most of which were certainly not enacted with any anticipation that the powers they conferred would be utilized for such purpose. Thus non-compliant workers who happened to be subject to conscription were confronted with induction into the armed forces, or employers holding war contracts were ordered not to employ such workers; and non-compliant employers might be denied "priorities," or have their plants seized by the Government under legislation authorizing this to be done when "necessary production" lagged. But in the case of Montgomery Ward, which claimed to be engaged not in "production" but in "distribution" only, the applicability of the legislation just referred to was challenged by a non-compliant company, with the result of raising the question whether the President as "Commander-in-Chief in wartime" was vested by the Constitution itself with the power to make such a seizure. That a military commander has the right to requisition private property to meet an impelling military necessity, subject to the requirement that the property be paid for in due course, is well established; but the taking over of the Ward properties clearly fell outside the precedents. It has to be acknowledged, however, that just as the permeation of the North with disloyal opinions and activities during the Civil War made it difficult to set definite boundaries to the theater of military operations, so do the facts of Total War, which is as much of an industrial operation as it is a military one, make it difficult to maintain a hard and fast line between civilian and military activities and between the governmental powers which are respectively applicable to each. Total War has completely destroyed International Law so far as it formerly attempted to set limits to methods of warfare. Its effect on Constitutional Limitations could be equally disastrous.[8] Some solace may be derived from the knowledge that the Court is quite prepared to limit the Commander-in-Chief in these matters when the warfare is less than total. During the Korean hostilities, the Court held with respect to President Truman's seizure of steel mills: "Even though 'theater of war' be an expanding concept, we cannot with faithfulness to our constitutional system hold that the Commander in Chief of the Armed Forces has the ultimate power as such to take possession of private property in order to keep labor disputes from stopping production. This is a job for the Nation's lawmakers, not for its military authorities."[9]

While the President customarily delegates supreme command of the forces in active service, there is no constitutional reason why he should do so; and he has been known to resolve personally important questions of military policy. Lincoln early in 1862 issued orders for a general advance in the hope of stimulating McClellan to action; Wilson in 1918 settled the

*Military Powers of the President*

---

[8] On the above paragraph *see* Judge Sullivan's informative opinion dismissing the Government's petition for an injunction and declaratory opinion against Montgomery Ward & Co., U.S. *v.* Montgomery Ward, 58 F. Supp. 408 (1945); *reversed* 150 F. 2d. 369 (1945); judgment of the Circuit Court was vacated and the cause remanded to the District Court with directions to dismiss the cause as moot, 326 U.S. 690 (1945). Presumably, the Administration had decided discretion was the better part of valor and chose not to persist in the matter. Executive Order 9370, 8 *Fed. Reg.*, 164 (1943); Employers Group of Motor Freight Carriers, Inc. *v.* NWLB 143 F. 2d. 145 (1944); Steuart and Bro., Inc. *v.* Bowles, 322 U.S. 398 (1944); John Lord O'Brian and Manly Fleischman, "The War Production Board, Administrative Policies and Procedures," 13 *George Washington Law Review*, 1 (1944); Thomas J. Graves, "The Enforcement of Priorities, Conservation and Limitation Orders of the War Production Board, 1942-1944" (Princeton University Ph.D. thesis); *also* United States *v.* Macintosh, 283 U.S. 605, 622 (1931).

[9] Youngstown Co. *v.* Sawyer, 343 U.S. 579, 587 (1952); *cf.* dissent of Chief Justice Vinson, *ibid.* 683-700.

question of an independent American command on the Western Front; Truman in 1945 ordered that the bomb be dropped on Hiroshima and Nagasaki. As against an enemy in the field the President possesses all the powers which are accorded by International Law to any supreme commander. "He may invade the hostile country, and subject it to the sovereignty and authority of the United States."[10] In the absence of attempts by Congress to limit his power, he may establish and prescribe the jurisdiction and procedure of military commissions, and of tribunals in the nature of such commissions, in territory occupied by Armed Forces of the United States, and his authority to do this sometimes survives cessation of hostilities.[11] He may employ secret agents to enter the enemy's lines and obtain information as to its strength, resources, and movements.[12] (He may, at least with the assent of Congress, authorize intercourse with the enemy.[13] He may also requisition property and compel services from American citizens and friendly aliens who are situated within the theatre of military operations when necessity requires, thereby incurring for the United States the obligation to render "just compensation."[14] By the same warrant he may bring hostilities to a conclusion by arranging an armistice, stipulating conditions which may determine to a great extent the ensuing peace.[15] He may not, however, effect a permanent acquisition of territory,[16] though he may govern recently acquired territory until Congress sets up a more permanent regime.[17] He is the ultimate tribunal for the enforcement of the rules and regulations which Congress adopts for the government of the forces, and which are enforced through courts-martial.[18] Indeed, until 1830, courts-

[10] Fleming v. Page, 9 How. 603, 615 (1850).
[11] Madsen v. Kinsella, 343 U.S. 341, 348 (1952). *See also* Johnson v. Eisentrager, 339 U.S. 763, 789 (1950).
[12] Totten v. U.S., 92 U.S. 105 (1876).
[13] Hamilton v. Dillin, 21 Wall. 73 (1875).
[14] Mitchell v. Harmony, 13 How. 115 (1852); United States v. Russell, 13 Wall. 623 (1871); Totten v. U.S. note 12 above, 40 *Op. Atty. Gen.* 251-253 (1942).
[15] *Cf.* the Protocol of August 12, 1898, which largely foreshadowed the Peace of Paris; *and* President Wilson's Fourteen Points, which were incorporated in the Armistice of November 11, 1918.
[16] Fleming v. Page, 9 How. 603, 615 (1850).
[17] Santiago v. Nogueras, 214 U.S. 260 (1909). As to temporarily occupied territory, *see* Dooley v. U.S., 182 U.S. 222, 230-231 (1901).
[18] Swaim v. U.S. 165 U.S. 553 (1897); and cases there reviewed. *See also* Givens v. Zerbst, 255 U.S. 11 (1921). Nonetheless, in a case in which a *habeas corpus* petition was sought to annul a court-martial murder conviction, the Supreme Court, while denying the writ, said: "the constitutional guarantee of due process is meaningful enough, and sufficiently adaptable, to protect

martial were convened solely on his authority as Commander-in-Chief.[19] Such rules and regulations are, moreover, it would seem, subject in wartime to his amendment at discretion.[20] Similarly, the power of Congress to "make rules for the government and regulation of the law and naval forces" (Art. I, §8, cl. 14) did not prevent President Lincoln from promulgating in April 1863 a code of rules to govern the conduct in the field of the armies of the United States which was prepared at his instance by a commission headed by Francis Lieber and which later became the basis of all similar codifications both here and abroad.[21] All of which notwithstanding, the Commander-in-Chief remains in the contemplation of the Constitution a civilian official.[22]

Legally, the President is limited in choosing his principal military subordinates, whose grades and qualifications are determined by Congress and whose appointment is ordinarily made by and with the advice and consent of the Senate, though undoubtedly Congress could if it wished vest their appointment in "the President alone."[23] Also, the President's power to dismiss an officer from the service, once unlimited, is today confined by statute to require a trial by court-martial

---

soldiers—as well as civilians—from crude injustices of a trial so conducted that it becomes bent on fixing guilt by dispensing with rudimentary fairness rather than finding truth through adherence to those basic guarantees which have long been recognized and honored by the military courts as well as the civil courts." Burns *v.* Wilson, 346 U.S. 137, 142-143 (1953). Also, with respect to the Selective Service Act, a Federal Court recently held that "the only 'lawmakers' who could explicitly authorize denial of counsel in hearings before the local draft boards are Congress, not the President. . . ." U.S. *v.* Weller, 309 F. Supp. 50 (1969).

[19] On the President's authority over courts-martial and military commissions, *see* Clinton Rossiter, *The Supreme Court and the Commander-in-Chief* (Ithaca, 1951), 102-120; *also* Burns *v.* Wilson, 346 U.S. 137 (1953).

[20] *Ex parte* Quirin, 317 U.S. 1, 28-29 (1942).

[21] General Orders, No. 100, *Official Records, War of Rebellion*, ser. III, vol. III; April 24, 1863.

[22] Interesting in this connection is the holding of the Surrogate's Court of Dutchess County, New York, that the estate of Franklin D. Roosevelt was not entitled to certain tax benefits that are extended by statute to persons dying in the military service of the United States, *New York Times*, July 26, 1950, 27.

[23] *See* e.g., Mimmack *v.* U.S., 97 U.S. 426, 437 (1878); United States *v.* Corson, 114 U.S. 619 (1885). However, in practice the President does pick them and Senate approval is virtually automatic. This is not to imply that the President plays a lone hand in selection. Normally, he consults and accepts the advice of civilian and military leaders in the Defense Establishment. There have been occasions, however, when Presidents have made selections for heads of Services or other important assignments that were very personal choices. Past practice, of course, does not preclude the Senate's playing a stronger role by virtue of its consent power if it so chooses.

if the officer contends that "he has been wrongfully dismissed" and requests one in writing.[24] But the provision is not regarded by the Court as preventing the President from displacing an officer of the Army or Navy by appointing with the advice and consent of the Senate another person in his place.[25] The President's power of dismissal in time of war Congress has never attempted to limit.

As to the President's constitutional power to relieve a military commander, there should have been no question. But when President Truman relieved General MacArthur in April 1951, there were great cries of outrage and anguish from certain quarters in Congress. Ultimately, a Joint Senate Committee on Armed Services and Foreign Relations after a searching inquiry was unanimous in the view that the President clearly had the power, although some of them felt he had exercised it unwisely.[26]

In recent years a naval officer who had been summarily removed from command of a ship by his superiors afforded a Federal court the opportunity to hold that: "military decisions concerning internal duty assignments and promotions must be left, absent Congressional regulation to the contrary, to the judgment of the chain of command under the President as Commander-in-Chief. If reviewable at all by the federal court, the only possible question would be whether . . . certain procedural Navy Regulations were violated."[27]

The President's Cabinet

"The principal officers" "of the executive departments" have, since Washington's day, composed the President's Cabinet, a body utterly unknown to the Constitution. They are customarily of the President's own party, and loyalty to the President is usually an indispensable qualification which, however, has been at times exhibited in very curious ways; and, of course, such loyalty may not be carried to the extent of violating the law.[28]

It has been frequently suggested, twice indeed by commit-

[24] 10 U.S.C. 804.

[25] Mullan *v.* U.S., 140 U.S. 240 (1891); Wallace *v.* U.S. 257 U.S. 541 (1922).

[26] For good accounts of the fascinating story, *see* Richard Lowitt, ed., *The Truman-MacArthur Controversy* (Chicago, 1967), and John Spanier, *The Truman-MacArthur Controversy and the Korean War* (Cambridge, 1959).

[27] Arnheiter *v.* Ignatius, 292 F. Supp. 911 (1968); *affirmed*, 435 F. 2d. 691 (1970).

[28] *See* generally Richard F. Fenno, Jr., *The President's Cabinet* (Cambridge, 1959).

tees of Congress, that the members of the Cabinet should be given seats on the floors of Congress, and permitted to speak there.[29] There is obviously nothing in the Constitution which stands in the way of this being done at any time.

Nor, for that matter, is there anything to prevent the President from making his Cabinet up out of the chairmen of the principal committees of the House of Representatives or the Senate, for a Cabinet post is not *as such* a "civil office under the authority of the United States"; nor does a member of the Cabinet *as such* "hold any office under the United States" *(see* p. 26ff.). At a time when there is a great deal of soul-searching for ways to involve Congress more in the making of foreign policy and in the disposition of the Armed Forces there is much to recommend such a proposal.[30] Such a step might eventually lead to something akin to the British system of Cabinet government.

As a practical matter, the extent to which Presidents have employed the principal officers of the executive departments as a Cabinet has varied widely in accordance with the style and ideas of particular Presidents. Like some other Presidents, President Eisenhower made extensive use of Cabinet meetings; President Kennedy, on the other hand, like some other Presidents and as the Cuban Missile Crisis attests, relied instead on ad hoc gatherings of selected advisers chosen on the basis of what expertise they could contribute irrespective of the offices they held.

The only constitutional question which has arisen concerning the Cabinet is whether or not it can meet on the call of the Secretary of State in the President's absence. It is an interesting footnote to history that President Wilson strenuously objected on constitutional grounds when his Secretary of State Lansing called a meeting in his absence. With all deference to that great constitutional scholar-President, as vexing as it might have been to have a subordinate take liberties, it does not seem at that stage of the power struggle a *constitutional* issue.[31]

[29] *See* generally Stephen Horn, *The Cabinet and Congress* (New York, 1960).

[30] For a detailed discussion of the proposal and its merits, *see* Edward S. Corwin, "Wanted: A New Type of Cabinet," *New York Times Magazine*, Oct. 10, 1948, p. 14.

[31] Corwin, *The President, Office and Powers*, 3rd. ed., 402. (The description of this event is not found in the 4th. ed.)

The A "reprieve" suspends the penalties of the law; a "pardon"
Pardoning remits them.
Power "Offenses against the United States" are offenses against the
national laws, not State laws. The term also includes acts of so-
called "criminal contempt," in defiance of the national courts
or their processes.[32]

Pardons may be absolute or conditional and may be conferred upon specific individuals or upon classes of offenders,
as by amnesty.

It was formerly supposed that a special pardon, to be effective, must be accepted by the person to whom it was prof-
fered.[33] In 1927, however, in sustaining the right of the President to commute a sentence of death to one of life imprisonment, against the professed will of the prisoner, the Court
abandoned this view. "A pardon in our days," it said, "is not
a private act of grace from an individual happening to possess
power. It is a part of the constitutional scheme. When granted
it is the determination of the ultimate authority that the public
welfare will be better served by inflicting less than what the
judgment fixed."[34]

Pardons may issue at any time after the offense pardoned
has been actually committed but not before then, for that
would be to give the President a power to set the laws aside,
that is, a dispensing power,[35] for asserting the like of which
James II lost his throne.

It is sometimes said that a pardon "blots out of existence the
guilt" of the offender, but such a view, although applicable in
the case of one who was pardoned *before* conviction, is extreme as to one whose offense was established by due process
of law. A pardon cannot qualify such a man for a post of trust
from which those convicted of crime are by law excluded. In
such case the pardoned man is in precisely the same situation
as a man who has served his sentence. The law will punish him
no further for his past offense, but neither will it ignore altogether the fact that he committed it.[36] But a pardon is effica-

---

[32] *Ex parte* Grossman, 267 U.S. 87 (1925). Note that the constitutional
provision itself excepts "cases of impeachment."
[33] United States *v.* Wilson, 7 Pet. 150 (1833); Burdick *v.* U.S., 236 U.S.
79 (1915).
[34] Biddle *v.* Perovich, 274 U.S. 480, 486 (1927).
[35] 1 *Op. Atty. Gen.* 342 (1820); United States *v.* Wilson, cited above;
*ex parte* Garland, 4 Wall. 333 (1866); United States *v.* Klein, 13 Wall. 128
(1872).
[36] *See* Samuel Williston, "Does a Pardon Blot Out Guilt?" 28 *Harvard*

cious to restore a convicted person's civil rights even when completion of his sentence would not have been.

Although Congress may not interfere with the President's exercise of the pardoning power, it may itself, under the "necessary and proper" clause, enact amnesty laws remitting penalties incurred under the national statutes. Recently, the present Senator Taft proposed just such an amnesty for draft-evaders who left the country during the Vietnam conflict and who would be willing to perform certain kinds of social services upon repatriation.[38]

Congressional Amnesties

¶2. *Clause* 1. He shall have power, by and with the advice and consent of the Senate, to make treaties, provided two-thirds of the Senators present concur;

The Treaty-Making Power

It is usual to regard the process of treaty-making as falling into two parts, negotiation and ratification, and to assign the former to the President exclusively and the latter exclusively to the Senate. In fact, it will be observed, the Constitution makes no such division of the subject, but the President and the Senate are associated throughout the entire process of "making" treaties. Originally, indeed, Washington tried to take counsel with the Senate even regarding the negotiation of treaties, but he early abandoned this method of procedure as unsatisfactory.[39] Thus what was intended to be *one* authority consisting of two closely collaborating organs became split into *two*, usually rival and often antagonistic, authorities, performing sharply differentiated functions. In consequence, in 1816, the Senate created the Committee on Foreign Relations as a standing committee, and through this medium most Presidents have managed to keep more or less in touch with Senatorial sentiment regarding pending negotiations, but not always with the result of conciliating it.[40] Today the actual initiation and nego-

---

*Law Review*, 647-663 (1915); *also* Carlesi *v.* New York 233 U.S. 51 (1914); Reed Cozart, "The Benefits of Executive Clemency," 32 *Federal Probation*, No. 2, p. 33 (1968).

[37] Brown *v.* Walker, 161 U.S. 591 (1896).

[38] Edward B. Fiske, "To Forgive or Not To Forgive Dissenters?" *New York Times*, Feb. 20, 1972; 117 *Cong. Rec.*, No. 196, S21588 (1971). *Also see* Louis Lusky, "Amnesty: Question Isn't If, but How and When?" *Washington Post*, Jan. 16, 1972.

[39] Corwin, *The President, Office and Powers*, 255-257.

[40] Edward S. Corwin, *The Constitution and World Organization* (Princeton, 1944), ch. III.

tiation of treaties is, by the vast weight of both practice and opinion the President's alone.[41]

Although it is popularly thought that the Senate ratifies treaties, ratification also belongs to the President alone. But he may not ratify a treaty with the result of *making* it, unless the Senate by a two-thirds vote of the members present, there being at least a quorum, advises such ratification and consents to it.[42] And since the Senate may or may not consent, it may consent conditionally, stating its conditions in the form of amendments to the proposed treaty or of reservations to the proposed act of ratification, the difference between the two being, that whereas amendments, if accepted by the President and the other party or parties to the treaty, change it for all parties, reservations merely limit the obligations of the United States thereunder. Amendments are accordingly resorted to in the case of bilateral treaties, and reservations in the case of general international treaties, like the Hague Conventions or the United Nations Charter.

Of course, if the President is dissatisfied with the conditions laid down by the Senate to ratification he may refuse to proceed further with the matter, as may also the other party or parties to the proposed treaty.[43] With well over 1000 treaties submitted by Presidents to the Senate from 1789 through 1971, it is a good calculation that the Senate amended about 14 per cent, and rejected or so tampered with about 12 per cent that

41 United States *v.* Curtiss-Wright Corp., 299 U.S. 304, 319 (1936).

42 The statement that consent of the Senate must be given by a two-thirds vote of a *quorum of the Senate* has apparently not always been true. Senator H. Alexander Smith of New Jersey, a member of the Foreign Relations Committee, wrote to Edward S. Corwin August 14, 1957, as follows: "Replying to your letter of August 11th with regard to the making of treaties—a few years ago we were very lax in this matter and treaties were frequently ratified by voice vote. We adopted the rule then, however, that there must be a full quorum present, and two-thirds of the Senators present must concur. This means two-thirds of a quorum, of course. Under the present practice we have a quorum call first, and then a roll call vote, with the vote announced and a statement from the chair that two-thirds of a quorum being present and having voted, etc., the treaty is agreed to."

43 "Obviously the treaty must contain the whole contract between the parties, and the power of the Senate is limited to a ratification of such terms as have already been agreed upon between the President, acting for the United States, and the commissioners of the other contracting power. The Senate has no right to ratify the treaty and introduce new terms into it, which shall be obligatory upon the other power, although it may refuse its ratification, or make such ratifications conditional upon the adoption of amendments to the treaty." Fourteen Diamond Rings *v.* U.S., 183 U.S. 176, 183 (1901).

either the President or the other contracting party declined to
go on with them.[44]

The power to make treaties is bestowed upon the United *The Scope*
States in general terms and extends to all proper subjects of *of the*
negotiation between nations. It should be noted, however, *Power*
that a treaty to which the United States is party is not only an
international compact but also "law of the land," in which latter respect it may not override the higher law of the Constitution. Therefore, it may not change the character of the government which is established by the Constitution nor require an
organ of that government to relinquish its constitutional
powers.[45]

How broad the scope of the treaty-making power is, is well
illustrated by the treaty of 1916 between the United States and
Canada providing for the reciprocal protection of migatory

[44] Charles H. McLaughlin, "The Scope of the Treaty Power," 43 *Minnesota Law Review*, 651, 659-678 (1959). To the tables constructed by Mc-
Laughlin, the Department of State was kind enough to provide this
addendum bringing his figures up to date:

TABULATION
SUPPLEMENTING THE TABLE IN McLAUGHLIN'S ARTICLE (PAGE 660)

| Treaty | 1945-1949 | 1950-1954 | 1955-1959 | 1960-1964 | 1965-1969 | 1970-1971 | Total |
|---|---|---|---|---|---|---|---|
| Submitted to Senate | 79 | 93 | 53 | 59 | 69 | 29 | 382 |
| Approved, no Change | 46 | 61 | 45 | 49 | 61 | 20 | 282 |
| Amended | 13 | 24 | 4 | 3 | 4 | 1 | 49 |
| Rejected | 0 | 0 | 0 | 0 | 0 | 0 | 0 |
| No Final Action | 4 | 0 | 2 | 3 | 3 | 8 | 20 |
| Withdrawn | 16 | 8 | 2 | 4 | 1 | 0 | 31 |
| Transmitted for Information Only | 0 | 0 | 0 | 0 | 0 | 0 | 0 |

| | |
|---|---|
| Approved without change | 282 |
| Amended | 49 |
| Rejected | 0 |
| No final action by Senate | 20 |
| Withdrawn | 31 |
| Submitted for information only | 0 |
| Total number of treaties submitted to Senate | 382 |

[45] *See* e.g. Geofroy *v.* Riggs, 133 U.S. 258, 267 (1890); Doe *v.* Braden,
16 How. 635, 657 (1853); The Cherokee Tobacco, 11 Wall. 616, 620-621
(1870); United States *v.* Minn., 270 U.S. 181, 207-208 (1926).
[46] 252 U.S. 416 (1920).

131

birds which make seasonal flights from the one country to the other. Congress passed a law putting this treaty into effect and authorizing the Secretary of Agriculture to draw up regulations to govern the hunting of such birds, any violation of these regulations to be subject to certain penalties; and, in the case of Missouri *v.* Holland,[46] the treaty and the law were sustained by the Supreme Court, the latter as a law "necessary and proper" to put the treaty into effect.

The Supremacy of Treaties over States Rights

In the 1950's, the decision in Missouri *v.* Holland was vehemently assailed as putting the treaty-making power beyond all constitutional metes and bounds, but more especially as invading States Rights; and various constitutional amendments were proposed (including the famed Bricker Amendment) in the tenor of the one proposed by the American Bar Association in 1952 that "A provision of a treaty which conflicts with any provision of this Constitution shall not be of any force or effect. . . ."[47]

Actually, Justice Holmes's opinion for the Court in Missouri *v.* Holland did not bear out the more sweeping charge. It is true that at one point the Justice indulged in some speculation as to whether "authority of the United States means more than the formal acts prescribed to make the convention," but he straightway added: "We do not mean that there are no qualifications to the treaty-making power," and pointed out that the convention before the Court did "not contravene any directly prohibitory words of the Constitution"; also that it dealt with "a national interest of very nearly the first magnitude," and one that could "be protected only by national action in concert with that of another power."[48] In short, it was made *bona fide*, and not for the purpose of aggrandizing the powers of the National Government.

On the other hand, the argument that the treaty impaired States Rights the Justice disparaged, and quite warrantably in view of the unambiguous terms of the supremacy clause. In this respect, indeed, the case only confirmed familiar doctrine and practice. From the time of the Jay Treaty (1794) down to the present, the National Government has entered into many treaties extending to the nationals of other governments the

47 For further discussion and analysis of these proposals *see* the superb articles by McLaughlin, "The Scope of the Treaty Power in the United States," 42 *Minnesota Law Review*, 705 (1958), and 43 *Minnesota Law Review*, 651 (1959), especially the latter, pp. 704-715.
48 252 U.S. 416, 433-435 (1920).

right to inherit, hold, and dispose of real property in the States, although the tenure of such property and its modes of disposition were conceded to be otherwise within the exclusive jurisdiction of the States.[49] Missouri v. Holland simply follows the pattern of these precedents.

In other words, it was proposed in the attempts at constitutional amendment to strip the treaty-making power of the right to enter into conventions of a kind which have thereafter furnished the ordinary grist of the treaty-making process— conventions extending to the nationals of other countries the right to engage in certain businesses in the States, to hold property there, to enjoy access to the courts thereof on terms of equality with American citizens, and so on, all in return for like concessions to our nationals residing abroad. More than that, however, it was proposed that that whole area of power which today rests, in the cases, on the mutual support that the treaty-making power and the power of Congress under the "necessary and proper" clause lend one another shall be expunged from the map of national power. Thus the right of Congress to accord judicial powers to foreign consuls in the United States[50] would have become at least doubtful; so also would have its right to confer judicial powers upon American consuls abroad;[51] its right to provide for the extradition of fugitives from justice;[52] its right to penalize acts of violence within a State against aliens;[53] and so on and so forth.[54] The treaty-making power would have been demoted from the rank of a substantive power of the United States to that of a mere auxiliary power to the other delegated powers. Consequently, it is surprising that the Bricker Amendment was only one vote short of two-thirds approval by the U.S. Senate when it was voted on in 1954.

How is a treaty enforced? Being "law of the land" the provisions of a treaty may, if they do not intrude upon Congress's domain and it was the design of the treaty-making body to put them into effect without reference to Congress, be enforced in court like any other law when private claims are based

How Treaties Are Enforced

---

[49] See McCormick v. Sullivant, 10 Wheat. 192, 202 (1825); United States v. Fox, 94 U.S. 315, 320 (1876); cf. Hauenstein v. Lynham, 100 U.S. 483 (1879).
[50] 22 U.S.C. 256.      [51] In re Ross, 140 U.S. 453 (1891).
[52] 18 U.S.C. 3181-3195.
[53] Baldwin v. Franks, 120 U.S. 678, 683 (1887).
[54] See Neely v. Henkel, 180 U.S. 109, 121 (1901).

upon them; and by the President, when the other contracting sovereignty bases a claim upon them. An example of the former case would be where an alien claimed the right to own land in the United States or to engage in business under a provision of a treaty, of the kind above mentioned, between the United States and his home country.[55] An instance of the latter would be a request by a party to the consultative pact which issued from the Inter-American Conference for Peace at Buenos Aires in December, 1936, for a further conference regarding inter-American relations. To agree to such a conference would be well within the President's diplomatic powers.

*The Power of Congress over Treaties* But it frequently happens that treaty provisions contemplate supplementary action by Congress, as did the treaty with Canada above referred to; and this is necessarily the case where money is needed to carry a treaty into effect (*see* Article I, Section IX, ¶7). Does, however, the same rule apply generally in the case of treaty provisions the enforcement of which involves executive and/or judicial action in the area of *Congress's enumerated powers*, its power for instance to declare war, its power to regulate foreign commerce, etc.? While there are a few judicial *dicta* which assert that the maxim "*leges posteriores priores contrarias abrogant* (later laws repeal earlier contradictory ones)" operates reciprocally as between treaties and acts of Congress, and hence carry the implication that the treaty-making power is capable of imparting to its engagements the quality of "law of the land" enforceable by the courts *within the area of Congress's powers*, yet only in one instance has a treaty provision ever been found to effect such a repeal.[56] Moreover, the trend of practice has been from an early date toward an affirmative answer to the above question, a development which is registered in the United Nations Participation Act of 1945. By this measure the steps to be taken to fulfill our engagements under the United Nations Charter in the matter of furnishing armed forces for use at the behest of the Security Council were all to be subject to the approval of Congress.[57] The frustration of this mode of

[55] Hauenstein *v*. Lynham, 100 U.S. 483 (1879); Jordan *v*. Tashiro, 278 U.S. 123 (1928); Nielson *v*. Johnson, 279 U.S. 47 (1929); Kolovrat *v*. Oregon, 366 U.S. 187 (1961); Zschernig *v*. Miller, 389 U.S. 429 (1968).

[56] *See* e.g. Whitney *v*. Robertson, 124 U.S. 190 (1888); United States *v*. Lee Yen Tai, 185 U.S. 213 (1902); Pigeon River Improvement, etc. Co. *v*. Cox, 291 U.S. 138 (1934); *and* Cook *v*. U.S., 288 U.S. 102 (1933)—which is the exceptional and exceptionable—holding.

[57] 59 *Stat.* 613 (1945).

procedure by the circumstances of our involvement in Korea in 1950 is dealt with later. (*See* p. 155.)

It is also by act of Congress that officers and employees of the United Nations have been accorded various diplomatic immunities, and their incomes exempted from taxation.[58]

But is Congress *obliged* to carry out a treaty which it alone may carry out? The answer would seem to be that it is not *legally* obliged to do so, since the Constitution generally leaves it full discretion as to whether or not it shall exercise its powers. But morally it would be obliged to carry out the pledges of the United States duly entered into unless in the specific situation before it an honorable nation would be morally justified in breaking its word.

Treaties of the United States may be terminated in accordance with their own provisions or by agreement with the other contracting party; or as "law of the land" they may be repealed by act of Congress, or denounced by the President or the President and Senate; but any such one-sided procedure still leaves the question of their international obligation outstanding.[59] The United States has the same right as any other nation has, and no more, to determine the scope of its obligations under International Law. *The Termination of Treaties*

Besides treaties proper, the President frequently negotiates agreements with other governments which are not referred to the Senate for its advice and consent. These are of two kinds: those which he is authorized by Congress to make, or which he lays before Congress for approval and implementation; and those which he enters into by virtue simply of his diplomatic powers and powers as Commander-in-Chief.[60] As early as 1792 *Executive Agreements by Authorization of Congress*

---

[58] 59 *Stat.* 669 (1945).

[59] Head Money cases, 112 U.S. 580 (1884). *See also* The Cherokee Tobacco, 11 Wall. 616 (1871); United States *v.* Forty-Three Gallons of Whiskey, 108 U.S. 491, 496 (1883); Botiller *v.* Dominguez, 130 U.S. 238 (1889); Chae Chan Ping *v.* U.S., 130 U.S. 581, 600 (1889); Whitney *v.* Robertson, 124 U.S. 190, 194 (1888); Fong Yue Ting *v.* U.S., 149 U.S. 698, 721 (1893); "Congress by legislation, and so far as the people and authorities of the United States are concerned, could abrogate a treaty made between this country and another country which had been negotiated by the President and approved by the Senate." La Abra Silver Mining Co. *v.* U.S., 175 U.S. 423, 460 (1899). *Cf.* Reichart *v.* Felps, 6 Wall. 160, 165-166 (1868), where it is stated obiter that "Congress is bound to regard the public treaties, and it had no power . . . to nullify [Indian] titles confirmed many years before. . . ."

[60] *See* Corwin, *The President, Office and Powers*, 259-264; McLaughlin, 42 *Minnesota Law Review*, 764-771, and 43 *Minnesota Law Review*, 678-693, 720-755. For the period 1938-1957, McLaughlin reports that 160 of

Congress authorized the Postmaster-General to enter into postal conventions; in 1934 it authorized the President to enter into foreign-trade agreements and to lower customs rates as much as fifty per cent on imports from the other contracting

2,687 executive agreements (about 5.9%) were neither authorized nor approved; virtually all the other executive agreements in that period were authorized in advance by treaty or Statute, 43 *Minnesota Law Review*, 721. The Department of State was kind enough to provide the following data to bring the McLaughlin tables up-to-date. Note, however, that the Department uses a somewhat different set of classifications. . . . "Executive Agreements (international agreements other than treaties) may, according to their respective legal bases, be . . . classified as those (A) based on prior legislation, (B) made effective through subsequent legislation, (C) within the framework of treaties and made effective, in whole or in part, in accordance with legislation, (D) made under treaties, (E) made in part on the basis of prior or subsequent legislation and/or in part on treaties and in part on the President's constitutional authority. . . ."

By Department of State reckoning then, from 1947-1968 only about 1% of executive agreements were based on the President's constitutional authority alone and 338, or another 7%, were based in part on the President's authority.

INTERNATIONAL AGREEMENTS OTHER THAN TREATIES, 1946-1968,
TABULATED ACCORDING TO TOTALS IN THE SEVERAL CATEGORIES
ON A YEAR-BY-YEAR BASIS

| | A | B | C | D | E | F | Totals |
|---|---|---|---|---|---|---|---|
| 1946 | 110 | 6 | 5 | | 16 | 2 | 139 |
| 1947 | 106 | 3 | 4 | 1 | 26 | 4 | 144 |
| 1948 | 135 | 2 | 3 | | 36 | 2 | 178 |
| 1949 | 117 | 1 | 3 | | 24 | 3 | 148 |
| 1950 | 143 | | 5 | 1 | 7 | 1 | 157 |
| 1951 | 180 | | 15 | 2 | 14 | 2 | 213 |
| 1952 | 257 | | 10 | 1 | 22 | 1 | 291 |
| 1953 | 135 | | 11 | 3 | 9 | 5 | 163 |
| 1954 | 179 | | 9 | 2 | 14 | 2 | 206 |
| 1955 | 270 | | 14 | 2 | 10 | 1 | 297 |
| 1956 | 208 | | 13 | 2 | 10 | | 233 |
| 1957 | 200 | | 8 | | 10 | 1 | 219 |
| 1958 | 174 | | 6 | | 15 | 1 | 196 |
| 1959 | 204 | 1 | 15 | 2 | 26 | | 248 |
| 1960 | 238 | 3 | 16 | 2 | 6 | 1 | 266 |
| 1961 | 234 | 3 | 11 | 1 | 7 | 3 | 259 |
| 1962 | 300 | 2 | 6 | 1 | 9 | | 318 |
| 1963 | 204 | | 11 | 3 | 13 | 2 | 233 |
| 1964 | 193 | 4 | 9 | | 13 | 1 | 220 |
| 1965 | 172 | 3 | 14 | | 11 | 2 | 202 |
| 1966 | 200 | 1 | 14 | 1 | 8 | 8 | 232 |
| 1967 | 170 | 1 | 11 | 5 | 17 | 5 | 209 |
| 1968 | 133 | 1 | 3 | 1 | 15 | 2 | 155 |
| Total | 4,262 | 31 | 216 | 30 | 338 | 49 | 4,926 |

countries in return for equivalent concessions. Present law reflecting more concern about increasing rates still authorizes the President to make agreements.[61] Similarly, the Lend-Lease Act of March 11, 1941, was the fountainhead of the numerous agreements with our allies and associates in World War II under which our government first and last furnished them more than forty billions worth of munitions of war and other supplies. Nor is the validity of such agreements and compacts today open to serious question in view of repeated decisions of the Court.[62]

Instances of "treaty making" by the President without the aid or consent of either Congress or the Senate are much fewer in number but some of them have dealt with issues of considerable magnitude. One was the exchange of notes in 1817 between the British Minister Bagot and Secretary of State Rush for the limitation of naval forces on the Great Lakes. Not till a year later was it submitted to the Senate, which promptly ratified it. Of like character was the protocol of August 12, 1898, between the United States and Spain, by which the latter agreed to relinquish all title to Cuba and cede Puerto Rico and her other West Indian possessions to the United States; the exchange of notes between the State Department and various European governments in 1899 and 1900 with reference to the "Open Door" in China; the exchange in 1908 of so-called "identic notes" with Japan concerning the maintenance of the integrity of China; the "Gentlemen's Agreement," first drawn in 1907, by which Japanese immigration to this country was long regulated; the *modus vivendi* by which after the termination of the Treaty of Washington in 1885 American fishing rights off the coast of Canada and Newfoundland were defined for more than a quarter of a century; the protocol for ending the Boxer Rebellion in 1901; the notorious Lansing-Ishii agreement of November 2, 1917, recognizing Japan to have "special rights" in China; the armistice of November 11, 1918—to say nothing of the entire complexus of conventions and understandings by which our relations with our "Associates" in World War I and our "Allies" in World War II were determined, of the latter of which those labelled "Yalta" and "Potsdam" have come to achieve special notoriety. More re-

*Executive Agreements Pure and Simple*

[61] 19 U.S.C. 1351.
[62] The leading cases are Field *v*. Clark, 143 U.S. 649 (1892); and Hampton, Jr. & Co. *v*. U.S., 276 U.S. 394 (1928). For Lend-Lease, *see* 55 *Stat*. 31 (1941).

137

cently, President Nixon revived and renewed an executive agreement with Portugal allowing the United States to refuel military planes in the Azores and granting $435 million in economic aid to Portugal without consulting Congress.[63]

Obviously, the line between such agreements and treaties which have to be submitted to the Senate for its approval is not an easily definable one. So when the Senate refused in 1905 to ratify a treaty which the first Roosevelt had entered into with the government of Santo Domingo for putting its customs houses under United States control, the President simply changed the "treaty" into an "agreement" and proceeded to carry out its terms, with the result that a year or so later the Senate capitulated and ratified the "agreement," thereby converting it once more into a "treaty." Furthermore, by recent decisions of the Supreme Court, an "executive agreement" within the power of the President to make is law of the land which the courts must give effect to, any State law or judicial policy to the contrary notwithstanding.[64] This, undoubtedly, is going rather far. It would be more accordant with American ideas of government by law to require, before a purely executive agreement be applied in the field of private rights, that it be supplemented by a sanctioning act of Congress. And that Congress, which can repeal any treaty as "law of the land or authorization," can do the same to executive agreements, would seem to be obvious. Yet, significance must be attached to the fact that when constitutional amendments were being prepared in the 1950's to limit the President's power to make executive agreements, they were rejected.[65] However, currently the Senate is manifesting renewed interest in finding ways to require Congressional consideration of executive agreements.[66]

Nor is the "executive agreement," whether made with or without the sanction of Congress, the only inroad which practice under the Constitution has made upon the original role of

[63] *New York Times* (editorial), Dec. 26, 1971.
[64] United States *v.* Belmont, 301 U.S. 324 (1937); United States *v.* Pink, 315 U.S. 203 (1942).
[65] McLaughlin, 43 *Minnesota Law Review*, 715-718.
[66] 1972 *Cong. Quart. Weekly Report*, 219, 1006, 1220. On March 3, 1972, the Senate passed a resolution stating that "any agreement with Portugal or Bahrain for military bases or foreign assistance should be submitted as a treaty to the Senate for advice and consent." Subsequent efforts to reverse that resolution were defeated in the Senate. 118 *Cong. Rec.* No. 99, S9639ff. (1972).

the Senate in treaty-making. Not only, as was pointed out above, is the business of negotiation today within the President's exclusive province, but Congress has come into possession of a quite indefinite power to legislate with respect to external affairs. The annexation of Texas in 1845 by joint resolution is the leading precedent. The example thus set was followed a half century later in the case of Hawaii; and of similar import are the Joint Resolution of July 2, 1921, by which war with the Central Powers was brought to a close, and the Joint Resolution of June 19, 1934, by which the President was enabled to accept membership for the United States in the International Labor Organization.[67] Such precedents make it difficult to state any limit to the power of the President and Congress, acting jointly, to implement effectively any foreign policy upon which they agree, no matter how "the recalcitrant third-plus-one-man" of the Senate may feel about the matter. Nonetheless, the Supreme Court has held that a Status of Forces Agreement (i.e. an agreement authorized by treaty made with a country in which U.S. troops are based) could not be used to sustain implementing legislation which abridged constitutional guarantees of the Bill of Rights.[68]

¶2. Clauses 2 and 3. And he shall nominate, and, by and with the advice and consent of the Senate, shall appoint ambassadors, other public ministers and consuls, judges of the Supreme Court and all other officers of the United States, whose appointments are not herein otherwise provided for, and which shall be established by law; but the Congress may by law vest the appointment of such inferior officers, as they think proper, in the President alone, in the courts of law, or in the heads of departments.

*The National Executive Establishment*

Evidently, the Framers of the Constitution assumed that all officials of the United States would be appointive and fall into two classes: the so-called "Presidential officers" and "inferior officers." They, of course, had no way of knowing, and, indeed probably would have been astounded that one day there would be a Federal bureaucracy of well over two million people. The total population in the country at that time was less than four million. Consequently, constitutional provisions for

---

[67] 42 *Stat.* 105; 49 *Stat.* 2741.
[68] Reid *v.* Covert, 354 U.S. 1 (1957); *but see* Wilson *v.* Girard, 354 U.S. 524 (1957).

only those two classes were not adequate for the long haul of history. Eventually, Congress by law provided for officials whose appointments were not made in accordance with Section II. In 1879, the Supreme Court held that an official who is not appointed in the manner prescribed in the Constitution "is not an *officer*, though he may be an agent or employé working for the government and paid by it, as nine-tenths of the persons rendering service to the government undoubtedly are, without thereby becoming its officers."[69] What the Court said in effect is that Congress could provide for appointment of officials in a manner inconsistent with the appointment provisions of the Constitution and those who were so appointed by definition were not "officers." Current law on the subject reflects the distinction made by the Court. "Officers" are defined as those "required by law to be appointed in the civil service by one of the following acting in an official capacity— (A) the President; (B) a court of the United States; (C) the head of an Executive agency; or (D) the Secretary of a military department." An "employee" is defined as one appointed by other specified officials as well as the President when he is appointing "in an official capacity" but not in pursuance of a requirement by law.[70] In sum, this constitutional provision has been interpreted to conform with the realities of the need for a large bureaucracy operating under some kind of merit system.

One other crucial distinction should be made at this point. The term "Civil Service" consists "of all appointive positions in the executive, judicial and legislative branches"; the terms "Competitive Service" and "Classified Service" indicate those who are covered by the merit system, including its job protection. Those outside the merit system are in the "Excepted Service"; or "Unclassified Civil Service." These include, most importantly, the so-called "Political officers" like Secretaries, Under Secretaries, and Assistant Secretaries who are appointed by the President with the advice and consent of the

---

[69] U.S. *v.* Germaine, 99 U.S. 508, 509 (1879).

[70] 5 U.S.C. 2104 and 2105. In an interesting opinion rendered in 1907, the Attorney General stated that "A fortiori it would seem clear that the recognition in a Federal statute of a person in public employ as an officer of the United States constitutes the person such officer. . . . If it be assumed, argumenti gratia, that the method of their appointment would be unconstitutional if they are officers, it does not seem that this fact constitutes any bar to their classification, so long as they continue to be recognized as officers de facto." 26 *Op. Atty. Gen.* 364, 370 (1907).

Senate, who do not have to take Civil Service examinations and who do not have the job protections of those in the "Competitive Service."

The steps of appointment provided for in the first clause are, first, their nomination by the President; second, their appointment "by and with the advice and consent of the Senate," the latter of which may not be, as in the case of treaties, qualified by conditions;[71] third, their commissioning, which is also by the President[72] (*see* Section III). As recent monumental battles over Supreme Court appointments suggest, obtaining the consent of the Senate is not always a *pro forma* matter.[73]

The offices of "ambassador," "public minister" and "consul" being recognized by the Law of Nations, it was at first thought that the President might nominate to them as occasion arose in our intercourse with foreign nations, but since 1855 Congress has asserted its right to restrict such appointments, which it is able to do through its control of the purse.

Besides "ambassadors" and "public ministers" there has sprung up in the course of time a class of "personal agents" of the President, in whose appointment the Senate does not participate. Theoretically these do not usually have diplomatic quality, but if their identity is known they will be ordinarily accorded it in the countries to which they are sent.[74]

"Shall be established by law": All civil offices of the United States except those of President, Vice-President, Ambassadors, Public Ministers and Consuls, and possibly of Justices of the Supreme Court, are supposed to be the creations of Congress. The great majority, however, of the alphabetical agencies, like WPB, WLB, WMC, ODT, and so on, through which World War II was conducted on the home front, were created by the President as ramifications of the OEM (Office of Emergency Management), also his creation; but most of them eventually received Congress's blessing and approval in the shape of appropriations or in legislation augmenting or regulating their powers. OPA (successor to Presidentially created OPACS) was brought into existence by Congress.

*The War Agencies*

[71] 3 *Op. Atty. Gen.* 188 (1837); Story, *Commentaries*, II, §1531; Gaillard Hunt, ed., *Writings of James Madison* (New York, 1900-1910) IX, 111-113.
[72] Marbury v. Madison, 1 Cr. 137 (1803).
[73] For a detailed description of the appointing process generally *see* Harold W. Chase, *Federal Judges, The Appointing Process* (Minneapolis, 1972).
[74] Corwin, *The President, Office and Powers*, 251-253.

When Congress creates offices it does so by virtue of its powers under the "necessary and proper" clause; and by the same authorization it may also stipulate what qualifications appointees to them shall have.[75]

**Congressional Regulation of Offices and Officers**

Furthermore, Congress has very broad power to regulate the conduct in office, especially regarding their political activities, of officers and employees of the United States. All such persons, and members of Congress as well, are forbidden to receive or solicit any contribution to be used for a political purpose.[76] By the Hatch Act of 1939[77] all persons in the executive branch of the Government, or any department or agency thereof, except the President and Vice-President and certain "policy determining" officers, are forbidden to "take an active part in political management or political campaigns," although they are still permitted to "express their opinions on all political subjects and candidates"; and by the Hatch Act of 1940[78] these regulations were extended to employees of State and local governments who were engaged in activities financed in whole or part by national funds. Although there has been a change in these laws, it is significant that in their original form both acts were sustained by the Court, the former on the ground that the conduct banned by it was "reasonably deemed by Congress to interfere with the efficiency of the public service."[79]

Will the Court take the same view with a recently enacted law which renders a person ineligible for a position with the Federal Government if he is convicted for "inciting, organizing, promoting, encouraging, or participating in a riot or civil disorder"?[80] A lower court has struck down as unconstitutional, a statute which denies Federal employment to an individual who among other things advocates overthrow of the Government or "asserts the right to strike against the Government."[81] But the law in that case did not require a conviction.

---

[75] *Ibid.*, 363-365.
[76] 18 U.S.C. 602.
[77] 53 *Stat.* 1147.
[78] 54 *Stat.* 767-772.
[79] United Public Workers v. Mitchell, 330 U.S. 75 (1947); Oklahoma v. C.S. Comm., *ibid.*, 127 (1947). *See also, ex parte* Curtis, 106 U.S. 371 (1882); United States v. Wurzbach, 280 U.S. 396 (1930). The current law can be found in 5 U.S.C. 7324. In 1972 a three-judge Federal district court held that the provisions banning political activities "are impermissibly vague and overbroad." National Assoc. of Letter Carriers v. Civil Service Com'n, 41 *LW* 2069 (1972); *rev. granted* 41 *LW* 3324 (1972).
[80] 5 U.S.C. 7313.
[81] Stewart v. Washington, 301 F. Supp. 610 (1969).

Also, Congress may, and usually does, limit the term for which an appointment to office may be made; while as to those officers who are instruments and agents only of the constitutional powers of Congress, the latter may limit drastically their removability during such terms. If, however, an officer *is an agent of the President in the exercise of any of his powers*—whether constitutional or statutory—such officer is for that reason removable at the will of the President.[82]

Chief Justice Taft, a former President not known for his assertions of Presidential power while in that office, speaking for the majority in the celebrated Myers case asserted that "The power to remove superior officers, is an incident of the power to appoint them, and is in its nature an executive power."[83] For about a decade following that decision it was thought that the President's power to remove was more sweeping than it turned out to be. In another celebrated case decided in 1935, the Court held: "Whether the power of the President to remove an officer shall prevail over the authority of Congress to condition the power by fixing a definite term and precluding a removal except for cause, will depend upon the character of the office; the *Myers* decision, affirming the power of the President alone to make the removal, is confined to purely executive officers" and that a Federal Trade Commissioner was not such an officer.[84] Later, it was determined that a War Claims Commissioner was not "an Executive Officer."[85] These decisions do not alter the fact that all non-judicial officers of the United States are subject to disciplinary removal by the President for good cause, by virtue of his duty to "take care that the laws be faithfully executed."[86]

On the other hand, Presidents have more than once had occasion to stand in a protective relation to their subordinates, assuming their defense in litigation brought against them[87] or pressing litigation in their behalf,[88] refusing a call for papers from one of the Houses of Congress which might be used, in their absence from the seat of government, to their disadvan-

*Power to Remove as an Incident of the Power to Appoint*

*The Power of the President to Protect Subordinates*

---

[82] *Cf.* Myers *v.* U.S. ("Oregon Postmaster Case"), 272 U.S. 52 (1926); Humphrey's Executor *v.* U.S., 295 U.S. 602 (1935); Wiener *v.* U.S., 357 U.S. 349 (1958); Kandall *v.* U.S., 186 Ct. Cl. 900 (1969).
[83] 272 U.S. 52 at 161 (1926).
[84] Humphrey's Executor *v.* U.S., 295 U.S. 602, 631-632 (1935).
[85] Wiener *v.* U.S., 357 U.S. 349 (1958).
[86] Corwin, *The President, Office and Powers*, 102-104.
[87] 6 *Op. Atty. Gen.*, 220 (1853); *in re* Neagle, 135 U.S. 1 (1890).
[88] United States *v.* Lovett, 328 U.S. 303 (1946).

tage[89] challenging the constitutional validity of legislation which the President deemed detrimental to their interests.[90] There is one matter, moreover, as to which he is able to spread his own official immunity to them. The courts may not require them to divulge confidential communications from or to the President, that is, communications which they choose to regard as confidential.[91]

The
Executive
Privilege

Whether a Congressional committee is similarly powerless is an interesting question which has not been adjudicated. There seems to be a substantial basis for concluding that the "separation of powers" principle which is believed to preclude compelling a President to testify would cover those who would be asked to testify about what the President said or wrote to them on a confidential basis. But this opens up the broader issue involved with respect to "executive privilege." More and more over the years the executive officers have refused to testify before Congressional committees, usually on the grounds that to do so would endanger national security. Some Congressmen suspect that more often than not the Administration is merely trying to prevent embarrassment through the exposure of misjudgments and inefficiencies. And even if the national security is involved, it can be persuasively argued that in a democratic society Congressmen should be given any information they need to know to legislate intelligently and that it can be done safely in executive session. But it has become conventional wisdom, based in part on the opinions of a succession of Attorneys General, that there was no point in Congressmen trying to settle the matter in the courts.[92] Consequently, a resolution to the issue seems to have been worked

---

[89] Richardson, *Messages and Papers of the Presidents*, II, 847 (January 10, 1825).

[90] *See* U.S. *v.* Lovett, 328 U.S. 303, 313 (1946).

[91] Marbury *v.* Madison, 1 Cr. 137, 144-145 (1803).

A ruling by Attorney General Jackson, dated April 20, 1941, holds that all FBI investigative reports are confidential documents that the President is entitled in the public interest to withhold from Congressional investigating committees. Early in 1944 an administrative assistant to the President refused to answer questions put to him by a Senate sub-committee, but later yielded on the President's order to do so. *New York Times*, February 29 and March 1, 5, and 10, 1944. *And see* generally Charles Warren, "Presidential Declarations of Independence," 10 *Boston University Law Review*, 1 (1930); *also* Attorney General Brownell's Memorandum, *New York Times*, May 18, 1954.

[92] *See* generally the brilliant articles by Raoul Berger, "Executive Privilege *v.* Congressional Inquiry," 12 *U.C.L.A. Law Review*, 1044 and 1288 (1965). He argues persuasively that the conventional wisdom is wrong.

out through the political process. In a carefully staged scenario in 1962 stemming from a dispute over whether or not a Senate sub-committee was entitled to know the names of Defense Department officials who had censored speeches of Generals and Admirals, Secretary of Defense McNamara appeared before the sub-committee and read a letter to him from President Kennedy directing him (McNamara) not to testify about certain matters. Among other things the Kennedy letter stated that "the principle which is at stake here cannot be automatically applied to every request for information. Each case must be judged on its merits. . . ." Senator Stennis, the Chairman of the sub-committee, obviously prepared for the event, "read from prepared notes and annotated transcripts of court decisions and Congressional hearings to justify his ruling" to accept the President's plea.[93] Subsequent events indicate that the precedent has been set. If the President himself indicates in writing that he does not want his subordinate to testify, the Congressional committee will usually let the matter drop there.[94]

But, during the recent donnybrook over the confirmation of Richard G. Kleindienst as Attorney General, when some Senators wanted White House aide Peter Flanigan to testify contrary to President Nixon's wishes, they had (and used) some unusual political leverage. They could and did put pressure on the President by threatening to hold up confirmation unless Flanigan testified.[95] Ultimately, a compromise was effected by which Flanigan would testify only as to certain events. During his testimony, several Senators angrily objected to Flanigan's refusal to answer questions that he thought were beyond the scope of the agreement. In terms of developing the meaning of the Constitution, perhaps the most significant event in the controversy was the Senate Judiciary Committee's refusal to subpoena Flanigan. A motion to that effect was defeated by a 6-6 tie vote and thus precluded a possible court test.[96]

"Inferior officers" are evidently officers subordinate to the heads of departments or the courts of law, but many classes of such officers are still appointed by the President with the

"Inferior Officers"

[93] *New York Times*, Feb. 9, 1962.

[94] 1971 *Cong. Quart. Weekly Report*, 1786 and 1873.

[95] Fred P. Graham, "Again the Clash Over Who Should Testify," *New York Times*, April 16, 1972.

[96] 1972 *Cong. Quart. Weekly Report*, 846 and 913; *New York Times*, April 13, 1972.

advice and consent of the Senate because Congress has never vested their appointment elsewhere. Also, there is good reason for believing that the Federal court judges other than the Supreme Court justices are "inferior officers."[97]

By the Oregon Postmaster case, one who is vested under this clause with the power to appoint an inferior officer is at the same time vested with the power to remove him, the power of removal being a part of the appointing power.

¶3. The President shall have power to fill up all vacancies that may happen during the recess of the Senate, by granting commissions which shall expire at the end of their next session.

There has been considerable argument throughout our history as to what the word "happen" means in this context. Some have argued that the President could fill any vacancy which happened to *exist* during recess; others have contended that he could only fill those which happened to *occur* during the recess.[98] In practice Presidents have tended to take the broader view. This practice received judicial sanction in 1962 from the United States Court of Appeals for the Second Circuit.[99] It was pointed out that if a vacancy existed on account of inaction in the Senate it would have to continue throughout the recess, and in this way the work of government might be greatly impeded. The power to make recess appointments gives the President an advantage in a contest with the Senate over an appointment. Once someone is in a post, even temporarily, it is more difficult to oppose confirmation.[100] Consequently, Congress as early as 1863 sought to discourage Presidents from making frequent use of the recess appointment by enacting a provision reading: "nor shall any money be paid out of the Treasury of the United States, as salary, to any person appointed during the recess of the Senate, to fill a vacancy in any existing office . . . until such appointee shall have been con-

---

97 Article III, Section I speaks of "inferior courts." For further discussion of this point *see* Chase, *Federal Judges: The Appointing Process*, p. 5.

98 Joseph Harris, *The Advice and Consent of the Senate* (New York, 1953), 255-257.

99 U.S. *v.* Alloco, 395 F. 2d. 704 (1962); *cert. denied*, 371 U.S. 964 (1963).

100 For further elaboration, *see* Chase, *Federal Judges: The Appointing Process*, pp. 14-16.

firmed by the Senate."[101] Current law on the subject is more
carefully drawn to withhold salary payment, with some exceptions, from a recess appointee who was picked to fill a vacancy
which "existed while the Senate was in session and was by law
required to be filled by and with the advice and consent of the
Senate,[102] until such appointee has been confirmed by the Senate. . . ." Thus there is financial risk in accepting an appointment to a vacancy which *existed while the Senate was in
session.*[103]

## SECTION III

¶He shall from time to time give to the Congress information
of the state of the Union, and recommend to their consideration such measures as he shall judge necessary and expedient;
he may, on extraordinary occasions, convene both houses, or
either of them, and in case of disagreement between them
with respect to the time of adjournment, he may adjourn
them to such time as he shall think proper; he shall receive
ambassadors and other public ministers; he shall take care
that the laws be faithfully executed, and shall commission all
the officers of the United States.

Prior even to recent Administrations, the duty conferred by
the opening clause of this section had come to be, at the hands
of outstanding Presidents like Washington, Jefferson, Theodore Roosevelt, and Wilson a tremendous power of legislative
leadership.[1] The President is not, on the other hand, obliged
by this clause to impart information which, in his judgment,
the public interest requires should be kept secret.[2]

*Legislative Leadership of the President*

The President has frequently summoned Congress into what
is known as "special session." His power to adjourn the houses
has never been exercised.

The power to "receive ambassadors and other public ministers" includes the power to dismiss them for sufficient cause;
and the exercise of the latter power may, as in the case
of Count Bernstorff early in 1917, result in a breach of diplo-

[101] 12 *Stat.* 646 (1863).     [102] 5 U.S.C. 5503.
[103] 41 *Op. Atty. Gen.* 463 (1960).

[1] Louis W. Koenig, *The Chief Executive* (New York, 1968), ch. 6, and
Joseph E. Kallenbach, *The American Chief Executive* (New York, 1966),
chs. 10 and 11.
[2] *See* pp. 144-145 above.

matic relations leading eventually to hostilities. The same power also carries with it the power to recognize new governments or to refuse them recognition, also a very important power sometimes, as was shown by President Wilson's success in thus bringing about the downfall of President Huerta of Mexico in 1916.

Finally, it may be said that it is the President's power under this clause, taken together with his power in connection with treaty-making and with the appointment of the diplomatic representatives of the United States, that gives him his large initiative in determining the foreign policies of the United States. In the words of Jefferson, although, characteristically, he did not always choose to abide by their consequences, "the transaction of business with foreign nations is executive altogether."[3] Moreover, as Chief Executive the President is protector of American rights and interests abroad, a capacity which has become progressively more and more difficult to demark *vis à vis* Congress's power "to declare war."

It is worth noting in passing, at a time when it has become common for self-appointed negotiators to seek to end the fighting in Vietnam and/or the return of prisoners of war, there has been legislation (the Logan Act) on the books since 1798 which makes it a crime for "any citizen" without authority of the United States to carry on "any correspondence or intercourse with any foreign government or of any officer or agent thereof in relation to any disputes or controversies with the United States."[4]

The President, be it noted, does not enforce the laws himself, but sees to it that they are enforced, and this is so even in the case of those laws which confer powers upon the President directly rather than upon some head of department or bureau.[5] But a Circuit Court has held that "the function of initiating a judicial proceeding for the enforcement of a legislative enactment is not the exercise of a prerogative exclusively reserved to the President" and that administrative bodies, such as the Interstate Commerce Commission could do so without violating the Constitution.[6]

[3] "Opinion on the Question Whether the Senate Has the Right," etc., April 24, 1790, Saul K. Padover, *The Complete Jefferson* (New York, 1943), 138.

[4] For the current law, *see* 18 U.S.C. 953.

[5] Williams *v.* U.S., 1 How. 290 (1843), and cases there cited.

[6] I.C.C. *v.* Chatsworth Cooperative Marketing Ass'n., 347 F. 2d. 821, 822 (1965); *cert. denied*, 382 U.S. 938 (1965).

Frequently, of course, statutes give power to specific officers to perform certain duties. This raises the question of what the President may do if he does not believe that an officer is executing a law faithfully. Ultimately, that answer must ride on the President's removal power. Whomever he can remove, he can force to do his bidding or replace him. With those he cannot remove, he can only contest. (*See* p. 143 and the cases cited therein.) Commonly Presidents have been exercised about actions of chairmen of the Board of the Federal Reserve System, for example; none has found a means for bringing them to heel except persuasion.

Because of his duty "to take care that laws be faithfully executed," the President has the right to take any necessary measures which are not forbidden by statute to protect against impending danger those great interests which are entrusted by the Constitution to the National Government. He may order a marshal to protect a Justice of the Supreme Court whose life has been threatened, and his order will be treated by the courts as having the force of law.[7] He may dispatch troops to points at which the free movement of the mails and of interstate commerce is being impeded by private combinations, or through the Department of Justice he may turn to the courts and ask them to employ the powers which the statutes regulating their jurisdiction afford them to forbid such combinations.[8] And, generally, from an early date he has been authorized by statute to employ available military forces against "combinations too powerful to be suppressed by the ordinary course of judicial proceedings or by the power vested in the marshals."[9]

It was under such statutes that President Eisenhower ordered troops to Arkansas in 1957, and President Kennedy to Mississippi and Alabama in 1962 and 1963.[10] However, these statutes require that "Whenever the President considers it necessary to use the militia or the armed forces under this chapter, he shall, by proclamation, immediately order the insurgents to disperse and retire peaceably to their abodes within a limited time." For that reason we queried the Justice Department as to why President Nixon did not do so during the May Day confrontation of 1971. We quote from the reply: "No

*Presidential Powers in Law Enforcement*

[7] *In re* Neagle, 135 U.S. 1 (1890).
[8] *In re* Debs, 158 U.S. 564 (1895); United States *v.* U.M.W., 330 U.S. 258 (1947); 61 *Stat.* 136, 155-156 (1947), the "Taft-Hartley Act."
[9] 1 *Stat.* 264, 424 (1795); 2 *Stat.* 443 (1807).
[10] 10 U.S.C. 332, 333, 334.

proclamation was issued by the President. However, as you know, the admitted purpose of the May Day demonstrations was to halt the functioning of the federal government. The President has the inherent power and the duty under the Constitution as Chief Executive to insure the continued functioning of the government and to protect government property. The troops were used to insure that federal employees had access to their places of employment so that they could carry on the government's work and to protect the government's property."

Two Kinds of Martial Law   In cases of "necessity," the President, or his subordinates at the scene of action, may proclaim martial law, of which two grades are today recognized—*preventive* and *punitive*. The latter, which is equivalent to *military government* is not, by the *Milligan* case,[11] allowable when the civil courts are open and properly functioning, nor in the presence of merely "threatened invasion. The necessity must be actual and present; the invasion real." And it was by applying this test literally that a divided Court held in 1946 that the President had had no constitutional power to institute military government in the Territory of Hawaii following the Japanese assault on Pearl Harbor, or to continue it after that date.[12] The Achilles heel of the decision consists in the fact that it was not rendered till after the war was over and the danger past. For Total War, when "home front" activities are only an extension of the battlefront and when crippling and demoralizing attacks by air may be launched from bases hundreds of miles away, the test set by the above-quoted dictum is inadequate.

Under "preventive martial law," so-called because it authorizes "preventive" arrests and detentions, the military acts as an adjunct of the civil authorities but not necessarily subject to their orders. It may be established whenever the executive organ, State or national, deems it to be necessary for the restoration of good order. The concept, being of judicial origin, is of course for judicial application, and ultimately for application by the Supreme Court, in enforcement of the "due process" clauses.[13] (*See also*, Section III of this Article, and Article IV, Section IV.)

[11] 4 Wall. 2 (1866).
[12] Duncan *v.* Kahanamoku and White *v.* Steer, 327 U.S. 304 (1946).
[13] Moyer *v.* Peabody, 212 U.S. 78 (1909); Sterling *v.* Constantin, 287 U.S. 378 (1932). The Great Depression produced an epidemic of declarations of "martial law" in some ill-defined sense of the term, by governors of States.

Another way in which the President's executive powers have been enlarged in recent years is by the growing practice by Congress of passing laws in broad, general terms, which have to be supplemented by regulations drawn up by a head of department under the direction of the President. Under legislation which Congress passed during World War I, the following powers, among others, were vested in the President: to control absolutely the transportation and distribution of foodstuffs; to fix prices; to license importation, exportation, manufacture, storage, and distribution of the necessaries of life; to operate the railroads; to issue passports; to control cable and telegraph lines; to declare embargoes; to determine priority of shipments; to loan money to foreign governments; to enforce Prohibition; to redistribute and regroup the executive bureaus; and in carrying these powers into effect the President's authorized agents put in operation a huge number of executive regulations having the force of law; and the two War Powers Acts and other legislation repeated this pattern in World War II.[14]

Delegations of Legislative Power to the President

Meantime, however, the Court had held that Congress in enacting the NIRA in 1933 had parted with its own powers somewhat too lavishly, and for the first time in the history of the country an act of Congress was set aside, in the "Hot Oil" cases of 1934,[15] as violative of the maxim that "the legislature may not delegate its powers." Congress, the Court argued, had

---

"The records of the War Department show that in the fiscal year 1934, twenty-seven States mobilized the Guard for emergency duty, and in the next year the number reached thirty-two. The occasions have often been small, even trivial in compass." Charles Fairman, "Law of Martial Rule and the National Emergency," 55 *Harvard Law Review*, 1253 (1942), at p. 1275. In recent years, the calling out of the Guard has again reached epidemic proportions. When Governor Faubus of Arkansas called out the Guard to maintain the peace in Little Rock and prevented Black children from attending a school which had been ordered to integrate, the occasion was afforded the Supreme Court to decide an important constitutional issue. The Court held that "law and order are not here to be preserved by depriving the Negro children of their constitutional rights." Cooper *v.* Aaron, 358 U.S. 1, 16 (1958). In short, courts will not usually challenge the governor's judgment in calling out the Guard, but they will require that when he does so, he must use it to uphold the exercise of constitutional rights. *See* Wilson and Company *v.* Freeman, 179 F. Supp. 520 (1959). (Note in that case the Court did challenge the governor's judgment.)

14 *See* especially Yakus *v.* U.S., 321 U.S. 414 (1944), in which the Emergency Price Control Act of January 30, 1942, was sustained against the objection that it delegated legislative power unconstitutionally to OPA.

15 Panama Refining Co. *v.* Ryan, 293 U.S. 388 (1935). *See also* Schechter Bros. *v.* U.S., 295 U.S. 495 (1935).

failed to lay down sufficient "standards" to guide executive action, and without doubt it had acted with unnecessary haste. Even so, subsequent decisions upholding broad delegations of power to various administrative agencies of the Government make it plain that, as the sphere of national power expands and the problems confronting the National Government become more complex, Congress will encounter ever lessening judicial resistance to its developing policy of leaving the details of legislative projects to be filled in by such agencies, which are able to carry on constant researches in their respective fields and to adapt their measures to changing conditions with comparative ease.[16] For example, we are currently living under a Presidential wage and price freeze stemming from a statute which reads: "The President is authorized to issue such orders and regulations as he may deem appropriate to stabilize prices, rents, wages, and salaries at levels not less than those prevailing on May 25, 1970. Such orders and regulations may provide for the making of such adjustments as may be necessary to prevent gross inequities."[17] Shades of NIRA!

Moreover, in United States v. Curtiss-Wright Export Corporation,[18] the Court, speaking by Justice Sutherland, used language implying that there is virtually no constitutional limit to Congress's power to delegate to the President authority which is "cognate" to his own constitutional powers, and especially his powers in the diplomatic field. The Lend-Lease Act,[19] while we were still formally at peace, authorized the President for a stated period (it was afterward renewed) to manufacture or "otherwise procure" to the extent of available funds "defense articles" (i.e., anything judged by him to be such), and lease, lend, exchange, or "otherwise dispose" of them, on terms "satisfactory" to himself, to any government, if he deemed that in so doing he was aiding the defense of the United States.

In brief, the President's duty "to take care that the laws be faithfully executed" becomes often a power to make the laws. Furthermore, as was pointed out earlier, his duty also embraces the defense of American rights and interests abroad,

16 See especially Justice Roberts's dissenting opinion in Hood & Sons v. U.S., 307 U.S. 588, 603 (1939); Opp Cotton Mills v. Administrator, etc., 312 U.S. 126 (1941); and the Yakus case, cited above.
17 84 Stat. 799 (1970). See Executive Order No. 11627 promulgated Oct. 16, 1971, 36 Fed. Reg. 20139.
18 299 U.S. 304, 327 (1936).      19 55 Stat. 31 (1941).

since he is, *vis à vis* other governments, the Chief Executive of its treaties and of International Law. The function is one the discharge of which it sometimes becomes difficult to demark from the war-making power of Congress. Nor was this unforeseen by the Framers.

Thus when it was proposed in the Federal Convention, on August 17, 1787, to authorize Congress "to make war," Madison and Gerry "moved to insert 'declare,' striking out 'make' war, leaving to the Executive the power to repel sudden attacks," and the motion carried.[20] Early in Jefferson's first administration, the question arose whether the President had the right to employ naval forces to protect American shipping against the Tripolitan pirates. The President himself was so doubtful on the point that he instructed his commander, that if he took any prisoners he should release them; also, that while he could disarm captured vessels in self-defense, he must release those too. These scruples excited the derision of Hamilton, who advanced the contention that if we were attacked we were *ipso facto* at war willy-nilly, and that Congress's prerogative was exclusive only when it came to putting the country into a state of war *ab initio*.[21] At the time Jefferson's view prevailed, Congress formally voting him war powers against the Bey of Tripoli.[22] Later developments have favored Hamilton's thesis. Commenting on the action of Lieutenant Hollins in 1854 in ordering the bombardment of Greytown, Nicaragua, in default of reparations from the local authorities for an attack by a mob on the United States consul stationed there, Justice Nelson, on circuit, said: "As respects the interposition of the Executive abroad for the protection of the lives or property of the citizen, the duty must, of necessity rest in the discretion of the President . . . under our system of government the citizen abroad is as much entitled to protecttion as the citizen at home,"[23] words which were endorsed by the Supreme Court in 1890. The President's duty, said Justice Miller, is not limited "to the enforcement of acts of Congress or of treaties of the United States according to their express terms," but includes "the rights, duties and obligations grow-

*Presidential War-Making*

---

[20] Max Farrand, ed., *The Records of the Federal Constitution of 1787*, II (New Haven, 1937), 318-319.
[21] Corwin, *The President, Office and Powers*, 242-243.
[22] Act of February 6, 1802.
[23] Durand *v.* Hollins, 4 Blatch. 451, 454 (1860).

ing out of the Constitution itself, our international relations, and all the protection implied by the nature of the Government under the Constitution."[24]

In his small volume on *World Policing and the Constitution*[25] Mr. James Grafton Rogers listed 149 episodes similar to the Greytown affair, stretching between the undeclared war with France in 1798 and Pearl Harbor. While inviting some pruning, the list demonstrates beyond peradventure that Presidents as Chief Executives and Commanders-in-Chief, have for a long time exercised the power to judge whether a situation requires the use of available forces to protect American rights of persons and property outside the United States and to take action in harmony with that decision. Such employment of the forces has, it is true, been usually justified as acts of self-defense rather than acts of war, but the countries where they occurred were entitled to treat them as acts of war nevertheless, although they were generally too feeble to assert their prerogative in this respect, and sometimes actually chose to turn the other cheek. Thus when in 1900 President McKinley, without consulting Congress, contributed a sizable contingent to the joint forces that went to the relief of the foreign legations in Peking, the Chinese Imperial Government agreed that this action had not constituted war.[26]

**President and Congress and the Atlantic Pact**

And Article V of the North Atlantic Treaty was built on such precedents. The novel feature was its enlarged conception of defensible American interests abroad. In the words of the published abstract of the Report of the Committee on Foreign Relations on the Pact, "Article 5 records what is a fact, namely, that an armed attack within the meaning of the treaty would in the present-day world constitute an attack upon the entire community comprising the parties to the treaty, including the United States. Accordingly, the President and the Congress, each within their sphere of assigned constitutional responsibilities, would be expected to take all action necessary and appropriate to protect the United States against the consequences and dangers of an armed attack committed against

---

[24] *In re* Neagle, 135 U.S. 1, 64.

[25] (Boston, 1945). *See also,* for the period 1811 to 1934, J. Reuben Clark's Memorandum as Solicitor of the Department of State entitled *Right to Protect Citizens in Foreign Countries by Landing Forces* (Washington, D.C. 1934). The great majority of the landings were for "the simple protection of American citizens in disturbed areas," and only about a third involved belligerent action.

[26] Moore, *International Law Digest,* V, 478-510, *passim.*

any party to the treaty."[27] But from the very nature of things, the discharge of this obligation against overt force will ordinarily rest with the President in the first instance, just as has the discharge in the past of the like obligation in the protection of American rights abroad. Furthermore, in the discharge of this obligation the President will ordinarily be required to use force and perform acts of war. Such is the verdict of history, a verdict which was confirmed by our intervention in Korea under the auspices of the United Nations. It is not surprising, therefore, that, as indicated earlier (pp. 83-84), challenges to the legality of Presidential actions with respect to Vietnam have been unavailing.[28] (For discussion of Congressional concern over President's power, *see* p. 84.)

"The aggregate of powers" available to the President in the absence of controlling legislation is, therefore, impressive, a fact which was dramatically advertised when, in April 1952, President Truman, in order to avert a nationwide strike of steel workers, directed the Secretary of Commerce to seize and operate most of the steel mills of the country.[29] The President cited no specific statutory warrant for this step, but urged the requirements of national defense at home and of our allies abroad, and cited generally "the authority vested in me by the Constitution and laws of the United States." Before he could execute the order, the Secretary was stopped by an injunction which, in due course, the Supreme Court affirmed.[30]

The *Steel Seizure Case of* 1952

The pivotal proposition of "the opinion of the Court" by Justice Black was that, inasmuch as Congress could have ordered the seizure of the mills, the President lacked power to do so without its authorization. In support of this position, which purported to have the endorsement of four other members of the Court, Justice Black invoked the principle of the Separation of Powers, but otherwise adduced no proof from previous decisions or from governmental practice. The opin-

[27] U.S., 81st Congress, 1st Sess., Senate, Document 123 (1949). 63 *Stat.* 2244. *Note also* Article IV of the Southeast Asia Collective Defense Treaty. 6 UST 82, 83 (1954).

[28] For another view *see* the "Yale Paper," "Indo-China: The Constitutional Crisis" Part I in 116 *Cong. Rec.* S7117-S7123 (daily ed. May 13, 1970); Part II in 116 *Cong. Rec.* S7591-7593 (May 21, 1970). For view upholding President's power, *see* William H. Rehnquist's remarks in Lockhart, Kamisar, Choper, *Constitutional Law Supplement 1971* (St. Paul, 1971), 20-25.

[29] Executive Order 10340, 17 *Fed. Reg.* 3139.

[30] Youngstown Sheet & Tube Co. *v.* Sawyer, 343 U.S. 579 (1952).

ion bears, in fact, the earmarks of hasty improvisation, and is unquestionably contradicted by a considerable record of Presidential pioneering in territory that was eventually occupied by Congress.

**Presidential Pioneering in the Legislative Field**

Thus Washington in 1793 issued the first Neutrality Proclamation. The year following Congress, at the President's suggestion, enacted the first neutrality statute.[31] In 1799 the elder Adams extradited the first fugitive from justice under the Jay Treaty, and was successfully defended by Marshall in the House of Representatives for his course.[32] Not till 1848 did Congress provide another method.[33] Also in 1799, an American naval vessel seized a Danish craft trading in the West Indies. Although it disallowed the seizure as violative of an act of Congress, the Court, by Chief Justice Marshall, voiced the opinion that but for the act, the President could in the circumstances have ordered it by virtue of his duty "to take care that the laws be faithfully executed" and of his power as commander of the forces.[34] That the President may, in the absence of legislation by Congress, control the landing of foreign cables in the United States and the passage of foreign troops through American territory, has been shown repeatedly.[35] Likewise, until Congress acts, he may govern conquered territory[36] and, "in the absence of attempts by Congress to limit his power," may set up military commissions in territory occupied by the armed forces of the United States.[37] That during the Civil War Lincoln's suspensions of the writ of *habeas corpus* paved the way to authorizing legislation was pointed out above (*see* p. 121). Similarly, Lincoln's action in seizing the railroad and telegraph lines between Washington and Baltimore in 1861 was followed early in 1862 by an act of Congress generally authorizing such seizures when dictated by military necessity.[38]

---

[31] 1 *Stat.* 381 (1794). For Washington's suggestion, *see* his Message of December 5, 1793, Richardson, *Messages and Papers of the President*, I, 139.

[32] 343 U.S. 579, 684 (1952), citing 10 *Annals of Congress* 619.

[33] *Rev. Stat.* §§5270-5279 (1878).

[34] Little *v.* Barreme, 2 Cr. 170, 177 (1804).

[35] 22 *Op. Atty. Gen.* 13 (1898); Tucker *v.* Alexandroff, 183 U.S. 424, 435 (1902). An act passed May 27, 1921, 42 *Stat.* 8, requires Presidential license for the landing and operation of cables connecting the United States with foreign countries. Quincy Wright, *The Control of American Foreign Relations* (New York, 1922), p. 302 n. 75.

[36] Santiago *v.* Nogueras, 214 U.S. 260 (1909).

[37] Madsen *v.* Kinsella, 343 U.S. 341 (1952).

[38] 12 *Stat.* 334.

On the specific issue of seizures of industrial property, Jus- Presidential
tice Frankfurter incorporated much pertinent data in an ap- Seizures of
pendix to his concurring opinion.[39] Of statutes authorizing Property
such seizures he listed eighteen between 1916 and 1951; and
of Presidential seizures without specific statutory authorization he listed eight for the World War I period and eleven for
the World War II period, several of which occurred before
the outbreak of hostilities. In the War Labor Disputes Act of
June 25, 1943,[40] such seizures were put on a statutory basis;
and in United States v. Pewee Coal Co., Inc.,[41] they were, in
implication, sustained as having been validly made.[42]

In consequence of the evident belief of at least four of the
Justices who concurred in the judgment in Youngstown that
Congress had exercised its powers in the premises of the case
in opposition to seizure, by the procedures which it had laid
down in the Taft-Hartley Act, the lesson of the case is somewhat blurred. But that the President does possess, in the absence of restrictive legislation, a residual or resultant power
above, or in consequence of his granted powers, to deal with
emergencies which he regards as threatening the national security, is explicitly asserted by Justice Clark,[43] and was evidently held, with certain qualifications, by Justices Frankfurter and Jackson, and was the essence of the position of the dissenting Justices.[44] The lesson of the case, therefore, if it has a
lesson, is that escape from Presidential autocracy today is to
be sought along the legislative route rather than that of judicial review.[45] But any impression that the American President

[39] 343 U.S. 579, 615-626 (1952).    [40] 57 *Stat.* 163.
[41] 341 U.S. 114 (1951).
[42] This is because damages were awarded in the Pewee case, implying
the Court's acceptance of the idea that the seizure had been a governmental act. *See* Hooe v. United States, 218 U.S. 322, 335-336 (1910); United
States v. North American Co., 253 U.S. 330, 333 (1920). *Cf.* Larson v. Domestic and Foreign Corp., 337 U.S. 682, 701-702 (1949).
[43] 343 U.S. at 662-663.
[44] A notable feature of Chief Justice Vinson's opinion for himself and
Justices Reed and Minton is a long passage extracted from the Government's brief in United States v. Midwest Oil Co., 236 U.S. 459 (1915). It
emphasizes and illustrates the proposition that there "are fields [of power]
which are common to both [Congress and the President] in the sense that
the Executive may move within them until they shall have been occupied
by legislative action." 343 U.S. 574, 691 (1952). The authors of the brief
were Solicitor General John W. Davis and Assistant Attorney General
Knaebel. The former, ironically, was Youngstown's principal counsel.
[45] This conclusion is emphasized by the division of the Court in the
case of Cole v. Young, 351 U.S. 536 (1956), which exhibited even more

has become a modern incarnation of Caesar, as has been alleged from time to time, does not conform to reality, despite the President's enormous legal powers described above. A distinction should be recognized and acknowledged between a President's power with respect to foreign affairs and domestic affairs. The President's role in foreign affairs is much more conclusive than his role in domestic affairs. In a television interview in which President Kennedy discussed his first two years in office, he described at length the inordinate difficulty a President, any President, has in getting a program through Congress. He concluded by saying: "So that they are two separate offices and two separate powers, the Congress and the Presidency, there is bound to be conflict, but they must cooperate to the degree that is possible. But that is why no President's program is *ever* put in. *The only time a President's program is put in quickly and easily is when the program is insignificant. But* if it is significant and affects important interests and is controversial, therefore, then there is a fight, and the President is never wholly successful (emphasis supplied)."[46] The best explanation for why this is so was provided by Professor James M. Burns: "We have been too much entranced by the Madisonian model of government. . . . This model was the product of the gifted men who gathered in Philadelphia over 175 years ago, and it deserves much of the admiration and veneration we have accorded it. But this is also the system of checks and balances and interlocked gears of government that requires the consensus of many groups and leaders before the nation can act; and it is a system that exacts the heavy price of delay and devitalization that I have noted."[47] In addition, Professor Richard Neustadt has provided a graphic account of just how difficult it is for a President in practice to have his wishes translated into action on the home front.[48]

For those disenchanted with the American System in the 1970's, seeking solutions to the problems of war, civil rights, pollution, poverty, safety in the streets among others, the an-

clearly than the opinions in Youngstown the schizophrenia that is apt to seize upon the Court when confronted with Presidential pretensions, and to cloud its common sense.

[46] Harold W. Chase and Allen H. Lerman, *Kennedy and the Press* (New York, 1965), 353.

[47] James M. Burns, *The Deadlock of Democracy* (Englewood Cliffs, N.J., 1963), 6.

[48] Richard E. Neustadt, *Presidential Power: The Politics of Leadership* (New York, 1960).

swers may well lie in finding ways to reduce the checks and balances with respect to domestic action and finding some with respect to the conduct of foreign affairs.

## SECTION IV

¶The President, Vice-President and all civil officers of the United States shall be removed from office on impeachment for and conviction of treason, bribery, or other high crimes and misdemeanors.

As indicated earlier, pp. 13-14, there have been important impeachments in our history, but as former Senator Joseph D. Tydings has so eloquently pointed out: "Even in the early years of the Republic the inadequacy of this process was recognized. As early as 1819, Thomas Jefferson said: 'Experience has already shown that the impeachment the Constitution has provided is not even a scarecrow. It is a cumbersome, archaic process. . . .' "[1] Besides their liability to the impeachment process (*see* Article I, Section III, ¶s 6 and 7), the President's principal subordinates are answerable to him, since as the law has stood from the beginning of the National Government, except for a brief period after the Civil War, he has had a practically unrestricted power of removal; but Congress may qualify this power in the case of agencies whose powers are derived solely from Congress, and especially is this true as to agencies like the Interstate Commerce Commission, the Federal Trade Commission, and so on, which are often required to proceed in a semi-judicial manner.[2]

The Legal Responsibility of Inferior Officers

Furthermore, all officers below the President, including such "independent commissions," are responsible to the courts in various ways. Indeed, an order of the President himself not in accordance with law will be set aside by the courts if a case involving it comes before them.[3] Also, while the President may not be prohibited by writ of injunction from doing a threatened illegal act, or be compelled by writ of mandamus to perform a duty definitely required by law,[4] his subordinates

[1] U.S., 89th Congress, 2d. Sess., Senate, Committee on the Judiciary, *Hearing*, "Judicial Fitness," Feb. 15, 1966, pp. 3-4.
[2] Humphrey's Executor *v.* U.S., 295 U.S. 602 (1935); Wiener *v.* U.S., 357 U.S. 349 (1958).
[3] Kendall *v.* U.S., 12 Pet. 524 (1838); United States *v.* Lee, 106 U.S. 196 (1882).
[4] Mississippi *v.* Johnson, 4 Wall. 475 (1866).

do not share his immunity, suits against them being usually brought in the United States District Court for the District of Columbia.[5] Also, by common law principles, a subordinate executive officer is personally liable under the ordinary law for any act done in excess of authority.[6] Indeed, district courts of the United States are bound to entertain suits for damages arising out of alleged violation of plaintiff's constitutional rights, even though as the law now stands the court is often times powerless to award damages.[7] But Congress may, in certain cases, exonerate the officer by a so-called act of indemnity;[8] while as the law stands at present, any officer of the United States who is charged with a crime under the laws of a State for an act done "under the authority of the United States" is entitled to have his case transferred to the national courts.[9]

The extent of the President's own liability under the ordinary law, while he is clothed with official authority, is a matter of some doubt. Impeachment aside, his principal responsibility seems to be simply his accountability, as Chief Justice Marshall expressed it, "to his country in his political character, and to his own conscience."[10]

[5] United States *v.* Schurz, 102 U.S. 378 (1880); United States *v.* Black, 128 U.S. 40 (1888); Riverside Oil Co. *v.* Hitchcock, 190 U.S. 316 (1903).

[6] Little *v.* Barreme, 2 Cr. 170 (1804); United States *v.* Lee, cited above; Spalding *v.* Vilas, 161 U.S. 483 (1896).

[7] Bell *v.* Hood, 327 U.S. 678 (1946). 28 U.S.C. 2331 and 28 U.S.C. 2680. *See* particularly Bivens *v.* Six Unknown Named Agents of Fed. Bur. of Narc., 409 F. 2d. 718 (1969), *cert. denied,* 397 U.S. 928 (1970).

[8] Mitchell *v.* Clark, 110 U.S. 633 (1884).

[9] 28 U.S.C. 1442; Willingham *v.* Morgan, 395 U.S. 402 (1969).

[10] Marbury *v.* Madison, 1 Cr. 137, 166-167 (1803).

# ARTICLE III

This article completes the framework of the National Government by providing for "the judicial power of the United States."

## SECTION I

¶The judicial power of the United States shall be vested in one Supreme Court, and in such inferior courts as the Congress may from time to time ordain and establish. The judges, both of the Supreme and inferior courts, shall hold their offices during good behavior, and shall, at stated times, receive for their services a compensation which shall not be diminished during their continuance in office.

"Judicial power" is the power to decide "cases" and "controversies" in conformity with law and by the methods established by the usages and principles of law.[1] It should not be confused with "jurisdiction," which is the authority of a court to exercise "judicial power" in a particular case. The Constitution vests the "judicial power" in the courts; Congress cannot, of course, change that, short of a constitutional amendment. But as shown below, Congress has considerable power under the Constitution to define the "jurisdiction" of the courts.

Like "legislative" and "executive power" under the Constitution, "judicial power," too, is thought to connote certain incidental or "inherent" attributes. One of these is the ability to interpret the standing law, whether the Constitution, acts of Congress, or judicial precedents, with an authority to which both the other departments are constitutionally obliged to defer.[2] But "political questions" often afford an exception to this general rule,[3] as also do so-called "questions of fact," which are often left to administrative bodies, although their determination may affect the scope of the authority of such bodies very materially.[4] And closely related to this attribute of judi-

*Inherent Elements of "Judicial Power"*

---

[1] Prentis v. Atl. Coast Line Co., 211 U.S. 210, 226 (1908). *See also* Muskrat v. U.S., 219 U.S. 346, 361 (1911); Securities & Exc. Com'n v. Medical Com. for Human Rights, 404 U.S. 403 (1972).

[2] *See* e.g., Federal Power Com'n v. Pacific Power and L. Co., 307 U.S. 156 (1939).

[3] On "political questions," *see* p. 171 below.

[4] Apparently, both Congress and the Supreme Court do not feel that leaving "questions of fact" primarily to administrative agencies and broad-

cial power is another, which may be termed power of "finality of decision." The underlying idea is that when a court of the United States is entrusted with the determination of any question *whether* of law or of fact, its decision of such question cannot constitutionally be made reviewable except by a higher *court*, that is, cannot be made reviewable by either of the other two departments, or any agency thereof.[5] Thus, so long as the decisions of the Court of Claims as to amounts due claimants against the Government were subject to disallowance by the Secretary of the Treasury, it was held not to be a "court," with the result that the Supreme Court could not take appeals from it.[6] But the principle is not an altogether rigid one, for the Court of Claims is today regarded as a true court, stemming from Article III, Section I, of the Constitution, despite the fact that its judgments have to be satisfied out of sums which only Congress can appropriate.[7] Also, the courts of the United States are today generally required to serve as adjuncts in the work of such administrative bodies as the Interstate Commerce Commission, the Federal Trade Commission, the National Labor Relations Board, etc., by backing up the valid findings of such tribunals with orders which those to whom they are addressed must obey if they do not want to go to jail for "contempt of court."[8]

Which calls attention to a third "inherent" judicial attribute, namely, the power of a court to vindicate its dignity

---

ening the concept of what is a "question of fact" as opposed to a "question of law" is an abrogation of "judicial power." Consolo v. Federal Maritime Commission, 383 U.S. 607 (1966); Universal Camera Corp. v. Labor Board, 340 U.S. 474 (1951); 5 U.S.C. 706. For a thorough explication of this issue *see* Kenneth C. Davis, *Administrative Law Treatise* (St. Paul, 1958) and Supplement (St. Paul, 1970), ch. 30 in both.

[5] For the start of this doctrine, *see* Hayburn's case, decided in 1792, 2 Dall. 409, and especially the reporter's notes. However, as the Supreme Court has pointed out "To give due weight to . . . congressional declarations is not of course to compromise the authority or responsibility of this Court as the ultimate expositor of the Constitution." Glidden Company v. Zdanok, 370 U.S. 530, 542-543 (1962).

[6] *See* Gordon v. U.S., 117 U.S., appendix (1864).

[7] DeGroot v. U.S., 5 Wall. 419 (1867); 67 *Stat.* 26 (1953); Glidden Company v. Zdanok, 370 U.S. 530 (1962).

[8] The great leading case is Interstate Com. Com'n v. Brimson, 154 U.S. 447 (1894). A 1946 decision inferentially sustains the right of Congress to confer the subpoena power upon administrative agencies. Justice Murphy dissented, saying he was "unable to approve the use of non-judicial subpoenas issued by administrative agents," but his protest was based on the great growth of administrative law "in the past few years," and not on the ground that the subpoena power was inherently or exclusively judicial. Oklahoma Press Pub. Co. v. Walling, 327 U.S. 186 (1946).

and authority in the way just mentioned. This power was defined in general terms in the Judiciary Act of 1789 and further restricted by the Act of 1831, which limited punishable contempt to disobedience to any judicial process or decree and to misbehavior in the presence of the Court, "or so near thereto as to obstruct the administration of justice."[9] The purpose of the last clause was to get rid of a doctrine of the common law which, although it has the sanction of Blackstone, is otherwise of dubious authenticity, that criticism reflecting on the conduct of a judge in a pending case constituted contempt because of its tendency to draw into question the impartiality of the court and to "scandalize justice."[10] Eighty-five years later, nevertheless, the Supreme Court largely restored the discredited doctrine by an enlarged interpretation of the "so near thereto" clause.[11] But not only was this decision overturned in 1941,[12] but the Court a little later, by a vote of five Justices to four, ruled that for an utterance to be held in contempt simply in reliance on the common law, it must offer an "extremely serious" threat of causing a miscarriage of justice or of obstructing its orderly administration, otherwise the constitutional guaranty of freedom of press would be invaded.[13]

> Contempt of Court

In recent years, the Supreme Court has been sharply divided over another aspect of the contempt power—the extent to which judges are entitled to punish for contempt *summarily.* There is no quarrel with the idea that judges must have the power to *cite* people for contempt. In 1970, the Supreme Court was unanimous in the belief that: "It is essential to the proper administration of criminal justice that dignity, order, and decorum be the hallmarks of all court proceedings in our country. The flagrant disregard in the courtroom of elementary standards of proper conduct should not and cannot be tolerated. We believe trial judges confronted with disruptive, contumacious, stubbornly defiant defendants must be given sufficient discretion to meet the circumstances of each case. No one formula for maintaining the appropriate courtroom atmosphere will be best in all situations. We think there are at least

---

[9] 4 *Stat.* 487 (1831); *ex parte* Robinson, 19 Wall. 505 (1874).
[10] *See* the bibliographical data in Justice Douglas's opinion for the Court in Nye *v.* U.S., 313 U.S. 33 (1941).
[11] Toledo Newspaper Co. *v.* U.S., 247 U.S. 402 (1918).
[12] *See* note 10 above.
[13] Bridges *v.* Calif., 314 U.S. 252 (1941); followed in Pennekamp *v.* Fla., 328 U.S. 331 (1946).

three constitutionally permissible ways for a trial judge to handle an obstreperous defendant . . . (1) bind and gag him, thereby keeping him present; (2) cite him for contempt; (3) take him out of the courtroom until he promises to conduct himself properly."[14] In 1958, Justice Black dissenting and speaking for Chief Justice Warren and Justice Douglas as well as himself bitterly complained: "The power of a judge to inflict punishment for criminal contempt by means of a summary proceeding stands as an anomaly in the law. In my judgment the time has come for a fundamental and searching reconsideration of the validity of this power which has aptly been characterized . . . as, 'perhaps, nearest akin to despotic power of any power existing under our form of government.' Even though this extraordinary authority first slipped into the law as a very limited and insignificant thing, it has relentlessly swollen, at the hands of not unwilling judges, until it has become a drastic and pervasive mode of administering criminal justice usurping our regular constitutional methods of trying those charged with offenses against society."[15] Justice Black ultimately won the day. In 1968, the Court held that the constitutional guarantees of a jury trial extended to "serious" criminal contempts[16] and in 1971 the Court held that, in those criminal contempt cases which can still be tried without jury and which involve behavior contemptuous of a judge, due process requires that a defendant "should be given a public trial before a judge other than the one reviled by the contemnor."[17]

Another limitation on the contempt power is that it exists for the protection of the processes of the Court, and thereby of justice. "The judge," the Court has said, "must banish the slightest personal impulse to reprisal, but he should not bend backward and impair the authority of the Court by too great leniency."[18] In Sacher *v.* United States,[19] an outgrowth of the

[14] Illinois *v.* Allen, 397 U.S. 337, 343 (1970).

[15] Green *v.* U.S., 356 U.S. 165, 194 (1958).

[16] Bloom *v.* Illinois, 391 U.S. 194 (1968). The Court explicitly refused to set the exact location of the line between petty offenses and "serious crimes" but went on to add "a crime punishable by two years in prison is . . . a serious crime." *Ibid.,* 211. *See* McGowan *v.* State, 258 So. 2d. 801 (1972). *See also* 18 U.S.C. 402 and 2691.

[17] Mayberry *v.* Pennsylvania, 400 U.S. 455 (1971).

[18] Cooke *v.* U.S., 267 U.S. 517, 539 (1925).

[19] Sacher *v.* U.S., 343 U.S. 1, 13-14 (1952); Dennis *v.* U.S., 341 U.S. 494 (1951).

trial of the so-called Eleven Communists, this rule was adhered to. Here counsel for the defense engaged in practices designed to break down the judge and break up the trial. In order not to further the latter objective Judge Harold Medina deferred calling them to account until the termination of the proceedings, and was sustained by the Court in so doing.

Two other restraints on the contempt power are, first, the provisions in recent Civil Rights legislation which grant the right to jury trial in contempt proceedings in situations where the alleged contempt might fall short of being of a "serious" crime.[20] Second, as was mentioned earlier, the President's pardoning power (*see* p. 128).

In contrast to certain State courts, no court of the United States possesses the power, *in the absence of authorization by Congress*, to suspend the sentence of a convicted offender,[21] clemency being under the Constitution an executive function.

Also, it would seem that the Supreme Court regards itself as having the inherent power to determine whether an appointment to it was constitutionally valid, although such power may be invoked only by one who is able to show that "he has sustained or is in danger of sustaining a direct injury" as a result of the challenged appointment.[22]

*Varying Size of the Supreme Court*

Although *a* Supreme Court is provided for by the Constitution, the organization of the existing Court rests on an act of Congress. The size of the Court is also a matter for legislative determination at all times, subject to the requirement that existing incumbents shall not be thrown out of office. Originally the Court had six members; today it has nine, any six of whom constitute a quorum.[23] At one time during the Civil War it had ten members, an enlargement which was partly occasioned by the fact that the unfavorable attitude of several of the Justices toward the war was thought to endanger the Government's policies.[24] Again, in 1870, at the time of the decision in Hepburn v. Griswold,[25] setting aside the Legal Tender Act of 1862, the two vacancies then existing in the Court's mem-

[20] 42 U.S.C. 1995 and 2000h.
[21] *Ex parte* United States, 242 U.S. 27 (1916); Holiday v. Johnston, 313 U.S. 342 (1941). Congress has in fact given such authorization, 18 U.S.C. 3651.
[22] *Ex parte* Albert Levitt, Petitioner, 302 U.S. 633 (1937).
[23] 28 U.S.C. 1.
[24] C. B. Swisher, *Roger B. Taney* (New York, 1935), 566.
[25] 8 Wall. 603.

bership were filled by appointees who were known to disapprove of that decision, and fifteen months later the decision was reversed by the new majority.[26] Though possessing all the formal attributes of a judicial tribunal, the Court today exercises such vast, and such undefined powers, in the censorship of legislation, both national and State, and in interpretation of the former, that the social philosophies of suggested appointees to it are quite legitimately a matter of great concern to the appointing authority, the President and Senate.[27]

The "inferior courts" covered by this section comprise today eleven Circuit Courts of Appeals and 91 District Courts, the Court of Claims, the Court of Customs and Patent Appeals and the Custom Court[28] with over 500 judges serving on them. Since they rest upon act of Congress alone, they may be abolished by Congress at any time; but whether their incumbents may be thus thrown out of office is at least debatable. When in 1802 Congress repealed an act of the previous year creating certain Circuit Courts of the United States, it also threw their judges out of office; but the Act of 1913, abolishing the Commerce Court, left its judges still judges of the United States.

The territorial courts, e.g., those of Guam, the Virgin Islands, and the Canal Zone do not exercise "judicial power of the United States," but a special judicial power conferred upon them by Congress, by virtue of its sovereign power over these places (*see* Article IV, Section III, ¶2). Their judges accordingly have a limited tenure and are removable by the President.[29]

---

[26] Sidney Ratner, "Was the Supreme Court Packed by President Grant?" in 50 *Political Science Quarterly*, 343 (1935); Knox *v*. Lee, 12 Wall. 457 (1871).

[27] This was well understood by the Senatorial opponents of Mr. Hughes's appointment as Chief Justice. *See New York Times*, February 12-15, 1930; *and see* the data compiled by the late Senator Robinson in his answer to Senator Borah, respecting President Roosevelt's Court Proposal of February 5, 1937. *Ibid.*, March 31, 1937. The avowed utilization of "sociological data" by the Court in the *Desegregation* cases confirms Senator Robinson's argument. In the recent battle over the nomination of William H. Rehnquist, President Nixon and some Senators understood that the issue was a question of social philosophies. Leon Friedman, "Rehnquist: He Was an Elusive Target," *New York Times*, Dec. 12, 1971.

[28] The Supreme Court in an earlier day held that the latter three courts were Article I courts. In the 1950's, Congress "Pronounced its disagreement by providing as to each that 'such court is hereby declared to be a court established under article III . . .' " The Supreme Court acquiesced. Glidden Co. *v*. Zdanok, 370 U.S. 530, 531-532 (1962). For a brief description of these courts, *see* U.S. Cong. House, Committee on the Judiciary, *The United States Courts: Their Jurisdiction and Work* (Washington, 1971).

Also, there are certain courts exercising jurisdiction over a limited class of cases, like the Tax Court of the United States and the Court of Military Appeals, which are regarded as "legislative," *not* "constitutional" courts. The powers of such courts sometimes embrace non-judicial elements, but any purely "judicial" determination by them may be made appealable, if Congress wishes, to the regular national courts. Nevertheless, since they do not participate in "the judicial power of the United States" within the sense of this section, the tenure of their judges rests solely on act of Congress.[30]

*"Legislative Courts"*

The word "diminished" in this section was considered above in connection with Article II, Section I, ¶7.

It has been contended that legislation permitting non-unanimous jury verdicts intrudes upon "judicial power."[31] Apparently the Supreme Court regards the contention as being without merit.[32]

## SECTION II

¶1. The judicial power shall extend to all cases, in law and equity, arising under this Constitution, the laws of the United States, and treaties made, or which shall be made, under their authority; to all cases affecting ambassadors, other public ministers, and consuls; to all cases of admiralty and maritime jurisdiction; to controversies to which the United States shall be a party; to controversies between two or more States; between a State and citizens of another State; between citizens of different States; between citizens of the same State claiming lands under grants of different States, and between a State, or the citizens thereof, and foreign States, citizens, or subjects.

The "cases" and "controversies" here enumerated fall into two categories; first, those over which jurisdiction "depends on the character of the cause," that is to say, the law to be enforced; second, those over which jurisdiction "depends entire-

Categories of "Cases" and "Controversies"

---

Note that that publication speaks of 93 district courts. However, the judges in the Canal Zone, Guam and the Virgin Islands are not appointed for life. Therefore, we use the figure of 90 plus 1 newly added, *ibid.*, 6-7.

[29] American Ins. Co. *v.* Canter, 1 Pet. 511 (1828) is still the leading case on the constitutional status of territorial courts.

[30] *Ex parte* Bakelite, 279 U.S. 438 (1929). *See* 10 U.S.C. 867 and 26 U.S.C. 7443; *see also* Palmore *v.* U.S., 290 A. 2d, 573 (1972).

[31] State *v.* Jackson, 254 So. 2d. 259 (1971).

[32] Apodaca *v.* Oregon, 406 U.S. 404 (1972).

ly on the character of the parties."[1] In both instances, however, the jurisdiction described is only *potential*, except as to the *original* jurisdiction of the Supreme Court. Thus the lower Federal courts derive *all* their jurisdiction immediately from acts of Congress, and the same is true of the Supreme Court as to its *appellate* jurisdiction.[2] Also, all writs by which jurisdiction is asserted or exercised are authorized by Congress.

Require-
ments of
Same

"Controversies" are civil actions or suits;[3] "cases" may be either civil or criminal. The connotations of these terms are otherwise substantially the same. Outstanding is the requirement of adverse litigants presenting an honest and antagonistic assertion of rights. Thus it was said in an earlier day to be "well settled" that "the Court will not pass upon the constitutionality of legislation . . . , upon the complaint of one who fails to show that he is injured by its operation, . . ."; also that, "litigants may challenge the constitutionality of a statute only insofar as it affects them."[4]

But, as it has in so many other areas, the Supreme Court in recent years has done much soul-searching on the question of "standing" i.e., who will be permitted to maintain a suit in a Federal court. In the landmark case, Flast *v.* Cohen, 1968, the Supreme Court expanded considerably old judicial notions of who could properly claim standing. Based on a Supreme Court decision of 1923, it was long assumed, for example, that Federal courts could not entertain taxpayer suits.[5] Speaking for the Court in 1968, Chief Justice Warren wrote: "Thus, in terms of Article III limitations on federal court jurisdiction, the question of standing is related only to whether the dispute sought to be adjudicated will be presented in an adversary context and in a form historically viewed as capable of judicial resolution. It is for that reason that the emphasis in standing problems is on whether the party invoking federal court juris-

[1] Cohens *v.* Va., 6 Wheat. 264, 378 (1821).
[2] Turner *v.* Bk. of No. Am., 4 Dall 8 (1798); Kline *v.* Burke Constr. Co., 226 U.S. 266 (1922); Durousseau *v.* U.S. 6 Cr. 307 (1810); *ex parte* McCardle, 7 Wall. 506 (1869); *The Francis Wright*, 105 U.S. 381 (1881); St. Louis and Iron Mountain R.R. *v.* Taylor, 210 U.S. 281 (1908); *also* Robert J. Harris, Jr., *The Judicial Power of the United States* (Baton Rouge, 1940), ch. II, for a review of controversies on this point.
[3] Smith *v.* Adams, 130 U.S. 167, 173-174 (1889).
[4] Fleming *v.* Rhodes, 331 U.S. 100, 104 (1947). *See also* Blackmer *v.* U.S., 284 U.S. 421, 442 (1932); Virginian R. Co. *v.* System Federation, 300 U.S. 515 (1937); Carmichael *v.* Southern Coal & Coke Co., 301 U.S. 495, 513 (1937).
[5] Frothingham *v.* Mellon, 262 U.S. 447 (1923).

diction has 'a personal stake in the outcome of the controversy,' . . . and whether the dispute touches upon 'the legal relations of parties having adverse legal interests.' . . . A taxpayer may or may not have the requisite personal stake in the outcome, depending upon the circumstances of the particular case. Therefore, we find no absolute bar in Article III to suits by federal taxpayers challenging allegedly unconstitutional federal taxing and spending programs." He went on to add "We have noted that, in deciding the question of standing, it is not relevant that the substantive issues in the litigation might be nonjusticiable. However, our decisions establish that, in ruling on standing, it is both appropriate and necessary to look to the substantive issues for another purpose, namely, to determine whether there is a logical nexus between the status asserted and the claim sought to be adjudicated. For example, standing requirements will vary in First Amendment religion cases depending upon whether the party raises an Establishment Clause claim or a claim under the Free Exercise Clause. . . . Such inquiries into the nexus between the status asserted by the litigant and the claim he presents are essential to assure that he is a proper and appropriate party to invoke federal judicial power. Thus, our point of reference in this case is the standing of individuals who assert only the status of federal taxpayers and who challenge the constitutionality of a federal spending program. Whether such individuals have standing to maintain that form of action turns on whether they can demonstrate the necessary stake as taxpayers in the outcome of the litigation to satisfy Article III requirements."[6]

Another element of a "case" or "controversy" formerly much insisted upon is the doctrine that the party initiating it must be asking the Court for a remedy or "execution" not just an advisory opinion. This no longer represents the position of the Court; and by an act passed by Congress on June 14, 1934, courts of the United States were authorized, "in cases of actual controversy," "to declare rights and other legal relations

*Advisory Opinions*

---

[6] Flast *v.* Cohen, 392 U.S. 83, 101-102 (1968). To fully appreciate the complexities of the "standing" issue, this decision deserves to be read in its entirety. Particularly enlightening is the section on the relationship between "standing" and "justiciability," which is discussed below. *See also* Jenkins *v.* McKeithen, 395 U.S. 411 (1969).

The Supreme Court has further demonstrated its expanding view of who may legitimately claim to have standing in two exceptionally interesting cases, Eisenstadt *v.* Baird, 405 U.S. 438 (1972) and Sierra Club *v.* Morton, 407 U.S. 926 (1972).

of any interested party petitioning for such declaration, whether or not further relief is or could be requested and such declaration shall have the force and effect of a final judgment or decree and be reviewable as such."[7] But the Supreme Court is extraordinarily careful at times to ensure that declaratory judgments are issued only where there is a real controversy. To illustrate, when some resident alien fishermen wanted to know whether or not, if they left to take temporary work in Alaska, they would be treated as "aliens entering the United States for the first time" under the law, the Supreme Court took a hard-nosed position. Frankfurter wrote for the Court: "Appellants in effect asked the District Court to rule that a statute the sanctions of which had not been set in motion against individuals on whose behalf relief was sought, because an occasion for doing so had not arisen, would not be applied to them if in the future such a contingency should arise. That is not a lawsuit to enforce a right; it is an endeavor to obtain a court's assurance that a statute does not govern hypothetical situations that may or may not make the challenged statute applicable. Determination of the scope and constitutionality of legislation in advance of its immediate adverse effect in the context of a concrete case involves too remote and abstract an inquiry for the proper exercise of the judicial function. . . ."[8] Justice Black's dissent seemed more in accord with reality and compassion: "This looks to me like the very kind of 'case or controversy' courts should decide. With the abstract principles of law relied on by the majority for dismissing the case, I am not in disagreement. Of course federal courts do not pass on the meaning or constitutionality of statutes as they might be thought to govern mere 'hypothetical situations. . . .' Nor should courts entertain such statutory challenges on behalf of persons upon whom adverse statutory effects are 'too remote and abstract an inquiry for the proper exercise of the judicial function.' But as I read the record it shows that judicial action is absolutely essential to save a large group of wage earners on whose behalf this action is brought from irreparable harm due to alleged lawless enforcement of a federal statute."[9]

[7] 28 U.S.C. 2201; Aetna Life Ins. Co. v. Haworth, 300 U.S. 227 (1937); Alvater v. Freeman, 319 U.S. 359 (1943); Alabama State Federation of Labor v. McAdory, 325 U.S. 450 (1945).
[8] Longshoremen's Union v. Boyd, 347 U.S. 222, 223-224 (1954). See Securities & Exch. Com'n v. Medical Com. for Human Rights, 404 U.S. 403 (1972).
[9] Ibid., 224.

Whether a case is one "in law" or "in equity" is a mere matter of history, and depends today on the kind of remedy that is asked for. Criminal prosecutions and private actions for damages are cases "in law," since these were early decided in England in the regular law courts. An application for an injunction, on the other hand, was passed upon by the Lord Chancellor, as a matter of grace, and so is a *suit* "in equity." Heretofore the distinction between the two kinds of cases has been maintained in the field of national jurisdiction, as it is in most of the States, although the same courts dispense both "law" and "equity." By the Act of June 19, 1934, however, the Supreme Court was empowered to merge the two procedures "so as to secure one form of civil action . . . for both" in the District Courts of the United States and the Courts of the District of Columbia, and it has since adopted rules for this purpose.[10]

A case is one "arising under this Constitution, the laws of the United States, and treaties" of the United States, when an interpretation of one or the other of these is required for its final decision.[11] But while the "judicial power" extends to *all* such cases, there is a certain category of them in which the Court does not usually claim full liberty of decision. These are cases involving so-called "political questions," the best example of which is furnished by questions respecting the rights of duties of the United States in relation to other nations. When the "political departments," Congress and the President, have passed upon such questions, the Court will generally accept their determinations as binding on itself in deciding cases.

[10] 48 *Stat.* 1064 (1934); 28R U.S.C. 1 and 81.

[11] Cohens *v.* Va., 6 Wheat. 264, 379 (1821). Willoughby, *The Constitutional Law of the United States*, III, 1326-1329. The cases fall into several categories, some of which touch the problem of constitutional interpretation more directly than others: (1) Those that raise the issue of what proof is required that a statute has been enacted, or a constitutional amendment ratified; (2) questions arising out of the conduct of foreign relations; (3) the termination of wars, or rebellions; (4) the question of what constitutes a "republican form of government" and the right of a State to protection against invasion or domestic violence; (5) questions arising out of political actions of States in determining the mode of choosing Presidential Electors, State officials, and Congressional reapportionment; (6) suits brought by States to test their sovereign rights. *See* Melville Fuller Weston, "Political Questions," 38 *Harvard Law Review*, 296 (1925). Some outstanding cases are Foster *v.* Neilson, 2 Pet. 253 (1929); Luther *v.* Borden, 7 How. 1 (1849); Georgia *v.* Stanton, 6 Wall. 50 (1868); Coleman *v.* Miller, 307 U.S. 433 (1939); Colegrove *v.* Green, 328 U.S. 549 (1946), with which *cf.* McDougall *v.* Green, 335 U.S. 281 (1948); South *v.* Peters, 339 U.S. 276 (1950); National City Bank *v.* Republic of China, 348 U.S. 356 (1955).

Historically, precise understanding of what kinds of questions were political and what the Court actually did with respect to political questions has been lacking. In 1962, the Court endeavored to remedy that situation. Speaking through Justice Brennan, the Court said: "The District Court was uncertain whether our cases withholding federal judicial relief rested upon a lack of federal jurisdiction or upon the inappropriateness of the subject matter for judicial consideration—what we have designated 'nonjusticiability.' The distinction between the two grounds is significant. In the instance of nonjusticiability, consideration of the cause is not wholly and immediately foreclosed; rather, the Court's inquiry necessarily proceeds to the point of deciding whether the duty asserted can be judicially identified and its breach judicially determined, and whether protection for the right asserted can be judicially molded. In the instance of lack of jurisdiction the cause either does not 'arise under' the Federal Constitution, laws or treaties (or fall within one of the other enumerated categories of Art. III, §2), or is not a 'case or controversy' within the meaning of that section; or the cause is not one described by any jurisdictional statute."[12] It went on to add later: "We have said that 'In determining whether a question falls within the [political question] category, the appropriateness under our system of government of attributing finality to the action of the political departments and also the lack of satisfactory criteria for a judicial determination are dominant considerations.' . . . The nonjusticiability of a political question is primarily a function of the separation of powers. Much confusion results from the capacity of the 'political question' label to obscure the need for case-by-case inquiry. Deciding whether a matter has in any measure been committed by the Constitution to another branch of government, or whether the action of that branch exceeds whatever authority has been committed, is itself a delicate exercise in constitutional interpretation, and is a responsibility of this Court as ultimate interpreter of the Constitution."[13] Of course, it rests with the Supreme Court to say finally whether a question is "a political question" in this sense. (*See also* Article IV, Section IV.)

In this connection, in an extraordinary proceeding after the Court had recessed for the summer of 1972, the Supreme

12 Baker *v.* Carr, 369 U.S. 186, 198 (1962).
13 *Ibid.*, 210-211.

Court rendered a dramatic decision with respect to the dispute over the seating of delegates at the Democratic National Convention. The Court concluded in a *per curiam* decision that "it cannot in this limited time give to these issues the consideration warranted for final decision on the merits; we therefore take no action on the petitions for certiorari at this time." Nonetheless, the Court said: "We must consider the absence of authority supporting the Court of Appeals in intervening in the internal determinations of a national political party, on the eve of its convention, regarding the seating of delegates. No case is cited to us in which any federal court has undertaken to interject itself into the deliberative processes of a national political convention; no holding of this Court up to now gives support for judicial intervention in the circumstances presented here, involving as they do, relationships of great delicacy and essentially political in nature." And the Court granted the stays of the judgments of the Court of Appeals.[14]

Cases "arising under this Constitution" are cases in which the validity of an act of Congress or a treaty or of a legislative act or constitutional provision of a State, or of any official act whatsoever which purports to stem directly from the Constitution, is challenged with reference to it. This clause, in alliance with the Supremacy Clause (Article VI, ¶2), furnishes the constitutional warrant for that highly distinctive feature of American Government, Judicial Review. The initial source of judicial review, however, is much older than the Constitution and indeed of any American constitution. It traces back to the common law, certain principles of which were earlier deemed to be "fundamental" and to comprise a "higher law" which even Parliament could not alter. "And it appears," wrote Chief Justice Coke in 1610, in his famous dictum in Bonham's case, "that when an act of Parliament is against common right and reason . . . the common law will control it and adjudge such act to be void."[15] This idea first commended itself to Americans as offering an available weapon against the pretensions of Parliament in the agitation leading to the Revolution.[16] Thus in 1765 the royal governor of Massachusetts Province wrote his government that the prevailing argument against the Stamp Act was that it contravened "Magna Charta

"Judicial Review": Its Origin

---

[14] O'Brien *v.* Brown, 92 S. Ct. 2718 (1972).

[15] 8 Reps. 107, 118 (1610).

[16] *See* Josiah Quincy, *Reports of Cases* (Early Massachusetts cases) (Boston, 1865), 469-488.

and the natural rights of Englishmen and therefore, according to Lord Coke," was "null and void";[17] and on the eve of the Declaration of Independence Judge William Cushing, later one of Washington's appointees to the original bench of the Supreme Court, charged a Massachusetts jury to ignore certain acts of Parliament as "void and inoperative," and was congratulated by John Adams for doing so. In fact, the Cokian doctrine was invoked by the Supreme Court of the United States as late as 1874.[18]

With, however, the establishment of the first written constitutions, a new basis for judicial review was suggested, the argument for which was elaborated by Hamilton, with the pending Federal Constitution in mind, in *The Federalist*, No. 78, as follows: "The interpretation of the laws is the proper and peculiar province of the courts. A constitution is in fact, and must be regarded by the judges as, a fundamental law. It therefore belongs to them to ascertain its meaning as well as the meaning of any particular act proceeding from the legislative body, and, in case of irreconcilable difference between the two, to prefer the will of the people declared in the constitution to that of the legislature as expressed in statute."

The Constitutional Basis of Judicial Review    The attention of the Federal Convention was drawn to judicial review as offering a means for securing the conformity of State laws and constitutional provisions with "the Supreme Law of the Land," comprising "this Constitution and the laws of Congress made in pursuance thereof, and the treaties made . . . under the authority of the United States," of which the State judiciaries were made the first line of defense, with, presumably, a final appeal to the Supreme Court.[19] Nor has judicial review on this basis ever been seriously contested.[20] Judicial review of acts of Congress has had a more difficult row to hoe, although it is clearly predicated in the clause of Article III now under discussion; and at any rate significant debate on the subject was concluded by Marshall's famous ruling in 1803, in Marbury *v.* Madison.[21] Not only has this deci-

---

[17] *Ibid.*, 527.

[18] Loan Assoc. *v.* Topeka, 20 Wall. 655, 662 (1874).

[19] *See* Cohens *v.* Va., 6 Wheat. 264 (1821).

[20] The right of the Supreme Court, however, to take appeals from the State judiciaries in cases covered by the Supremacy Clause was for a time disputed by the Virginia Court of Appeals. *See* preceding note; and Martin *v.* Hunter's Lessee, 1 Wheat. 304 (1816).

[21] 1 Cr. 137 (1803).

sion never been disturbed, its influence soon spread into the States, with the result that long before the Civil War judicial review by State courts of local legislation was established under the local constitutions, and usually with far less textual support than the Constitution of the United States affords judicial review of acts of Congress.[22]

Inasmuch as judicial review is exercised only in connection with the decision of *cases* and for the purpose of "finding the law of the case," it is intrinsically subject to the limitations adhering to the judicial function as such (*see* pp. 167-172). Hence the Court will not render advisory opinions at the request of the coordinate departments; and a self-denying ordinance which it adopted in 1793 to this effect has, perhaps with one exception, been observed ever since.[23]

Also, the Court has announced from time to time certain other self-restraining maxims which were evoked rather by its recognition of the extraordinary nature of judicial review than by judicial decorum as such. Thus it has said that it will intervene only in "clear cases" and only when the constitutional issue cannot be avoided.[24] The latter doctrine has sometimes led it to construe the challenged statute so narrowly as to impair greatly its intended operation;[25] the former doctrine is fre-

*Maxims Governing Its Exercise*

[22] On State judicial review prior to the Civil War, *see* Edward S. Corwin, *Doctrine of Judicial Review* (Princeton, 1914), 75-78.

[23] In 1793 the Supreme Court refused to grant the request of President Washington and Secretary of State Jefferson to construe the treaties and laws of the United States pertaining to questions of International Law arising out of the wars of the French Revolution. Warren, *The Supreme Court in United States History*, I, 110-111. For the full correspondence *see* Henry P. Johnston, ed., *Correspondence and Public Papers of John Jay* (New York and London, 1890-1893), III, 486. According to E. F. Albertsworth, "Advisory Functions in Federal Supreme Court," 23 *Georgetown Law Journal*, 643, 644-647 (1935), the Court rendered an advisory opinion to President Monroe in response to a request for legal advice on the power of the Government to appropriate Federal funds for public improvements, by responding that Congress might do so under the war and postal powers. *See also* Chief Justice Hughes's letter to Senator Wheeler *in re* F.D.R.'s "Court packing" plan. Merlo Pusey, *Charles Evans Hughes*, II (New York, 1951), 756-757.

[24] Willoughby, *Constitutional Law*, I, 25-33, *passim*.

[25] *See* in this connection United States *v.* E. C. Knight Co. ("The *Sugar Trust* Case"), 156 U.S. 1 (1895); United States *v.* Delaware and Hudson Co., 213 U.S. 366 (1909); and First Employers' Liability Cases, 207 U.S. 463 (1908). The Court may also treat an act of Congress as "severable" and sustain a part of it, while holding the rest void. Pollock *v.* Farmers' Loan & Trust Co., 157 U.S. 429 (1895). But on one occasion it disregarded a statement, thrice repeated in a statute, that certain sections of it were severable, and thereby contrived to overturn the entire act. Carter *v.* Carter Coal Co., 298 U.S. 238 (1936).

quently equivocal, the application of it turning on the Court's "philosophy." Thus the Court has never exercised its censorship of legislation, whether national or State, more energetically than during the half century between 1887 and 1937, when its thinking was strongly colored by *laissez faire* concepts of the role of government. This point of view, translated into congenial constitutional doctrines, like that of "liberty of contract" and the exclusive right of the States to govern industrial relations, brought hundreds of State laws to grief, as well as an unusual number of Congressional enactments. Two persistent dissenters from this tendency were Justices Holmes and Brandeis, both of whom thrust forward maxims of judicial self-restraint in vain. The Court had converted judicial review, declared Justice Brandeis, into the power of "a super-legislature," while Justice Holmes complained that he could discover "hardly any limit but the sky" to the power claimed by the Court to disallow State acts "which may happen to strike a majority" of its members "as for any reason undesirable."[26] Conversely, the so-called "Constitutional Revolution" of 1937 connotes a distinct lightening of judicial censorship in the *economic* realm, based on a new set of constitutional values. When in recent times civil liberties issues came to the forefront on the Supreme Court's docket, there was a revival of judicial activism predicated on the argument that when it came to "preferred freedoms" (those of the First Amendment, particularly), the usual presumptions about constitutionality of legislation could not attach in the face of guarantees of at least the First Amendment. There is further discussion of this development on pp. 238-240 and 245-248.[27] In short, judicial review is at any particular period a "function" of its own product, the constitutional law of the period. Surely, there must be a lesson in the story of Justice Frankfurter, who came on the Court after the 1937 "revolution" hailed by liberals and feared by conservatives because he was an articulate practitioner of judicial self-restraint. Years later, when he retired from the bench, now the *most* articulate practitioner of judicial self-restraint, he was admired by conservatives and denigrated by liberals.

All of which considerations raise the question of the impor-

Effect of *Laissez Faire* on

[26] Burns Baking Co. *v.* Bryan, 264 U.S. 504, 534 (1924); Baldwin *v.* Mo., 281 U.S. 586, 595 (1930).
[27] *See* Harold W. Chase, *Security and Liberty* (New York, 1955), ch. II.

tance of the doctrine of *stare decisis* as an element of Constitutional Law. Story was strongly of the opinion that it was fully operative in that field. Whether, however, because of the difficulty of amending the Constitution or for cautionary reasons, the Court took the position as early as 1851 that it would reverse previous decisions on constitutional issues when convinced that they were "erroneous."[28] An outstanding instance of this nature was the decision in the Legal Tender cases, in 1870, reversing the decision which had been rendered in Hepburn *v.* Griswold fifteen months earlier;[29] and no less shattering to the prestige of *stare decisis* in the constitutional field was the Income Tax decision of 1895,[30] in which the Court, accepting Joseph H. Choate's invitation to "correct a century of error," greatly expanded its interpretation of the "direct tax" clauses.

The "Constitutional Revolution" of 1937, just alluded to, produced numerous reversals of earlier precedents on the ground of "error," some of them, Congressman James M. Beck complained, without "the decent obsequies of a funeral oration."[31] In 1944 Justice Reed cited fourteen cases decided between March 27, 1937, and June 14, 1943, in which one or more prior constitutional decisions were overturned.[32] On the same occasion Justice Roberts expressed the opinion that adjudications of the Court were rapidly gravitating "into the same class as a restricted railroad ticket, good for this day and train only."[33]

*Stare Decisis in Constitutional Law*

There is much to be said for Chief Justice Stone's dictum that "To give blind adherence to a rule or policy that no decision of this Court is to be overruled would be itself to overrule many decisions of the Court which do not accept that view. But the rule of *stare decisis* embodies a wise policy because it is often more important that a rule be settled than that it be settled right."[34] In rejoinder we have Justice Black's later observation: "Ordinarily it is sound policy to adhere to prior de-

[28] The pioneer case on the point was *The Genessee Chief*, 12 How. 443 (1851) overturning *The Thomas Jefferson*, 10 Wheat. 428 (1825). *See* especially Chief Justice Taney's opinion, 12 How. at p. 456.
[29] 8 Wall. 603 (1869); Knox *v.* Lee, 12 Wall. 457 (1871).
[30] Pollock *v.* Farmers' Loan & Trust Co., 157 U.S. 429 and 158 U.S. 601 (1895).
[31] 78 *Cong. Rec.* 5358 (1934).
[32] Smith *v.* Allwright, 321 U.S. 649, 665 note 10 (1944).
[33] *Ibid.*, 669.
[34] U.S. *v.* Underwriters Ass'n., 322 U.S. 533, 579 (1944).

cisions but this practice has quite properly never been a blind, inflexible rule."[35] Note the common denominator between the two points of view—*stare decisis* is "ordinarily" sound policy. Courts do not take lightly the matter of overruling precedent.

Two other doctrinal limitations on judicial review are one which limits the *occasions* for judicial review and one which limits the *effect* of its exercise. The former is the doctrine of Political Questions, dealt with earlier (*see* p. 171 above). The latter is the doctrine, or theory, of Departmental Construction, which stems from the contention, advanced by Jefferson and Jackson and endorsed by Lincoln, that while the Court is undoubtedly entitled to interpret the Constitution independently in the decision of cases, by the same token the other two "equal" branches of the Government are entitled to the like freedom in the exercise of their respective functions.[36] Actually, this claim was not pushed—some mythology to the contrary notwithstanding—to the logical extreme of exonerating the President from the duty of enforcing the Court's decisions, and ordinarily acts of Congress also, unless and until they have been held by the Court to be "void."[37] Its intention was to assert for the President and Congress in their *legislative* capacity the right to shape new legislation in accordance with their independent views of constitutional requirements, unembarrassed by the judicial gloss. The brittleness of *stare decisis* in the Constitutional Law field goes far to support this contention.

Congres-
sional Re-
straints on
Judicial
Review

The chief external restraint upon judicial review arises from Congress's unlimited control over the size of the Supreme Court and its equally unlimited control over the Court's appellate jurisdiction, as well as of the total jurisdiction of the lower federal courts. By virtue of the latter, Congress is in position to restrict the actual exercise of judicial review at times, or even to frustrate it altogether. Thus in 1869 it prevented the Court from passing on the constitutionality of the Reconstruction Acts by repealing the latter's jurisdiction over a case which had already been argued and was ready for decision,[38]

---

[35] Green *v.* U.S., 356 U.S. 165, 195 (1958).

[36] The classic statement of the doctrine of Departmental Construction occurs in President Jackson's famous Veto Message of July 10, 1832. Richardson, *Messages and Papers of the President*, II, 582.

[37] Warren, *The Supreme Court in United States History*, II, 221-224, where it is asserted that Andrew Jackson never said, "John Marshall has made his decision, now let him enforce it."

[38] *Ex parte* McCardle, 7 Wall. 506.

and in World War II it confined the right to challenge the
validity of provisions of the Emergency Price Control Act
and of orders of the OPA under it to a single Emergency
Court of Appeals and to the Supreme Court upon review of
that court's judgments and orders.[39] There is good reason to
believe that the nearly successful effort in Congress to with-
draw certain kinds of cases from the Supreme Court's appellate jurisdiction in the 1950's caused the Court to pull in its
horns.[40] In that bitter controversy there was never any real
question raised about Congress's power to diminish the
Court's appellate jurisdiction, only the wisdom of doing so.

It frequently happens that cases "arising under this Constitution, the laws of the United States, and treaties" of the
United States are first brought up in a State court, in consequence of a prosecution by the State itself under one of its
own laws or of an action by a private plaintiff claiming something under a law of the State. If in such a case the defendant
sets up a counter-claim under the Constitution or laws or treaties of the United States, thereupon the case becomes one
"arising under this Constitution," etc.[41] By the famous 25th
Section of the Judiciary Act of 1789, the substance of which
still remains on the statute books, such a case may be appealed
to the Supreme Court if the decision of the highest State court
to which under the law of the State it can come affirms the
claim based on State law,[42] while by an act passed in 1914 the
Supreme Court may by writ of *certiorari* bring the kind of
case described before itself for final review even if the claim
which was based on State law was rejected by the State court
in deference to national law.[43] It should be emphasized, however, that there must be a *Federal* question involved for the
Court to review since its mandate rides on the words "arising
under this Constitution etc."[44]

*Judicial
Review and
National
Supremacy*

[39] 56 *Stat.* 23, 31 and 32 (1942). Lockerty *v.* Phillips, 319 U.S. 182 (1943);
Yakus *v.* U.S., 321 U.S. 414 (1944); Bowles *v.* Willingham, 321 U.S. 503
(1944).
[40] Walter F. Murphy, *Congress and the Court* (Chicago, 1962).
[41] Cohens *v.* Va., 6 Wheat. 264 (1821).
[42] 28 U.S.C. 1257; Pope *v.* Atlantic Coast Line Co., 345 U.S. 379, 381-382
(1953); Sibron *v.* N.Y., 392 U.S. 40, 58-59 (1968); Mills *v.* Alabama, 384
U.S. 214, 217-218 (1966); Atlantic Coast Line Co. *v.* Engineers, 398 U.S.
281, 294-296 (1970).
[43] 28 U.S.C.A. 1257, *see* Historical and Revision Note: Street *v.* N.Y.,
394 U.S. 576, 583 (1969).
[44] Fay *v.* Noia 372 U.S. 391, 428-429 (1963); NAACP *v.* Alabama, 357
U.S. 449 (1958).

"All cases affecting ambassadors, other public ministers and consuls": The word "all" is used here in a rather Pickwickian sense, as we learn from a case in which the Supreme Court refused to pass on the marital difficulties of the, then, Roumanian vice-consul stationed at Cleveland, Ohio.[45]

"Admiralty and Maritime Jurisdiction"

"Cases in admiralty and maritime jurisdiction": These largely overlapping terms embody a broader content than they possessed in England,[46] but connote the peculiarities of English admiralty procedure, subject to modification by Congress: to wit, proceedings *in rem*, against the vessel; and the trial of both law and facts by a judge without the aid of a jury. Today this jurisdiction embraces, first, cases involving acts on the high seas or in navigable waters, including prize cases, and torts or other injuries; second, those involving contracts and transactions connected with shipping employed on the high seas or in navigable waters.[47] In the first category the *locality* of the act is the determinative element; in the second, *subject-matter* is the decisive factor.

What is meant by "navigable waters" in this connection? The English rule confined the term to the high seas and to rivers as far as the ebb and flow of the tide extended, and in the case of *The Thomas Jefferson*,[48] decided in 1825, the Court, speaking by Justice Story, followed this rule. Twenty-seven years later, in the case of *The Genessee Chief*,[49] the Court, speaking by Chief Justice Taney, overruled this holding, on the ground that it was not adapted to American conditions, and sustained an act of Congress giving the Federal courts jurisdiction over the Great Lakes and connecting waters. Later decisions have brought within the term canals, waters wholly within a single State but forming a connecting link in interstate commerce, waters navigable in their normal condition, and finally waterways capable of being rendered navigable by "reasonable improvement."[50] Throughout this devel-

---

[45] Ohio *ex rel.* Popovich *v.* Agler, 280 U.S. 379 (1930); U.S. *v.* Fitzpatrick, 214 F. Supp. 425 (1963); U.S. *v.* Egorov, 222 F. Supp. 106 (1963).
[46] New Jersey Steam Nav. Co. *v.* Merchants' Bk., 6 How. 344 (1848); Erastus C. Benedict, *The Law of American Admiralty, Revised* (New York, 1970), I., 1-7.
[47] Waring *v.* Clarke, 5 How. 441 (1847); *ex parte* Easton, 95 U.S. 68 (1877); North Pacific S.S. Co. *v.* Hall Brothers M. R. & S. Co., 249 U.S. 119 (1919); Grant Smith-Porter Ship Co. *v.* Rohde, 257 U.S. 469 (1922).
[48] 10 Wheat. 428 (1825).
[49] 12 How. 443 (1852).
[50] *The Daniel Ball*, 10 Wall. 557 (1871); *ex parte* Boyer, 109 U.S. 629 (1884); United States *v.* Appalachian Elec. P. Co., 311 U.S. 377 (1940);

opment the catalytic effect of the commerce clause clearly appears.

Despite assertions to the contrary in our early history, it was settled in 1874 that Congress may amend the maritime law.[51] Justice Bradley speaking for the Court gave an exceptionally clear explanation of the meaning and operation of maritime law. "But it is hardly necessary to argue that the maritime law is only so far operative as law in any country as it is adopted by the laws and usages of that country. In this respect it is like international law or the laws of war, which have the effect of law in no country any further than they are accepted and received as such; . . . The adoption of the common law by the several States of this Union also presents an analogous case. It is the basis of all the State laws; but is modified as each sees fit. Perhaps the maritime law is more uniformly followed by commercial nations than the civil and common laws are by those who use them. But, like those laws, however fixed, definite, and beneficial the theoretical code of maritime law may be, it can have only so far the effect of law in any country as it is permitted to have. But the actual maritime law can hardly be said to have a fixed and definite form as to all the subjects which may be embraced within its scope. . . . But no nation regards itself as precluded from making occasional modifications suited to its locality and the genius of its own people and institutions, especially in matters that are of merely local and municipal consequence and do not affect other nations. . . ."[52] But Congress wisely has largely left to the Supreme Court "the responsibility for fashioning the controlling rules of admiralty law."[53]

Nor does the Constitution forbid the States to create rights enforcible in Federal admiralty proceedings. In 1940 a Florida statute whereby a cause of action for personal injury due to another's negligence survives the death of the tort-feasor against his estate was enforced in a proceeding *in rem* in

*Powers of Congress Over*

---

Southern S.S. Co. *v.* N.L.R.B., 316 U.S. 31 (1942). Evidently, there are limits, however. A Federal court recently held that: "We cannot find substance to plaintiff's argument that Conneaut Lake is navigable under the admiralty definition because it was once connected by a feeder channel conveying water from the lake to the Erie Extension Canal. The canal system has been gone for almost a century." Doran *v.* Lee, 287 F. Supp. 807, 812 (1968).

[51] *The Lottawanna*, 88 U.S. 558 (1874).

[52] *Ibid.*, 572-573.

[53] Fitzgerald *v.* U.S., 374 U.S. 16, 20 (1963).

a United States district court, and the holding was sustained by the Supreme Court.[54]

Even so, the Court held in 1917, five Justices to four, that a New York Workmen's Compensation statute was unconstitutional when applied to employees engaged in maritime work, being destructive, it said, of "the very uniformity in respect to maritime matters which the Constitution was designed to establish";[55] and three years later it stigmatized an attempt by Congress to save such claimants their rights and remedies under State law as an "unconsitutional delegation of legislative power to the States."[56]

Just *when* "uniformity" is disturbed by this species of legislation is therefore difficult to say. Speaking for the Court in 1942 in sustaining the applicability of a Washington "death act," in an action brought by the widow of a harbor worker who was drowned in a navigable stream, Justice Black hinted that the choice presented the Justices by the precedents was about a 50-50 one.[57] That problem continues to plague the Court, but its latest decisions continue to uphold the application of State wrongful death statutes.[58] Significantly, in late 1971 the Supreme Court held that a suit brought by a longshoreman injured on a dock was governed by State law and not Federal maritime law.[59]

"Controversies to which the United States shall be a party": It is a universally accepted maxim of public law that the sovereign may not be sued except on his own consent. In Chisholm *v.* Georgia,[60] decided in 1792, the Court held that the States of the United States were not "sovereign" within the sense of this principle—a ruling which was soon "recalled" by the adoption of the Eleventh Amendment (*see* p. 375 below). On the same occasion Chief Justice Jay voiced the opinion that the United States, i.e., the National Government, was "sovereign" in this sense, and this opinion has always been adhered to in theory.

[54] Just *v.* Chambers, 312 U.S. 383 (1941).
[55] Southern Pacific Co. *v.* Jensen, 244 U.S. 205, 215-218 (1917).
[56] Knickerbocker Ice Co. *v.* Steward, 253 U.S. 149, 163-166 (1920).
[57] Davis *v.* Dept. of Labor, 317 U.S. 249, 252-253 (1942).
[58] The Tungus *v.* Skovgaard, 358 U.S. 588 (1959); United Pilots Ass'n. *v.* Halecki; 358 U.S. 613 (1959); Hess *v.* U.S. 361 U.S. 314 (1960). For related issues *see* Kossick *v.* United Fruit Co., 365 U.S. 731 (1961); Moragne *v.* States Marine Lines, Inc., 398 U.S. 375 (1970); 42 *Op. Atty. Gen.* 25 (1966).
[59] Victory Carriers Inc. *v.* Law, 404 U.S. 202 (1971).
[60] 2 Dall. 419 (1793).

It follows that the "controversies" mentioned above are Suability of either those in which the United States appears as party plain- the United tiff or those in which it has, through Congress, consented to be States sued. By the so-called Tucker Act of 1887 the United States did consent to be sued, in the Court of Claims at Washington, on all claims founded upon any contract "express or implied"; while by the Federal Tort Claims Act of 1946 it consented to be sued for injuries "caused by the negligent or wrongful act or omission of any employee . . . acting within the scope of his office or employment." Excluded were claims for damage caused by loss of mails, false imprisonment, operations in war-time of the armed forces, etc. These laws have survived.[61] In contrast to these acts of generosity, the United States may spread its immunity to corporations created by it to act as in-strumentalities of its powers, but its intention to do so must be clear.[62] The Supreme Court has generally given a broad, if at times uneven interpretation to those entitled to recover under the law.[63] (Re suability of States, *see* p. 376.)

The right of the government in actions against it to with-hold evidence alleged to reveal military secrets is very broad.[64] However, with the Supreme Court leading the way in the highly controversial Jencks case, a combination of statute and Court decisions have made government files a lot less sacro-sanct.[65]

How is it as to suits brought against Federal officials? Under Suability of the common law an officer of government who acts in excess Federal of his lawful authority loses his official character and becomes Officers legally responsible. Following this rule, the Supreme Court in 1882 held, by a vote of five to four, in the famous case of United States *v.* Lee,[66] that ejectment proceedings could be brought against army officers whom it found to be in "illegal" possession of the Arlington estate of the Lee family, under an "unlawful" order of the President. But the Court was destined to learn that the issue was much too complicated to be serv-

[61] 28 U.S.C. 1346, 2680, 1481.
[62] Larson *v.* Domestic and For. Corp., 337 U.S. 682 (1949).
[63] Indian Towing Co. *v.* U.S., 350 U.S. 61 (1955); U.S. *v.* Muniz, 374 U.S. 150 (1963); Rayonier, Inc. *v.* U.S., 352 U.S. 315 (1957), *cf.* Dalehite *v.* U.S., 346 U.S. 15 (1953).
[64] United States *v.* Reynolds, 345 U.S. 1 (1953).
[65] This fascinating, complicated story is well told by the Court in Pa-lermo *v.* U.S., 360 U.S. 343 (1959); *see also* Rosenberg *v.* U.S., 360 U.S. 367 (1959); Campbell *v.* U.S., 365 U.S. 85 (1961); Clancy *v.* U.S., 365 U.S. 312 (1961); U.S. *v.* Augenblick, 393 U.S. 348 (1969).
[66] 106 U.S. 196, 207-208 (1882).

iced by a simple rule. As Justice Frankfurter pointed out in a notable dissent in 1949, there are really four different kinds of cases which arise in this area: " (1) Cases in which the plaintiff seeks an interest in property which concededly, even under the allegation of the complaint, belongs to the government, or calls for an assertion of what is unquestionably official authority. (2) Cases in which action to the legal detriment of a plaintiff is taken by an official justifying his action under an unconstitutional statute. (3) Cases in which a plaintiff suffers a legal detriment through action of an officer who has exceeded his statutory authority. (4) Cases in which an officer seeks shelter behind statutory authority or some other sovereign command for the commission of a common-law tort."[67] He concluded his analysis with these words: "The matter boils down to this. The federal courts are not barred from adjudicating a claim against a governmental agent who invokes statutory authority for his action if the constitutional power to give him such a claim of immunity is itself challenged. Sovereign immunity may, however, become relevant because the relief prayed for also entails interference with governmental property or brings the operation of governmental machinery into play. The Government then becomes an indispensable party and without its consent cannot be implicated."[68] And there is much truth to the dictum of Justice Douglas that in this type of case "The question of jurisdiction is dependent on decision on the merits."[69]

"Controversies between two or more States": From the outset the Court has generally construed its jurisdiction in this field liberally. In earlier years its principal grist comprised State boundary disputes, which were held to be justiciable, not political in nature.[70] Later arose a succession of suits in which the plaintiff State prayed that defendant State be enjoined from diverting or polluting the former's water resources.[71] "A

---

[67] Larson v. Domestic & Foreign Corp., 337 U.S. 682, 709-710 (1949).

[68] Ibid., 715. See also the opinion of highly regarded Judge Friendly in Knight v. N.Y., 443 F. 2d. 415 (1971).

[69] Land v. Dollar, 330 U.S., 731, 735 (1947); Hawaii v. Gordon, 373 U.S. 57 (1963).

[70] Rhode Island v. Mass., 12 Pet. 657, 721, 736-737 (1838). On the whole subject see Charles Warren, The Supreme Court and Sovereign States (Princeton, 1924).

[71] Missouri v. Ill. and Sanitary Dist. of Chicago, 180 U.S. 208 (1901); Nebraska v. Wyo., 325 U.S. 589 (1945).

river," said Justice Holmes, "is more than an amenity, it is a treasure."[72] In 1911, in Virginia *v.* West Virginia[73] the Court undertook to determine the proportion of the public debt of the original State of Virginia which West Virginia ought to shoulder. Speaking again by Justice Holmes, it said: "The case is to be considered in the untechnical spirit proper for dealing with a quasi-international controversy, remembering that there is no municipal code governing the matter, and that this Court may be called on to adjust differences that cannot be dealt with by Congress or disposed of by the legislature of either State alone."[74] It was also at a later stage of these same proceedings that Chief Justice White, for the Court, asserted with much emphasis that the National Government possessed adequate authority to enforce the Court's decrees against any State which failed to comply with them—an announcement which stimulated West Virginia to abandon dilatory tactics and vote the sum which the Court had held to be due Virginia.[75]

In recent years, where the problem of use of scarce water resources has been much aggravated, the Supreme Court has been deeply involved, for as the Court has said: ". . . this Court does have serious responsibility to adjudicate cases where there are actual, existing controversies over how interstate streams should be apportioned among the States."[76]

Latterly the Court has shown itself disinclined to exercise its *original* jurisdiction over "controversies between two or more States" as a shortcut method whereby the citizens of a State may secure a determination of their alleged rights against the legislative policies of another State or of the National Government, such as the recent effort of Massachusetts to have the Supreme Court find the war in Vietnam illegal.[77] Nor may a State make itself a collection agency of debts due

---

[72] New Jersey *v.* N.Y., 283 U.S. 336, 342 (1931).
[73] 220 U.S. 1 (1911).     [74] *Ibid.*, 27.
[75] Virginia *v.* W. Va., 246 U.S. 565 (1918).
[76] Arizona *v.* California, 373 U.S. 546 (1963); Arizona *v.* California, 383 U.S. 268 (1966); Recently, there have been several other interesting cases involving controversies between States, Arkansas *v.* Tennessee, 397 U.S. 88 (1970) and Ohio *v.* Wyandotte Chemicals Corp., 401 U.S. 493 (1971).
[77] Massachusetts *v.* Laird, 400 U.S. 886 (1970). *See* the Douglas dissent. *See* Hawaii *v.* Standard Oil Co., 405 U.S. 251 (1972) particularly Justice Douglas's dissent. *See also* Alabama *v.* Ariz., 291 U.S. 286 (1934); Massachusetts *v.* Mo., 308 U.S. 1, 17 (1939); Massachusetts *v.* Mellon, 262 U.S. 447 (1923).

its citizens from another State and expect the Supreme Court to further the transaction by its original jurisdiction; but an outright assignment of such debts to the plaintiff State is a horse of another color.[78]

Judicial Invasion of State Power

By the terms of the Eleventh Amendment "controversies between a State and citizens of another State" include only such controversies as are commenced by a State. But the restrictive force of this limitation had been in earlier decades greatly broken down by the practice of the United States District Courts in entertaining applications for injunctions against State officers, and especially State public utility commissions, forbidding them to attempt to enforce State laws or regulations which were claimed by the applicant to be unconstitutional, with the result often of postponing the actual going into effect of such laws or regulations until—if ever—their constitutionality was sustained by the Supreme Court. Sometimes a period of several years—in one case fifteen years—had elapsed before the State measure involved, although it was finally held to be valid, was allowed to go into operation.[79] Certain statutory restraints have been laid upon this practice from time to time,[80] but even more important in curbing it today are the present Supreme Court's enlarged views of State power in the regulation of public utility rates. (*See* pp. 390-391 below.)

Judicial Protection of State Interests

Even so, the grounds upon which such controversies, commenced by the State itself, may be based still remain broad; the Court having recognized repeatedly within recent years the right of a State government to intervene in behalf of important interests of its citizens, or a considerable section of them, and to ask the Court to protect such interests against the tortious acts of outside persons and corporations of other States. Thus, in the leading case the Court granted the petition of Georgia for an injunction against certain copper companies in Tennessee, forbidding them to discharge noxious gases from their works in Tennessee over the adjoining counties of Georgia; and it was on this precedent that Governor Arnall relied chiefly in his successful appeal to the Court in 1945 to concede Georgia's right to maintain before it an original suit un-

[78] *Cf.* New Hampshire *v.* La., 108 U.S. 76 (1883), and South Dakota *v.* N.C., 192 U.S. 286 (1904).

[79] Justice Brandeis, concurring, in St. Joseph Stockyards Co. *v.* U.S., 298 U.S. 38, 90-91 (1936).

[80] For example, *see* 28 U.S.C. 1342 and 2281.

der the Sherman Act to enjoin an alleged conspiracy of some twenty railroads to fix discriminatory rates from which, he claimed, Georgia and the South generally suffered grave economic detriment.[81] On the question of merits, however, Georgia eventually lost out in the latter case.[82] But in 1971, the Court declined to exercise its jurisdiction in a case involving Ohio's complaint against companies allegedly polluting Lake Erie, explaining that the issues were bottomed on local law, which Ohio courts are competent to consider.[83]

The judicial power of the United States is extended to the kinds of controversies already mentioned because there is no other tribunal for such controversies. It is extended to controversies "between citizens of different States" for a quite different reason, namely, to make available a tribunal for such cases which shall be free from local bias. In this field, accordingly, Congress has felt free to leave the States a concurrent jurisdiction, and as the statute now stands, the United States District Courts have original jurisdiction of controversies between citizens of different States in which ten thousand dollars or more is involved, while controversies of the same pecuniary importance, if brought by a plaintiff in a court of a State of which defendant is not a resident, may be removed by the latter to the nearest United States District Court.[84] It was long the doctrine of the Court that the national courts were free to decide cases of this description in accordance with their own notions of "general principles of common law," but later decisions overrule this view, holding that the substantive law enforced must be that laid down by the courts of the State where the cause of action arose, a rule which applies equally to suits in equity and actions at law.[85]

The word "citizens" in this clause, as well as other clauses of this paragraph, has come practically to include corporations, since the Court, by an extended course of judicial legislation which was completed prior to the Civil War, has estab-

*The Diversity of Citizenship Jurisdiction*

[81] Georgia *v.* Tenn. Copper Co., 206 U.S. 230 (1907); Georgia *v.* Pa. R.R. Co., 324 U.S. 439 (1945).

[82] *See* 340 U.S. 889.

[83] Ohio *v.* Wyandotte Chemicals Corp., 401 U.S. 493 (1971). *See also* Hawaii *v.* Standard Oil Co., 405 U.S. 251 (1972).

[84] 28 U.S.C. 1332.

[85] Erie R.R. Co. *v.* Tompkins, 304 U.S. 64 (1938); Prima Paint *v.* Flood & Conklin, 388 U.S. 395, 404 (1967). The cases overruled are headed by Swift *v.* Tyson, 16 Pet. 1 decided in 1842.

lished the "jurisdictional fiction" that the stockholders of a corporation are all citizens of the State which chartered it, even when the corporation is being sued by a stockholder from another State.[86]

On the other hand, the word "State" in the clause was held by the Court, speaking by Chief Justice Marshall, in 1805, to be confined to "the members of the American confederacy," with the consequence that a citizen of the District of Columbia could not sue a citizen of Virginia on the ground of diversity of citizenship.[87] At the same time, the Chief Justice indicated that the subject was one for "legislative, not for judicial consideration"; and, apparently relying on this dictum, Congress in 1940 adopted an amendment to the Federal Judicial Code to extend the jurisdiction of Federal district courts to civil actions involving no Federal question "between citizens of different States or citizens of the District of Columbia . . . and any State or Territory."[88] This act was sustained by five Justices, but for widely different reasons, with the result that while the District of Columbia is still not a "State," its citizens may sue citizens of States in the absence of a Federal question, not on the basis of any statable constitutional principle, but through the grace of what Justice Frankfurter has called "conflicting minorities in combination."[89]

*The Diversity Clause and the D. of C.*

*Clashes between Federal and State Courts*

Not surprisingly, the presence within the same territory of two autonomous jurisdictions has produced numerous clashes between them. In the vast majority of such cases the State courts involved have, since the boisterous days of Worcester *v.* Georgia, come off second best, thanks to the Supreme Court's vigorous application of the principle of National Supremacy. Nor have occasional legislative efforts to protect the local interest proved especially successful. By an act passed in 1793[90] Congress forbade the Federal courts to enjoin proceedings in State courts, but that act is today honeycombed with exceptions. First, it has been held that an injunction will lie against proceedings in a State court to protect the lawfully acquired jurisdiction of a Federal court against impairment or

[86] Dodge *v.* Woolsey, 18 How. 331 (1855); Ohio and Miss. R.R. Co. *v.* Wheeler, 1 Bl. 286 (1861); Ross *v.* Bernhard, 396 U.S. 531, 534 (1970).
[87] Hepburn *v.* Ellzey, 2 Cr. 445 (1805).
[88] 54 *Stat.* 143; 28 U.S.C. 1332.
[89] National Mutual Ins. Co. *v.* Tidewater Transfer Co., 337 U.S. 582, 655 (1949); Metlakatla Indians *v.* Egan, 363 U.S. 555, 558 (1960).
[90] 1 *Stat.* 355 (1793); 28 U.S.C. 2283 and 2281.

defeat.[91] This exception is notably applicable to cases where the Federal court has taken possession of property which it may protect by injunction from interference by State courts.[92] Second, in order to prevent irreparable damage to persons and property the Federal courts may restrain the legal officers of a State from taking proceedings to State courts to enforce State legislation alleged to be unconstitutional.[93] Also Federal courts may issue injunctions restraining the execution of judgments in State courts obtained by fraud,[94] and restraining proceedings in State courts in cases which have been removed to the federal courts.[95] And, for a time, Federal courts could restrain proceedings in State courts to relitigate issues previously adjudicated and finally settled by decrees of a Federal court.[96] Congressional unhappiness with these decisions led to enactment of the requirement that these kinds of injunctions could only be issued by a three-judge court.[97]

To say that Federal courts may, and do to this day, step in to restrain proceedings in State courts is not to suggest that they do it often and blithely. Judicial unease over the perceived necessity to do it on occasion was reflected very well in a recent opinion written for the Court by Justice Black:

"Since the beginning of this country's history Congress has, subject to few exceptions, manifested a desire to permit state courts to try state cases free from interference by federal courts. In 1793 an Act unconditionally provided: [N]or shall a writ of injunction be granted to stay proceedings in any court of a state. . . . A comparison of the 1793 Act with its present-day successor, graphically illustrates how few and minor have been the exceptions granted from the flat, prohibitory

[91] Freeman *v.* Howe, 24 How. 450 (1861); Julian *v.* Central Trust Co., 193 U.S. 93 (1904); Riverdale Cotton Mills *v.* Ala. & Ga. Mfg. Co., 198 U.S. 188 (1905); Looney *v.* Eastern Texas R. Co., 247 U.S. 214 (1918).

[92] Farmers' Loan & Trust Co. *v.* Lake St. Elev. R. Co., 177 U.S. 51 (1900); Riverdale Cotton Mills *v.* Ala. & Ga., Mfg. Co., 198 U.S. 188 (1905); Julian *v.* Central Trust Co., 193 U.S. 93 (1904); Kline *v.* Burke Construction Co., 260 U.S. 226 (1922). For a discussion of this rule *see* Toucey *v.* New York Life Ins. Co., 314 U.S. 118, 134-136 (1941).

[93] *Ex parte* Young, 209 U.S. 123 (1908), is the leading case.

[94] Arrowsmith *v.* Gleason, 129 U.S. 86 (1889); Marshall *v.* Holmes, 141 U.S. 589 (1891); Simon *v.* Southern R. Co., 236 U.S. 115 (1915).

[95] French *v.* Hay, 22 Wall. 231 (1875); Dietzsch *v.* Huidekoper, 103 U.S. 494 (1881); Madisonville Traction Co. *v.* St. Bernard Mining Co., 196 U.S. 239 (1905).

[96] The earlier cases are Root *v.* Woolworth, 150 U.S. 401 (1893); Prout *v.* Starr, 188 U.S. 537 (1903); Julian *v.* Central Trust Co., 193 U.S. 93 (1904).

[97] 18 U.S.C. 2281.

language of the old Act. During all this lapse of years from 1793 to 1970 the statutory exceptions to the 1793 congressional enactment have been only three: (1) except as expressly authorized by Act of Congress; (2) where necessary in aid of its jurisdiction; and (3) to protect or effectuate its judgments. In addition, a judicial exception to the longstanding policy evidenced by the statute has been made where a person about to be prosecuted in a state court can show that he will, if the proceeding in the state court can show that he will, if the proceeding in the state court is not enjoined, suffer irreparable damages. *See ex parte* Young, 209 U.S. 123 (1908).

"The precise reasons for this longstanding public policy against federal court interference with state court proceedings have never been specifically identified but the primary sources of the policy are plain. One is the basic doctrine of equity jurisprudence that courts of equity should not act, and particularly should not act to restrain a criminal prosecution, when the moving party has an adequate remedy at law and will not suffer irreparable injury if denied equitable relief. . . . This underlying reason for restraining courts of equity from interfering with criminal prosecutions is reinforced by an even more vital consideration, the notion of 'comity,' that is, a proper respect for state functions, a recognition of the fact that the entire country is made up of a Union of separate state governments, and a continuance of the belief that the National Government will fare best if the States and their institutions are left free to perform their separate functions in their separate ways. . . . The concept does not mean blind deference to 'States' Rights' any more than it means centralization of control over every important issue in our National Government and its courts. The Framers rejected both these courses. What the concept does represent is a system in which there is sensitivity to the legitimate interests of both State and National Governments, and in which the National Government, anxious though it may be to vindicate and protect federal rights and federal interests, always endeavors to do so in ways that will not unduly interfere with the legitimate activities of the States."[98] Yet, in its understandable and commendable zeal to safeguard important civil liberties from violation at the State level, the Supreme Court has in recent years made inroads on the in-

[98] Younger *v.* Harris, 401 U.S. 37 (1971).

violability of a doctrine it had long employed, the "abstention doctrine."[99] "Abstention," according to the Court's own description, "is a judge-fashioned vehicle for according appropriate deference of the state and federal court systems. Its recognition of *the role of state courts as the final expositors of state law* implies no disregard for the primacy of the federal judiciary in deciding questions of federal law. Accordingly, we have on several occasions explicitly recognized that abstention 'does not, of course, involve the abdication of federal jurisdiction, but only the postponement of its exercise' " (emphasis supplied).[100] The Abstention Doctrine

Significantly, in June 1972 the Supreme Court held that the statute which authorizes a suit in equity to redress the deprivation "under color" of State law "of any rights, privileges, or immunities secured by the Constitution" was within the exceptions of the Federal anti-injunction statute which provides among other things that a Federal court may not enjoin State court proceedings "except as expressly authorized by Act of Congress."[101]

In recent years, moreover, a new source of interference by Federal courts in the domain of State judicial process has emerged in consequence, first, of the impact of the expanding concept of due process upon enforcement by the States of their criminal laws, and, second, of the almost complete freedom claimed by the Supreme Court today "to decline to review decisions which, right or wrong, do not present questions of sufficient gravity." The natural product of these cooperating factors has been a vast increase in the number of petitions filed in Federal district courts for the writ of *habeas corpus*, in the name of persons accused or convicted of crime in the States, in alleged violation of their constitutional rights. In a case decided in 1948 Justice Murphy, while favoring this increased availability of the writ, revealed that in the fiscal years 1944, 1945, and 1946 an average of 451 *habeas corpus* petitions were filed each year in Federal district courts by persons in State custody, although an average of only six per cent resulted in a reversal of the conviction and release of the petitioner.[102] The *Habeas Corpus* Problem

[99] Dombrowski *v.* Pfister, 380 U.S. 479 (1965); England *v.* Medical Examiners, 375 U.S. 411 (1964).

[100] England *v.* Medical Examiners, 375 U.S. 411, 415-416 (1964).

[101] Mitchum *v.* Foster, 407 U.S. 225 (1972). The statutes referred to above are contained in 42 U.S.C. 1983 and 28 U.S.C. 2283, respectively.

[102] Wade *v.* Mayo, 334 U.S. 672, 682 (1948).

Based on these figures Justice Frankfurter observed in 1953 that "the writ has possibilities for evil as well as good," that abuse of it "may undermine the orderly administration of justice," the responsibility for which "rests largely with the States," and in consequence "weakening the forces of authority that are essential for civilization."[103] Imagine how the minds of those two Justices would boggle to learn that in 1969 there were *12,000* such petitions.[104]

Retro-
activity
    In the wake of its landmark decisions with respect to right to counsel, illegal search and seizures, and involuntary confessions (discussed below under the Bill of Rights), the Warren Court was forced to wrestle with another trying problem respecting judicial review. Once the Court decides that the Constitution requires right to counsel in a criminal case, what happens to all those languishing in jail who had been denied that right? It hardly seems justice to let them remain there. But if we allow them to take steps to freedom, what of the felon who was convicted on the basis of good evidence which was illegally obtained? Once the Court decides to deny the use of such evidence to prevent illegal police activity in the future, does it change the likelihood that those already convicted were guilty? The Court's answer to these questions fashioned in a series of cases is this: "Relying on prior cases, we firmly rejected the idea that all new interpretations of the Constitution must be considered always to have been the law and that prior constructions to the contrary must always be ignored. Since that time, we have held to the course that there is no inflexible constitutional rule requiring in all circumstances either absolute retroactivity or complete prospectivity for decisions construing the broad language of the Bill of Rights. Nor have we accepted as a dividing line the suggested distinction between cases on direct review and those arising on collateral attack. Rather we have proceeded to weigh the merits and demerits in each case by looking to the prior history of the rule in question, its purpose and effect, and whether retrospective operation will further or retard its operation.

"Where the major purpose of new constitutional doctrine is to overcome an aspect of the criminal trial which substan-

---

103 Brown *v.* Allen, 344 U.S. 443 (1953). All quoted passages are from Justice Frankfurter's supplementary opinion, *ibid.*, 488-513.
104 George C. Doub, "The Case Against Modern Federal *Habeas Corpus*," 57 *ABA Journal*, 323, 325 (1971).

tially impairs its truth-finding function and so raises serious questions about the accuracy of guilty verdicts in past trials, the new rule has been given complete retroactive effect. Neither good-faith reliance by state or federal authorities on prior constitutional law or accepted practice, nor severe impact on the administration of justice has sufficed to require prospective application in these circumstances.

"It is quite different where the purpose of the new constitutional standard proscribing the use of certain evidence or a particular mode of trial is not to minimize or avoid arbitrary or unreliable results but to serve other ends. In these situations the new doctrine raises no question about the guilt of defendants convicted in prior trials. Mapp *v.* Ohio cast no doubt on the relevance or probity of illegally seized evidence but excluded it from criminal trials to deter official invasions of individual privacy protected by the Fourth Amendment."[105]

The short of the matter is that the Court has made the right-to-counsel decision retroactive but has refused to do so as a general proposition with respect to "Fourth Amendment cases and new interpretations of the Fifth Amendment's privilege against compelled self-incrimination."[106]

¶2. In all cases affecting ambassadors, other public ministers and consuls, and those in which a State shall be party, the Supreme Court shall have original jurisdiction. In all the other cases before mentioned the Supreme Court shall have appellate jurisdiction, both as to law and fact, with such exceptions and under such regulations as the Congress shall make.

Jurisdiction is either original or appellate. In Marbury *v.* Madison, the case in which the Court first pronounced an act of Congress unconstitutional, it was held that Congress could not extend the original jurisdiction of the Supreme Court to other cases than those specified in the first sentence of this paragraph.[107] But, if a case "in which the State is party" is also one

---

[105] Williams *v.* U.S., 401 U.S. 646, 651-653, 1151-1153 (1971).

[106] *Ibid.*, 655 note 7. *See also* Linkletter *v.* Walker, 381 U.S. 618 (1965); Desist *v.* U.S., 394 U.S. 244 (1969); Tehan *v.* U.S., 382 U.S. 406 (1966); Johnson *v.* N.J., 384 U.S. 719 (1966); Mackey *v.* U.S., 401 U.S. 667 (1971).

[107] 1 Cr. 137 (1803). This holding was anticipated by Chief Justice Ellsworth in his opinion in Wiscart *v.* Dauchy, 3 Dall. 321 (1796).

"arising under the Constitution and laws of the United States," it may, if Congress so enacts, be brought elsewhere in the first instance. In face of the express words of Section II, ¶2, of the Constitution this may seem a little surprising but Chief Justice Marshall explained it this way: "The words of the constitution are, 'in all cases affecting ambassadors, other public ministers, and consuls, and those in which a State shall be a party, the Supreme Court shall have original jurisdiction. In all the other cases before mentioned, the Supreme Court shall have appellate jurisdiction.'

"This distinction between original and appellate jurisdiction excludes, we are told, in all cases, the exercise of the one where the other is given.

"The constitution gives the Supreme Court original jurisdiction in certain enumerated cases, and gives it appellate jurisdiction in all others. Among those in which jurisdiction must be exercised in the appellate form are cases arising under the constitution and laws of the United States. These provisions of the constitution are equally obligatory, and are to be equally respected. If a State be a party, the jurisdiction of this Court is original; if the case arise under a constitution or a law, the jurisdiction is appellate. But a case to which a State is a party may arise under the constitution or a law of the United States. What rule is applicable to such a case? What, then, becomes the duty of the Court? Certainly, we think, so to construe the constitution as to give effect to both provisions, as far as it is possible to reconcile them, and not to permit their seeming repugnancy to destroy each other. We must endeavour so to construe them as to preserve the true intent and meaning of the instrument."[108]

Whatever the intent of the Framers, Justice Douglas, speaking for the Court, recently explained that "It has long been this Court's philosophy that 'our original jurisdiction should be invoked sparingly' . . . to make it obligatory only in appropriate cases." According to Douglas, what constitutes appropriateness depends upon "the seriousness and dignity of the claim" and "beyond that it necessarily involves the availability of another forum where there is jurisdiction over the named parties, where the issues tendered may be litigated, and where

---

[108] Cohens v. Va., 6 Wheat. 264, 392-393 (1821); Ames v. Kan., 111 U.S. 449 (1884); United States v. Calif., 297 U.S. 175 (1936).

appropriate relief may be had." He further explained: "We incline to a sparing use of our original jurisdiction so that our increasing duties with the appellate docket will not suffer."[109] Even in so important a matter as a complaint against automobile manufacturers alleging a conspiracy "to restrain the development of motor vehicle air pollution control equipment" in which eighteen States were the plaintiffs, the Court refused in 1972 to take original jurisdiction. Admitting that "our jurisdiction over the controversy cannot be disputed," Justice Douglas, speaking for the Court, stated that "corrective remedies for air pollution . . . necessarily must be considered in the context of localized situations," and concluded, therefore, that the cases should first be heard in the appropriate Federal district courts.[110] In assessing the Court's wisdom in this decision, one must bear in mind that in practical terms it may be as much as ten years before the issue is fully litigated.

The Court's appellate jurisdiction Congress may, as indicated earlier (p. 168), enlarge or diminish at will so long as it does not exceed the catalogue of "cases" and "controversies" given in ¶1, above. The appellate jurisdiction of the Supreme Court as to fact in "cases of law" is much curtailed by Amendment VII. Even so, the Court will always review findings of fact by a State court, or by an administrative agency, to any extent necessary to vindicate rights claimed under the Constitution.[111]

¶3. The trial of all crimes, except in cases of impeachment, shall be by jury; and such trial shall be held in the State where the said crimes shall have been committed: but when not committed within any State, the trial shall be at such place or places as the Congress may by law have directed.

In spite of its mandatory form the opening clause of this paragraph, like the parallel provision on the same subject in Amendment VI, only establishes trial by jury as a privilege of accused persons, which such persons may accordingly waive

[109] Illinois *v.* City of Milwaukee, 406 U.S. 91 (1972).

[110] Washington *v.* General Motors Corp., 406 U.S. 109 (1972).

[111] This does not contradict what was said on p. 161. To determine whether or not a determination of facts is supported by "substantial evidence" requires a review of those facts.

if they choose[112] and the government consents. The substance of the other two clauses is also covered by that amendment. (*See* p. 340 for discussion.)

## SECTION III

¶1. Treason against the United States shall consist only in levying war against them, or in adhering to their enemies, giving them aid and comfort. No person shall be convicted of treason unless on the testimony of two witnesses to the same overt act, or on confession in open court.

"Levying war" consists, in the first place, in a combination or conspiracy to effect a change in the laws or the government by force, but a war is not "levied" until the treasonable force is actually assembled.[1]

One "adheres" to the enemies of the United States, "giving them aid and comfort," when he knowingly furnishes them with assistance of any sort.[2]

Vicissitudes of the "Treason" Clause

"Overt act" means simply open act, that is to say, an act which may be testified to, and not a mere state of consciousness. Otherwise, the precise force of this requirement is still a matter of some doubt. At the common law, treason by levying war involved a conspiracy, so that if an overt act of war in pursuance of the conspiracy took place, all the conspirators were equally liable for it at the place where it occurred; and in the *Bollman* case early in 1807 Chief Justice Marshall followed the common law doctrine. A few weeks later, however, while presiding at Richmond over the trial of Aaron Burr for treason, he turned his back on this doctrine completely by holding that Burr must be linked with the conspiracy by an overt act of his own. And in 1945 the Court held, five to four, that in a prosecution for treason by giving "aid and comfort," the overt act or acts testified to must be of themselves sufficient to establish treasonable intent. This holding, based in part on an error of history, has since been abandoned for something more nearly approaching the older doctrine, that

---

[112] Patton *v.* U.S., 281 U.S. 276 (1930); U.S. *v.* Harris 314 F. Supp. 437 (1970); Goldstein *v.* Pavlikowski, 489 P. 2d. 1159 (1971); *ex parte* Quirin, 317 U.S. 1 (1942); U.S. *v.* National City Lines, 334 U.S. 573 (1948); Reid *v.* Covert, 354 U.S. 1 (1957).

[1] *Ex parte* Bollman, 4 Cr. 75 (1807).
[2] Charles Warren, "What is Giving Aid and Comfort to the Enemy?" 27 *Yale Law Journal*, 331 (1918); Tomoya Kawakita *v.* U.S. 343 U.S. 717 (1952).

a traitor may be convicted on any kind of admissible evidence into which the testimony of two witnesses to an overt act enters.[3]

¶2. The Congress shall have power to declare the punishment of treason, but no attainder of treason shall work corruption of blood or forfeiture except during the life of the person attainted.

Some years ago, the Supreme Court said all that needs to be said on this provision:

"In England, attainders of treason worked corruption of blood and perpetual forfeiture of the estate of the person attainted, to the disinherison of his heirs, or of those who would otherwise be his heirs. Thus innocent children were made to suffer because of the offence of their ancestor. When the Federal Constitution was framed, this was felt to be a great hardship, and even rank injustice. For this reason, it was ordained that no attainder of treason should work corruption of blood or forfeiture, except during the life of the person attainted. No one ever doubted that it was a provision introduced for the benefit of the children and heirs alone; a declaration that the children should not bear the iniquity of the fathers."[4]

[3] *Cf.* the *Bollman* case, cited above; Beveridge, *Marshall*, III, 618-626; Willoughby, *Constitutional Law*, II, 1125-1133; Cramer *v.* U.S.325 U.S. 1 (1945); Haupt *v.* U.S., 330 U.S. 631 (1947). The error referred to was Justice Jackson's mistaken idea that the two-witness requirement originated in the Constitution. It comes from the Treason Trials Act of 1696 (7 and 8 Wm. III, c. 3). David Hutchison, *The Foundations of the Constitution* (New York, 1928), 215.

[4] Wallick *et al. v.* Van Riswick, 92 U.S. 202, 210 (1875).

# ARTICLE IV

This article, sometimes called "the Federal Article," defines in certain important particulars the relations of the States to one another and of the National Government to the States.

## SECTION I

¶Full faith and credit shall be given in each State to the public acts, records, and judicial proceedings of every other State. And the Congress may by general laws prescribe the manner in which such acts, records, and proceedings shall be proved, and the effect thereof.

In accordance with what is variously known as Conflict of Laws, Comity, or Private International Law, rights acquired under the laws or through the courts of one country may often receive recognition and enforcement in the courts of another country, and it is the purpose of the above section to guarantee that this shall be the case among the States in certain instances.[1]

Article IV, Section I, has had its principal operation in relation to judgments. The cases fall into two groups: First, those in which the judgment involved was offered as a basis of proceedings for its own enforcement outside the State where rendered, as for example, when an action for debt is brought in the courts of State B on a judgment for money damages rendered in State A; secondly, those in which the judgment involved was offered in conformance with the principle of *res judicata*, in defense in a new or "collateral" proceeding growing out of the same facts as the original suit, as for example, when a decree of divorce granted in State A is offered as barring a suit for divorce by the other party to the marriage in the courts of State B.

Operation of the "Full Faith and Credit" Clause on Judgments

By an act of Congress passed in 1790, and still on the statute books, "the records and judicial proceedings of the Courts of any State . . . shall have such faith and credit given to them in every court within the United States as they have by law or usage in the courts of the State from which they are taken."[2] In the pioneer cases of Mills *v.* Duryee and Hampton *v.* Mc-

[1] T. M. Cooley, *Principles of Constitutional Law* (Boston, 1898), 3rd ed., 196-206.
[2] 28 U.S.C. 1738.

199

Connel this language was given literal application by the Marshall Court, and the judgments there involved were held to be entitled in the courts of sister States to the validity of final judgments.[3] In 1839, however, in McElmoyle v. Cohen,[4] the Court, then in the grip of States' Rights prepossessions, ruled that the Constitution was not intended "materially to interfere with the essential attributes of the *lex fori*" ("the forum State"); that the act of Congress only established a rule of evidence—of conclusive evidence to be sure, but still of evidence only—and that it was necessary, in order to carry into effect in a State the judgment of a court of a sister State, to institute a fresh action in a court of the former, in strict compliance with its laws; and that consequently, when remedies were sought in support of the rights accruing in another jurisdiction, they were governed by the *lex fori*.

One consequence of this arrant nullification of the Act of 1790 was that for a time the Court was occasionally confronted with the contention that a State need not provide a forum for some particular type of judgment from a sister State that it chose to disrelish—a contention which the Court rejected categorically at least by 1945 when it said: "But the Clause does not make a sister State judgment a judgment in another State. The proposal to do so was rejected by the Philadelphia Convention. To give it the force of a judgment in another state, it must be made a judgment there. M'Elmoyle v. Cohen. It can be made a judgment there only if the court purporting to render the original judgment had power to render such a judgment. *A judgment in one State is conclusive upon the merits in every other State*, but only if the court of the first State had power to pass on the merits—had jurisdiction, that is, to render the judgment (emphasis supplied)."[5] The Court has never since that time found occasion to backtrack and other courts accept this statement as the law without question.[6]

The Juris-
dictional
Question

The important and lasting consequence of the Court's partial nullification of the Act of 1790 has been the spawn of cases it has bred raising the question whether the judgment for which recognition was being sought under the "full faith and

[3] 7 Cr. 485 (1813); 3 Wheat. 234.

[4] McElmoyle v. Cohen, 13 Pet. 312, 326 (1839).

[5] Williams v. N.C., 325 U.S. 226, 229 (1945).

[6] For examples *see* Western Auto Supply Co. v. Dillard, 172 S.E. 2d. 388, 394 (1970); State *ex. rel.* Lynn v. Eddy, 163 S.E. 2d. 472 (1968). Contentions to the contrary generally cite cases decided prior to 1945.

credit" clause was rendered "with jurisdiction," i.e. in accordance with some test or standard alleged not to have been observed by the court rendering it. Foreshadowed in a dissenting opinion in 1813,[7] this doctrine was definitely accepted by the Court in 1850 as to judgments *in personam*,[8] and in 1874 as to judgments *in rem*,[9] and in 1878 was transferred from the shadowy realm of "fundamental principles of justice" to the more solid contours of the "due process clause" of Amendment XIV where it still remains.[10]

What the law and doctrine of these cases boils down to is this: A judgment of a State court, in a civil, not a penal, cause within its jurisdiction, and against a defendant lawfully summoned, or against lawfully attached property of an absent defendant, is entitled to as much force and effect against the person summoned or the property attached, when the question is presented for decision in a court in another State, as it has in the State in which it was rendered.[11]

The Court still maintains that with respect to *in personam* judgments, "the consistent constitutional rule has been that a court has no power to adjudicate a personal claim or obligation unless it has jurisdiction over the person of the defendant."[12] But this holding must be read against the backdrop of a previous holding that: "Since *Pennoyer v. Neff*, this Court has held that the Due Process Clause of the Fourteenth Amendment places some limit on the power of state courts to enter binding judgments against persons not served with process within their boundaries. But just where this line of limitation falls has been the subject of prolific controversy, particularly with respect to foreign corporations. In a continuing process of evolution this Court accepted and then abandoned 'consent,' 'doing business,' and 'presence' as the standard for measuring the extent of state judicial power over such corporations. . . . More recently in *International Shoe Co. v. Washington* the Court decided that 'due process requires only that in order to subject a defendant to a judgment *in per-*

---

[7] *See* Mills *v.* Duryee, 7 Cr. 481, 486-487.
[8] D'Arcy *v.* Ketchum, 11 How. 165 (1850).
[9] Thompson *v.* Whitman, 18 Wall. 457 (1874).
[10] Pennoyer *v.* Neff, 95 U.S. 714 (1878); *see also* Milliken *v.* Meyer, 311 U.S. 457 (1940); International Shoe Co. *v.* Washington, 326 U.S. 310, 316 (1945); McGee *v.* International Life Insurance Co., 355 U.S. 220 (1957).
[11] McGee *v.* International Life Insurance Co., 355 U.S. 220, 223 (1957).
[12] Zenith Corp. *v.* Hazeltine, 395 U.S. 100, 110 (1969).

*sonam,* if he be not present within the territory of the forum, he have certain minimum contacts with it such that the maintenance of the suit does not offend traditional notions of fair play and substantial justice.' "[13]

Today, the jurisdictional question comprises the principal grist of cases arising under Article IV, Section I, but is most copiously illustrated in divorce cases, particularly in those in which the respondent to a suit for divorce has offered in defense an earlier divorce from the courts of some sister State, most likely Nevada.

Divorce Cases: a Judicial Tilting Field

By the almost universally accepted view prior to 1906, a proceeding in divorce was one against the marriage status, i.e. *in rem,* and hence might be validly brought by either party in any State where he or she was *bona fide* domiciled;[14] and, conversely, when the plaintiff did not have a *bona fide* domicile in the State, a court could not render a decree binding in other States even if the nonresident defendant entered a personal appearance.[15] That year, however, the Court discovered, by a vote of five-to-four, a situation in which a divorce proceeding is one *in personam.*

The case referred to is Haddock *v.* Haddock,[16] while the earlier rule is illustrated by Atherton *v.* Atherton,[17] decided five years previously. In the latter it was held, in the former denied, that a divorce granted a husband without personal service upon the wife, who at the time was residing in another State, was entitled to recognition under the "full faith and credit" clause and the acts of Congress; the difference between the cases consisting solely in the fact that in the Atherton case the husband had driven the wife from their joint home by his conduct, while in the *Haddock* case he had deserted her. The Court which granted the divorce in Atherton *v.* Atherton was held to have had jurisdiction of the marriage status, with the result that the proceeding was one *in rem* and hence required only service by publication upon the respondent. Haddock's suit, on the contrary, was held to be as to the wife *in personam,* and so to require personal service upon her, or her voluntary

[13] McGee *v.* International Life Insurance Co., 355 U.S. 220, 222, (1957).
[14] Cheever *v.* Wilson, 9 Wall. 108 (1870).
[15] Andrews *v.* Andrews, 188 U.S. 14 (1903). *See also* German Savings Society *v.* Dormitzer, 192 U.S. 125 (1904).
[16] 201 U.S. 562 (1906). *See also* Thompson *v.* Thompson, 226 U.S. 551 (1913).
[17] 181 U.S. 155, 162 (1901).

appearance, neither of which had been had; although, notwithstanding this, the decree in the latter case was held to be valid as to the State where obtained on account of the State's inherent power to determine the status of its own citizens. The upshot was a situation in which a man and a woman, when both were in Connecticut, were divorced; and when both were in New York, were married; and when the one was in Connecticut and the other in New York, the former was divorced and the latter married. In Atherton *v.* Atherton the Court had earlier acknowledged that "a husband without a wife, or a wife without a husband, is unknown to the law."

Nor, in overruling Haddock *v.* Haddock in 1942, did the Court clarify the situation materially. For while holding that any State is entitled to divorce anybody who is "*bona fide* domiciled*" within its borders even though the other spouse, being outside the State, was not personally served, yet it has since handed down another ruling, the logic of which appears to expose to the danger of going to jail anybody who, having left his home State, gets a divorce in another State, remarries, and then returns to State No. 1, or *goes to some third State,* provided a jury of his last place of residence can be persuaded that his residence in the divorcing State lacked "domiciliary intent," that is to say, the intention of remaining there from then on.[18] Quite evidently this contravenes the Act of 1790, the divorce being conceded to be valid in the State where granted.

How can one account for this abrupt backing and filling? At first glance it appears to stem from an ideological quarrel between Justices who set great store by the principle of *res judicata,* as the "full faith and credit" clause itself does, and other Justices who swear by the principle of domicile as a kind of substitute for the due process of law requirement. This, however, would be a superficial account of the matter. A divorce case may involve other questions than that merely of the marital status of the party holding the divorce. It may also involve issues connected with the right of a divorced wife to support, with the custody of the children of the dissolved partnership, with the ownership of property, etc.; and when this happens, first one and then the other of the opposed concepts may appear best adapted to do the tangled situation essential justice.

[18] Williams *v.* N.C., 317 U.S. 287 (1942); Williams *v.* N.C., 325 U.S. 226 (1945)—"Williams I" and "Williams II."

"Divisible    Recognizing this fact, the Court, sought to strike a working
Divorce"    compromise, as it were, between *res judicata* and domicile.
The leading case is Estin *v.* Estin, decided in 1948.[19] Here,
while conceding the validity of an *ex parte* Nevada decree obtained by a husband, the Court held that New York had not
denied full faith and credit to said decree when, subsequently
thereto, it granted the wife a judgment for arrears in alimony
founded upon a decree of separation previously awarded to
her when both she and her husband were domiciled in New
York. The Nevada decree issued to the husband after he had
resided there a year, and upon constructive notice to the wife
in New York who entered no appearance, was held to be effective to change the marital status of both parties in all States of
the Union but ineffective on the issue of alimony. Divorce, in
other words, was viewed as being divisible; and Nevada, in
the absence of acquiring jurisdiction over the wife, was held
incapable of adjudicating the rights of the wife in the prior
New York judgment awarding her alimony. Such a result was
justified as accommodating the interests of both New York and
Nevada in the broken marriage by restricting each State to
matters of dominant concern to it, the concern of New
York being that of protecting the abandoned wife against
impoverishment.

The doctrine of divisible divorce is now well established.[20]
And on that basis it seems safe to assert that an *ex parte* divorce, founded upon acquisition of domicile by one spouse in
the State which granted it, is effective to destroy the marital
status of both parties in the State of domiciliary origin and
probably in all other States and therefore to preclude subsequent prosecutions for bigamy, but not to alter rights as to
property, alimony, or custody of children in the State of domiciliary origin of a spouse who was neither served nor personally appeared.[21]

[19] 334 U.S. 541 (1948).
[20] Vanderbilt *v.* Vanderbilt, 354 U.S. 416 (1957) *but see* Justice Harlan's
dissent; Simons *v.* Miami Beach Nat. Bank, 381 U.S. 81 (1965); *see also*
Justice Harlan's concurring opinion; Edwards *v.* Edwards, 481 P. 2d. 432
(1971); *see* Stucky *v.* Stucky, 185 N.W. 2d. 656, 661 (1971). The Iowa Supreme Court recently ruled that full faith and credit need only be accorded final judgments, saying that "an interlocutory decree does not come
within the ambit of the [full faith and credit clause]." Morris *v.* Morris,
197 N.W. 2d. 357 (1972).
[21] Harold W. Chase, "The Lawyers Need Help with 'the Lawyer's
Clause,' " in Gottfried Dietze, ed., *Essays on the American Constitution*

As to the extrastate protection of rights which have *not matured into final judgments*, the unqualified rule prior to the Civil War was that of the dominance of local policy over the rules of comity.[22] This was stated by Justice Nelson in the Dred Scott case, as follows: "No State, . . . can enact laws to operate beyond its own dominions, . . . Nations, from convenience and comity, . . . , recognizes [sic] and administer the laws of other countries. But, of the nature, extent, and utility, of them, respecting property, or the state and condition of persons within her territories, each nation judges for itself; . . ." He added that it was the same as to a State of the Union in relation to another. It followed that even though Dred had become a free man in consequence of his having resided in the "free" State of Illinois, he had nevertheless upon his return to Missouri, which had the same power as Illinois to determine its local policy respecting rights acquired extraterritorially, reverted to servitude under the laws and decisions of that State.[23]

*Extraterritorial Operation of State Laws*

In a case decided in 1887, however, the Court remarked: "Without doubt the constitutional requirement, Art. IV, §1, that 'full faith and credit shall be given in each State to the public acts, records and judicial proceedings of every other State,' implies that the public acts of every State shall be given the same effect by the courts of another State that they have by law and usage at home."[24] And this proposition was later held to extend to State constitutional provisions.[25] Later this doctrine was stated in a much more mitigated form, the Court saying that where statute or policy of the forum State is set up as a defense to a suit brought under the statute of another State or territory, or where a foreign statute is set up as a defense to a suit or proceedings under a local statute, the conflict is to be resolved, not by giving automatic effect to the full faith and credit clause, thereby compelling courts of each State to subordinate its own statutes to those of others, but by

---

(Englewood Cliffs, N.J. 1964), 110-116. *See* Gunther *v.* Gunther, 478 S.W. 2d. 821 (1972).

22 Bank of Augusta *v.* Earle, 13 Pet. 519, 589-596 (1839). *See* Kryger *v.* Wilson, 242 U.S. 171 (1916); Bond *v.* Hume, 243 U.S. 15 (1917).

23 19 How. 393, 460 (1857). *Cf.* Bonaparte *v.* Tax Court, 104 U.S. 592 (1882), where it was held that a law exempting from taxation certain bonds of the enacting State did not operate extraterritorially by virtue of the full faith and credit clause.

24 Chicago & Alton R. Co. *v.* Wiggins Ferry, 119 U.S. 615, 622 (1887).

25 Smithsonian Institution *v.* St. John, 214 U.S. 19 (1909).

appraising the governmental interest of each jurisdiction and deciding accordingly.[26] Obviously this doctrine endows the Court with something akin to an arbitral function in the decision of cases to which it is applied, just as does the concept of divided divorce. Take for example, the *Pearson* case, which attracted so much attention several years ago.[27] A widow, whose husband had been killed in an airplane crash in Massachusetts, was granted a $160,000 award by a jury in a New York court. Although the crash occurred in Massachusetts, the husband had bought the ticket in New York and the plane had taken off from La Guardia Airport in New York. Since a Massachusetts statute limited recovery in such cases to $15,000 at that time and New York's law did not, the airline appealed the decision on the grounds that Massachusetts law should have been controlling in this case. A three-judge panel of the United States Court of Appeals, Second Circuit, reversed the decision and remanded the case. When the case came again to the Court of Appeals, the full court heard the case, explaining that "The issue being one of great significance—the constitutional power of the states to develop conflict of laws doctrine—it was ordered upon application by the plaintiff appellee and the affirmative vote of a majority of the active judges of this circuit, that the appeal be reheard *en banc*." This time the court reversed itself. It cited with approval the reasoning of a lower court in a parallel case: "An air traveler from New York may in a flight of a few hours' duration pass through several commonwealths. His plane may meet with disaster in a state he never intended to cross but into which the plane has flown because of bad weather or other unexpected developments, or an airplane's catastrophic descent may begin in one state and end in another. The place of injury becomes entirely fortuitous."[28] Eventually the case was brought to the United States Supreme Court which denied *certiorari*.[29] The case is recalled here not for the outcome on the merits but rather to make the point that at the late date of 1962, lawyers and judges were still not quite sure which State's law would apply in such a sit-

[26] Alaska Packers Asso. *v.* Industrial Acci. Commission, 294 U.S. 532 (1935); Bradford Electric Light Co. *v.* Clapper, 286 U.S. 145 (1932); Crider *v.* Zurich Ins. Co., 380 U.S. 39 (1965); D.R.-T. *v.* O.M., 244 So. 2d. 752, 756 (1971); Application of Schatz, 497 P. 2d. 153 (1972).
[27] Pearson *v.* Northeast Airlines, 309 F. 2d. 553 (1962).
[28] *Ibid.*, 561, note 10.
[29] 372 U.S. 912 (1963).

uation and the case was not resolved until it went all the way
to the Supreme Court.

It is today "the settled rule" that the defendant in a transitory action is entitled to all the benefits resulting from whatever material restrictions the statute under which plaintiff's
right of action originated sets thereto, except that courts of sister States cannot be thus prevented from taking jurisdiction
in such cases.[30] Nor is it alone to defendants in transitory actions that the "full faith and credit" clause is today a shield
and a buckler. Some legal relationships are so complex, the
Court holds, that the law under which they were formed
ought always to govern them as long as they persist.[31] One
such relationship is that of a stockholder and his corporation;[32]
another is the relationship which is formed when one takes out
a policy in a "fraternal benefit society."[33] Stock and mutual insurance companies and mutual building and loan associations,
on the other hand, are beings of a different stripe;[34] as to them
the *lex fori* controls. Finally, the relationship of employer and
employee, so far as the obligations of the one and the rights of
the other under workmen's compensation acts are concerned,
is, in general, governed by the law of the State under which
the relationship was created.[35]

The question arises whether the application to date of the
full faith and credit clause can be said to have met the expectations of its framers. A partial answer is that there are few
clauses of the Constitution, the literal possibilities of which
have been so little developed as the full faith and credit clause.
Congress has the power under the clause to decree the effect
that the statutes of one State shall have in other states. This being so, it does not seem extravagant to argue that Congress
may under the clause describe a certain type of divorce and
say that it shall be granted recognition throughout the Union,
and that no other kind shall. Or, to speak in more general

Unrealized
Possibilities
of the
Clause

[30] Northern Pacific R.R. *v.* Babcock, 154 U.S. 190 (1894); Atchison, T. &
S.F.R. Co. *v.* Sowers, 213 U.S. 55, 67 (1909).

[31] Modern Woodmen of Am. *v.* Mixer, 267 U.S. 544 (1925).

[32] Converse *v.* Hamilton, 224 U.S. 243 (1912); Selif *v.* Hamilton, 234 U.S.
652 (1914).

[33] Royal Arcanum *v.* Green, 237 U.S. 531 (1915), ff'd in Modern Woodmen *v.* Mixer, cited above; Order of Travelers *v.* Wolfe, 331 U.S. 586, 588-
589, 637 (1947).

[34] National Mutual Building and Loan Asso. *v.* Brahan, 193 U.S. 635
(1904); Pink *v.* A.A.A. Highway Express, 314 U.S. 201, 206-208 (1941).

[35] Bradford Electric Co. *v.* Clapper, 286 U.S. 145, 158 (1932) is the leading case.

terms, Congress has under the clause power to enact standards whereby uniformity of State legislation may be secured
as to almost any matter in connection with which interstate
recognition of private rights would be useful and valuable.[36]

## SECTION II

¶ 1. The citizens of each State shall be entitled to all privileges
and immunities of citizens in the several States.

Four
Theories
of the
Clause

This is a compendious, although not especially lucid, redaction
of Article IV of the Articles of Confederation. First and last,
some four theories have been offered as to its real intention
and meaning. The first is that the clause is a guaranty to the
citizens of the different States of equal treatment by Congress
—is, in other words, a species of equal protection clause binding on the National Government. The second is that the clause
is a guaranty to the citizens of each State of all the privileges
and immunities of citizenship that are enjoyed in any State by
the citizens thereof—a view which, if it had been accepted at
the outset, might well have endowed the Supreme Court with
a reviewing power over restrictive State legislation as broad
as that which it later came to exercise under the Fourteenth
Amendment. The third theory of the clause is that it guarantees to the citizen of any State the rights which he enjoys as
such even when sojourning in another State, that is to say, enables him to carry with him his rights of State citizenship
throughout the Union, without embarrassment by State lines.
Finally, the clause is interpreted as merely forbidding any
State to discriminate against citizens of other States in favor
of its own. Though the first theory received some recognition
in one of the opinions in the Dred Scott case,[1] it is today obsolete. Theories 2 and 3 have been specifically rejected by the
Court;[2] the fourth has become a settled doctrine of Constitutional Law.[3]

Yet even this theory is not all-inclusive. For there are certain
privileges and immunities for which a State, as *parens patriae,*

---

[36] Chase, "The Lawyers Need Help With 'the Lawyer's Clause.'"

[1] Scott *v.* Sandford, 19 How. 393, 527-529 (1857).
[2] McKane *v.* Durston, 153 U.S. 684, 687 (1894); Detwit *v.* Osborne, 135
U.S. 492, 498 (1890).
[3] The Slaughter-House cases, 16 Wall. 36, 77 (1873).

may require a previous residence, like the right to fish in its streams, to hunt game in its fields and forests, to divert its waters, even to engage in certain businesses of a quasi-public nature, like that of insurance.[4] Furthermore, universal practice has established another exception to which the Court has given approval in the following words: "A State may, by a rule uniform in its operation as to citizens of the several States, require residence within its limits for a given time before a citizen of another State who becomes a resident thereof shall exercise the right of suffrage or become eligible to office."[5]

Nor does the term "citizens" include corporations.[6] Thus a corporation chartered elsewhere may enter a State to engage in local business only on such terms as the State chooses to lay down, provided these do not deprive the corporation of its rights under the Constitution—of its right, for instance, to engage in interstate commerce, or to appeal to the national courts, or, once it has been admitted into a State, to receive equal treatment with corporations chartered by the latter.[7]

Also, while a State may not substantially discriminate between residents and non-residents in the exercise of its taxing power,[8] yet what may at first glance appear to be a discrimination may turn out not to be when the entire system of taxation prevailing in the enacting State is considered. Nor are occasional or accidental inequalities to a non-resident taxpayer sufficient to defeat a scheme of taxation whose operation, in the judgment of the Court, is generally equitable.[9]

In an exceptionally important case decided in 1969, the Su-

4 McCready *v.* Va., 94 U.S. 391 (1877); Geer *v.* Conn., 161 U.S. 519 (1896); Hudson County Water Co. *v.* McCarter, 209 U.S. 349 (1908); La Tourette *v.* McMaster, 248 U.S. 465 (1919). In the case of Toomer *v.* Witsell, 334 U.S. 385, 403 (1948), the Court refused to follow the above rule as to free-swimming fish caught in the three-mile belt off South Carolina. *See also* Mullaney *v.* Anderson, 342 U.S. 415 (1952) in which the Toomer case was followed. In 1971, a Florida court held that a continued residency requirement for retention of a real estate broker's license was reasonable and constitutional. Hall *v.* King 254 So. 2d. 223 (1971).
5 Blake *v.* McClung, 172 U.S. 239, 256 (1898).
6 Paul *v.* Va., 8 Wall. 168 (1868).
7 International Paper Co. *v.* Mass., 246 U.S. 135 (1918); Terral *v.* Burke Constr. Co., 257 U.S. 529 (1922). *See also* Crutcher *v.* Ky., 141 U.S. 47 (1891).
8 Ward *v.* Md., 12 Wall. 418, 424 (1871); Travis *v.* Yale and Towne Mfg. Co., 252 U.S. 60, 79-80 (1920).
9 Travelers' Ins. Co. *v.* Conn., 185 U.S. 364, 371 (1902); Maxwell *v.* Bugbee, 250 U.S. 525 (1919).

preme Court struck down State and District of Columbia laws which denied welfare assistance to persons who had not been resident in the State for one year.[10]

It seemed to be an appropriate case to invoke the privileges and immunities clause of Article IV. However, in spelling out the "right to travel interstate," the Court said that it had no occasion "to ascribe the source of this right . . . to a particular constitutional provision." It pointed out that the privilege and immunities clause of the Fourteenth Amendment and the commerce clause had also been invoked in the past as a basis for the right to travel. In a pregnant footnote, the Court cautioned that this decision was limited to the issues in the case at hand, that "We imply no view of the validity of waiting-period or residence requirements determining eligibility to vote, eligibility for tuition-free education, to obtain a license to practice a profession, to hunt or fish, and so forth. Such requirements may promote compelling state interests on the one hand, or, on the other, may not be penalties upon the exercise of the constitutional right of interstate travel."[11] In short, for those who would see this particular provision as a possible vehicle for asserting "rights" not already found to be guaranteed elsewhere in the Constitution, this decision does not hold out much promise. But those who are disappointed that the Court did not use this case as an opportunity to read *more* meaning into Article IV, Section II, ¶1, should ponder the thought expressed by Justice Douglas in a concurring opinion some years ago, that the privileges and immunities safeguarded by the Fourteenth Amendment are *national* whereas those safeguarded under Article IV are *State*. The implication, of course, is that if there is to be an expansion of "rights," it would be more easily done under the Fourteenth Amendment.[12]

¶2. A person charged in any State with treason, felony, or other crime, who shall flee from justice, and be found in another State, shall, on demand of the executive authority

10 Shapiro *v.* Thompson, 394 U.S. 618, 630 (1969).
11 *Ibid.*, 638 note 21. *See also* Hall *v.* King, 254 So. 2d. 223 (1971).
12 Edwards *v.* California, 314 U.S. 160, 180-181 (1941). Recently, in an interesting New York State case, it was held that a statute establishing a procedure for residents' obtaining permits for having weapons but which did not provide a procedure for travelers to do so was not a violation of this clause. People *v.* Percy, 325 N.Y.S. 2d. 183 (1971).

of the State from which he fled, be delivered up, to be removed to the State having jurisdiction of the crime.

The word "crime" here includes "every offense forbidden and made punishable by the laws of the State where the offense is committed."[13] The performance of the duty which is cast by this paragraph upon the States was imposed by an act of Congress passed February 12, 1793, upon the governors thereof, but the Supreme Court shortly before the Civil War ruled that, while the duty is a legal duty, it is not one the performance of which can be compelled by writ of mandamus,[14] and in consequence governors of States have often refused compliance with a demand for extradition when in their opinion substantial justice required such refusal. On the other hand, the Act of 1793 does not prevent a State from surrendering one who is not a fugitive within its terms, nor from trying a fugitive for a different offense than the one for which he was surrendered.[15]

As was pointed out earlier, the deficiencies of this clause have been today partly remedied by compacts among the States and by uniform State legislation, as well as by national legislation under the commerce clause. Especially important in the latter connection is the Act of May 18, 1934, which makes it an offense against the United States for a person to flee from one State to another in order to avoid prosecution or the giving of testimony in certain cases.[16] But this raises an interesting question about what Federal officials do when they apprehend such a fugitive. In that connection, a recent newspaper story regarding extradition caught the authors' eyes. The *New York Times* reported:

". . . With the arrival here of the California warrants, Miss [Angela] Davis and her attorney, John Abt, were summoned once again to the [Federal] Commissioner's office where Mr. Bishop revoked her bail and released her on her own recognizance. Her Federal handcuffs were removed.

"Then Detective Alfred C. Hatalkts of the city's safe and loft squad stepped forward and said, 'Miss Davis, you're under ar-

Interstate Extradition on a Voluntary Basis

---

13 Kentucky v. Dennison, 24 How. 66, 99 (1861).
14 *Ibid.; cf.* Virginia v. W. Va., 246 U.S. 565 (1918).
15 Lascelles v. Ga., 148 U.S. 537 (1893); Innes v. Tobin, 240 U.S. 127 (1916). *See* 18 U.S.C. 3182; Ray v. Warden, Baltimore City Jail, 281 A. 2d. 125 (1971); Hidaleo v. Purcell, 488 P. 2d. 858 (1971).
16 18 U.S.C. 1073.

rest,' and placed her hands in city handcuffs."[17] Curious to know the legal basis for what seemed an unusual performance, we queried the Justice Department. Here is their explanation:

"Miss Davis was arrested in New York City by the Federal Bureau of Investigation on the basis of a federal warrant for unlawful flight to avoid prosecution, Title 18, United States Code, Section 1073. It is our practice to turn over a fugitive to local authorities at the place where the fugitive is apprehended. The statute serves basically as a device to locate and apprehend fugitives from justice. It is not generally used as a substitute for State extradition proceedings nor is it generally used for the purpose of prosecution for the substantive offense."[18]

¶3. No person held to service or labor in one State, under the laws thereof, escaping into another, shall, in consequence of any law or regulation therein, be discharged from such service or labor, but shall be delivered up on claim of the party to whom such service or labor may be due.

"Person held to service or labor" meant slave or apprentice. The paragraph is now of historical interest only.

### SECTION III

¶1. New States may be admitted by the Congress into this Union; but no new State shall be formed or erected within the jurisdiction of any other State; nor any State be formed by the junction of two or more States or parts of States, without the consent of the legislatures of the States concerned as well as of the Congress.

"A Union of Equal States" The theory which the Supreme Court has adopted in interpretation of the opening clause of this paragraph is that when new States are admitted into "this Union" they are admitted on a basis of equality with the previous members of the Union. By the Joint Resolution of December 29, 1845, Texas "was admitted into the Union on an equal footing with the original States in all respects whatever."[1] Again and again, in adjudi-

---

[17] *New York Times*, Oct. 15, 1970.
[18] An obliging U.S. Attorney was kind enough to provide a more detailed explanation; *see* 1973 Supplement to this edition.

[1] Justice Harlan, speaking for the Court in United States *v.* Tex., 143 U.S. 621, 634 (1892); 9 *Stat.* 108. For an interesting recent affirmation of

cating the rights and duties of States admitted after 1789, the Supreme Court has referred to the condition of equality as if it were an inherent attribute of the Federal Union.[2] In 1911, it invalidated a restriction on the change of location of the State capital, which Congress had imposed as a condition for the admission of Oklahoma, on the ground that Congress may not embrace in an enabling act conditions relating wholly to matters under State control.[3] In an opinion, from which Justice Holmes and McKenna dissented, Justice Lurton argued: "The power is to admit 'new States into *this* Union.' 'This Union' was and is a union of States, equal in power, dignity and authority, each competent to exert that residuum of sovereignty not delegated to the United States by the Constitution itself."

Sovereignty is one thing, however, property a different thing. Holding that a "mere agreement in reference to property" involved "no question of equality of status," the Supreme Court upheld, in Stearns *v.* Minnesota,[4] a promise exacted from Minnesota upon its admission to the Union which was interpreted to limit its right to tax lands held by the United States at the time of admission and subsequently granted to a railroad. The "equal footing" doctrine has had an important effect, however, on the property rights of new States to soil under navigable waters. In Pollard *v.* Hagan,[5] the Court held that the original States had reserved to themselves the ownership of the shores of navigable waters and the soils under them, and that under the principle of equality the title to the soils of navigable waters passes to a new State upon admission. This was in 1845. The Court refused, 102 years later, to extend the same rule to the three-mile marginal belt along the coast,[6] and shortly after applied the principle of the Pollard case in reverse, as it were, in United States *v.* Texas.[7] Since the orig-

State Proprietorship versus Federal Dominion

the Doctrine, *see* Cherokee Nation or Tribe of Indians *v.* Oklahoma, 402 F. 2d. 739 (1968).

[2] Permoli *v.* New Orleans, 3 How. 589, 609 (1845); McCabe *v.* Atchison, T. & S. F. R. Co., 235 U.S. 151 (1914); Illinois Central R. Co. *v.* Illinois, 146 U.S. 387, 434 (1892); Knight *v.* United Land Asso., 142 U.S. 161, 183 (1891); Weber *v.* State Harbor Comrs., 18 Wall. 57, 65 (1873).

[3] Coyle *v.* Smith, 221 U.S. 559, 567 (1911).

[4] 179 U.S. 223, 245 (1900).

[5] 3 How. 212, 223 (1845). *See also* Martin *v.* Waddell, 16 Pet. 367, 410 (1842).

[6] United States *v.* Calif., 332 U.S. 19, 38 (1947); United States *v.* La., 339 U.S. 699 (1950).

[7] 339 U.S. 699, 707, 716 (1950).

inal States had been found not to own the soil under the three-mile belt, Texas, which concededly did own this soil before its annexation to the United States, was held to have surrendered its dominion and sovereignty over it, upon entering the Union on terms of equality with the existing States. To this extent, the earlier rule that, unless otherwise declared by Congress, the title to every species of property owned by a territory passes to the State upon admission has been qualified.[8] However in 1953, Congress passed the Submerged Lands Act of 1953 declaring it to be in the public interest to turn over to the States "title to and ownership of the lands beneath navigable waters within the boundaries of the respective states."[9] By definition in the law this included lands covered by tidal waters up to three miles seaward *"and to the boundary line of each such State where in any case as it existed at the time such State became a member of the Union . . . extends seaward (or into the Gulf of Mexico) beyond three geographical miles."* When the act was challenged in part on the basis that it violated the "equal footing" doctrine, the motions were simply denied by the Court, which said: "The power of Congress to dispose of any kind of property belonging to the United States 'is vested in Congress without limitation.' "[10]

¶2. The Congress shall have power to dispose of and make all needful rules and regulations respecting the territory or other property belonging to the United States; and nothing in this Constitution shall be so construed as to prejudice any claims of the United States or of any particular State.

What Property Congress May Dispose of

Congress's control of the public lands is derived from this paragraph. The relation of the National Government to such of its public lands as lie within the boundaries of States is not, however, that of simple proprietorship, it is more, for it includes many of the elements of sovereignty. The States may not tax such lands;[11] and Congress may punish trespassers upon them, "though such legislation may involve the exercise

8 Brown *v.* Grant, 116 U.S. 207, 212 (1886).
9 43 U.S.C. 1311.
10 Alabama *v.* Texas, 347 U.S. 272, 273 (1954); *see also,* U.S. *v.* Louisiana, 363 U.S. 1 (1960); U.S. *v.* California, 381 U.S. 139, 184 (1965); Sierra Club *v.* Hickel, 433 F. 2d. 24, 28 (1970); *affirmed,* 405 U.S. 727 (1972).
11 Van Brocklin *v.* Tenn., 117 U.S. 151 (1886). *Cf.* Wilson *v.* Cook, 327 U.S. 474 (1946).

of the police power."[12] Furthermore, in disposing of such lands, Congress may impose conditions on their future alienation or that of the water power thereon which the State where the lands are may not alter.[13]

Although "other property" undoubtedly includes warships, this fact did not, as we saw earlier, deter President Roosevelt from handing over to Great Britain, in September 1940, in return for leases from the latter of certain sites for naval bases in the west Atlantic, fifty newly conditioned destroyers without consulting Congress. But as Congress later appropriated money for the construction of the said bases, it may perhaps be thought to have ratified the arrangement.

The debts of various nations of Europe to the United States are also "property belonging to the United States," so that Congress's ratification had to be obtained to agreements for their settlements after World War I. Likewise, electrical power developed at a dam of the United States is "property belonging to the United States."

But the above clause is also important for another reason— it is the source to which has sometimes been traced the power of the United States to govern territories, though, as we have seen, this and the power to acquire territory can be ascribed simply to the sovereignty inherent in the National Government as such;[14] as is also the power to cede territory to another government, as for example, the Philippine Islands to the Philippine Republic.

And while the United States may, through the treaty-making power acquire territory, its incorporation in the United States ordinarily waits upon action by Congress. Such incorporation may be effected either by admitting the territory into "this Union" as new States or, less completely, by extending the Constitution to it.[15] Until territory is thus incorporated into the United States, persons born therein are not citizens of the United States under the Fourteenth Amendment, though Congress may admit them to citizenship, as in fact it has done in several instances (*see* pp. 64-65); and the power of Con-

*"Incorporated" and "Unincorporated" Territories*

---

[12] Camfield *v.* U.S., 167 U.S. 518 (1897).

[13] United States *v.* San Francisco, 310 U.S. 16 (1940). This case involved the famous "Hetch-Hetchy" grant by the Raker Act of December 19, 1913.

[14] American Insurance Co. *v.* Canter, 1 Pet. 511, 542 (1928).
The entire subject of the power to acquire and govern territories is comprehensively treated in Willoughby, *Constitutional Law*, I, chs. 23-32.

[15] Downes *v.* Bidwell, 182 U.S. 244 (1901). *Cf.* Duncan *v.* Louisiana, 391 U.S. 145 (1968). *See also*, p. 237 note 5.

gress in legislating for such unincorporated territory is limited only by "fundamental rights" of the individual, of which trial by jury was in an earlier day not one.[16] Incorporation, however, makes the inhabitants of territories citizens of the United States, and extends to them full protection of the Constitution. Since Alaska and Hawaii became States, there are no "incorporated" territories in this nomenclature; Guam is an example of an "unincorporated" territory.[17] Puerto Rico has an unique status of "commonwealth"—an experiment decidedly worth study.[18] Conquered territory may be governed temporarily by the President by virtue of his power as Commander-in-Chief of the Army and Navy, but Congress may at any time supplant such government with one of its own creation.[19]

## SECTION IV

¶The United States shall guarantee to every State in this Union a republican form of government, and shall protect each of them against invasion, and on application of the legislature, or of the executive (when the legislature cannot be convened), against domestic violence.

National Guaranties to the States: a "Political Question"

"The United States" here means the governing agency created by the Constitution, but especially the President and Congress; for the Court has repeatedly declared that what is a "republican form of government" is "a political question," and one finally for the President and the houses to determine within their respective spheres.[1] Thus Congress may approve of the government of a new State by admitting it into the Union, or the houses of Congress may indicate their approval by seating the Senators and Representatives of the State, or the President may do the same by furnishing a State with military assistance in cases where he is authorized so to act.

Inasmuch as the adoption of the initiative, referendum, and recall by many States some decades back appears not to have imperiled their standing with Congress, it must be concluded

16 Dorr *v.* U.S., 195 U.S. 138 (1904). In view of recent Supreme Court decisions on trial by jury, it is unlikely that today a jury trial would not be regarded as a fundamental right in like circumstances. *See* pp. 343-348. Also *see* 1968 amendment to Guam's Bill of Rights, which expressly provides for jury trial. 48 U.S.C. 1421b.
17 48 U.S.C. 1421a.                    18 48 U.S.C. 731.
19 Santiago *v.* Nogueras, 214 U.S. 260 (1909).

1 *See*, for example, Luther *v.* Borden, 7 How. 1 (1849).

that a considerable admixture of direct government does not make a government "unrepublican."[2]

Despite the Supreme Court's stance, Section IV still tempts those who are unhappy with what they regard as an "unrepublican" governmental institution, law, or practice to take their cause to the courts, invariably without success.[3] However, interestingly enough, a United States Court of Appeals observed in the course of a recent decision: "abrogation of judicial immunity by Congress would destroy the independence of the judiciary in the various States, and consequently deprive them of a republican form of government."[4]

The President is authorized by statute to employ the forces of the United States to discharge the duties of the United States under the second part of this paragraph, in which connection he may in proper cases proclaim martial law.[5] But this does not mean that a President must always await an invitation before employing troops, for this provision does not comprise the whole of the Chief Executive's power to send troops into a State.[6] (*See* pages 149-150 above.)

[2] Pacific States Tel. and Tel. Co. *v.* Ore., 223 U.S. 118 (1912).
[3] *See*, for example, Kohler *v.* Tugwell, 292 F. Supp. 978 (1968) *affirmed*, 393 U.S. 531 (1969) *and* O'Keefe *v.* Atascadero County Sanitation District, 98 Cal. Rptr. 878 (1971).
[4] Bauers *v.* Heisel, 361 F. 2d. 581, 588-589 (1966), *cert. denied*, 386 U.S. 1021 (1967).
[5] 10 U.S.C. 331.
[6] *In re* Debs, 158 U.S. 564 (1895). *Cf.* 10 U.S.C. 331 and 10 U.S.C. 332.

# ARTICLE V

¶ The Congress, whenever two-thirds of both houses shall deem it necessary, shall propose amendments to this Constitution, or, on the application of the legislatures of two-thirds of the several States, shall call a convention for proposing amendments, which in either case shall be valid to all intents and purposes as part of this Constitution, when ratified by the legislatures of three-fourths of the several States, or by conventions in three-fourths thereof, as the one or the other mode of ratification may be proposed by the Congress, provided that no amendment which may be made prior to the year one thousand eight hundred and eight shall in any manner affect the first and fourth clauses in the ninth section of the first article; and that no State, without its consent, shall be deprived of its equal suffrage in the Senate. *The Amending Power*

From the opinions filed in the case of Coleman *v.* Miller,[1] in 1939, in which certain questions were raised concerning the status of the proposed Child Labor Amendment (pending since 1924), it would seem that the Court today regards all questions relating to the interpretation of this article as "political questions," and hence as addressed exclusively to Congress. This is either because all such questions have been in the past effectually determined by Congressional action; or because the Court lacks adequate means of informing itself about them; or because the "judicial power" established by the Constitution does not extend to this part of the Constitution. Nevertheless, certain past decisions of the Court dealing with Article V may still be usefully cited for the light shed by their statement of the actual results, as well as the logical implications, of Congressional action in the past. *"Political Questions"*

"The Congress, whenever . . . both houses shall deem it necessary": The necessity of amendments to the Constitution is a question to be determined by the two houses alone, but not necessarily without suggestion or guidance from the President.[2]

"Two-thirds of both houses" means two-thirds of a quorum in both houses.[3] (*See* Article I, Section V, ¶ 1.)

---

[1] 307 U.S. 433 (1939).
[2] The National Prohibition Cases, 253 U.S. 350 (1920); Richardson, *Messages and Papers*, I, 53; *ibid.*, II, 447, 518, 557, 605; etc.
[3] *Ibid.*; Missouri Pac. R. Co. *v.* Kan., 248 U.S. 276 (1919).

"Legislatures" means the legislative assemblies of the States and does not include their governors, far less their voters. Moreover, when acting upon amendments proposed by Congress, the State legislatures—and doubtless the same is true of conventions within the States—do not act as representatives of the States or the populations thereof, but in performance of a "federal function" imposed upon them by this article of the Constitution.[4]

If a State legislature ratifies a proposed amendment may it later reconsider its vote, the amendment not having yet received the favorable vote of three-fourths of the legislatures? In Coleman v. Miller this question was answered "No," on the basis of Congressional rulings in connection with the adoption of the Fourteenth Amendment. May a legislature, after rejecting a proposed amendment, reconsider and ratify it? On the same basis, this question was answered "Yes" in Coleman v. Miller. Within what period may a proposal of amendment be effectively ratified? Within any period which Congress chooses to allow either in advance, or by finding that a proposed amendment has been ratified, is again the verdict of Coleman v. Miller.

Of the two methods here laid down for proposing amendments to the Constitution only the first has ever been successfully resorted to, and, prior to the proposal to repeal the Eighteenth Amendment, all proposals had been referred to the State legislatures.[5] In that instance, Congress prescribed that ratification should be by popularly elected conventions, chosen for the purpose, but left their summoning, as well as other details, to the several State legislatures. What ordinarily resulted was a popular referendum within each State, the conventions being made up almost entirely of delegates previously pledged to vote for or against the proposed amendment.[6] The term "convention," therefore, it must be presumed, does not today, if it ever did, denote a *deliberative* body; it is sufficient if it is representative of popular sentiment.

---

4 Hawke v. Smith, 253 U.S. 221 (1920).

5 It was contended in United States v. Sprague, 282 U.S. 716 (1931), that, as the Eighteenth Amendment affected the liberties of the people and the rights of the State, it ought to have been submitted to conventions in the States, but the Court rejected the contention.

6 *See* Everett S. Brown's valuable article on "The Ratification of the Twenty-First Amendment," 29 *American Political Science Review*, 1005 (1935).

The word "successfully" was used advisedly above. For in recent years there have been several attempts to get proposed amendments started through the State legislature route, one of very serious proportions under the aegis of the Council of State Governments. One of the three amendments they sought would have changed the mode of the amending process.[7] Also, Senator Dirksen led an effort to take this route for an amendment which would in effect modify the Court's rulings in reapportionment.[8] But more pertinent to the present discussion is the fact that it was discovered that the State legislature route might actually be much easier to use effectively than previously thought, and it held some strategic advantages for proposers of amendments. Protagonists could quietly make their pitch in the various State legislatures without attracting the attention and concern that a serious effort in Congress would.[9] It is an unfortunate fact of American politics that the work of State legislatures is not as carefully monitored by the press and public as the proceedings of Congress.

The recent efforts to have State legislatures apply to Congress for a convention highlighted another unresolved problem. Would such a convention be limited to consideration of specific amendments or would it be able to consider anything and possibly become, in the popular expression a "run-away" convention?[10]

Chief Justice Marshall characterized the constitution-amending machinery as "unwieldy and cumbrous." Undoubtedly it is, and the fact has had an important influence upon our institutions. Especially has it favored the growth of judicial review, since it has forced us to rely on the Court to keep the Constitution adapted to changing conditions. What is more, this machinery is, *prima facie* at least, highly undemocratic. A proposed amendment can be added to the Constitution by 38 States containing considerably less than half of the popula-

---

[7] Charles L. Black, Jr., "The Proposed Amendment of Article V: A Threatened Disaster," 72 *Yale Law Journal*, 957 (1963). For a measure of how seriously the effort was viewed, *see* report of the speech of Chief Justice Warren, *New York Times*, May 24, 1963.

[8] 1969 *Cong. Quart. Almanac* 1200; 1967 *Cong. Quart. Almanac* 461. The Dirksen effort only needed the approval of one more State legislature.

[9] *New York Times*, April 14, 1963.

[10] Morris D. Forkosch, "The Alternative Amending Clause in Article V: Reflections and Suggestions," 51 *Minnesota Law Review*, 1053, 1074-1077 (1967).

tion of the country, or can be defeated by 13 States containing less than one-twentieth of the population of the country.

Of the two exceptions to the amending power, the first is today obsolete. This does not signify, however, that the only change that the power which amends the Constitution may not make in the Constitution is to deprive a State without its consent of its "equal suffrage in the Senate." The amending, like all other powers organized in the Constitution, is in form a delegated, and hence a limited power, although this does not imply necessarily that the Supreme Court is vested with authority to determine its limits. The one power known to the Constitution which clearly is not limited by it is that which ordains it—in other words, the original, inalienable power of the people of the United States to determine their own political institutions.

# ARTICLE VI

¶1. All debts contracted and engagements entered into, before the adoption of this Constitution, shall be as valid against the United States under this Constitution as under the Confederation.

This paragraph, which is now of historical interest only, was intended to put into effect the rule of International Law that when a new government takes the place of an old one it succeeds to the latter's financial obligations.

¶2. This Constitution, and the laws of the United States which shall be made in pursuance thereof, and all treaties made, or which shall be made, under the authority of the United States, shall be the supreme law of the land; and the judges in every State shall be found thereby, anything in the Constitution or laws of any State to the contrary notwithstanding.

*The Supremacy Clause*

This paragraph has been called "the linch pin of the Constitution," and very fittingly, since it combines the National Government and the States into one governmental organization, one Federal State.

It also makes plain the fact that, while the National Government is for the most part one of enumerated powers, as to its powers it is supreme over any conflicting State powers whatsoever.[1] When, accordingly, a collision occurs between national and State law the only question to be answered is, ordinarily, whether the former was within a fair definition of Congress's powers. As Chief Justice Marshall so eloquently put it: "This government is acknowledged by all to be one of enumerated powers. ... If any one proposition could command the universal assent of mankind, we might expect it would be this—that the government of the Union, though limited in its powers, is supreme within its sphere of action."[2] Notwithstanding which the Court has at various periods proceeded on the view that the Tenth Amendment segregates to the control of the States certain "subjects," production for instance, with the result that the power of the States over such

---

[1] McCulloch *v.* Maryland, 4 Wheat. 316 (1819) *and* Gibbons *v.* Ogden, 9 Wheat. 1 (1824).
[2] McCulloch *v.* Maryland, 4 Wheat. 316, 405 (1819).

"subjects" constitutes a limitation on the granted powers of Congress. Obviously such a view cannot be logically reconciled with the supremacy clause. (*See* Tenth Amendment, pp. 369ff.)

In applying the supremacy clause to subjects which have been regulated by Congress, the primary task of the Court is to ascertain whether a challenged State law is compatible with the policy expressed in the Federal statute. When Congress condemns an act as unlawful, the extent and nature of the legal consequences of its doing so are Federal questions, the answers to which are to be derived from the statute and the policy thereby adopted. To the Federal statute and policy, conflicting State law and policy must yield.[3]

So when the United States performs its functions directly through its own officers and employees, State police regulations clearly are inapplicable. In reversing the conviction of the governor of a national soldiers' home for serving oleomargarine in disregard of State law, the Court said that the Federal officer was not "subject to the jurisdiction of the State in regard to those very matters of administration which are thus approved by Federal authority."[4] An employee of the Post Office Department is not required to submit to examination by State authorities concerning his competence and to pay a license fee before performing his official duty in driving a motor truck for transporting the mail.[5] To Arizona's complaint, in a suit to enjoin the construction of Hoover Dam, that her quasi-sovereignty would be invaded by the building of the dam without first securing approval of the State engineer as required by its laws, Justice Brandeis replied that, "if Congress has power to authorize the construction of the dam and reservoir, Wilbur [Secretary of the Interior] is under no obligation to submit the plans and specifications to the State Engineer for approval."[6]

**The Doctrine of Preemption and Supercession**

As to the question of what happens when State and Federal laws appear to conflict, Chief Justice Warren in 1956 provided

[3] Sola Electric Co. *v.* Jefferson Electric Co., 317 U.S. 173, 176 (1942). *See also* Francis *v.* Southern Pacific Co., 333 U.S. 445 (1948); Testa *v.* Katt, 330 U.S. 386, 391 (1947); Hill *v.* Fla., 325 U.S. 538 (1945); Amalgamated Assoc. *v.* Wis. Emp. Rels. Bd., 340 U.S. 383 (1951); Adams *v.* Md., 347 U.S. 179 (1954).
[4] Ohio *v.* Thomas, 173 U.S. 276, 283 (1899).
[5] Johnson *v.* Md., 254 U.S. 51 (1920).
[6] Arizona *v.* Calif., 283 U.S. 423, 451 (1931); California Commission *v.* U.S., 355 U.S. 534 (1958); U.S. *v.* Georgia Public Service Com'n., 371 U.S. 285 (1963).

the criteria used by the Court to decide such cases: "Where
. . . Congress has not stated specifically whether a federal
statute has occupied a field in which States are otherwise free
to legislate, different criteria have furnished touchstones for
decision. . . .

"*First*, [t]he scheme of federal regulation is so pervasive as
to make reasonable the inference that Congress left no room
for the States to supplement it. . . .

"*Second*, the federal statutes 'touch a field in which the
federal interest is so dominant that the federal system [must]
be assumed to preclude enforcement of state laws on the same
subject.' . . .

"*Third*, enforcement of state sedition acts presents a serious
danger of conflict with the administration of the federal program."[7] (*See also* discussion under Commerce Clause, pp.
54-64.)

Not only, however, is the "supremacy clause" important as
a sort of third dimension of national power, thrusting aside all
conflicting State powers; it is also of great significance as having been a source of private immunity, particularly from State
taxation. Thus, in the famous case of McCulloch *v.* Maryland,[8]
the Court under Chief Justice Marshall held that a State might
not tax an "instrumentality" of the National Government on
its operations; and it was later held that a State might not reach
by a general tax national bonds, national official salaries, incomes from national bonds, or lands owned by the National

Tax Exemp-
tion Again;
Its Rise and
Decline

---

[7] Pennsylvania *v.* Nelson, 350 U.S. 497, 501-505 (1956). This decision was
highly controversial and became the basis for much Congressional criticism
of the Court. See Murphy, *Congress and the Court.* Nonetheless, Warren's
criteria have been upheld in subsequent cases and followed by the lower
courts. *See* for example of the latter, Conant *v.* Hill, 326 F. Supp. 25, 27
(1971) *and* Mobil Oil Corp. *v.* Atty. General, 280 N.E. 2d. 406 (1972). *Also,*
"When there is an unavoidable conflict between the Federal and a State
Constitution, the supremacy clause, of course, controls." Reynolds *v.* Sims,
377 U.S. 533 (1964). Treaties, too, take precedence over State law in the
event of a conflict. *See* Mescalero Apache Tribe *v.* Jones, 489 P. 2d. 666,
669 (1971). For the latest Supreme Court decision with respect to the
supremacy clause, *see* Townsend *v.* Swank, 404 U.S. 282 (1971). The Court
did not cite the Nelson case in its decision but it nonetheless struck down
a state statute it found in conflict with Federal law. In 1972, a U.S. Court
of Appeals declared invalid a city ordinance prohibiting jet aircraft from
taking off at night on the grounds that Federal regulation of air commerce
was pervasive. Lockheed Air Terminal, Inc. *v.* City of Burbank, 457 F. 2d.
667 (1972).

[8] 4 Wheat. 316 (1819). Marshall's initial statement of the principle of
national supremacy, however, occurs in United States *v.* Fisher, 2 Cr. 358
(1805), where is asserted the priority of United States claims to debtor's
assets over those of a State. Spokane County *v.* U.S., 279 U.S. 80, 87 (1929),
follows this rule.

Government.[9] Then in a case decided in 1928 the Court ruled that a State tax on sales of gasoline might not be validly applied in the case of sales of the commodity to the National Government for use by its Coast Guard Fleet and a Veterans' Hospital,[10] thus prompting the query whether a butcher who sold meat to a Congressman would be subject validly to State taxation on such sales or on the profits thereof! But starting in the late 1930's, the Court has greatly curtailed the operation of the principle of tax exemption not only as a limitation on national power, but as a limitation on State power also, and especially in the field of income taxation. Thus in 1937 it held that a State may impose an occupation tax upon an independent contractor, measured by his gross receipts under contracts with the United States.[11] Previously it had sustained a gross receipts tax levied in lieu of a property tax upon the operator of an automobile stage line, who was engaged in carrying the mails as an independent contractor,[12] and an excise tax on gasoline sold to a contractor with the Federal Government and used to operate machinery in the construction of levees in the Mississippi River.[13] Subsequently it has approved State taxes on the net income of a government contractor,[14] and income[15] and social security[16] taxes on the operators of bath houses maintained in a national park under a lease from the United States; sales and use taxes on sales of beverages by a concessionaire in a national park;[17] taxes on purchases of materials used by a contractor in the performance of a cost-plus contract with the United States;[18] and a severance tax imposed on a

[9] Weston *v.* Charleston, 9 Wheat. 738 (1824); Dobbins *v.* Coms. of Erie City, 16 Pet. 435 (1842); Pollock *v.* Farmers' L. and T. Co., 157 U.S. 429 (1895); Van Brocklin *v.* Tenn., 117 U.S. 151 (1886). For the most recent exemplification of this principle, *see* First Federal Savings, etc. *v.* Bowers, 349 U.S. 143 (1955).
[10] Panhandle Oil Co. *v.* Miss., 277 U.S. 218 (1928); *cf.* Union Pac. R.R. Co. *v.* Peniston, 18 Wall. 5 (1873).
[11] James *v.* Dravo Contracting Co., 302 U.S. 134 (1937).
[12] Alward *v.* Johnson, 282 U.S. 509 (1931).
[13] Trinityfarm Const. Co. *v.* Grosjean, 291 U.S. 466 (1934).
[14] Atkinson *v.* Tax Commission, 303 U.S. 20 (1938).
[15] Superior Bath House Co. *v.* McCarroll, 312 U.S. 176 (1941).
[16] Buckstaff Bath House *v.* McKinley, 308 U.S. 358 (1939).
[17] Collins *v.* Yosemite Park & Curry Co., 304 U.S. 518 (1938). *See also* Humble Oil and Refining Co. *v.* Calvert, 478 S.W. 2d. 926 (1972) and Buck Act, 4 U.S.C. 105-110.
[18] Alabama *v.* King & Boozer, 314 U.S. 1 (1941), overruling Panhandle Oil Co. *v.* Knox, 277 U.S. 218 (1928) and Graves *v.* Texas Co., 298 U.S. 393 (1936). *See also* Curry *v.* U.S., 314 U.S. 14 (1941).

contractor who severed and purchased timber from lands owned by the United States.[19]

But Congress is still able, by virtue of the necessary and proper and supremacy clauses in conjunction, to exempt instrumentalities of the National Government, or private gains therefrom, from State or local taxation; but any person, natural or corporate, claiming such an exemption must ordinarily be able to point to an explicit stipulation by Congress to that effect. Moreover, Congress is always free to waive such exemptions when it can do so without breach of contract, and any such waiver will generally be liberally construed by the Court in favor of the taxing authority.[20]

Tax Exemption by Congressional Grant

A case illustrative of the Court's stance in this general field was the case in which the Court was confronted with an attempt on the part of Tennessee to apply its tax on the use within the State of goods purchased elsewhere to a private contractor for the Atomic Energy Commission and to vendors of such contractors.[21] This, the Court held, could not be done under Section 9b of the Atomic Energy Commission Act, which provides in part that: "The Commission, and the property, activities, and income of the Commission, are hereby expressly exempted from taxation in any manner or form by any State, county, municipality, or any subdivision thereof."[22] The power of exemption, said the Court, "stems from the power to preserve and protect functions validly authorized—the power to make all laws necessary and proper for carrying into execution the powers vested in Congress." The term, "activities," as used in the act, was held to be nothing less "than all of the functions of the Commission."[23]

In 1928 the Court went so far as to hold that a State could not tax as income royalties for the use of a patent issued by the United States.[24] This proposition was soon overruled in Fox

---

[19] Wilson v. Cook, 327 U.S. 474 (1946).

[20] Besides the leading case of Graves v. N.Y., 306 U.S. 466 (1939), *see also* Pittman v. HOLC, 308 U.S. 21 (1939); Tradesmen's National Bank v. Okla. Tax Com'n., 309 U.S. 560 (1940); Philadelphia Co. v. Dipple, 312 U.S. 168 (1941); and Cleveland v. U.S., 323 U.S. 329 (1945). *Cf.* Mayo v. U.S., 319 U.S. 441 (1943).

[21] Carson v. Roane Anderson Co., 342 U.S. 232 (1952).

[22] 60 *Stat.* 765; that law has since been amended to permit payments to the States in lieu of taxes. *See* 42 U.S.C. 2208.

[23] 342 U.S. 232, 234, 236. *See also* Kern-Limerick Inc. v. Scurlock, 347 U.S. 110 (1954).

[24] Long v. Rockwood, 277 U.S. 142 (1928).

Film Corp. *v.* Doyal,[25] where a privilege tax based on gross income and applicable to royalties from copyrights was upheld. Likewise a State may lay a franchise tax on corporations, measured by the net income from all sources, including income from copyright royalties.[26]

Immunity of National Official Action from State Control

It would seem elementary that a State court cannot interfere with the functioning of a Federal tribunal. Nevertheless, this proposition has not always gone unchallenged. Shortly before the Civil War, the Supreme Court of Wisconsin, holding the Federal Fugitive Slave Law invalid, ordered a United States marshal to release a prisoner who had been convicted of aiding and abetting the escape of a fugitive slave. In an act of further defiance, the State court instructed its clerk to disregard and refuse obedience to the writ of error issued by the United States Supreme Court. Strongly denouncing this interference with Federal authority, Chief Justice Taney held that when a State court is advised, on the return of a writ of *habeas corpus,* that the prisoner is in custody on authority of the United States, it can proceed no further.[27] To protect the performance of its functions against interference by State tribunals, Congress may constitutionally authorize the removal to a Federal court of a criminal prosecution commenced in a State court against a revenue officer of the United States on account of any act done under color of his office.[28] In the celebrated case of *In re* Neagle,[29] a United States marshal who, while assigned to protect Justice Field, killed a man who had been threatening the life of the latter, was charged with murder by the State of California. Invoking the supremacy clause, the Supreme Court held that a person could not be guilty of a crime under State law for doing what it was his duty to do as an officer of the United States.

¶3. The Senators and Representatives before mentioned, and the members of the several State legislatures, and all executive and judicial officers, both of the United States

---

[25] 286 U.S. 123 (1932).

[26] Educational Films Corp. *v.* Ward, 282 U.S. 379 (1931).

[27] Ableman *v.* Booth, 21 How. 506, 523 (1859). *See also* United States *v.* Tarble, 13 Wall. 397 (1872). The Court's opinions in both of these cases invoked the doctrine of Dual Federalism as well as that of National Supremacy, but rather inconsistently.

[28] Tennessee *v.* Davis, 100 U.S. 257 (1880); *see also* Maryland *v.* Soper, 270 U.S. 36 (1926).

[29] 135 U.S. 1 (1890).

and of the several States, shall be bound by oath or affirmation, to support this Constitution; but no religious
test shall ever be required as a qualification to any office
or public trust under the United States.

Congress may require no other oath of fidelity to the Constitution, but it may superadd to this oath such other oath of office
as its wisdom may require.[30] It may not, however, prescribe
a test oath as a qualification for holding office, such an act being in effect an *ex post facto* law;[31] and the same rule holds in
the case of the States.[32]

In a noteworthy case decided in 1972, the Supreme Court
declared constitutional a Massachusetts law requiring that
"every person entering the employ of the commonwealth" to
affirm an oath which in addition to the words of the usual oath
(*see* p. 119) added "and that I will oppose the overthrow of the
government of the United States of America or of this Commonwealth by force, violence, or by any illegal or unconstitutional method."[33]

Commenting in *The Federalist* No. 27 on the requirement
that State officers, as well as members of the State legislatures,
shall be bound by oath affirmation to support this Constitution, Hamilton wrote: "Thus the legislatures, courts and magistrates, of the respective members, will be incorporated into
the operations of the national government *as far as its just and
constitutional authority extends*, and will be rendered auxiliary to the enforcement of its laws." The younger Pinckney
had expressed the same idea on the floor of the Philadelphia
Convention: "They [the States] are the instruments upon
which the Union must frequently depend for the support and
execution of their powers, . . ."[34] Indeed, the Constitution itself
lays many duties, both positive and negative, upon the different organs of State government,[35] and Congress may frequently add others, provided it does not require the State authorities to act outside their normal jurisdiction. Early Congres-

*State Aid in National Law Enforcement*

[30] McCulloch *v.* Maryland, 4 Wheat. 316, 416 (1819); Cole *v.* Richardson, 405 U.S. 676 (1972).
[31] *Ex parte* Garland, 4 Wall. 333, 337 (1867).
[32] Cummings *v.* Mo., 4 Wall. 227, 323 (1867).
[33] Cole *v.* Richardson, 405 U.S. 676 (1972).
[34] Max Farrand, ed., *The Records of the Federal Convention of 1787*, I (New Haven, 1937), 404.
[35] *See* Art. I, Sect. III, Par. 1; Sect. IV, Par. 1; Sect. X; Art. II, Sect. I, Par. 2; Art. III, Sect. II, Par. 2; Art. IV, Sects. I and II; Art. V; Amendments XIII, XIV, XV, XVII, and XIX.

sional legislation contains many illustrations of such action by Congress.

The Judiciary Act of 1789[36] left the State courts in sole possession of a large part of the jurisdiction over controversies between citizens of different States and in concurrent possession of the rest. By other sections of the same act State courts were authorized to entertain proceedings by the United States itself to enforce penalties and forfeitures under the revenue laws, while any justice of the peace or other magistrate of any of the States was authorized to cause any offender against the United States to be arrested and imprisoned or bailed under the usual mode of process. Even as late as 1839, Congress authorized all pecuniary penalties and forfeitures under the laws of the United States to be sued for before any court of competent jurisdiction in the State where the cause of action arose or where the offender might be found.[37] Pursuant also of the same idea of treating State governmental organs as available to the National Government for administrative purposes, the act of 1793 entrusted the rendition of fugitive slaves in part to national officials and in part to State officials and the rendition of fugitives from justice from one State to another exclusively to the State executives.[38] Certain later acts empowered State courts to entertain criminal prosecutions for forging paper of the Bank of the United States and for counterfeiting coin of the United States,[39] while still others conferred on State judges authority to admit aliens to national citizenship and provided penalties in case such judges should utter false certificates of naturalization—provisions which are still on the statute books.[40]

With the rise of the doctrine of States Rights and of the equal sovereignty of the States with the National Government, the availability of the former as instruments of the latter The States in the execution of its power, came to be questioned.[41] In Prigg Rights *v.* Pennsylvania,[42] decided in 1842, the constitutionality of the Reaction provision of the act of 1793 making it the duty of State magis-

[36] 1 *Stat.* 73 (1789).　　　　　　　　[37] 5 *Stat.* 322 (1839).
[38] 1 *Stat.* 303 (1793).　　　　　　　[39] 2 *Stat.* 404 (1806).
[40] *See* Kent, *Commentaries*, II, 64-65; 34 *Stat.* 596, 602 (1906); 8 U.S.C. 1421 and 18 U.S.C. 1426; 18 U.S.C. 471 and 485; *also* Holmgren *v.* U.S., 217 U.S. 509 (1910).
[41] For the development of opinion especially on the part of State courts, adverse to the validity of the above-mentioned legislation, *see* Kent, *Commentaries*, I, 396-404.
[42] 16 Pet. 539 (1842).

trates to act in the return of fugitive slaves was challenged; and in Kentucky *v.* Dennison,[43] decided on the eve of the Civil War, similar objection was leveled against the provision of the same act which made it "the duty" of the Chief Executive of a State to render up a fugitive from justice upon the demand of the Chief Executive of the State from which the fugitive had fled. The Court sustained both provisions, but upon the theory that the cooperation of the State authorities was purely voluntary. In the *Prigg* case the Court, speaking by Justice Story, said: ". . . state magistrates may, if they choose, exercise the authority [conferred by the act], unless prohibited by state legislation."[44] In the *Dennison* case, "the duty" of State executives in the rendition of fugitives from justice was construed to be declaratory of a "moral duty." Said Chief Justice Taney for the Court: "We think it clear, that the Federal Government, under the Constitution, has no power to impose on a State officer, as such, any duty whatever, and compel him to perform it; for if it possessed this power, it might overload the officer with duties which would fill up all his time, and disable him from performing his obligations to the State, and might impose on him duties of a character incompatible with the rank and dignity to which he was elevated by the State."[45]

Eighteen years later, in *ex parte* Siebold,[46] the Court sustained the right of Congress, under Article I, Section IV, ¶1 of the Constitution, to impose duties upon State election officials in connection with a Congressional election and to prescribe additional penalties for the violation by such officials of their duties under State law. The outlook of Justice Bradley's opinion for the Court is decidedly nationalistic rather than dualistic, as is shown by the answer made to the contention of counsel "that the nature of sovereignty is such as to preclude the joint cooperation of two sovereigns, even in a matter in which they are mutually concerned." To this Justice Bradley replied: "As a general rule, it is no doubt expedient and wise that the operations of the State and national governments should as far as practicable, be conducted separately, in order to avoid undue jealousies and jars and conflicts of jurisdiction and power. But there is no reason for laying this down as a rule of universal application. It should never be made to override the plain and manifest dictates of the Con-

*Return to Earlier Views*

---

[43] 24 How. 66 (1861).  [44] 16 Pet. 539, 622.
[45] 24 How. 66, 107-108.  [46] 100 U.S. 371 (1880).

stitution itself. We cannot yield to such a transcendental view of State sovereignty. The Constitution and laws of the United States are the supreme law of the land, and to these every citizen of every State owes obedience, whether in his individual or official capacity."[47] Three years earlier the Court, speaking also by Justice Bradley, sustained a provision of the Bankruptcy Act of 1867 giving assignees a right to sue in State courts to recover the assets of a bankrupt. Said the Court: "The statutes of the United States are as much the law of the land in any State as are those of the State; and although exclusive jurisdiction for their enforcement may be given to the federal courts, yet where it is not given, either expressly or by necessary implication, the State courts having competent jurisdiction in other respects, may be resorted to."[48]

The Selective Service Act of 1917[49] was enforced to a great extent through State "employees who functioned under State supervision";[50] and State officials were frequently employed by the National Government in the enforcement of National Prohibition.[51] Nowadays, there is constant cooperation, both in peacetime and in wartime, in many fields between National and State officers and official bodies.[52] This relationship obviously calls for the active fidelity of both categories of officialdom to the Constitution.

A "Religious Test"

A "religious test" is one demanding the avowal or repudiation of certain religious beliefs. No religious test may be required as a qualification for office under the United States. In 1961, the Supreme Court held that to enforce a State constitutional requirement which required a belief in God as a qualification for office was unconstitutional.[53] However, an indulgence in immoral practices claiming the sanction of religious belief, such as polygamy, may be made a disqualification.[54]

[47] Ibid., 392.

[48] Claflin v. Houseman, 93 U.S. 130, 136, 137 (1876); followed in Second Employers' Liability Cases, 223 U.S. 1, 55-59 (1912).

[49] 40 Stat. 76 (1917).

[50] Jane Perry Clark, The Rise of a New Federalism (New York, 1938), 91.

[51] See James Hart in 13 Virginia Law Review, 86 (1926) discussing President Coolidge's order of May 8, 1926, for Prohibition enforcement.

[52] W. Brooke Graves, American Intergovernmental Relations (New York, 1964); Morton Grodzins, The American System (Chicago, 1966).

[53] Torasco v. Watkins, 367 U.S. 488 (1961).

[54] Reynolds v. U.S., 98 U.S. 145 (1878) and Mormon Church v. U.S., 136 U.S. 1 (1890), both support this proposition, assuming they are still law of the land.

Contrariwise, alleged religious beliefs or moral scruples do not furnish ground for evasion of the ordinary duties of citizenship, like the payment of taxes or military service, although, of course, Congress may of its own volition grant exemptions on such grounds. The related subject of "religious freedom" is discussed immediately below.

"Oath or affirmation": This option was provided for the special benefit of Quakers.

# ARTICLE VII

¶The ratification of the conventions of nine States shall be sufficient for the establishment of this Constitution between the States so ratifying the same.

The Articles of Confederation provided for their own amendment only by the unanimous consent of the thirteen States, given through their legislatures. The provision made for the going into effect of the Constitution upon its ratification by *nine* States, given through *conventions* called for the purpose, clearly indicates the establishment of the Constitution to have been, in the legal sense, an act of revolution.

The Constitution an Act of Revolution

¶Done in convention by the unanimous consent of the States present, the seventeenth day of September, in the year of our Lord one thousand seven hundred and eighty-seven, and of the independence of the United States of America the twelfth.

In witness whereof we have hereunto subscribed our names.

George Washington, President, and Deputy from Virginia.
New Hampshire—John Langdon, Nicholas Gilman.
Massachusetts—Nathaniel Gorham, Rufus King.
Connecticut—William Samuel Johnson, Roger Sherman.
New York—Alexander Hamilton.
New Jersey—William Livingston, David Brearly, William Paterson, Jonathan Dayton.
Pennsylvania—Benjamin Franklin, Thomas Mifflin, Robert Morris, George Clymer, Thomas Fitzsimons, Jared Ingersoll, James Wilson, Gouverneur Morris.
Delaware—George Read, Gunning Bedford, Jr., John Dickinson, Richard Bassett, Jacob Broom.
Maryland—James McHenry, Daniel of St. Thomas Jenifer, Daniel Carroll.
Virginia—John Blair, James Madison, Jr.
North Carolina—William Blount, Richard Dobbs Spaight, Hugh Williamson.
South Carolina—John Rutledge, Charles Cotesworth Pinckney, Charles Pinckney, Pierce Butler.
Georgia—William Few, Abraham Baldwin.

ATTEST:                                    WILLIAM JACKSON, *Secretary.*

# AMENDMENTS[1]

The "Bill of Rights"

The first ten amendments make up the so-called Bill of Rights of the National Constitution. They were designed to quiet the fears of mild opponents of the Constitution in its original form and were proposed to the State legislatures by the first Congress which assembled under the Constitution. They bind only the National Government and in no wise limit the powers of the States of their own independent force;[2] but the rights which they protect against the National Government are, nevertheless, today not infrequently claimable against State authority under the Court's interpretation of the "due process" clause of the Fourteenth Amendment.[3]

Also, the efficacy of the Bill of Rights as a restriction on the National Government is confined to the territorial limits of the United States, including within that term the "incorporated" territories (*see* p. 215), except when "fundamental rights" are involved, it being for the Supreme Court to say what rights are "fundamental" in this sense.[4] The right to trial by jury, an inherited feature of Anglo-America jurisprudence, was at one

[1] The first ten amendments were proposed in 1789 and adopted in 810 days. The Eleventh Amendment was proposed in 1794 and adopted in 339 days. The Twelfth Amendment was proposed in 1803 and adopted in 229 days. The Thirteenth Amendment was proposed in 1865 and adopted in 309 days. The Fourteenth Amendment was proposed in 1866 and adopted in 768 days. The Fifteenth Amendment was proposed in 1869 and adopted in 356 days. The Sixteenth Amendment was proposed in 1909 and adopted in 1278 days. The Seventeenth Amendment was proposed in 1912 and adopted in 359 days. The Eighteenth Amendment was proposed in 1917 and adopted in 396 days. The Nineteenth Amendment was proposed in 1919 and adopted in 444 days. The Twentieth Amendment was proposed in 1932 and adopted in 327 days. The Twenty-first Amendment was proposed in 1933 and adopted in 286 days. For these statistics, which were compiled by Hon. Everett M. Dirksen of Illinois, *see* the *New York Times*, February 21, 1937. Several of the amendments were, however, the outcome of many years of agitation.

[2] Barron *v.* Balt., 7 Pet. 243 (1833). According to Mr. Warren, "In at least twenty cases between 1877 and 1907, the Court was called upon to rule upon this point and to reaffirm Marshall's decision of 1833." "The New 'Liberty' under the Fourteenth Amendment," 39 *Harvard Law Review*, 431, 436 (1926).

[3] *See* Gitlow *v.* N.Y., 268 U.S. 652 (1925); Near *v.* Minn., 283 U.S. 697 (1931); Powell *v.* Ala., 287 U.S. 45 (1932); Palko *v.* Conn., 302 U.S. 319 (1937).

[4] Downes *v.* Bidwell, 182 U.S. 244 (1901).

time not considered to be such a right;[5] immunity from "cruel and unusual punishment" is.[6]

## THE WARREN COURT AND THE SECOND CONSTITUTIONAL REVOLUTION

Any meaningful consideration of the civil liberties protections premised in the amendments to the Constitution must be prefaced with some discussion of the work of the Supreme Court under Chief Justice Earl Warren, for it was the Warren Court (1953-1969) with its judicial activism, intermittent at first in the 'fifties, more constant and sure-footed in its last eight years, that left an indelible imprint on their scope and meaning. Yet, for all its impact, the attachment of the Supreme Court to the vindication of civil liberties did not spring full-blown with the accession of Earl Warren as Chief Justice. Its roots are deep in the changing contours of judicial policy-making evident during the preceding decade and a half.

### THE LEGACY OF THE ROOSEVELT COURT

The Constitutional Revolution of 1937 had been a supreme victory for those styled as "liberals" in the 'thirties and 'forties. By 1941, with the departure of Justice McReynolds, the last of the old conservatives, the Bench had been shoved considerably to the Left. This transition, however, had bequeathed three significant trends which were to fracture the cohesion of the new Roosevelt appointees. First, it ended the activism of the Court in the area of economic regulation and transferred the policy-making interest of the High Bench to the area of civil liberties. Second, it rekindled the debate over activism and self-restraint among the new liberal Justices, virtually all of whom had been openly critical of the vigor of the old Court. Finally, it signalled the acceptance of the "balancing of interests" approach to adjudication over the old legal method known as "mechanical jurisprudence."[1] No longer did

---

[5] Dorr v. U.S., 195 U.S. 138 (1904). However, in 1968 the Supreme Court held that trial by jury in a criminal case is a fundamental right which is guaranteed as against the States. Duncan v. Louisiana 391 U.S. 145 (1968). See p. 343 below. Presumably, that decision by inference guarantees the right to a jury trial in a criminal case in unincorporated territories now and in the future. See 1968 amendment to Guam's Bill of Rights, 48 U.S.C. 1421b.
[6] Weems v. U.S., 217 U.S. 349 (1910).

[1] Cf. United States v. Butler, 297 U.S. 1 (1936) and Carter v. Carter Coal Co., 298 U.S. 238 (1936) with Steward Machine Co. v. Davis, 301 U.S.

the Court seem bent on presenting the image that judges were merely the instruments through which law spoke neutrally and impartially and where syllogistic reasoning and literal interpretation were viewed as the life of the law. Instead, the new Justices avowed a legal method which indicated a more sophisticated awareness of the political implications of the value choices they made. They saw themselves as decision-makers who deliberately weigh the conflicting claims of competing interests in the society in the context of some broad policy goals.

### THE PREFERRED FREEDOMS CONCEPT

The activist response to the vacuum existing in the Court's policy-making role found its rationale in the "preferred freedoms" concept.[2] This approach sought, first, to expand civil liberties protections by reading through the word "liberty" in the due process clause of the Fourteenth Amendment, and thereby also making applicable against State infringement guarantees emanating from certain freedoms in the Bill of Rights.[3] Second, it provided a rigorous three-pronged test to evaluate whether governmental action was, in any given instance, violative of these specially regarded liberties: (1) where legislation on its face abridged a preferred freedom, the presumption would be with unconstitutionality, the burden lying with the Government to convincingly demonstrate the contrary; (2) the Government would have to prove that the exercise of freedom in this context presented a clear and imminent danger; and (3) the Government would have to show that the remedy espoused was confined to the eradication of the immediate evil and was not some scatter-gun approach which imperiled additional liberties by its overbreadth.[4]

The justification for this concept of incorporation and its companion test of infringement lay in what was asserted to be the requisite of certain freedoms to the conduct of the democratic process (especially insofar as this concept protected the

---

548 (1937); South Carolina State Highway Dept. *v.* Barnwell Bros., 303 U.S. 177 (1938); *and* Southern Pacific Co. *v.* Ariz., 325 U.S. 761 (1945).

[2] *See* Justice Frankfurter's catalog of the instances where the Court used the preferred freedoms test to 1945 in Kovacs *v.* Cooper, 336 U.S. 77, 90-94 (1949).

[3] Palko *v.* Conn., 302 U.S. 319 (1937).

[4] Thomas *v.* Collins, 323 U.S. 516 (1945).

articulation of views and demands by minorities in the society) and the maintenance of individual dignity.[5] With this preferred freedoms doctrine, Justices Murphy, Rutledge, Douglas, and Black sought to respond to the questions which the revolution of 1937 had left unanswered. Recognizing that freedom was the rule and restraint the exception, they had constructed a balancing framework with a built-in bias against governmental interference, one which justified activism to its former critics, and a doctrine which shifted the focus of the Court's policy-making by recognizing that civil liberties, and not economic liberties, were essential to the maintenance of human dignity and the democratic enterprise.

### JUDICIAL SELF-RESTRAINT AND CIVIL LIBERTIES

Prominent among those Justices who remained unconvinced by the preferred freedoms concept was Felix Frankfurter. Starting from the premise that the use of judicial review by an appointed, life-tenured Court was "an undemocratic aspect of our scheme of government,"[6] Frankfurter argued that its active use "serves to prevent the full play of the democratic process."[7] The remedy for unwise legislation lay in the main with "an informed, civically militant electorate" and the ultimate articulation of its demands through the ballot box.[8] Judicial review was to be exercised only when laws were clearly arbitrary or discriminatory, when legislative choices went patently beyond the bounds of what one might presume a collection of reasonable men might rationally choose.

Beyond his attack on activism in general, Frankfurter saw specific liabilities in its articulation via the preferred freedoms concept. First, any distinction between civil liberties and economic liberties that would justify putting the former on a higher plane and thus warrant reversing the usual presumption of constitutionality in laws regulating those freedoms was textually undemonstrable.[9] The Fifth Amendment secured all human rights equally—life, liberty, *and property*—and none was to be taken away without due process of law. The same philosophy of constitutional interpretation must therefore apply in all instances. Second, Frankfurter decried the creation

[5] United States *v.* Carolene Products Co., 304 U.S. 144, 152 note 4 (1938).
[6] W.Va. State Bd. of Educ. *v.* Barnette, 319 U.S. 624, 650 (1943).
[7] *Ibid.*
[8] Baker *v.* Carr, 369 U.S. 186, 270 (1962).
[9] W.Va. State Bd. of Educ. *v.* Barnette, 319 U.S. 624, 648-649 (1943).

of such a rigid test for evaluating the constitutionality of legislation. He feared that facile tests, such as the "clear and present danger" component, were an invitation to return to the mechanical approach of yesteryear.[10] He felt that the tendency to pigeonhole legislation in neat categories, using oversimplified standards, obscured the real function of a judge, which was to carefully weigh the competing claims and interests presented in each case. Finally, Frankfurter was concerned that such constant, active vindication of individual rights flew in the face of majority rule. The use of judicial review to invalidate legislation on the grounds that it offended the scruples of a minority had the effect of creating a specially privileged group, for it was tantamount to saying that "the consciences of a minority are more sacred and more enshrined in the Constitution than the consciences of a majority."[11]

### JUSTICE BLACK AND THE ABSOLUTIST APPROACH

The third approach, absolutism, generally comes to mind as a particular test for the guaranty of First Amendment freedoms, yet the term can also be used to describe a theory of comprehensive incorporation whereby all of the provisions contained in the first eight amendments are read through the Fourteenth to apply against State action, as well as an entire outlook on constitutional interpretation. Espoused by only one member of the recent Court, Justice Hugo Black, this doctrinaire approach reflects, personally, a repudiation of the self-restraint and preferred freedoms approaches, each of which he had consecutively endorsed in his early years on the Court,[12] and, methodologically, a return to a mechanical technique and uncompromising literalism reminiscent of the old Court.

Justice Black first articulated his view of total incorporation in his dissent from the decision in a 1947 case[13] which upheld a State law permitting "the court, counsel, and jury to comment upon and consider the failure of defendant 'to explain or deny by his testimony any evidence or facts in the case against him' "[14] over the claim that the statute infringed the defend-

10 Kovacs *v.* Cooper, 336 U.S. 77, 96 (1949).
11 W.Va. State Bd. of Educ. *v.* Barnette, 319 U.S. 624, 662 (1943).
12 *See* Minersville School Dist. *v.* Gobitis, 310 U.S. 586 (1940) *and* Thomas *v.* Collins, 323 U.S. 516 (1945).
13 Adamson *v.* Calif., 332 U.S. 46 (1947).
14 *Ibid.*, 50.

ant's privilege against self-incrimination under the Fifth Amendment. Based upon exhaustive historical research which he presented in considerable detail in his opinion and an accompanying appendix, Black concluded that it was the manifest intent of the Framers of the Fourteenth Amendment to substantially alter the Federal system by applying all of the provisions of the Bill of Rights in their entirety to the States. Perfectly consistent with this position, Black has since argued that the Fourteenth Amendment guarantees no more rights than those contained in the first eight amendments.[15]

As a corollary to this theory of total incorporation, Justice Black has asserted his belief that the scope of these protections, as intended by the Framers of the Constitution, must remain inviolate. The Court, except where explicitly permitted (as, for example, in determining what is an "unreasonable search and seizure" under the Fourth Amendment) may not balance competing claims in civil liberties cases because the Constitution, in his view, has already struck the balance. Thus, where the First Amendment provides that "Congress shall make no law" abridging the specific freedoms contained therein, it literally means "Congress shall make *no* law."[16]

Justice Black's legal approach, in civil liberties cases and in those of a non-civil liberties character alike,[17] is uniquely marked by a rejection of judicial discretion in an attempt to divine the true and exact meaning of the Framers' words and to apply that interpretation literally. Nowhere does the essence of his outlook seem more succinctly mirrored than in this passage from his dissent in a recent narcotics case: "The Framers of our Constitution and Bill of Rights were too wise, too pragmatic, and too familiar with tyranny to attempt to safeguard personal liberty with broad, flexible words and phrases like 'fair trial,' 'fundamental decency' and 'reasonableness.' Such stretchy, rubberlike terms would have left judges constitutionally free to try people charged with crime under will-o'-the-wisp standards improvised by different judges for different defendants. Neither the due process clause nor any other constitutional language vests any judge with such power. Our Constitution was not written in the sands to be washed away by each wave of new judges blown in by each successive

---

[15] Griswold v. Conn., 381 U.S. 479, 507-527 (1965).
[16] Hugo L. Black, "The Bill of Rights," 35 *New York University Law Review*, 865 (1960).
[17] *See* El Paso v. Simmons, 379 U.S. 497, 517 (1965).

political wind which brings new political administrations into temporary power. Rather, our Constitution was fashioned to perpetuate liberty and justice by marking clear, explicit, and lasting constitutional boundaries for trials. One need look no further than the language of that sacred document itself to be assured that defendants charged with crime are to be accorded due process of law—that is, they are to be tried as the Constitution and the laws pursuant to it prescribe and not under arbitrary procedures that a particular majority of sitting judges may see fit to label as 'fair' or 'decent.' I wholly, completely, and permanently reject the so-called 'activist' philosophy of some judges which leads them to construe our Constitution as meaning what they now think it should mean in the interest of 'fairness and decency' as they see it."[18]

## THE STONE AND VINSON COURTS

If there has been one validated hypothesis which has served to characterize the Court's treatment of civil liberties it has been the proposition that the scope of those protections—Justice Black to the contrary notwithstanding—has hung indeed on "each wave of new judges blown in by each successive political wind." The ability of preferred freedoms or self-restraint to hold sway at a given time in the post-1937 era is directly traceable to the different composition of the Stone and Vinson Courts, respectively. This observation about the relation of the prevailing doctrine to the complexion of the Court applies equally well to the early and later Warren Courts, though in reverse sequence.

Dominated by the four preferred freedoms advocates (who usually managed to pick up the additional vote needed to make a majority from among Stone, Frankfurter, or Jackson),[19] the Court presented a marked libertarian image from 1943 until the deaths of Justices Murphy and Rutledge in the summer of 1949. It very closely scrutinized governmental attempts to harness political and religious expression[20] and moved to in-

[18] Turner v. U.S., 396 U.S. 398, 426 (1970).
[19] See C. Herman Pritchett, The Roosevelt Court (New York, 1948).
[20] Jones v. Opelika, 316 U.S. 584 (1942); Murdock v. Pa., 319 U.S. 105 (1943); Martin v. Struthers, 319 U.S. 141 (1943); W.Va. State Bd. of Educ. v. Barnette, 319 U.S. 624 (1943); Prince v. Mass., 321 U.S. 158 (1944); Follett v. McCormick, 321 U.S. 573 (1944); Thomas v. Collins, 323 U.S. 516 (1945); Marsh v. Ala., 326 U.S. 501 (1946); Pennekamp v. Fla., 328 U.S. 331 (1946); Craig v. Harney, 331 U.S. 367 (1947); Saia v. N.Y., 334 U.S. 558 (1948); Terminello v. Chicago, 337 U.S. 1 (1949).

validate prior restraint on publication.[21] The Court struck out at racial discrimination,[22] and it sought to reform some of the brutalities in criminal procedure.[23] Finally, it advanced the incorporation process by adding the "establishment clause" of the First Amendment[24] and the right to be free from unreasonable searches and seizures under the Fourth[25] to the list of those rights contained in the first eight amendments which required national protection via the due process clause of the Fourteenth Amendment because they were found to be "of the very essence of a scheme of ordered liberty."[26]

Even though Chief Justice Vinson was appointed in 1946, the character of the Court did not change until Justices Clark and Minton took their seats three years later. The stodgy conservatism of the Truman appointees contrasted sharply with the libertarian outlook of the Court during most of the 'forties. Deeply embedded in the philosophy of judicial self-restraint, most of the Justices—excepting Black and Douglas—turned a deaf ear to the perils of civil liberties in an era racked by the issues of Communism and subversion. With a finger on the scales, they balanced with a heavy bias favoring national security over personal liberty.[27] The Court upheld governmental action inhibiting the speech process,[28] prying into the right of individuals to freely associate,[29] intruding on people in their private beliefs,[30] and punishing alleged conspiracies to overthrow the Government at some uncertain time in the future.[31] Amid growing suspicion and hysteria, the Vinson Court, in what may be the classic example of its inaction, elevated legis-

[21] Winters v. N.Y., 333 U.S. 507 (1948).

[22] Smith v. Allwright, 321 U.S. 649 (1944); Morgan v. Va., 328 U.S. 373 (1946); Sipuel v. Okla., 332 U.S. 631 (1948); Bob-Lo Excursion Co. v. Mich., 333 U.S. 28 (1948); Shelley v. Kraemer, 334 U.S. 1 (1948).

[23] Ashcraft v. Tenn., 322 U.S. 143 (1944); Screws v. U.S., 325 U.S. 91 (1945); Haley v. Ohio, 332 U.S. 596 (1948); *but cf.* Louisiana v. Resweber, 329 U.S. 459 (1947).

[24] Everson v. Bd. of Educ., 330 U.S. 1 (1947).

[25] Wolf v. Colo., 338 U.S. 25 (1949).

[26] Palko v. Conn., 302 U.S. 319, 325 (1937).

[27] *See* C. Herman Pritchett, *Civil Liberties and the Vinson Court* (Chicago, 1954) and Harold W. Chase, *Security and Liberty* (Garden City, 1955).

[28] Feiner v. N.Y., 340 U.S. 315 (1951).

[29] Amer. Communications Assn. v. Douds, 339 U.S. 382 (1950); Adler v. Bd. of Educ., 342 U.S. 485 (1952); *cf.* Wieman v. Updegraff, 344 U.S. 183 (1952).

[30] Gerende v. Bd. of Elections, 341 U.S. 56 (1951); Garner v. Bd. of Public Works, 341 U.S. 716 (1951).

[31] Dennis v. U.S., 341 U.S. 494 (1951).

lative intent and administrative finality to new heights in the face of real hardship visited upon aliens and naturalized citizens alike by the Immigration and Naturalization Service.[32] Such was the legacy of passivity bequeathed by the Vinson Court when the new Chief Justice took his center seat at the beginning of the October 1953 term.

## THE SECOND CONSTITUTIONAL REVOLUTION

The phrase "constitutional revolution" seems almost certainly no exaggeration to describe the cumulative effect of the Warren Court's expansive interpretations of the Bill of Rights and the Fourteenth Amendment. The Court's work of the 'fifties and 'sixties was genuinely as revolutionary as that of the Hughes Court in the late 'thirties; in both instances the Court acted to integrate what had heretofore been out-groups into the political system and to extend to them fuller protection and participation in society. In the days of the New Deal, these groups had been labor and the urban-based ethnic minorites—the working class generally; in the second constitutional revolution of the twentieth century, these groups were Black people, poor people, radicals, urbanites, juveniles, people accused of crime, and religious dissenters. There was, however, a significant difference in the role of the Court in these two constitutional revolutions. In the first, the Court acted as legitimator—surrendering to what was already a *fait accompli*; in the second, the Court became the catalyst itself— initiating change rather than responding to the pressures applied by other branches of the Government.

The theme of constitutional development which emerges from the nearly sixteen-year tenure of the Warren Court can perhaps best be characterized as the application of libertarian precepts in an equalitarian context. That is to say, while the Court agreed with the general premise of the balancing approach that it ought to maximize the claims of as many people as possible in the cases which came before it, it was more deeply committed to the belief that the vindication of fundamental liberties for peripheral groups in the society took

[32] Ludecke *v.* Watkins, 335 U.S. 160 (1948); United States *ex rel.* Knauff *v.* Shaughnessy, 338 U.S. 537 (1950); Carlson *v.* Landon, 342 U.S. 524 (1952); Harisiades *v.* Shaughnessy, 342 U.S. 580 (1952); Shaughnessy *v.* U.S. *ex rel.* Mezei, 345 U.S. 206 (1953).

precedence over the extension of any additional rights to the larger in-groups.[33]

## PREFERRED FREEDOMS AND SELF-RESTRAINT
### IN WARREN COURT

Given the concern of the Warren Court for the status of those individuals to be found living at society's margins, it is not surprising that the constitutional doctrine which came to have controlling influence in the disposition of civil liberties cases generally was the preferred freedoms concept. Yet this was not consistently true, largely because, as we have noted before, the outlook of the Court is contingent upon its membership, and the Warren Court did not always have an activist majority. At this point it may be well to remember that, while we may talk of the Stone, Vinson, and Warren Courts and their orientations toward civil liberties as reflecting activism or self-restraint, Courts are nevertheless not monolithic. They are composed of men who frequently differ greatly with one another. When we speak, then, of the affinity of the Warren Court for the preferred freedoms approach, we intend nothing more than a kind of shorthand characterization of the prevailing outlook of a majority of the Justices sitting at a particular time and denoted according to the man who presided over them (whether or not he was their driving force). And that majority may be a tenuous one indeed, as was that of the activists on the Court from 1943 to 1949, for example.

The overall cast of the decisions rendered by the Warren Court in its first five years suggests a distinctly libertarian trend. Beginning with the School Desegregation Cases, which consumed much of its attention during the 1953 and 1954 terms,[34] the Court rapidly expanded its activism to other areas in which it saw personal rights under assault, principally against governmental shortcuts at both the State and national levels aimed at exposing and punishing those engaged in allegedly subversive activities[35] and against abuses of the crimi-

---

[33] For development of this position, *see* Christian Bay, *The Structure of Freedom* (Stanford, 1958), and John Rawls, *A Theory of Justice* (Cambridge, Mass., 1971).

[34] Brown *v.* Topeka, 347 U.S. 483 (1954); Bolling *v.* Sharpe, 347 U.S. 497 (1954); Brown *v.* Topeka, 349 U.S. 294 (1955).

[35] Pennsylvania *v.* Nelson, 350 U.S. 497 (1956); Slochower *v.* Bd. of Educ., 350 U.S. 551 (1956); Cole *v.* Young, 351 U.S. 536 (1956); Schware *v.* Bd. of Bar Examiners, 353 U.S. 232 (1957); Konigsberg *v.* State Bar of Calif., 353 U.S. 252 (1957); Jencks *v.* U.S., 353 U.S. 657 (1957); Watkins *v.*

nal process.[36] This movement was greatly facilitated by the appointment of an activist, William Brennan, in 1956 to replace the retiring Sherman Minton, a devotee of self-restraint.

Enraged by what it saw as a judicial fifth-column movement, a coalition of Southern Democrats and conservative Republicans responded in the 1958 Congressional session with several pieces of legislation designed to curb the Court by withdrawing some of its appellate jurisdiction. The legislative effort failed, but by rather close votes.[37] Justices Frankfurter and Harlan, both restraintists at heart, who had joined the activists (Black, Douglas, Warren, and Brennan) only on a case-by-case basis, became sensitized by this display of Congressional and public dissatisfaction.[38] They backed off and carried a majority of the Court with them, so that, for approximately the next three years, the Court's activism was somewhat tempered by judicial self-restraint in the offending areas—notably by the Court's modest retreat in the area of governmental attempts to deal with the Red issue, specifically in its treatment of legislative investigations,[39] associational inquiries,[40] and proscribed-group registration and membership.[41] The Court, however, stood fast on the matter of racial discrimination.[42]

Prefaced a year earlier with the sudden stirring of Justices Stewart and Clark,[43] both of whom had heretofore been regarded as rather firmly attached to the philosophy of self-restraint, the Warren Court began its second and uninterrupted period of activism with the retirement of Justices Whittaker and Frankfurter and the appointment of their more lib-

---

U.S., 354 U.S. 178 (1957); Sweezey v. N.H., 354 U.S. 234 (1957); Yates v. U.S., 354 U.S. 298 (1957); Service v. Dulles, 354 U.S. 363 (1957).

[36] Rea v. U.S., 350 U.S. 214 (1956); Kremen v. U.S., 353 U.S. 346 (1957); Mallory v. U.S., 354 U.S. 449 (1957).

[37] For a thorough treatment of the controversy, see Walter Murphy, *Congress and the Court* (Chicago, 1962). An excellent discussion of the work of the Warren Court and its critics is also contained in G. Theodore Mitau, *Decade of Decision* (New York, 1967).

[38] Cf. Watkins v. U.S., 354 U.S. 178 (1957) *with* Barenblatt v. U.S., 360 U.S. 109 (1959).

[39] Uphaus v. Wyman, 360 U.S. 72 (1959); Barenblatt v. U.S., 360 U.S. 109 (1959); Nelson v. Los Angeles, 362 U.S. 1 (1960); Wilkinson v. U.S., 365 U.S. 399 (1961); Braden v. U.S., 365 U.S. 431 (1961).

[40] Beilan v. Bd. of Educ., 357 U.S. 399 (1958); Lerner v. Casey, 357 U.S. 468 (1958); Konigsberg v. State Bar of Calif., 366 U.S. 36 (1961).

[41] Communist Party v. S.A.C.B., 367 U.S. 1 (1961); Scales v. U.S., 367 U.S. 203 (1961).

[42] N.A.A.C.P. v. Ala., 357 U.S. 449 (1958); Cooper v. Aaron, 358 U.S. 1 (1958); U.S. v. La., 364 U.S. 500 (1960).

[43] See Mapp v. Ohio, 367 U.S. 643 (1961).

eral replacements, White and Goldberg, in 1962. Fueled with a solid liberal majority of five Justices (the four activists of the early Warren Court plus Goldberg), enhanced from time to time with the additional votes of Stewart and White, the Court moved vigorously and consistently up until Chief Justice Warren's retirement in 1969 to restore the preferred freedoms concept as controlling doctrine. In addition to its expansive interpretations of the Bill of Rights and the due process clause of the Fourteenth Amendment, the Court bore down heavily against discrimination on political and economic fronts as well as social with its increased reliance upon the equal protection clause.

With these perspectives on constitutional development behind us, we turn now to a brief overview of the labors of the Warren Court in specific areas of constitutional rights.

### RACIAL INEQUALITY

Surely what must be regarded as the most significant decision of the Warren Court was virtually its first. When it handed down its unanimous ruling of May 1954 in the School Desegregation cases, overturning the fifty-eight year old "separate but equal" doctrine,[44] and when it ruled a year later that desegregation in public education must proceed with "all deliberate speed"[45] (regardless of the fact that it did not), the Court began to sketch out a new era for itself and for Black people to whom it remained unfailingly sympathetic. In the face of enormous community pressure applied to the Federal district judges charged with enforcement of the ruling,[46] endless attempts at avoidance, evasion, and delay via court appeals, pupil placement laws, school closings, armed resistance and terror,[47] and an explicitly stated Presidential neutrality,[48] the Court not only remained steadfast but expanded the attack on other forms of racial discrimination.

Under the equal protection clause of the Fourteenth Amendment, the Court also widened the meaning of "state action" to prohibit even the remotest support given to private discrimi-

---

[44] Brown v. Topeka, 347 U.S. 483 (1954).
[45] Brown v. Topeka, 349 U.S. 294 (1955).
[46] See Jack W. Peltason, Fifty-Eight Lonely Men (New York, 1961).
[47] For an excellent description, see Albert P. Blaustein and Clarence C. Ferguson, Desegregation and the Law (2nd ed.) (New York, 1962).
[48] Public Papers of the Presidents: Dwight D. Eisenhower, 1958 (Washington, 1959), 625.

nation by a State,[49] it struck down statutes which forbade racially mixed marriages,[50] and it invalidated the vote of a popular majority which had, through a referendum, overturned a State open housing law.[51] The Court, applying the Thirteenth Amendment, moved to outlaw *all* discrimination in the sale and rental of property—private as well as public.[52] And finally, in a not unrelated action, the Court upheld Congressional legislation designed to assure all racial groups equal access to public accommodations despite the personal view of some of the Justices that such legislation ought to have been based on the Fourteenth Amendment rather than the commerce clause.[53]

### POLITICAL DISCRIMINATION

As it fought racial inequality, so the Warren Court attacked political inequality in voting rights and legislative apportionment, and it found that the two varieties of discrimination frequently overlapped as, for example, in the case of the racially inspired gerrymander.[54] Though it had earlier acknowledged that a literacy test, like an age requirement, was not logically unrelated to the casting of an intelligent vote,[55] the Court readily sustained Congressional action eliminating it except under the closest Federal scrutiny.[56] A year before, the Court had declared invalid the invidious Constitution interpretation tests as patently vague and discriminatory.[57] The Warren Court also sought to open up the electoral process by striking down State poll tax[58] and property qualifications,[59] unreasonable residency requirements,[60] and burdensome obstacles to getting third parties on the ballot.[61]

Reversing its precedents for non-intervention in the area of

---

[49] Burton *v.* Wilmington Parking Auth., 365 U.S. 715 (1961).
[50] Loving *v.* Va., 388 U.S. 1 (1967); *see also* McLaughlin *v.* Fla., 379 U.S. 184 (1964).
[51] Reitman *v.* Mulkey, 387 U.S. 369 (1967).
[52] Jones *v.* Mayer Co., 392 U.S. 409 (1968).
[53] Heart of Atlanta Motel *v.* U.S., 379 U.S. 241 (1964); Katzenbach *v.* McClung, 379 U.S. 294 (1964).
[54] Gomillion *v.* Lightfoot, 364 U.S. 339 (1960).
[55] Lassiter *v.* Northampton County Bd. of Elections, 360 U.S. 45 (1959).
[56] South Carolina *v.* Katzenbach, 383 U.S. 301 (1966).
[57] Louisiana *v.* U.S., 380 U.S. 145 (1965).
[58] Harper *v.* Va. Bd. of Elections, 383 U.S. 663 (1966).
[59] Kraemer *v.* Union Free School Dist., 395 U.S. 621 (1969).
[60] Carrington *v.* Rash, 380 U.S. 89 (1965).
[61] Williams *v.* Rhodes, 393 U.S. 23 (1968).

legislative malapportionment, the Court, after deciding that a diluted vote constituted a justiciable cause of action under the Equal Protection Clause,[62] elevated this recognition of a political right to a constitutional command by its later ruling that only State legislative apportionments reflecting this "one man-one vote" premise were valid.[63] In subsequent decisions, the Court extended the application of this standard to the local level as well.[64] Moreover, by placing the burden on the State to demonstrate a strongly convincing countervailing interest where apportionment deviated from absolute equality,[65] the Court seemed, indeed, quite clearly to regard this as a preferred freedom.

### EQUAL PROTECTION AND THE INDIGENT

In addition to upholding the claims of Black people and city dwellers to share in those rights already possessed by society's in-groups, the Warren Court pressed hard against the kind of discrimination, especially in the criminal process, which made second-class citizens of poor people and significantly reduced their chances for justice. On the trial court level, the Warren Court moved to assure that, in all felony cases, the accused would have counsel provided for him if he could not so afford.[66] Moreover, the Court ruled that indigent defendants could not be denied the chance to appeal their cases[67] or to participate fully in post-conviction proceedings[68] because of a lack of funds to procure the necessary transcripts[69] or to hire counsel. With these rulings, the Warren Court sought to maintain for poor people that parity between the defense and the prosecution prescribed by the adversary system of criminal justice.

The Warren Court also sought to remove other kinds of discrimination visited upon the poor and socially outcast. In 1969,

---

62 Baker v. Carr, 369 U.S. 186 (1962).

63 Reynolds v. Sims, 377 U.S. 533 (1964).

64 Avery v. Midland County, 390 U.S. 474 (1968).

65 Swann v. Adams, 385 U.S. 443 (1967); Kilgarlin v. Hill, 386 U.S. 120 (1967).

66 Gideon v. Wainwright, 372 U.S. 335 (1963); Miranda v. Ariz., 384 U.S. 436 (1966).

67 Douglas v. Calif., 372 U.S. 353 (1963); Lane v. Brown, 372 U.S. 477 (1963).

68 Smith v. Bennett, 365 U.S. 708 (1961).

69 Griffin v. Ill., 351 U.S. 12 (1956); Long v. Dist. Court, 385 U.S. 192 (1966).

it struck down one-year State residency requirements for welfare aid as arbitrary and an infringement upon the right of people to travel freely unjustified by any "compelling state interest."[70] One year earlier, the Court invalidated as invidiously and irrationally discriminatory a Louisiana statute which sought to deny illegitimate children certain legal rights already shared by other children.[71]

## RESUMING NATIONALIZATION OF THE BILL OF RIGHTS

Not since 1949, when a bare majority of the Justices absorbed the Fourth Amendment's protection against unreasonable searches and seizures into the Fourteenth, had the process of incorporation advanced. In 1961, the Warren Court picked up the process exactly at the point where it had left off by reading the exclusionary rule into the Fourteenth as a necessary adjunct to those Fourth Amendment rights.[72] The theme of the incorporation process at the hands of the Warren Court rapidly became clear—the absorption of basic procedural guarantees. In quick succession, there followed the incorporation of the right against cruel and unusual punishment in the Eighth Amendment,[73] the right to counsel in the Sixth expanded to include all felonies,[74] the right against self-incrimination in the Fifth,[75] and the rights to confront witnesses[76] and to a jury trial in all criminal cases,[77] both Sixth Amendment guarantees.

These incremental advances in the nationalization of the Bill of Rights, while doubtless pleasing to Justice Black, nevertheless demonstrated the Warren Court's attachment to the preferred-freedoms concept rather than a commitment to total incorporation. What was not pleasing to Justice Black was the Court's willingness, as indicated by its handling of the 1965 Connecticut birth control case,[78] to go substantially beyond the scope and literal meaning of the first eight amendments. In that decision the Court incorporated into the Fourteenth

---

[70] Shapiro v. Thompson, 394 U.S. 618 (1969).
[71] Levy v. La., 391 U.S. (1968).
[72] Mapp v. Ohio, 367 U.S. 643 (1961).
[73] Robinson v. Calif., 370 U.S. 660 (1962).
[74] Gideon v. Wainwright, 372 U.S. 335 (1963).
[75] Malloy v. Hogan, 378 U.S. 1 (1964); Murphy v. Waterfront Comm., 378 U.S. 52 (1964).
[76] Pointer v. Tex., 380 U.S. 400 (1965).
[77] Duncan v. La., 391 U.S. 145 (1968).
[78] Griswold v. Conn., 381 U.S. 479 (1965).

Amendment a latent "right of privacy" which, it held, emanated from penumbras of the First, Third, Fourth, Fifth Amendments and the heretofore unmentioned Ninth Amendment.

### CRIMINAL PROCEDURE

In one of his dissents, Justice Robert Jackson wrote, "Let it not be over-looked that due process of law is not for the sole benefit of an accused. It is the best insurance for the Government itself against those blunders which leave lasting stains on a system of justice. . . ."[79] No court showed greater regard for this belief than did the Warren Court by its revolutionary decisions to make the routine process of criminal justice square with the Anglo-American ideal of the adversary system. Not only did the Warren Court extend the right to counsel at the courtroom level to all those individuals accused of felonies,[80] it pushed the right to counsel back into the pre-trial and investigatory stages of the process.[81] The Court acted to protect the individual under suspicion from being forced to incriminate himself also by demanding speedy arraignment[82] and by throwing out convictions based upon coerced confessions.[83] The Warren Court extended these same basic procedural safeguards to juvenile offenders[84] and, as we have noted before, assured them on an equal basis to the indigent.

The Warren Court also sought to subordinate the police bureaucracy to the rule of law in the execution of searches and seizures by interposing the courts as neutral third parties who would oversee law enforcement activities. The Court put an end to vaguely justified and overbroad "evidence hunts"[85] by narrowing the kinds of searches which could be conducted without a warrant,[86] demanding that police officers put for-

[79] Shaughnessy *v.* U.S. *ex rel.* Mezei, 345 U.S. 206, 224-225 (1953).

[80] Gideon *v.* Wainwright, 372 U.S. 335 (1963).

[81] Escobedo *v.* Ill., 378 U.S. 478 (1964); Miranda *v.* Ariz., 384 U.S. 436 (1966).

[82] Mallory *v.* U.S., 354 U.S. 449 (1957).

[83] Spano *v.* N.Y., 360 U.S. 315 (1959); Rogers *v.* Richmond, 365 U.S. 534 (1961); Lynnum *v.* Ill., 372 U.S. 528 (1963); Haynes *v.* Wash., 373 U.S. 503 (1963); Massiah *v.* U.S., 377 U.S. 201 (1964); Jackson *v.* Denno, 378 U.S. 368 (1964).

[84] *In re* Gault, 387 U.S. 1 (1967).

[85] Kremen *v.* U.S., 353 U.S. 346 (1957).

[86] *Ibid.*; Chapman *v.* U.S., 365 U.S. 610 (1961); Preston *v.* U.S., 376 U.S. 364 (1964); Camara *v.* Municipal Court, 387 U.S. 523 (1967); Sibron *v.* N.Y., 392 U.S. 40 (1968).

ward concrete and persuasive evidence of probable cause as a prerequisite to getting a warrant,[87] and limiting the scope of a search which could be conducted persuant to a warrant or in an exceptional circumstance.[88] Consistent with its preferred freedoms outlook, it invalidated evidence in several wiretapping cases for overbreadth and vagueness in the procedures authorizing such activity.[89] To enforce Fourth Amendment requirements, the Court applied the exclusionary rule both against direct infractions and against the admission of evidence obtained from a tip disclosed through a prior illegal search or coerced confession.[90] Finally, the Court expanded these Fourth and Fifth Amendment guarantees against infringement by governmental agents other than the police.[91]

## FREEDOMS OF THOUGHT, ASSOCIATION, AND EXPRESSION

During the 'sixties, the Warren Court heard renewed challenges to governmental attempts aimed at probing the beliefs and past associations of public employees. After the modifications of the Court's membership in 1962, the majority of Justices began again to assert the preferred-freedoms doctrine against vagueness and overbreadth in compulsory loyalty oaths and membership disclosures.[92] However, the radical and politically unorthodox were not the only targets of these measures; in the South, the organization of Black people was viewed likewise as subversive. There the Court moved to invalidate attempts to inhibit the functioning of the N.A.A.C.P.[93] (especially in its ability to aid Black litigants), to expose

[87] Giordenello *v.* U.S., 357 U.S. 480 (1958); Draper *v.* U.S., 358 U.S. 307 (1959); Henry *v.* U.S., 361 U.S. 98 (1959); Jones *v.* U.S., 362 U.S. 257 (1960); Aguilar *v.* Tex., 378 U.S. 108 (1964); United States *v.* Ventresca, 380 U.S. 102 (1965); Spinelli *v.* U.S., 393 U.S. 410 (1969).

[88] Kremen *v.* U.S., 353 U.S. 346 (1957); Schmerber *v.* Calif., 384 U.S. 57 (1966); Warden *v.* Hayden, 387 U.S. 294 (1967); Chimel *v.* Calif., 395 U.S. 752 (1969).

[89] Berger *v.* N.Y., 388 U.S. 41 (1967); Katz *v.* U.S., 389 U.S. 347 (1967).

[90] Wong Sun *v.* U.S., 371 U.S. 471 (1963); Miranda *v.* Ariz., 384 U.S. 436 (1966).

[91] Camara *v.* Municipal Court, 387 U.S. 523 (1967); See *v.* Seattle, 387 U.S. 541 (1967).

[92] Cramp *v.* Bd. of Public Instruction, 368 U.S. 278 (1961); Baggett *v.* Bullitt, 377 U.S. 360 (1964); Elfbrandt *v.* Russell, 384 U.S. 11 (1966); Keyishian *v.* Bd. of Regents, 385 U.S. 589 (1967).

[93] N.A.A.C.P. *v.* Ala., 357 U.S. 449 (1958); N.A.A.C.P. *v.* Button, 371 U.S. 415 (1963).

its members,[94] and to deny them opportunity for public employment.[95]

For the first time in American history, the Supreme Court declared unconstitutional legislation passed by Congress which infringed a First Amendment freedom by its holding in a 1965 case[96] which invalidated a Federal statute requiring the Post Office Department to detain and destroy Communist propaganda unless the recipient to whom it was addressed filled out a form declaring that he wanted to receive such materials. Speaking for the majority, Justice Douglas concluded that the statute was clearly unconstitutional because it placed the burden on the wrong party. The following year, the Court invalidated an action of the Georgia House of Representatives excluding Julian Bond, one of its duly elected members, where the legislators concluded that his anti-war and anti-draft sentiments made it impossible, in their judgment, for him conscientiously to swear to support the Constitution.[97] In 1969, the Warren Court struck down the Ohio Criminal Syndicalism statute on the ground that it infringed the First Amendment by punishing mere speech because it failed to distinguish specifically between action and expression.[98]

Finally, the later Warren Court was confronted with cases, chiefly involving Black people and people disenchanted with the Vietnam war, raising issues of constitutionality in the emerging forms of public protest. In the case of mass demonstrations, the Court decided that the right to public expression did not prevail unfettered everywhere. The right to petition the Government, while in a preferred position, nevertheless had to be carefully weighed against competing interests of preserving public order and considered in the light of the protestors' right to be in a given place. By very narrow votes, the Court distinguished the legitimacy of demonstrating at a State capitol,[99] in the streets,[100] or sitting-in at a lunch counter[101]

---

[94] N.A.A.C.P. *v.* Ala., 357 U.S. 449 (1958); Bates *v.* Little Rock, 361 U.S. 516 (1960); Gibson *v.* Fla. Leg. Inv. Comm., 372 U.S. 539 (1963).

[95] Shelton *v.* Tucker, 364 U.S. 479 (1960).

[96] Lamont *v.* Postmaster Gen., 381 U.S. 301 (1965).

[97] Bond *v.* Floyd, 385 U.S. 116 (1966).

[98] Brandenburg *v.* Ohio, 395 U.S. 444 (1969).

[99] Edwards *v.* S.C., 372 U.S. 229 (1963).

[100] Cox *v.* La., 379 U.S. 559 (1965).

[101] Peterson *v.* Greenville, 373 U.S. 244 (1963); Lombard *v.* La., 373 U.S. 267 (1963); *see also* Robinson *v.* Fla., 378 U.S. 153 (1964).

from assembling outside a courthouse, a jail,[102] or in a library.[103] Moreover, while the Court was quick to strike down a municipal parade ordinance because of its vague licensing guidelines,[104] the majority of Justices made it equally clear that they would not tolerate having the right to speak determined in the streets by the willful violation of injunctions even if those court orders were later overturned.[105] On the matter of symbolic speech, the Court sought to determine, in acts of draft card[106] and flag[107] burning, where speech and action became so thoroughly intertwined that symbolic speech might be regulated. It did so with mixed results. The Court, however, had less difficulty in upholding the First Amendment rights of three high and and junior high school students to express their opposition to the Vietnam war by wearing black arm bands to school.[108]

## FREEDOM OF THE PRESS

The Warren Court's treatment of constitutional issues bearing upon freedom of the press reflected overall a similar commitment to basic libertarian values. While a majority of the Justices was not prepared to categorically reject the constitutionality of all censorship,[109] the Court did indicate that any system of prior restraint would come to the Court bearing a heavy presumption of invalidity.[110] Indeed, the Warren Court upheld censorship only where consideration of allegedly offensive material was prompt and under circumstances which afforded full play to procedural safeguards.[111]

The Court, by contrast, had considerably greater difficulty defining what it was that the State and national governments had the right to censor. Obscenity proved a very elusive concept for the Court largely because the Court failed to offer

[102] Adderley *v.* Fla., 385 U.S. 39 (1966).
[103] Brown *v.* La., 383 U.S. 131 (1966).
[104] Shuttlesworth *v.* Birmingham, 394 U.S. 147 (1969).
[105] Walker *v.* Birmingham, 388 U.S. 307 (1967).
[106] United States *v.* O'Brien, 391 U.S. 367 (1968).
[107] Street *v.* N.Y., 394 U.S. 576 (1969).
[108] Tinker *v.* Des Moines Ind. Community School Dist., 393 U.S. 503 (1969).
[109] Times Film Corp. *v.* Chicago, 365 U.S. 43 (1961).
[110] Bantam Books, Inc. *v.* Sullivan, 372 U.S. 58 (1963).
[111] *Cf.* Kingsley Books *v.* Brown, 354 U.S. 436 (1957) *with* Freedman *v.* Md., 380 U.S. 51 (1965).

any justification for its suppression (and thus provided no foundation for the standards it enunciated) beyond its superficial conclusion that obscenity is not protected by the First Amendment because, unlike speech, it is without redeeming social importance.[112] The Justices incrementally developed a tripartite standard[113] based upon what they discerned as the elements common to all types of obscenity, an approach which produced the conclusion that the Court, in effect, sought to proscribe only "hard-core pornography."[114] Because of its serious shortcomings, however, this initial tack was modified in favor of a variable approach.[115] Though the Court retained the standards which had evolved, it significantly modified their application by hinging its judgment on two contextual factors: the primary audience to whom the material was directed[116] and the nature of the appeal made to that audience.[117] The Court thus came around to the view, articulated earlier by Chief Justice Warren,[118] that obscenity is a relative concept.

Consistent with its general application of the preferred freedoms doctrine to open up discussion in the political system, the Warren Court sought to reduce the chilling effects of State libel laws. It acted initially to broaden what might be considered "fair comment" about a public official by insisting that awards for damage to his reputation be predicated on more than a showing of factual inaccuracy in the statements made. Statutes allowing such compensation would be sustained only if a false statement were made with " 'actual malice'—that is, with knowledge that it was false or with reckless disregard of whether it was false or not."[119] In addition, the Court expanded press immunity in this area by enlarging the concept of public official to include "public figures" who were "involved in issues

112 Roth *v.* U.S., 354 U.S. 476, 484 (1957).

113 Roth *v.* U.S., 354 U.S. 476 (1957); Manual Ent. *v.* Day, 370 U.S. 478 (1962); Jacobellis *v.* Ohio, 378 U.S. 184 (1964); Memoirs *v.* Atty. Gen., 383 U.S. 413 (1966).

114 William B. Lockhart and Robert C. McClure, "Censorship of Obscenity: The Developing Constitutional Standards," 45 *Minnesota Law Review* 5, 58-68 (1960).

115 For the authoritative discussion of the concepts of "constant" and "variable" obscenity, *see ibid.* at 68 *et seq.*

116 Mishkin *v.* N.Y., 383 U.S. 502 (1966); Ginsberg *v.* N.Y., 390 U.S. 629 (1968).

117 Ginzburg *v.* U.S., 383 U.S. 563 (1966).

118 Roth *v.* U.S., 354 U.S. 476, 495-496 (1957).

119 New York Times Co. *v.* Sullivan, 376 U.S. 254 (1964).

in which the public has a justified and important interest."[120] Aside from the vagueness inherent in these terms, the Court's expansive holding created severe conflict with the correlative right to privacy.[121]

The Warren Court, on the other hand, was markedly less enthusiastic about the robust exercise of First Amendment rights when they conflicted with rights guaranteed in the Sixth Amendment and imperiled the prospect of a fair trail. The Court overturned convictions of defendants in three cases involving extensive pre-trial publicity and interviews.[122] In one of those cases, the press and media coverage assumed such gigantic proportions that the trial itself was characterized by Justice Clark as having a "carnival atmosphere."[123] In reviewing the trial of Billie Sol Estes, a majority of the Justices indicated that they took a very dim view of televised proceedings.[124] Situations like these, in which constitutional rights directly conflicted with one another, made the real-world application of Justice Black's absolutism difficult indeed.

## FREEDOM OF RELIGION

The necessity of resolving similar collisions in constitutional rights marked the Warren Court's decisions on religious freedom. In cases involving interpretation of the establishment clause, the problem was one of steering a middle course, neither denying a legitimate opportunity for the practice of a religious belief on the one hand nor establishing a religion on the other. Thus the Court struck down Bible-reading[125] and the recitation of a State-written prayer[126] in the public schools, even on a voluntary basis, but upheld, with qualifications, State aid to religious schools.[127] The Court also upheld Sunday Closing laws,[128] but only on utilitarian grounds.

[120] Curtis Pub. Co. *v.* Butts, 388 U.S. 130, 134 (1967); *see also* Associated Press *v.* Walker, considered together with the Curtis Publishing case; Rosenblatt *v.* Baer, 383 U.S. 75 (1966); Time, Inc. *v.* Hill, 385 U.S. 374 (1967); Pickering *v.* Bd. of Educ., 391 U.S. 563 (1968).
[121] Time, Inc. *v.* Hill, 385 U.S. 374 (1967).
[122] Irvin *v.* Dowd, 366 U.S. 717 (1961); Rideau *v.* La., 373 U.S. 723 (1963); Sheppard *v.* Maxwell, 384 U.S. 333 (1966).
[123] Sheppard *v.* Maxwell, 384 U.S. 333 (1966).
[124] Estes *v.* Tex., 381 U.S. 532 (1965).
[125] Abington School Dist. *v.* Schempp, 374 U.S. 203 (1963).
[126] Engel *v.* Vitale, 370 U.S. 421 (1962).
[127] Board of Education *v.* Allen, 392 U.S. 236 (1968).
[128] McGowan *v.* Md., 366 U.S. 420 (1961).

The Court was confronted with a second dilemma in the application of the free exercise clause when the unfettered practice of one's religious beliefs collided with the concept of equal protection. Adhering to the preferred-freedoms concept that favored vindicating the rights of religious dissenters and non-conformists, the Court struck down a provision of the Maryland constitution requiring the declaration of a belief in God as a prerequisite to holding public office,[129] and held that South Carolina could not deny unemployment benefits to a Seventh Day Adventist who had refused a job offer because of her religious belief against working on Saturday.[130] The Court also widened the rights of religious dissenters and non-conformists by its 1965 holding that one need not believe in a Supreme Being to be eligible for conscientious objector status, but only that the belief be meaningful and sincere and that it occupy a position in the life of the draft registrant parallel to that of the more orthodox conception.[131] Finally, while the Court sustained a Pennsylvania Sunday Closing law which, in effect, forced an Orthodox Jew to choose between his religion and his livelihood, it made clear its holding that the statute was upheld only because the State had, again consistent with the preferred freedoms doctrine, demonstrated a compelling interest which outweighed the First Amendment infringement.[132]

## THE END OF THE WARREN COURT

The depth of the Warren Court's impact upon civil liberties in the American system will, most probably, be without parallel. The measure of a revolution, however, is not only in its depth but also in its permanence.

In the spring of 1968, the struggle to maintain the activism of the Warren Court began. Liberals were heartened by the early initiative of the Chief Justice, then 77, who announced his retirement effective upon the appointment of a successor. President Johnson, moving quickly with an eye toward maintaining a solid liberal majority on the Court, nominated Justice Fortas to succeed Warren and U.S. District Judge Homer Thornberry of Texas to fill Fortas's old seat. A Senate coalition

---

129 Torcaso *v.* Watkins, 367 U.S. 488 (1961).
130 Sherbert *v.* Verner, 374 U.S. 398 (1963).
131 United States *v.* Seeger, 380 U.S. 163 (1965).
132 Braunfeld *v.* Brown, 366 U.S. 599 (1961).

of Republicans and Southern Democrats frustrated this attempt. Refusing to acquiesce in such swift confirmations only months before a new President would be chosen, many of the conservatives claimed that no vacancy on the bench existed because no one could "conditionally resign" from any office. These opponents of the Warren Court were successful not only in stalling the nominations and skillfully using the nomination hearings as forums from which to criticize the Court's activism, but also to deliver a stunning counterblow to the liberals by revealing through investigations that Justice Fortas, while on the bench, had maintained involvement with a Las Vegas enterprise which allegedly had connections with the underworld. Fortas resigned subsequently.[133]

As the "law and order" tone of the 1968 Presidential campaign became increasingly shrill, the work of the Warren Court came under repeated attack, especially by those candidates who counted on a large share of the vote contributed by "Middle America"—that broad segment of average men and women—unblack, unpoor, and unyoung. Harassed by minority and youth protest, bewildered by assassinations, frustrated by an aimless war, victimized by mounting crime, and threatened by wide-spread rioting, the average American thought society was coming apart at its seams and he felt powerless to do anything about it.[134] Where the Court had pursued increased tolerance, the advocates of sterner stuff saw increasing permissiveness, and the Court, in their view, was partly to blame for it. Richard Nixon, first as candidate, then as President, verbalized the dissatisfaction: "As a judicial conservative, I believe some Court decisions have gone too far in weakening the peace forces as against the criminal forces in our society."[135] The decisions he criticized most dealt with criminal procedure,[136] specifically Escobedo v. Illinois[137] and Miranda v. Arizona,[138] but he also attacked other judicial actions, notably the use of busing to achieve racial desegregation of the schools.[139] He promised that his appointments to the

---

[133] See Robert Shogan, A Question of Judgment: The Fortas Case and the Struggle for the Supreme Court (Indianapolis, 1972).
[134] See Theodore H. White, The Making of the President 1968 (New York, 1969).
[135] New York Times, Oct. 22, 1971.
[136] 1968 Congressional Quarterly Weekly Report, 2159-2160.
[137] 378 U.S. 478 (1964).        [138] 384 U.S. 436 (1966).
[139] 1968 Congressional Quarterly Weekly Report, 2160.

Court would be different. "As far as judicial philosophy is concerned, it is my belief that it is the duty of a judge to interpret the Constitution, and not to place himself above the Constitution or outside the Constitution. He should not twist or bend the Constitution in order to perpetuate his personal, political and social views."[140]

### THE EMERGENCE OF THE BURGER COURT

Redeeming his pledge "to nominate to the Supreme Court individuals who share my judicial philosophy which is basically a conservative philosophy,"[141] President Nixon had a greater opportunity to redesign the Court in his first term than any Chief Executive since Warren Harding. New faces appeared on the bench with each succeeding term of the Court: Warren Burger replaced the out-going Chief Justice in June 1969; Harry Blackmun, the President's third nominee to fill the still-vacant Fortas seat was sworn in during June 1970, after Senate liberals had twice defeated attempts to name Southern judges Clement Haynsworth and G. Harrold Carswell to the bench;[142] Lewis Powell and William Rehnquist were seated in January 1972, to replace Justices Black and Harlan, who retired the previous fall. The solid liberal majority was gone.

By the midpoint of its October 1971 term, the Court appeared divided into three blocs—a configuration that bore an uncanny resemblance to the Hughes Court, which generated the Constitutional Revolution of 1937.[143] There was a conservative bloc composed of the four Nixon appointees; a liberal bloc comprised Justices Douglas, Brennan, and Marshall, the three remaining stalwarts of the Warren Court's activism; and a center bloc of Justices Stewart and White. As the Nixon appointees appeared, power on the bench gravitated to the center. The fate of the Warren Court's work lay increasingly in the hands of the two men who, in the past, had been only its ambivalent supporters.

### PRUDENCE, PRAGMATISM, AND CAUTIOUS ADVANCE

If the Burger Court, in its first three terms, seemed less visibly wedded to the ideology of preferred freedoms than its

---

[140] *New York Times*, Oct. 22, 1971.    [141] *Ibid.*
[142] *See* Richard Harris, *Decision* (New York, 1971).
[143] *See* Glendon Schubert, *Quantitative Analysis of Judicial Behavior* (Glencoe, Ill., 1959), pp. 192-210.

predecessor, it by no means followed that it was willing to repudiate those values. Indeed, underneath all the rhetoric of modification and tinkering, not only did the nightmares of some liberals fail to materialize—that the Burger Court would somehow turn the clock back—but the Burger Court, on balance, wound up expanding upon the work of the Warren Court. To be sure one could find instances where the Burger Court had clipped and pruned Warren Court policies, notably in criminal procedure, and one could find cases, particularly in race relations, in which the advance was probably not what it would have been had the Warren Court decided them, but it was more true that the Burger Court handed down some shattering new precedents—things one would have thought the Warren Court more capable of doing—and that it maintained as well, in most of the routine cases, some sense of progress and advance in the application of liberal values. If Justices Stewart and White had viewed the galloping liberalism of the Warren Court with a wary eye, they seemed much more wary of quickly abandoning it.

### THE BURGER COURT AND RACE RELATIONS

Although the Burger Court has, at times, been soft around the edges of racial equality, particularly in assuring Black people service from public[144] and private[145] facilities, the Court has resolutely set itself against discrimination in jury selection,[146] toward applying the Thirteenth Amendment to private conspiracies to deprive Black people of their civil liberties,[147] and, most of all, to ending school segregation. Like its predecessor, the Burger Court's initial decision on school desegregation came early, unanimously, and aggressively. The Court demanded immediate compliance with the decision in *Brown*,[148] and, two years later, positively endorsed busing[149] and the redrawing of school attendance zones[150] as means to

[144] *See* Evans *v.* Abney, 396 U.S. 435 (1970); and Palmer *v.* Thompson, 403 U.S. 217 (1971).

[145] *See* Moose Lodge No. 107 *v.* Irvis, 407 U.S. 163 (1972).

[146] Alexander *v.* La., 405 U.S. 625 (1972); Peters *v.* Kiff, 407 U.S. 493 (1972).

[147] Griffin *v.* Breckenridge, 403 U.S. 88 (1971).

[148] Alexander *v.* Holmes County Bd. of Educ., 396 U.S. 19 (1969).

[149] North Carolina State Board of Education *v.* Swann, 402 U.S. 43 (1971); Davis *v.* Bd. of School Com'rs. of Mobile County, 402 U.S. 33 (1971).

[150] Swann *v.* Charlotte-Mecklenburg Bd. of Educ., 402 U.S. 1 (1971); McDaniel *v.* Barresi, 402 U.S. 39 (1971); Davis *v.* Bd. of School Com'rs. of Mobile County, 402 U.S. 33 (1971).

achieve the goal of racial desegration. During the third term of the Burger Court, however, the unanimity of determination with which the Court had traditionally met the problem of dual systems of education disappeared, though a majority of the Justices stood their ground in striking down State-sanctioned and locally constructed obstacles to desegregation.[151] The attempt to turn the clock back has come from President Nixon, not the Burger Court. In a message to the Congress that smacked of the old and discredited "separate but equal" doctrine, the President asked Congress to enact legislation which would severely limit if not preclude Court-ordered busing to achieve racial balance. As part of the package, more funds would be appropriated to up-grade poorer, inner-city schools.[152] When Congress replied by passing compromise legislation putting a temporary moratorium on busing and increasing substantially educational appropriations,[153] the President responded by saying that the anti-busing provisions were inadequate and that he would seek stiffer and more specific legislation, perhaps a constitutional amendment.[154]

### THE BURGER COURT ON CRIMINAL PROCEDURE

The most salient issue on which the Nixon appointees and the remaining members of the Warren Court were expected to disagree was that of criminal procedure, the largest area of the Court's business. The Burger Court thus far, however, has remained attached overall to the work of the Warren Court— a natural consequence of the new Court's tendency to dispose of cases with closer attention to their specific factual conditions than enthusiasm for generating broad new rules. In search and seizure cases (*see* pp. 301-309), the Court has stuck closely to the facts, departing only rarely to endorse stern general rules as, for example, its holding that domestic political surveillance still demanded a warrant.[155]

On another matter of criminal procedure, the expansion of

---

[151] Wright *v.* Council of the City of Emporia, 407 U.S. 451 (1972); United States *v.* Scotland Neck City Bd. of Educ., 407 U.S. 484 (1972).

[152] 1962 *Congressional Quarterly Weekly Report*, 642-648.

[153] The compromise legislation was contained in amendments to the 1972 Higher Education Bill, which subsequently became Public Law 92-318.

[154] *New York Times*, June 24, 1972; 1972 *Congressional Quarterly Weekly Report*, 1584-1585.

[155] United States *v.* U. S. Dist. Court, East. Mich., 407 U.S. 297 (1972).

the privilege against self-incrimination was brought to a halt around its fringes, notably in cases involving alleged pressures impinging on the defendant in plea-bargaining[156] and under the self-report obligations of auto hit-and-run statutes.[157] The Burger Court also closed many of the doors which *Miranda* had left open *(see* pp. 355-356), but the Court made no attempt to overturn that decision.

While the outlook of the Burger Court on issues of criminal justice has been more conservative than that of its predecessor, it has been only moderately so and inconstant even then. Using a balancing approach strikingly akin to that associated with Frankfurter, the Burger Court has pragmatically endeavored to make both the punishment and the procedure[158] fit the crime. The Court continues to pick and choose the rights applicable to juvenile defendants.[159] In a decision which one might have thought more characteristic of the Warren Court, the Burger Court expanded the right of counsel to defendants in all criminal cases involving the prospect of a jail term.[160] The Court upheld granting only limited immunity to a witness who was compelled to give testimony,[161] and ruled that guilty verdicts in non-capital cases might be returned with less than unanimity if a given State so chose to allow.[162] The Court then turned around and, after three years of toying with the notion,[163] declared by the tender margin of 5-4 that unqualified imposition of the death penalty violated the Eighth Amendment's prohibition on cruel and unusual punishment.[164] In sum, one might say that the Burger Court has brought the momentum of the Warren Court to a halt at least in criminal procedure cases. It has not undone the work of the Warren Court, but it has moved toward retrenchment.

[156] Brady *v.* U.S., 397 U.S. 742 (1970); Parker *v.* N.C., 397 U.S. 790 (1970).
[157] California *v.* Byers, 402 U.S. 424 (1971).
[158] *See* e.g., Baldwin *v.* N.Y., 399 U.S. 66 (1970).
[159] *In re* Winship, 397 U.S. 358 (1970); McKeiver *v.* Pa., 403 U.S. 528 (1971).
[160] Argersinger *v.* Hamlin, 407 U.S. 25 (1972).
[161] Kastigar *v.* U.S., 406 U.S. 441 (1972); Zicarelli *v.* N.J. State Com'n of Investig., 407 U.S. 472 (1972).
[162] Johnson *v.* La., 406 U.S. 356 (1972); Apodaca *v.* Ore., 406 U.S. 404 (1972).
[163] *See* Maxwell *v.* Bishop, 398 U.S. 262 (1970); and McGautha *v.* Calif., 402 U.S. 183 (1971).
[164] Furman *v.* Ga., 408 U.S. 238 (1972).

EQUAL PROTECTION AND THE BURGER COURT

The Burger Court's performance, on the other hand, seemed virtually indistinguishable from what one might have expected of the Warren Court in cases involving political equality and the opening up of the electoral process. The Burger court pursued with equal fervor the continued expansion of the "one man-one vote" doctrine, but sometimes diluted its application.[165] It struck down prohibitive filing fees as a prerequisite to candidate participation in a primary election[166] and invalidated unjustifiably restrictive residency requirements imposed by States as a requirement to vote.[167] The effect of an additional action by the Court upholding the eighteen-year-old vote in National but denying it in State and local elections[168] was subsequently overturned by the adoption of the Twenty-Sixth Amendment.

In the social and economic sphere, the Burger Court proceeded, if sometimes haltingly, to expand the scope of equal rights. The Court sporadically continued to strike out at irrational and highly punitive State laws, principally Louisiana's, which deprived illegitimate children of certain legal rights.[169] The Court struck down an Idaho statute which preferred men over women in the appointment of executors for the administration of estates.[170] It also invalidated the use of standardized intelligence tests and seemingly high educational requirements not directly pertinent in the hiring of an individual for a given job because such standards unduly and unjustifiably discriminated against Black applicants.[171]

Less successful were the poor. The Court did move to eradicate discriminatory practices of State criminal law which made a convicted person's freedom largely dependent on his ability to bear the cost of a fine,[172] and assured to the indigent the provision of a free transcript for the appeal of trial court

165 Hadley *v.* Jr. College Dist., 397 U.S. 50 (1970); Phoenix *v.* Kolodziejski, 399 U.S. 204 (1970); *but cf.* Abate *v.* Mundt, 403 U.S. 182 (1971).
166 Bullock *v.* Carter, 405 U.S. 134 (1972).
167 Dunn *v.* Blumstein, 405 U.S. 330 (1972).
168 Oregon *v.* Mitchell, 400 U.S. 112 (1970).
169 Weber *v.* Aetna Cas. & Sur. Co., 406 U.S. 164 (1972); *but cf.* Labine *v.* Vincent, 401 U.S. 532 (1971).
170 Reed *v.* Reed, 404 U.S. 71 (1972).
171 Griggs *v.* Duke Power Co., 401 U.S. 424 (1971).
172 Williams *v.* Ill., 399 U.S. 235 (1970); Tate *v.* Short, 401 U.S. 395 (1971).

decisions even in non-felony cases.[173] Yet the Burger Court ruled against the interests of the poor in at least three significant instances. The Court delivered a blow to the cause of low-income public housing by upholding a California law which provided that such housing receive majority approval by the voters before construction could begin in any community.[174] The Court also ruled that tenants could not withhold their rent while the alleged negligence of their landlord was being litigated.[175] Finally, the Court refused to invalidate the notorious "midnight visits" by social workers to the homes of welfare mothers to determine if there was a man in the house.[176] The Court, however, did overturn State legislation which discriminated against aliens in determining welfare eligibility.[177]

## THE BURGER COURT AND FIRST AMENDMENT FREEDOMS

Unlike the area of criminal procedure where the Burger Court has most notably endeavored to distinguish present cases from Warren Court precedents so as to work modifications at the margins of constitutional policy, the Burger Court has been more loyal to the application of the preferred freedoms concept in the interpretation of First Amendment rights. It has consistently upheld the rights of anti-war protestors to peacefully and publicly assemble,[178] to distribute literature advancing their cause,[179] and to enunciate their opposition to established policy in a most uninhibited manner.[180] Despite the degree to which some segments of the public have occasionally felt offended at the forcefulness of such expression, the Burger Court has held that regulation can be permitted only with the most specific and stringent safeguards—mere offensiveness is not the test; expression must be truly tantamount to using "fighting words."[181] The Court, however, has limited the applicability of these rights to public places—private property is not a public forum.[182] The Court has also

[173] Mayer v. Chicago, 404 U.S. 189 (1972).
[174] James v. Valtierra, 402 U.S. 137 (1971).
[175] Lindsey v. Normet, 405 U.S. 56 (1972).
[176] Wyman v. James, 400 U.S. 309 (1971).
[177] Graham v. Richardson, 403 U.S. 365 (1971).
[178] Coates v. Cinn., 402 U.S. 611 (1971).
[179] Flower v. U.S., 407 U.S. 197 (1972).
[180] Cohen v. Calif., 403 U.S. 15 (1971).
[181] Gooding v. Wilson, 405 U.S. 518 (1972).
[182] Lloyd Corp., Ltd. v. Tanner, 407 U.S. 551 (1972); Central Hardware Co. v. N.L.R.B., 407 U.S. 539 (1972).

swept away any sanction of constitutionality from the vague and overbroad provisions of archaic vagrancy statutes[183] and anti-picketing ordinances.[184] Finally, while the Court has validated some loyalty oaths, it has demanded, consistent with the tenets of preferred freedoms, that such oaths be specific in their referents[185] and that they be divorced entirely from attempts to ferret out the past political associations and the perhaps unorthodox beliefs of their signatories.[186]

In matters of freedom of the press, the Burger Court has been marginally more conservative than that of its predecessor. Reiterating a stern libertarian position against prior restraint, the Court upheld newspaper publication of the celebrated "Pentagon Papers," a collection of stolen, once-secret memoranda of the executive branch tracing the development of American involvement in the Vietnam conflict.[187] The Burger Court also continued to push back the preserve of protected private interests guarded by State libel laws by enlarging still further the degree of fair comment about private persons allowed through the media.[188] On the other hand, the Court narrowed press freedoms with its holding that the First Amendment does not protect a newspaper reporter's sources where they might furnish relevant information in a grand jury investigation.[189] Finally, in an area which received a great deal less notoriety from the Burger Court than it got from the Warren Court, the Justices turned their attention from attempts to describe the content of material or the behavior of the defendant as relevant factors in defining obscenity to those of delimiting constitutionally protected versus non-protected areas where one might view allegedly objectionable materials. The Court upheld the sanctity of viewing materials in the home, but was quick to point out that some degree of government regulation was justified in public.[190] The Court also sought to protect the interests of the unwilling recipient of

183 Papachristou *v*. Jacksonville, 405 U.S. 156 (1972); *see also* Palmer *v*. City of Euclid, 402 U.S. 544 (1971).
184 Chicago Police Dept. *v*. Mosley, 408 U.S. 92 (1972).
185 Law Students Civil Rights Research Council *v*. Wadmond, 401 U.S. 154 (1971); Cole *v*. Richardson, 405 U.S. 676 (1972).
186 Baird *v*. State Bar of Ariz., 401 U.S. 1 (1971); Connell *v*. Higginbotham, 403 U.S. 207 (1971).
187 New York Times Co. *v*. U.S., 403 U.S. 713 (1971).
188 Rosenbloom *v*. Metromedia, Inc., 403 U.S. 29 (1971).
189 Branzburg *v*. Hayes, 408 U.S. 665 (1972).
190 United States *v*. Reidel, 402 U.S. 363 (1971); Rabe *v*. Wash., 405 U.S. 313 (1972).

provocative material by upholding Federal legislation designed to prevent subsequent deliveries of such material as well as so-called "junk mail" if the intended recipient complained.[191]

### THE BURGER COURT ON CHURCH AND STATE

Matters involving religion are separated in this overview from the Burger Court's treatment of other First Amendment freedoms because of the Court's very different approach to them. Although it is undeniably true that the Court has continued to defend the right of individuals with strict moral scruples from being entirely socialized by the State's educational process[192] or from being compelled to serve in the military where one is opposed to what the State is doing in principle not in instance,[193] the Court has clearly set itself in the direction of much closer relations between church and state, especially where the State is acting to aid a religious institution. In his opinion for the Court, upholding the tax-exempt status of religious institutions, Chief Justice Burger characterized this new policy as one of "a benevolent neutrality."[194] Decrying "the considerable internal inconsistency in the opinions of the Court"[195] in the past, which resulted from "what . . . may have been too sweeping utterances on aspects of these [Free-Exercise and Establishment] clauses that seemed clear in relation to the particular cases but have limited meaning as general principles,"[196] Burger has appealed to the Court to take a more pragmatic balancing approach. It has followed this exhortation to a more case-by-case tack with confusing and mixed results. With rationales that may seem dubious in the distinctions they draw,[197] the Burger Court, in three 1971 cases, simultaneously voided Pennsylvania and Rhode Island laws providing financial support for the teaching of secular subjects in parochial schools at the primary and secondary level[198] and sustained construction grants to four Roman Catholic institutions of higher learning under the Higher Edu-

[191] Rowan v. U.S. Post Off. Dept., 397 U.S. 728 (1970).
[192] Wisconsin v. Yoder, 406 U.S. 205 (1972).
[193] Gillette v. U.S., 401 U.S. 437 (1971); *see also* Welsh v. U.S., 398 U.S. 333 (1970).
[194] Walz v. Tax Comm., 397 U.S. 664, 669 (1970).
[195] *Ibid.*, 668.     [196] *Ibid.*
[197] *See* Donald A. Giannella, "Lemon and Tilton: The Bitter and the Sweet of Church-State Entanglement," 1971 *Supreme Court Review* 147.
[198] Lemon v. Kurtzman, 403 U.S. 602 (1971).

cation Facilities Act.[199] It is difficult to tell if more fluid balancing will provide the doctrinal remedy the Chief Justice suggests, but it clearly greases the skids for greater potential government support of religious institutions. Whether this becomes "excessive entanglement"[200] will, most probably, depend upon the future composition of the Court. This point, however, is clear: the Burger Court looks upon the Warren Court precedent first sustaining educational aid to religious schools[201] as an invitation to cooperation and not a breach in the wall that was intended to separate church and state.

### THE BURGER COURT AND THE FUTURE

Despite the seating of the four Nixon appointees in three years, the Burger Court has not yet become the Nixon Court. Just as one Presidential election did not undo the conservatives' grip on the old Court of the 'thirties, neither has one Presidential election undone the work of the Warren Court. In one respect, then, that time lag which is part and parcel of the judicial institution seems to smile with equal favor on both liberals and conservatives. Whatever will be the legacy of the Warren Court, it is too soon to tell; the outcome of the 1972 election likely furnishes a clue. But even if the second constitutional revolution should survive intact, the central dilemmas confronting the guarantee of civil liberties will be only a little abated. For the next great libertarian Court will have to confront—and with some urgency—the real puzzle only uncovered by the contributions of the Warren Court: reconciling the freedoms contained in the amendments, not with the demands of governmental power, but with the conflicting demands of each other.[202]

---

[199] Tilton v. Richardson, 403 U.S. 672 (1971).

[200] The Court suggested this as the applicable standard in Walz v. Tax Comm., 397 U.S. 664 (1970).

[201] Board of Education v. Allen, 392 U.S. 236 (1968).

[202] While the provisions of the amendments contain many conflicting guarantees (such as that, for example, between fair trial and free press), it is likely that the most severe conflict will come in the collision of these guarantees with the Court's self-generated "right of privacy." For articulations of that general right, see Griswold v. Conn., 381 U.S. 479 (1965); and Eisenstadt v. Baird, 405 U.S. 438 (1972).

# AMENDMENT I

Congress shall make no law respecting an establishment of religion, or prohibiting the free exercise thereof; or abridging the freedom of speech or of the press; or the right of the people peaceably to assemble, and to petition the government for a redress of grievances.

In the case of Gitlow *v.* New York, decided in 1925,[1] the Court, while affirming a conviction for violation of a State statute prohibiting the advocacy of criminal anarchy, declared: "For present purposes we may and do assume that freedom of speech and of the press—which are protected by the First Amendment from abridgment by Congress—are among the fundamental personal rights and 'liberties' protected by the due process clause of the Fourteenth Amendment from impairment by the States."[2] This dictum became, two years later, accepted doctrine when the Court invalidated a State law on the ground that it abridged freedom of speech contrary to the "due process clause" of Amendment XIV.[3] Subsequent decisions have brought the other rights safeguarded by the First Amendment—freedom of religion,[4] freedom of the press,[5] and the right of peaceable assembly[6]—within the protection of the Fourteenth. (*See* pp. 391-399.) In consequence of this development, cases dealing with the safeguarding of these rights against infringement by the States are included in the ensuing discussion of the First Amendment.

*Extension of the "Freedoms" of Amendment I to the States*

"An establishment of religion": Two theories regarding the meaning and intention of this clause have confronted each other in decisions of the Court. According to one, what the clause bans is the *preferential* treatment of any particular religion or sect by government in the United States. This theory has the support of Story, except for the fact that he regarded Congress as still free to prefer the Christian religion over other religions.[7] It is also supported by Cooley in his *Principles of Constitutional Law*, where it is said that the clause forbids "the setting up or recognition of a state church, or at least the

*Two Views of "Establishment of Religion"*

---

[1] 268 U.S. 652 (1925).    [2] *Ibid.*, 666.
[3] Fiske v. Kan., 274 U.S. 380 (1927).
[4] Cantwell v. Conn., 310 U.S. 296 (1940).
[5] Near v. Minn., 283 U.S. 697 (1931).
[6] DeJonge v. Ore., 299 U.S. 353 (1937).
[7] Joseph Story, *Commentaries on the Constitution*, II (Cambridge, Mass. 1833) §§ 1870-1879.

conferring upon one church of special favors and advantages which are denied to others."[8] This conception of the clause is, moreover, foreshadowed in the Northwest Ordinance of 1787, the third article of which reads: "Religion, morality, and knowledge being necessary to good government and the happiness of mankind, schools and the means of education shall forever be encouraged."[9] In short, religion as such is not excluded from the legitimate concerns of government, but quite the contrary.

The other theory was first voiced by Jefferson in a letter which he wrote a group of Baptists in Danbury, Connecticut, in 1802. Here it is asserted that it was the purpose of the First Amendment to build "a wall of separation between Church and State."[10] Seventy-seven years later Chief Justice Waite, in speaking for the unanimous Court in the first Mormon Church case, in which the right of Congress to forbid polygamy in the territories was sustained, characterized this statement by Jefferson as "almost an authoritative declaration of the scope and effect of the amendment."[11]

In the first of a series of recent cases, a sharply divided Court, speaking by Justice Black, sustained, in 1947, the right of local authorities in New Jersey to provide free transportation for children attending parochial schools,[12] but accompanied its holding with these warning words, which appear to have had, at that time, the approval of most of the Justices: "The 'establishment of religion' clause of the First Amendment means at least this: Neither a state nor the Federal Government can set up a church. Neither can pass laws which aid one religion, aid all religions, or prefer one religion over another. Neither can force nor influence a person to go to or to remain away from church against his will or force him to profess a belief or disbelief in any religion. No person can be punished for entertaining or professing religious beliefs or disbeliefs, for

[8] Cooley, *Principles*, 224-225.
[9] H. S. Commager, ed., *Documents of American History* (New York, 1947), 128, 131.
[10] Padover, ed., *The Complete Jefferson*, 518-519.
[11] Reynolds *v.* U.S., 98 U.S. 145, 164 (1879). In his second Inaugural Address, Jefferson expressed a very different, and presumably more carefully considered opinion upon the purpose of Amendment I: "In matters of religion, I have considered that its free exercise is placed by the Constitution independent of the powers of the general government." This was said three years after the Danbury letter. Richardson, *Messages and Papers*, I, 379.
[12] Everson *v.* Board of Education, 330 U.S. 1 (1947).

church attendance or non-attendance. No tax in any amount, large or small, can be levied to support any religious activities or institutions, whatever they may be called, or whatever form they may adopt to teach or practice religion. Neither a state nor the Federal Government can, openly or secretly, participate in the affairs of any religious organizations or groups and *vice versa.*"[13] And a year later a nearly unanimous Court overturned on the above grounds a "released time" arrangement under which the Champaign, Illinois, Board of Education agreed that religious instruction should be given in the local schools to pupils whose parents signed "request cards." By this plan the classes were to be conducted during regular school hours in the school building by outside teachers furnished by a religious council representing the various faiths, subject to the approval or supervision of the superintendent of schools. Attendance records were kept and reported to the school authorities in the same way as for other classes; and pupils not attending the religious-instruction classes were required to continue their regular secular studies.[14] Said Justice Black, speaking for the Court: "Here not only are the State's tax-supported public school buildings used for the dissemination of religious doctrines. The State also affords sectarian groups an invaluable aid in that it helps to provide pupils for their religious classes through use of the State's compulsory public school machinery. This is not separation of Church and State."[15]

Justice Frankfurter presented a supplementary, affirming opinion for himself and three other Justices, the purport of which was that public-supported education must be kept secular.[16] In a dissenting opinion, Justice Reed pointed out that "the Congress of the United States has a chaplain for each House who daily invokes divine blessings and guidance for the proceedings. The armed forces have commissioned chaplains from early days. They conduct the public services in accordance with the liturgical requirements of their respective faiths, ashore and afloat, employing for the purpose property belonging to the United States and dedicated to the services of religion. Under the Servicemen's Readjustment Act of 1944, eligible veterans may receive training at government expense for

"Released Time." Its Ups and Downs

---

13 *Ibid.*, 15, 16.
14 McCollum *v.* Board of Education, 333 U.S. 203 (1948).
15 *Ibid.*, 212.        16 *Ibid.*, 212ff.

the ministry in denominational schools. The schools of the District of Columbia have opening exercises which 'include a reading from the Bible without note or comment, and the Lord's Prayer.' "[17]

Justice Reed's views were not without effect. In 1952 the Court, six Justices to three, sustained a New York City "released time" program under which religious instruction must take place off the school grounds and numerous other features of the Champaign model were avoided.[18] Speaking for the majority, Justice Douglas said: "We are a religious people whose institutions presuppose a Supreme Being. We guarantee the freedom to worship as one chooses. We make room for as wide a variety of beliefs and creeds as the spiritual needs of man deem necessary. We sponsor an attitude on the part of government that shows no partiality to any one group and that lets each flourish according to the zeal of its adherents and the appeal of its dogma. When the state encourages religious instruction or cooperates with religious authorities by adjusting the schedule of public events to sectarian needs, it follows the best of our traditions. For it then respects the religious nature of our people and accommodates the public service to their spiritual needs. To hold that it may not would be to find in the Constitution a requirement that the government show a callous indifference to religious groups. That would be preferring those who believe in no religion over those who do believe. We find no constitutional requirement which makes it necessary for government to be hostile to religion and to throw its weight against efforts to widen the effective scope of religious influence."[19]

Concessions to the Religious Interest Farther back, in 1899, the Court held that an agreement between the District of Columbia and the directors of a hospital chartered by Congress for erection of a building and treatment of poor patients at the expense of the District was valid despite the fact that the members of the corporation belonged to a monastic order or sisterhood of a particular church.[20] It has also sustained a contract made at the request of Indians to whom money was due as a matter of right, under a treaty, for the payment of such money by the Commissioner of Indian

---

[17] *Ibid.*, 253-254.
[18] Zorach *v.* Clauson, 343 U.S. 306 (1952).
[19] *Ibid.*, 313-314. Justices Black, Frankfurter, and Jackson dissented.
[20] Bradfield *v.* Roberts, 175 U.S. 291 (1899).

Affairs for the support of Indian Catholic schools.[21] In 1930 the use of public funds to furnish nonsectarian textbooks to pupils in parochial schools of Louisiana was sustained,[22] and in 1947, as we have seen, the use of public funds for the transportation of pupils attending such schools in New Jersey.[23] In the former case the Court cited the States's interest in secular education even when conducted in religious schools, in the latter its concern for the safety of school children on the highways; and the National School Lunch Act,[24] which aids all school children attending tax-exempt schools, can be similarly justified. (The most notable financial concession to religion, however, is not to be explained in this way—the universal practice of exempting religious property from taxation. This unquestionably traces back to the idea expressed in the Northwest Ordinance that government has an interest in religion as such, as will be seen below.)

The Court continues to wrestle with the problem of where to draw the line between constitutionally permissible and impermissible financial aid to religious schools. In one recent case, the Court held that a New York statute authorizing the loan of textbooks to students attending parochial schools did not offend the establishment clause.[25] Nor did the Court find that the Higher Education Facilities Act of 1963, which provided grants for the construction of academic facilities to religious institutions, generally unconstitutional, although it did strike down one provision of the act which limited to twenty years the recipients' obligation not to use Federally financed facilities for sectarian instruction or religious worship. With respect to that provision, the Court said "Limiting the prohibition for religious use of the structure to 20 years obviously opens the facility to use for any purpose at the end of that period. It cannot be assumed that a substantial structure has no value after that period and hence the unrestricted use of a valuable property is in effect a contribution of some value to a religious body."[26] At the same time, in a pair of cases decided together the Court struck down a Rhode Island statute providing salary supplements to teachers of secular subjects in non-

---

[21] Quick Bear v. Leupp, 210 U.S. 50 (1908).
[22] Cochran v. Louisana State Board of Education, 281 U.S. 370 (1938).
[23] Everson v. Board of Education, 330 U.S. 1 (1947).
[24] 60 Stat. 230 (1946).
[25] Board of Education v. Allen, 392 U.S. 236 (1968).
[26] Tilton v. Richardson, 403 U.S. 672, 683 (1971).

public schools operated for the benefit of parochial schools and a Pennsylvania statute providing reimbursement to nonpublic schools for teachers' salaries, textbooks, and instructional materials used in the teaching of secular subjects, because both statutes involved excessive entanglements of State with church in the matter of implementation.[27] As Chief Justice Burger explained it:

"Every analysis in this area must begin with consideration of the cumulative criteria developed by the Court over many years. Three such tests may be gleaned from our cases. First, the statute must have a secular legislative purpose; second, its principal or primary effect must be one that neither advances nor inhibits religion; finally, the statute must not foster 'an excessive government entanglement with religion'. . . .

"This is not to suggest, however, that we are to engage in a legalistic minuet in which precise rules and forms must govern. A true minuet is a matter of pure form and style, the observance of which is itself the substantive end. Here we examine the form of the relationship for the light that it casts on the substance.

"In order to determine whether the government entanglement with religion is excessive we must examine the character and purposes of the institutions that are benefited, the nature of the aid that the State provides, and the resulting relationship between the government and the religious authority. . . . Here we find that both statutes foster an impermissible degree of entanglement."[28]

With respect to taxation of property, the Court found constitutional a New York statute exempting from a real property tax, real estate owned by an association organized and used exclusively for religious purposes, saying: "Few concepts are more deeply embedded in the fabric of our national life, beginning with pre-Revolutionary colonial times, than for the government to exercise at the very least this kind of benevolent neutrality toward churches and religious exercise generally so long as none was favored over others and none suffered interference."[29]

---

[27] Lemon v. Kurtzman and Early v. DiCenso, 403 U.S. 602 (1971).

[28] Ibid., 612-615. See Hunt v. McNair, 187 S.E. 2d. 645 (1972) and State v. Nebraska Bd. of Ed., 195 N.W. 2d. 161 (1972). The Court has not favored the so-called tax-credit idea. Essex v. Wolman, 40 LW 2724 (1971); aff'd, 41 LW 3167 (1972).

[29] Walz v. Tax Com'n, 397 U.S. 664, 676 (1970).

Seldom have decisions of the Court produced more criticism and cries of outrage than the Court's decisions in the so-called "prayer" and "bible-reading" cases.[30] Ultimately, opposition to those decisions led to a serious and prolonged effort at constitutional amendment lasting into the 1970's.[31] In 1962, the Court held that the state officials could not constitutionally compose a prayer and require that it be recited each school day, even though the prayer was non-denominational and pupils who did not want to participate would be excused. Then, in 1963 the Court said that to require a reading from the Bible or a recitation of the Lord's Prayer was also constitutionally impermissible. In the uproar over these decisions, critics of the Court seemed to overlook the fact that the Court did not forbid study of the Bible. On the contrary, the Court specifically said: "Nothing we have said here indicates that . . . study of the Bible or religion, when presented objectively as part of a secular program of education, may not be effected consistently with the First Amendment."[32] Also, overlooked was the fact that in the "prayer" case, what was involved was a prayer written by government officials. Surely, this must have been precisely the kind of action the framers of the First Amendment wanted to preclude. In the Court's words: "It is neither sacrilegious nor antireligious to say that each separate government in this country should stay out of the business of writing or sanctioning official prayers and leave that purely religious function to the people themselves and to those the people choose to look to for religious guidance."[33]

*Bible-Reading and Prayer in Public Schools*

As pointed out earlier (pp. 86-87), the interesting cases in recent years involving conscientious objectors to service in the Armed Forces have been decided primarily on statutory interpretation. However, Justice Harlan in a concurring opinion in 1970 indicated that he, at least, thought there was an Establishment question in these cases: "The constitutional question that must be faced . . . is whether a statute that defers to the individual's conscience only when his views emanate from adherence to theistic religious beliefs is within the power of Congress. Congress, of course, could entirely consistent with the requirements of the Constitution, eliminate *all* exemptions for

*Conscientious Objectors*

30 Engel *v.* Vitale, 370 U.S. 421 (1962); Abington School District *v.* Schempp, 374 U.S. 203 (1963).
31 1971 *Cong. Quart. Weekly Report*, 2290 ff. and 2307.
32 Abington School District *v.* Schempp, 374 U.S. 203, 225 (1963).
33 Engel *v.* Vitale, 370 U.S. 421, 435 (1962).

conscientious objectors. . . . However, having chosen to exempt, it cannot draw the line between theistic or nontheistic religious beliefs on the one hand and secular beliefs on the other. Any such distinctions are not, in my view, compatible with the Establishment Clause of the First Amendment."[34]

Sunday Closing Laws

As helpful at it is to separate out the two religious clauses of the First Amendment for analysis and explication, it may inhibit understanding to do so. As the Supreme Court recently pointed out:

"The Court has struggled to find a neutral course between the two Religion Clauses, both of which are cast in absolute terms, and either of which, if expanded to a logical extreme, would tend to clash with the other. . . .

"The course of constitutional neutrality in this area cannot be an absolutely straight line: rigidity could well defeat the basic purpose of these provisions, which is to insure that no religion be sponsored or favored, none commanded, and none inhibited. The general principle deducible from the First Amendment and all that has been said by the Court is this: that we will not tolerate either governmentally established religion or governmental interference with religion. Short of those expressly proscribed governmental acts there is room for play in the joints productive of a benevolent neutrality which will permit religious exercise to exist without sponsorship and without interference."[35]

This difficulty is exemplified in the so-called "Sunday Closing Laws" cases. Curiously, in view of our history, the Court found that laws proscribing certain business activities on Sundays was not necessarily based on religion and thus were not laws "respecting an establishment of religion."[36] But when Orthodox Jews protested the application of such a law to them on the grounds that they were thus required to be closed for business two days, Sunday and their own Sabbath, the Court came up with what appears less than a Solomon-like judgment that:

"Furthermore, the law's effect does not inconveneince all members of the Orthodox Jewish faith but only those who be-

[34] Welsh v. U.S., 398 U.S. 333, 356 (1970). For a more recent dialogue on this point, see Justice Douglas's dissent in Wisconsin v. Yoder, 406 U.S. 205, 248-249 (1972) and Chief Justice Burger's opinion at 215.
[35] Walz v. Tax Commissioner, 397 U.S. 664, 669 (1970).
[36] McGowan v. Maryland, 366 U.S. 420 (1961); Two Guys v. McGinley, 366 U.S. 582 (1961).

lieve it necessary to work on Sunday. And even these are not faced with as serious a choice as forsaking their religious practices or subjecting themselves to criminal prosecution. Fully recognizing that the alternatives open to appellants and others similarly situated—retaining their present occupations and incurring economic disadvantage or engaging in some other commercial activity which does not call for either Saturday or Sunday labor—may well result in some financial sacrifice in order to observe their religious beliefs, still the option is wholly different than when the legislation attempts to make a religious practice itself unlawful."[37] Yet two years later, the Court decided that a State could not constitutionally deny unemployment compensation benefits to a woman who had refused employment because that employment would have required her to work on Saturday and "from conscientious scruples she would not take Saturday work."[38]

"Free exercise thereof": The religious freedom here envisaged has two aspects. It "forestalls compulsion by law of the acceptance of any creed or the practice of any form of worship," and conversely it "safeguards the free exercise of the chosen form of religion."[39] But "the free exercise thereof" does not embrace actions which are "in violation of social duties or subversive of good order"; hence it was within Congress's power to prohibit polygamy in the territories.[40] So it was held in 1878, and sixty-two years later the Court added these words of qualification to a decision setting aside a State enactment as violative of religious freedom: "Nothing we have said is intended even remotely to imply that, under the cloak of reli-

*[marginal note: Limitations upon the "Free Exercise" of Religion]*

[37] Braunfeld *v.* Brown, 366 U.S. 599, 605-606 (1961); Gallagher *v.* Crown Kosher Market, 366 U.S. 617 (1961).

[38] Sherbert *v.* Verner, 374 U.S. 398 (1963).

[39] Justice Roberts for the Court in Cantwell *v.* Conn., 310 U.S. 296 at 303 (1940). As Justice Jackson so eloquently stated in writing the Court's opinion on the famous "Flag Salute" case: "If there is any fixed star in our constitutional constellation, it is that no official, high or petty, can prescribe what shall be orthodox in politics, nationalism, religion or other matters of opinion or force citizens to confess by word or act their faith therein." W.Va. Board of Education *v.* Barnette, 319 U.S. 624, 642 (1943).

[40] Reynolds *v.* U.S., 98 U.S. 145 (1878). *See also* Davis *v.* Beason, 133 U.S. 333 (1890); and Mormon Church *v.* U.S., 136 U.S. 1 (1890). It was never intended that the First Amendment to the Constitution "could be invoked as a protection against legislation for the punishment of acts inimical to the peace, good order, and morals of society." 133 U.S. at 342. *But see* Justice Douglas's dissent in Wisconsin *v.* Yoder, 406 U.S. 205, 247 (1972).

gion, persons may, with impunity, commit frauds upon the public."[41] Yet four years later, when the promoters of a religious sect, whose founder had at different times identified himself as Saint Germain, Jesus, George Washington, and Godfre Ray King, were convicted of using the mails to defraud by obtaining money on the strength of having supernaturally healed hundreds of persons, they found the Court in a softened frame of mind. Although the trial judge, carefully discriminating between the question of the truth of defendants' pretensions and that of their good faith in advancing them, had charged the jury that it could pass on the latter but not the former, this caution did not avail with the Court, which contrived on another ground ultimately to upset the verdict of "guilty." Chief Justice Stone, speaking for himself and Justices Roberts and Frankfurter, dissented: "I cannot say that freedom of thought and worship includes freedom to procure money by making knowingly false statements about one's religious experiences."[42]

In 1945, the Supreme Court did not think that it was a violation of religious freedom to deny conscientious objectors the right to practice law.[43] However, the 1961 decision mentioned earlier that struck down as unconstitutional a requirement that a State officer must declare his belief in the existence of God (*see* p. 258) as well as a recent decision finding unconstitutional efforts to deny people the right to practice law because of unpopular beliefs would indicate that the 1945 decision is no longer good law.[44]

In 1972, in its decision holding that the First and Fourteenth Amendments prevented Wisconsin from compelling Amish parents to have their children attend formal high school, the Court declared that ". . . to agree that religiously grounded conduct must often be subject to the broad police power of

---

[41] Cantwell *v.* Connecticut, 310 U.S. 296, 306 (1940). Conversely, a Florida court recently held that an ordinance proscribing the sale of non-kosher foods as kosher did not violate either the establishment or free exercise provisions of the First Amendment. The court said "Rather than to prohibit the free exercise of the religion, the ordinance serves to safeguard the observance of its tenets, and to prohibit actions which improperly would interfere therewith." Sossin Systems, Inc. *v.* City of Miami Beach, 262 So. 2d. 28, 29 (1972).

[42] United States *v.* Ballard, 322 U.S. 78 (1944). The interstate transportation of plural wives by polygamous Fundamentalists is punishable under the Mann Act. Cleveland *v.* U.S., 329 U.S. 14 (1946); 18 U.S.C. 2421.

[43] *In re* Summers, 325 U.S. 561 (1945).

[44] Baird *v.* State Bar of Arizona, 401 U.S. 1 (1971).

the State is not to deny that there are areas of conduct protected by the Free Exercise Clause of the First Amendment and thus beyond the power of the State to control, even under regulations of general applicability."[45] But, in dissenting in part, Justice Douglas saw the deprivation of religious freedom in this case in a different light: "If the parents in this case are allowed a religious exemption, the inevitable effect is to impose the parents' notions of religious duty upon their children. Where the child is mature enough to express potentially conflicting desires, it would be an invasion of the child's rights to permit such an imposition without canvassing his views." And Justice Douglas concluded that "if an Amish child desires to attend high school, and is mature enough to have that desire respected, the State may well be able to override the parents' religiously motivated objections."[46] But the majority felt that "there is no reason for the Court to consider that point since it is not an issue in the case."[47] Predictably, in an age where young people are asserting themselves, a case will one day arise where a mature child wants to go to high school contrary to his parents' religious scruples; it would be a good bet that the courts would uphold State support of the child's right. In this respect some recent State court decisions respecting claims for the exercise of religious freedom are most instructive. The Superior Court of Pennsylvania recently upheld actions aimed at providing blood transfusions to a sixteen-year-old child over the mother's objections based on religious scruples.[48] The Supreme Court of Kansas found that a regulation requiring a medical examination, contrary to applicant's religious beliefs, as a condition for receiving disability benefits was not a violation of freedom of religion.[49] A Connecticut court found that the free exercise clause was not a bar to a mandatory sex education course in school, where the statute permitted parents the option of providing equivalent education in the home or in private schools, including parochial schools.[50] The Court of Appeals of New York held that a State statute providing for the placement of a child with adoptive

[45] Wisconsin v. Yoder, 406 U.S. 205 (1972).
[46] Ibid., 1546.
[47] Ibid., 1541.
[48] In re Green, 286 A. 2d. 681 (1971).
[49] Powers v. State Department of Social Welfare, 493 P. 2d. 590 (1972).
[50] Hopkins v. Hamden Board of Education, 289 A. 2d. 914 (1971).

parents of the same religion did not deny prospective adoptive parents their freedom of religion.[51] And a Federal Court of Appeals in June of 1972 held that compulsory chapel attendance at the U.S. military academies is an unconstitutional violation of the First Amendment's guarantee of religious freedom.[52]

**Prisoners' Rights** In a noteworthy decision rendered in 1972, the Supreme Court cautioned that prisons must be careful not to trench on the religious freedom of prisoners. The Court said that "Federal Courts sit not to supervise prisons but to enforce the constitutional rights of all 'persons' which include prisoners. We are not unmindful that prison officials must be accorded latitude in the administration of prison affairs, and that prisoners necessarily are subject to appropriate rules and regulations."[53] But the Court went on to stress that persons in prison do have rights.

**Church Disputes** Over the years a number of cases have come to the Supreme Court involving church disputes, particularly over property. The Court has held strictly to the line that civil courts ought not to determine ecclesiastical questions and has been equally limiting with respect to state legislation touching on doctrine and church governing bodies.[54]

Finally, it is worth noting that in the last few years, there have been a number of actions in the lower courts protesting as violations of both religion clauses the exhibition of religious symbols and displays by one or another governmental body; the redoubtable Madalyn Murray O'Hair went to court to restrain NASA from "further directing or permitting religious activities or ceremonies and especially the reading of the Sectarian Christian religion Bible and from prayer recitation in space and in relation to all future space flight activity." Such petitions have not usually met with success.[55]

"Freedom of speech or of the press": According to Black-

---

[51] Dickens *v*. Ernesto, 330 N.Y.S. 2d. 346 (1972).

[52] Anderson *v*. Laird, 466 F. 2d. 283 (1972); *cert. denied*, 41 *LW* 3341 (1972).

[53] Cruz *v*. Beto, 405 U.S. 319 (1972). *But see* Justice Rehnquist's stinging dissent, *ibid.*, 323.

[54] Md. & Va. Churches *v*. Sharpsburg Ch., 396 U.S. 367 (1970); Presbyterian Church *v*. Hull Church, 393 U.S. 440 (1969); Kedroff *v*. St. Nicholas Cathedral, 344 U.S. 94 (1952); Kreshik *v*. St. Nicholas Cathedral, 363 U.S. 190 (1960). *See also* Draskovich *v*. Pasalich, 280 N.E. 2d. 69 (1972) for a review of pertinent cases.

[55] O'Hair *v*. Paine, 312 F. Supp. 434 (1969). *See also*, for example, Paul *v*. Dade County, 419 F. 2d. 10 (1969), *cert. denied*, 397 U.S. 1065 (1970).

stone, who was the oracle of the common law when the First Amendment was framed, "liberty of the press consists in laying no *previous* restraints upon publications, and not in freedom from censure for criminal matter when published. Every freeman," he asserted, "has an undoubted right to lay what sentiments he pleases before the public; to forbid this is to destroy the freedom of the press; but if he publishes what is improper, mischievous, and illegal, he must take the consequences of his own temerity. . . . To punish (as the law does at present) any dangerous or offensive writings, which, when published, shall on a fair and impartial trial be adjudged of a pernicious tendency, is necessary for the preservation of peace and good order, of government and religion, the only solid foundations of civil liberty."[56] Also, as the law stood at that time, the question whether a publication or oral utterance was of "a pernicious tendency" was, in a criminal trial, a question not for the jury but for the judge; nor was the truth of the utterance a defense.

The Blackstonian Conception of "Freedom of Speech or of the Press"

While it was originally no intention of the authors of Amendment I to revise the common law, as set forth by Blackstone, on the subject of freedom of the press,[57] there was one feature of it which early ran afoul of the facts of life in America. This was the common law of "seditious libel," which operated to put persons in authority beyond the reach of public criticism. The first step was taken in the famous, or infamous, Sedition Act of 1798, which admitted the defense of truth in prosecutions brought under it, and submitted the general issue of defendant's guilt to the jury.[58] But the Act of 1798 still retained the substantive doctrine of "seditious libel," a circumstance which put several critics of President Adams in jail, and thereby considerably aided Jefferson's election as President in 1800. Once in office, nevertheless, Jefferson himself appealed to the discredited principle against partisan critics. Writing his friend Governor McKean of Pennsylvania in 1803 anent such critics, Jefferson said: "The federalists having failed in destroying freedom of the press by their gag-law, seem to have attacked it in an opposite direction; that is by pushing its li-

The Doctrine of Seditious Libel

Jefferson vs. Hamilton on Freedom of Press

[56] Sir William Blackstone, *Commentaries on the Laws of England*, edited by Warren Carey Jones, IV (San Francisco, 1916), 151.
[57] *See* Justice Frankfurter's opinion in Dennis *v.* U.S., 341 U.S. 494, 521-525 (1951); citing Robertson *v.* Baldwin, 165 U.S. 275, 281 (1897).
[58] These two improvements upon the common law were, in fact, adopted from Fox's Libel Act, passed by Parliament in 1792.

centiousness and its lying to such a degree of prostitution as to deprive it of all credit. . . . This is a dangerous state of things, and the press ought to be restored to its credibility if possible. The restraints provided by the laws of the States are sufficient for this, if applied. And I have, therefore, long thought that a few prosecutions of the most prominent offenders would have a wholesome effect in restoring the integrity of the presses. Not a general prosecution, for that would look like persecution; but a selected one."[59]

The sober truth is that it was that archenemy of Jefferson and of democracy, Alexander Hamilton, who made the greatest single contribution toward rescuing this particular freedom as a political weapon from the coils and toils of the common law, and that in connection with one of Jefferson's "selected prosecutions." The reference is to Hamilton's many-times-quoted formula in the Croswell case in 1804: "The liberty of the press is the right to publish with impunity, truth, with good motives, for justifiable ends though reflecting on government, magistracy, or individuals."[60] Equipped with this brocard, which is today embodied in twenty-four State constitutions, our State courts working in co-operation with juries, whose attitude usually reflected the robustiousness of American political discussion before the Civil War, gradually wrote into the common law of the States the principle of "qualified privilege," which is a notification to plaintiffs in libel suits that if they are unlucky enough to be office holders or office seekers, they must be prepared to shoulder the almost impossible burden of showing defendant's "special malice."[61] (*See* p. 286.)

Blackstone Accepted, then Rejected

In 1907 the Court, speaking by Justice Holmes, rejected the contention that the Fourteenth Amendment rendered applicable against the States "a prohibition similar to that in the First," and at the same time endorsed Blackstone, in words drawn from an early Massachusetts case: "The preliminary freedom [i.e., from censorship] extends as well to the false as

[59] Paul L. Ford, *The Writings of Thomas Jefferson*, IX (New York, 1892-1899), 451-452.
[60] People *v.* Croswell, 1 N.Y. Common Law Reports 717 (1804).
[61] *See* Edward S. Corwin, *Liberty against Government* (Baton Rouge, 1948), 157-159n; Cooley, *Constitutional Limitations*, ch. 12; Samuel A. Dawson, *Freedom of the Press, A Study of the Doctrine of "Qualified Privilege"* (New York, 1924). *See also* New York Times Co. *v.* Sullivan, 376 U.S. 254 (1964).

to the true; the subsequent punishment may extend to the true as to the false."[62] Even as late as 1922 Justice Pitney, speaking for the Court, said: "Neither the Fourteenth Amendment nor any other provision of the Constitution of the United States imposes upon the States any restriction about 'freedom of speech' or the 'liberty of silence.' . . ."[63] Gitlow *v*. New York, in which this position was abandoned, came three years later.

Meantime the so-called "clear and present danger doctrine" had made its appearance. The original formulation of that doctrine was a simple assertion that before an utterance can be penalized by government it must, ordinarily, have occurred "in such circumstances or have been of such a nature as to create a clear and present danger" that it would bring about "substantive evils" within the power of government to prevent.[64] The question whether these conditions exist is one of law for the courts, and ultimately for the Supreme Court, in enforcement of the First and/or the Fourteenth Amendment,[65] and in exercise of its power of review in these premises the Court is entitled to review broadly findings of facts of lower courts, whether State or Federal.[66]

The *The "Clear and Present Danger" Shibboleth*

The formula emerged in the course of a decision in 1919, holding that the circulation of certain documents constituted an "attempt," in the sense of the Espionage Act of 1917, to cause insubordination in the armed forces and to obstruct their recruitment.[67] Said Justice Holmes, speaking for the Court: "We admit that in many places and in ordinary times the defendants in saying all that was said in the circular would have been within their constitutional rights. But the character of every act depends upon the circumstances in which it is done. . . . The most stringent protection of free speech would not protect a man in falsely shouting fire in a theatre and causing a panic. It does not even protect a man from an injunction against uttering words that have all the effect of force. . . . The question in every case is whether the words used are used in such circumstances and are of such a nature as to create a clear and present danger that they will bring about the sub-

---

[62] Patterson *v*. Colo., 205 U.S. 454, 461-462 (1907).
[63] Prudential Life Ins. Co. *v*. Cheek, 259 U.S. 530, 543 (1922).
[64] Schenck *v*. United States, 249 U.S. 47 (1919).
[65] *See* Justice Brandeis's concurring opinion in Whitney *v*. Calif., 274 U.S. 357 (1927); and cases reviewed below.
[66] Fiske *v*. Kansas, 274 U.S. 380 (1927).
[67] Note 54 above.

stantive evils that Congress has a right to prevent. It is a question of proximity and degree."[68]

Whether Justice Holmes actually intended here to add a new dimension to constitutional freedom of speech and press may be seriously questioned, inasmuch as in two similar cases following shortly after, in which he again spoke for the Court, and in which prosecutions under the Espionage Act were sustained, he did not allude to the formula.[69] Moreover, when a case did arise in which the formula might have made a difference, seven Justices declined to follow it.[70] This time, however, Justice Holmes, accompanied by Justice Brandeis, dissented on the ground that defendants' utterances did not create a clear and present danger of substantive evils. From this time forth in the course of the next twenty years, these two Justices filed numerous opinions, sometimes in dissent, sometimes in affirmation, of rulings of the Court in freedom of speech cases in which the "clear and present danger" test was urged, but without convincing any of their brethren of its soundness.[71] The majority employed the "bad tendency" test (that is, "that a state in the exercise of its police power may punish those who abuse this freedom by utterances inimicable to the welfare, tending to corrupt morals, incite to a crime, or disturb the public peace."

Then suddenly in 1940, the stone rejected by the builders suddenly appeared at the head of the column, and along with it the further tenet that freedom of speech and press occupied "a preferred position" in the scale of constitutional values.[72] As indicated earlier (p. 239), the libertarians on the Court made of Holmes' formulation a *method* for dealing with First Amendment cases.

From 1937 through 1948, a majority of the Court applied this method in fourteen cases. In each of these the Court assumed that the governmental action at issue was invalid. This is not to say that in every case the Court assumed that a particular statute was unconstitutional; in some cases the Court

---

[68] 249 U.S. 47, 52.

[69] The reference is to Frohwerk *v.* U.S., 249 U.S. 204 (1919); *and* Debs *v.* U.S., 249 U.S. 211 (1919).

[70] Abrams *v.* U.S., 250 U.S. 616 (1919).

[71] *See* Schaefer *v.* U.S., 251 U.S. 466 (1920); Gitlow *v.* N.Y., 268 U.S. 652 (1925); Whitney *v.* Calif., 274 U.S. 357 (1927).

[72] Thornhill *v.* Ala., 310 U.S. 88 (1940); *and* Cantwell *v.* Conn., 310 U.S. 296 (1940) are especially referred to. *Cf.* Herndon *v.* Lowry, 301 U.S. 242 (1937).

assumed that only the particular application of a broadly drawn statute was unconstitutional. This stand of the Court, in each case, compelled the States or their agents to attempt to prove that the exercise of liberty did *in fact* present a "clear and present danger." In the three cases where the Court, after an inquiry into the facts, found that a clear and present danger did exist, it inquired into the appropriateness of the remedy.

In eleven of the fourteen cases, the Court's decision favored the rights of the individual. In one of the cases where the Court decided against the individuals, there was actual violence involved.[73] In another, it was found that child labor *per se* was an evil.[74] The Court, in a third case, found that, where an ice peddlers' union sought to picket in an effort to force wholesale distributors into an illegal agreement to sell their goods exclusively to union members, there was a danger to the nation in such a use of free speech.[75] That the Court should have found for the individual in eleven out of fourteen cases should not be regarded as surprising or disproportionate, for as James Madison pointed out in *Federalist* No. 10, in a representative government there is more danger of infringement of individual rights by the majority than *vice versa*.

Both the growing concern over the "Communist Problem" and personnel changes on the Court contributed to the demise of clear and present danger as a useful formulation. Had the Court employed the doctrine as method in the case of the "Eleven Communist Leaders" who were convicted in 1949 under the Smith Act, it would have felt compelled to overturn the conviction.[76] That conviction was reviewed first in the Appeals Court in which the venerable Judge Learned Hand sat. It was he who gave the Court a new approach. Hand had written: "In each case they [the courts] must ask whether the gravity of the 'evil,' discounted by its improbability, justifies such invasion of free speech as is necessary to avoid the danger. We have purposely substituted 'improbability' for 'remoteness,' *because that must be the right interpretation*" (emphasis supplied).[77] When the case came to it, the Supreme

*Clear and Probable Danger Test*

[73] Milk Drivers Union *v.* Meadomoor Dairies Inc., 312 U.S. 287 (1941).
[74] Prince *v.* Massachusetts, 321 U.S. 158 (1944).
[75] Giboney *v.* Empire Storage, 336 U.S. 490 (1949).
[76] Chase, *Security and Liberty*, ch. 2. *See also* Yates *v.* U.S., 354 U.S. 298 (1957).
[77] U.S. *v.* Dennis, 183 F. 2d. 201, 212 (1950).

Court specifically endorsed the Hand opinion, adding that: "Overthrow of the Government by force and violence is certainly a substantial enough interest for the Government to limit speech. Indeed, this is the ultimate value of our society, for if a society cannot protect its very structure from armed internal attack, it must follow that no subordinate value can be protected."[78]

**The Balancing Approach** From that point on, the Court's majority, whoever has composed it, has refrained from seeking a doctrine or formulation that will cover all free speech cases, evidently leaving it to the dissenters and some professors to do so.[79] Instead, they take each case on its own merits and balance "the competing private and public interests."[80] Needless to say, several of the more libertarian Justices who had been devotés of the clear and present danger doctrine were not happy with this development. Justice Black's attack on the balancing approach is worthy of study.[81] But, interestingly enough, Justices Douglas and Black took the occasion in 1969 to indicate that their objection to the clear and present danger test was that it did not give *enough* protection to individual rights.[82]

The catalogue of recent cases dealing with free speech which are the fruits of the non-doctrinaire approach was presented earlier (pp. 253-255). What remains here to be stated is where the case law on free speech leaves us at this moment. Apparently, one is free to say pretty much what he pleases, provided the speech is not tied in with a call to violent or other illegal action.[83] True, there are situations when it becomes a subjective judgment as to whether or not there has been a call to action.[84] And the Court has not always opted for the libertarian position. But on the whole, the right of free speech

[78] Dennis *v.* U.S., 341 U.S. 494 (1951).

[79] For a superb effort of that kind, *see* Thomas I. Emerson "Toward a General Theory of the First Amendment," 72 *Yale Law Journal*, 877 (1963).

[80] Barenblatt *v.* U.S., 360 U.S. 109, 126 (1959). For a more recent expression of the balancing process used in First Amendment cases, *see* Wisconsin *v.* Yoder, 405 U.S. 205, 214 (1972).

[81] *Ibid.*, 140-145.

[82] Brandenburg *v.* Ohio, 395 U.S. 444, 450-457 (1969).

[83] Yates *v.* U.S., 354 U.S. 298 (1957); Scales *v.* U.S., 367 U.S. 203 (1960); Noto *v.* U.S., 367 U.S. 290; Brandenburg *v.* Ohio, 395 U.S. 444 (1969); Gooding *v.* Wilson, 405 U.S. 518 (1972). *See* State *v.* Cappon, 285 A. 2d. 287 (1971).

[84] *Ibid., see also* Street *v.* N.Y., 394 U.S. 576 (1969). In this connection, see the interesting court decisions with respect to urging "blockbusting"; State *v.* Wagner, 291 A. 2d. 161 (1972) and Summer *v.* Teaneck, 251 A. 2d. 761 (1969).

*qua* speech as a practical matter seems thoroughly secure. Further, certain symbolic acts like wearing armbands, will in certain circumstances be regarded as symbolic free speech and as such be entitled to the full protection of the First Amendment.[85] But burning the American flag or a draft card in the face of a statute making it a crime will not be so regarded,[86] for, the Court has said: "We cannot accept the view that an apparently limitless variety of conduct can be labeled 'speech' whenever the person engaging in the conduct intends thereby to express an idea."[87]

The issues of *where* and *when* limitations on the exercise of Free Speech are permissible will be dealt with below under Assembly.

Five other items respecting Free Speech are worthy of mention. First, there has long been a concept of "fighting words"; in Justice Murphy's description: "There are certain well-defined and narrowly limited classes of speech the prevention of which have never thought to raise any Constitutional problem. These include the lewd, the obscene, the profane, the libelous, and the insulting or 'fighting' words those which by their very utterance inflict injury or tend to incite an immediate breach of the peace."[88] The concept is still very much alive, although the Court is generally more permissive as to what actually constitute "fighting words."[89]

Fighting Words

85 Tinker *v.* Des Moines School Dist., 393 U.S. 503 (1969). A California court recently held the wearing of a beard a symbolic expression and consequently ruled that a man who lost his job because he refused to give up his beard was entitled to unemployment insurance, where the state did not show how it would be "adversely affected if benefits were granted" and, if, it did, it must show that "no conceivable alternatives would preclude the adverse results without 'infringing First Amendment rights.'" King *v.* Cal. Unemployment Insurance Appeals Bd., 101 Cal. Rptr. 660 (1972).

86 U.S. *v.* O'Brien, 391 U.S. 367 (1968) *and see* Warren's dissent in Street *v.* N.Y., 394 U.S. 576, 594 (1969). In recent years there has been a rash of state cases involving flag desecrations, almost invariably the desecrators have been punished; in one Texas jurisdiction a flag-burner was sentenced to four years in the penitentiary. Deeds *v.* State 474 S.W. 2d. 718 (1972). *See* Commonwealth *v.* Goguen, 279 N.E. 2d. 666 (1972); State *v.* Zimmelman, 287 A. 2d. 474 (1972); State *v.* Saulino, 277 N.E. 2d. 580 (1971); People *v.* Keogh, 329 N.Y.S. 2d. 80 (1972), *but cf.* State *v.* Hodson, 289 A. 2d. 635 (1972). *See also* Joyce *v.* U.S., 454 F. 2d. (1971), *cert. den.* 92 S. Ct. 1188 (1972).

87 U.S. *v.* O'Brien, 391 U.S. 367, 376 (1968); State *v.* Saulino, 277 N.E. 2d. 580 (1971).

88 Chaplinsky *v.* New Hampshire, 315 U.S. 568 (1942).

89 Cohen *v.* California, 403 U.S. 15, 20-27 (1971); Gooding *v.* Wilson, 405 U.S. 518 (1972), *see* particularly Justice Blackman's dissent, *ibid.,* 534.

"Chilling Effect"    A relatively new expression has found its way into First Amendment cases, Free Speech cases particularly. Those words "chilling effect" are applied to government actions which inhibit the exercise of First Amendment freedoms. To the extent the "chill" is real, it will render the action unconstitutional.[90] However, in 1972, five of the nine Supreme Court Justices were unsympathetic to a claim that the Army's civilian surveillance program had a "chilling" effect on those who had initially brought the suit.[91] The Court held that "Allegations of a subjective 'chill' are not an adequate substitute for a claim of specific present objective harm or a threat of specific future harm; 'the federal courts ... do not render advisory opinions.'" The Court spelled out its holding in these words: "We, of course, intimate no view with respect to the propriety or desirability, from a policy standpoint, of the challenged activities of the Department of the Army; our conclusion is a narrow one, namely, that on this record the respondents have not presented a case for resolution by the courts."

Picketing    In the early 1940's the Court, according to Justice Frankfurter, ". . . broadly assimilated peaceful picketing in general to freedom of speech, and as such protected against abridgement by the Fourteenth Amendment."[92] But ultimately, as Justice Douglas complained, the Court came to view picketing as something more than just an exercise of Free Speech: "State courts and state legislatures cannot fashion blanket prohibitions on all picketing. But . . . State courts and state legislatures are free to decide whether to permit or suppress any particular picket line for any reason other than a blanket policy against all picketing."[93]

Loyalty Oaths    Despite their doubtful efficacy, some legislatures have for years been enamoured by the use of loyalty oaths as a means

[90] *See,* for example, Dombrowski *v.* Pfister, 380 U.S. 479, 494 (1965).

[91] Laird *v.* Tatum, 408 U.S. 1 (1972); *but see* report of a district court decision refusing to dismiss a challenge to police surveillance of protest activities. *N.Y. Times,* Oct. 29, 1972. Recently, the American Civil Liberties Union filed a suit challenging the constitutionality of the Bank Secrecy Act which requires disclosure on Treasury order of certain bank transactions. The ACLU contended that this would have a chilling effect on rights of association since it might make people chary of contributing to organizations. *New York Times,* July 2, 1972. The court, however, declared the law unconstitutional on Fourth Amendment grounds. 41 *LW* 2132 (1972).

[92] Teamsters Union *v.* Vogt, Inc., 354 U.S. 284 (1957).

[93] *Ibid.,* 297.

for combatting subversion.[94] Since some of the oaths require the oath-taker to affirm that he will not *advocate* overthrow of the government, on their face they constitute an abridgment of freedom of speech. Loyalty oaths have had a checkered career before the Supreme Court. That career was recently succinctly described by the Court itself when, in 1972, the Court endeavored to indicate what kinds of oaths were permissible and which impermissible and for what reasons. "We have made clear that neither federal nor state governments may condition employment on taking oaths which impinge rights guaranteed by the First and Fourteenth Amendments respectively, as for examples those relating to political beliefs. ... Nor may employment be conditioned on an oath that one has not engaged, or will not engage, in protected speech activities such as the following: criticizing institutions of government; discussing political doctrine that approves the overthrow of certain forms of government; and supporting candidates for political office. ... Employment may not be conditioned on an oath denying past, or abjuring future associational activities within constitutional protection; such protected activities include membership in organizations having illegal purposes unless one knows of the purpose and shares a specific intent to promote the illegal purpose. ... And, finally, an oath may not be so vague that 'men of common intelligence must necessarily guess at its meaning and differ as to its application, [because such an oath] violates the first essential of due process of law.' ... Several cases recently decided by the Court stand out among our oath cases because they have upheld the constitutionality of oaths, addressed to the future, promising constitutional support in broad terms. These cases have begun with a recognition that the Constitution itself prescribes comparable oaths in two articles [Article II, Section I, cl. 7, and Article VI, cl. 3]. ..."[95]

One of the most distressing manifestations of protest on our college and university campuses of recent memory has been the shouting down of speakers and the use of other forms of derision to prevent people from speaking. Clearly, the First Amendment does not itself prohibit private persons from

*Private Abridgements of Free Speech*

---

[94] Chase, *Security and Liberty*, 60-61; A. W. Griswold, "Loyalty: An Issue of Academic Freedom," *New York Times Magazine*, Dec. 20, 1959, p. 18.

[95] Cole *v.* Richardson, 405 U.S. 676, 680-681 (1972). *See also* Socialist Labor Party *v.* Gilligan, 406 U.S. 583 (1972).

attempting to abridge Free Speech. At the same time, the Constitution does not forbid Government from endeavoring to insure that the freedom can be exercised. For example, a carefully drawn State law making it a crime to prevent any one from exercising his freedom of speech would not only be constitutional but seem highly desirable. In implementing such a law, care would have to be taken not to prevent protesters to a speech from exercising *their* freedom to speak. But this does not seem a hard practical problem, protesters could protest outside a meeting (exercising their freedom) but not inside someone else's meeting.

Freedom
of the
Press

The framers of the First Amendment, of course, equated press and the printed word. But as radio, movies, and television became important parts of the so-called "media," the Court has expanded the meaning of "press" to cover them.

By and large, freedom of the press has been co-extensive with freedom of speech. When the Court was using a special test like "bad tendency" or "clear and present danger," it applied it to all First Amendment freedoms. The special application of clear and present danger to the press came in a series of cases where the Court upheld members of the press against contempt charges laid on them by irate judges whom they had criticized.[96] There are, however, several constitutional doctrines which have been specially tailored to meet problems peculiar to the operation of a Free Press. The first of these is the doctrine of no-previous restraints which basically forbids censorship of the press *previous* to publication. Although there have been instances where the Supreme Court has upheld a previous restraint, it is rare.[97] As recently as the Pentagon Papers case, the Supreme Court took for granted that "any system of prior restraint of expression comes to this Court bearing a heavy presumption against its constitutional validity."[98] Justice Warren has spelled out the special vice of prior censorship in this way: "The censor performs free from all the procedural safeguards afforded litigants in a court of law."[99]

[96] Bridges v. California, 314 U.S. 252 (1941); Pennekamp v. Florida, 328 U.S. 331 (1946); Craig v. Harney, 331 U.S. 367 (1947).
[97] Times Film Corp. v. Chicago, 365 U.S. 43 (1961).
[98] New York Times Co. v. U.S., 403 U.S. 713 (1971).
[99] Times Film Corp. v. Chicago, 365 U.S. 43, 68 (1961). As to another kind of censorship problem, a U.S. Court of Appeals recently held that the city of West Palm Beach could not foreclose the use of its auditorium for a production of "Hair" since the auditorium was used for other productions. Southeastern Productions Ltd. v. City of West Palm Beach, 457 F. 2d. 1016 (1972).

The doctrine does not preclude holding members of the press responsible for what they do. Once they do something allegedly illegal, they can be so charged and tried. But in all save unusual circumstances, they must be permitted to publish, exhibit or broadcast.

The other special doctrines deal with libel and obscenity and were discussed earlier along with a brief discussion of the Court's most recent postures on these matters. (*See* pp. 255-257.)

Congress has some special controls with respect to the press by virtue of its control of the mails. Few newspapers or periodicals can profitably circulate except locally unless they enjoy the "second class privilege" that is, the privilege of specially low rates—and this privilege, being a gratuity, is under the nearly absolute control of Congress, notwithstanding which Congress's delegate in the matter, the Postmaster General, may not, in carrying out Congress's expressed will that the privilege be confined to publications "originated and published for the dissemination of information of a public character, or devoted to literature, the sciences, arts, or some special industry," set himself up as a censor, for if he does the Court will over-rule him and bring his decrees to naught.[100] Moreover, Congress may banish from the mails altogether, as well as from the channels of interstate commerce, obscene and fraudulent matter.[101] For there can be no right to circulate what there is no right to publish, circulation indeed being only an incident of publication. Nor, as we have seen, is it an invasion of freedom of the press to require a newsgathering agency to treat its employees in the same way as other employers are required to treat theirs; or to subject it to the antimonopoly provisions of the Sherman Anti-Trust Act.[102]

As Justice White, speaking for the Court, explained: "The Federal Communication Commission has for many years imposed on radio and television broadcasters the requirement

*Congressional Control of the Press*

*The Constitutionality of the "Equal Time" and the "Fairness" Doctrines*

---

[100] United States *ex rel.* Milwaukee Soc. Dem. Pub. Co. *v.* Burleson, 255 U.S. 407 (1921), and cases there cited; Hannegan *v.* Esquire, Inc., 327 U.S. 146 (1946); 39 U.S.C. 4354.

[101] *In re* Rapier, 143 U.S. 110 (1892); Public Clearing House *v.* Coyne, 194 U.S. 497 (1904); Lewis Pub. Co. *v.* Morgan, 229 U.S. 288 (1913). 39 U.S.C. 4001; Ginzburg *v.* U.S., 383 U.S. 463 (1966).

[102] Associated Press *v.* NLRB, 301 U.S. 103 (1937); Associated Press *v.* U.S., 326 U.S. 1 (1945). In 1972, a U.S. court of appeals upheld a provision of the Civil Rights Act prohibiting publishing discriminatory notices regarding sale or rental of housing. U.S. *v.* Hunter, 459 F. 2d. 205 (1972).

that discussion of public issues be presented on broadcast stations, and that each side of those issues must be given fair coverage. This is known as the fairness doctrine, which originated very early in the history of broadcasting and has maintained its present outlines for some time. It is an obligation whose content has been defined in a long series of FCC rulings in particular cases, and which is distinct from the statutory requirement of . . . the Communications Act of 1934, 48 Stat. 1081, as amended 47 U.S.C. 301 that equal time be allotted all qualified candidates for public office."[103]

In a challenge to the constitutionality of the "fairness doctrine" in 1969 the Court held: "In view of the scarcity of broadcast frequencies, the Government's role in allocating those frequencies, and the legitimate claims of those unable without governmental assistance to gain access to those frequencies for expression of their views, we hold the regulations and ruling at issue here are both authorized by statute and constitutional."[104] In the course of its opinion, the Court also made clear it viewed the equal-time requirement constitutional also.[105] Needless to say, implementation of these doctrines is fraught with difficulties, a fact recognized by the Federal Communication Commission. Significantly, on June 11, 1971, the commission released a Notice of Inquiry "instituting a broad-ranging study of the Fairness Doctrine and related public interest policies" and later ordered that panel discussions be held in Washington, D.C., for a three-day period commencing March 27, 1972, and that oral argument be held "before the Commission 'en banc' on March 30, 1972."[106] On June 22, 1972 the commission issued its first report providing some guidelines for broadcasters but raising more problems than it resolved and pointing to where Congress might take appropriate action to resolve some of the issues discussed.[107]

What of the Newsgatherer's Privilege? In a trio of cases decided together in 1972, the Supreme Court came to grips with an issue long debated and litigated. As the Court recounted it: "Petitioners Branzburg and Pappas and respondent Caldwell press First Amendment claims that may be simply put: that to gather news it is often necessary to agree either not to identify the source of information published or to publish only part of the facts revealed, or both;

---

103 Red Lion Broadcasting Co. v. FCC, 395 U.S. 367, 369-370 (1969).
104 *Ibid.*, 400-401.  105 *Ibid.*, 391.
106 37 *Fed. Reg.* 4978 (1972).  107 37 *Fed. Reg.* 12744 (1972).

that if the reporter is nevertheless forced to reveal these confidences to a grand jury, the source so identified and other confidential sources of other reporters will be measurably deterred from furnishing publishable information, all to the detriment of the free flow of information protected by the First Amendment. Although petitioners do not claim an absolute privilege against official interrogation in all circumstances, they assert that the reporter should not be forced either to appear or to testify before a grand jury or at trial until and unless sufficient grounds are shown for believing that the reporter possesses information relevant to a crime the grand jury is investigating, that the information the reporter has is unavailable from other sources, and that the need for the information is sufficiently compelling to override the claimed invasion of First Amendment interests occasioned by the disclosure."[108]

Pointing out that, although some states have provided a statutory privilege to newsmen, most along with the Federal Government have not, the Court said it was being asked to interpret "the First Amendment to grant newsmen a testimonial privilege that other citizens do not enjoy. This we decline to do." But the Court did go on to assert that newsgathering "is not without its First Amendment protections, and grand jury investigations if instituted or conducted other than in good faith, would pose wholly different issues for resolution under the First Amendment." Specifically, the Court suggested that a grand jury proceeding for the purpose of disrupting a reporter's relationship with his news sources "would have no justification."

For discussion of the Press's claim to a "right to know" and the free press-fair trial, issue, see pp. 341-342.

Historically, the right of petition is the primary right, the right peaceably to assemble a subordinate and instrumental right, as if Amendment I read: "the right of the people peaceably to assemble" *in order to* "petition the government."[109] To-

Expansion of the Right to Assemble and to Petition

---

[108] Branzburg *v.* Hayes (and companion cases), 408 U.S. 665 (1972). In a noteworthy California case, where an even greater privilege was claimed i.e. that a stolen goods statute interpreted "to prohibit receipt of stolen documents by newsmen for purposes of publication . . . abridges the freedom of the press . . . ," the court citing a host of previous decisions stressed that there was no unrestrained right to gather information. People *v.* Kunkin, 100 Cal. Rptr. 845 (1972). *See* particularly its discussion of New York Times Co. *v.* U.S. (1971), *ibid.*, 862.

[109] United States *v.* Cruikshank, 92 U.S. 542, 552 (1876).

day, however, the right of peaceable assembly is the language of the Court, "cognate to those of free speech and free press and is equally fundamental. . . . [It] is one that cannot be denied without violating those fundamental principles of liberty and justice which lie at the base of all civil and political institutions—principles which the Fourteenth Amendment embodies in the general terms of its due process clause. . . . The holding of meetings for peaceable political action cannot be proscribed. Those who assist in the conduct of such meetings cannot be branded as criminals on that score. The question . . . is not as to the auspices under which the meeting is held but as to its purposes; not as to the relations of the speakers, but whether their utterances transcend the bounds of the freedom of speech which the Constitution protects."[110] Even so, the right is not unlimited. Under the common law any assemblage was unlawful which aroused the apprehensions of "men of firm and rational minds with families and property there," and it is not unlikely that the First Amendment takes this principle into account.[111]

In recent years, "confrontation politics" has given the Court new and urgent occasion to divine the meaning of the right to assemble and petition. The prevailing view was stated by Justice Goldberg in 1965:

"From these decisions certain clear principles emerge. The rights of free speech and assembly, while fundamental in our democratic society, still do not mean that every one with opinions or beliefs to express may address a group at any public place and at any time. The constitutional guarantee of liberty implies the existence of an organized society maintaining public order, without which liberty itself would be lost in the excesses of anarchy. The control of travel on the streets is a clear example of governmental responsibility to insure this necessary order. A restriction in that relation, designed to promote the public convenience in the interest of all, and not susceptible to abuses of discriminatory application, cannot be disregarded by the attempted exercise of some civil right which, in other circumstances, would be entitled to protection. One would not be justified in ignoring the familiar red light be-

---

[110] De Jonge v. Ore., 299 U.S. 353, 364-365 (1937). *See also* Hague v. Com. for Indust'l Organization, 307 U.S. 496 (1939).

[111] People v. Kerrick, 261 Pac. Rep. 756 (1927); *and* State v. Butterworth, 104 N.J.L. 579 (1928), are two relatively early cases on the subject which were thoroughly argued and carefully decided.

cause this was thought to be a means of social protest. Nor could one, contrary to traffic regulations, insist upon a street meeting in the middle of Times Square at the rush hour as a form of freedom of speech or assembly. Governmental authorities have the duty and responsibility to keep their streets open and available for movement. A group of demonstrators could not insist upon the right to cordon off a street, or entrance to a public or private building, and allow no one to pass who did not agree to listen to their exhortations."[112]

But Justice Douglas has made a strong case for permitting petitioners wide latitude in choosing where to assemble and how to petition: "The right to petition for the redress of grievances has an ancient history and is not limited to writing a letter or sending a telegram to a congressman; it is not confined to appearing before the local city council, or writing letters to the President or Governor or Mayor. Conventional methods of petitioning may be, and often have been, shut off to large groups of our citizens. Legislators may turn deaf ears; formal complaints may be routed endlessly through a bureaucratic maze; courts may let the wheels of justice grind very slowly. Those who do not control television and radio, those who cannot afford to advertise in newspapers or circulate elaborate pamphlets may have only a more limited type of access to public officials. Their methods should not be condemned as tactics of obstruction and harassment as long as the assembly and petition are peaceable. . . ."[113] The late Justice Black confounded his libertarian supporters by the position he took in such cases. Some thought he was backtracking on his absolutist approach to freedom of speech. Black simply explained his views this way:

"While I have always believed that under the First and Fourteenth Amendments neither the State nor the Federal Government has any authority to censor the content of speech, I have never believed that any person has a right to give speeches or engage in demonstrations where he pleases and when he pleases."[114]

Five very recent cases illustrate that the Court is still having difficulty in determining precisely where and when the exercise of First Amendment freedoms is permissible. Over

[112] Cox *v.* Louisiana, 379 U.S. 536, 554 (1965).
[113] Adderley *v.* Florida, 385 U.S. 39, 50-51 (1966).
[114] Tinker *v.* Des Moines School District, 393 U.S. 503, 517 (1969).

the dissent of three Justices, the Court decided *per curiam* that a member of the American Friends Service Committee had been wrongly arrested for distributing leaflets on an avenue within the limits of Fort Sam Houston because "The Fort Commander chose not to exclude the public from the street where petitioner was arrested."[115] In short order, with a different set of dissenters, the Court held that arresting a student who failed to leave the scene where a State policeman was issuing a traffic ticket to someone else and who continued to engage the officer in conversation did not violate First Amendment rights. Justice White, speaking for the Court, said "the State has a legitimate interest in enforcing its traffic laws and its officers were entitled to enforce them free from possible interference or interruption from by-standers, even those claiming a third-party interest in the transaction."[116]

In a six-three decision, the Court directed a lower court to reconsider its decision that a company that operated two retail stores could not forbid solicitations on its parking lots. Justice Powell, speaking for the majority, said "Before an owner of private property can be subjected to the commands of the First and Fourteenth Amendments the privately owned property must assume to some significant degree the functional attributes of public property devoted to public use. The First and Fourteenth Amendments are limitations on state action, not on action by the owner of private property used only for private purposes."[117]

In another case, a majority of five held that the corporate owner of a large shopping center could forbid handbilling in the center. Again, Justice Powell, speaking for the majority, pointed out "It is true that facilities at the Center are used for certain meetings and for various promotional activities. The obvious purpose, recognized widely as legitimate and responsible business activity, is to bring potential shoppers to the Center. . . . There is no open-ended invitation to the public to use the Center for any and all purposes, however incompatible with the interests of both the stores and the shoppers whom

---

[115] Flower *v.* U.S., 407 U.S. 197, 198 (1972).

[116] Colton *v.* Kentucky, 407 U.S. 104, 109 (1972). The California Supreme Court recently made short shrift of the contention that "the operations of a roller skating rink are entitled to First Amendment protection." Sunset Amusement Co. *v.* Bd. of Police Com'rs., 496 P. 2d. 840 (1972).

[117] Central Hardware Co. *v.* NLRB, 407 U.S. 539 (1972).

they serve."[118] All the members of the Court but Justice Douglas upheld as constitutional a city ordinance that read: "No person, while on public or private grounds adjacent to any building in which a school or any class thereof is in session, shall willfully make or assist in the making of any noise or diversion which disturbs or tends to disturb the peace or good order of such school session or class thereof. . . ."[119]

In a day when it is fashionable in some quarters to speak of how repressive America has become, it is reassuring to see to what great lengths the governments in the United States actually go to permit people to exercise the constitutional rights to peaceably assemble and petition even in the face of provocation and threatened illegal activity.[120]

The application of the penumbra theory to the First Amendment is mentioned below, p. 368. At least two important liberties have been found by the Court in the shadow of the First Amendment. Fifteen years ago the Court held that "It is beyond debate that freedom to engage in association for the advancement of beliefs and ideas is an inseparable aspect of the 'liberty' assured by the Due Process Clause of the Fourteenth Amendment, which embraces freedom of speech [First Amendment]."[121] And a fine scholar assures us with evidence that the Court has accepted Justice Frankfurter's inclusion of academic freedom within the ambit of First Amendment protections.[122] In a *concurring* opinion in 1952 well worth a full reading, Justice Frankfurter asserted "But, in view of the nature of the teacher's relation to the effective exercise of the rights which are safeguarded by the Bill of Rights and by the Fourteenth Amendment, inhibition of freedom of thought, and of action upon thought, in the case of teachers brings the safeguards of those amendments vividly into operation."[123]

With respect to the right of association, the Supreme Court in an important decision in 1972 reversed a lower court decision which had upheld the denial of recognition as a campus

*Applicability of the Penumbra Theory: Freedom of Association and Academic Freedom*

[118] Lloyd Corp. *v.* Tanner, 407 U.S. 551 (1972).
[119] Grayned *v.* Rockford, 408 U.S. 104 (1972). *See* U.S. *v.* Crowthers, 456 F. 2d. 1074 (1972), where a U.S. court of appeals held that Pentagon officials could not discriminate against peace protesters in authorizing use of the Pentagon's concourse for "events."
[120] *See,* for example, preparations for the "May Day" demonstration in Washington, D.C., 1971 *Cong. Quart. Weekly Report,* 959ff., and 1015ff.
[121] N.A.A.C.P. *v.* Alabama, 357 U.S. 449, 460 (1958).
[122] Milton R. Konvitz, *Expanding Liberties* (New York, 1966), ch. III.
[123] Wieman *v.* Updegraff, 344 U.S. 183, 195 (1952).

organization to a group seeking to establish a chapter of Students for Democratic Society (SDS) at Central Connecticut State College.[124] Justice Powell, speaking for the Court, stated that "At the outset we note that state colleges and universities are not enclaves immune from the sweep of the First Amendment" and that "Among the rights protected by the First Amendment is the right of individuals to associate to further their personal beliefs." But in remanding the case to the lower court, the Supreme Court significantly indicated "that we are unable to conclude that no basis exists upon which nonrecognition might be appropriate." The Court went on to say that if the reason for nonrecognition was based on the organization's activities rather than its philosophy and "were factually supported by the record" it would "provide a basis for considering the propriety of nonrecognition. The critical line heretofore drawn for determining the permissibility of regulation is the line between mere advocacy and advocacy 'directed to inciting or producing imminent lawless action and . . . likely to incite or produce such action.' "

[124] Healy *v.* James, 408 U.S. 169 (1972).

# AMENDMENT II

A well-regulated militia being necessary to the security of a free state, the right of the people to keep and bear arms shall not be infringed.

The expression "a free state" is obviously here used in the generic sense, and refers to the United States as a whole rather than to the several states (*see* Article I, Section VIII, ¶s 15 and 16).

The amendment does not cover concealed weapons, the right "to bear arms" being the right simply to bear them openly. Nor will the Court apply it to sawed-off shot-guns, being unable to say of its own knowledge that their possession and use furthers in any way the preservation of a "well regulated militia."[1] Moreover, this right, being a right of citizenship rather than of person, may be denied aliens, at least on reasonable grounds.[2] Nor will the amendment prevent a State from making it unlawful for men to associate in a paramilitary organization, or to drill or parade with arms unless authorized by law.[3] Indeed, there are several State court decisions of recent vintage which hold that this amendment, unlike some others in the Bill of Rights, applies only to the National Government and not to the States,[4] and thus no bar in and of itself to State action.

"Arms"

[1] United States *v.* Miller, 307 U.S. 174 (1939), sustaining the National Firearms Act of June 26, 1934 (26 U.S.C. 5811), which levies a virtually prohibitive tax on the transfer of such weapons and requires their registration. Justice McReynold's opinion for the Court in this case contains interesting historical data regarding the antecedents of Amendment II. For an interesting discussion of coverage of present law, *see* 1960 *U.S. Code Cong. and Adm. News,* 2112ff.
[2] Patsone *v.* Pa., 232 U.S. 139 (1914) deals with a closely analogous point. *See also* Presser *v.* Ill., 116 U.S. 252 (1886). Recent decisions regarding denial of rights to aliens cast some doubt as to whether such a holding would pass muster today. Graham *v.* Richardson, 403 U.S. 365 (1971); Leger *v.* Sailer, 321 F. Supp. 250 (1970).
[3] Presser *v.* Illinois, 116 U.S. 252, 265 (1886).
[4] Burton *v.* Sills, 248 A. 2d. 462 (1967), appeal dismissed, 394 U.S. 812 (1969); Hardison *v.* State, 437 P. 2d. 868 (1968); Harris *v.* State, 432 P. 2d. 929 (1967).

299

# AMENDMENT III

No soldier shall, in time of peace, be quartered in any house without the consent of the owner, nor in time of war, but in a manner to be prescribed by law.

This and the following amendment sprang from certain grievances which contributed to bring about the American Revolution. They recognize the principle of the security of the dwelling which was embodied in the ancient maxim that a man's house is his castle. There has never been an instance of an attempted violation of the prohibition. There was, however, a novel challenge to the Federal Housing and Rent Act of 1947[1] on the grounds that the act "as amended and extended is and always was the incubator and hatchery of swarms of bureaucrats to be quartered as storm troopers upon the people in violation of Amendment III." A Federal District Court found the challenge without merit.[2]

[1] 61 *Stat.* 193 (1947).
[2] U.S. *v.* Valenzuela, 95 F. Supp. 363 (1951).

## AMENDMENT IV

The right of the people to be secure in their persons, houses, papers and effects, against unreasonable searches and seizures, shall not be violated, and no warrants shall issue but upon probable cause, supported by oath or affirmation, and particularly describing the place to be searched, and the persons or things to be seized.

*"Unreasonable Searches and Seizures"*

This amendment reflected the abhorrence of the times against so-called "general warrants," from which the Colonists had suffered more or less.[1] Today it derives its chief importance from the doctrine the beginnings of which were laid down by the Court in 1886 in Boyd *v.* United States,[2] that the above provisions must be read in conjunction with the self-incrimination clause of Amendment V, so that when any seizure of papers or things is "unreasonable" in the sense of the Fourth Amendment, such papers and things may not, under the Fifth Amendment, be received by any court, Federal or State, in evidence against the person from whom they were seized.

For years, the commonly accepted definition of "arrest" was "the taking of a person into custody in order that he may be forthcoming to answer for the commission of an offense."[3] The Supreme Court expanded the concept abruptly and emphatically in 1968: "There is some suggestion in the use of such terms as 'stop' and 'frisk' that such police conduct is outside the purview of the Fourth Amendment because neither action arises to the level of a 'search' or 'seizure' within the meaning of the Constitution. We emphatically reject this notion. It is quite plain that the Fourth Amendment governs 'seizures' of the person which do not eventuate in a trip to the station house and prosecution for crime—'arrests' in traditional terminology. *It must be recognized that whenever a police officer accosts an individual and restrains his freedom to walk away, he has 'seized' that person"[4]* (emphasis supplied).

*Arrest and "Stop" and "Frisk"*

The Court's expanded definition of "arrest" would on its face seem thereafter to require an "arrest" warrant. Previously, the Court had held that the Fourth Amendment did not

*Probable Cause*

---

[1] Hutchinson, *Foundations of the Constitution*, 293-298.
[2] 116 U.S. 616.
[3] Caleb Foote, "The Fourth Amendment: Obstacle or Necessity in the Law of Arrest," 51 *J. Crim., L.C. & P.S.* 402 (1960).
[4] Terry *v.* Ohio, 392 U.S. 1, 16 (1968).

require it.[5] But the Court went on to say in the 1968 decision: "We do not retreat from our holdings that the police must, whenever practicable, obtain advance judicial approval of searches and seizures through the warrant procedure. . . . But we deal here with an entire rubric of police conduct—necessarily swift action predicated upon the on-the-spot observations of the officer on the beat—which historically has not been, and as a practical matter could not be, subjected to the warrant procedure."[6] Consequently, arrests can and continue to be made for "probable cause." As the Court has seen it: "In dealing with probable cause, . . . as the very name implies, we deal with probabilities. These are not technical; they are the factual and practical considerations of everyday life in which reasonable and prudent men, not legal technicians act."[7] Also that probable cause exists where "the facts and circumstances within [the arresting officers'] knowledge and of which they had reasonably trustworthy information [are] sufficient in themselves to warrant a man of reasonable caution in the belief that" an offense has been or is being committed.[8] Clearly, "probable cause" is a very subjective judgment which law enforcement officers must sometimes make on the run. But the Court assures us that it is not as bad as it sounds:

"The scheme of the Fourth Amendment becomes meaningful only when it is assured that at some point the conduct of those charged with enforcing the laws can be subjected to the more detached, neutral scrutiny of a judge who must evaluate the reasonableness of a particular search or seizure in light of the particular circumstances. And in making that assessment it is imperative that the facts be judged against an objective standard: would the facts available to the officer at the moment of the seizure or the search warrant a man of reasonable caution in the belief that the action taken was appropriate? Anything less would invite intrusions upon constitutionally guaranteed rights based on nothing more substantial than inarticulate hunches, a result this Court has consistently refused to sanction. And simple 'good faith on the part of the arresting

5 Ker v. California, 374 U.S. 23, 41 (1963). See also U.S. v. Hall, 348 F. 2d. 837, 841-842 (1965); Ford v. U.S., 352 F. 2d. 927, 922 (1965).
6 Terry v. Ohio, 392 U.S. 1, 20 (1968).
7 Brinegar v. U.S., 338 U.S. 160, 175 (1919); Draper v. U.S. 358 U.S. 307, 313 (1959).
8 Carroll v. U.S., 267 U.S. 132, 162 (1925); Draper v. U.S., 358 U.S. 307, 313, (1959).

officer is not enough.' . . . If subjective good faith alone were the test, the protections of the Fourth Amendment would evaporate, and the people would be 'secure in their persons, houses, papers, and effects,' only in the discretion of the police."[9]

Predictably, the Court has had great difficulty in etching out a clear picture of what in effect constitutes "probable cause." In a recent round with that concept, as applied to a warrant, the Court was split in several directions.[10] There, Chief Justice Burger reviewed the leading cases on the subject and then said "We cannot conclude that a policeman's knowledge of a suspect's reputation—something that policemen frequently know . . . is not a 'practical consideration of everyday life' upon which an officer (or a magistrate) may properly rely in assessing the reliability of an informant's tip."[11]

But in a more recent case dealing with a Jacksonville, Florida, vagrancy ordinance (*see* p. 352), the Court inveighed against arrests on suspicion: "We allow our police to make arrests only on 'probable cause.' . . . Arresting a person on suspicion, like arresting a person for investigation, is foreign to our system, even when the arrest is for past criminality."[12] The Court then offered some astounding statistics revealing that the notion that such arrests are "foreign to our system" is more honored in the breach than the observance. In three years, 1968 through 1970, over 300,000 people in the United States were arrested on vagrancy charges and well over 200,000 on suspicion.[13]

With respect to the propriety of a law officer frisking someone he has stopped, the Court in the very case where it minted the new broader definition of "arrest" admitted that there is still some difference between stopping someone and arresting him:

"The crux of this case, however, is not the propriety of Officer McFadden's taking steps to investigate petitioner's suspicious behavior, but rather *whether there was justification for McFadden's invasion of Terry's personal security by searching him for weapons in the course of that investigation.* We are now concerned with more than the governmental interest in

9 Terry *v.* Ohio, 392 U.S. 1, 21-22 (1968).
10 U.S. *v.* Harris, 403 U.S. 573 (1971).
11 *Ibid.,* 583.
12 Papachristou *v.* City of Jacksonville, 405 U.S. 156, 169 (1972).
13 *Ibid.*

investigating crime; in addition, there is the more immediate interest of the police officer in taking steps to assure himself that the person with whom he is dealing is not armed with a weapon that could unexpectedly and fatally be used against him. Certainly it would be unreasonable to require that police officers take unnecessary risks in the performance of their duties. American criminals have a long tradition of armed violence, and every year in this country many law enforcement officers are killed in the line of duty, and thousands more are wounded. Virtually all of these deaths and a substantial portion of the injuries are inflicted with guns and knives.

"In view of these facts, we cannot blind ourselves to the need for law enforcement officers to protect themselves and other prospective victims of violence in situations where they may lack probable cause for an arrest. When an officer is justified in believing that the individual whose suspicious behavior he is investigating at close range is armed and presently dangerous to the officer or to others, it would appear to be clearly unreasonable to deny the officer the power to take necessary measures to determine whether the person is in fact carrying a weapon and to neutralize the threat of physical harm.

"We must still consider, however, the nature and quality of the intrusion on individual rights which must be accepted if police officers are to be conceded the right to search for weapons in situations where probable cause to arrest for crime is lacking. Even a limited search of the outer clothing for weapons constitutes a severe, though brief, intrusion upon cherished personal security, and it must surely be an annoying, frightening, and perhaps humiliating experience.

"Our evaluation of the proper balance that has to be struck in this type of case leads us to conclude that there must be a narrowly drawn authority to permit a reasonable search for weapons for the protection of the police officer, where he has reason to believe that he is dealing with an armed and dangerous individual, regardless of whether he has probable cause to arrest the individual for a crime. The officer need not be absolutely certain that the individual is armed; the issue is whether a reasonably prudent man in the circumstances would be warranted in the belief that his safety or that of others was in danger. And in determining whether the officer acted reasonably in such circumstances, due weight must be given, not to inchoate and unparticularized suspicion or 'hunch' but to the specific reasonable inferences which he is entitled to draw from the facts in light of his experience.[14] This view was vigorously reinforced by the Court in June 1972.[15]

In 1972, the Supreme Court had occasion to address the question of *who* could issue arrest warrants. The Charter of the city of Tampa, Florida, authorizes the clerks of the Municipal Court to issue certain arrest warrants. It was contended that the Fourth Amendment requires that a "judicial officer" determine whether or not probable cause exists for issuing a warrant. The Court held that there was no constitutional reason that "all warrant authority must reside exclusively in a judge or lawyer." The Court said that "an issuing magistrate must meet [only] two tests. He must be neutral and detached, and he must be capable of determining whether probable cause exists for the requested arrest or search."[16]

It has long been axiomatic that a search may be made without warrant when it is incident to a lawful arrest.[17] But the Court has recently held that such a search must be limited to the person "and the area from within which he might have obtained either a weapon or something that could have been used as evidence against him."[18] Conversely, however, the Court has recognized that there are unusual circumstances where a search without warrant must be made even though there is no arrest: "The Fourth Amendment does not require police officers to delay in the course of an investigation if to do so would gravely endanger their lives or the lives of others."[19]

*Searches Without Warrant*

14 Terry *v.* Ohio, 392 U.S. 1, 25-27 (1968). For a good summary of a suspect's right to defend himself from the use of excessive force by an arresting officer, *see* State *v.* Ramsdell, 285 A. 2d. 399 (1971).

15 Adams *v.* Williams, 407 U.S. 143 (1972). *Cf.* the decision of the California Supreme Court in The People *v.* the Superior Court, 496 P. 2d. 1205 (1972).

16 Shadwick *v.* Tampa, 407 U.S. 345 (1972).

17 Edward W. Nottingham, "Scope of Searches Incident to Arrest," 43 *Colorado Law Review*, 63 (1971). *See also* State *v.* Gustafson, 258 So. 2d. 1 (1972).

18 Chimel *v.* California, 395 U.S. 752 (1969) and cases discussed therein; Vale *v.* Louisiana, 399 U.S. 30 (1970); Chamber *v.* Maroney, 399 U.S. 42 (1970); Coolidge *v.* New Hampshire, 403 U.S. 443 (1971). For a discussion of the interesting and complex question of who has "standing" to challenge search of an automobile, *see* Palmer *v.* State, 286 A. 2d. 572 (1972) and Kurtz *v.* People, 294 P. 2d. 97 (1972).

19 Warden *v.* Hayden, 387 U.S., 294, 299 (1967). But there must be an "exigent situation." People *v.* Miller, 496 P. 2d. 1228 (1972) *and* People *v.* Smith, 496 P. 2d. 1261 (1972). One state court has held that "a search by

For a time certain kinds of administrative inspections encompassed generally in municipal fire, health, and housing inspection programs were regarded as at most touching only at the periphery of the "important interest safeguarded by the Fourteenth Amendment's protection against official intrusion,"[20] and as not requiring a warrant. The landmark case of that genre was expressly overruled in 1967. In that year the Court held that the Fourth Amendment bars prosecution of a person who refused to permit a warrantless code-enforcement inspection of his personal residence.[21] However, in 1971, the Supreme Court held that the home visitation provided for in the New York law in connection with the AFDC program is a reasonable administrative tool which does not violate the Fourth and Fourteenth Amendments.[22] The Court distinguished this case from the one previously mentioned on the grounds that in the earlier case, the Court was dealing with a pending criminal prosecution whereas in this case "The *only* consequence of her refusal [to allow the visit] is that the payment of benefits ceases" (emphasis supplied).

And in 1972, the Court, over a bitter dissent of Justice Douglas, upheld a warrantless search of a gun dealer's locked storeroom during business hours.[23] This kind of search is explicitly authorized under the Gun Control Act of 1968.[24] Justice White, speaking for the Court, explained: "We have little difficulty in concluding that where, as here, regulatory inspections further urgent *federal* interest and the possibilities of abuse and threat to privacy are not of impressive dimensions, the inspection may proceed without a warrant, *where specifically authorized by statute*" (emphasis supplied).[25] There seems to be a suggestion here that the Court will give greater deference to Congressional determinations as to when search

---

a parole or probation officer [of probationers and parolees] need not satisfy completely the usual test of 'probable cause.' " State *v.* Davis, 496 P. 2d. 923 (1972).

[20] Frank *v.* Maryland, 359 U.S. 360 (1959); Eaton *v.* Price, 364 U.S. 263 (1960).

[21] Camara *v.* Municipal Court, 387 U.S. 523 (1967). *See also* Colonnade Corp. *v.* U.S., 397 U.S. 72 (1970). *Cf.* Bennett *v.* Commonwealth, 188 S.E. 2d. 215 (1972).

[22] Wyman *v.* James, 400 U.S. 309 (1971).

[23] U.S. *v.* Biswell, 406 U.S. 311 (1972).

[24] *Ibid.*, 317. *See also* Justice Douglas's dissent, *ibid.*, 317.

[25] *Ibid.*, 317. The same Fourth Amendment standards of probable cause are applicable to arrests as well as to searches. Commonwealth *v.* Stevens, 283 N.E. 2d. 673 (1972) and cases cited therein.

warrants can be dispensed with than it will to determinations of local and State officials.

As the constitutional provision makes plain, warrants for searches shall be issued only for "probable cause." All that has been said above about "probable cause" with respect to arrest has application here. One troublesome question with respect to search warrants is how quickly must they be executed to meet the constitutional test of reasonableness. The New York Appeals Court recently had occasion to canvass the problem, and it held that the State law which required "forthwith execution . . . does not mean immediately, but is qualified by the practicalities and exigencies that the executing officer faces in the performance of duty."[26]

Searches With Warrants

The frequent and fearsome plane hijackings have undoubtedly had a heavy impact on judicial as well as public attitudes with respect to searches, at least at airports. A secret system has been devised for spotting potential hijackers so that they can be searched before they board the aircraft. In view of past decisions dealing with searches generally, it would seem that such a system would face heavy sledding in the courts. Yet, in 1972, in a highly unusual proceeding in prestigious United States Court of Appeals for the Second Circuit heard a challenge to the system behind closed doors.[27] The court was very uneasy about the secrecy, stating that "While secret proceedings are, of course, odious and smack of ideologies as repugnant to the founders as they are today, there is precedent for the proposition that limited exceptions are constitutionally permissible." The court justified the search on the grounds of the need to protect passengers and justified the secrecy of the profile used for determining whom to search on the grounds that it would be "relatively simple for the prospective hijacker to avoid the initial designation were any of the norms employed to become generally known."

A Special Problem: Airport Searches

As indicated at the outset of this discussion of the Fourth Amendment, in 1914 the Court barred in a Federal prosecution the use of evidence secured through an illegal search and seizure (the "exclusionary rule").[28] In 1949 when the question

The Exclusionary Rule

[26] People v. Glen, 331 N.Y.S. 2d. 656 (1972).
[27] The Bell case, N.Y. Times, July 9, 1972. Also see U.S. v. Epperson, 454 F. 2d. 769 (1972). But see "Ruling Restricts Airport Searches," N.Y. Times, Dec. 10, 1972.
[28] Weeks v. U.S., 232 U.S. 383 (1914).

was raised as to whether or not States should likewise be barred from using such evidence, Justice Frankfurter speaking for the Court explained that the earlier decision "was not derived from the explicit requirements of the Fourth Amendment; it was not based on legislation expressing Congressional policy in the enforcement of the Constitution. The decision was a matter of judicial implication. Since then it has been frequently applied and we stoutly adhere to it. . . ."[29] Then in what looked like an invitation for Congress to act on the matter, Frankfurter concluded by saying: "And though we have interpreted the Fourth Amendment to forbid the admission of such evidence, a different question would be presented if Congress under its legislative powers were to pass a statute purporting to negate [the exclusionary] doctrine. We would then be faced with the problem of the respect to be accorded the legislative judgment on an issue as to which, in default of that judgment, we have been forced to depend upon our own. Problems of a converse character, also not before us, would be presented should Congress under §5 of the Fourteenth Amendment undertake to enforce the rights guaranteed by attempting to make the [exclusionary] doctrine binding upon the States."[30]

The arrangement, whereby the Federal jurisdiction used the exclusionary rule and some thirty States did not, created some predictable difficulties. Some Federal law enforcement officials turned over evidence they could not use to State officials if they could use it to establish the commission of a State crime. This practice became common enough to be honored in the "silver-platter doctrine" used by courts to justify the use of such evidence. It also covered the situation where State officials gave Federal officials evidence that the latter could not have used had they obtained it themselves in the manner in which State officials had.[31]

Then in 1961 in a ringing decision the Court held that: "Since the Fourth Amendment's right of privacy has been declared enforceable against the States through the Due Process Clause of the Fourteenth, it is enforceable against them by the

29 Wolf v. Colorado, 338 U.S. 25 (1949).
30 *Ibid.*, 33.
31 The zany history of the Silver Platter doctrine is described in a decision that put a stop to it. Elkins v. U.S., 364 U.S. 206 (1960).

same sanction of exclusion as is used against the Federal Government."[32]

One of the fascinating questions of American constitutional law is, *why* an exclusionary rule? Evidence is evidence. A gun found in an illegal search may very well link a defendant to a murder beyond a reasonable doubt. Why not use it? And, if it was procured illegally, punish those who acted illegally, don't discard the evidence, some have said. Protagonists of the rule have argued that only by excluding the evidence can you get law enforcement officials to behave. Other remedies just do not work.

A notable dissent from Chief Justice Burger in 1971 indicates that the last word may not have been spoken on the exclusionary rule. "I do not question the need for some remedy to give meaning and teeth to the constitutional guarantees against unlawful conduct by government officials. . . . But the hope that this objective could be accomplished by the exclusion of reliable evidence from criminal trials was hardly more than a wistful dream. Although I would hesitate to abandon it until some meaningful substitute is developed, the history of the Suppression Doctrine demonstrates that it is both conceptually sterile and practically ineffective in accomplishing its stated objective. Some clear demonstration of the benefits and effectiveness of the Exclusionary Rule is required to justify it in view of the high price it extracts from society—the release of countless guilty criminals. . . . But there is no empirical evidence to support the claim that the rule actually deters illegal conduct of law enforcement officials."[33]

The history of the Supreme Court's handling of the issue arising from wiretapping and electronic surveillance is as complicated as it is fascinating.[34] The short of the history pertinent

*Wiretapping and Electronic Surveillance*

[32] Mapp *v.* Ohio, 367 U.S. 643 (1961). The New Hampshire Supreme Court has held that where evidence is gained by private individuals acting on their own and not as agents of the police, it is not a violation of the Fourth Amendment, State *v.* Salsman, 290 A. 2d. 618 (1972). Miramontes *v.* Superior Court, 102 Calif. Rptr. 182 (1972); People *v.* Mangiefico, 102 Calif. Rptr. 449 (1972); U.S. *v.* Knox, 458 F. 2d. 612 (1972).

[33] Bivens *v.* Six Unknown Named Agents, 403 U.S. 388, 415 (1971). The Pennsylvania Supreme Court recently held that the State may not introduce at trial the testimony of a witness whose existence was solely come upon as the result of an illegal search. Commonwealth *v.* Cephas, 291 A. 2d. 106 (1972).

[34] Justice Clark provided a good short history in his opinion for the Court in Berger *v.* N.Y., 388 U.S. 41 (1967).

here is that from 1928 until the late 1960's, the Court held that the Fourth Amendment did not cover these activities except when electronic snooping was accomplished by a "physical trespass," like putting a foot-long spike with a microphone attached into the heating duct of a house. After 1934, cases involving the old-fashioned type of wiretapping were decided on the basis of the meaning of the Communications Act of 1934,[35] which on its face seemed to prohibit wiretapping, but clumsy wording made it an arguable proposition that only wiretapping *and* divulging the contents was forbidden, not wiretapping alone. But all the subtle distinctions, all the formidable rhetoric ("fruit of the poisonous tree") which emerged from these cases were overtaken by events. In a pair of cases decided in 1967, the Court finally swept away past distinctions and held that both wiretapping and electronic surveillance through a "bug" or other device are now covered by the Fourth Amendment.[36] That does not mean therefore that they cannot be used, for, as we have already seen, searches are permissible if done under a warrant issued for probable cause. Subsequently, Congress passed the Omnibus Crime Control and Safe Streets Act of 1968[37] providing an elaborate procedure under which "the Attorney General, or any Assistant Attorney General specially designated by the Attorney General, may authorize an application to a Federal Judge of competent jurisdiction for and such judge may grant . . . an order authorizing or approving the interception of wire or oral communications by the Federal Bureau of Investigation, or a Federal agency having responsibility for the investigation of an offense as to which application is made. . . ."

While still Attorney General, John Mitchell took the position that, in dealing with the threat of domestic subversion, the government needs and has the inherent power to use wiretaps and other devices to maintain surveillance. Mitchell quickly received a verbal thrashing in the courts. A United States Court of Appeals said in answer to him: "The government has not pointed to, and we do not find, one written phrase in the Constitution, in the statutory law, or in the case

[35] 48 *Stat.* 1102.
[36] Berger *v.* N.Y., 388 U.S. 41 (1967); Katz *v.* U.S., 389 U.S. 347 (1967); U.S. *v.* White, 401 U.S. 745 (1971). U.S. courts of appeals recently have held that wiretaps do not violate the Fourth Amendment "when one party consents but the other party has no knowledge of the phone tap." U.S. *v.* Quintana, 457 F. 2d. 874, 878 (1972) and cases cited therein.
[37] 18 U.S.C. 2510 *et seq.*

law of the United States, which exempts the President, the Attorney General, or federal law enforcement from the restrictions of the Fourth Amendment in the case at hand: . . . that in dealing with the threat of domestic subversion, the Executive Branch of our government, including the Attorney General and the law enforcement agents of the United States, is subject to the limitations of the Fourth Amendment to the Constitution when undertaking searches and seizures for oral communications by wire."[38] In more restrained language, the Supreme Court itself by a vote of 8-0 (Justice Rehnquist not participating) recently rejected Mitchell's contention, saying: "Thus, we conclude that the Government's concerns do not justify departure in this case from the customary Fourth Amendment requirement of judicial approval prior to initiation of a search or surveillance. Although some added burden will be imposed upon the Attorney General, this inconvenience is justified in a free society to protect constitutional values. Nor do we think the Government's domestic surveillance powers will be impaired to any significant degree. A prior warrant establishes presumptive validity of the surveillance and will minimize the burden of justification in post-surveillance judicial review. By no means of least importance will be the reassurance of the public generally that indiscriminate wiretapping and bugging of law-abiding citizens cannot occur.

"We emphasize, before concluding this opinion, the scope of our decision. As stated at the outset, this case involves only the domestic aspects of national security. We have not addressed, and express no opinion as to, the issues which may be involved with respect to activities of foreign powers or their agents. Nor does our decision rest on the language of §2511 (3) or any other section of Title III of the Omnibus Crime Control and Safe Streets Act of 1968. That Act does not attempt to define or delineate the powers of the President to meet domestic threats to the national security."[39] A few days later, the Court ruled in a 5-4 decision, with the non-Nixon appointees constituting the majority, that grand jury witnesses could, in an adjudication for civil contempt for refusing to answer questions before a Federal grand jury, invoke as a de-

[38] U.S. *v.* U.S. District Court for E.D. of Mich., 444 F. 2d. 651, 665-667 (1971).
[39] U.S. *v.* U.S. District Court, 407 U.S. 297 (1972). For statistics on use of Federal wiretapping *see* Justice Douglas's dissent, *ibid.*

fense that the interrogation would be based on illegal wire-taps.[40] The majority pointed out that Federal law provides that the contents of wiretapping "may not be received in evidence in any proceeding in or before . . . any grand jury, . . . if disclosure of that information would be in violation of this chapter." Justice Rehnquist, speaking for the dissenters, protested bitterly the majority's interpretation of the statute, asserting that "The Court has at least figuratively stood on its head both the language and the legislative history of this section [of the statute] in order to conclude that it was intended to expand the rights of criminal defendants." Despite its importance, it should be noted that this decision involves statutory and not constitutional interpretation.

Interestingly enough, in an interview following the earlier wiretap decision, Attorney General Kleindienst said that the decision would reduce the Government's intelligence activity into subversive activities "but not to an extent that will damage national security."[41]

**Non-retro-activity of Fourth Amendment Decisions** As pointed out earlier (pp. 192-193), recent Supreme Court decisions with respect to the Fourth Amendment are generally not retroactive in application.

**Waiver of Fourth Amendment Rights** Like other important rights, the rights to be free from unreasonable search and seizures can be waived. But as the California Supreme Court recently put it, those rights "where reasonably related to the achievement of a proper purpose, may be waived as a condition to gaining some other advantage, but the waiver must appear of record to have been knowingly and intelligently made."[42]

**A Novel Contention Rejected** In a recent Connecticut court challenge to a compulsory sex education course in school, one of the contentions of the parent-plaintiffs was that they feared that their children would disclose private family activities or conversations which had taken place in their homes. The court held that "Disclosures of this nature are not constitutionally protected and do not constitute an unlawful invasion of privacy under the fourth amendment . . . nor under any other law known to the court."[43]

40 Gelbard *v.* U.S., 408 U.S. 41 (1972).
41 Fred P. Graham, "Wiretap Ruling Called No Danger to Security," *The Dallas Morning News*, June 24, 1972.
42 People *v.* Myers, 494 P. 2d. 684 (1972). *Cf.* Himmage *v.* State, 496 P. 2d. 763 (1972).
43 Hopkins *v.* Hamden Bd. of Ed., 289 A. 2d. 914, 924 (1971). *But see* p. 288, n. 91.

# AMENDMENT V

No person shall be held to answer for a capital or otherwise infamous crime, unless on a presentment or indictment of a grand jury, except in cases arising in the land or naval forces, or in the militia, when in actual service in time of war or public danger; nor shall any person be subject for the same offense to be twice put in jeopardy of life or limb; nor shall be compelled in any criminal case to be a witness against himself, nor be deprived of life, liberty or property, without due process of law; nor shall private property be taken for public use without just compensation.

Amendments IV, V, VI, and VIII constitute a "bill of rights" for accused persons. For the most part they were compiled from the Bills of Rights of the early State constitutions, and in more than one respect they represented a distinct advance upon English law of that time and indeed for many years afterward.

"Infamous crime" is one rendered so by the penalty attached to it. Any offense punishable by imprisonment, or loss of civil or political privileges, or hard labor, is, the Court has held, "infamous" in the sense of the Constitution.[1] But "what punishments shall be considered infamous may be affected by the changes of public opinion from one age to another. In former times, being put in the stocks was not considered as necessarily infamous. . . . But at the present day [it] might be thought an infamous punishment."[2]

"Presentment or indictment": A presentment is returned upon the initiative of the grand jury; an indictment is returned upon evidence laid before that body by the public prosecutor.

The "grand jury" here stipulated for is the grand jury as it was known to the common law, and so consists of at least twelve and not more than twenty-three persons chosen from the community by a process prescribed by law. Once constituted it has large powers of investigation, but its presentments or indictments must have the support of at least twelve members. Despite the fact that much of the Bill of Rights has been incorporated into the Fourteenth Amendment, it has been

[1] *Ex parte* Wilson, 114 U.S. 417 (1885); United States *v.* Moreland, 258 U.S. 433 (1922). *But see* Harvin *v.* U.S., 445 F. 2d. 675 (1971).
[2] *Ex parte* Wilson, 114 U.S. 417, 427-428 (1885).

held that States are not required to employ grand juries as long as the process they employ is a fair one.[3]

The use of grand juries to combat crime and to have the power to make reports is controversial and interesting but beyond the scope of a discussion of the meaning of this particular constitutional provision. For those interested in pursuing that subject see citation below.[4]

The Case
of the
Saboteurs

"The land and naval forces" are, of course, subject to military law, administered through the court-martial (see Article I, Section VIII, ¶14). But the exception also for a time served a broader purpose, namely, "to authorize the trial by court-martial of the members of the armed forces for all that class of crimes which under the Fifth and Sixth Amendments might otherwise have been deemed triable in the civil courts."[5] The term "land and naval forces" included at one time camp followers as well as enrollees[6] but all that has been changed by recent decisions as described earlier on pp. 88-90.

In the Case of the Saboteurs[7] who landed on our shores in June 1942 from German submarines and were later picked up in civilian dress in New York City and Chicago by the FBI, the Court declined to say that it included enemy personnel who were found in disguise within our lines and so were charged with violating the laws of war. The Court's position was that such cases had never been deemed to fall within the guaranties of the amendments, citing in this connection Section 2 of the Act of Congress of April 10, 1806, which, following the Resolution of the Continental Congress of August 21, 1776, imposed the death penalty on alien spies "according to the law and usage of nations, by sentence of a general court martial."[8] The trial of the saboteurs by military commission was conse-

---

[3] ". . . we are unable to say that the substitution for a presentment or indictment by a grand jury of the proceeding by information, after examination and commitment by a magistrate, certifying to the probable guilt of the defendant, with the right on his part to aid of counsel, and to the cross-examination of the witness produced for prosecution, is not due process of law." Hurtado v. Cal., 110 U.S. 516, 538 (1884); Alexander v. Louisiana, 405 U.S. 625, 633 (1972); Gasaway v. Page, 303 F. Supp. 391 (1969), Freeman v. Page, 443 F. 2d. 493, 495 (1971).

[4] Senator John L. McClellan, "The Organized Crime Act or Its Critics: Which Threatens Civil Liberties?" 46 Notre Dame Lawyer, 55 (1970).

[5] Ex parte Quirin, 317 U.S. 1, 43 (1942).

[6] Charles K. Burdick, Law of the American Constitution (N.Y., 1922), 264, and cases there cited.

[7] Note 5 above.

[8] 317 U.S. 1, 41. The famous case of Major André during the Revolution was a prototype of the Case of the Saboteurs. Ibid., 31, note 9.

quently held to be within the merged powers of the President and Congress; but inasmuch as they were really conducting a hostile operation against the United States, in a way forbidden by the laws of war, it would have been reasonable to hold that they were answerable to the President simply in his capacity as Supreme Commander. This, in fact, was the result which was later arrived at by the Court in General Yamashita's case, the doctrine of which is summed up by Justice Rutledge, in his dissent, as follows: "That there is no law restrictive upon these proceedings other than whatever rules and regulations may be prescribed for their government by the executive authority or the military."[9] The charge against Yamashita was that he had systematically violated the laws of war.

"In time of war or public danger" took on new meaning in 1968 as a result of the important case, O'Callahan v. Parker. There the Court held that "We have concluded that the crime to be under military jurisdiction must be service connected, lest 'cases arising in the land or naval forces, or in the Militia, when in actual service in time of War or public danger,' as used in the Fifth Amendment, be expanded to deprive every member of the Armed services of the benefits of an indictment by a grand jury and a trial by a jury of his peers."[10] Previously, it was assumed that all servicemen on active duty were subject to court-martial *at all times,* as were members of the militia in times of war or public danger.[11] The explicit exception for men in service, makes clear that as to all other persons, the Fifth Amendment is designed for times of war as well as for times of peace. But it is obvious that in order to enforce its provisions, as well as those of the following amendment, the courts must be open and functioning properly.[12]

[9] *In re* General Yamashita, 327 U.S. 1, 81 (1946). For a latitudinarian view of the jurisdiction of courts-martial, *see* Charles Warren, "Spies and the Power of Congress to Subject Certain Classes of Civilians to Trial by Court Martial," *American Law Review,* 195-228 (March-April, 1919); also Article 106 of the Uniform Code of Military Justice: "Any person who in time of war found lurking or acting as a spy in or about any of the fortifications, posts, quarters, or encampments of any of the armies of the United States, or elsewhere [N.B.] shall be tried by a general court-martial or by a military commission, and shall, on conviction thereof, suffer death." 10 U.S.C. 906.

[10] O'Callahan v. Parker, 395 U.S. 258, 272-273 (1969).

[11] Johnson v. Sayre, 158 U.S. 109 (1895); Lee v. Madigan, 358 U.S. 228, 232-235 (1959).

[12] *Ex parte* Milligan, 4 Wall. 2 (1866). The attempt of counsel of the Saboteurs to invoke this case in behalf of their clients was countered by the Court pointing out that Milligan had not surrendered his civilian status.

315

When
"Jeopardy"
Arises

"Twice in jeopardy": For years, because of legal complexities this phrase did not seem to mean the comprehensive protection it appears to mean on its face.[13] Furthermore, it was held for a long time that this provision was not applicable to the States.[14] All that has been changed by recent decisions. The Court in 1968 held that the provision did indeed apply to the States, going on to say: "The fundamental nature of the guarantee against double jeopardy can hardly be doubted. Its origins can be traced back to Greek and Roman times and it became established in the common law of England long before this Nation's independence. . . . As this Court put it in Green v. U.S. . . . (1957), 'the underlying idea . . . is that the State with all its resources and power should not be allowed to make repeated attempts to convict an individual for an alleged offense, thereby subjecting him to embarrassment, expense and ordeal compelling him to live in a continuing state of anxiety and insecurity, as well as enhancing the possibility that even though innocent he may be found guilty.' "[15] In subsequent cases, the Supreme Court has viewed with critical eye any governmental action which smacks of double jeopardy within *one system* of government be it State or Federal.[16] These decisions have caused some observers to wonder about the future survival of previous decisions which permitted successive prosecutions by Federal and State governments for the same crime on the theory that they were separate sovereigns. Thus far the Supreme Court has not had occasion to overrule them.[17] Whatever the Court does in the future on that issue, it is highly unlikely that it will alter three other well-settled propositions. One, if a jury cannot agree, or if it is illegally constituted, there is no trial, and so no jeopardy, under the clause; and the same result follows where a verdict of conviction is set aside on appeal by the accused.[18] (A declaration of mistrials for other reasons is more complicated in present

13 For extended discussion of one of these complexities *see* Ashe v. Swenson, 397 U.S. 436 (1970).

14 Palko v. Conn., 302 U.S. 319 (1937).

15 Benton v. Maryland, 395 U.S. 784, 795-796 (1969). *See* People v. Rushin, 194 N.W. 2d. 718 (1971). *See also* Simpson v. Florida, 403 U.S. 384 (1971).

16 Waller v. Florida 397 U.S. 387 (1970); Ashe v. Swenson, 397 U.S. 436 (1970); Simpson v. Florida, 403 U.S. 384 (1971).

17 *See* Bartkus v. U.S., 359 U.S. 121 (1959); Abbate v. U.S., 359 U.S. 187 (1959).

18 U.S. v. Perez, 9 Wheat. 579 (1824); Trono v. U.S., 199 U.S. 521 (1905).

law.[19] As the Court states it: "The trial judge must recognize that lack of preparedness by the government to continue the trial directly implicates policies underpinning both the double jeopardy provision and the speedy trial guarantee. Alternatively, the judge must bear in mind the potential risks of abuse by the defendant of society's unwillingness to unnecessarily subject him to repeated prosecution. Yet in the final analysis, the judge must always temper the decision whether or not to abort a trial by considering the importance to the defendant of being able, once and for all, to conclude his confrontation with society through the verdict of a tribunal he might believe to be favorably disposed to his fate.")[20]

Two, if government seeks to "impose both a civil and criminal sanction in respect to the same act or omission," this is not precluded because the clause refers only to criminal liability.[21]

Three, the judgment of a court-martial rendered with jurisdiction is entitled to the same finality as to the issues involved as the judgment of a civil court in cases within its jurisdiction. Hence a soldier, acquitted of a charge of homicide by a court-martial of competent jurisdiction was not subsequently triable by a civil court exercising authority in the same place.[22]

Another complicated issue with which the Court has had to deal under "double jeopardy" is, in the event of a retrial, may the sentence in the second trial be more severe without doing violence to the constitutional provision. The Court's answer: "Due process of law requires that vindictiveness against a defendant for having successfully attacked his first conviction must play no part in the sentence he receives after a new trial. And since the fear of such vindictiveness may unconstitutionally deter a defendant's exercise of the right to appeal or collaterally attack his first conviction, due process also requires that a defendant be freed of apprehension of such a retaliatory motivation on the part of a sentencing judge.

"In order to assure the absence of such a motivation, we have concluded that whenever a judge imposes a more severe

[19] *See* U.S. *v.* Jorn, 400 U.S. 470 (1971).
[20] *Ibid.*, 486. *See also* State *v.* White, 285 A. 2d. 832 (1972); Commonwealth *v.* Shaffer, 288 A. 2d. 727 (1972); Baker *v.* State, 289 A. 2d. 348 (1972.)
[21] Helvering *v.* Mitchell, 303 U.S. 391 (1938); U.S. *v.* Hees, 317 U.S. 537 (1943); *but see* McKeehan *v.* U.S., 438 F. 2d. 739, 744 (1971).
[22] Grafton *v.* U.S., 206 U.S. 333 (1907). *See also* Hiatt *v.* Brown, 339 U.S. 103 (1950); Johnson *v.* Eisentrager, 339 U.S. 763 (1950); Waller *v.* Florida, 397 U.S. 387, 393-394 (1970).

sentence upon a defendant after a new trial, the reasons for his doing so must affirmatively appear."[23]

"Life or limb" has come to mean, since drawing and quartering have gone out of style, life or liberty.

Source of the Self-Incrimination Clause

"Nor shall be compelled in any criminal case to be a witness against himself":

The source of this clause was the maxim that "no man is bound to accuse himself (*nemo tenetur prodere*—or *accusare —seipsum*)," which was brought forward in England late in the sixteenth century in protest against the inquisitorial methods of the ecclesiastical courts. What the advocates of the maxim meant was merely that a person ought not to be put on trial and compelled to answer questions to his detriment unless he had first been properly accused, i.e., by the grand jury. But the idea once set going gained headway rapidly, especially after 1660, when it came to have attached to it most of its present-day corollaries.[24]

Its Modern Application

Under the clause as it is today administered by the Supreme Court, a *witness* in *any* governmental proceeding whatsoever including legislative investigations, in which testimony is legally required may refuse to answer any question his answer to which might be used against him in a future criminal proceeding, or which might uncover further evidence against him.[25] But the witness must explicitly claim his constitutional immunity or he will be considered to have waived it;[26] and he is not the final judge of the validity of his claim.[27] Moreover, the privilege exists solely for the protection of the witness himself,

---

[23] North Carolina *v.* Pearce, 395 U.S. 711, 725-726 (1969). *Cf.* Roberson *v.* State, 258 So. 2d. 257 (1972).

[24] *See generally* J. H. Wigmore, *Evidence in Trials at Common Law,* IV (Boston, 1923), Section 2250; *also* Edward S. Corwin, "The Supreme Court's Construction of the Self-Incrimination Clause," 29 *Michigan Law Review,* 1-27, 195-207 (1930).

[25] McCarthy *v.* Arndstein, 266 U.S. 34, 40 (1924). *See also* Boyd *v.* U.S., 116 U.S. 616 (1886) Counselman *v.* Hitchcock, 142 U.S. 547 (1892); Brown *v.* Walker, 161 U.S. 591 (1896); U.S. *v.* Kordel, 397 U.S. 1, 6 (1970); California *v.* Byers, 402 U.S. 424, 437 (1971). It was on this ground that one Johnny Dio invoked the Fifth Amendment 140 times in the course of a two-hour appearance before a Senate investigating committee, *New York Times,* August 9, 1957.

[26] Rogers *v.* U.S., 340 U.S. 367, 370 (1951); United States *v.* Monia, 317 U.S. 424, 427 (1943); California *v.* Byers, 402 U.S. 424 (1971).

[27] Hoffman *v.* U.S., 341 U.S. 479, 486 (1951); Mason *v.* U.S., 244 U.S. 362, 365 (1917); Mackey *v.* U.S., 401 U.S. 667, 704-705 (1971); California *v.* Byers, 402 U.S. 424, 432, 435 (1971).

and may not be claimed for the benefit of third parties.[28] Nor does the clause impair the obligation of a witness to testify if a prosecution against him is barred by lapse of time, by statutory enactment, or by a pardon.[29]

Several times in our history Congress has passed immunity acts which granted an individual immunity from criminal prosecution on the basis of what he said in the compelled testimony. In 1970 Congress passed a sweeping law of this kind: "Whenever a witness refuses, on the basis of the privilege against self-incrimination, to testify or provide other information in a proceeding before or ancillary to—(1) a court or grand jury of the United States (2) an agency of the United States, or (3) [Congressional Committees] and the person presiding over the proceeding communicates to the witness an order issued under this part, the witness may not refuse to comply with the order on the basis of his privilege against self-incrimination; but no testimony or other information compelled under the order (or any information directly or indirectly derived from such testimony or other information) may be used against the witness in any criminal case, except a prosecution for perjury, giving a false statement, or otherwise failing to comply with the order."[30] There are some procedural safeguards in the law. Court decisions in cases involving earlier immunity statutes make plain that such a statute is constitutional (for Congress under the necessary and proper clause) provided the immunity applies to *both* Federal and State jurisdictions.[31] And so the Court held in 1972 with respect to the present law.[32] In addition the Court resolved a continuing controversy of many years about the *scope* of the immunity that had to be granted. The broad view was that a person could not be prosecuted or subject to any penalty "for or on account of any transaction, matter or thing, concerning which he may testify." The narrow view was the one spelled out in the 1970 statute that "no testimony or other information compelled . . . (or any information directly or indirectly de-

---

[28] Rogers *v.* U.S., 340 U.S. 367, 371 (1951); United States *v.* Murdock, 284 U.S. 141, 148 (1931); Minor *v.* U.S., 396 U.S. 87, 93 (1969).
[29] Brown *v.* Walker, 161 U.S. 591, 598-599 (1896).
[30] 18 U.S.C. 6002.
[31] Ullmann *v.* U.S., 350 U.S. 422 (1956); Murphy *v.* N.Y. Waterfront Commission, 378 U.S. 52 (1964).
[32] Kastigar *v.* U.S., 406 U.S. 441, 444 (1972).

rived from such testimony or other information) may be used. . . ." The Court made the narrow view the law of the land in 1972. The Court reasoned that: "such immunity from use and derivative use is coextensive with the scope of the privilege against self-incrimination, and therefore is sufficient to compel testimony over a claim of the privilege. While a grant of immunity must afford protection commensurate with that afforded by the privilege, it need not be broader. Transactional immunity, which accords full immunity from prosecution for the offense to which the compelled testimony related, affords the witness considerably broader protection than does the Fifth Amendment privilege. The privilege has never been construed to mean that one who invokes it cannot subsequently be prosecuted. Its sole concern is to afford protection against being 'forced to give testimony leading to the infliction of penalties affixed to . . . criminal acts.' Immunity from the use of compelled testimony and evidence derived directly and indirectly therefrom affords this protection. It prohibits the prosecutorial authorities from using the compelled testimony in *any* respect, and it therefore insures that the testimony cannot lead to the infliction of criminal penalties on the witness."[33]

As indicated above, the immunity may be waived, but if an accused takes the stand in his own behalf, he must submit to cross-examination;[34] if he does not take the stand, the Court has held that the Fifth Amendment (plus the Fourteenth in State cases) "forbids either comment by the prosecution on the accused's silence or instructions by the court that such silence is evidence of guilt."[35]

One of the continuing perplexing problems growing out of the privilege against self-incrimination has been the problem

[33] *Ibid.*, 1661. *But see* Justice Douglas's dissent, *ibid.*, 1666. *See also* Zicarelli *v.* N.J. State Com'n., 92 S. Ct. 1670 (1972). Recently, a state court held that under a state immunity statute a person compelled to testify in a civil case could not later be prosecuted in a criminal case on the basis of the compelled testimony. Smith *v.* Superior Court, Pima County, 495 P. 2d. 519 (1972). But the Illinois Supreme Court has held that where an attorney testified at the trial of a judge under a grant of immunity, that testimony could be used as basis for disbarment proceeding. *In re* Schwarz, 282 N.E. 2d. 689 (1972).

[34] United States *v.* Murdock, 284 U.S. 141, 149 (1931).

[35] Griffin *v.* California, 380 U.S. 609, 615 (1965). The Court went on to say that it reserved "decision on whether an accused can require . . . that the jury be instructed that his silence must be disregarded." *Ibid.*, 615, note 6. *But see* Bowles *v.* U.S., 439 F. 2d. 536, 542 (1970) and Commonwealth *v.* Greene, 285 A. 2d. 865, 867 (1971).

of whether or not public employees who invoked the privilege in hearings concerning their performance of duties could constitutionally be dismissed from their jobs for so doing. The guidelines wrought by the Supreme Court through a series of difficult cases are these: "public employees are entitled, like all other persons, to the benefit of the Constitution, including the privilege against self-incrimination. At the same time, . . . public employees, subject themselves to dismissal if they refuse to account for their performance of their public trust, *after proper proceedings, which do not involve an attempt to coerce them to relinquish their constitutional rights"* (emphasis supplied).[36] But these guidelines defy easy application as cases in this area clearly demonstrate.[37]

Until 1964, the Supreme Court employed a double standard with respect to involuntary confessions. From 1897 the standard employed with respect to Federal prosecutions was that laid down by the Court in the case, Bram v. United States, decided that year. There, the Court held that: "in criminal trials, in the courts of the United States, wherever a question arises whether a confession is incompetent because not voluntary, the issue is controlled by that portion of the Fifth Amendment to the Constitution of the United States commanding that no person 'shall be compelled in any criminal case to be a witness against himself.' "[38] As Justice Brennan pointed out in 1964 such a standard means "The constitutional inquiry is not whether the conduct of . . . officials in obtaining the confession was shocking, but whether the confession was 'free and voluntary; that is, it must not be extracted by any sort of threats or violence, nor obtained by any direct or implied promises, however slight, by the exertion of any improper influence. . . .' In other words the person must not have been compelled to incriminate himself. We have held inadmissible even a confession secured by so mild a whip as the refusal, under certain

*Involuntary Confessions* (margin note)

---

[36] Sanitation Men v. Sanitation Comm'r, 392 U.S. 280 (1968).

[37] For a good résumé of the appropriate cases, *see* decision of the Supreme Court of the State of Washington, Seattle Police Officers' Guild v. Seattle, 494 P. 2d. 485 (1972). *See also* Napolitano v. Ward, 457 F. 2d. 279 (1972), a case involving a State court judge who was dismissed after invoking the self-incrimination clause before a grand jury. With respect to a parallel problem, a New York court recently held that a driver's license could not be suspended for exercising the privilege where he could have been subject to criminal prosecution. Jackson v. Commissioner, 328 N.Y.S. 2d. 547 (1972).

[38] Bram v. U.S., 168 U.S. 532, 542-543 (1897).

circumstances, to allow a suspect to call his wife until he confessed."[39] Decisions with respect to the use of involuntary confessions in State prosecutions were rendered under the Due Process Clause, i.e. "inquiring whether the proceedings below met the demands of fundamental fairness which due process embodies."[40] It is true as Justice Brennan pointed out that, even before 1964, there had been a "marked shift to the federal standard in state cases . . ."[41] But whatever difference there was, it was extinguished by the Court's pronouncement in Malloy *v.* Hogan (1964): "We hold today that the Fifth Amendment's exception from compulsory self-incrimination is also protected by the Fourteenth Amendment against abridgment by the States."[42] The Court, as Justice Brennan's words above indicate, is quick to see compulsion in the maneuvers of law enforcement officials.[43] Perhaps, the greatest significance of the Court's holding in Malloy *v.* Hogan is its impact on another important right—right to counsel. If an accused must be protected from all kinds of subtle coercion to incriminate himself then he is going to need a lawyer to protect him even in the early stages of an investigation. That issue is explored below, pp. 355-356.

The Schmerber Distinction and Implied Consent Laws

In view of the Court's posture with respect to compulsory self-incrimination, it has puzzled many that State "Implied Consent Laws" like this one of California have survived court tests:

"Any person who drives a motor vehicle on a highway is deemed to have given his consent to a chemical test of his blood, breath, or urine to determine the alcoholic content of his blood if lawfully arrested for any offense allegedly committed while he was driving a motor vehicle under the influence of intoxicating liquor. The test must be incidental to a lawful arrest and administered at the direction of a peace officer having reasonable cause to believe the person was driving while under the influence of intoxicating liquor. The person arrested may have his choice of whether the test shall be of his blood, breath, or urine. Where the person is dead, unconscious, or otherwise in a condition rendering him incapable of refusing the test, he shall not be deemed to have withdrawn

---

[39] Malloy *v.* Hogan, 373 U.S. 1, 7 (1964).
[40] From Justice Harlan's dissent, *ibid.*, 28.
[41] *Ibid.*, 7.　　　　　　[42] *Ibid.*, 6.
[43] Haynes *v.* Washington, 378 U.S. 503 (1963); Miranda *v.* Arizona, 384 U.S. 436 (1966).

his consent thereto. If the person arrested refuses to submit to a chemical test, the department of motor vehicles must suspend his driving privilege for a period of six months after notifying him in writing of the suspension and on providing him, on his written request, with a hearing to determine whether the peace officer had reasonable cause to believe he had been driving while under the influence of intoxicating liquor, whether he was placed under arrest, whether he refused to submit to the test, and whether he had been advised that his driving privilege would be suspended if he refused."[44] In the important case of Schmerber v. California (1966), the Court professed to see a difference in kind between an involuntary confession and an involuntary blood test: "We therefore must now decide whether the withdrawal of blood and admission in evidence of the analysis involved in this case violated petitioner's privilege against self-incrimination. We hold that the privilege protects an accused only from being compelled to testify against himself, or otherwise provide the state with evidence of a testimonial or communicative nature, and that withdrawal of blood and uses of the analysis in question in this case did not involve compulsion to these ends."[45] In response to a complaint in a dissent that the report of the blood test was indeed testimonial in nature, the Court replied: "It is clear that the protection of the privilege reaches an accused's communications, whatever form they might take, and the compulsion of responses which are also communications, for example, compliance with a subpoena to produce one's papers. On the other hand, both federal and state courts have usually held that it offers no protection against compulsion to submit to fingerprinting, photographing, or measurements, to write or speak for identification, to appear in court, to stand, to assume a stance, to walk, or to make a particular gesture."[46]

[44] Cal. Jur. 2d. 372. See also Taft A. McKinstry, "Kentucky's 'Implied Consent' Statute," 59 Kentucky Law Journal, 536 (1970). See also People v. Superior Court of Kern County, 493 P. 2d. 1145 (1972).

[45] Schmerber v. California, 384 U.S. 757, 761 (1966).

[46] Ibid., 763-764. For some instructive State court decisions in this area, see Heichelbach v. State, 281 N.E. 2d. 102 (1972); State v. Heston, 280 N.E. 2d. 376 (1972); State v. Ostrowski, 282 N.E. 2d. 359 (1972); State v. Tew, 195 N.W. 2d. 615 (1972). State courts have also held that wiretapping "In the absence of compulsion by the authorities does not bring the right against self-incrimination into play." State v. Siegel, 285 A. 2d. 671 (1971); Dudley v. State, 186 S.E. 2d. 875 (1972).

Keeping
Records
and
Registering

Government has long required that people keep records, file forms, and register with respect to certain activities. That requirement quite naturally raises the question of whether or not the Government can do that without violating the Self-Incrimination Clause. For example, an individual might argue that if he has acquired income by illicit means, he might expose himself to criminal prosecution by making out an income tax return. In dealing with such a case, some years ago, Justice Holmes said: "He could not draw a conjurer's circle around the whole matter by his own declaration that to write any word on the government blank would bring him in danger of the law."[47] Also, the Court upheld the requirement under the Emergency Price Control Act of 1942 that certain merchants keep records.[48] But in 1968, it struck down a statute which required gamblers to register and to submit monthly detailed information concerning their wagering activities.[49] The Court carefully distinguished these latter decisions from the earlier decision in the case involving the Price Control Act (Shapiro v. U.S.) concluding: "We think that neither *Shapiro* nor the cases upon which it relied are applicable here. . . . Moreover, we find it unnecessary for present purposes to pursue in detail the question, left unanswered in *Shapiro*, of what 'limits . . . the government cannot constitutionally exceed in requiring the keeping of records. . . .' It is enough that there are significant points of difference between the situations here and in *Shapiro* which in this instance preclude, under any formulation, an appropriate application of the 'required records' doctrine."[50] One of the differences stressed by the Court was that "the requirements at issue in *Shapiro* were imposed in 'an essentially non-criminal and regulatory area of inquiry' while those here are directed to a 'selective group inherently suspect of criminal activities.' "[51] And the Court recently upheld California's "hit and run" statute, which requires the driver of a motor vehicle involved in an accident to stop at the scene and give his name and address, concluding that "the disclosure of inherently illegal activity is inherently risky. . . . But

47 U.S. *v.* Sullivan, 274 U.S. 259, 263-264 (1927).
48 Shapiro *v.* U.S., 335 U.S. 1 (1948).
49 Marchetti *v.* U.S., 390 U.S. 39 (1968); Grosso *v.* U.S., 390 U.S. 62 (1968). *See also* Mackey *v.* U.S., 401 U.S. 667 (1971).
50 Marchetti *v.* U.S., 390 U.S. 39, 56 (1968). For elaboration of the Marchetti decision *see* Williams *v.* State, 287 A. 2d. 803 (1972) and State *v.* Braun, 495 P. 2d. 1000 (1972).
51 *Ibid.*, 57.

disclosures with respect to automobile accidents simply do not entail the kind of substantial risk involved in [the gambler's cases]. Furthermore, the statutory purpose is noncriminal and self-reporting is indispensable to its fulfillment."[52]

The privilege of witnesses is a purely personal one, and hence may not be claimed by an agent or officer of a corporation either in its behalf or in his own behalf as regards books and papers of the corporation;[53] and the same rule holds in the case of the custodian of the records of a labor union;[54] nor does the Communist Party enjoy any immunity as to its books and records.[55] Taken in connection with the interdiction of the Fourth Amendment against unreasonable searches and seizures, the clause protects an individual from the compulsory production of private papers which would incriminate him.[56] The scope of this latter privilege was, however, narrowed by the *Shapiro* decision, in which as pointed out above, the Court held that the privilege against self-incrimination does not extend to books and records which an individual is required to keep to evidence his compliance with lawful regulations.[57]

*Personal Character of the Immunity*

In the ensuing discussion of "due process of law" under the Fifth Amendment, it must be borne in mind that there is also a "due process" clause in the Fourteenth Amendment. The Fifth, of course, applies to the National Government and the Fourteenth to the State governments. However, in the history of conceptualization of "due process" both clauses were inextricably entwined. Consequently, the story of that history can only be traced by dealing with them jointly. Nonetheless, specific applications of "due process" can be separated out in a meaningful way. Consequently, here we will deal with the conceptualization of due process with primary emphasis on its application to the National Government; its application to the State governments is discussed under the Fourteenth Amendment.

[52] California *v.* Byers, 402 U.S. 424 (1971).
[53] Hale *v.* Henkel, 201 U.S. 43 (1906); Wilson *v.* U.S., 221 U.S. 361 (1911); Oklahoma Press Pub. Co. *v.* Walling, 327 U.S. 186 (1946); McPaul *v.* U.S., 364 U.S. 372 (1960); U.S. *v.* Fleischman, 339 U.S. 349 (1950); *in re* Mal Bros. Contracting Co., 444 F. 2d. 615 (1971); People *v.* Pintozzi, 277 N.E. 2d. 844 (1972).
[54] United States *v.* White, 322 U.S. 694 (1944).
[55] Rogers *v.* U.S., 340 U.S. 367-373 (1951).
[56] *See* pp. 301ff.
[57] Shapiro *v.* U.S., 335 U.S. 1 (1948). *See also* People *v.* Pintozzi, 277 N.E. 2d. 844 (1972).

Source and
Develop-
ment of
"Due
Process
of Law"

The phrase "due process of law" comes from chapter 3 of 28 Edw. III (1335), which reads: "No man of what state or condition he be, shall be put out of his lands or tenements nor taken, nor disinherited, nor put to death, without he be brought to answer by due process of law." This statute, in turn, harks back to the famous chapter 29 of Magna Carta (issue of 1225), where the King promises that "no free man (*nullus liber homo*) shall be taken or imprisoned or deprived of his freehold or his liberties or free customs, or outlawed or exiled, or in any manner destroyed, nor shall we come upon him or send against him, except by a legal judgment of his peers or by the law of the land (*per legem terrae*)."[58] Whichever phraseology is used always occurs in close association with other safeguards of accused persons, just as does the clause here under discussion in Amendment V. As a limitation on legislative power, in short, the due process clause originally operated simply to place certain procedures, and especially the grand jury–petit jury process, beyond its reach, but this has not remained its sole importance, or its principal importance.[59]

The absorptive powers of the law of the land clause, the precursor in the original State constitutions, of the due process clause, was foreshadowed as early as 1819 in a dictum by Justice William Johnson of the United States Supreme Court: "As to the words from Magna Charta . . . after volumes spoken and written with a view to their exposition, the good sense of mankind has at length settled down to this: that they were intended to secure the individual from the arbitrary exercise of the powers of government, unrestrained by the established principles of private rights and distributive justice."[60] Thirty-eight

[58] *See* Sir Edward Coke, *Institutes of the Laws of England* (1669) (First American Edition, Philadelphia, 1853), Part 2, 50-51.
[59] On the above *see* especially Justice Harlan's dissenting opinion in Hurtado *v.* Calif., 110 U.S. 516, 538 (1884); *also* Den *ex dem.* Murray *v.* Hoboken Land & Improvement Co., 18 How. 272, 280 (1856); Twining *v.* New Jersey, 211 U.S. 78 (1908); Corwin, *Liberty Against Government*, ch. 3.
[60] B'k of Columbia *v.* Okely, 4 Wheat. 235, 244 (1819). *See also* Edward S. Corwin "Due Process of Law before the Civil War," 24 *Harvard Law Review* 366, 460 (1911), and Clinton Rossiter, ed., *Higher Law Background of American Constitutional Law* (Ithaca, 1953); C. W. Collins, *The Fourteenth Amendment and the States* (Boston, 1912); R. L. Mott, *Due Process of Law* (Indianapolis, 1926); Willoughby, *Constitutional Law*, III, chs. xci-cv; Benjamin F. Wright, *The Growth of American Constitutional Law* (Boston, 1942); Carl B. Swisher, *American Constitutional Development* (Boston, 1943).

years later the prophecy of these words was realized in the famous *Dred Scott* case,[61] in which Section 8 of the Missouri Compromise, whereby slavery was excluded from the territories, was held void under the Fifth Amendment, not on the ground that the procedure for enforcing it was not due process of law, but because the Court regarded it as unjust to forbid people to take their slaves, or other property, into the territories, the common property of all the States.

Meanwhile, the previous year the recently established Court of Appeals of New York had, in the landmark case of Wynehamer *v.* People,[62] set aside a state-wide Prohibition law as comprising, with regard to liquors in existence at the time of its going into effect, an act of destruction of property not within the power of Government to perform "even by the forms of due process of law." The term "due process of law," in short, simply drops out of the clause, which comes to read "no person shall be deprived of property," period. And subsequently two other terms of the clause have undergone a comparable enlargement. At the common law, "property" signified ownership, which was "exercised in its primary and fullest sense over physical objects only, and more especially over land."[63] In Court decisions, it came to cover each and all of the valuable elements of ownership, and moreover tended at times to merge with the more indefinite rights of "liberty." "Liberty" at the common law meant little more than the right not to be physically restrained except for good cause. Whether the cause was good or not would be inquired into by a court, in connection with an application for a writ of *habeas corpus*, or in connection with an action for damages for false imprisonment.[64] About seventy-five years ago, however, the Court, following the urging of influential members of the American Bar and the lead given by certain of the State courts, adopted the view that the word "liberty" as used here and in the Fourteenth Amendment was intended to protect the "freedom of contract" of adults engaged in the ordinary employments, especially when viewed from the point of view of would-be

*Expanded Conceptions of "Liberty," and "Property"*

[61] Scott *v.* Sandford, 19 How. 393 (1857).
[62] 13 N.Y. 378 (1856).
[63] T. E. Holland, *Elements of Jurisprudence*, 211 (Oxford, 1924), 13th ed.; Blackstone, *Commentaries*, VII, ch. 1.
[64] C. E. Shattuck, "The True Meaning of the Term 'Liberty,'" 4 *Harvard Law Review*, 365-392 (1891).

employers.[65] Then in 1925 the Court took the further step of extending the term as it is used in the Fourteenth Amendment to certain of the rights, described as "fundamental," which were already protected against the National Government by the more specific language of the Bill of Rights, among these being freedom of speech and press.[66] Later, the Court, responding to the social teachings of the New Deal, came practically to dismiss the conception of "freedom of contract" as a definition of "liberty" and to substitute for it a special concern for "the rights of labor," its right to organize, and to strike and picket so long as too obvious violence was avoided.

The Heyday of Substantive Due Process    In brief, this clause, for a time (roughly from 1900-1937), was employed frequently to challenge the *substantive* content of legislation, or in other words to require that Congress exercise its powers "reasonably," that is to say, *reasonably in the judgment of the Court.* A similar requirement was laid upon the State legislatures by the Fourteenth Amendment but with two differences which operated to Congress's advantage. In the first place, whereas the "police power" of the States is an indefinite power to provide for "the public health, safety, morals, and general welfare," most of Congress's powers are defined by reference to a specified subject-matter, like "post offices and post roads," "commerce among the States," etc., and this difference is sufficient to invoke in Congress's favor and against the States the rule of legal interpretation that the specific is to be preferred to the general. In the second place, the Fifth Amendment contains no "equal protection" clause, although this does not signify that the Court would not pass upon the soundness of the factual justification urged in support of a specially drastic discrimination by the National Government against a particular class of its citizens, as, for example, that which characterized its policies toward the West Coast Japanese early in World War II. (*See* pp. 79-80).

Relying upon public policy and its supervisory authority over federal courts, the Court in the 1940's reached results similar to those arrived at under the Equal Protection Clause

---

[65] Allgeyer *v.* La., 165 U.S. 578 (1897); Holden *v.* Hardy, 169 U.S. 366 (1898); Lochner *v.* N.Y., 198 U.S. 45 (1905). For the Bar's connection with this development, *see* Benjamin R. Twiss, *Lawyers and the Constitution: How Laissez Faire Came to the Supreme Court* (Princeton, 1942).

[66] *See* Charles Warren, "The New Liberty under the Fourteenth Amendment," 39 *Harvard Law Review,* 431 (1926); also Gitlow *v.* N.Y., 268 U.S. 652 (1925).

of the Fourteenth Amendment, in refusing to enforce restrictive covenants in the District of Columbia,[67] and in reversing a judgment of a Federal District Court because of the exclusion of day laborers from the jury panel;[68] and in 1944 the Railway Labor Act was construed to require a collective bargaining representative to act for the benefit of all members of the craft without discrimination on account of race.[69] Chief Justice Stone indicated that any other construction would raise grave constitutional doubts,[70] while in a concurring opinion Justice Murphy asserted unequivocally that the act would be inconsistent with the Fifth Amendment if the bargaining agent, acting under color of Federal authority, were permitted to discriminate against any of the persons he was authorized to represent.[71]

In another respect, national and State legislation stood much more nearly on a parity with each other, since in the case of both the Court was apt to have available from its own past decisions two widely different approaches to the question of the "reasonableness" of a challenged legislative measure, and hence of its conformity with the "due process of law" requirement. One approach was furnished by the proposition that a legislative act is presumed to be valid, and, deduced from this, the further one that if facts could exist which would render the legislation before it "reasonable," it must be assumed by the Court that they did exist.[72] The other, on the contrary, invoked the idea that "liberty is the rule and restraint is the exception," and hence demanded that special justification be adduced in support of any new inroad upon previous freedom of action, as almost any law was bound to be.[73]

In other words, under the latter rule the Court did some-

---

[67] Hurd *v.* Hodge, 334 U.S. 24 (1948).
[68] Thiel *v.* Southern Pacific Co., 328 U.S. 217 (1946).
[69] Steele *v.* L. & N. R. Co., 323 U.S. 192 (1944).
[70] *Ibid.*, 198, 199.
[71] *Ibid.*, 208-209. *Cf.* the following sentence from the concurring opinion of Justice Jackson in Railway Express Agency, Inc. *v.* New York, 336 U.S. 106, 112 (1949): "I regard it as a salutary doctrine that cities, States and the Federal Government must exercise their powers so as not to discriminate between their inhabitants except upon some reasonable differentiation fairly related to the object of regulation."
[72] Munn *v.* Ill., 94 U.S. 113, 132 (1876); Powell *v.* Pa., 127 U.S. 678 (1888). *See also* Justice Stone, in United States *v.* Carolene Products Co., 304 U.S. 144 (1938).
[73] Adkins *v.* Children's Hospital, 261 U.S. 525, 546.

thing very like what Congress did in the first place, in balancing the apparent detriments of the statute from the point of view of "liberty" or "property" as against its anticipated benefits from the point of view of "public policy." And it was from this approach that the Court in 1923, being then very much under the influence of *laissez-faire* concepts of governmental power, set aside as "unreasonable" and "arbitrary" an act of Congress establishing a minimum wage for women industrially employed in the District of Columbia[74]—a decision which it overturned in 1936[75] under the influence of the New Deal ideology.[76]

The Demise of Substantive Due Process in Economic Realm

After the New Deal had become ensconced, the Supreme Court came to eschew the role it had assumed during the heyday of substantive due process particularly with respect to economic matters. Justice Black summarized the Court's recent views on the matter in a case in 1963 which dealt with a State statute making it a misdemeanor to engage in the debt adjustment business:

"We refuse to sit as a 'superlegislature to weigh the wisdom of legislation,' and we emphatically refuse to go back to the time when courts used the Due Process Clause 'to strike down state laws, regulatory of business and industrial conditions, because they may be unwise, improvident, or out of harmony with a particular school of thought.' . . . Whether the legislature takes for its textbook Adam Smith, Herbert Spencer, Lord Keynes, or some other is no concern of ours."[77]

Substantive Due Process Still Lives

There has been a tendency among observers of the Court's work to believe that the concept of substantive due process as a useful judicial doctrine is dead. Granted, it has lost importance with respect to economic regulation, but it does have vitality still with respect to civil liberties and civil rights.[78] Consider what the Supreme Court did in the companion case

---

[74] *Ibid.*

[75] West Coast Hotel *v.* Parrish, 300 U.S. 379 (1937).

[76] *See* Swisher, *American Constitutional Development* (Boston, 1943), chs. 34 and 35.

[77] Ferguson *v.* Skrupa, 372 U.S. 726, 731-732 (1963) and cases cited therein.

[78] The current Court may yet reassert a stronger role in "safeguarding" economic rights. In a recent decision Justice Stewart speaking for the Court said, "that the dichotomy between personal liberties and property rights is a false one. Property does not have rights. People have rights. The right to enjoy property without unlawful deprivation, no less than the right to speak or the right to travel is, in truth, a 'personal right. . . .'" Lynch *v.* Household Finance Corp., 405 U.S. 538 (1972).

to the momentous *Brown* case, in which it found segregation in public schools a violation of "equal protection." Since it could not use "equal protection" with respect to schools in the District of Columbia, the Court was compelled to find another basis for the result it desired to achieve. The Court reasoned: "Although the Court has not assumed to define 'liberty' with great precision, that term is not confined to mere freedom from bodily restraint. Liberty under law extends to the full range of conduct which the individual is free to pursue, and it cannot be restricted except for a proper governmental objective. Segregation in public education is not reasonably related to any proper governmental objective, and thus it imposes on Negro children of the District of Columbia a burden that constitutes an arbitrary deprivation of their liberty in violation of the Due Process Clause."[79] That, surely, is a use of the concept of substantive due process. Also, to the extent that Court continues to assume that the substantive rights of the First Amendment are safeguarded against the States by the Fourteenth, however that incorporation is justified, it is a manifestation of the continued vitality of the idea of substantive due process.

In an important decision rendered in 1972, the Supreme Court held that two State laws permitting conditional sales contracts which "simply provided that upon default the seller 'may take back,' 'may retake,' or 'may repossess' merchandise" were unconstitutional on due process grounds. The Court insisted that, before a person could be deprived of his property, there must be notice and a hearing at a "meaningful time" and in a "meaningful manner." The Court said, "The constitutional right to be heard is a basic aspect of the duty of government to follow a fair process of decision making when it acts to deprive a person of his possessions. The purpose of this requirement is not only to ensure abstract fair play to the individual. Its purpose, more particularly, is to protect his use and possession of property from arbitrary encroachment, to minimize substantively unfair or mistaken deprivations of property, a danger that is especially great when the State seizes goods simply upon the application of and for the benefit of a private party."[80] As to the exact nature of hearings that would meet the due process requirement the Court was not very specific.

*[margin note: Procedural Requirements with Respect to Deprivation of Property]*

[79] Bolling *v.* Sharpe, 347 U.S. 497, 499-500 (1954).
[80] Fuentes *v.* Shevin, 407 U.S. 67, 80 (1972).

331

"The nature and form of such prior hearings . . . are legitimately open to many potential variations and are a subject, at this point, for legislation, not adjudication. Since the essential reason for the requirement of a prior hearing is to prevent unfair and mistaken deprivations of property, however, it is axiomatic that the hearing must provide a real test."[81]

Procedural Requirements with Respect to Law Enforce- Because the specific procedural rights with respect to law enforcement on the national level are spelled out in other Bill of Rights Amendments, the development of the meaning of due process with respect to law enforcement procedures has chiefly centered on efforts to secure these same rights, right to counsel, protection from unreasonable searches and seizures, trial by jury, etc., against the States by incorporating them into the due process clause of the Fourteenth Amendment. In the course of this development, there has been much soul-searching about the meaning of due process. One classic position on the meaning is described by Justice Frankfurter: "Regard for the requirements of the Due Process Clause 'inescapably imposes upon this Court an exercise of judgment upon the whole course of proceedings [resulting in a conviction] in order to ascertain whether they offend those canons of decency and fairness which express the notions of justice of English-speaking peoples even to those charged with the most heinous offenses.' These standards of justice are not authoritatively formulated anywhere as though they were specifics. Due process of law is a summarized constitutional guarantee of respect for those personal immunities which . . . are 'so rooted in the traditions and conscience of our people as to be ranked as fundamental' or are 'implicit in the concept of ordered liberty.' "[82] In practice, for Frankfurter, this meant that any procedure which "shocks the conscience" violates due process.[83] The opposing position has been best articulated by Justice Black, who argued that due process in the Fourteenth Amendment means *only* the procedural guarantees in the Bill of Rights.[84] As he saw it, the "shock the conscience" test was "a test which depends, not on the language of the Constitution, but solely on the views of a majority of the Court as to what is 'fair' and decent."[85]

[81] *Ibid.*, 96.
[82] Rochin *v.* California, 342 U.S. 165, 169 (1952).
[83] *Ibid.*, 172.
[84] His dissent in Adamson *v.* California, 332 U.S. 46 (1947).
[85] Williams *v.* Florida, 399 U.S. 78, 107 (1970).

With the expanded reach of the specific procedural guarantees with respect to law enforcement by the National Government, described above and below, plus the fact that the Court
has long held that it had an inherent "supervisory authority
over the administration of criminal justice in the Federal
courts,"[86] it is difficult to visualize what kinds of cases could
arise in the future which would test the meaning of procedural
due process in the *Fifth Amendment* in law enforcement. A
recent case suggests some possibilities. With respect to the
question whether or not, in a State proceeding with a juvenile
"proof beyond a reasonable doubt" was a requirement of due
process, the Court decided it was.[87] Such a case could conceivably have arisen within Federal jurisdiction. Also, Congress
could conceivably pass laws with respect to procedures which
go counter to those established by the Court under its supervisory role, and this would set the basis for a possible test on
due process grounds. In this connection, it is worth pondering
some words contained in Justice Black's dissent in the case just
mentioned: "I admit a strong, persuasive argument can be
made for a standard of proof beyond a reasonable doubt in
criminal cases—and the majority has made that argument well
—but it is not for me as a judge to say that Congress or the
States are without constitutional power to establish another
standard that the Constitution does not otherwise forbid. It is
quite true that proof beyond a reasonable doubt has long been
required in federal criminal trials. It is also true that this requirement is almost universally found in the governing laws
of the States. . . . But when, as here, a State through its duly
constituted legislative branch decides to apply a different
standard, then that standard, unless it is otherwise unconstitutional, must be applied to insure that persons are treated according, to 'the law of the land.' The State of New York has
made such a decision, and nothing in the Due Process Clause
invalidates it."[88]

Apparently, the Court still has work to do in determining

---

[86] McNabb *v.* U.S., 318 U.S. 332, 341 (1943).

[87] *In re* Winship, 397 U.S. 358 (1970). In a recent noteworthy case, the
Court held that the cognovit, an "ancient legal device by which the
debtor consents in advance to the holder's obtaining a judgment without
notice or hearing" did not offend due process. The Court said "the due
process rights to notice and hearing prior to a civil judgment are subject
to waiver." D. H. Overmyer Co., Inc. *v.* Frick Co., 405 U.S. 174, 185 (1972).
*See also* Stanley *v.* Illinois, 405 U.S. 645 (1972).

[88] *Ibid.*, 385-386.

the meaning of the Fourteenth Amendment's due process clause with respect to law enforcement procedures in State jurisdictions. In three important decisions on the question in 1972, the Court held the following as violations of Fourteenth Amendment due process: (1) The holding of a convictee in a mental hospital beyond the time of his sentence, where his original commitment was effected on the basis of an *ex parte* order committing him to observation without the safeguards commensurate with a long-term commitment.[89] (2) The revocation of paroles without a hearing. The Court held that "the revocation of parole is not part of a criminal prosecution and the full panoply of rights due a defendant in such proceeding does not apply to parole revocations," but "what is needed [for due process] is an informal hearing structured to assure that the finding of parole violation will be based on verified facts and that the exercise of discretion will be informed by an accurate knowledge of the parolee's behavior."[90] (3) But in the third case, where it was contended that, when the defense moved for disclosure of all written statements taken by the police from any witness, six items were withheld by the State, the Supreme Court (5-4) held that "We know of no constitutional requirement that the prosecution must make a complete and detailed accounting to the defense of all police investigating work on a case."[91] The Court then went on to state its allegiance to the standard of due process set in an earlier case that the prosecution could not suppress evidence "in the face of a defense production request, where the evidence is favorable to the accused and is material either to guilt or to punishment." Clearly, the Court felt that the withheld information in the 1972 case did not fit this description.

Due Process in Administrative Proceedings    In administrative proceedings, which are today an important feature of government, both State and national, the significance of the term "due process" has been elaborated by the Court. Thus Congress has delegated to the Interstate Commerce Commission the power to set "reasonable rates," and when the Commission orders a carrier to observe a certain rate as "reasonable," the Court will sustain its order as having been set by "due process of law," provided the Commission

---

[89] McNeil *v.* Director, Patuxent Institution, 407 U.S. 245 (1972). *Cf.* Murel *v.* Baltimore City Criminal Court, 407 U.S. 355 (1972).
[90] Morrissey and Booher *v.* Brewer, 408 U.S. 471 (1972).
[91] Moore *v.* Illinois, 408 U.S. 786 (1972).

did not act "arbitrarily" but gave the carrier an opportunity to be heard, that it observed all the rules of law which the Court has laid down for such cases, and finally that its findings of fact were sustained by "substantial evidence."[92]

Judicial decisions in this field frequently turn on whether the Court regards the question before it to be one "of fact" and so within the power of an administrative body to determine, or one "of law" and so within the power of the Court to determine on review. The same question (as, e.g., whether a given rate is "reasonable") may be of either sort, depending on the angle from which it is viewed. Nowadays the Court seems generally to treat such "mixed questions" as "questions of fact."[93]

Congress, of course, is free at any time to add to the bare constitutional requirements of "due process of law" others which must be observed by administrative agencies, and has done so in its Administrative Procedure Act of 1946.[94] Significantly, persons appearing before administrative agencies are not afforded all the protections they would have in a court proceeding (*see* p. 357).[95] It should be noted, however, that there are certain inherent limitations to judicial review of administrative determinations—those which arise out of the vast bulk of facts which a regulatory agency often brings into court and those which arise from the necessity of getting a case decided. State regulation of public utility rates had been at one period rendered largely farcical by the idea that the courts ought to retry from the ground up administrative findings of fact.[96] Finally, whatever the scope of judicial review, before there is any judicial review the administrative remedy generally must be exhausted.[97]

Troubles on the campus and the more vigorous assertion of rights by individuals in recent years ultimately led to Supreme

*Hearings For Non-Tenured Teachers Whose Contracts Are Not Renewed*

92 Interstate Com. Com'n. *v.* Un. P. R. R. Co., 222 U.S. 541 (1912); Interstate Com. Com'n. *v.* L. & N. R. R. Co., 227 U.S. 88 (1913); Consolidated Edison Co. *v.* NLRB, 305 U.S. 197 (1938); Opp Cotton Mills *v.* Administrator of Wage and Hr. Div. etc., 312 U.S. 126 (1941); Sniadach *v.* Family Finance Corp., 395 U.S. 337 (1969); Goldberg *v.* Kelly, 397 U.S. 254 (1970); Wisconsin *v.* Constantine, 400 U.S. 433 (1971). For cases involving suspension of drivers' licenses, *see* Bell *v.* Burson, 402 U.S. 535 (1971); Jennings *v.* Mahoney, 404 U.S. 25 (1971).
93 *See* pp. 161-163 *supra.*
94 5 U.S.C. 551-559.
95 *See* Gerace *v.* County of Los Angeles, 100 Cal. Rptr. 917 (1972).
96 *See* pp. 42-43 *supra.*
97 Myers *v.* Bethlehem Shipbuilding Corp., 303 U.S. 41 (1938); Levers *v.* Anderson, 326 U.S. 219 (1945); *cf.* Oestereich *v.* Selective Service Board, 393 U.S. 233 (1968).

Court decisions in 1972 on the question of whether or not non-tenured teachers were entitled to a hearing prior to non-renewal of contract. In one such case, the Court decided 5-3 that a teacher hired for one year only was not "deprived of liberty or property protected by the Fourteenth Amendment." Consequently, no hearing was constitutionally required, although the Court hinted it might be good policy to grant one.[98] But in another case, the Court held that a non-tenured professor who had been employed for ten years was another matter.[99] Since the complaining professor "alleged that the college had a *de facto* tenure program, and that he had tenure under that program," the Court held that if he could prove that, he was entitled to a hearing. "Proof of such a property interest would not, of course, entitle him to reinstatement. But such proof would obligate college officials to grant a hearing at his request, where he could be informed of the grounds for his non-retention and challenge their sufficiency."

**The Eminent Domain Power of the National Government**    The power which the government exerts when it "takes private property" for "public use" is called the power of eminent domain. Before the Civil War it was generally denied that the National Government could exercise the power of eminent domain within a State without the consent of the State.[100] (*See* Article I, Section VIII, ¶17.) Today, however, it is well settled that the National Government may take property by eminent domain whenever it is "necessary and proper" for it to do so in order to carry out any of the powers of the National Government; and that it may, in proper cases, vest this power in corporations chartered by it.[101]

**When Property is "Taken"**    Property is "taken," generally speaking, only when title to it is transferred to the Government or the Government takes over or assumes to control its valuable uses, or when, in the case of land, it commits a deliberate and protracted trespass, as by the repeated and persistent discharge of heavy guns across the grounds of a summer resort, with the natural result of frightening off the public; or the frequent flight at low altitudes of military planes over a commercial chicken farm, with the natural result of destroying the value of the property for

[98] Board of Regents *v.* Roth, 408 U.S. 564 (1972).
[99] Perry *v.* Sindermann, 408 U.S. 593 (1972).
[100] *See* Edward S. Corwin, *National Supremacy* (N.Y., 1913), 262-263.
[101] Kohl *v.* U.S., 91 U.S. 367 (1875); California *v.* Pac. Cent. R.R. Co., 127 U.S. 1 (1888); Luxton *v.* No. R. Bridge Co., 153 U.S. 525 (1894).

that use.[102] On the other hand, jet aircraft operations which raise havoc with ordinary home activities but do not make private homes uninhabitable do not constitute a taking of an interest for which compensation must be paid.[103] But the Supreme Court of California created a stir in 1972 when it decided that people could seek damages for injuries alleged to have been suffered in consequence of the operation of an airport on the grounds of nuisance, negligence, and zoning violations but not on the grounds that it constituted "a taking."[104]

Property is not "taken simply because its value declines in consequence of an exertion of lawful power by the Government."[105] Thus, Congress may lower the tariff, cheapen the currency, or declare war, and so forth and so on, without having to compensate those who suffer losses as a result of its action. Nor is the destruction of private property by the Army to prevent its falling into enemy hands a compensable loss.[106]

What is a "public use"? Existing precedents yield a broad definition of this term in connection with both the taxing power and the power of eminent domain, when these are exercised by the States;[107] and in the case of the National Government determination of the issue rests with Congress "unless shown to involve an impossibility."[108]

[102] United States *v.* Great Falls Mfg. Co., 112 U.S. 645 (1884); Portsmouth Harbor Land & Hotel Co. *v.* U.S., 260 U.S. 327 (1922); United States *v.* Causby, 328 U.S. 256 (1946); United States *v.* Dickinson, 331 U.S. 745 (1947); Aris Gloves Inc. *v.* U.S., 420 F. 2d. 1386 (1970).

[103] Batten. v. U.S., 292 F. 2d. 144 (1961); *cert. denied*, 371 U.S. 955 (1963); *rehearing denied*, 372 U.S. 925 (1963).

[104] Nestle *v.* City of Santa Monica, 101 Cal. Rptr. 568 (1972). "Manager Would Close L.A. Airport if It Is Warranted," *Los Angeles Times*, May 4, 1972; "Los Angeles Seeks Legislation to Keep Airport Open," *Washington Post*, May 5, 1972.

[105] New Haven Inclusion Cases, 399 U.S. 392, 491-493 (1970).

[106] Knox *v.* Lee, 12 Wall. 457 (1871); Omnia Com'l Co. *v.* U.S., 261 U.S. 502 (1923); United States *v.* Caltex, 344 U.S. 149 (1952); YMCA *v.* U.S., 395 U.S. 85 (1969).

[107] The Supreme Court of Michigan upheld a city's taking of property to be resold to private persons for redevelopment saying: "The *controlling* purpose of the city's plan is to rehabilitate a blighted area. The property is acquired, not for the purpose of redevelopment at a profit to the city or any private developer, but to protect the health, safety, morals and general welfare of the municipality. Since the controlling purpose is public use, the circumstance of a private developer's benefit would not change its character." *In re* City of Center Line, 196 N.W. 2d. 144 (1972).

[108] Green *v.* Frazier, 253 U.S. 233 (1920); United States *v.* Gettysburg Elec. R. Co., 160 U.S. 668 (1896); United States *ex rel.* TVA *v.* Welch, 327 U.S. 546, 552 (1946).

"Just compensation" must be determined by an impartial body, not necessarily a court or a jury; nor necessarily, in the case of land, in advance of the taking, so long as the owner is guaranteed the opportunity of being heard sooner or later, but not too late, on the question of value.[109] Theoretically, what the term signifies is the full and perfect equivalent in money of the real property taken,[110] the measure whereof is the owner's loss, not the Government's gain.[111] More concretely, where the property taken has a determinable "market value," in other words, "what a willing buyer would pay in cash to a willing seller,"[112] that is the measure of recovery,[113] which may reflect not only the use to which the property is currently devoted, but also that to which it may be readily converted.[114] Such is the language of the cases. It cannot be said, however, that the Court has displayed impressive unanimity of opinion in its efforts to apply these principles in cases which grew out of the facts of World War II.[115]

Which Department the Clause Binds

To which branch of the National Government is the duty to render just compensation addressed when the National Government is involved in taking property? Undoubtedly to Congress, since it alone has the power to appropriate money for the purpose. But this does not imply that Congress must in all instances have authorized the taking in the first place. Thus, in passing upon a seizure of American-owned property by an American military commander operating in Mexico during the Mexican War, the Court said, that if the exigencies of war

---

[109] United States v. Great Falls Mfg. Co., 112 U.S. 645 (1884); Bauman v. Ross, 167 U.S. 548 (1897); Bailey v. Anderson, 326 U.S. 203 (1945). Where land is taken by the United States under the eminent domain power without compensation proceedings, the owner may, under the Tucker Act, bring suit for compensation in the Court of Claims or in a district court sitting as a court of claims. United States v. Great Falls Co., above; Jacobs v. U.S., 290 U.S. 13 (1933).

[110] Monongahela Nav. Co. v. U.S., 148 U.S. 312, 326 (1893); Acton v. U.S., 401 F. 2d. 896 (1968); cert. denied, 395 U.S. 945 (1969).

[111] United States v. Chandler-Dunbar Co., 229 U.S. 53 (1913); United States ex rel. TVA v. Powelson, 319 U.S. 266, 281 (1943).

[112] United States v. Miller, 317 U.S. 369, 374 (1943). Cf. Kimball Laundry Co. v. U.S., 338 U.S. 1 (1949).

[113] United States v. Powelson, 319 U.S. 266, 275 (1943).

[114] Boom Co. v. Patterson, 98 U.S. 403 (1879); McCandless v. U.S., 298 U.S. 342 (1936).

[115] Cf. United States v. Felin & Co., 334 U.S. 624 (1948); United States v. Cors, 337 U.S. 325, 333 (1949); United States v. Toronto Nav. Co., 338 U.S. 396 (1949); United States v. Commodities Trading Corp., 339 U.S. 121 (1950).

clearly warranted the act, the Government was "bound to make full compensation; but the officer is not a trespasser,"[116] doctrine which it reiterated years later with respect to a similar taking in the course of the Civil War.[117]

[116] Mitchell *v.* Harmony, 13 How. 115 (1852).
[117] United States *v.* Russell, 13 Wall. 623 (1871). *See also* note 70 above; and United States *v.* Pewee Coal Co., 341 U.S. 114 (1951).

# AMENDMENT VI

In all criminal prosecutions the accused shall enjoy the right
to a speedy and public trial, by an impartial jury of the State
and district wherein the crime shall have been committed,
which district shall have been previously ascertained by law,
and to be informed of the nature and cause of the accusation; to be confronted with the witnesses against him; to
have compulsory process for obtaining witnesses in his favor, and to have the assistance of counsel for his defense.

Speedy and  As a consequence of its decision in 1967 that the Fourteenth
Public  Amendment incorporated the right to a "speedy trial," en-
Trial  forceable against the States,[1] the Supreme Court had recent
occasion to attempt to spell out what a "speedy trial" meant.
The Court supplied some handsome rhetoric but no real
guidelines when it said: "The right to a speedy trial is not a
theoretical or abstract right but one rooted in hard reality in
the need to have charges promptly exposed. If the case for the
prosecution calls on the accused to meet charges rather than
rest on the infirmities of the prosecution's case, as is the defendant's right, the time to meet them is when the case is fresh.
Stale claims have never been favored by the law, and far less
so in criminal cases. Although a great many accused persons
seek to put off confrontation as long as possible, the right to a
prompt inquiry into criminal charges is fundamental and the
duty of the charging authority is to provide a prompt trial."[2]
But what exactly is a "prompt trial"? State courts have struggled with that question since the Supreme Court's decision.[3]
Indeed, the Supreme Court itself in 1972 acknowledged the
need "to set out the criteria by which a speedy trial right is to
be judged," but ended up in frustration, saying "A balancing
test necessarily compels courts to approach speedy-trial cases
on an *ad hoc* basis. We can do little more than identify some
of the factors which courts should assess in determining
whether a particular defendant has been deprived of his right.
Though some might express them in different ways, we iden-

[1] Klopfer *v.* North Carolina, 386 U.S. 213 (1967).
[2] Dickey *v.* Florida, 398 U.S. 30, 37-38 (1970).
[3] For a particularly enlightening state court decision, *see* the decision of
the North Carolina Supreme Court in State *v.* Harrell, 187 S.E. 2d. 789
(1972). *See also* Tennessee *v.* McCullough, 470 S.W. 2d. 50 (1971); Commonwealth *v.* Bunter, 282 A. 2d. 705 (1971); State *v.* Lawless, 283 A. 2d.
160 (1971); Thompson *v.* State, 290 A. 2d. 565 (1972).

tify four such factors: Length of delay, the reason for delay, the defendant's assertion of his right, and prejudice to the defendant."[4]

Also, Congress has endeavored to step into the breach. With respect to the Interstate Agreement on Detainers Act of 1970, the Senate Report accompanying the bill tells us what the act provides with respect to detainers: "If the prisoner is not brought to trial within the 180-day limit, the charges are dismissed with prejudice and the detainer is no longer valid. The time limit can be extended for good cause shown in open court with the prisoner or his counsel present."[5] Pending before the Congress currently is a Speedy Trial Bill which would guarantee trials in Federal criminal cases within 60 days of the indictment or the dropping of charges.[6] Presumably the judgments of Congress will bear great weight with the Court if there are future challenges on the grounds that the time frame set by Congress does not provide a "speedy trial."

With respect to a "public trial" undoubtedly the framers of this amendment were impelled by the reasons recited by Justice Black some years ago: "The traditional Anglo-American distrust for secret trials has been variously ascribed to the notorious use of this practice by the Spanish Inquisition, to the excesses of the English Court of Star Chamber, and to the French monarchy's abuse of the *lettre de cachet*. . . . Whatever other benefits the guarantee to an accused that his trial be conducted in public may confer upon our society. The guarantee has always been recognized as a safeguard against any attempt to employ our courts as instruments of persecution."[7] In addition, no doubt, there was also the idea that an accused should be able to have some of his friends in the courtroom for the putative protection their presence would afford.

For years, some members of the press have claimed that the public has a "right to know" what its government is doing and, that the press serving as the public's agent should be permitted to cover trials virtually as they see fit to do so within the bounds of a little decorum. The Supreme Court does not recognize the full measure of such a claim. As the Court put

*The Press's Claim of a "Right to Know"*

---

[4] Barker *v.* Wingo, 407 U.S. 514 (1972).

[5] 1970 *U.S. Cong. & Adm. News*, 4864ff. For the law itself *see ibid.*, 1630.

[6] 1971 *Cong. Quart. Weekly Report*, 1560, 1607, 1990. For the views of Chief Justice Burger, *see* "The Image of Justice," 55 *Journal of the American Judicature Society*, 200 (1971).

[7] *In re* Oliver, 333 U.S. 257, 268-270 (1948).

it in 1965: "The free press has been a mighty catalyst in awakening public interest in governmental affairs, exposing corruption among public officers and employees, and generally including court proceedings. While maximum freedom must be allowed the press in carrying on this important function in a democratic society its exercise must necessarily be subject to the maintenance of absolute fairness in the judicial process."[8] Consequently, the Court has forbidden the televising of criminal cases. After a long recital of how televising a trial inhibits fairness, the Court went on to say: "It is said that the ever-advancing techniques of public communication and adjustment of the public to its presence may bring about a change in the effect of telecasting upon the fairness of criminal trials. But we are not dealing here with future developments in the field of electronics. Our judgment cannot be rested on the hypothesis of tomorrow but must take the facts as they are presented today."[9] Furthermore, the Court had been quick to point out earlier in its opinion: "Nor can the Courts be said to discriminate where they permit the newspaper reporter access to the courtroom. The television and radio reporter has the same privilege. They are entitled to the same rights as the general public. The press reporter is not permitted to bring his typewriter or printing press. When the advances in these arts permit reporting by printing press or by television without their present hazards to a fair trial we will have another case."[10]

Does Plea-Bargaining Subvert the Right to Trial? The time-honored custom of "plea-bargaining," i.e. where counsel for the defendant negotiates with the prosecutor to see if he can obtain a reduced charge at the price of pleading guilty, raises a severe question of whether or not the defendant is not in effect being enticed to bargain away his right to a trial. Justice White speaking for the Court in 1970 said: "But we cannot hold that it is unconstitutional for the State to extend a benefit to a defendant who in turn extends a substantial benefit to the State and who demonstrates by his plea that he is ready and willing to admit his crime and to enter the correctional system in a frame of mind which affords hope for

---

[8] Estes *v.* Texas, 381 U.S. 532, 539 (1965).
[9] *Ibid.*, 551-552.
[10] *Ibid.*, 540. For an interesting state court decision involving a judge closing the courtroom to press and public, *see* Oliver *v.* Poste, 331 N.Y.S. 2d. 407 (1972).

success in rehabilitation over a shorter time than might otherwise be necessary." But he went on to show that he was not unmindful of the dangers involved: "This is not to say that guilty plea convictions hold no hazards for the innocent or that the methods of taking guilty pleas presently employed in this country are necessarily valid in all respects. This mode of conviction is no more foolproof than full trials to the court or to the jury. Accordingly, we take great precautions against unsound results, and we should continue to do so, whether conviction is by plea or by trial."[11]

In 1968, the Supreme Court held that the right to trial by jury in criminal cases was guaranteed as against the States.[12] Then, in what may fairly be characterized as a surprising decision—surprising in view of history—the Court held in 1970 "that the 12-man panel is not a necessary ingredient of 'trial by jury,' and the respondent's refusal to impanel more than six members provided for by Florida law did not violate petitioner's Sixth Amendment rights as applied to the States through the Fourteenth."[13] With respect to the widely accepted practice of requiring a unanimous verdict, the Court wrote "We intimate no view whether or not the requirement of unanimity is an indispensable element of the Sixth Amendment jury trial."[14] But to the suggestion that "the 12-man jury gives a defendant a greater advantage since he has more 'chances' of finding a juror who will insist on acquittal and thus prevent conviction," the Court answered: ". . . The advantage might just as easily belong to the State, which also needs only one juror out of twelve insisting on guilt to prevent acquittal. What few experiments have occurred—usually in the civil area—indicate that there is no discernible difference between the results reached by the two different-sized juries."[15]

Later, in 1972, when it was squarely confronted with the issue of whether or not the Sixth Amendment required a unanimous verdict of the jury, the Court held that the requirement of unanimity "was not of constitutional stature."[16] The Court

An Impartial Jury

---

[11] Brady *v.* U.S., 397 U.S. 742 (1970). *See also* Peter L. Zimroth, "101,000 Defendants Were Convicted of Misdemeanors Last Year, 98,000 of Them Pleaded Guilty—To Get Reduced Sentences," *New York Times Magazine,* May 28, 1972, p. 14.
[12] Duncan *v.* Louisiana, 391 U.S. 145 (1968).
[13] Williams *v.* Florida, 399 U.S. 78, 86 (1970).
[14] *Ibid.,* 100, note 46.        [15] *Ibid.,* 101.
[16] Apodaca *v.* Oregon, 406 U.S. 404, 406 (1972).

reasoned that "the purpose of trial by jury is to prevent oppression by the Government by providing a 'safeguard against the corrupt or overzealous prosecutor and against the compliant, biased, or eccentric judge.' " Consequently, it pointed out that "a requirement of unanimity does not materially contribute" to the exercise of the jury's "commonsense judgment." Further, "a jury will come to such a judgment as long as it consists of a group of laymen representative of a cross section of the community who have the duty and the opportunity to deliberate, free from outside attempts at intimidation, on the question of a defendant's guilt. In terms of this function we perceive no difference between juries required to act unanimously and those permitted to convict or acquit by votes of 10 to two or 11 to one. Requiring unanimity would obviously produce hung juries in some situations where non-unanimous juries will convict or acquit. But in either case, the interest of the defendant in having the judgment of his peers interposed between himself and the officers of the State who prosecute and judge him is equally well served."[17] In a significant concurring opinion, Justice Blackmun wrote, "I do not hesitate to say . . . that a system employing a seven-five standard, rather than a nine-three or 75% minimum, would afford me great difficulty."[18] Also, Justice Blackmun made clear that he did not think that non-unanimous verdicts were wise policy: "My vote means only that I cannot conclude that the system is constitutionally offensive. Were I a legislator, I would disfavor it as a matter of policy."

With respect to the composition of juries, the Court has held that "[The] right does not entitle one accused of a crime to a jury tailored to the circumstances of the particular case, whether relating to the sex or other condition of the defendant, or to the nature of the charges tried. It requires only that the jury be indiscriminantly drawn from among those eligible in the community for jury service, untrammelled by any arbitrary and systematic exclusions."[19] Consequently, the Court has upheld a Florida law which provides that no woman shall be taken for jury duty unless she volunteers[20] as well as a State statute which provides for challenges in murder trials of jurors

---

[17] *Ibid.*, 410.　　　　　[18] *Ibid.*, 366.

[19] Hoyt *v.* Florida, 368 U.S. 57, 59 (1961). *See also*, Apodaca *v.* Oregon, 406 U.S. 404, 410 (1972).

[20] *Ibid.*, Strangely, the Court has in recent years avoided deciding whether or not women may be excluded as a class from jury rolls. In his

who admit conscientious scruples against capital punishment.[21] In the latter case, the Court explained "We simply cannot conclude, either on the basis of the record now before us or as a matter of judicial notice, that the exclusion of jurors opposed to capital punishment results in an unrepresentative jury on the issue of guilt or substantially increases the risk of conviction. In light of the presently available information, we are not prepared to announce a *per se* constitutional rule requiring the reversal of every conviction returned by a jury selected as this one was."[22]

But in 1972 the Supreme Court decided a case involving a scheme for empaneling a grand jury in Lafayette Parish of Louisiana, which had the effect of keeping Negro representation well under its percentage of the Parish's population. The Court held that a *prima facie* case of invidious discrimination had been established that the State did not satisfactorily rebut. The Court explained: "This Court has never announced mathematical standards for the demonstration of 'systematic' exclusion of blacks but has rather emphasized that a factual inquiry is necessary in each case which takes into account all possible explanatory factors. The progressive decimation of potential Negro grand jurors is indeed striking here, but we do not rest our conclusion that petitioner has demonstrated a *prima facie* case of invidious racial discrimination on statistical improbability alone, for the selection procedures themselves were not racially neutral."[23]

A very divided Court held in 1971 that "the Due Process Clause of the Fourteenth Amendment" did not assure "the right of a trial by jury in the adjudicative phase of a state juvenile court delinquency proceeding."[24] Justice Blackmun rea-

Jury Trial and Juveniles

---

concurring opinion in Alexander *v.* Louisiana, 405 U.S. 625, 635 (1972). Justice Douglas complained: "I believe the time has come to reject the dictum in Strauder *v.* West Virginia . . . that a State 'may confine' jury service 'to males.' I would here reach the question we reserved in Hoyt *v.* Florida . . . and hold that [the statute] as applied to exclude women as a class from . . . jury rolls, violated petitioner's constitutional right to an impartial jury drawn from a group representative of a cross section of the community."

21 Witherspoon *v.* Illinois, 391 U.S. 510 (1968).

22 *Ibid.*, 517-518.

23 Alexander *v.* Louisiana, 405 U.S. 625, 630 (1972). *See also* Morris *v.* State, 184 S.E. 2d. 82 (1971); Commonwealth *v.* Fisher, 290 A. 2d. 262 (1972); State *v.* Silva, 259 So. 2d. 153 (1972); *and cf.* State *v.* Kilbourne, 256 So. 2d. 630 (1972).

24 McKeiver *v.* Pennsylvania, 403 U.S. 528, 530 (1971).

soned that "accepting 'the proposition that the Due Process Clause has a role to play' . . . our taste here with respect to trial by jury, as it was in *Gault* [*see* p. 252] with respect to other claimed rights, 'is to ascertain the precise impact of the due process requirement.' "[25] In that context, Justice Blackmun concluded that "If the formalities of the criminal adjudicative process are to be superimposed upon the juvenile court system, there is little need for its separate existence. Perhaps that ultimate disillusionment will come one day, but for the moment we are disinclined to give impetus to it."[26] And as Justice Blackmun said earlier in his opinion "the applicable due process standard in juvenile proceedings . . . is fundamental fairness."[27]

Trial by Media
One of the most vexing problems inherent in the requirement of an impartial jury is how to keep a jury free from the impact of the enormous pretrial and trial publicity the news media usually lavish on the juicier criminal cases, often aided and abetted by prosecutors and defense counsels who see advantage in taking their case to the media. To fully appreciate what this kind of publicity can do to a trial, one must read the Supreme Court's almost unbelievable account of what went on at the highly publicized trial of Dr. Sheppard some few years ago.[28] In its opinion in that case, the Court made emphatically clear that courts have an obligation to do their utmost to minimize the impact of publicity on the outcome of a trial:

"From the cases coming here we note that unfair and prejudicial news comment on pending trials has become increasingly prevalent. Due process requires that the accused receive a trial by an impartial jury free from outside influences. Given the pervasiveness of modern communications and the difficulty of effacing prejudicial publicity from the minds of the jurors, the trial courts must take strong measures to ensure that the balance is never weighed against the accused. And appellate tribunals have the duty to make an independent evaluation of the circumstances. Of course, there is nothing that proscribes the press from reporting events that transpire in the courtroom. But where there is a reasonable likelihood that prejudicial news prior to trial will prevent a fair trial, the judge should continue the case until the threat abates, or

[25] *Ibid.*, 541.  [26] *Ibid.*, 551.
[27] *Ibid.*, 543.
[28] Sheppard v. Maxwell, 384 U.S. 333 (1966).

346

transfer it to another county not so permeated with publicity. In addition, sequestration of the jury was something the judge should have raised *sua sponte* with counsel. If publicity during the proceedings threatens the fairness of the trial, a new trial should be ordered. But we must remember that reversals are but palliatives; the cure lies in those remedial measures that will prevent the prejudice at its inception. The courts must take such steps by rule and regulation that will protect their processes from prejudicial outside interferences. Neither prosecutors, counsel for defense, the accused, witnesses, court staff nor enforcement officers coming under the jurisdiction of the court should be permitted to frustrate its function. Collaboration between counsel and the press as to information affecting the fairness of a criminal trial is not only subject to regulation, but is highly censurable and worthy of disciplinary measures."[29]

Despite the Supreme Court's guidelines and the heroic work of a Committee of the American Bar Association which, wrestling with the problem, produced the highly regarded but controversial Reardon report[30] suggesting means for mitigating it, Professor John E. Stanga reports: "How does one assess the impact of the line of cases culminating in *Sheppard*? Obviously, they (and the work of groups like the American Bar Association) have had some effect: Convictions have been reversed because of the probability that prejudice might result from press comment or coverage. Protections such as change of venue have been given greater attention, and court rules to protect the accused from prejudicial publicity have been adopted in some jurisdictions. But a more comprehensive examination requires a qualified assessment of the *Rideau, Estes* and *Sheppard* line, for in the vast majority of cases the criminal justice system goes on as before, with or without press comment, and the reversal of a conviction on prejudicial press publicity grounds is the exception. Of 202 cases involving publicity issues decided over a period of about three years beginning in 1966, only 12 resulted in the setting aside or reversal of convictions."[31]

[29] *Ibid.*, 362-363.
[30] ABA Project on Minimum Standards For Criminal Justice, *Fair Trial and Free Press* (1966).
[31] John E. Stanga, Jr., "Judicial Protection of the Criminal Defendant Against Adverse Press Coverage," 13 *William and Mary Law Review*, 1 (1971).

Perhaps, it is too soon to conclude that no more will be done. The Reardon report standards were not incorporated into the new A.B.A. code of professional responsibility which became effective for its members on 1 January 1970.[32]

Judge and Jury At the common law the court was judge of the "law" and the jury was judge of the "facts"; nor could either call the other to account for its determinations within its proper sphere.[33] In actual practice, nevertheless, the judge had great freedom in advising the jury as to the merits of a case, the weight of the evidence, the reliability of witnesses, and so on.[34] And while this feature of jury trial, too, is an element of the institution as it is embodied in the Constitution, a Federal judge must always make it clear to the jury that the final determination of all matters of fact rests with them, and that his remarks on such matters are advisory only.[35] The right to trial by jury may be waived as to any offense,[36] while except by allowance of Congress it does not extend to petty offenses.[37] However, the Court has recently held: "In light of the Constitution's emphasis on jury trial, we find it difficult to understand . . . the bald proposition that to compel a defendant in a criminal case to undergo a jury trial against his will is contrary to his right to a fair trial or to due process. A defendant's only constitutional right concerning the method of trial is to an impartial trial by jury. We find no constitutional impediment to conditioning a waiver of this right on the consent of the prosecuting attorney and the trial judge when, if either refuses to consent, the result is simply that the defendant is subject to an impartial trial by jury—the very thing that the Constitution guarantees him."[38]

[32] *Ibid.*, 144. *Also see* his Addendum, *ibid.*, 69ff.

[33] Coke, *Institutes of England*, Sect. 234; Bushell's Case (1670); J. B. Thayer, *Preliminary Treatise on Evidence* (Boston, 1898), 166-169. For the early history of the jury, see *ibid.*, ch. 2; A. W. Scott, *Fundamentals of Procedure* (New York, 1922), ch. 3.

[34] Thayer, *Preliminary Treatise*, ch. 3, passim. Thayer declares it "impossible to conceive" of jury trial existing at any stage of English history in a form that "would withhold from the jury the assistance of the court in dealing with facts. Trial by jury, in such a form as that, is not trial by jury in any historic sense of the words." *Ibid.*, 188n. "The jury works well in England because the bench is stronger than the bar." W. S. Holdsworth, *Some Lessons from Our Legal History* (New York, 1928), 85.

[35] Quercia *v.* U.S., 289 U.S. 466 (1933). *See also* Glasser *v.* U.S., 315 U.S. 60 (1942); U.S. *v.* Dunmore, 446 F. 2d. 1214 (1971); U.S. *v.* Wyatt, 442 F. 2d. 858 (1971).

[36] Patton *v.* U.S., 281 U.S. 276 (1930).

[37] Schick v. U.S., 195 U.S. 65 (1904).

[38] Singer *v.* U.S., 380 U.S. 24 (1965); Goldstein *v.* Paulikowski, 489 P. 2d. 1159 (1971).

Also, it should be recalled here that in recent years the right to trial by jury has been extended to some who were previously subject to courts-martial. (*See* pp. 88-90.)

"State and district": The jury must be drawn from the vicinage of the crime, it being assumed that this will ordinarily be the residence of the accused, who will thus be guaranteed a trial by his neighbors. But in modern conditions the vicinage of the crime may run over and beyond the boundaries of several States, and there was a time when persons charged with conspiring to violate the laws of the United States or to defraud the National Government could be dragged to the remotest parts of the Union on account of something done there by somebody else.[39] Not that Congress or the Government ever really had *carte blanche*. For as the Court had explained in 1944: "If an enactment of Congress equally permits the underlying spirit of the constitutional concern for trial in the vicinage to be respected rather than disrespected, construction should go in the direction of constitutional policy even though not commanded by it."[40] Starting in 1947, the Federal Rules of Criminal Procedure have set stricter guidelines for determining the venue of a Federal trial as well as the basis for granting or withholding a request for a change of venue by a defendant.[41] For example, the Rules state among other things that "the court upon motion of the defendant shall transfer the proceeding as to him to another district . . . if the court is satisfied that there exists in the district where the prosecution is pending so great a prejudice against the defendant that he cannot obtain a fair and impartial trial at any place fixed by law for holding court in that district."[42] In short, a defendant does have the right under the Rules to seek a change of venue to avoid prejudice and "for the convenience of parties and witnesses, and in the interest of justice" and Federal courts have been meticulous in considering claims to that statutory right.[43] This does not mean, however, that the defendant always gets his way, for as the Supreme Court said in 1964, in considering

---

[39] *See* United States *v*. Johnson, 323 U.S. 273 (1944). For a succinct history *see* Justice Holmes, dissenting, in Hyde *v*. U.S., 225 U.S. 347 at 384 (1912); Jones *v*. Gasch, 404 F. 2d. 231, 234-235 (1967), *cert. denied* 390 U.S. 1414 (1968).

[40] United States *v*. Johnson, 323 U.S. 273, 276 (1944).

[41] 18R U.S.C. 18, 20, 21.      [42] *Ibid.*, 21.

[43] Jones *v*. Gasch, 404 F. 2d. 1231 (1967); U.S. *v*. Sweig, 316 F. Supp. 1148, 1161-1162 (1970); U.S. *v*. Price, 447 F. 2d. 23, 26 (1971).

"the interest of justice," valid factors include: " (1) location of
corporate defendant; (2) location of possible witnesses; (3)
location of events likely to be in issue; (4) location of documents and records likely to be involved; (5) disruption of defendant's business unless the case is transferred; (6) expense
to the parties; (7) location of counsel; (8) relative accessibil-
ity of place of trial; (9) docket condition of each district or division involved; and (10) any other special elements which
might affect the transfer."[44]

For offenses against Federal laws not committed within any
State, Congress has the sole power to prescribe the place of
trial; such an offense is not local and may be tried at any place
Congress designates.[45]

Nothing in the foregoing should becloud the fact that where
all elements of an alleged crime take place in a particular State
and district and the defendant insists on it, he has the constitutional right to be tried in that State and district. In the struggle to vindicate the civil rights of Blacks in the South, this fact
has created difficulties. Too often in the past it was virtually
impossible to get juries to convict those who transgressed the
rights of Blacks. This led the Government at times to attempt
to bypass jury trials by seeking remedies that would invoke
the use of a judge's power to punish summarily for contempt.
The problems that such an approach raises were described
above (pp. 163-165). Suffice it to point out here that the constitutional requirement has had at least one adverse impact on
justice that the framers of the amendment had not anticipated.
It was undoubtedly never intended to be a means for encouraging lawlessness.

"Nature and cause of the accusation": That is to say, the law
must furnish a reasonably definite standard of guilt.[46] Applying the sense of this requirement in interpretation of the due
process clause of the Fourteenth Amendment, the Court in
1939 set aside a New Jersey statute which penalized "gang-
sters," but later upheld a Minnesota statute which authorized
proceedings against "psychopathic personalities." In the latter
case the material term had been closely defined by judicial

*Venue as a Bar to Vin- dicating Civil Rights*

*Indefinite Charges and Illegal Presump- tions*

---

[44] Platt *v.* Minnesota Mining & Mfg. Co., 376 U.S. 240, 243-244 (1964).
*See also,* State *v.* Niccum, 190 N.W. 2d. 815 (1971).

[45] Jones *v.* U.S., 137 U.S. 202, 211 (1890); United States *v.* Johnson, 323
U.S. 273 (1944); 18 U.S.C. 3238.

[46] United States *v.* Cohen Grocery Co., 255 U.S. 81 (1921); Coates *v.*
City of Cincinnati, 402 U.S. 611, 616 (1971).

interpretation; in the former it had not.[47] Statutes prohibiting the coercion of employers to hire "unneeded" employees,[48] establishing "minimum" wages and "maximum" hours of service for persons engaged in the production of goods for interstate commerce,[49] or forbidding "undue" or "unreasonable" restraints of trade,[50] have been held to be sufficiently definite to be constitutional. Nor is a provision of the Immigration Act,[51] which makes it a felony for an alien against whom a specified order of deportation is pending to "willfully fail or refuse to make timely application in good faith for travel or other documents necessary to his departure," void, on its face, for indefiniteness.[52]

More recently in upholding obscenity legislation, the Court held that "Many decisions have recognized that these terms of obscenity statutes are not precise. This Court, however, has consistently held that lack of precision is not itself offensive to the requirements of due process. . . . 'The Constitution does not require impossible standards'; all that is required is that the language 'conveys sufficiently definite warning as to the proscribed conduct when measured by common understanding and practices. . . .' "[53] Nor did the Court find the words "under color of law" too vague to uphold indictments for a conspiracy to deprive three young civil rights workers of their Fourteenth Amendment rights by setting them up for murder.[54] In 1971, however, the Court struck down a Cincinnati ordinance which read in part: "It shall be unlawful for three or more persons to assemble except at a public meeting of citizens, on any of the sidewalks . . . and there conduct themselves in a manner annoying to persons passing by, or occupants of adjacent buildings." The Court explained: "In our opinion this ordinance is unconstitutionally vague because it subjects the exercise of the right to assemble to an unascertainable

[47] Lanzetta v. N.J., 306 U.S. 451 (1939); Minnesota v. Probate Court, 309 U.S. 270 (1940).
[48] United States v. Petrillo, 332 U.S. 1 (1947).
[49] United States v. Darby, 312 U.S. 100, 125 (1941).
[50] Nash v. U.S., 229 U.S. 373 (1913).
[51] 8 U.S.C. 1252 (3).
[52] United States v. Spector, 343 U.S. 169 (1952).
[53] Roth v. U.S., 354 U.S. 476, 491 (1957).
[54] U.S. v. Price, 383 U.S. 787, 806 note 20 (1966). Evidently, the Federal government officials felt that a murder charge in a State court would be to no avail. Consequently, to take the case to a Federal court, they had to proceed on the basis of a Federal law; that is why the indictment was framed as it was.

standard, and unconstitutionally broad because it authorizes the punishment of constitutionally protected conduct."[55]

In a 1972 decision,[56] the Supreme Court made all so-called "vagrancy laws" constitutionally suspect when it struck down as unconstitutionally vague a particularly odious law contained in the Jacksonville, Florida, Ordinance Code which read as follows:

"Rogues and vagabonds, or dissolute persons who go about begging, common gamblers, persons who use juggling or unlawful games or plays, common drunkards, common night walkers, thieves, pilferers or pickpockets, traders in stolen property, lewd, wanton and lascivious persons, keepers of gambling places, common railers and brawlers, persons wandering or strolling around from place to place without any lawful purpose or object, habitual loafers, disorderly persons, persons neglecting all lawful business and habitually spending their time by frequenting houses of ill fame, gaming houses, or places where alcoholic beverages are sold or served, persons able to work but habitually living upon the earnings of their wives or minor children shall be deemed vagrants and upon conviction in the Municipal Court shall be punished as provided for Class D offenses." As Justice Douglas speaking for the Court so eloquently put it: "A presumption that people who might walk or loaf or loiter or stroll or frequent houses where liquor is sold, or who are supported by their wives or who look suspicious to the police are to become future criminals is too precarious for a rule of law."

As to the indictment, the Federal Rules of Criminal Procedure require that the indictment "be a plain, concise and definite written statement of the essential facts constituting the offense charged."[57] The Supreme Court has held to the following standard for years:

"The true test of the sufficiency of an indictment is not whether it could have been made more definite and certain, but whether it contains the elements of the offense intended to be charged, 'and sufficiently apprises the defendant of what he must be prepared to meet, and, in any case any other proceedings are taken against him for a similar offence, whether

[55] Coates *v.* City of Cincinnati, 402 U.S. 611, 614 (1971).
[56] Papachristou *et al. v.* City of Jacksonville, 405 U.S. 156 (1972).
[57] 8R U.S.C. 7 (c).

the record shows with accuracy to what extent he may plead a former acquittal or conviction.' "[58]

As the Court has said: "Certain principles have remained relatively immutable in our jurisprudence. One of these is that where government action seriously injures an individual, and the reasonableness of the action depends on fact findings, the evidence used to prove the Government's case must be disclosed to the individual so that he has an opportunity to show that it is untrue. While this is important in the case of documentary evidence, it is even more important where the evidence consists of the testimony of individuals whose memory might be faulty or who, in fact, might be perjurers of persons motivated by malice, vindictiveness, intolerance, prejudice, or jealousy. We have formalized these protections in the requirements of confrontation and cross-examination. They have ancient roots. They find expression in the Sixth Amendment which provides that in all criminal cases the accused shall enjoy the right 'to be confronted with the witnesses against him.' This Court has been zealous to protect these rights from erosion. It has spoken out not only in criminal cases, . . . but also in all types of cases where administrative and regulatory actions were under scrutiny."[59] And in recent years there has been precious little niggling about confrontation in criminal trials.[60] Either the Government must produce the witnesses and evidence or drop the case. For example, the Supreme Court held in 1968 that "the admission of a confession of a codefendant who did not take the stand deprived the defendant of his rights under the Sixth Amendment Confrontation Clause."[61] Nonetheless, there has "traditionally been an exception to the confrontation requirement where a witness is un-

*Confrontation*

[58] U.S. v. Anderson, 447 F. 2d. 833 (1971); Cochrane and Sayre v. U.S., 157 U.S. 286 (1895); Rosen v. U.S., 161 U.S. 29 (1896); Hagner v. U.S., 285 U.S. 427 (1932); U.S. v. Debrow, 346 U.S. 374 (1953).
[59] Greene v. McElroy, 360 U.S. 474, 496 (1959).
[60] Cf. Illinois v. Allen, 397 U.S. 337 (1970), where it was held that privilege may be lost by misconduct.
[61] Bruton v. U.S., 391 U.S. 123 (1968). In 1972, the Supreme Court held that a violation of Bruton rule could be considered harmless error where there was overwhelming evidence of guilt and a relatively insignificant impact of the co-defendant's statement. The Court pointed out that in Bruton it had said "a defendant is entitled to a fair trial but not a perfect one." Schneble v. Florida, 405 U.S. 427 (1972). But see dissent of Justice Marshall with whom Justices Douglas and Brennan joined. Cf. Dutton v. Evans, 400 U.S. 74 (1970).

available and has given testimony at previous judicial proceedings against the same defendant which was subject to cross-examination by the defendant. . . . This exception has been justified on the ground that the right of cross-examination initially afforded provides substantial compliance with the purposes behind the confirmation requirement."[62] In reaffirming this exception in 1972, the Court stressed again that the witness must truly be unavailable and that the trier of fact must be afforded "a satisfactory basis for evaluating the truth of the prior statement."[63]

The interesting problems which have come up regarding confrontation in recent years are whether or not due process requires confrontation in administrative or legislative proceedings. The short of the matter is that the majority of the Supreme Court, over some bitter dissents, has not found that the Constitution compels the right of confrontation in these kinds of proceedings. As Chief Justice Warren put it:

"Therefore, as a generalization, it can be said that due process embodies the differing rules of fair play, which through the years, have become associated with differing types of proceedings. Whether the Constitution requires that a particular right obtain in a specific proceeding depends upon a complexity of factors. The nature of the alleged right involved, the nature of the proceeding, and the possible burden on that proceeding, are all considerations which must be taken into account. An analysis of these factors demonstrates why it is that the particular rights claimed by the respondents need not be conferred upon those appearing before purely investigative agencies, of which the Commission on Civil Rights is one."[64]

"Compulsory process for obtaining witnesses": The right is not as absolute as the language of the amendment suggests. Speaking of the application of Federal Rule 17b, which deals with "defendants unable to pay the fees of witnesses," an Appeals Court said: "Obviously, the right given the defendant is not absolute, but is to be governed by the sound discretion of

---

[62] Barber v. Page, 390 U.S. 719, 722 (1968); California v. Green, 399 U.S. 149 (1970). See also Dutton v. Evans, 400 U.S. 74 (1970) for a discussion of distinction between the requirements of hearsay rules and the confrontation clause.

[63] Mancusi v. Stubbs, 408 U.S. 204 (1972).

[64] Hannah v. Larche, 363 U.S. 420, 442 (1960). See also Richardson v. Perales, 402 U.S. 389 (1971); Goldberg v. Kelly, 397 U.S. 254 (1970); Flemming v. Nestor, 363 U.S. 603 (1960).

the trial judge, which will not be disturbed by an appellate court unless exceptional and compelling circumstances clearly indicate an abuse of discretion."[65] Even in upholding such an important right, judges, of course, must be able to refuse patently frivolous requests in order to prevent a trial from becoming a farce.

In 1963, in the much discussed case of Gideon *v.* Wainwright, the Supreme Court held the right to counsel was obligatory upon the States by the Fourteenth Amendment.[66] Actually, the Supreme Court, even before *Gideon*, had held that due process alone required the right to counsel in many State cases because of particular fact situations.[67] For example, "ignorance and illiteracy of the defendants, their youth, the circumstances of public hostility . . . and above all that they stood in deadly peril of their lives" had caused the Court to find "that the state court had a duty to assign counsel for the trial as a necessary requisite of due process of law." In retrospect, the greatest impact of the *Gideon* decision was not that it made assistance of counsel mandatory on States but the kind of soul searching it inspired on the question of what is the significance of right to counsel *in the trial* if a defendant has suffered all the disadvantages of not having counsel at the earlier stages of the investigation that preceded the trial.

Protagonists for extending the right to counsel were as plentiful as they were persuasive. Yale Kamisar, Professor of Criminal Law at the University of Michigan Law School, was particularly forceful and provocative.[68] The result of the ferment has been the extension of the right to counsel to the point where "the investigation is no longer a general inquiry into an unsolved crime but has begun to focus on a particular suspect," and "the suspect has been taken into police custody." To deny the suspect the right to counsel at that stage is to deny him his Sixth Amendment right to counsel.[69] This led inexorably to the *Miranda* decision, with the Court saying: "As for the procedural safeguards to be employed, unless other fully effective

*Right to Counsel*

---

[65] Wagner *v.* U.S., 416 F. 2d. 558, 564 (1969); *cert. denied*, 397 U.S. 923 (1970); People *v.* Nieto, 190 N.W. 2d. 579 (1971).

[66] Gideon *v.* Wainwright, 372 U.S. 335 (1963).

[67] *Ibid.*, Justice Harlan's concurring opinion.

[68] *See,* for example, his "Equal Justice in the Gatehouses and Mansions of American Criminal Procedure," in *Criminal Justice in our Time* (1965), 653.

[69] Escobedo *v.* Illinois, 378 U.S. 478 (1964).

means are devised to inform accused persons of their right of silence . . . the following measures are required. Prior to any questioning, the person must be warned that he has a right to remain silent, that any statement he does make may be used as evidence against him, and that he has a right to the presence of an attorney, either retained or appointed. The defendant may waive effectuation of these rights, provided the waiver is made voluntarily, knowingly and intelligently. If, however, he indicates in any manner and at any state of the process that he wishes to consult with an attorney before speaking there can be no questioning."[70] Today there is scarcely a jurisdiction in which law enforcement officers do not carry a "Miranda card" from which they read to a suspect what his constitutional rights are, making clear, of course, that he has right to counsel.

In 1967, the Supreme Court specifically extended right to counsel to *post*-indictment police lineups.[71] In the ensuing years some lower courts extended the right to counsel to lineups in pre-arrest situations.[72] In 1972, when the Supreme Court was confronted precisely with the question of extending the exclusionary rule to "identification testimony based upon a police station showup that took place before the defendant had been indicted or otherwise formally charged with any criminal offense," it was sharply split.[73] But at least four of the majority held that "it has been firmly established that a person's right to counsel attaches only at or after the time that adversary judicial proceedings have been initiated against him."[74] But they cautioned that "What has been said is not to suggest that there may not be occasions during the course of a criminal investigation when the police do abuse identification procedures. Such abuses are not beyond the reach of the Constitution. . . . The Due Process Clause of the Fifth and Fourteenth Amendments forbids a lineup that is unnecessarily suggestive and conducive to irreparable mistaken identification."[75] While the current Court was limiting right to counsel to only the time "that adversary judicial proceedings have been ini-

---

[70] Miranda *v.* Arizona, 384 U.S. 436 (1966). *But see* Commonwealth *v.* Bartlett, 288 A. 2d. 796 (1972).

[71] U.S. *v.* Wade, 388 U.S. 218 (1967); *see* Neil *v.* Biggers, 41 *LW* 4064 (1972); *cf.* Stovall *v.* Denno, 388 U.S. 293 (1967).

[72] State *v.* Oliver, 288 A. 2d. 81 (1971) and the cases cited therein. *But see* Zeigler *v.* Commonwealth, 186 S.E. 2d. 38 (1972).

[73] Kirby *v.* Illinois, 406 U.S. 682 (1972).

[74] *Ibid.*, 688.   [75] *Ibid.*, 690.

tiated," it extended the right markedly where the proceedings were begun.[76] In 1972 the Court held that, "absent a knowing and intelligent waiver, no person may be imprisoned for any offense, whether classified as petty, misdemeanor or felony, unless he is represented by counsel at his trial."[77] The justices manifested a concern for the difficulties this decision would make for the administration of justice in the states. But Chief Justice Burger undoubtedly bespoke the hope of most of them in his separate opinion, where he said "The holding of the Court today may well add large new burdens on a profession already overtaxed, but the dynamics of the profession have a way of rising to the burdens placed on it."[78]

No Constitutional Right to Counsel in Legislative and Administrative Proceedings

Despite the growth of right to counsel with respect to criminal law enforcement, the Court has been reluctant to find that the *Constitution* requires that legislative and administrative proceedings provide the right to counsel even where those proceedings may "lay a witness open to criminal charges."[79]

As indicated earlier, (pp. 192-193), the Court has generally been favorably disposed to its right-to-counsel decisions having retroactive application.

Retroactivity of Right to Counsel Decisions

[76] Argensinger *v.* Hamlin, 407 U.S. 25 (1972).
[77] *Ibid.*, 37.          [78] *Ibid.*, 44.
[79] Hannah *v.* Larche, 363 U.S. 420, 445 and Appendix (1960); *in re* Groban, 352 U.S. 330 (1957).

# AMENDMENT VII

In suits at common law, where the value in controversy shall exceed twenty dollars, the right of trial by jury shall be preserved, and no fact tried by a jury, shall be otherwise reexamined in any court of the United States, than according to the rules of the common law.

The primary purpose of this amendment was to preserve the historic line separating the province of the jury from that of the judge in civil cases, without at the same time preventing procedural improvements which did not transgress this line. Elucidating this formula, the Court has achieved the following results: It is constitutional for a Federal judge, in the course of trial, to express his opinion upon the facts, provided all questions of fact are ultimately submitted to the jury;[1] to call the jury's attention to parts of the evidence he deems of special importance,[2] being careful to distinguish between matters of law and matters of opinion in relation thereto;[3] to inform the jury when there is not sufficient evidence to justify a verdict, that such is the case;[4] to direct the jury, after plaintiff's case is all in, to return a verdict for the defendant on the ground of the insufficiency of the evidence;[5] to set aside a verdict which in his opinion is against the law or the evidence, and order a new trial;[6] to refuse defendant a new trial on the condition, accepted by plaintiff, that the latter remit a portion of the damages awarded him[7] but not, on the other hand, to deny

[1] Vicksburg & Railroad Co. v. Putnam, 118 U.S. 545, 553 (1886); United States v. Reading Railroad, 123 U.S. 113, 114 (1887); Ray v. U.S., 367 F. 2d. 258 (1966).

[2] 118 U.S. 545; where are cited Carver v. Jackson ex dem. Astor et al., 4 Pet. 1, 80 (1830); Magniac v. Thompson, 7 Pet. 348, 390 (1833); Mitchell v. Harmony, 13 How. 115, 131 (1852); Transportation Line v. Hope, 95 U.S. 297, 302 (1877); see also Ray v. U.S., 367 F. 2d. 258 (1966).

[3] Games v. Dunn, 14 Pet. 322, 327 (1840); Boeing Co. v. Shipman, 411 F. 2d. 365, 380 (1969).

[4] Sparf v. U.S., 156 U.S. 51, 99-100 (1895); Pleasants v. Fant, 22 Wall. 116, 121 (1875); Randall v. Baltimore & Ohio R.R. Co., 109 U.S. 478, 482 (1883); Meehan v. Valentine, 145 U.S. 611, 625 (1892); Coughran v. Bigelow, 164 U.S. 301 (1896); Belton v. U.S., 382 F. 2d. 150 (1967).

[5] Treat Mfg. Co. v. Standard Steel & Iron Co., 157 U.S. 674 (1895); Randall v. Baltimore & Ohio R.R. Co., 109 U.S. 478, 482 (1883) and cases there cited.

[6] Capital Traction Co. v. Hof, 174 U.S. 1, 13 (1899); Southern Pacific Co. v. Guthrie, 186 F. 2d. 926 (1951).

[7] Arkansas Land & Cattle Co. v. Mann, 130 U.S. 69, 74 (1889); Gorsalitz v. Olin Corp., 429 F. 2d. 1033, 1043 (1970).

plaintiff a new trial on the converse condition, although defendant accepted it.[8] From this point on, the line is not always easy to trace. In general, the Court has held that Federal courts of appeal must remand for retrial cases in which they reverse the verdict of a lower court, and may not substitute a judgment of their own on the merits, although more recent cases somewhat mitigate this rule, which obviously favors the law's delays.[9]

One of the liveliest disputes among Supreme Court Justices in recent decades has been whether or not the Court should review cases arising under the Federal Employers' Liability Act, cases which, when they come to the Court, generally boil down to a dispute over lower court judges' withholding cases from juries or setting aside verdicts—juries being notoriously more generous in making awards to disabled employees than are judges. An angry Justice Douglas sought to put the matter in perspective in 1959:

"It is apparent from the decisions where we refused to review cases in which lower courts withheld cases from the jury or set aside jury verdicts (or where, having granted certiorari, we sustained the lower courts in that action) that the system of judicial supervision still exists in this as in other types of cases.

"It is suggested that the Court has consumed too much of its time in reviewing these FELA cases. An examination of the 33 cases in which the Court has granted certiorari during the period of over 10 years . . . reveals that 16 of these cases were summarily reversed without oral argument and without full opinions. Only 17 cases were argued during this period of more than a decade and, of these, 5 were disposed of by brief *per curiam* opinions. Only 12 cases in over 10 years were argued, briefed and disposed of with full opinions by the Court. We have granted certiorari in these cases on an average of less than 3 per year and have given plenary consideration to slightly more than 1 per year. Wastage of our time is therefore a false issue.

[8] Dimick *v.* Schiedt, 293 U.S. 474, 476-478 (1935); Gorsalitz *v.* Olin Corp., 429 F. 2d. 1033, 1043 (1970).
[9] Slocum *v.* N.Y. Life Ins. Co., 228 U.S. 364 (1913); Dimick *v.* Schiedt, above; Baltimore & C. Line *v.* Redman, 295 U.S. 654 (1935); Smith *v.* Illinois Central R.R. Co., 394 F. 2d. 254 (1968); Hartnett *v.* Brown & Bigelow, 394 F. 2d. 438 (1968).

"The difference between the majority and minority of the Court in our treatment of FELA cases concerns the degree of vigilance we should exercise in safeguarding the jury trial—guaranteed by the Seventh Amendment and part and parcel of the remedy under this Federal Act when suit is brought in state courts. . . ."[10]

Limited Application of the Amendment

The amendment governs only courts which sit under the authority of the United States,[11] including courts in the territories and the District of Columbia.[12] It does not apply to a State court even when it is enforcing a right created by Federal statute.[13] Materially it is "limited to rights and remedies peculiarly legal in their nature,"[14] the term "common law" being used in contradistinction to suits in which equitable rights alone were recognized at the time of the framing of the amendment.[15] Nor does it apply to cases in admiralty and maritime jurisdiction, in which the trial is by a court without a jury;[16] nor to suits to enforce claims against the United States;[17] nor to suits to cancel a naturalization certificate for fraud;[18]

---

[10] Harris v. Penn. R. R. Co., 361 U.S. 15, 17 (1959). *See also* Rogers v. Missouri Pacific R.R.Co., 352 U.S. 500 (1957); Harrison v. Missouri Pacific R.R. Co., 372 U.S. 248 (1963); Basham v. Penn. R.R. Co., 372 U.S. 699 (1963); Barboza v. Texaco, Inc., 434 F. 2d. 121 (1970).

[11] Pearson v. Yewdall, 95 U.S. 294, 296 (1877). *See also* Edwards v. Elliott, 21 Wall. 532, 557 (1874); Justices v. U.S. *ex rel.* Murray, 9 Wall. 274, 277 (1870); Walker v. Sauvinet, 92 U.S. 90 (1875); St. Louis & K.C. Land Co. v. Kansas City, 241 U.S. 419 (1916); *in re* Advisory Opinion to Senate, 278 A. 2d. 852, 854 (1971); Williams v. Williams, 186 S.E. 2d., 210 (1972).

[12] Webster v. Reid, 11 How. 437, 460 (1851); Kennon v. Gilmer, 131 U.S. 22, 28 (1889); Glidden v. Zdanok, 370 U.S. 530, 572 (1962).

[13] Minneapolis & St. L.R. Co. v. Bombolis, 241 U.S. 211 (1916), which involved the Federal Employers Liability Act of 1908. The ruling is followed in four other cases in the same volume. *See ibid.*, 241, 261, 485 and 494; Mills v. Louisiana, 360 U.S. 230, 237 (1959); Sharpe v. State, 448 P. 2d. 301 (1968), *cert. denied*, 394 U.S. 904 (1969).

[14] Shields v. Thomas, 18 How. 253, 262 (1856); Glidden Co. v. Zdanok, 370 U.S. 530, 572 (1962).

[15] Parsons v. Bedford, 3 Pet. 433, 447 (1830); Barton v. Barbour, 104 U.S. 126, 133 (1881). "It is now fundamental, though, that when legal and equitable claims are tried together, common questions of fact must be decided by the jury in order to preserve the integrity of the Seventh Amendment guarantee." Heyman v. Kline, 456 F. 2d. 123 (1972), and cases cited therein.

[16] Parsons v. Bedford, above; Waring v. Clarke, 5 How. 441, 460 (1847). *See also* The "Sarah," 8 Wheat. 390, 391 (1823), and cases there cited.

[17] McElrath v. U.S., 102 U.S. 426, 440 (1880). *See also* Galloway v. U.S., 319 U.S. 372, 388 (1943); Glidden Co. v. Zdanok, 370 U.S. 530, 572 (1962).

[18] Luria v. U.S., 231 U.S. 9 (1913).

to orders of deportation of an alien;[19] to suits under the Long-shoremen's and Harbor Workers Compensation Act.[20] In short, the Court, in its application of the amendment, until recently has followed the historic pattern of the common law. Now, substantial change may be in store as a consequence of a Supreme Court decision in 1970. The story starts back in 1934 when Congress granted the Supreme Court the power to prescribe rules for Federal courts in "civil actions at law." Congress empowered the Court to "at any time unite the general rules prescribed for cases in equity with those in actions at law so as to secure one form of civil action and procedure for both: *Provided, however,* that in such union of rules the right of trial by jury as at common law and declared by the Seventh Amendment to the Constitution shall be preserved to the parties inviolate."[21] Subsequently, the Federal Rules did provide for one form of civil action.[22] Justice White, speaking for the Court in 1970, pointed out that "Actions are no longer brought as actions at law or suits in equity. Under the Rules there is only one action—a 'civil action'—in which all claims may be joined and all remedies are available. Purely procedural impediments to the presentation of any issue by any party, based on the difference between law and equity were destroyed. . . ."[23] Consequently, the Court held that "Under the rules law and equity are procedurally combined; nothing turns now upon the form of the action or the procedural devices by which the parties happen to come before the court . . . ."[24] Three Justices sharply dissented, pointing out:

"In holding as it does that the plaintiff in a shareholder's derivative suit is constitutionally entitled to a jury trial, the Court today seems to rely upon some sort of ill-defined combination of the Seventh Amendment and the Federal Rules of Civil Procedure. Somehow the Amendment and the Rules magically interact to do what each separately was expressly

[19] Gee Wah Lee *v.* U.S., 25 F. 2d. 107 (1928); *cert. denied,* 277 U.S. 608 (1928). Filer & S. Co. *v.* Diamond Iron Works, 270 Fed. 489 (1921); *cert. denied,* 256 U.S. 691 (1921).
[20] Crowell *v.* Benson, 285 U.S. 22, 45, 49 (1932). The Court held that "As the Act relates solely to injuries occurring upon the navigable waters of the United States, it deals with maritime law, applicable to matters that fall within the admiralty and maritime jurisdiction. . . ." *ibid.,* 39.
[21] 48 *Stat.* 1064 (1934).      [22] 28R U.S.C. Rule 2.
[23] Ross *v.* Bernhard, 396 U.S. 531, 539 (1970).
[24] *Ibid.*

intended not to do, namely, to enlarge the right to a jury trial in civil actions brought in the courts of the United States.

"The Seventh Amendment, by its terms, does not extend, but merely *preserves* the right to a jury trial '[i]n Suits at common law.' All agree that this means the reach of the Amendment is limited to those actions that were tried to the jury in 1791 when the Amendment was adopted. Suits in equity, which were historically tried to the court, were therefore unaffected by it. Similarly, Rule 38 of the Federal Rules has no bearing on the right to a jury trial in suits in equity, for it simply preserves inviolate '[t]he right of trial by jury as declared by the Seventh Amendment.' Thus this Rule, like the Amendment itself, neither restricts nor enlarges the right to jury trial. Indeed nothing in the Federal Rules can rightly be construed to enlarge the right of jury trial, for in the legislation authorizing the Rules, Congress expressly provided that they 'shall neither abridge, enlarge, nor modify the substantive rights of any litigant.' I take this plain, simple, and straightforward language to mean that after the promulgation of the Federal Rules, as before, the constitutional right to a jury trial attaches only to suits at common law. So, apparently, has every federal court that has discussed the issue. Since, as the Court concedes, a shareholder's derivative suit could be brought only in equity, it would seem to me to follow by the most elementary logic that in such suits there is no constitutional right to a trial by jury. Today the Court tosses aside history, logic, and over 100 years of firm precedent to hold that the plaintiff in a shareholder's derivative suit does indeed have a constitutional right to a trial by jury. This holding has a questionable basis in policy and no basis whatever in the Constitution."[25] Clearly, if the majority's holding continues to prevail, the right to trial by jury in civil cases will be extended considerably.

[25] *Ibid.*, 543-544.

# AMENDMENT VIII

Excessive bail shall not be required, nor excessive fines imposed, nor cruel and unusual punishments inflicted.

The Supreme Court has had little to say with reference to excessive fines or bail. In an early case it held that it had no appellate jurisdiction to revise the sentence of an inferior court, even though the excessiveness of the fine was apparent on the face of the record.[1] Nearly one hundred and twenty years later, in 1951, however, it ruled that bail must not be excessive, that its purpose was to make reasonably sure of a defendant's appearance for trial but not so heavy that he could not give it and thereby secure his liberty for the purpose of preparing his defense.[2] According to one Federal court, the prohibition against excessive bail applies to the States.[3]

In recent years, the whole bail system has come under close scrutiny and criticism from a host of responsible persons and groups.[4] Nonetheless, interpretation of the constitutional command remains what the Supreme Court said it was in 1951.[5]

The ban against "cruel and unusual punishments" has received somewhat greater attention. In Wilkerson v. Utah[6] the Court observed that "difficulty would attend the effort to define with exactness the extent of the constitutional provision which provides that cruel and unusual punishments shall not be inflicted," but that it was "safe to affirm that punishment of torture, ... and all others in the same line of unnecessary cruelty, are forbidden by that Amendment . . .";[7] but that shooting as a mode of executing the death penalty was not "cruel and unusual" within the intention of the amendment. Thirty years later a divided court condemned a Philippine statute prescribing fine and imprisonment of from twelve to twenty years for entering a known false statement in a public record, on the ground that the gross disparity between this punishment and that imposed for other more serious offenses

"Cruel and Unusual Punishments"

[1] Ex parte Watkins, 7 Pet. 568, 574 (1832).
[2] Stack v. Boyle, 342 U.S. 1 (1951); 18R U.S.C. Rule 46; Kinney v. Lenon, 447 F. 2d. 596 (1971); U.S. v. Smith, 444 F. 2d. 61 (1971).
[3] Pilkington v. Circuit Court, 324 F. 2d. 45, 46 (1963).
[4] See People v. Jones, 489 P. 2d. 596, 598 (1971) and works cited therein.
[5] People v. Jones, 489 P. 2d. 596, 598 (1971); State ex. rel. Ghiz v. Johnson, 183 S.E. 2d. 703 (1971); McDermott v. Superior Court, 97 Cal. Rptr. 171 (1971).
[6] 99 U.S. 130 (1879).          [7] Ibid., 135.

made it cruel and unusual, and as such, repugnant to the Bill of Rights.[8] But no constitutional infirmity was discovered in a measure punishing as a separate offense each act of placing a letter in the mails in pursuance of a single scheme to defraud.[9] Nor was it "cruel and unusual punishment," in the opinion of a divided Court, to subject one convicted of murder to electrocution after an accidental failure of equipment had rendered a previous attempt unsuccessful.[10]

In June 1972, the Supreme Court rendered its long-awaited decision with respect to the death penalty. How intense were the feelings and divisions on the Court is manifested by the fact that each Justice, whether part of the five-man majority or the four-man dissent, filed a separate opinion.[11] The short *per curiam* decision simply stated that "The Court holds that the imposition and carrying out of the death penalty in these cases constitutes cruel and unusual punishment in violation of the Eighth and Fourteenth Amendments." But at least two of the Justices composing the majority (Stewart and White) indicated that they did not think the Constitution prohibited the death penalty *per se*. As Justice Stewart worded it: "I simply conclude that the Eighth and Fourteenth Amendments cannot tolerate the infliction of a sentence of death under legal systems that permit this unique penalty to be so wantonly and so freakishly imposed." And as Justice White said, "In joining the Court's judgment, therefore, I do not at all intimate that the death penalty is unconstitutional *per se* or that there is no system of capital punishment that would comport with the Eighth Amendment." Presumably, a fair system of capital punishment, if one can, indeed, be devised, would be held constitutional by a majority of the current Court. One factor worth pondering is how heavily it must have weighed on some Justices' minds that the immediate and ultimate fate of 700 men and women in the nation's death rows was in their hands.[12]

In recent years, in keeping with the greater concern manifested for civil liberties, there have been some novel contentions as to what constitutes cruel and unusual punishments. A Georgia court of appeals held that requiring a probationer to

8 Weems *v.* U.S., 217 U.S. 349, 371, 389 (1910).
9 Donaldson *v.* Read Magazine, 333 U.S. 178, 191 (1948).
10 Louisiana *v.* Resweber, 329 U.S. 459 (1947).
11 Furman *v.* Georgia (and companion cases), 408 U.S. 238 (1972).
12 Fred P. Graham, "700 Await Court's Verdict," *New York Times,* Jan. 23, 1972.

keep his hair cut short was a violation of the First, Eighth, and Fourteenth Amendments.[13] The Supreme Court of Minnesota, however, found that a statute which did not authorize marriage between persons of the same sex did not offend the Eighth Amendment.[14] Nor did the Virginia Supreme Court find that the forfeiture of a $8,700 automobile for the owner's driving after his license was revoked an unusual punishment.[15] Nor did the Supreme Court of the United States find that a conviction for *public* drunkenness was a cruel and unusual punishment.[16]

Not surprisingly, in view of the saliency of the nation's prison and drug problems, our State courts have been dealing currently with a flurry of cases in which it is claimed that solitary confinement of prisoners and long prison sentences for sellers of marijuana do violence to the Eighth Amendment. The courts have upheld the use of solitary confinement, but, in doing so, one court held that a "prison inmate is entitled to relief by habeas corpus if he alleges and proves that 'excessive punishment was inflicted upon him in violation of his fundamental and basic rights' " and that, where a prisoner is segregated "under conditions of maximum security," prison authorities must offer facts to justify it.[17]

State court decisions manifest our national confusion about whether or not marijuana is a dangerous drug. The Supreme Court of Ohio held that a 20-40 year sentence imposed for the sale of marijuana did not constitute cruel or unusual punishment;[18] a Texas court did not find a sentence of 15 years for the sale of one-half ounce excessive.[19] But the Michigan Su-

---

13 Inman *v.* State, 183 S.E. 2d. 413 (1971).

14 Baker *v.* Nelson, 191 N.W. 2d. 185 (1971); *appeal dismissed*, 41 *LW* 3167 (1972).

15 Commonwealth *v.* One 1970, 2 Dr. H. T. Lincoln Auto, 186 S.E. 2d. 279 (1972).

16 Powell *v.* State of Texas, 392 U.S. 514 (1968). For other cases *see* McLaughlin *v.* Minnesota, 190 N.W. 2d. 867 (1971); City of Portland *v.* Juntunen, 488 P. 2d. 806 (1971); Arizona *v,* Burns, 488 P. 2d. 998 (1971).

17 *In re* Hutchinson, 100 Cal. Rptr. 124, 127-128 (1972); Levier *v.* State, 497 P. 2d. 265 (1972). *Cf. In re* Henderson, 101 Cal. Rptr. 479 (1972). *See also* State *v.* Coiner, 186 S.E. 2d. 220 (1972); State *v.* Scott, 496 P. 2d. 609 (1972). For a case involving alleged mistreatment other than solitary confinement, *see* Hawthorne *v.* People 328 N.Y.S. 2d. 488 (1971). *See also* Rosecki *v.* Gaughan, 459 F. 2d. 6 (1972).

18 State *v.* Chaffin, 282 N.E. 2d. 46 (1972).

19 Lovett *v.* State, 479 S.E. 2d. 287 (1972). *See also* Trammel *v.* State, 186 S.E. 2d. 438 (1971) *and* State *v.* Conaty, 187 S.E. 2d. 119 (1972).

preme Court held that a penalty of 20 years imprisonment for the sale of marijuana was excessive.[20] And in a subsequent decision, some of its justices lectured long and hard on the foolishness of current legal approaches to its sale and use.[21]

[20] People *v.* Lorentzen, 194 N.W. 2d. 827 (1972).
[21] People *v.* Sinclair, 194 N.W. 2d. 878 (1972).

# AMENDMENT IX

The enumeration in the Constitution of certain rights shall not be construed to deny or disparage others retained by the people.

In other words, there are certain rights of so fundamental a character that no free government may trespass upon them whether they are enumerated in the Constitution or not.[1] In point of fact, the course of our constitutional development has been to reduce fundamental rights to rights guaranteed by the sovereign from the natural rights that they once were—a development reflected especially in the history of the Due Process of Law Clause. *Rights Anterior to the Constitution*

In an intriguing concurring opinion in the noteworthy "birth control" case, involving the constitutionality of a Connecticut statute making it a crime for any person to use any drug or article to prevent conception, Justice Goldberg tried to breathe vitality into the Ninth Amendment:

"While this Court has had *little occasion* to interpret the Ninth Amendment '[i]t cannot be presumed that any clause in the Constitution is intended to be without effect.' . . . In interpreting the Constitution, 'real effect should be given to all the words it uses.' . . . The Ninth Amendment to the Constitution may be regarded by some as a recent discovery and may be forgotten by others, but since 1791 it has been a basic part of the Constitution which we are sworn to uphold. To hold that a right so basic and fundamental and so deep-rooted in our society as the right of privacy in marriage may be infringed because that right is not guaranteed in so many words by the first eight amendments to the Constitution is to ignore the Ninth Amendment and to give it no effect whatsoever. Moreover, a judicial construction that this fundamental right is not protected by the Constitution because it is not mentioned in explicit terms by one of the first eight amendments or elsewhere in the Constitution would violate the Ninth

---

[1] *See* the language of Justice Chase, in Calder *v.* Bull, 3 Dall. 386, 387-389 (1798); *also* Justice Miller, for the Court, in Savings and Loan Asso. *v.* Topeka, 20 Wall. 655, 662-663 (1874); "We accept appellant's contention that the nature of political rights reserved to the people by the Ninth and Tenth Amendments are [sic] involved. The right claimed as inviolate may be stated as the right of a citizen to act as a party official or worker to further his own political views," Justice Reed, for the Court, in United Public Workers *v.* Mitchell, 330 U.S. 75, 94-95 (1947).

Amendment, which specifically states that '[t]he enumeration in the Constitution, of certain rights shall not be construed to deny or disparage others retained by the people' (emphasis added)."[2]

The Penumbra Theory Justice Goldberg's argument has never commanded the assent of a majority of the Court, however. And the Ninth Amendment continues in a state of "benign neglect." Undoubtedly, the most important factor contributing to this neglect is the development of the penumbra theory of Justice Douglas, which has won the assent of a majority of the Court. Evidently, any important liberty not specifically safeguarded by the Bill of Rights can be found in the penumbra, or shadow, of a specific guarantee and thus be constitutionally protected as part of that guarantee. Let Justice Douglas explain it:

"The foregoing cases suggest that specific guarantees in the Bill of Rights have penumbras, formed by emanations from those guarantees that help give them life and substance. . . . Various guarantees create zones of privacy. The right of association contained in the penumbra of the First Amendment is one, as we have seen. The Third Amendment in its prohibition against the quartering of soldiers 'in an house' in time of peace without the consent of the owner is another facet of that privacy. The Fourth Amendment explicitly affirms the 'right of the people to be secure in their persons, houses, papers, and effects, against unreasonable searches and seizures.' The Fifth Amendment in its Self-Incrimination Clause enables the citizen to create a zone of privacy which government may not force him to surrender to his detriment. The Ninth Amendment provides: 'The enumeration in the Constitution, of certain rights, shall not be construed to deny or disparage others retained by the people.'

"The Fourth and Fifth Amendments were described in Boyd v. United States, . . . as protection against all governmental invasions 'of the sanctity of a man's home and the privacies of life.' We referred in Mapp v. Ohio, . . . to the Fourth Amendment as creating a 'right to privacy, no less important than any other right carefully and particularly reserved to the people.' "[3]

[2] Griswold v. Connecticut 381 U.S. 479, 490-492 (1965).
[3] Ibid., 484-485. The penumbra theory has received elucidation in several U.S. courts of appeals, which in dealing with school dress codes were hard put patently determined to find constitutional protections for boys who wanted to wear their hair long. Stull v. School Bd., 459 F. 2d. 339 (1972) and cases cited therein.

## AMENDMENT X

The powers not delegated to the United States by the Constitution, nor prohibited by it to the States, are reserved to the States respectively, or to the people.

"The Tenth Amendment was intended to confirm the understanding of the people at the time the Constitution was adopted, that powers not granted to the United States were reserved to the States or to the people. It added nothing to the instrument as originally ratified. . . ."[1] That this provision was not conceived to be a yardstick for measuring the powers granted to the Federal Government or reserved to the States was clearly indicated by its sponsor, James Madison, in the course of the debate which took place while the amendment was pending concerning Hamilton's proposal to establish a national bank. He declared that: "Interference with the powers of the States was no constitutional criterion of the power of Congress. If the power was not given, Congress could not exercise it; if given, they might exercise it, although it should interfere with the laws, or even the Constitution of the States."[2] Nevertheless, for approximately a century, from the death of Marshall until 1937, the Tenth Amendment was frequently invoked to curtail powers expressly granted to Congress, notably the powers to regulate interstate commerce, to enforce the Fourteenth Amendment, and to lay and collect taxes.

The first, and logically the strongest, effort to set up the Tenth Amendment as a limitation on Federal power was directed to the expansion of that power by virtue of the necessary and proper clause. In McCulloch v. Maryland,[3] the Attorney General of Maryland cited the charges made by the enemies of the Constitution that it contained ". . . a vast variety of powers, lurking under the generality of its phraseology, which would prove highly dangerous to the liberties of the people, and the rights of the states, . . ."; and he cited the adoption of the Tenth Amendment to allay these apprehensions, in support of his contention that the power to create corporations was reserved by that amendment to the States.[4] Stressing the fact that this amendment, unlike the cognate section of the Articles of Confederation, omitted the word "ex-

*"Reserved" Rights of the States versus National Supremacy*

---

[1] United States v. Sprague, 282 U.S. 716, 733 (1931).
[2] II Annals of Congress, col. 1897 (1791).
[3] 4 Wheat. 316 (1819).    [4] *Ibid.*, 372.

pressly" as a qualification of the powers granted to the National Government, Chief Justice Marshall declared that its effect was to leave the question "whether the particular power which may become the subject of contest has been delegated to the one government, or prohibited to the other, to depend upon a fair construction of the whole instrument."[5]

The States Rights Bench which followed Marshall took a different view, and from that time forth for a full century the Court proceeded at discretion on the theory that the amendment withdrew various matters of internal police from the rightful reach of power committed to Congress. This view, which elevated the Court to the position of a quasi-arbitral body standing over and above two competing sovereignties, was initially invoked in behalf of the constitutionality of certain State acts which were alleged to have invaded the national field.[6] Not until after the Civil War was the idea that the reserved powers of the States comprise an independent qualification of otherwise constitutional acts of the Federal Government actually applied to nullify, in part, an act of Congress. This result was first reached in a tax case—Collector v. Day.[7] Holding that a national income tax, in itself valid, could not be constitutionally levied upon the official salaries of State officers, Justice Nelson made the sweeping statement that ". . . The States within the limits of their powers not granted, or, in the language of the Tenth Amendment, 'reserved,' are as independent of the general government as that government within its sphere is independent of the States."[8] In 1939, Collector v. Day was expressly overruled.[9]

Outside the field of taxation, the Court proceeded more hesitantly. A year before Collector v. Day it held invalid, except as applied in the District of Columbia and other areas over which Congress has exclusive authority, a Federal statute penalizing the sale of dangerous illuminating oils.[10] It did not, however, refer to the Tenth Amendment. Instead, it asserted that the ". . . express grant of power to regulate commerce

---

[5] *Ibid.*, 406.
[6] *See* especially New York *v.* Miln, 11 Pet. 102 (1837); License Cases, 5 How. 504, 573-574 (1847).
[7] 11 Wall. 113 (1871).
[8] *Ibid.*, 124.
[9] Graves *v.* O'Keefe, 306 U.S. 466 (1939).
[10] United States *v.* Dewitt, 9 Wall. 41 (1870).

among the States has always been understood as limited by its terms; and as a virtual denial of any power to interfere with the internal trade and business of the separate States; except, indeed, as a necessary and proper means for carrying into execution some other power expressly granted or vested."[11] Similarly, in the Employers' Liability cases,[12] an act of Congress making every carrier engaged in interstate commerce liable to "any" employee, including those whose activities related solely to intrastate activities, for injuries caused by negligence, was held unconstitutional by a closely divided court, without explicit reliance on the Tenth Amendment. At last, however, in the famous case of Hammer v. Dagenhart,[13] a narrow majority of the Court amended the amendment by inserting the word "expressly" before the word "delegated," and on this basis ruled that an act of Congress which prohibited the transportation of child-made goods in interstate commerce was not a regulation of "commerce among the States" but an invasion of the reserved powers of the States.

*Judicial Amendment of the Tenth Amendment*

During the twenty years following this decision, a variety of measures designed to regulate economic activities, directly or indirectly, were held void on similar grounds. Excise taxes on the profits of factories in which child labor was employed,[14] on the sale of grain futures on markets which failed to comply with federal regulations,[15] on the sale of coal produced by non-members of a coal code established as a part of a Federal regulatory scheme,[16] and a tax on the processing of agricultural products, the proceeds of which were paid to farmers who complied with production limitations imposed by the Federal Government,[17] were all found to invade the reserved powers of the States. And in Schechter Poultry Corporation v. United States[18] the Court, holding that the commerce power did not extend to local sales of poultry brought from without the State, invoked the amendment in support of the proposition that Congress could not regulate local matters which af-

[11] *Ibid.*, 44.

[12] 207 U.S. 463 (1908). *See also* Keller v. U.S., 213 U.S. 138 (1909).

[13] 247 U.S. 251 (1918).

[14] Bailey v. Drexel Furniture Co., 259 U.S. 20, 36, 38 (1922).

[15] Hill v. Wallace 259 U.S. 44 (1922). *See also* Trusler v. Crooks, 269 U.S. 475 (1926).

[16] Carter v. Carter Coal Co., 298 U.S. 238 (1936).

[17] United States v. Butler, 297 U.S. 1 (1936).

[18] 295 U.S. 495 (1935).

fected interstate commerce only "indirectly." The maintenance of this rule, said Chief Justice Hughes, was essential to the maintenance of the Federal system itself.[19]

On the other hand, both before and after Hammer *v.* Dagenhart, the Court sustained Federal laws penalizing the interstate transportation of lottery tickets,[20] of women for immoral purposes,[21] of stolen automobiles,[22] of tick-infested cattle,[23] of prison-made goods.[24] Thus with some sacrifice of consistency, it still has managed to be always on the side of the angels.

Triumph of the Supremacy Clause

At last, in 1941 the Court came full circle in its exposition of Amendment X. Having returned to the position of John Marshall four years earlier when it sustained the Social Security[25] and National Labor Relations Acts,[26] it explicitly restated Marshall's thesis in upholding the Fair Labor Standards Act in the United States *v.* Darby.[27] Speaking for a unanimous court, Chief Justice Stone wrote: "The power of Congress over interstate commerce 'is complete in itself, may be exercised to its utmost extent, and acknowledges no limitations other than are prescribed in the Constitution.' . . . That power can neither be enlarged nor diminished by the exercise or non-exercise of state power. . . . It is no objection to the assertion of the power to regulate interstate commerce that its exercise is attended by the same incidents which attend the exercise of the police power of the states. . . . Our conclusion is unaffected by the Tenth Amendment which . . . states but a truism that all is retained which has not been surrendered."[28] Hammer *v.* Dagenhart was expressly overruled.[29]

Today it is apparent that the Tenth Amendment does not

[19] *Ibid.*, 529.

[20] Champion *v.* Ames, 188 U.S. 321 (1903).

[21] Hoke *v.* U.S., 227 U.S. 308 (1913).

[22] Brooks *v.* U.S., 267 U.S. 432 (1925).

[23] Thornton *v.* U.S., 271 U.S. 414 (1926).

[24] Kentucky Whip & Collar Co. *v.* Illinois C.R. Co., 299 U.S. 334 (1937).

[25] Steward Machine Co. *v.* Davis, 301 U.S. 548 (1937); Helvering *v.* Davis 301 U.S. 619 (1937).

[26] National Labor Relations Board *v.* Jones & Laughlin Steel Corp., 301 U.S. 1 (1937).

[27] 312 U.S. 100 (1941). *See also* United States *v.* Carolene Products Co., 304 U.S. 144, 147 (1938); Case *v.* Bowles, 327 U.S. 92, 101 (1946).

[28] 312 U.S. 100, 114, 123, 124 (1941). *See also* Fernandez *v.* Wiener, 326 U.S. 340, 362 (1945).

[29] 312 U.S. 100, 116-117.

shield the States nor their political subdivisions from the impact of any authority affirmatively granted to the Federal Government. It was cited to no avail in Case *v.* Bowles,[30] where a State officer was forbidden to sell timber on school lands at a price in excess of the maximum prescribed by the Office of Price Administration; and when California violated the Federal Safety Appliance Act in the operation of the State Belt Railroad as a common carrier in interstate commerce, it was held liable for the statutory penalty.[31] Years earlier, indeed, the Sanitary District of Chicago was enjoined, at the suit of the Attorney General of the United States, from diverting water from Lake Michigan in excess of a specified amount. On behalf of a unanimous Court, Justice Holmes wrote: "This is not a controversy among equals. The United States is asserting its sovereign power to regulate commerce and to control the navigable waters within its jurisdiction. . . . There is no question that this power is superior to that of the States to provide for the welfare or necessities of their inhabitants."[32] Similarly, under its superior power of eminent domain, the United States may condemn land owned by a State even where the taking will interfere with the State's own project for water development and conservation.[33] Nor are rights reserved to the States invaded by a statute which requires a reduction in the amount of a Federal grant-in-aid of the construction of highways upon failure of a State to remove from office a member of the State Highway Commission found to have violated Federal law by participating in a political campaign.[34]

In its most recent reference to the Tenth Amendment the Court said in 1968: "Indeed, appellants do not contend that labor conditions in all schools and hospitals are without the reach of the commerce power, but only that the Act may not be constitutionally applied to state-operated institutions because that power must yield to state sovereignty in the performance of governmental functions. This argument is simply not tenable. There is no general 'doctrine implied in the Federal Constitution that the two governments, national and state,

[30] 327 U.S. 92, 102 (1946).
[31] United States *v.* Calif., 297 U.S. 175 (1936).
[32] Sanitary District of Chicago *v.* U.S., 266 U.S. 405, 425, 426 (1925).
[33] Oklahoma *v.* Atkinson Co., 313 U.S. 508, 534 (1941).
[34] Oklahoma *v.* U.S. Civil Service Commission, 330 U.S. 127, 142-144 (1947). *See also* Adams *v.* Md., 347 U.S. 179 (1954).

are each to exercise its powers so as not to interfere with the free and full exercise of the other.' Case *v.* Bowles. . . ."[35]

"United States" means primarily the political branches of the National Government; but the term may be comprehensive enough to include any authority which was created by and which rests upon the Constitution, as for instance, the power of amending it (*see* Article V).

The States in International Law "States" means the State governments and the people of the States, and sometimes the States territorially. In a case decided by the Supreme Court which raised the question whether the National Government or the coastal States held title to the oil lands underlying coastal submerged lands between low-water mark and the three-mile limit, numerous judicial dicta favored the State claim, but fundamental principle was on the side of the United States, and the Court held with the latter.[36] By International Law, sovereignty, which includes paramount ownership over tidewater lands, is an attribute of nationality, and so far as International Law is concerned the States do not exist.[37]

"The people" means the people of the United States as constituting one sovereign political community; that is, the same people who ordained and established the Constitution (*see* Preamble).

[35] Maryland *v.* Wirtz, 392 U.S. 183, 195 (1968).

[36] United States *v.* Calif., 332 U.S. 19 (1947). The Court held, however, that Congress could, as it did, cede to the States its right to the tidelands oil. *See* p. 214. Alabama *v.* Texas, 347 U.S. 272 (1954).

[37] *See* Holmes *v.* Jennison, 14 Pet. 540, 573-576 (1840); United States *v.* Calif., 332 U.S. 19 (1947). *Cf.* Skiriotes *v.* Fla., 313 U.S. 69, 78-79 (1941).

# AMENDMENT XI

The judicial power of the United States shall not be construed to extend to any suit in law or equity, commenced or prosecuted against one of the United States by citizens of another State, or by citizens or subjects of any foreign State.

The action of the Supreme Court in accepting jurisdiction of a suit against a State by a citizen of another State in 1793, in Chisholm *v.* Georgia,[1] provoked such angry reactions in Georgia and such anxieties in other States that at the first meeting of Congress after this decision what became the Eleventh Amendment was proposed by an overwhelming vote and ratified with "vehement speed."[2] The protection afforded the States by the amendment against suits for debt extends, however, not only to those instituted "by citizens of another State," or "the citizens or subjects of a foreign State," but also those brought by the State's own citizens, or by a foreign state.[3]

Otherwise, the amendment has proved comparatively ineffective as a protection of States Rights against Federal judicial power. For one thing, a suit is not "commenced or prosecuted" against a State by the appeal of a case which was instituted by the State itself against a defendant who claims rights under the Constitution or laws or treaties of the United States[4] (*see* Article III, Section II, ¶1). Nor may an officer of a State who is acting in violation of rights protected by the Constitution or laws or treaties of the United States claim the protection of the amendment, inasmuch as in so acting he loses his official and representative capacity.[5] Indeed, nowadays the amendment does not forbid the Federal courts from enjoining temporarily a State official from undertaking to enforce a State statute alleged to be unconstitutional until it has been determined finally whether the statute is constitutional or not.[6]

State Official Immunity

[1] 2 Dall. 419 (1793).
[2] Justice Frankfurter, dissenting in Larson *v.* Domestic and Foreign Corp., 337 U.S. 682, 708 (1949).
[3] Hans *v.* La., 134 U.S. 1 (1890); Monaco *v.* Miss., 292 U.S. 313 (1934); Kirker *v.* Moore, 308 F. Supp. 615 (1970); Knight *v.* New York, 443 F. 2d. 415 (1971); Parden *v.* Terminal Railway, 377 U.S. 184 (1964).
[4] Cohens *v.* Va., 6 Wheat. 264, 411-412 (1821).
[5] Osborn *v.* B'k of U.S., 9 Wheat. 738, 858-859, 868 (1824).
[6] *Ex parte* Young, 209 U.S. 123 (1908). *See also* Home Tel. & Tel. Co. *v.* Los Angeles, 227 U.S. 278 (1913); Terrace *v.* Thompson, 263 U.S. 197 (1923); Alabama Com. *v.* Southern R. Co., 341 U.S. 341 (1951); Georgia R. *v.* Redwine, 342 U.S. 299, 304-305 (1952); Perez *v.* Ledesma, 401 U.S. 82, 85, 106-108 (1971).

On the other hand, suits against the officers of a State involving what is conceded to be State property or suits asking for relief which clearly calls for the exercise of official authority cannot be maintained. Thus, in the leading case of Louisiana v. Jumel,[7] in which a holder of State bonds sought to compel the State treasurer to apply a sinking fund that had been created under an earlier constitution for the payment of the bonds to such purpose after a new constitution had abolished this provision for retiring the bonds, the proceeding was held to be a suit against the State. "The relief asked," said the Court, "will require the officers against whom the process is issued to act contrary to the positive orders of the supreme political power of the State, whose creatures they are, and to which they are ultimately responsible in law for what they do. They must use the public money in the treasury and under their official control in one way, when the supreme power has directed them to use it in another, and they must raise more money by taxation when the same power has declared that it shall be done."[8] But mandamus proceedings to compel a State official to perform a "ministerial duty," which admits of no discretion, are held not to be suits against the State since the official is regarded as acting in his individual capacity in failing to act according to law.[9]

The immunity of a State from suit is a privilege which it may waive at pleasure by voluntary submission to suit,[10] as distinguished from appearing in a similar suit to defend its officials,[11] and by general law consenting to suit in the Federal courts. Such consent must be clear and specific and consent to suit in its own courts does not imply a waiver of immunity to

7 107 U.S. 711 (1883). See also Christian v. Atlantic & N.C.R. Co., 133 U.S. 233 (1890); Knight v. New York, 443 F. 2d. 415 (1971).

8 107 U.S. 711, 721.

9 Board of Liquidation v. McComb, 92 U.S. 531, 541 (1876). This was a case involving an injunction, but Justice Bradley regarded mandamus and injunction as correlative to each other in cases where the official unlawfully commits or omits an act. See also Rolston v. Missouri Fund Commissioners, 120 U.S. 390, 411 (1887), where it is held that an injunction would lie to restrain the sale of a railroad on the ground that a suit to compel a State official to do what the law requires of him is not a suit against the State.

10 Clark v. Barnard, 108 U.S. 436, 447 (1883); Ashton v. Cameron County Water Improvement Dist., 298 U.S. 513, 531 (1936); Knight v. New York, 443 F. 2d. 415 (1971). But see P.T. & L. Const. Co. v. Commissioner, 288 A. 2d. 574 (1972).

11 Farish v. State Banking Board, 235 U.S. 498 (1915); Missouri v. Fiske, 290 U.S. 18 (1933); Ford Co. v. Dept. of Treasury, 323 U.S. 459, 470 (1945).

suit in the federal courts.[12] In short, in consenting to be sued, the States, like the National Government, may attach such conditions as they deem fit.[13]

In 1972, the Supreme Court reaffirmed that "an action brought by one State against another violates the Eleventh Amendment if the plaintiff State is actually suing to recover for injuries to designated individuals."[14]

[12] Murray *v.* Wilson Distilling Co., 213 U.S. 151, 172 (1909); citing Smith *v.* Reeves, 178 U.S. 436 (1900); Great Northern Life Ins. Co. *v.* Read, 322 U.S. 47 (1944); Kennecott Copper Corp. *v.* St. Tax Comm., 327 U.S. 573 (1946).

[13] The California Supreme Court has engendered skepticism about the concept of the doctrine of governmental immunity. *See* the brief description of the Court's and the legislature's actions in recent years in Nestle *v.* City of Santa Monica, 101 Cal. Rptr. 568, 575-578 (1972). *See also* Justice Traynor's brilliant and seminal opinion in Muskopf *v.* Corning Hospital District, 359 P. 2d. 457 (1961).

[14] Hawaii *v.* Standard Oil Co. of California, 405 U.S. 251, 258 note 12 (1972).

# AMENDMENT XII

The "College of Electors" So-called

¶1. The electors shall meet in their respective States and vote by ballot for President and Vice-President, one of whom, at least, shall not be an inhabitant of the same State with themselves; they shall name in their ballots the person voted for as President, and in distinct ballots the person voted for as Vice-President, and they shall make distinct lists of all persons voted for as President and of all persons voted for as Vice-President, and of the number of votes for each; which lists they shall sign and certify, and transmit sealed to the seat of the government of the United States, directed to the President of the Senate. The President of the Senate shall, in the presence of the Senate and House of Representatives, open all the certificates and the votes shall then be counted. The person having the greatest number of votes for President shall be the President, if such number be a majority of the whole number of electors appointed; and if no person have such majority, then from the persons having the highest numbers not exceeding three on the list of those voted for as President, the House of Representatives shall choose immediately, by ballot, the President. But in choosing the President the votes shall be taken by States, the representation from each State having one vote; a quorum for this purpose shall consist of a member or members from two-thirds of the States, and a majority of all the States shall be necessary to a choice. And if the House of Representatives shall not choose a President whenever the right of choice shall devolve upon them, before the fourth day of March next following, then the Vice-President shall act as President as in the case of the death or other constitutional disability of the President.

¶2. The person having the greatest number of votes as Vice-President shall be the Vice-President, if such number be a majority of the whole number of electors appointed; and if no person have a majority, then from the two highest numbers on the list the Senate shall choose the Vice-President; a quorum for the purpose shall consist of two-thirds of the whole number of Senators, and a majority of the whole number shall be necessary to a choice. But no person constitutionally ineligible to the office of President shall be eligible to that of Vice-President of the United States.

This amendment, which supersedes ¶3 of Section I of Article II of the original Constitution, was inserted on account of the tie between Jefferson and Burr in the election of 1800. The difference between the procedure which it defines and that which was laid down in the original Constitution is in the provision it makes for a separate designation by the Electors of their choices for President and Vice-President, respectively. The final sentence of ¶1, above, has been in turn superseded today by Amendments XX and XXV.

In consequence of the disputed election of 1876, Congress, by an act passed in 1887, has laid down the rule that if the vote of a State is not certified by the governor under the seal thereof, it shall not be "counted" unless both houses of Congress are favorable.[1]

It was early supposed that the House of Representatives would be often called upon to choose a President, but the political division of the country into two great parties has hitherto always prevented this, except in 1800 and 1824. Should, however, a strong third party appear, the election might be frequently thrown into Congress, with the result, since the vote would be by States, of enabling a small fraction of the population of the country to choose the President from the three candidates receiving the highest electoral vote. The situation obviously calls for a constitutional amendment.

It should be noted that no provision is made by this amendment for the situation which would result from a failure to choose either a President or Vice-President, an inadequacy which Amendment XX undertakes to cure.

"The mode of appointment of the Chief Magistrate of the United States," Hamilton wrote in *Federalist* No. 68, "is almost the only part of the system of any consequence, which has escaped without severe censure, or which has received the slightest mark of approbation from its opponents." Hamilton himself did not "hesitate . . . to affirm that if the manner of it be not perfect, it is at least excellent," being designed to guarantee that the choice of President should be by "a small number of persons" eminently fit to make a wise selection and to avoid "cabal, intrigue, and corruption." Actually, the so-called "College of Electors"—a college which never meets—had come by the time that Amendment XII became a part of the Constitution, to consist of party marionettes who have never exercised the least individual freedom of choice in circum-

*Original Expectations*

[1] 3 U.S.C. 17.

stances that made their doing so a matter of the least importance in the world. Indeed, in 1872 the Democratic Electors
from three States automatically cast their votes for the party
candidate, Horace Greeley, on the very day he was carried to
his grave.

The
Actuality
In Ray *v.* Blair,[2] decided April 15, 1952, the Court
had occasion to comment on the theory of the constitutional
independence of the Elector, which it did in these words:
"History teaches that the Electors were expected to support
the party nominees. Experts in the history of government recognize the long-standing practice. Indeed, more than twenty
States do not print the names of the candidates for Electors on
the general election ballot." In view of such facts, the Court
declined to rule that it was "unconstitutional" for one seeking
nomination as an Elector in a party primary to announce his
choice for President beforehand, thereby pledging himself.
Justice Jackson's dissent in this case was particularly noteworthy: "No one faithful to our history can deny that the plan
originally contemplated, what is implicit in its text, that electors would be free agents to exercise an independent and non-
partisan judgment as to the men best qualified for the Nation's
highest offices. Certainly under that plan no state law could
control the elector in performance of his federal duty, any
more than it could a United States Senator who also is chosen
by, and represents, the State.

"This arrangement miscarried. Electors, although often personally eminent, independent, and respectable, officially became voluntary party lackeys and intellectual nonentities to
whose memory we might justly paraphase a tuneful satire:

They always voted at their Party's call
And never thought of thinking for themselves at all.

As an institution the Electoral College suffered atrophy almost
indistinguishable from *rigor mortis* . . . if custom were sufficient authority for amendment of the Constitution by Court
decree, the decision in this matter would be warranted. Usage
may sometimes impart changed content to constitutional generalities, such as 'due process of law,' 'equal protection' or
'commerce among the states.' But I do not think powers or dis-

2 343 U.S. 214, 218-219, 228-231 (1962). *See* Penton *v.* Humphrey, 264
F. Supp. 250, 252 note 1 (1967).

cretions granted to federal officials by the Federal Constitution can be forfeited by the Court for disuse. A political practice which has its origin in custom must rely upon custom for its sanctions."[3] *(See also* the discussion on p. 447.)

[3] *Ibid.,* 233-234. *See also* Irish *v.* DFL Party of Minnesota, 287 F. Supp. 794 (1968). The Supreme Court's reluctance to permit the courts to interject themselves in the business of the political parties was further manifest in its decision with respect to the challenge to delegate seating at the Democratic National Convention in 1972. O'Brien *v.* Brown, 92 S.Ct. 2718 (1972). *See* p. 173, *supra.*

# AMENDMENT XIII

## SECTION I

Neither slavery nor involuntary servitude, except as a punishment for crime whereof the party shall have been duly convicted, shall exist within the United States, or any place subject to their jurisdiction.

The historical importance of this amendment consists in the fact that it completed the abolition of African slavery in the United States, but that has not been its sole importance. The amendment is not, in the words of the Court, "a declaration in favor of a particular people. It reaches every race and every individual, and if in any respect it commits one race to the Nation, it commits every race and every individual thereof. Slavery or involuntary servitude of the Chinese, of the Italian, of the Anglo-Saxon are as much within its compass as slavery or involuntary servitude of the African."[1]

Peonage Outlawed

Moreover, "the words 'involuntary servitude' have for a long time had larger meaning than slavery."[2] Especially does this phrase ban peonage, "the essence of which is compulsory service in the payment of a debt."[3] Consequently, an Alabama statute which imposed a criminal liability and subjected to imprisonment farm laborers who abandoned their employment to enter into similar employment with other persons, was held to violate Amendment XIII, as well as national legislation forbidding peonage.[4] So it was held in 1905; and six years later the Court overturned another Alabama statute which made the refusal "without just cause" to perform the labor called for in a written contract or to refund the money advanced therefor, *prima facie* evidence of an intent to defraud and punishable as a criminal offense.[5] Subsequently other statutes of like tendency, emanating from Southern legislatures, have similarly succumbed to the Court's conception of "involuntary servitude."[6]

---

[1] Hodges v. U.S., 203 U.S. 1, 16-17 (1906); Bailey v. Ala., 219 U.S. 219, 240-241 (1911).
[2] Slaughter House Cases, 16 Wall. 36, 69 (1873).
[3] Bailey v. Ala., 219 U.S. 219, 242 (1911).
[4] Clyatt v. U.S., 197 U.S. 207 (1905); Act of March 2, 1867, 14 *Stat.* 546.
[5] Bailey v. Ala., above.
[6] United States v. Reynolds, 235 U.S. 133 (1914); Taylor v. Ga., 315 U.S. 25 (1942); Pollock v. Williams, 322 U.S. 4 (1944).

Interestingly enough the reserve system in baseball, which requires a player to play with a certain team or not play at all has not yet been regarded by the courts as "involuntary servitude."[7] As one Federal Court reasoned:

"A showing of compulsion is thus prerequisite to proof of involuntary servitude. Concededly, plaintiff is not compelled by law or statute to play baseball for Philadelphia. We recognize that, under the existing rules of baseball, by refusing to report to Philadelphia plaintiff is by his own act foreclosing himself from continuing a professional baseball career, a consequence to be deplored. Nevertheless, he has the right to retire and to embark upon a different enterprise outside organized baseball. The financial loss he might thus sustain may affect his choice, but does not leave him with 'no way to avoid continued service. . . .' "[8]

The Court for a time rejected what it regarded as over-extended conceptions of "involuntary servitude." Thus, the denial of admission to public places such as inns, restaurants, and theaters, or the segregation of races in public conveyances did not fall under the condemnation of Amendment XIII for many years.[9] However, in 1968 in upholding the provisions of the Civil Rights Act of 1968 to prohibit all racial discrimination, private and public, in the sale and rental of property, the Court broadened the scope of the Thirteenth Amendment by holding:

"Negro citizens, North and South, who saw in the Thirteenth Amendment a promise of freedom—freedom to 'go and come at pleasure' and to 'buy and sell when they please'— would be left with 'a mere paper guarantee' if Congress were powerless to assure that a dollar in the hands of a Negro will purchase the same thing as a dollar in the hands of a white man. At the very least, the freedom that Congress is empowered to secure under the Thirteenth Amendment includes the freedom to buy whatever a white man can buy, the right to live wherever a white man can live. If Congress cannot say that be-

---

[7] Flood *v.* Kuhn, 316 F. Supp. 271, 281 (1970); *affirmed,* 443 F. 2d. 264 (1971). In its review of the case, the Supreme Court did not speak to the contention that the reserve clause resulted in involuntary servitude. Flood *v.* Kuhn, 407 U.S. 258 (1972).

[8] 316 F. Supp. 271, 281 (1970).

[9] Civil Rights Cases, 109 U.S. 3 (1883); Plessy *v.* Ferguson, 163 U.S. 537 (1896).

ing a free man means at least this much, then the Thirteenth Amendment made a promise the Nation cannot keep."[10]

Things Not Outlawed

Contracts for certain services which have from time immemorial been treated as exceptional, although involving to a certain extent the surrender of personal liberty[11] still do not fall under the condemnation of the Thirteenth Amendment; nor does "enforcement of those duties which individuals owe the State, such as service in the army, militia, on the jury, etc."[12] (But *see* pp. 85-87 for discussion of forced military service.) Hence, "a State has inherent power to require every able-bodied man within its jurisdiction to labor for a reasonable time on public roads near his residence without compensation."[13] Nor was Mr. James C. Petrillo subjected to "involuntary servitude" when he was forbidden under the Federal Communications Act "to coerce, compel, or constrain" licensees under the act to employ unneeded persons in the conduct of their broadcasting activities.[14] And a State court recently held that a State separate maintenance statute which denied the husband "the advantages of marriage or the privileges of divorce" did not violate Amendment XIII.[15]

## SECTION II

Congress shall have power to enforce this article by appropriate legislation.

[10] Jones *v.* Mayer Co., 392 U.S. 409, 443 (1968); Griffin *v.* Breckenridge, 403 U.S. 88, 104-107 (1971); *cf.* Palmer *v.* Thompson, 403 U.S. 217, 226-227 (1971).

[11] Robertson *v.* Baldwin, 165 U.S. 275, 282 (1897).

[12] Butler *v.* Perry, 240 U.S. 328, 333 (1916); Draper *v.* Rhay, 315 F. 2d. 193, 197 (1963), *cert. denied,* 375 U.S. 915 (1963).

Wilson *v.* Kelley, 294 F. Supp. 1005, 1012 (1968). *See also* Arver *v.* U.S. (Selective Draft Cases), 245 U.S. 366, 390 (1918). "Work or fight" laws, such as States enacted during World War I, which required male residents to be employed during the period of that war were sustained on similar grounds, as were municipal ordinances, enforced during the depression, which compelled indigents physically able to perform manual labor to serve the municipality without compensation as a condition of receiving financial assistance. State *v.* McClure, 7 Boyce (Del.) 265 (1919); Commonwealth *v.* Pauliot, 292 Mass. 229 (1935). For a recent case involving conscientious objector *see* U.S. *v.* O'Brien, 391 U.S. 367, 377 (1968).

[13] Butler *v.* Perry, 240 U.S. 328 (1916).

[14] United States *v.* Petrillo, 332 U.S. 1 (1947); Act of June 19, 1934, as amended April 16, 1946; 47 U.S.C. 506; *see also* Trustees of Cal. St. Colleges *v.* Local 1352, 92 Cal. Rptr. 134 (1970); Jefferson County Teachers *v.* Bd. of Ed., 463 S.W. 2d. 627 (1971).

[15] Reese *v.* Reese, 278 N.E. 2d. 122 (1971).

It should be noted that this amendment, in contrast to the opening section of the Fourteenth Amendment, just below, lays down a rule of action for private persons no less than for the States. In other words, it is legislative in character, as was the Eighteenth Amendment; and accordingly, in enforcing it, Congress may enact penalties for the violation of its provisions by private persons and corporations without paying any attention to State laws on the same subject.[1]

As the Court said in 1968: "Thus, the fact that the Congressional statute operates upon the unofficial acts of private individuals, whether or not sanctioned by state law, presents no constitutional problem. If Congress has power under the Thirteenth Amendment to eradicate conditions that prevent Negroes from buying and renting property because of their race or color, then no federal statute calculated to achieve that objective can be thought to exceed the constitutional power of Congress simply because it reaches beyond state action to regulate the conduct of private individuals. The constitutional question in this case, therefore, comes to this: Does the authority of Congress to enforce the Thirteenth Amendment 'by appropriate legislation' include the power to eliminate all racial barriers to the acquisition of real and personal property? We think the answer to that question is plainly yes."[2]

[1] Clyatt v. U.S., 197 U.S. 207 (1905).
[2] Jones v. Mayer Co., 392 U.S. 409, 438-439 (1968); Griffin v. Breckenridge, 403 U.S. 88, 104-107 (1971); cf. Palmer v. Thompson, 403 U.S. 217, 226-227 (1971).

## SECTION I

"The
Great Four-
teenth
Amend-
ment"

All persons born or naturalized in the United States, and subject to the jurisdiction thereof, are citizens of the United
States and of the State wherein they reside. No State shall
make or enforce any law which shall abridge the privileges
or immunities of citizens of the United States; nor shall any
State deprive any person of life, liberty or property, without
due process of law; nor deny to any person within its jurisdiction the equal protection of the laws.

The opening clause of this section makes national citizenship
primary and State citizenship derivative therefrom. The definition it lays down of citizenship "at birth" is not, however,
exhaustive, as was pointed out in connection with Congress's
power to "establish an uniform rule of naturalization."

"Subject to the jurisdiction thereof": The children born to
foreign diplomats in the United States are not subject to the
jurisdiction of the United States, and so are not citizens of the
United States. With this narrow exception all persons born in
the United States are, by the principle of the Wong Kim Ark
case, entitled to claim citizenship of the United States.[1]

Judicial Re-
peal of the
"Privileges
and Im-
munities"
Clause

"The privileges or immunities of citizens of the United
States" were held in the famous Slaughter House cases, decided soon after the Fourteenth Amendment was added to the
Constitution, to comprise only those privileges and immunities
which the Constitution, the laws, and the treaties of the United
States confer, such as the right to engage in interstate and foreign commerce, the right to appeal in proper cases to the national courts, the right to protection abroad, etc.; but not "the
fundamental rights," which were said still to adhere exclusively to State citizenship.[2]

Following this line of reasoning, which renders the clause
tautological, the Court ruled in 1920, in United States v.
Wheeler,[3] that the right to reside quietly within the State of
one's domicil is not a right which the National Government
may protect against local mobs—plainly a most anomalous

[1] 169 U.S. 649 (1898).
[2] 16 Wall. 36, 71, 77-79 (1873). See also Twining v. N.J., 211 U.S. 78, 97
(1908).
[3] 254 U.S. 281 (1920).

result. In Hague *v.* Committee for Industrial Organization,[4] however, in which a Jersey City ordinance requiring a permit for any assembly in the streets, parks, or public buildings of the city was held void, two of the Justices based their opinion on this clause. The "privilege and immunity" which they found to be infringed was the right of workingmen who are at the same time citizens of the United States to assemble for the purpose of discussing their newly acquired rights under the National Labor Relations Act; and in Edwards *v.* California four Justices agreed in 1941 that a State enactment which sought to exclude from the State indigent persons from the rest of the Union was, as to citizens of the United States, an abridgment of their privileges and immunities as such.[5] As a matter of history, there can be little question that it was the intention of the framers of the clause to transmute all the ordinary rights of citizenship in a free government into rights of national citizenship, and thereby in effect to transfer their regulation and protection to the National Government.[6] (For further discussion of "privileges and immunities," *see* pp. 208-210).

"Nor shall any State deprive any person of life, liberty, or property without due process of law": By "State" is meant not only all agencies of State government but those of local government as well[7] when acting under color of official authority, even though in a manner that is contrary to State law.[8] More will be said about what constitutes "State action" below, pp. 416-418. **Due Process Clause**

While, in a general way, this clause imposes on the powers of the State the same kinds of limitations that the corresponding clause of Amendment V does on the powers of the National Government, there have been conspicuous differences historically which will be spelled out below. **Effect of Amendment XIV on State Criminal Law**

The earlier discussion of substantive due process under the

---

[4] 307 U.S. 496 (1939); *cf.* Davis *v.* Mass., 167 U.S. 43 (1897).

[5] 314 U.S. 160 (1941), where the decision overturning the State statute was based by a majority of the Court on the commerce clause. For a temporary flare-up of the "privileges and immunities" clause of Amendment XIV which was soon quenched, *cf.* Colgate *v.* Harvey, 296 U.S. 404 (1935); and Madden *v.* Ky., 309 U.S. 83 (1940).

[6] Horace Flack, *The Adoption of the Fourteenth Amendment* (Baltimore, 1908), *passim*.

[7] *Ex parte* Virginia, 100 U.S. 339 (1879); Yick Wo *v.* Hopkins, 118 U.S. 356 (1886). *See also* Trenton *v.* N.J., 262 U.S. 182 (1923).

[8] United States *v.* Classic, 313 U.S. 299 (1941); Screws *v.* U.S., 325 U.S. 91 (1945). *Cf.* Barney *v.* City of N.Y., 193 U.S. 430 (1904).

<table>
<tr><td>

Applica-
tion of
Substan-
tive Due
Process

Judicial
Supervi-
sion of the
"Police
Power"
under
Amend-
ment XIV

</td><td>

Fifth Amendment (pp. 327-331) should be read as a backdrop to the present discussion. The concept that due process required legislatures to exercise their powers "reasonably," historically had much greater impact on State legislation than on Congressional enactments. For, as pointed out earlier, the State "police power" is not so circumscribed as the power of the National Government. The "police power" is the power of the State "to promote the public health, safety, morals, and general welfare"; or, as it has been more simply and comprehensively described, "the power to govern men and things."[9]

Under the 1900-1937 interpretation of "liberty," "property," and "due process of law," this power was confronted at every turn by the Court's power of judicial review. Some statistics are pertinent in this connection. During the first ten years of the Fourteenth Amendment, hardly a dozen cases came before the Court under all of its clauses put together. During the next twenty years, when the *laissez-faire* conception of governmental functions was being translated by the Bar into the phraseology of Constitutional Law, and gradually embodied in the decisions of the Court, more than two hundred cases arose, most of them under the Due Process of Law Clause. During the ensuing twelve years this number was more than doubled—a ratio which still holds substantially.[10]

</td></tr>
</table>

During this later period, moreover, an increasing rigor was to be discerned in the Court's standards, especially where legislation on social and economic questions was concerned. Prior to 1912 the Court had decided 98 cases involving this kind of legislation. "In only six of these did the Court hold the legislation unconstitutional. From 1913 to 1920 the Court decided 27 cases of this type and held seven laws invalid"; while between 1920 and 1930, out of 53 cases, the Court held against the legislation involved in fifteen.[11]

The same result appears from another angle when we compare an early case in this field of judicial review with a later

---

[9] License Cases, 5 How., 504, 583 (1847). *See also* Charles River Bridge Co. *v.* Warren Bridge, 11 Pet. 420, 547-548 (1837); the Slaughter House cases, cited above in note 2; Barbier *v.* Connelly, 113 U.S. 27 (1885), and scores of other cases.

[10] Charles W. Collins, *The Fourteenth Amendment and the States* (Boston, 1912), 188-206. *See also* Benjamin R. Twiss, *Lawyers and the Constitution: How Laissez Faire Came to the Supreme Court* (Princeton, 1942), chs. II-VII.

[11] Professor (later Justice) Felix Frankfurter, "The Supreme Court and the Public," *Forum*, 333 (June 1930).

one. In Powell *v.* Pennsylvania,[12] decided in 1888, the Court
sustained an act prohibiting the manufacture and sale of oleomargarine, taking the ground that it could not say, "from anything of which it may take judicial cognizance," that oleomargarine was not injurious to the health, and that this being
the case the legislative determination of facts was conclusive.
Thirty-six years later we find the Court setting aside a Nebraska statute requiring that bread be sold in pound and half-
pound loaves, on its own independent finding that the allowance made by the statute for shrinkage of the loaves was too
small. Entering upon an elaborate discussion of the entire
process of bread-making the Court pronounced the act "unnecessary" for the protection of buyers against fraud, and "essentially unreasonable and arbitrary."[13] In short, the case furnishes a perfect example of what was above characterized as
"broad review," and that in a connection with a case which
had no apparent wide-reaching implications of any sort.

Commenting upon this general development, Professor Kales
once suggested that attorneys arguing "due process cases" before the Court ought to address the justices not as "Your
Honors," but as "Your Lordships."[14] Similarly Senator Borah,
in the Senate debate on Mr. Hughes's nomination for Chief
Justice, declared that the Supreme Court had become, under
the Fourteenth Amendment, "economic dictator in the United
States,"[15] and in the Bread case, just mentioned, Justice
Brandeis, dissenting, characterized the Court as "a superlegislature," while similar views were expressed by Justice Holmes
shortly before his retirement from the Court.

*(margin: The Supreme Court as "a Super-legislature")*

No doubt there was an element of exaggeration in some, or
even all, of these expressions—no doubt, too, it would be rather difficult to indicate very precisely just wherein the exaggeration lay. The Court, of course, has no power to initiate legislation; and even before it can "veto" an act it must wait for
a case to arise under it. Yet a case is sure to arise sooner or
later, and as a practical matter sooner *rather* than later. One
difference which lawyers are apt to stress between the point
of view of a court exercising the power of judicial review and
an executive exercising the veto power, is that which is sup-

12 127 U.S. 678 (1888).
13 Burns Baking Co. *v.* Bryan, 264 U.S. 504 (1924). *See also* Weaver *v.*
Palmer Bros., 270 U.S. 402 (1926).
14 12 *American Political Science Review*, 241 (1918).
15 *New York Times*, February 12, 1930.

posed to result from the doctrine of *stare decisis*. A court, it is said, is apt to reflect that a present decision will be a future precedent. But then, executives are apt so to reflect too; while the fact is that in the field of Constitutional Law the doctrine of *stare decisis* is today very shaky. (*See* pp. 175-178.)

"Social Philoso-phies" of the Justices
The really distinctive thing about the Supreme Court considered as a governing body is that its make-up usually changes very gradually, so that for considerable intervals it will be found to be under the sway of a particular "social philosophy," the operation of which in important cases becomes a matter of fairly easy prediction on the part of those who follow the Court's work with some care. The Court which set aside the Income Tax Act of 1894 and which retired the Sherman Act into disuse for some years by its decision in the Sugar Trust case[16] was also the Court which ten years later in Lochner *v*. New York[17] held void as "unreasonable and arbitrary" an act regulating the hours of labor in bakeries. But another decade, and a "liberal" Court sustained without apparent effort a general ten-hour law[18] and upheld compulsory workmen's compensation.[19] Then from 1920 followed a Court of conservative outlook, a Court prone to take a decidedly astringent view of all governmental powers except its own, and to frown upon legislative projects, whether State or national, which were calculated to curtail freedom of business judgment. The outlook of the present Court, on the other hand, stems from "the Constitutional Revolution" of 1937, and is in general favorable to governmental activity at all levels. In fact, since 1940 the Court has revamped our Constitutional Law pretty thoroughly as the foregoing pages so well illustrate.

Summing up: In consequence of the doctrine of due process of law as "reasonable law," *judicial review ceased to have definite, statable limits*; and while the extent to which the Court would recanvass the factual justification of a statute under the "due process" clauses of the Constitution often varied considerably as between cases, yet this was a matter which in the last analysis depended upon the Court's own discretion, and on nothing else.

In the famous case of Munn *v*. Illinois[20] which was decided

16 United States *v*. E. C. Knight Co., 156 U.S. 1 (1895).
17 198 U.S. 45 (1905).
18 Bunting *v*. Ore., 243 U.S. 426 (1917).
19 New York Central R. R. Co. *v*. White, 243 U.S. 188 (1917).
20 94 U.S. 113.

in 1876, the Court ruled that the State's police power extended to the regulation of the prices set by "businesses affected with a public interest"; and it later held that whether a business was of this character depended on circumstances. Thus the rental of houses in the City of Washington during wartime was held to be such a business, as was the insurance business normally.[21] Later, however, the Court virtually contracted the term to public utilities,[22] holding, as we saw earlier, that their charges were subject to regulation so long as the price fixed by public authority yielded "a fair return on the value of that which is used for the benefit of the public" (see pp. 42-43). Then in Nebbia v. New York,[23] which was decided early in 1934, the Court, again altering its approach, laid down the doctrine that there is no closed category of "businesses affected with a public interest," but that the State by virtue of its police power may regulate prices whenever it is "reasonably necessary" for it to do so in the public interest; and on this basis was sustained a New York statute providing for the regulation of milk prices in that State. Commenting at the time on this decision, the Hon. James M. Beck declared, with some exaggeration, however, that the Court had "calmly discarded its decisions of fifty years," without even paying "those decisions the obsequious respect of a funeral oration."[24] Subsequent decisions further illustrate the new outlook.[25]

*Rate and Price Regulation*

Ultimately, as explained earlier (pp. 330-332), the Supreme Court declined to use substantive due process as a check on economic regulation by legislatures.

During and after the first World War many State legislatures passed acts imposing restraints upon freedom of speech, press, and teaching and learning. In deciding the question whether such measures were within the police power the Court came early to adopt the theory that the word "liberty" of the Fourteenth Amendment covers such freedoms and hence protects them against "unreasonable" State acts. A statute forbidding the teaching of subjects in any but the Eng-

*Incorporation of the Substantive Freedoms of the First Amendment*

21 Block v. Hirsh, 256 U.S. 135 (1921); German Alliance Co. v. Lewis, 233 U.S. 389 (1914).
22 Wolff Packing Co. v. C't of Indust'l Relations, 262 U.S. 522 (1923).
23 291 U.S. 502 (1934).
24 78 Cong. Rec. 5358 (1934).
25 Highland Farms Dairy v. Agnew, 300 U.S. 608 (1937); Townsend v. Yeomans, 301 U.S. 441 (1937); Olsen v. Neb., 313 U.S. 236 (1941); Federal Power Commission v. Hope Natural Gas Co., 320 U.S. 591 (1944).

lish language was held void as to private schools,[26] as was also an act which, by requiring that all children attend the public schools, practically forbade their attending private schools.[27] On the other hand, the Court sustained legislation penalizing advocacy of the use of violence to bring about social and political change,[28] but, in doing so, the Court said "For present purposes we may and do assume that freedom of speech and of the press—which are protected by the First Amendment from abridgment by Congress—are among the fundamental personal rights and 'liberties protected by the due process clause of the Fourteenth Amendment from impairment by the States.' "[29] Thus began the process of selective incorporation of the Bill of Rights into the Fourteenth Amendment.

Due Process Procedures
Before that development reached full flower, the Due Process Clause of the Fourteenth Amendment had an interesting history of its own with respect to law enforcement procedures. For example, it was thought that the clause did *not* subject State criminal procedure to the detailed requirements which the Fifth and Sixth Amendments lay upon the National Government. For this reason the States remained free to remodel their procedural practices, so long as they retained the essence of "due process of law," that is a fair trial in a court having jurisdiction of the case.[30] So, the mere forms of a fair trial did not suffice if the substance was lacking, as in a trial which proceeded to its foreordained conclusion under mob domination;[31] or one in which a plea of guilty or confession was obtained by misrepresentation or recourse to "third degree" methods. In judging these matters, the Court went fully into the factual record made in the trial court.[32] Likewise the Court inquired closely whether the accused was denied assistance of counsel unfairly, although whether this was because Amendment XIV adopted the "assistance of counsel" requirement of Amendment VI outright or only to the extent that such

26 Meyer *v.* Neb., 262 U.S. 390 (1923).
27 Pierce *v.* Society of Sisters, 268 U.S. 510 (1925).
28 Gitlow *v.* N.Y., 268 U.S. 652 (1925); Whitney *v.* Calif., 274 U.S. 357 (1927).
29 *Ibid.*, 666.         30 *See* notes 31-34 below.
31 Moore *v.* Dempsey, 261 U.S. 86 (1923).
32 Brown *v.* Miss., 297 U.S. 278 (1936); Chambers *v.* Fla., 309 U.S. 227 (1940); White *v.* Tex., 310 U.S. 530 (1940); Smith *v.* O'Grady, 312 U.S. 329 (1941); Ashcraft *v.* Tenn., 322 U.S. 143 (1944); Malinski *v.* N.Y., 324 U.S. 401 (1945). Whether a confession of an accused was coerced could be left to the jury to decide. Stein *v.* N.Y., 346 U.S. 156 (1953).

assistance was requisite to a "fair trial" remained somewhat uncertain.[33] The latter, more flexible test seemed to dispense with any or all of those ancient muniments of "Anglo-Saxon liberties"—indictment by grand jury, trial by jury, and immunity from self-incrimination. The Fourteenth Amendment was found not to stand in the way, provided the method of trial guaranteed, in the judgement of the Court, a fair trial.[34]

The approach just described went by the boards once the Fifth and Sixth Amendments were incorporated into the Fourteenth. But that takes a little explaining.

A good place to begin that explanation is with the opinion of the Court, written by Justice Cardozo in the case of Palko v. Connecticut in 1937: ". . . the due process clause of the Fourteenth Amendment may make it unlawful for a state to abridge by its statutes the freedom of speech which the First Amendment safeguards against encroachment by Congress, . . . or like freedom of the press, . . . or the free exercise of religion, . . . or the right of peaceable assembly, without which speech would be unduly trammeled, . . . or the right of one accused of crime to the benefit of counsel. . . . In these and other situations immunities that are valid as against the federal government by force of the specific pledges of particular amendments have been found to be implicit in the concept of ordered liberty, and thus, through the Fourteenth Amendment, become valid as against the states."[35] It seems pretty clear that neither the Court nor Cardozo at that time was suggesting a wholesale incorporation of the Bill of Rights.[36] After all in this very case they said: "The right to trial by jury and the immunity from prosecution except as the result of an indictment may have value and importance. Even so, they are not of the very essence of a scheme of ordered liberty. To abolish them is not to violate a 'principle of justice so rooted in the traditions and conscience of our people as to be ranked

*Development of the Doctrine of Selective Incorporation*

---

[33] Powell v. Ala., 287 U.S. 45 (1932) *and* Avery v. Ala., 308 U.S. 444 (1939) illustrate the care with which the Court would at times go into the facts of such cases. In Betts v. Brady, 316 U.S. 455 (1942) a divided Court found that a State was not required in every case to provide counsel for an indigent defendant. *See also* Gibbs v. Burke, 337 U.S. 773, 780-781 (1949).

[34] Hurtado v. Calif., 110 U.S. 516 (1884); Maxwell v. Dow, 176 U.S. 581 (1900); Twining v. N.J., 211 U.S. 78 (1908); Adamson v. Calif., 332 U.S. 46 (1947); *and note* particularly Justice Cardozo's words in Palko v. Conn., 302 U.S. 319 (1937).

[35] 302 U.S. 319, 324-325 (1937).

[36] Louis Henkin, " 'Selective Incorporation' in the Fourteenth Amendment," 73 *Yale Law Journal*, 74 (1963).

as fundamental.' " The Court went on to hold with respect to the double jeopardy involved in the case at hand: "Is that kind of double jeopardy to which the statute has subjected them a hardship so acute and shocking that our polity will not endure it? Does it violate those 'fundamental principles of liberty and justice which lie at the base of all our civil and political institutions'? . . . The answer surely must be 'no.' " Whatever their intent, the Court and Cardozo provided a concept and a rhetoric upon which others could build, i.e. "immunities that are valid as against the federal government . . . thus through the Fourteenth Amendment, become valid as against the States."

In 1947, in an attempted *tour de force*, Justice Black argued that the Court should incorporate all of the Bill of Rights into the Fourteenth Amendment. He asserted that "history conclusively demonstrates that the language of the first section of the Fourteenth Amendment, taken as a whole, was thought by those responsible for its submission, sufficiently explicit to guarantee that thereafter no state could deprive its citizens of the privileges and protections of the Bill of Rights. Whether this Court ever will, or whether it now should, in the light of past decisions, give full effect to what the Amendment was intended to accomplish is not necessarily essential to a decision here. However that may be, our prior decisions, do not prevent our carrying out that purpose, at least to the extent of making applicable to the states, not a mere part, as the Court has, but the full protection of the Fifth Amendment's provision against compelling evidence from an accused to convict him of crime."[37] However, Justice Black was unable to convince a majority of the Court to go along with him. He concluded his dissent with a telling statement of intent: "If the choice must be between the selective process of the *Palko* decision applying some of the Bill of Rights to the States, or the *Twining* rule applying none of them, I would choose the *Palko* selective process. But rather than accept either of these choices, I would follow what I believe was the original purpose of the Fourteenth Amendment—to extend to all the people of the nation the complete protection of the Bill of Rights. To hold that this Court can determine what, if any, provisions of the Bill of Rights will be enforced, and if so to what degree is to frustrate

[37] Adamson *v.* California, 332 U.S. 46, 74-75 (1947).

the great design of a written Constitution." He soon realized
he had no choice but to use the selective process of *Palko*. And
so for the next two decades he labored hard to convince a majority of the Court that the specific guarantees of the Bill of
Rights each, one by one, was "implicit in the concept of ordered liberty." After all, the specifics of the concept are a subjective judgment, and, for Black, there was no reason to believe that the judgments of Cardozo and the Court of 1937
were any better than his. Black was inordinately successful in
that enterprise.

Unfortunately, the rationale for incorporating the various
guarantees has been difficult to divine, perhaps a predictable
difficulty of the *ad hoc* approach. Did the Court read these
guarantees into the word "liberty"? or "due process"? It took
an erudite scholar, Professor Louis Henkin of the Columbia
Law School, to find some pattern in what the Court had actually done:

"In fact, it should be clear, the Court has not read 'due process of law' as a short-hand way of referring to specifics of the
Bill of Rights. (It could hardly have so read a clause which re-
states, identically, only one single provision of only one of the
early amendments.) To find in that phrase any limitations at
all it had to give meaning and content to the phrase 'due process of law.' It found protection for 'liberty,' including the liberties mentioned in the first and fourth amendments, in notions of 'substantive due process,' and, in regard to procedural
due process, the Court held that the 'process' that is 'due'—
say, in criminal proceedings—is what is required by the conscience of mankind. *That is the essentail link* between the constitutional language and purport and all the procedural limitations which the Court applies to the states under this provision.
So far as here relevant, then, all that is required of the states
is that which is due because it is 'fundamental,' because its denial would shock the conscience of mankind. There is no relation—historical, linguistic or logical—between that standard
and the specific provisions, or any specific provision, of the Bill
of Rights. At bottom, it is difficult even to ask meaningfully
whether a specific of the Bill of Rights is incorporated in
ordered liberty. That a particular procedure or action is required of, or forbidden to, the federal government by a provision of the Bill of Rights is some evidence that it may be required, or forbidden, by the conscience of mankind. But this

indirect relevance of the Bill of Rights to determine the content of 'due process of law' cannot support the view that any provision of the Bill of Rights, in its total federal import, is either all in, or all out of, this standard of ordered liberty. Some specifics of the Bill of Rights, in all their manifestations, may indeed be 'process' which is required by the conscience of mankind; others may not. Some elements or aspects of a specific may be required by the conscience of mankind; others may not."[38] Whatever the rationale, the results are clear: incorporation of the right against cruel and unusual punishment in the Eighth Amendment, the right to counsel in the Sixth, the right against self-incrimination in the Fifth, and the rights to confront witnesses and to a jury trial in all criminal cases, both Sixth Amendment guarantees. (For citations to cases, *see* p. 251.)

Breadth of an Incorporated Guarantee    From 1947 on, Justice Black took the position that when a guarantee was incorporated into the Fourteenth Amendment it was swallowed whole. Thus, once Free Speech became part of the Fourteenth, all the protections afforded that right against the National Government applied equally to the States. In Black's own words: "Now it appears that at least some of the provisions of the Bill of Rights in their very terms satisfy the Court as sound and meaningful expressions of fundamental liberty. If the Fifth Amendment's protection against self-incrimination be such an expression of fundamental liberty, I ask, and have not found a satisfactory answer, why the Court today should consider that it should be 'absorbed' in part but not in full? . . . Nothing in the *Palko* opinion requires that when the Court decides that a Bill of Rights' provision is to be applied to the States, it is to be applied piecemeal. Nothing in the *Palko* opinion recommends that the Court apply part of an amendment's established meaning and discard that part which does not suit the current style of fundamentals."[39] That has been the nearly unanimous view of the members of the Court in the decade in which most of the incorporations have been accomplished.

At least three Justices have felt compelled to challenge this position. In 1952, Justice Jackson wrote: "The assumption of other dissents is that the 'liberty' which the Due Process Clause of the Fourteenth Amendment protects against denial

---

[38] Louis Henkin, " 'Selective Incorporation' . . . ," p. 78.
[39] Adamson *v.* California, 332 U.S. 46, 86 (1947).

by the States is the literal and identical 'freedom of speech or of the press' which the First Amendment forbids only Congress to abridge. The history of criminal libel in America convinces me that the Fourteenth Amendment did not 'incorporate' the First, that the powers of Congress and of the States over this subject are not of the same dimensions, and that because Congress probably could not enact this law it does not follow that the States may not."[40]

Later in 1957, Justice Harlan wrote a separate opinion in an obscenity case: "In judging the constitutionality of this conviction, we should remember that our function in reviewing state judgments under the Fourteenth is a narrow one. We do not decide whether the policy of the State is wise, or whether it is based on assumptions scientifically substantiated. We can inquire only whether the state action so subverts the fundamental liberties implicit in the Due Process Clause that it cannot be sustained as a rational exercise of power. . . . The States' power to make printed words criminal is, of course, confined by the Fourteenth Amendment, but only insofar as such power is inconsistent with our concepts of 'ordered liberty.' "[41] Generally, the other Justices have not been persuaded by the arguments of Jackson and Harlan.

However, in 1970 Justice Stewart erupted in volcanic fashion (note his language): "I substantially agree with the separate opinion Mr. Justice Harlan has filed in these cases—an opinion that fully demonstrates some of the basic errors in a mechanistic 'incorporation' approach to the Fourteenth Amendment. I cannot subscribe to his opinion in its entirety, however, if only for the reason that it relies in part upon certain dissenting and concurring opinions in previous cases in which I did not join.

"The 'incorporation' theory postulates the Bill of Rights as the substantive metes and bounds of the Fourteenth Amendment. I think this theory is incorrect as a matter of constitutional history, and that as a matter of constitutional law it is both stultifying and unsound. It is, at best, a theory that can lead the Court only to a Fourteenth Amendment dead end. And, at worst, the spell of the theory's logic compels the Court either to impose intolerable restrictions upon the constitutional sovereignty of the individual States in the administration of their own criminal law, or else intolerably to relax the explicit

[40] Beauharnais v. Illinois, 343 U.S. 250, 288 (1952).
[41] Roth v. U.S., 354 U.S. 476, 501 (1957).

restrictions that the Framers actually did put upon the Federal Government in the administration of criminal justice. All this, and much more is elaborated in Mr. Justice Harlan's separate opinion . . . .

"The architect of the contemporary 'incorporation' approach to the Fourteenth Amendment is, of course, Mr. Justice Black. . . . And the separate opinion my Brother Black has filed today . . . could serve as Exhibit A to illustrate the extraordinary habits of thought into which some of us have fallen in conditioned reflex to that erroneous constitutional doctrine. 'Incorporation' has become so Pavlovian that my Brother Black barely mentions the Fourteenth Amendment in the course of an 11-page opinion dealing with the procedural rule the State of Florida has adopted for cases tried in Florida courts under Florida's criminal laws. His opinion relies instead upon the 'plain and obvious meaning' of the 'specific words' of the Fifth Amendment and other 'provisions of the Bill of Rights' which, together with 'the history surrounding the adoption of those provisions,' make clear that '[t]he Framers . . . designed' those rights 'to shield the defendant against state power.'

"Though I admire the rhetoric, I submit with all deference that those statements are, to quote their author, 'plainly and simply wrong as a matter of fact and law. . . .' If the Constitution forbids the Florida alibi-defense procedure, it is because of the Fourteenth Amendment, and not because of either the 'specific words' of the Bill of Rights or 'the history surrounding' their adoption. For as every schoolboy knows, the Framers 'designed' the Bill of Rights not against 'state power,' but against the power of the Federal Government.

"Surely Mr. Justice Harlan is right when he says it is time for the Court to face up to reality."[42]

Justice Black's rejoinder: "My Brother Harlan, . . . charges that the Court's decision . . . is evidence that the 'incorporation doctrine,' through which the specific provisions of the Bill of Rights are made fully applicable to the States under the same standards applied in federal courts will somehow result in a 'dilution' of the protections required by those provisions. He asserts that this Court's desire to relieve the States from the rigorous requirements of the Bill of Rights is bound to cause

[42] Williams *v.* Florida, 399 U.S. 78, 143-145 (1970).

re-examination and modification of prior decisions interpreting those provisions as applied in federal courts in order simultaneously to apply the provisions equally to the State and Federal Governments and to avoid undue restrictions on the States. This assertion finds no support in today's decision or any other decision of this Court. We have emphatically 'rejected the notion that the Fourteenth Amendment applies to the States only a "watered-down, subjective version of the individual guarantees of the Bill of Rights." . . .' Today's decision is in no way attributable to any desire to dilute the Sixth Amendment in order more easily to apply it to the States, but follows solely as a necessary consequence of our duty to re-examine prior decisions to reach the correct constitutional meaning in each case."[43] As things currently stand, the Black position prevails.

In two classes of cases "due process of law" has the meaning of *jurisdiction,* the general idea being that a State has normally no right to attempt to exercise its governmental powers upon persons and property situated beyond its boundaries.

"Due Process of Law" as Jurisdiction

The first class embraces cases in which a defendant in a personal action in a State court challenges the validity of a judgment rendered against him on the ground that, not having been within the forum State at the time, he was not served there with the proper papers. Once such a judgment was *ipso facto* void as having been rendered without jurisdiction.[44] But over a century ago, the force of this rule was broken as regards "foreign" corporations (those chartered by other States) by the doctrine that since a State may absolutely exclude such "persons," it ought to be presumed that those admitted by it had consented to be sued in its courts.[45] Then somewhat later this doctrine became impaired in turn by the doctrine that a State may not exclude "foreign" corporations from engaging in interstate commerce; while as regards natural persons who are citizens of sister States, it was never applicable anyway on account of the right of entry which is accorded them by Article IV, Section II. The result is that within the last few decades the Court has developed a much more flexible principle regarding service of process in personal actions, both those in-

---

[43] *Ibid.,* 106-107.
[44] *See* e.g. Pennoyer *v.* Neff, 95 U.S. 714 (1877).
[45] Lafayette Ins. Co. *v.* French, 18 How. 404 (1855); Arrowsmith *v.* United Press Int., 320 F. 2d. 219, 228-229 (1963).

volving corporate defendants and those involving natural persons. This principle is that nowadays due process requires only that, in order to subject a defendant to a judgment *in personam*, if he be not present within the territory of the forum, he must have certain minimum contacts with it such that the maintenance of the suit does not offend "traditional notions of fair play and substantial justice." Such contacts existing, "substituted service" (i.e. other than personal service) will satisfy the requirements of the due process clause, provided "it is reasonably calculated to give him [the defendant] actual notice of the proceedings and an opportunity to be heard."[46]

Substituted Service
Substituted service is also adequate in an action concerning land which is the property of a non-resident, since such actions are *in rem* and the *res* is within the court's jurisdiction. Also, a State may by statute make non-residents operating motor vehicles within its borders liable to suit for any damage they do there, provided a designated State officer is served with the proper papers and a reasonable effort is made to notify the non-resident defendant of the proceedings and an opportunity thus given him to be heard.[47]

As we saw earlier, it is possible for a State court to assert jurisdiction over a suit brought by a non-resident for divorce so far as the due process clause is concerned, but without at the same time satisfying the requirements of the "full faith and credit" clause. (*See* p. 199.)

Jurisdiction in Taxation
The second class of cases referred to apply the jurisdictional principle in the field of taxation. All realty is, of course, within the taxing jurisdiction of the State where situated. Tangible personalty, or "movables," on the other hand, were once deemed attached to the person of the owner (*mobilia personam sequuntur*), and hence to be taxable at the place of his residence, but in the philosophy of the Court this is no longer so. Today such things are taxable under the due process clause only where they have "taxable *situs*"—a point not always easy to determine.

---

[46] Milliken *v.* Meyer, 311 U.S. 457 (1940); International Shoe Co. *v.* Wash., 326 U.S. 310 (1945); Polizzi *v.* Cowles Mag. Inc., 345 U.S. 663 (1953); Scanapico *v.* RF&P R. R. Co., 439 F. 2d. 17, 19 (1970).

[47] Hess *v.* Pawloski, 274 U.S. 352 (1927); Wuchter *v.* Pizzutti, 276 U.S. 13 (1928). Chief Justice Taft's opinion in the latter case is valuable for its exposition of the law of substituted service. *See also* Worthley *v.* Rockville Lease Car, Inc., 328 F. Supp. 185 (1971).

As the Court held in 1962: "Nor does the Due Process Clause confine the domiciliary State's taxing power to such proportion of the value of the property being taxed as is equal to the fraction of the tax year which the property spends within the State's borders. Union Refrigerator Transit Co. *v.* Kentucky, 199 U.S. 194, held only that the Due Process Clause prohibited ad valorem taxation by the owner's domicile of tangible personal property permanently located in some other State. Northwest Airlines, Inc., *v.* Minnesota, 322 U.S. 292, reaffirmed the principle established by earlier cases that tangible property for which no tax situs has been established elsewhere may be taxed to its full value by the owner's domicile. . . . If such property has had insufficient contact with States other than the owner's domicile to render any one of these jurisdictions a 'tax situs,' it is surely appropriate to presume that the domicile is the only State affording the 'opportunities, benefits, or protection' which due process demands as a prerequisite for taxation. . . . Accordingly, the burden is on the taxpayer who contends that some portion of its total assets are beyond the reach of the taxing power of its domicile to prove that the same property may be similarly taxed in another jurisdiction. . . ."[48]

As to intangibles, the Court sought for a time, in an effort to eliminate "double taxation" of inheritances, to confine the power to tax them to the State where the decedent resided,[49] but has latterly been forced by the wealth of expedients devised to avoid taxation altogether which sprang up in the wake of this rule, to abandon it.[50] And State income taxation is frequently "double," or overlapping.[51] The State in which a man is resident may tax him on his total income, while other States may tax him on such portions of it as accrued to him from property situated, or business carried on, within their respec-

[48] Central R. R. Co. *v.* Penn., 370 U.S. 607, 612 (1962).

[49] Frick *v.* Pa., 268 U.S. 473 (1925); Blodgett *v.* Silberman, 277 U.S. 1 (1928); Farmers' Loan & T. Co. *v.* Minn., 280 U.S. 204 (1930); Baldwin *v.* Mo., 281 U.S. 586 (1930); First Nat'l Bk. *v.* Me., 284 U.S. 312 (1932).

[50] Curry *v.* McCanless, 307 U.S. 357 (1939); Graves *v.* Elliot, 307 U.S. 383 (1939); Tax Com'n *v.* Aldrich, 316 U.S. 174 (1942); Greenough *v.* Tax Assessors, 331 U.S. 486 (1947); Tabacalera Severiand Jorge, S. A. *v.* Standard Cigar Co., 392 F. 2d. 706, 715 (1968); State Loan & Finance Corp. *v.* D. C. 381 F. 2d. 895 (1967).

[51] Guaranty Trust Co. *v.* Va., 305 U.S. 19 (1938); Miller Bros. Co. *v.* Maryland, 347 U.S. 340, 345 (1954).

Due
Process as
Protection
Against
Arbitrari-
ness

tive limits; but, of course, such taxes must not be more onerous upon non-residents than upon residents.[52]

The due process clause performs yet another important function—to protect against the arbitrary action of State officials generally, where no specific constitutional guarantee affords protection. This function is best described by the Supreme Court's opinion in a case involving suspension of an automobile driver's license: "Once licenses are issued, as in petitioner's case, their continued possession may become essential in the pursuit of a livelihood. Suspension of issued licenses thus involved state action that adjudicates important interests of the licensees. In such cases the licenses are not to be taken away without that procedural due process required by the Fourteenth Amendment. . . . This is but an application of the general proposition that relevant constitutional restraints limit state power to terminate an entitlement whether the entitlement is denominated a 'right' or a 'privilege.' Sherbert *v.* Verner, 374 U.S. 398 (1963) (disqualification for unemployment compensation); Slochower *v.* Board of Education, 350 U.S. 551 (1956) (discharge from public employment); Speiser *v.* Randall, 357 U.S. 513 (1958) (denial of a tax exemption); Goldberg *v.* Kelly, 397 U.S. 254 (1970) (withdrawal of welfare benefits). . . .

"We turn then to the nature of the procedural due process which must be afforded the licensee on the question of his fault or liability for the accident. A procedural rule that may satisfy due process in one context may not necessarily satisfy procedural due process in every case. Thus, procedures adequate to determine a welfare claim may not suffice to try a felony charge. . . . Due process requires that when a State seeks to terminate an interest such as that here involved, it must afford 'notice and opportunity for hearing appropriate to the nature of the case' before the termination becomes effective."[53]

"Equal
Protection
of the
Laws" and
Legislative
Classifica-
tions

"Equal protection of the laws": This clause was originally intended for the benefit of the Negro freedmen; but in the famous case of Yick Wo *v.* Hopkins, decided in 1886, its protection was extended to Chinese residents of the United States,

[52] Shaffer *v.* Carter, 252 U.S. 37 (1920). A State may tax dividends declared outside its jurisdiction by a "foreign corporation" to the amount of the dividends which were earned within the State by the corporation. Wisconsin *v.* J. C. Penney Co., 311 U.S. 435 (1940); American Commuters' Association *v.* Levitt, 405 F. 2d. 1148, 1152 (1969).

[53] Bell *v.* Burson, 402 U.S. 535, 538-542 (1971).

and at about the same time corporations were also declared to be "persons" within the meaning of the amendment.[54] The clause does not automatically rule out legislative classifications. Indeed, substantially all legislation involves classification of some sort.[55] What the clause appears to require today is that *any* classification of "persons" shall be reasonably relevant to the recognized purposes of good government; and furthermore, that there shall be *no* distinction made on the sole basis of race or alienage as to certain rights. Thus, it was at one time considered reasonable as a measure for protecting game to deny aliens the use of shotguns, while it was considered not reasonable to deny them the right to work for a living.[56]

Clearly, these general propositions leave wide latitude for subjective judgment. In recent years the courts have been flooded with contentions of the denial of equal protection. In its last term, the Supreme Court held that the following contravened the requirement of equal protection: (1) the Texas primary filing fee system, which required candidates for local office to pay fees ranging as high as $8,900;[57] (2) a Tennessee law requiring would-be voters to have resided in the State for one year, and three months in the county;[58] (3) the denial to an unmarried father of a hearing on his fitness as a father, where under Illinois law other parents are accorded a hearing when custody of their children is challenged;[59] (4) a Massa-

---

[54] Yick Wo *v.* Hopkins, 118 U.S. 356 (1886); Santa Clara County *v.* So. Pac. R. R. Co., 118 U.S. 394 (1886).

[55] *See* e.g., Mo., Kan. and Tex. R. Co. *v.* May, 194 U.S. 267 (1904), *and* Lindsley *v.* Natural Carbonic Gas Co., 220 U.S. 61 (1911). *Also*, compare Buck *v.* Bell, 274 U.S. 200 (1927), *and* Skinner *v.* Okla., 316 U.S. 535 (1942). In the former a sterilization statute applicable to mental defectives in State institutions was sustained; in the latter a similar act applicable to triple offenders was held void.

[56] Patsone *v.* Pa., 232 U.S. 138 (1914); *cf.* Takahashi *v.* Fish and Game Commission, 334 U.S. 410 (1948); Truax *v.* Raich, 239 U.S. 33 (1915). In 1971, the Supreme Court held that State statutes denying welfare benefits to resident aliens violated the Equal Protection Clause. Graham *v.* Richardson, 403 U.S. 365. The Supreme Court of California recently held that a requirement of citizenship for admission to the bar offended the Equal Protection Clause. Raffaelli *v.* Committee of Bar Examiners, 101 Cal. Rptr. 896 (1972).

[57] Bullock *v.* Carter, 405 U.S. 134 (1972). But the Court did say: "It must be emphasized that nothing herein is intended to cast doubt on the validity of reasonable candidate filing fees or licensing fees in other contexts."

[58] Dunn *v.* Blumstein, 405 U.S. 330 (1972). *See* dissent of Chief Justice Burger. *Also see* decision of California Supreme Court, Young *v.* Gnoss, 496 P. 2d. 445 (1972).

[59] Stanley *v.* Illinois, 405 U.S. 645 (1972). This case involved a father

chusetts statute prohibiting single persons from obtaining contraceptives to prevent pregnancy while permitting married persons to do so;[60] (5) a Lafayette Parish, Louisiana grand jury selection system where a *prima facie* case was made that it discriminated against Negroes and the State failed "to rebut the presumption of unconstitutional action by showing that permissible racially neutral selection criteria and procedures have produced the monochromatic results";[61] (6) Louisiana's workmen's compensation statutes, which denied equal recovery rights to dependent, unacknowledged illegitimate children (Louisiana law affords the rights to illegitimate children "who have been acknowledged by their father";[62] (7) Indiana's system for pretrial commitment of incompetent criminal defendants, which subjects them "to a more lenient commitment standard and to a more stringent standard of release than those generally applicable to all others not charged with offenses, and by this condemning [them] in effect to permanent institutionalization without the showing required for commitment or the opportunity for release afforded [others by Indiana law]";[63] (8) State statutes which obligated indigent defendants to repay the State for expense of counsel and legal services without affording them the protective exemptions accorded to other civil judgment debtors;[64] (9) the systematic exclusion from the grand jury and the petit jury of Negroes even where the individual indicted and convicted was not himself a Negro (the Court explained: "The Court has also recognized that the exclusion of a discernible class from jury service injures not only those defendants who belong to the excluded class, but other defendants as well, in that it destroys the possibility that the jury will reflect a representative cross-section of the community");[65] (10) a city ordinance which exempted "peaceful labor picketing from its general prohibition of picketing next to a school." (The Court reasoned, "Necessarily, then, under the Equal Protection Clause, not to men-

---

who had lived intermittently with a woman for 18 years without marrying her. When she died, their children were placed with court-appointed guardians. (Under Illinois law the children of unwed fathers become wards of the State.)

[60] Eisenstadt v. Baird, 405 U.S. 438 (1972).
[61] Alexander v. Louisiana, 405 U.S. 625 (1972).
[62] Weber v. Aetna Casualty & Surety Co., 406 U.S. 164 (1972); *see also* Davis v. Richardson, 342 F. Supp. 588 (192); *affirmed*, 41 *LW* 3340 (1972).
[63] Jackson v. Indiana, 406 U.S. 715 (1972).
[64] James v. Strange, 407 U.S. 128 (1972).
[65] Peters v. Kiff, 407 U.S. 493 (1972).

tion the First Amendment itself, government may not grant the use of a forum to people whose views it finds acceptable, but deny use to those wishing to express less favored or more controversial views.")[66]

But the Supreme Court decided with respect to the Texas welfare system, which it was contended, discriminated against Blacks and Chicanos, who made up 87 per cent of those receiving AFDC aid, that: "We cannot say that Texas' decision to provide somewhat lower welfare benefits for AFDC recipients is invidious or irrational. Since budgetary constraints do not allow the payment of full standard of need for all welfare recipients, the State may have concluded that the aged and infirm are the least able of the categorical grant recipients to bear the hardships of an inadequate standard of living."[67]

State courts have had their share of equal protection cases to decide in recent times, including several of particular interest to the academic community. The New Hampshire Supreme Court decided that "it is not invidious discrimination to provide regulations on the use of the [State] university's inadequate parking facilities by the faculty who teach which differ from those applied to the students who attend to be taught."[68] State courts (and lower Federal courts as well) have upheld differentials in tuition rates between residents and non-residents at state colleges and universities.[69] The Minnesota Supreme Court held that the requirement of a minimum age for the holding of office above that of the age for voting was not a denial of equal protection.[70]

In 1896 it was held in Plessy v. Ferguson[71] that it was reasonable for a State to require, in the interest of minimizing occasions for race friction, that white and colored persons travelling by rail be assigned separate coaches, the quality of the accommodations afforded the two races being substantially equal; and in due course the same ruling was extended to public-supported institutions of learning.[72] This enlarged application of the "separate but equal" formula is, of course, no long-

School
Desegrega-
tion

---

[66] Chicago v. Mosley, 408 U.S. 92 (1972).
[67] Jefferson v. Hackney, 406 U.S. 535 (1972).
[68] Peters v. University of New Hampshire, 289 A. 2d. 396 (1972).
[69] Arizona Board of Regents v. Harper, 495 P. 2d. 453 (1972) and the cases cited therein.
[70] Opatz v. St. Cloud, 196 N.W. 2d. 298 (1972).
[71] 163 U.S. 537.
[72] Cumming v. C'ty B'd of Educ., 175 U.S. 528 (1899); Gong Lum v. Rice, 275 U.S. 78 (1927).

er law of the land. It was first repudiated by the Court as to professional schools and schools of higher learning on the ground that for financial and other reasons, such as scarcity of available teaching talent, it was impossible for certain States to provide equal facilities for the two races in these fields of instruction.[73] Moreover, said the Court, in 1950, speaking with reference to a segregated Negro law school, such an institution could not offer its students "those qualities which are incapable of objective measurement but which make for greatness in a law school."[74] In the celebrated *"Brown"* case, decided in 1954, it was held that like considerations "apply with added force to children in grade and high schools. To separate them," said Chief Justice Warren, speaking for a unanimous Court, "from others of similar age and qualifications solely because of their race generates a feeling of inferiority as to their status in the community that may affect their hearts and minds in a way unlikely ever to be undone. . . . We conclude that in the field of education the doctrine of 'separate but equal' has no place. Separate educational facilities are inherently unequal."[75]

[73] Missouri *ex rel.* Gaines *v.* Canada, 305 U.S. 337 (1938); Sipuel *v.* Okla., 332 U.S. 631 (1948); Sweatt *v.* Painter, 339 U.S. 629 (1950); McLaurin *v.* Okla. St. Regents, 339 U.S. 637 (1950).

[74] 339 U.S. 637, 634.

[75] Brown *v.* Topeka, 347 U.S. 483, 495. The cases originated in Kansas, South Carolina, Virginia, and Delaware. They first reached the Court in 1952 and were put over for reargument in the 1953 term. Of this reargument the Chief Justice remarked: "It was largely devoted to the circumstances surrounding the adoption of the Fourteenth Amendment in 1868. It covered, exhaustively, consideration of the Amendment in Congress, ratification by the states, then existing practices in racial segregation, and the views of proponents and opponents of the Amendment.

"This discussion and our own investigation convince us that, although these sources cast some light, it is not enough to resolve the problem with which we are faced.

"At best, they are inconclusive. The most avid proponents of the postwar Amendments undoubtedly intended them to remove all legal distinctions among 'all persons born or naturalized in the United States.'

"Their opponents, just as certainly, were antagonistic to both the letter and the spirit of the Amendments and wished them to have the most limited effect. . . .

"An additional reason for the inclusive nature of the Amendment's history with respect to segregated schools, is the status of public education at that time. In the South, the movement toward free common schools, supported by general taxation, had not yet taken hold. Education of white children was largely in the hands of private groups. Education of Negroes was almost nonexistent, and practically all of the race was illiterate. In fact, any education of Negroes was forbidden by law in some states.

"Today, in contrast, many Negroes have achieved outstanding success in the arts and sciences as well as in the business and professional world. It is true that public education has already advanced further in the North,

That the Court was headed for some such result without the
necessity of invoking "sociological data" is indicated by certain
earlier holdings, including those reached by it in implementing
the "separate but equal" rule (*see* note 73 *supra*). Thus, even
under the law as it stood when the Desegregation cases were
decided, the two races could not be segregated by public authority as to their places of abode; and while private covenants
forbidding the transfer of real property to persons of a designated race or color had been held to be "lawful,"[76] the enforcement thereof by a State through its courts, being a State act,
was held to violate the "equal protection" clause.[77] And, of
course, even at that time neither race could be denied the generally recognized "civil rights," the right to own and possess
property, to make contracts, to serve on juries,[78] etc.

---

but the effect of the Amendment on Northern States was generally ignored
in the Congressional debates.

"Even in the North, the conditions of public education did not ap-
proximate those existing today. The curriculum was usually rudimentary;
ungraded schools were common in rural areas; the school term was but
three months a year in many states; and compulsory school attendance was
virtually unknown.

"As a consequence, it is not surprising that there should be so little in
the history of the Fourteenth Amendment relating to its intended effect
on public education."

Later he adds: "Today, education is perhaps the most important function of state and local governments. Compulsory school attendance laws
and the great expenditures for education both demonstrate our recognition
of the importance of education to our democratic society. It is required in
the performance of our most basic public responsibilities, even service in
the armed forces. It is the very foundation of good citizenship. . . .

"Today, it is a principal instrument in awakening the child to cultural
values, in preparing him for later professional training, and in helping
him to adjust normally to his environment," citing the following works:
K. B. Clark, *Effect of Prejudice and Discrimination on Personality De-
velopment* (Midcentury White House Conference on Children and Youth,
1950): Witmer and Kotinsky, *Personality in the Making* (1952), ch. 6;
Deutscher and Chein, "The Psychological Effects of Enforced Segregation:
A Survey of Social Science Opinion," 26 *J. Psychol.*, 259 (1948); Chein,
"What Are the Psychological Effects of Segregation Under Conditions of
Equal Facilities?" 3 *Int. J. Opinion and Attitude Res.* 229 (1949); Brameld,
*Educational Costs in Discrimination and National Welfare* (McIver, ed.,
1949), 44-48; Frazier, *The Negro in the United States* (1949), 674-681; and
Myrdal, *An American Dilemma* (1944); 347 U.S. 483, 489-496.

A fifth case from the District of Columbia was disposed of in line with
the holdings in the State cases under the "due process" clause of Amendment V. *See* Bolling *v.* Sharpe, 347 U.S. 497 (1954).

[76] Buchanan *v.* Warley, 245 U.S. 60 (1917); Corrigan *v.* Buckley, 271
U.S. 323 (1926).

[77] Shelley *v.* Kramer, 334 U.S. 1 (1948); ff'd in Barrows *v.* Jackson, 346
U.S. 249 (1953).

[78] Strauder *v.* W. Va., 100 U.S. 303 (1880).

The story of the attempt to make good the promise of the Court's decision in the Brown case is not a pretty nor encouraging one. That story was concisely told by Justice Burger in 1971:

"Nearly 17 years ago this Court held, in explicit terms, that state-imposed segregation by race in public schools denies equal protection of the laws. At no time has the Court deviated in the slightest degree from that holding or its constitutional underpinnings. None of the parties before us questions the Court's 1955 holding in *Brown II*, that 'School authorities have the primary responsibility for elucidating, assessing, and solving these problems; courts will have to consider whether the action of school authorities constitutes good faith implementation of the governing constitutional principles. Because of their proximity to local conditions and the possible need for further hearings, the courts which originally heard these cases can best perform this judicial appraisal. Accordingly, we believe it appropriate to remand the cases to those courts.

" 'In fashioning and effectuating the decrees, the courts will be guided by equitable principles. Traditionally, equity has been characterized by a practical flexibility in shaping its remedies and by a facility for adjusting and reconciling public and private needs. These cases call for the exercise of these traditional attributes of equity power. At stake is the personal interest of the plaintiffs in admission to public schools as soon as practicable on a nondiscriminatory basis. To effectuate this interest may call for elimination of a variety of obstacles in making the transition to school systems operated in accordance with the constitutional principles set forth in our May 17, 1954, decision. Courts of equity may properly take into account the public interest in the elimination of such obstacles in a systematic and effective manner. But it should go without saying that the vitality of these constitutional principles cannot be allowed to yield simply because of disagreement with them.' Brown v. Board of Education, 349 U.S. 294, 299-300 (1955). It should be noted that it was in *Brown II* that the Court also said 'The . . . cases are remanded . . . to take such proceedings and enter such orders and decrees consistent with this opinion as are necessary and proper to admit to public schools on a racially nondiscriminatory basis *with all deliberate speed* the parties to these cases (emphasis supplied).'

"Over the 16 years since *Brown II*, many difficulties were

encountered in implementation of the basic constitutional requirement that the State not discriminate between public school children on the basis of their race. Nothing in our national experience prior to 1955 prepared anyone for dealing with changes and adjustments of the magnitude and complexity encountered since then. Deliberate resistance of some to the Court's mandates has impeded the good-faith efforts of others to bring school systems into compliance. The detail and nature of these dilatory tactics have been noted frequently by this Court and other courts.

"By the time the Court considered Green v. County School Board, 391 U.S. 430, in 1968, very little progress had been made in many areas where dual school systems had historically been maintained by operation of state laws. In *Green*, the Court was confronted with a record of a freedom-of-choice program that the District Court had found to operate in fact to preserve a dual system more than a decade after *Brown II*. While acknowledging that a freedom-of-choice concept could be valid remedial measure in some circumstances, its failure to be effective in *Green* required that:

" 'The burden on a school board today is to come forward with a plan that promises realistically to work . . . now . . . until it is clear that state-imposed segregation has been completely removed.' *Green, supra*, at 439.

"This was plain language, yet the 1969 Term of Court brought fresh evidence of the dilatory tactics of many school authorities. Alexander v. Holmes County Board of Education, 396 U.S. 19, restated the basic obligation asserted in Griffin v. School Board, 377 U.S. 218, 234 (1964), and *Green, supra*, that the remedy must be implemented forthwith."[79]

It was this dismal record which led Justice Black in an unprecedented television interview[80] to observe that in retrospect he felt that the Court should have decided *Brown I* like any other law case, make its decision, and let the other branches of government figure out how to vindicate the rights established by the decision rather than to endeavor to do it through the judicial process. Surely, the record shows how inadequate the judicial process is to the task. The judicial effort with all of the attendant difficulties led inexorably to the Supreme Court's effort to formulate guidelines for the lower

[79] Swann v. Board of Education, 402 U.S. 1, 11-13 (1971).
[80] For the text of the interview, *see* 1969 *Cong. Quart. Weekly Report*, 6-11.

courts in 1971. As Chief Justice Burger put it: "The problems encountered by the district courts and courts of appeals make plain that we should now try to amplify guidelines, however incomplete and imperfect, for the assistance of school authorities and courts."[81] In doing so, Chief Justice Burger continued: "This Court, in *Brown I*, appropriately dealt with the large constitutional principles; other federal courts had to grapple with the flinty intractable realities of day-to-day implementation of those constitutional commands. Their efforts of necessity, embraced a process of 'trial and error,' and our effort to formulate guidelines must take into account their experience."[82]

The guidelines which the Court set forth were these:

(1) "Racial Balances or Racial Quotas. . . . In sum, the very limited use made of mathematical ratios was within the equitable remedial discretion of the District Court."

(2) "One-race Schools. . . . The district judge or school authorities should make every effort to achieve the greatest possible degree of actual desegregation and will thus necessarily be concerned with the elimination of one-race schools. . . . An optimal majority-to-minority transfer provision has long been recognized as a useful part of every desegregation plan."

(3) "Remedial Altering of Attendance Zones. . . . We hold that the pairing and grouping of non-contiguous school zones is a permissible tool and such action is to be considered in light of the objectives sought."

(4) "Transportation of Students. . . . In these circumstances [situations in Charlotte, N.C. and Mobile, Ala.], we find no basis for holding that the local school authorities may not be required to employ bus transportation as one tool of school desegregation. Desegregation plans cannot be limited to the walk-in school."[83]

No one living in the United States in 1972 has to be reminded about the furor created by the Court's sanction of busing as a tool for desegration. What the ultimate outcome will be it is too soon to tell. But some significant events have already taken place. After an intense battle, undoubtedly exacerbated by the impact of the busing issue in the Democratic Presidential primaries of 1972 and some highly controversial lower

---

[81] Swann *v.* Board of Education, 402 U.S. 1, 11-13 (1971).
[82] *Ibid.*, 6.                    [83] *Ibid.*, 22-31.

court busing orders,[84] Congress inserted a "compromise" anti-busing provision in the Higher Education Act of 1972.[85] In the words of the *Congressional Quarterly Weekly Report*, the provisions of the compromise:

"Postponed until all appeals had been ruled on, or the time for them had expired, the effective date of all federal district court orders requiring the transfer or transportation of students to achieve racial balance. This provision expired Jan. 1, 1974.

"Limited the use of federal funds for busing (1) intended to overcome racial imbalance or (2) to desegregate a school system to instances when local officials requested federal funds for this use; barred busing where it would risk the health of the children or require that a student attend a school educationally inferior to the school he had formerly attended.

"Prohibited federal pressure on local school boards to induce them to undertake busing unless constitutionally required."[86]

President Nixon indicated his unhappiness with the provision when he signed the bill into law. He called it "inadequate, misleading and entirely unsatisfactory."[87] The "watering-down" of the "compromise" provision triggered off renewed effort by those who oppose busing to seek an anti-busing constitutional amendment. Chairman of the House Rules Committee, William H. Colmer of Mississippi, on June 29, 1972, issued an ultimatum to the Judiciary Committee to act on the proposed amendment by August 1 or risk losing jurisdiction.[88]

Whatever the outcome on the proposed constitutional amendment, clearly the present provision raises constitutional questions as to whether it constitutes a Congressional invasion of the exercise of "judicial power" and whether or not its application in specific cases permits States to engage in invidious discrimination. These questions will have to be resolved even-

[84] Ben Franklin, "A Decision That May Be a Real Blockbuster," *New York Times*, Jan. 16, 1972. *See* Bradley *v.* School Bd. of Richmond, 325 F. Supp. 828 (1971) *and* Bradley *v.* Milliken, 338 F. Supp. 582 (1971). In a noteworthy decision, the Pennsylvania Supreme Court held that there is no "inherent right, enforceable by parents, pupils and taxpayers, to a 'neighborhood school.'" Balsbaugh *v.* Rowland, 290 A. 2d. 85 (1972).

[85] 1972 *Cong. Quart. Weekly Report*, pp. 1241-1242, 1371.

[86] *Ibid.*, 1241.

[87] *New York Times*, June 24, 1972. For the President's full views on busing, see the report of his March 16, 1972 broadcast on the issue, *New York Times*, March 17, 1972 and report of his news conference of June 22, 1972, *New York Times*, June 23, 1972.

[88] *Ibid.*, June 30, 1972.

tually by the Supreme Court unless it is preempted from doing so by a constitutional amendment.

Even as the issue of busing hotted up in 1972, a 5-4 majority of the Court held in three cases that realignment of school districts could be enjoined "where its effect would be to impede the process of dismantling a dual system."[89]

Public School Financing and Equal Protection
Another momentous problem involving schools and equal protection surfaced in the early 'seventies. In 1971, both a Federal district court in Texas and the California Supreme Court held that a State school financing system which relied heavily on local property taxes was unconstitutional in that it results in invidious discrimination against the poor as to the quality of the schools which their children attend.[90] The Supreme Court has indicated that it will decide the Texas case in 1973.[91] Since all States but Hawaii rely heavily on local property taxes to finance their schools, the impact of the Court's decision may be considerable.

In the aftermath of *Brown I*, the Equal Protection Clause has been employed by the Court as a sharp sword to cut the many knots of invidious discrimination which had been woven into the social fabric of American life. (The reason for stressing the word "invidious" is made clear below in the discussion of the "benign quota.") The Court has operated on a premise which Chief Justice Warren articulated for the Court when it struck down a Virginia statute barring interracial marriages: "The clear and central purpose of the Fourteenth Amendment was to eliminate all official state sources of invidious racial discrimination in the States."[92] But, evidently, there are limits beyond which the Court will not go. In 1971 in deciding a case involving the contention that the City of Jackson, Mississippi, closed down all of its public swimming pools rather than desegregate them, the Court per Justice Black held: "Nothing in the history or the language of the Fourteenth Amendment nor in any of our prior cases persuades us that the closing of the Jackson swimming pools to all citizens constitutes a denial of 'the equal protection of the laws.' "[93]

[89] Wright *v.* City of Emporia, 407 U.S. 451 (1972); U.S. *v.* Scotland Neck City Board of Education (and companion case), 407 U.S. 484 (1972).
[90] Serrano *v.* Priest, 487 P. 2d. 1241 (1972) *and* Rodriguez *v.* San Antonio School Dist., 337 F. Supp. 280 (1971).
[91] 41 *LW* 3197 (1972).
[92] Loving *v.* Virginia, 388 U.S. 1, 10 (1967); Gilmore *v.* City of Montgomery, 337 F. Supp. 22 (1972).
[93] Palmer *v.* Thompson, 403 U.S. 217, 226 (1971).

As Chief Justice Burger explained in a concurring opinion: "We are, of course, not dealing with the wisdom or desirability of public swimming pools; we are asked to hold on a very meagre record that the Constitution requires that public swimming pools, once opened may not be closed. But all that is good is not commanded by the Constitution and all that is bad is not forbidden by it. We would do a grave disservice, both to elected officials, and to the public, were we to require that every decision of local governments to terminate a desirable service be subjected to a microscopic scrutiny for forbidden motives rendering the decision unconstitutional."[94] Four Justices dissented presumably on the grounds articulated by Justice White: "It is also my view, but apparently not that of the majority, that a state may not have an official stance against desegregating public facilities and implement it by closing those facilities in response to a desegregation order."[95]

In the struggle to eliminate *invidious* discrimination, officials have sometimes seen fit to establish quotas in various enterprises like housing, education, and employment to ensure a better representation of groups which are commonly discriminated against. For example, under the vaunted Philadelphia Plan, contractors who wanted contracts with the Federal Government were required to meet the following standards for manpower utilization:[96]

The Benign Quota

RANGE OF MINORITY GROUP EMPLOYMENT

| Identification of Trade | Until 12/31/70 | for 1971 | for 1972 | for 1973 |
|---|---|---|---|---|
| Ironworkers | 5%–9% | 11%–15% | 16%–20% | 22%–26% |
| Plumbers & Pipefitters | 5%–8% | 10%–14% | 15%–19% | 20%–24% |
| Steamfitters | 5%–8% | 11%–15% | 15%–19% | 20%–24% |
| Sheetmetal workers | 4%–8% | 9%–13% | 14%–18% | 19%–23% |
| Electrical workers | 4%–8% | 9%–13% | 14%–18% | 19%–23% |
| Elevator construction workers | 4%–8% | 9%–13% | 14%–18% | 19%–23% |

94 *Ibid.*, 228.

95 *Ibid.*, 240. The various opinions in this case contain a catalogue of Court decisions in which specific invidious discriminations have been struck down.

96 Contractors Ass'n *v.* Secretary of Labor, 442 F. 2d. 159, 164 (1971).

As can readily be seen, such standards are themselves discriminatory, since they discriminate against members of the majority group and are very troublesome constitutionally to some
people for that fact.[97] To be troubled about the constitutionality of the benign quota one must fail to recognize the distinction between "invidious" discrimination and discrimination
*per se.* If a particular discrimination has as its objective ending
invidious discrimination then it is a reasonable classification.
True, there will be times when it is difficult to determine purpose. On the other hand, judges are entitled to know what
everyone else knows, and purpose many times can be determined or measured by the facts. For those concerned, as we,
the writers are, with the need for neutral principles,[98] this distinction does not violate neutral principles, Professor Herbert
Wechsler's exposition of the idea notwithstanding.[99] We would
suggest that the neutral principle is that "invidious" discrimination is in all situations unconstitutional. Apparently, this
view will prevail in the courts. In the case dealing with the
Philadelphia Plan, the United States Court of Appeals, Third
Circuit, held: "Finally, the plaintiffs urge that its specific goals
specified by the Plan are racial quotas prohibited by the equal
protection aspect of the Fifth Amendment. [This case involved
the Federal Government, that is why the Fifth Amendment
was invoked. *See* pp. 330-331.] . . . The Philadelphia Plan is
valid Executive action designed to remedy the perceived evil
that minority tradesmen have not been included in the labor
pool available for the performance of construction projects in
which the federal government has a cost and performance interest. The Fifth Amendment does not prohibit such action."[100]
In late 1971, the Supreme Court denied certiorari in the
case.[101]

Women's    In what undoubtedly is a happy harbinger of things to
Rights

[97] See Professor Boris I. Bittker's very clever hypothetical case, "The Case
of the Checker-Board Ordinance: An Experiment in Race Relations," 71
*Yale Law Journal,* 1387 (1962).

[98] We are in accord with the idea first expounded by Professor Herbert
Wechsler that: "A principled decision . . . is one that rests on reasons with
respect to all issues in the case, reasons that in their generality and their
neutrality transcend any immediate result that is involved," Herbert
Wechsler, "Toward Neutral Principles of Constitutional Law," 73 *Harvard Law Review,* 1, 19 (1959).

[99] *Ibid.*

[100] Contractors Ass'n *v.* Secretary of Labor, 442 F. 2d. 159, 176-177 (1971).

[101] 404 U.S. 854 (1971). But there is indication that the Labor Dept.
plans to cut these quotas. *Washington Post,* Sept. 7, 1972.

come, the Supreme Court in 1971 held unconstitutional an Idaho statute which provided that, as between persons equally qualified to administer estates, males must be favored over females. The Court said: "To give a mandatory preference to members of either sex over members of the other, merely to accomplish the elimination of hearings on the merits, is to make the very kind of arbitrary legislative choice forbidden by the Equal Protection Clause of the Fourteenth Amendment; and whatever may be said as to the positive values of avoiding intrafamily controversy, the choice in this context may not lawfully be mandated solely on the basis of sex."[102]

As was remarked earlier, corporations are "persons" within the meaning of the Fourteenth Amendment, and so are entitled to the "equal protection of the laws." But for a "foreign" corporation to be entitled to equal treatment with the corporations chartered by a State it must be "subject to the jurisdiction thereof."[103] The importance, moreover, of this reading of the term, the historical validity of which has been disputed,[104] is much less than is sometimes supposed. It does not mean that the law may not exact special duties of corporations, but it does mean that such duties must bear some reasonable relation to the fact that they are corporations and to the nature of the business in which they are engaged. Thus, in view of the special dangers to which the railroad business exposes the public, railroad companies may be required to stand the heavy expense of elevating their grade crossings.[105] On the other hand, a railroad may not be required to carry selected commodities at a loss.[106]

*Corporations as "Persons"*

In the leading case concerning the application of equal protection to persons in the same business, the Court explained: "That the Equal Protection Clause does not require that every state regulatory statute apply to all in the same business is a truism. For example, where size is an index to the evil at which the law is directed, discriminations between the large and the small are permissible. . . . On the other hand, a statutory dis-

*Equal Protection as to Persons in the Same Business*

[102] Reed *v.* Reed, 404 U.S. 71, 76 (1971).
[103] Santa Clara County *v.* So. Pac. R.R. Co., 118 U.S. 394 (1886); Hanover Fire Ins. Co. *v.* Carr, 272 U.S. 494 (1926); *cf.* WHYY *v.* Glassboro, 393 U.S. 117 (1968).
[104] *See* the interesting dissenting opinion of Justice Black in Connecticut Gen. L. Ins. Co. *v.* Johnson, 303 U.S. 77 at 82 (1938), and references.
[105] Chicago & Alton R.R. Co. *v.* Tranbarger, 238 U.S. 67 (1915), and cases there cited. *Cf.* Robertson *v.* California, 328 U.S. 440 456-457 (1946).
[106] Northern Pacific Ry. *v.* No. Dak., 236 U.S. 585 (1915).

crimination must be based on differences that are reasonably related to the purposes of the Act in which it is found. . . .

"Of course, distinctions in the treatment of business entities engaged in the same business activity may be justified by genuinely different characteristics of the business involved. This is so even where the discrimination is by name. But distinctions cannot be so justified if the discrimination has no reasonable relation to these differences."[107] In that case, the Court held that an Illinois law which exempted the American Express Company from its provisions requiring currency exchanges to be licensed was unconstitutionally applied therefore to a small partnership in the same business because the classification (discrimination) was not reasonably related to the differences in business characteristics.

Taxation    The clause is least effective as a restraint on the taxing power of the States. Almost any classification made in a tax measure will be sustained by the Court, whether it is relevant to the business of raising revenue or proceeds from some ulterior motive.[108] As the Court said in 1959: "Of course, the States, in the exercise of their taxing power, are subject to the requirements of the Equal Protection Clause of the Fourteenth Amendment. But that clause imposes no iron rule of equality, prohibiting the flexibility and variety that are appropriate to reasonable schemes of state taxation. The State may impose different specific taxes upon different trades and professions and may vary the rate of excise upon various products. It is not required to resort to close distinctions or to maintain a precise, scientific uniformity with reference to composition, use or value. . . . But there is a point beyond which the State cannot go without violating the Equal Protection Clause. The State must proceed upon a rational basis and may not resort to a classification that is palpably arbitrary. . . ."[109]

Expansion    As we saw above, the term "State" in this clause meant for
of the    years any agency whereby the State exercised its powers. It
Concept    thus included any State or local official when acting under
of State
Action    [107] Morey *v.* Dodd, 354 U.S. 457, 464-466 (1957); Graham *v.* Richardson, 403 U.S. 365, 371 (1971); State *v.* Richardson, 285 A. 2d. 842 (1972).
    [108] *See* State Tax Com'rs *v.* Jackson, 283 U.S. 527 (1931); *and* Great Atlantic and Pacific Tea Co. *v.* Grosjean, 301 U.S. 412 (1937); and cases cited there.
    [109] Allied Stores of Ohio *v.* Bowers, 358 U.S. 522, 526-527 (1959); Flores *v.* Government of Guam, 444 F. 2d. 284, 288 (1971); State *v.* Kelly, 285 A. 2d. 571 (1972).

color of his office,[110] and in deciding whether a State has violated the above provisions, the Court has always been free to go behind the face of the law and inquire into the fairness of its actual enforcement.[111] This rule, originally laid down in Yick Wo v. Hopkins, was illustrated some years ago in one of the *Scottsboro* cases, where an indictment returned by a grand jury of whites in a county of Alabama in which no member of a considerable Negro population had ever been called for jury service, was held void, although the Alabama statute governing the matter contained no discrimination between the two races.[112]

In recent years, the concept of what constitutes State action has been broadened dramatically, though not suddenly. Case by case, the Court moved from its position in Shelley v. Kraemer (1948) that "action inhibited by the first section of the Fourteenth Amendment is only action which may fairly be said to be that of the States"[113] to its present position which is worth quoting at length: "Is there sufficient state action to prove a violation of petitioner's Fourteenth Amendment rights if she knows that Kress [S. H. Kress and Co.] refused her service because of a state-enforced custom compelling segregation of the races in Hattieburg restaurants?

"In analyzing this problem, it is useful to state two polar propositions, each of which is easily identified and resolved. On the one hand, the Fourteenth Amendment plainly prohibits a State itself from discriminating because of race. On the other hand, §1 of the Fourteenth Amendment does not forbid a private party, not acting against a backdrop of state compulsion or involvement, to discriminate on the basis of race in his personal affairs as an expression of his own personal predilections. As was said in Shelley v. Kraemer . . . §1 of '[t]hat Amendment erects no shield against merely private conduct however discriminatory or wrongful.'

"At what point between these two extremes a State's involvement in the refusal becomes sufficient to make the private

110 *Ex parte* Virginia, 100 U.S. 339 (1879); Screws v. U.S., 325 U.S. 91 (1945); Shelley v. Kraemer, 334 U.S. 1 (1948).
111 Yick Wo v. Hopkins, 118 U.S. 356 (1886); Reagan v. Farmers' Loan & T. Co., 154 U.S. 362 (1894); Tarrance v. Fla., 188 U.S. 519 (1903).
112 Norris v. Ala., 294 U.S. 587 (1935). To the same effect were Hale v. Ky., 303 U.S. 613 (1938); Pierre v. La., 306 U.S. 354 (1939); *and* Smith v. Tex., 311 U.S. 128 (1940); Avery v. Ga., 345 U.S. 559 (1953). *Cf.* Brown v. Allen, 344 U.S. 443 (1953).
113 Shelley v. Kraemer, 334 U.S. 1, 13 (1948).

refusal to serve a violation of the Fourteenth Amendment, is far from clear under our case law. If a State had a law requiring a private person to refuse service because of race, it is clear beyond dispute that the law would violate the Fourteenth Amendment and could be declared invalid and enjoined from enforcement. Nor can a State enforce such a law requiring discrimination through either convictions of proprietors who refuse to discriminate, or trespass prosecutions of patrons who, after being denied service pursuant to such a law, refuse to honor a request to leave the premises. . . .

"For state action purposes it makes no difference of course whether the racially discriminatory act by the private party is compelled by a statutory provision or *by a custom having the force of law*—in either case it is the State that has commanded the result by its law. Without deciding whether less substantial involvement of a State might satisfy the state action requirement of the Fourteenth Amendment, we conclude that petitioner would show an abridgment of her equal protection right, if she proves that Kress refused her service because of a state-enforced custom of segregating the races in public restaurants"[114] (emphasis supplied).

But the Court in 1972 narrowed somewhat the concept of what constitutes State action. In the attention-getting case involving the Negro guest who was denied service in a Moose Lodge, Justice Rehnquist speaking for the Court stated the view that "Our holdings indicate that where the impetus for discrimination is private, the State must have 'significantly involved itself with invidious discriminations,' in order for the discriminating action to fall within the ambit of the constitutional prohibition."[115] The Court did not find the act of liquor licensing (on which the contention of State action was based) such a significant involvement. As the Court saw it, with a minor exception the State Liquor Control Board "plays absolutely no part in establishing or enforcing the membership or guest policies of the club which it licenses to serve liquor."[116]

---

114 Adickes v. Kress and Co., 398 U.S. 144, 169-171 (1970).
115 Moose Lodge No. 107 v. Irvis, 407 U.S. 163, 173 (1972).
116 *Ibid.*, 1972. The Court was troubled by the fact that the Board did have regulations which required that "every club licensee shall adhere to all the provisions of its constitution and by-laws." Of course, this could have the effect of enforcing discriminations spelled out in the constitution and by-laws. But parties to the suit conceded that the purpose of these regulations was to keep public accommodations from masquerading as private clubs. Nonetheless, the Court held that the discriminated-against guest was entitled to a decree enjoining the enforcement of those regula-

The Equal Protection Clause served as the basis for the breakthrough in 1962 on the reapportionment issue. As pointed out earlier, p. 172, until then the matter of legislative districting was considered by the Court to be a "political question." As a practical matter this left it to the State legislatures and Congress to change a situation which would upset a political power balance in which many of the legislators were themselves beneficiaries.[117] And it was clear by the 1960's that it just would not be done.[118] Consequently, gross inequities in the worth of citizens' votes abounded throughout the political system.[119]

At length, in Baker v. Carr (1962), the Court held that: "the complaint's allegations of a denial of equal protection present a justiciable constitutional cause of action upon which appellants are entitled to a trial and a decision. The right asserted is within the reach of judicial protection under the Fourteenth Amendment."[120] Once the Court found that such complaints were justiciable, much of what followed with respect to having votes count equally was predictable. After all, it was the meaning of the *equal* protection clause which was being decided in most of the cases that followed. However, in the first case after Baker v. Carr, Wesberry v. Sanders (1964), the Court held with respect to Congressional districts "the command of Art. I §2 that the Representatives be chosen 'by the People of the several States' means that as nearly as practicable one man's vote in a congressional election is to be worth as much as another's," and explicitly said it was not deciding the issue on the basis of the Fourteenth Amendment.[121] This decision was followed quickly by Reynolds v. Sims (1964), in which the Court held that "the Equal Protection Clause guarantees the opportunity for equal participation by all voters in the election of state legislators. Diluting the weight of votes because of place of residence impairs basic constitutional rights just as much as invidious discriminations based upon factors such as

The Right to Have Votes Count Equally

---

tions, "He was entitled to no more." *Ibid.*, 179. Subsequently, the Pennsylvania Supreme Court upheld an order that the Harrisburg Moose Lodge drop a ban against serving Negro guests. 294 A. 2d 594 (1972); *appeal dismissed*, 41 *LW* 3324 (1972).

[117] Carl A. Auerbach, "The Reapportionment Cases: One person, One Vote-One Vote, One Value," 1964 *Supreme Court Review*, 1, 68-70.

[118] *Ibid.*

[119] Baker v. Carr, 369 U.S. 186, 253-255 (1962).

[120] *Ibid.*, 237.

[121] Wesberry v. Sanders, 376 U.S. 1, 8 and note 10 (1964).

race . . . or economic status. . . . We hold that, as a basic constitutional standard, the Equal Protection Clause requires that the seats in both houses of a bicameral state legislature must be apportioned on a population basis. Simply stated, an individual's right to vote for state legislators is unconstitutionally impaired when its weight is in a substantial fashion diluted when compared with votes of citizens living in other parts of the State."[122]

One can only wonder if the Court fully appreciated the difficulties in store for the courts of the United States in attempting to resolve the myriad of complex practical questions which would arise upon the interpretation that the equal protection clause required that one man's vote be worth the same as every other man's. They certainly would never be able to say that they were not warned. In a long, artful, and powerful dissent in Baker *v.* Carr, Justice Frankfurter had alerted them to the pitfalls:

"A hypothetical claim resting on abstract assumptions is now for the first time made the basis for affording illusory relief for a particular evil even though it foreshadows deeper and more pervasive difficulties in consequence. The claim is hypothetical and the assumptions are abstract because the Court does not vouchsafe the lower courts—state and federal —guidelines for formulating specific definite, wholly unprecedented remedies for the inevitable litigations that today's umbrageous disposition is bound to stimulate in connection with politically motivated reapportionments in so many States. In such a setting to promulgate jurisdiction in the abstract is meaningless. It is as devoid of reality as 'a brooding omnipresence in the sky,' for it conveys no intimation what relief, if any, a District Court is capable of affording that would not invite legislatures to play ducks and drakes with the judiciary. For this Court to direct the District Court to enforce a claim to which the Court has over the years consistently found itself required to deny legal enforcement and at the same time to find it necessary to withhold any guidance to the lower court how to enforce this turnabout, new legal claim, manifests an odd— indeed an esoteric—conception of judicial propriety. One of the Court's supporting opinions, as elucidated by commentary, unwittingly affords a disheartening preview of the mathematical quagmire (apart from divers judicially inappropriate and

[122] Reynolds *v.* Sims, 377 U.S. 533, 566-568 (1964).

elusive determinants) into which this Court today catapults the lower courts of the country without so much as adumbrating the basis for a legal calculus as a means of extrication. Even assuming the indispensable intellectual disinterestedness on the part of judges in such matters, they do not have accepted legal standards or criteria or even reliable analogies to draw upon for making judicial judgments. To charge courts with the task of accommodating the incommensurable factors of policy that underlie these mathematical puzzles is to attribute, however flatteringly, omnicompetence to judges."[123]

Three basic problems have plagued the courts with respect to reapportionment: (1) how much deviation from absolute equality will be permitted because of practical considerations? (2) what kinds of elections are required to pass the muster of equal protection? (3) what remedies should be applied by courts to force recalcitrant legislatures to reapportion?

As to the first problem, the Court's most recent pronouncement is that " 'Mathematical exactness or precision is hardly a workable constitutional requirement,' . . . but deviations from population equality must be justified by legitimate state considerations. . . ."[124] That, of course, still leaves it up to the courts to determine what is a legitimate State consideration and how much deviation to allow for it. Without defining the precise limits the Supreme Court has from time to time indicated what it considered to be excessive: *"De minimus deviations are unavoidable, but variations of* 30% *among senate districts and* 40% *among house districts can hardly be deemed de minimus and none of our cases suggests that differences of that magnitude will be approved without a satisfactory explanation grounded on acceptable state policy."*[125]

In 1970, the Supreme Court attempted to dispose of problem number two: "It has also been urged that we distinguish for apportionment purposes between elections for 'legislative' officials and those for 'administrative' officers. Such a suggestion would leave courts with an equally unmanageable princi-

---

123 Baker *v.* Carr, 369 U.S. 186, 267-268 (1962).
124 Abate *v.* Mundt, 403 U.S. 182, 185 (1971). *See also* Witcomb *v.* Chavis, 403 U.S. 124 (1971).
125 Swann *v.* Adams, 385 U.S. 440, 444 (1967). *See also* Kirkpatrick *v.* Preisler, 394 U.S. 526 (1969); J. Dudley McClain, Jr., "Reapportionment Recapitulated, 1960-1970," 7 *Georgia State Bar,* 191 (1970). For an attempt at a novel use of the *de minimus* approach, *see in re* Legislative Districting, 193 N.W. 2d. 784 (1972).

ple since governmental activities 'cannot easily be classified in the neat categories favored by civics texts,' . . . and it must also be rejected. We therefore hold today that as a general rule, whenever a state or local government decides to select persons by popular election to perform governmental functions, the Equal Protection Clause of the Fourteenth Amendment requires that each qualified voter must be given an equal opportunity to participate in that election, and when members of an elected body are chosen from separate districts, each district must be established on a basis that will insure, as far as is practicable, that equal numbers of voters can vote for proportionally equal numbers of officials. It is of course possible that there might be some case in which a State elects certain functionaries whose duties are so far removed from normal governmental activities and so disproportionately affect different groups that a popular election . . . might not be required. . . ."[126]

As was predictable, the courts have had great difficulty with legislatures which in Frankfurter's words have played "ducks and drakes with the judiciary." After canvassing what courts have used for remedies, Professor David R. Berman wrote in a splendid article: "By the end of March 1966, all indications were that the favorite form of positive judicial relief was the foundation of a court plan, with all the bi-partisan and non-partisan assistance possible."[127] One such plan devised by the U.S. District Court of Minnesota came a cropper in the Supreme Court. The District Court sharply reduced the size of the legislature in devising its apportionment order. The Supreme Court held *per curiam*: "We know of no federal constitutional principle or requirement that authorizes a federal reapportioning court to go as far as the District Court did and, thus, to by-pass the State's formal judgment as to the proper size of its legislative bodies. No case decided by this Court has gone that far and we have found no district court decision that has employed such radical surgery in reapportionment. There are cases where judicial reapportionment has effectuated minor changes in a legislature's size. . . . We do not disapprove

---

126 Hadley *v.* Junior College District, 397 U.S. 50, 55-56 (1970). The Supreme Court recently affirmed a lower court decision that the "one man, one vote" rule was inapplicable to judicial elections. 41 *LW* 3167 (1972).
127 1970 *Law and the Social Order*, 519, 536.

a court-imposed minor variation from a State's prescribed figure when that change is shown to be necessary to meet constitutional requirements."[128]

All in all, ten years after Baker *v.* Carr, apportionment inequities were far from eliminated.[129] It is noteworthy that fifteen States were operating under court-ordered reapportionment schemes. Where legislatures or special commissions were accomplishing the task, they were, of course, under the threat of challenge in the courts. The slow progress in reapportionment again raises the question of the efficacy of the judicial process for resolving certain kinds of problems as it did in the school desegregation issue. But here, there literally was no other way. As Justice Clark pointed out in Baker *v.* Carr:

"Although I find the Tennessee apportionment statute offends the Equal Protection Clause, I would not consider intervention by this Court into so delicate a field if there were any other relief available to the people of Tennessee. But the majority of the people of Tennessee have no 'practical opportunities for exerting their political weight at the polls' to correct the existing 'invidious discrimination.' Tennessee has no initiative and referendum. I have searched diligently for other 'practical opportunities' present under the law. I find none other than through the federal courts. The majority of the voters have been caught up in a legislative strait jacket. Tennessee has an 'informed, civically militant electorate' and 'an aroused popular conscience,' but it does not sear 'the conscience of the people's representatives.' This is because the legislative policy has riveted the present seats in the Assembly to their respective constituencies, and by the votes of their incumbents a reapportionment of any kind is prevented. The people have been rebuffed at the hands of the Assembly; they have tried the constitutional convention route, but since the call must originate in the Assembly, it, too, has been fruitless. They have tried Tennessee courts with the same result, and Governors have fought the tide only to flounder. It is said that there is recourse in Congress and perhaps that may be, but from a practical standpoint this is without substance. To date Congress has never undertaken such a task in any State. We

[128] Sixty-Seventh Minn. State Senate *v.* Beens, 406 U.S. 187, 198 (1972).
[129] 1971 *Cong. Quarterly Weekly Report*, 644ff., and The Council of State Governments, *The Book of the States* (Lexington, Ky., 1970-1971), 83-84.

therefore must conclude that the people of Tennessee are stymied and without judicial intervention will be saddled with the present discrimination in the affairs of their state government. . . ."[130]

Voting Restrictions on Bond Issues

In the course of attempting to equalize the worth of votes, the Supreme Court has had to face up to two common practices in American history: (1) limiting voting on bond issues to property holders and (2) requiring more than a majority to carry the day on such issues. In 1970, the Court held violative of equal protection a State statute permitting only real property taxpayers to vote on the issuance of general obligation bonds.[131] A year later, the Court held constitutional a State requirement that approval of 60% of the voters was needed on bond issues and increases in tax rates in its political subdivisions. The Court reasoned: "that so long as such provisions do not discriminate against or authorize discrimination against any identifiable class they do not violate the Equal Protection Clause. We see no meaningful distinction between such absolute provisions on debt, changeable only by constitutional amendment, and provisions that legislative decisions on the same issues require more than a majority vote in the legislature. On the contrary, these latter provisions may, in practice, be less burdensome than the amendment process. Moreover, the same considerations apply when the ultimate power, rather than being delegated to the legislature remains with the people, by way of a referendum."[132]

## SECTION II

Representatives shall be apportioned among the several States according to their respective numbers, counting the whole number of persons in each State, excluding Indians not taxed. But when the right to vote at any election for the choice of electors for President and Vice-President of the United States, Representatives in Congress, the executive and judicial officers of a State, or the members of the legislature thereof, is denied to any of the male inhabitants of

---

[130] Baker *v.* Carr, 369 U.S. 186, 259 (1962).

[131] Phoenix *v.* Kolodziejski, 399 U.S. 204 (1970); Vermilion *v.* Herbert, 245 So. 2d. 249 (1971), *cert. granted* and judgment reversed, 404 U.S. 807 (1971). The Washington State Supreme Court held unconstitutional an ordinance requiring candidates to a board to be freeholders, *see* Sorenson *v.* Bellingham, 496 P. 2d. 512 (1972).

[132] Gordon *v.* Lance, 403 U.S. 1, 7 (1971).

such State, being twenty-one years of age, and citizens of the United States, or in any way abridged, except for participation in rebellion, or other crime, the basis of representation therein shall be reduced in the proportion which the number of such male citizens shall bear to the whole number of male citizens twenty-one years of age in such State.

In the struggle to vindicate the legal rights of Black Americans, it was a natural reaction to attempt to breathe life into this provision of the Constitution, despite the fact that it had never been successfully implemented.[1] Senator Pat McNamara of Michigan led an abortive effort in the late 1950's to enact legislation designed to reduce the number of Representatives from States which restricted voting rights.[2] And in the 1960's there was an effort to include such a provision in the Civil Rights Act of 1964, an effort which failed.[3] As recently as 1965, a group of citizens went to a Federal district court seeking a declaratory judgment against the Secretary of Commerce and the Director of the Census Bureau to compile at the next census figures as to the denial of the right to vote and to figure the apportionment for the House of Representatives on the basis of those figures. Although the District Court held that the citizens who brought the case lacked standing it did go to the merits of the Fourteenth Amendment argument and cited with approval the language of a Circuit Court in an earlier case: "Irrespective of the Fourteenth Amendment's mandate the Congress, in the present state of the law, is not required to prescribe that census-takers ascertain information relative to disenfranchisement. . . . There was nothing unconstitutional in the omission from the census form of a question relating to disenfranchisement."[4]

Presumably, the efficacy of the other efforts to vindicate the right to vote, precludes any further effort to invoke this provision of the Constitution.[5] (*See* pp. 433-435.)

[1] George D. Zuckerman, "A Consideration of the History and Present Status of Section 2 of the Fourteenth Amendment," 30 *Fordham Law Review*, 93, 124 (1961).

[2] *Ibid.*, 120-124.

[3] 1964 U.S. *Cong. & Adm. News*, 2422ff.

[4] Lampkin *v.* Connor, 239 F. Supp. 757, 766 (1965), *affirmed*, 360 F. 2d. 505 (1966); U.S. *v.* Sharrow, 409 F. 2d. 77 (1962), *cert. denied*, 372 U.S. 949 (1963).

[5] *But see* Zuckerman, "A Consideration of the History and Present Status of Section 2 of the Fourteenth Amendment," pp. 128-135.

## SECTION III

No person shall be a Senator or Representative in Congress, or elector of President and Vice-President, or hold any office, civil or military, under the United States or under any State, who, having previously taken an oath as a member of Congress, or as an officer of the United States, or as a member of any State legislature, or as an executive or judicial officer of any State, to support the Constitution of the United States, shall have engaged in insurrection or rebellion against the same, or given aid or comfort to the enemies thereof. But Congress may, by a vote of two-thirds of each house, remove such disability.

## SECTION IV

The validity of the public debt of the United States, authorized by law, including debts incurred for payment of pensions and bounties for services in suppressing insurrection or rebellion, shall not be questioned. But neither the United States nor any State shall assume or pay any debt or obligation incurred in aid of insurrection or rebellion against the United States, or any claim for the loss or emancipation of any slave; but all such debts, obligations and claims shall be held illegal and void.

These sections are today, for the most part, of historical interest only.

## SECTION V

The Congress shall have power to enforce, by appropriate legislation, the provisions of this article.

Congressional Enforcement of the Amendment
The full extent of the powers of Congress under this section, in the regulation and protection of civil rights, has never been conclusively determined.[1] In the famous Civil Rights cases,[2] decided nearly three quarters of a century ago, the Court held void an act of Congress forbidding inns, railroads, and theaters to discriminate between persons on the ground of race, the basis of the decision being the proposition that the pro-

1 Griffin *v.* Breckenridge, 403 U.S. 88, 107 (1971).
2 109 U.S. 3 (1883).

hibitions of the opening section of the Fourteenth Amendment were intended to reach only positive acts of State authorities derogatory of the rights protected by the amendment—not acts of private individuals or acts of omission by the State itself. In the case of Truax *v.* Corrigan,[3] on the other hand, which was decided in 1921, the Court declared that the same clauses require a certain minimum of protection from the State for all classes and persons. In 1966, to the argument that "an exercise of congressional power under § 5 of the Fourteenth Amendment that prohibits the enforcement of a state law can only be sustained if the judicial branch determines that the state law is prohibited by the provisions of the Amendment that Congress sought to enforce," the Court said "We disagree. Neither the language nor history of § 5 supports such a construction. . . . 'Congress is authorized to *enforce* the prohibitions by appropriate legislation. Such legislation is contemplated to make the amendment fully effective.' A construction of § 5 that would require a judicial determination that the enforcement of the state law precluded by Congress violated the Amendment, as a condition of sustaining the congressional enactment, would depreciate both congressional resourcefulness and congressional responsibility for implementing the legislative power in this context to the insignificant role of abrogating only those state laws that the judicial branch was prepared to adjudge unconstitutional, or of merely informing the judgment of the judiciary by particularizing the 'majestic generalities' of § 1 of the Amendment."[4]

Nor is it only the Equal Protection Clause which Congress is empowered to implement by "appropriate legislation," but all the "provisions of this article." The outstanding legislation having this purpose was first enacted in 1866 and, as since amended, appears today in Title 18 of the United States Code.[5] It reads thus: "Whoever, under color of any law, statute, ordinance, regulation, or custom, willfully subjects . . . any inhabitant of any State, Territory, or District to the deprivation of any rights, privileges, or immunities secured or protected by the Constitution and laws of the United States, or to different punishments, pains, or penalties, on account of such inhabitant

3 257 U.S. 312 (1921).
4 Katzenbach *v.* Morgan, 384 U.S. 641, 648-649 (1966).
5 18 U.S.C. 242. *See also* 18 U.S.C. 371.

being an alien, or by reason of his color, or race, than are pre-scribed for the punishment of citizens shall be fined not more than $1,000, or imprisoned not more than one year, or both."

Re-suscitation of this Power After lying dormant for many years, this provision was re-suscitated and reanimated in 1941 by the decision in the *Classic* case (*see* p. 431). It was given added vitality by the Court's decision in the attention-getting case, Screws *v.* United States.[6] Speaking for the Court, Justice Douglas re-cited the circumstances of a case of extreme and wanton bru-tality by a Georgia sheriff and two assistants in effecting the arrest of a young Negro, who died in consequence of this treatment.

Screws and his co-defendants were indicted for having, un-der color of the laws of Georgia, "willfully" caused Hall to be deprived of "rights, privileges, or immunities secured or pro-tected" to him by the Fourteenth Amendment—the right not to be deprived of life without due process of law; the right to be tried upon the charge on which he was arrested by due process of law, and if found guilty to be punished in accord-ance with the laws of Georgia.

While the indictment was held to fall within the terms of the Federal law quoted above, the conviction of Screws and his companions was reversed on the ground that the trial judge should have charged the jury that to convict they must find the accused to have had the *"specific* intention" of depriving Hall of his constitutional rights. This charge being given in a sec-ond trial, the jury acquitted. Later decisions, however, quali-fied the requirement of "specific intention" with the doctrine of the common law, that "the intent is presumed and inferred from the result of the action."[7]

Significantly (and curiously in view of the Court's position with respect to Congress's power under the Thirteenth Amendment; *see* pp. 383-384), the Court in 1971 seemed to go out of its way to avoid deciding that Congress could impose liabilities on private persons under the Fourteenth Amend-ment. Because the case involved an assault on travelers on the highway, the Court was able to hold that "Our cases have firm-ly established that the right of interstate travel is constitution-

[6] 325 U.S. 91 (1945).
[7] *See* Williams *v.* U.S. 341 U.S. 97 (1951); Koehler *v.* U.S., 342 U.S. 852 (1951); *also* Robert L. Hale, "Unconstitutional Acts as Federal Crimes," 60 *Harvard Law Review*, 65 (1946). *But see* Griffin *v.* Breckenridge, 403 U.S. 88, 102 note 10 (1971).

ally protected, does not necessarily rest on the Fourteenth Amendment, and is assertable against private as well as governmental interference. . . ."[8] *(See* pp. 209-210.)

To emphasize its point, the Court concluded with this statement: "More specifically, the allegations of the complaint in this case have not required consideration of the scope of the power of Congress under § 5 of the Fourteenth Amendment."[9] A clue as to what bothered the Court about deciding once and for all and in the broadest terms, that the Fourteenth Amendment permitted Congress to reach private action can be found in the fears it expressed about having the particular law involved in the case become a general Federal tort law: "The constitutional shoals that would lie in the path of interpreting [the law] as a general federal tort law can be avoided. . . ."[10] The implication seems to be that unless the Court is careful in finding power for Congress under the Fourteenth Amendment, Congress could become involved in regulation of activities which have normally been regarded as State matters. The Court referred, for example, to punishing an assault committed by two or more persons within a State.[11] But the Court's own language in the case suggests that such fears are exaggerated. After all, the only warrant for Congressional action even under a broadened scope for § 5 would be that it comported with the purpose of the Fourteenth Amendment—to end invidious discrimination. It is one thing for Congress to pass a law making it a Federal crime to assault someone in an effort to keep him from exercising a constitutional right; it is quite another for Congress to attempt to pass a law making a simple assault occurring within a State a Federal crime.[12]

8 Griffin *v.* Breckenridge, 403 U.S. 88, 105 (1971).
9 *Ibid.*, 107.  10 *Ibid.*, 101.  11 *Ibid.*
12 *See* Justice Black's words in Oregon *v.* Mitchell, 400 U.S. 112, 128 (1970).

## SECTION I

The right of citizens of the United States to vote shall not be denied or abridged by the United States or by any State on account of race, color or previous condition of servitude.

An Affirmative Grant of Rights

At the outset the Court emphasized only the negative aspects of this amendment. "The Fifteenth Amendment," it asserted, did "not confer the right ... [to vote] upon any one," but merely "invested the citizens of the United States with a new constitutional right which is ... exemption from discrimination in the exercise of the elective franchise on account of race, color, or previous condition of servitude."[1] Within less than ten years, however, in *ex parte* Yarbrough,[2] the Court ventured to read into the amendment an affirmative as well as a negative purpose. Conceding "that this article" had originally been construed as giving "no affirmative right to the colored man to vote," and as having been "designed primarily to prevent discrimination against him," Justice Miller, in behalf of his colleagues, conceded "that under some circumstances it may operate as the immediate source of a right to vote. In all cases where the former slave-holding States had not removed from their Constitutions the words 'white man' as a qualification for voting, this provision did, in effect, confer on him the right to vote, because ... it annulled the discriminating word *white*, and thus left him in the enjoyment of the same right as white persons. And such would be the effect of any future constitutional provision of a State which should give the right of voting exclusively to white people, ... "

Disallowance of Nullifying Expedients

The early history (i.e. before 1957) of the Fifteenth Amendment was largely a record of belated judicial condemnation of various attempts by States to disfranchise the Negro either overtly through statutory enactment, or covertly through inequitable administration of their electoral laws or by toleration of discriminatory membership practices of political parties. Of several such devices, one of the first to be held uncon-

[1] United States *v.* Reese, 92 U.S. 214, 217-218 (1876); United States *v.* Cruikshank, 92 U.S. 542, 556 (1876).

[2] 110 U.S. 651, 665 (1884); citing Neal *v.* Delaware, 103 U.S. 370, 389 (1881). This affirmative view was later reiterated in Guinn & Beal *v.* U.S., 238 U.S. 347, 363 (1915).

stitutional was the "grandfather clause." Without expressly disfranchising the Negro, but with a view to facilitating the permanent placement of white residents on the voting lists while continuing to interpose severe obstacles upon Negroes seeking qualification as voters, several States, beginning in 1895, enacted temporary laws whereby persons who were voters, or descendants of voters on January 1, 1867, could be registered notwithstanding their inability to meet any literacy requirements. Unable because of the date to avail themselves of the same exemption, Negroes were thus left exposed to disfranchisement on grounds of illiteracy while whites no less illiterate were enabled to become permanent voters. With the achievement of this intended result, most States permitted their laws to lapse; but Oklahoma's grandfather clause was enacted as a permanent amendment to the State constitution; and when presented with an opportunity to pass on its validity, a unanimous Court condemned the standard of voting thus established as recreating and perpetuating "the very conditions which the [Fifteenth] Amendment was intended to destroy."[3] Nor, when Oklahoma in 1916 followed up this defeat with a statute which provided that all persons, except those who voted in 1914, who were qualified to vote in 1916 but who failed to register between April 30 and May 11, 1916 should be perpetually disfranchised, did the Court experience any difficulty in holding the same to be repugnant to the amendment.[4] That amendment, Justice Frankfurter declared, "nullifies sophisticated as well as simple-minded modes of discrimination. It hits onerous procedural requirements which effectively handicap exercise of the franchise by the colored race although the abstract right to vote may remain unrestricted as to race."[5]

When, however, it was first called upon to deal with the exclusion of Negroes from participation in primary elections, the Court displayed indecision. Prior to its becoming convinced that primary contests were in fact elections,[6] the Court had relied upon the Equal Protection Clause to strike down a Texas White Primary Law[7] and a subsequent Texas statute which

*Primaries as Elections*

---

[3] Guinn & Beal *v.* U.S., 238 U.S. 347, 360, 363-364 (1915).
[4] Lane *v.* Wilson, 307 U.S. 268 (1939).
[5] *Ibid.*, 275.
[6] United States *v.* Classic, 313 U.S. 299 (1941); Smith *v.* Allwright, 321 U.S. 649 (1944).
[7] Nixon *v.* Herndon, 273 U.S. 536 (1927).

contributed to a like exclusion by limiting voting in primaries to members of State political parties as determined by the central committees thereof.[8] When exclusion of Negroes was thereafter maintained by political parties acting not in obedience to any statutory command, this discrimination was for a time viewed as not constituting State action and so as not prohibited by either the Fourteenth or the Fifteenth Amendments.[9] Nine years later this holding was reversed when the Court, in Smith v. Allwright,[10] declared that where the selection of candidates for public office is entrusted by statute to political parties, a political party in making its selection at a primary election is a State agency, and hence may not under this amendment exclude Negroes from such elections.

Initially the Court held that literacy tests drafted so as to apply alike to all applicants for the voting franchise would be deemed to be fair on their face, and in the absence of proof of discriminatory enforcement could not be viewed as denying the equal protection of the laws guaranteed by the Fourteenth Amendment.[11] Later however, the Boswell amendment to the constitution of Alabama, which provided that only persons who understood and could explain the Constitution of the United States to the reasonable satisfaction of boards of registrars, was found, both in its object as well as in the manner of its administration, to be contrary to the Fifteenth Amendment. The legislative history of the Alabama provision disclosed, said the Court, that "the ambiguity inherent in the phrase 'understand and explain' . . . was purposeful . . . and . . . intended as a grant of arbitrary power in an attempt to obviate the consequences of" Smith v. Allwright.[12]

8 Nixon v. Condon, 286 U.S. 73, 89 (1932).
9 Grovey v. Townsend, 295 U.S. 45, 55 (1935).
10 321 U.S. 649 (1944). Notwithstanding that the South Carolina Legislature, after the decision in Smith v. Allwright, repealed all statutory provisions regulating primary elections and political organizations conducting them, a political party thus freed of control is not to be regarded as a private club and for that reason exempt from the constitutional prohibitions against racial discrimination contained in Amendment XV. Rice v. Elmore, 165 F. 2d. 387 (1947); cert. denied, 333 U.S. 875 (1948). A South Carolina political party, which excluded Negroes from membership, required that white as well as Negro qualified voters, as a prerequisite for voting in its primary, take an oath that they would support separation of the races. Not surprisingly, this ingenious (?) maneuver was held void. Terry v. Adams, 345 U.S. 461 (1953).
11 Williams v. Miss., 170 U.S. 213, 220 (1898).
12 Davis v. Schnell, 81 F. Supp. 872, 878, 880 (1949); affirmed, 336 U.S. 933 (1949).

Starting in 1957, Congress has taken a strong, positive, and leading role in the effort to vindicate voting rights, as will be shown below.

## SECTION II

The Congress shall have power to enforce this article by appropriate legislation.

In the protection of the right conferred by this amendment Congress passed the Enforcement Act of 1870, which, however, was largely nullified by a Supreme Court decision in 1876.[1] Congress finally endeavored to remedy the situation by enacting the Civil Rights Act of 1957. The measure created a Commission on Civil Rights, whose duty it is to investigate allegations that certain citizens of the United States are being deprived of the right to vote and have their votes counted on account of race, color, religion or national origin; and, when such allegations are found to be substantiated, the Attorney General may institute "a civil action or other proper proceeding for preventive relief," including under some circumstances prosecutions for criminal contempt by a judge acting without a jury.[2] (*See* p. 163.)

Continued State resistance forced Congress to seek constantly new and ingenious ways to vindicate the right to vote.[3] For example, in 1964 Congress made it a presumption (albeit a rebuttable presumption) "that any person who has not been adjudged an incompetent and who has completed the sixth grade in a public school . . . possesses sufficient intelligence to vote in any Federal election."[4] The purpose, of course, was to make it easier to register large numbers of voters quickly and put the burden on the States to show that particular individuals were not qualified after they were registered. More powerful medicine was administered by Congress in 1965. For example, the law passed that year contains this provision: "If in

---

[1] In the early case of United States *v.* Reese, 92 U.S. 214, 218 (1876), the Enforcement Act of 1870 (16 *Stat.* 140), which penalized State officers for refusing to receive the vote of any qualified citizen, was held to be constitutionally inapplicable to support a prosecution of such officers for having prevented a qualified Negro from voting.

[2] 71 *Stat.* 634 (1957).

[3] 74 *Stat.* 88 (1969); 78 *Stat.* 241 (1964); 79 *Stat.* 437 (1965). For a good, concise description of this effort, see 2 *U.S. Cong. & Admin. News*, 2437-2582 (1965).

[4] 78 *Stat.* 241 (1964).

a proceeding instituted by the Attorney General under any statute to enforce the guarantees of the fifteenth amendment in any State . . . the court finds that a test or device has been used for the purpose or with the effect of denying or abridging the right of any citizen . . . to vote on account of race or color, it shall suspend the use of tests and devices in such State . . . as the court shall determine is appropriate and for such period as it deems necessary."[5]

Then, in a provision which seems drastic on its face, Congress sought to put an end to State ingenuity in seeking new ways to restrict voting. States enacting or seeking "to administer any voting qualification . . . different from that in force or effect on November 1, 1964" are required literally to obtain approval by Federal authorities.[6] These Congressional efforts were, of course, challenged on constitutional grounds, but such challenges were unsuccessful.[7] But even so stout a protagonist of Civil Rights as Justice Black expressed concern about a "federal law which assumes the power to compel the States to submit in advance any proposed legislation they have for approval by federal agents." He said it "approaches dangerously near to wiping the States out as useful and effective units in the government of our country. I cannot agree to any constitutional interpretation that leads inevitably to such a result."[8] The majority held otherwise, however, concluding that "In the oft-repeated words of Chief Justice Marshall, referring to another specific legislative authorization in the Constitution, 'This power, like all others vested in Congress, is complete in itself, may be exercised to its utmost extent and acknowledges no limitations other than are prescribed in the constitution.' "[9]

Nor was the majority being cavalier in its holding. They recited the problems Congress had faced in attempting to vindicate voting rights and indicated the need for inventiveness: "Congress exercised its authority under the Fifteenth Amendment in an inventive manner when it enacted the Voting Rights Act of 1965. First: The measure prescribes remedies for voting discrimination which go into effect without any need for prior adjudication. This was clearly a legitimate response

---

[5] 79 *Stat.* 437 (1965).
[6] *Ibid.*, 439.
[7] South Carolina *v.* Katzenbach, 383 U.S. 301 (1966) and cases cited at 326; Katzenbach *v.* Morgan, 384 U.S. 641 (1966).
[8] South Carolina *v.* Katzenbach, 383 U.S. 301, 360 (1966).
[9] *Ibid.*, 327.

to the problem, for which there is ample precedent under other constitutional provisions. . . . Congress had found that case-by-case litigation was inadequate to combat widespread and persistent discrimination in voting, because of the inordinate amount of time and energy required to overcome the obstructionist tactics invariably encountered in these lawsuits. After enduring nearly a century of systematic resistance to the Fifteenth Amendment, Congress might well decide to shift the advantage of time and inertia from the perpetrators of the evil to its victims. The question remains, of course, whether the specific remedies prescribed in the Act were an appropriate means of combatting the evil, and to this question we shall presently address ourselves."[10]

In 1970 Congress amended the Voting Rights Act by banning until August 6, 1975, a literacy test in any national, State, or local election in any area of the United States where such a test is not already prescribed by the basic acts.[11] The Court unanimously upheld the constitutionality of that provision.[12]

[10] *Ibid.*       [11] 84 *Stat.* 314 (1970).
[12] Oregon *v.* Mitchell, 400 U.S. 112, 118 (1970).

# AMENDMENT XVI

A Judicial
Decision
"Re-
called" The Congress shall have power to lay and collect taxes on incomes, from whatever source derived, without apportionment among the several States, and without regard to any census or enumeration.

The ratification of this amendment was the direct consequence of the decision in 1895[1] whereby the attempt of Congress the previous year to tax incomes uniformly throughout the United States[2] was held by a divided court to be unconstitutional. A tax on incomes derived from property,[3] the Court declared, was a "direct tax" which Congress under the terms of Article I, Section II, clause 3, and Section XI, clause 4, could impose only by the rule of apportionment according to population; although scarcely fifteen years prior the Justices had unanimously sustained[4] the collection of a similar tax during the Civil War.[5]

Decisions Undermining the Pollack Case During the interim between the *Pollock* decision in 1895, and the ratification of the Sixteenth Amendment in 1913, the Court gave evidence of a growing awareness of the dangerous consequences to national solvency which that holding threatened, and partially circumvented it, either by taking refuge in redefinitions of "direct tax" or, and more especially, by emphasizing, virtually to the exclusion of the former, the history of excise taxation. In a series of cases, including Nicol v. Ames,[6] Knowlton v. Moore,[7] and Patton v. Brady,[8] the Court held the following taxes to have been levied merely upon one of the "incidents of ownership" and hence to be excises: a tax which involved affixing revenue stamps to memoranda evidencing the sale of merchandise on commodity exchanges, an inheritance tax, and a war revenue tax upon tobacco on which the hitherto imposed excise tax had already been paid and which was held by the manufacturer for resale.

[1] Pollock v. Farmers' Loan & Trust Co., 157 U.S. 429 (1895); 158 U.S. 601 (1895).

[2] 28 *Stat.* 509.

[3] The Court conceded that taxes on incomes from "professions, trades, employments, or vocations" levied by this act were excise taxes and therefore valid. The entire statute, however, was voided on the ground that Congress never intended to permit the entire "burden of the tax to be borne by professions, trades, employments, or vocations" after real estate and personal property had been exempted. 158 U.S. 601, 635 (1895).

[4] Springer v. U.S., 102 U.S. 586 (1881).

[5] 13 *Stat.* 223 (1864).

[6] 173 U.S. 509 (1899).     [7] 178 U.S. 41 (1900).     [8] 184 U.S. 608 (1902).

Thanks to these endeavors, the Court found it possible in 1911 to sustain a corporate income tax as an excise "measured by income" on the privilege of doing business in corporate form.[9] But while the adoption of the Sixteenth Amendment put a stop to speculation whether the Court would not eventually overrule *Pollock,* it is interesting to note that in its initial appraisal of the amendment it characterized income taxes as "inherently indirect" and hence subject to the rule of uniformity, the same as excises, duties and imports until they were "removed" therefrom and "placed under the direct class"—removed, that is, by the Court itself.[10]

Building upon definitions formulated in cases construing the Corporation Tax Act of 1909, the Court initially described income as the "gain derived from capital, from labor, or from both combined," inclusive of the "profit gained through a sale or conversion of capital assets."[11] Moreover, any gain not accruing prior to 1913 was held to be taxable income for the year in which it was realized by sale or conversion of the property to which it had accrued;[12] while corporate dividends in the shape of money or of the stock of another corporation were held to be taxable income of the stockholder for the year in which he received them, regardless of when the profits against which they were voted had accrued to the corporation.[13] A stock dividend issued against a corporate surplus, however, was held not to be "income" in the hands of the stockholder, since it left the stockholder's share of the surplus still under the control of the corporate management.[14] That decision, of course, narrowed the definition of "income" and has proved troublesome.[15] Nor has Congress in its efforts to mitigate the troubles been free to ignore the Court's holding for as the

*The Court's Interpretation of Amendment XVI*

[9] Flint *v.* Stone Tracey Co., 220 U.S. 107 (1911).
[10] Brushaber *v.* Union Pac. R. Co., 240 U.S. 1, 18-19 (1916). *See also* Stanton *v.* Baltic Min. Co., 240 U.S. 103, 112 (1916).
[11] Stratton's Independence *v.* Howbert, 231 U.S. 399, 415 (1914); Doyle *v.* Mitchell Bros. Co., 247 U.S. 179 (1918).
[12] Eisner *v.* Macomber, 252 U.S. 189 (1920); Bowers *v.* Kerbaugh-Empire Co., 271 U.S. 170 (1926).
[13] Lynch *v.* Hornby, 247 U.S. 339 (1918).
[14] Eisner *v.* Macomber, cited above. Helvering *v.* Griffiths, 318 U.S. 371 (1943), which maintained the rule laid down in Eisner *v.* Macomber, was based immediately on 53 *Stat.* 1, Sect. 115a (1): *see also* Moline Properties, Inc. *v.* Com'r of Int. Rev., 319 U.S. 436 (1943), where the corporate entity conception, which is basic to the decision in the *Eisner* holding, is endorsed. For recent citations to *Eisner see* Connor *v.* U.S., 439 F. 2d. 974, 980 (1971) and cases cited therein; Kem *v.* C.I.R., 432 F. 2d. 961, 962 (1970).
[15] *Ibid. Also* U.S. *v.* Davis, 397 U.S. 301, 308-311 (1970).

Court said in that decision: "Congress cannot by any definition it may adopt conclude the matter, since it cannot by legislation alter the Constitution, from which alone it derives its power to legislate, and within whose limitations alone that power can be lawfully exercised." That decision laid down in 1920 is still good law,[16] and Congress has endeavored to get around it by shifting liability from stockholders to the corporations.[17]

Although empowered to tax incomes "from whatever source derived," Congress is not precluded from leaving some incomes untaxed.[18] Conversely, it may "condition, limit or deny deductions from gross income to arrive at the net that it chooses to tax";[19] and in 1927 the Court ruled that gains derived from illicit traffic in liquor were taxable income under the Act of 1921.[20] Said Justice Holmes for the unanimous Court: "We see no reason . . . why the fact that a business is unlawful should exempt it from paying the taxes that if lawful it would have to pay."[21] However, in Commissioner v. Wilcox,[22] decided in 1946, Justice Murphy, speaking for a majority of the Court, held that embezzled money was not taxable income to the embezzler, although any gain he derived from the use of it would be. Justice Burton dissented on the basis of the Sullivan case; and in 1952, a sharply divided court, cutting loose from the metaphysics of the Wilcox case, held that Congress had the power under Amendment XVI to tax as income monies received by an extortioner.[23] In 1961, the Court expressly overruled Wilcox.[24]

While Congress's power to tax incomes is relieved by this amendment from the rule of apportionment, it still remains subject to the Due Process Clause of Amendment V, which would forbid any obviously arbitrary classification for this purpose. Thus an act of Congress which taxed incomes of Republicans at a higher rate than those of Democrats would, presumably, be invalid. But incomes of corporate persons may be

16 See notes 14 and 15 above.
17 Motor Fuel Carriers Inc. v. U.S., 420 F. 2d. 702, 704 (1970).
18 Brushaber v. Union Pac. R. Co., 240 U.S. 1 (1916); Moritz v. C.I.R., 55 T.C. 113, 115 (1970); Shinder v. C.I.R., 395 F. 2d. 222 (1968).
19 Helvering v. Independent L. Ins. Co., 292 U.S. 371, 381 (1934); Helvering v. Winmill, 305 U.S. 79, 84 (1938); Moritz v. C.I.R., 55 T.C. 113, 115 (1970); Shinder v. C.I.R., 395 F. 2d. 223 (1968).
20 United States v. Sullivan, 274 U.S. 259 (1927).
21 Ibid., 263.          22 327 U.S. 404 (1946).
23 Rutkin v. U.S., 343 U.S. 130 (1952).
24 James v. U.S., 366 U.S. 213 (1961). See also Urban v. U.S., 445 F. 2d. 641 (1971).

taxed on a different basis than those of natural persons, and large incomes may be, and are, taxed at progressively higher rates than smaller incomes. Also, Congress may, in order to compel corporations to distribute their profits and thereby render them taxable in the hands of stockholders, levy a special tax on such accumulated profits in the hands of the corporation, without transcending its powers under the Sixteenth Amendment,[25] or violating the Fifth Amendment. And Congress without violating the Fifth Amendment "may provide for retroactive operation of income tax legislation."[26]

The question has been occasionally mooted whether the separate incomes of a husband and wife may be taxed as one joint income and so, in effect, at a *higher rate* than incomes of the same size of unmarried persons, the tax being "progressive." Some years ago the Court overturned a Wisconsin tax of this description on the ground that the Due Process Clause of Amendment XIV forbade the taxation of one person's income or property by reference to those of another person. Three Justices, however, dissented in an opinion by Justice Holmes, which argued that such a tax was constitutional, first, in the light of "a thousand years of history," the reference being to the common law doctrine that the income and property of the wife were at the disposal of the husband; secondly, because husbands and wives do actually get the benefit of one another's income; thirdly, as a means of avoiding tax evasions.[27] The second and third reasons, at least, are persuasive that such a classification for purposes of income taxation would not be so utterly unreasonable as to fall under the ban of the Fifth Amendment, which, it should be remembered, does not contain an Equal Protection Clause, and a later decision which held that the entire value of a "community property" (property held in common by husband and wife) may be subjected to the Federal estate tax upon the death of either spouse, confirms this conclusion.[28]

It should be understood that as a general proposition most income tax litigation does not involve constitutional questions and, when it is contended that it does, the "long established

[25] Helvering *v.* National Grocery Co., 304 U.S. 282 (1938); Helvering *v.* National Steel Rolling Mills, Inc., 311 U.S. 46 (1940); Motor Fuel Carriers Inc. *v.* U.S., 420 F. 2d. 702, 704 (1970) and cases cited therein.
[26] Shanahan *v.* U.S., 447 F. 2d. 1082 (1971) and cases cited therein.
[27] Hoeper *v.* Tax Com. of Wis., 284 U.S. 206 (1931).
[28] Fernandez *v.* Wiener, 326 U.S. 340 (1945).

policy of the Court" is to defer, "where possible, to Congressional procedures in the tax field."[29]

As indicated earlier the requirement to keep tax records does not offend the Fifth Amendment's privilege against self-incrimination (p. 324). Recently, a Federal Court held that an embezzler was required to report embezzlement income despite his Fifth Amendment right not to be compelled to be a witness against himself.[30]

[29] Schlude *v.* C.I.R., 372 U.S. 129, 135 (1963).
[30] U.S. *v.* Milder, 329 F. Supp. 759 (1971).

# AMENDMENT XVII

¶1. The Senate of the United States shall be composed of two Senators from each State, elected by the people thereof, for six years; and each Senator shall have one vote. The electors in each State shall have the qualifications requisite for electors of the most numerous branch of the State legislatures.

¶2. When vacancies happen in the representation of any State in the Senate, the executive authority of such State shall issue writs of election to fill such vacancies: *Provided,* That the legislature of any State may empower the executive thereof to make temporary appointments until the people fill the vacancies by election as the legislature may direct.

¶3. This amendment shall not be so construed as to affect the election or term of any Senator chosen before it becomes valid as part of the Constitution.

This amendment, as was noted before, supersedes Article I, Section III, ¶1. Very shortly after its ratification the point was established that if a person possessed the qualifications requisite for voting for a Senator, his right to vote for such an officer was not derived merely from the constitution and laws of the State in which they are chosen but has its foundation in the Constitution of the United States.[1] Consistently with this view, Federal courts years ago declared that when local party authorities, acting pursuant to regulations prescribed by a party's State executive committee, refused to permit a Negro, on account of his race, to vote in a primary to select candidates for the office of United States Senator, they deprived him of a right secured to him by the Constitution and laws, in violation of this amendment.[2]

The politics of New York State gave rise to two recent cases involving interpretation of the Seventeenth Amendment. When Senator James Buckley won only a plurality in the three-cornered 1970 Senate race, the Committee for Fair Play for Voters went to Federal court contending that their right

[1] United States v. Aczel, 219 F. 917 (1915), citing *ex parte* Yarbrough, 110 U.S. 651 (1884).
[2] Chapman v. King, 154 F. 2d. 460 (1946); *cert. denied,* 327 U.S. 800 (1946).

under the Seventeenth Amendment "to be represented by a senator who is elected by a majority vote" had been abridged, they sought a run-off between the top two candidates. The court held that the Seventeenth Amendment contained no provision that a Senator must win a majority of the vote.[3]

When Senator Robert F. Kennedy was assassinated on June 6, 1968, groups of New York voters brought three suits seeking to have the vacancy filled in the November 1968 election. Under New York law, if there was less than 60 days left prior to New York's regular spring primary in an even-numbered year, the vacancy was to be filled by election in the next even-numbered year, which in this situation was November 1970. In the meantime, the Governor was empowered to make a temporary appointment. The Court held that "the Seventeenth Amendment's vacancy provision explicitly confers upon state legislatures discretion concerning the timing of vacancy elections" and dismissed the complaints.[4]

---

[3] Phillips *v.* Rockefeller, 321 F. Supp. 516 (1970), *affirmed*, 435 F. 2d. 976 (1970).
[4] Valenti *v.* Rockefeller, 292 F. Supp. 851 (1968), *affirmed*, 393 U.S. 405 (1969), *rehearing denied*, 393 U.S. 1124 (1969).

# AMENDMENT XVIII

## SECTION I

After one year from the ratification of this article the manufacture, sale or transportation of intoxicating liquors within, the importation thereof into, or the exportation thereof from the United States and all territory subject to the jurisdiction thereof for beverage purposes is hereby prohibited.

## SECTION II

The Congress and the several States shall have concurrent power to enforce this article by appropriate legislation.

## SECTION III

This article shall be inoperative unless it shall have been ratified as an amendment to the Constitution by the Legislatures of the several States, as provided in the Constitution, within seven years from the date of the submission hereof to the States by the Congress.

This final section was no proper part of the amendment but was really a part of the Congressional resolution of submission, and was rightly so treated by the Supreme Court.[1] How, indeed, could an inoperative amendment operate to render itself inoperative?

The entire amendment was repealed in 1933 by the Twenty-first Amendment (*see* below, pp. 448-449). Some of the questions, however, which were raised under Article V and the Fourth and Fifth Amendments by the efforts, first to enforce, and then to get rid of, National Prohibition, contributed significantly to the development of the meaning of those two amendments.[2]

In 1934, the Supreme Court held that "Upon ratification of the Twenty-first Amendment, the Eighteenth Amendment became inoperative. Neither the Congress nor the courts could give it continued vitality. The National Prohibition Act, to the extent that its provisions rested upon grant of authority to the Congress by the Eighteenth Amendment, immediately fell

[1] Dillon *v.* Gloss, 256 U.S. 368 (1921).
[2] Amos *v.* U.S., 255 U.S. 313 (1921); Carroll *v.* U.S., 267 U.S. 132 (1925); Taylor *v.* U.S., 286 U.S. 1 (1932); Hester *v.* U.S., 265 U.S. 57 (1924); Olmstead *v.* U.S., 277 U.S. 438 (1928).

with the withdrawal by the people of the essential constitutional support."[3] Consequently, even prosecution for acts committed while the law was in force could not be prosecuted after the date of adoption of the new amendment. "In case a statute is repealed or rendered inoperative, no further proceedings can be had to enforce it in pending prosecutions unless competent authority has kept the statute alive for that purpose."

[3] U.S. *v.* Chambers, 291 U.S. 217, 222-223 (1934).

# AMENDMENT XIX

The right of citizens of the United States to vote shall not be denied or abridged by the United States or by any State on account of sex.

Congress shall have power to enforce this article by appropriate legislation.

This amendment, which consummated a reform that had been long under way in the States, was passed by the House on May 21, 1919, and by the Senate on June 4, 1919. It was ratified by the required number of States in time for the Presidential election November 1920. An objection that the amendment by enlarging the electorate without a State's consent, destroyed its autonomy and hence exceeded the amending power, was overruled by the Court by pointing to the precedent created by the adoption of the Fifteenth Amendment.[1]

The Nineteenth Amendment has given rise to some novel contentions in Federal and State courts in recent years. One woman, protesting that there were only males on the ballot, contended that she had the right "to vote only for women candidates, and to withhold her vote from male candidates";[2] a seventeen-year-old male contended that a State delinquency law which defined a delinquent child as a male under 16 and a female under 18 years of age violated the Nineteenth Amendment.[3] The courts have made short shrift of such arguments. But a Federal court did give broader meaning to the Amendment than appears called for by its words in saying "Whatever the ancient doctrine [of domicile], a wife is capable of acquiring a domicile separate from that of her husband; at least to this extent legal equality of the sexes is embodied in the Fourteenth and Nineteenth Amendments."[4]

Patently, as a weapon against State discriminations other than on the basic right to vote, the Fourteenth Amendment is more effective than the Nineteenth Amendment.

[1] Leser v. Garnett, 258 U.S. 130 (1922).

[2] Boineau v. Thornton, 235 F. Supp. 175 (1964); affirmed, 379 U.S. 15 (1964).

[3] Coyle v. Oklahoma, 489 P. 2d. 223 (1971); Benson v. Oklahoma, 488 P. 2d. 383 (1971).

[4] Spindel v. Spindel, 283 F. Supp. 797 (1968).

# AMENDMENT XX

## SECTION I

The terms of the President and Vice-President shall end at noon on the 20th day of January, and the terms of Senators and Representatives at noon on the 3d day of January, of the years in which such terms would have ended if this article had not been ratified; and the terms of their successors shall then begin.

## SECTION II

The Congress shall assemble at least once in every year, and such meeting shall begin at noon on the 3d day of January, unless they shall by law appoint a different day.

## SECTION III

If, at the time fixed for the beginning of the term of the President, the President-elect shall have died, the Vice-President-elect shall become President. If a President shall not have been chosen before the time fixed for the beginning of his term or if the President-elect shall have failed to qualify, then the Vice-President-elect shall act as President until a President shall have qualified; and the Congress may by law provide for the case wherein neither a President-elect nor a Vice-President-elect shall have qualified, declaring who shall then act as President, or the manner in which one who is to act shall be selected, and such person shall act accordingly until a President or Vice-President shall have qualified.

## SECTION IV

The Congress may by law provide for the case of the death of any of the persons from whom the House of Representatives may choose a President whenever the right of choice shall have devolved upon them and for the case of death of any of the persons from whom the Senate may choose a Vice-President whenever the right of choice shall have devolved upon them.

## SECTION V

Sections 1 and 2 shall take effect on the 15th day of October following the ratification of this article.

## SECTION VI

This article shall be inoperative unless it shall have been ratified as an amendment to the Constitution by the legislatures of three-fourths of the several States within seven years from the date of its submission.

This, the so-called Norris "Lame Duck" Amendment, was proposed by Congress March 2, 1932, to the legislatures of the States, and was proclaimed by the Secretary of State February 6, 1933, having then been ratified by 39 States. By October 15, 1933, it had been ratified by all the States. Its primary purpose was to eliminate the so-called short session of Congress which used to follow after an election and in which defeated Congressmen ("Lame Ducks") participated. A constitutional amendment was required because adoption of the Amendment did in fact shorten the full constitutional terms of the President, Vice President, and Congressmen then in office.[1] The original date selected and used before this amendment, of course, reflected the rudimentary state of communications and transportation of a much earlier day.[2] (*See* p. 113.)

Congress has fulfilled its obligations under Section III by enacting from time to time legislation dealing with Presidential succession.[3] The latest version provides among other things that where a President-elect is not qualified the Speaker of the House will act as President until a President or Vice President qualifies.[4] One can only shudder at a prospect possible under the amendment and the law. Suppose an election goes to the House for resolution under the Twelfth Amendment and a wrangle ensues and for weeks none of the three candidates from which the House must select can command the necessary vote to be qualified (nor can a Vice President be chosen). Suppose a large number of the members of the House prefer the Speaker to the regular candidates! What would be their incentive to settle the election and qualify a President?[5]

---

[1] U.S., 72d Cong., 1st Sess., Senate, Report No. 26 (1932).
[2] *Ibid.*          [3] 3 U.S.C. 19.          [4] *Ibid.*
[5] 1947 *U.S. Cong. Serv.* 1310; Edward S. Corwin, *The President, Office and Powers*, pp. 56-58.

# AMENDMENT XXI

## SECTION I

The eighteenth article of amendment to the Constitution of the United States is hereby repealed.

## SECTION II

The transportation or importation into any State, Territory, or possession of the United States for delivery or use therein of intoxicating liquors, in violation of the laws thereof, is hereby prohibited.

## SECTION III

This article shall be inoperative unless it shall have been ratified as an amendment to the Constitution by conventions in the several States, as provided in the Constitution, within seven years from the date of the submission hereof to the States by the Congress.

This amendment was proposed by Congress February 20, 1933, to conventions to be called in the several States, and was proclaimed to be in effect December 5 of the same year, having been ratified by 36 States, a record for celerity.

Decisions Interpreting the Amendment Decisions interpreting the amendment to date fall into two general categories: decisions which assert the unlimited character of State power within the precincts marked out by Section II; decisions which define those precincts with greater particularity. On the one hand, the Court has said, the amendment authorizes a State to impose a license fee upon the importation into it of liquor from without;[1] to discriminate as to what liquors it shall permit to be imported;[2] to retaliate against such discriminations;[3] and in general to legislate, unfettered by "traditional Commerce Clause limitations" or any other clause of the Constitution, respecting liquor introduced into it from without.[4] On the other hand, the amendment does not, the Court holds, enable a State to regulate the sale of

[1] State Bd. of Equalization v. Young's Market Co., 299 U.S. 59 (1936).
[2] Mahoney v. Joseph Triner Corp., 304 U.S. 401 (1938).
[3] Indianapolis Brewing Co. v. Liquor Control Com'n of Mich., 305 U.S. 391 (1938).
[4] Hostetter v. Idlewild Bon Voyage Liquor Corp., 377 U.S. 324, 330 (1964); but see Justice Black's dissent, ibid., 334; Ziffrin v. Reeves, 308 U.S. 132 (1939); Joseph E. Seagram & Sons, Inc. v. Hostetter, 384 U.S. 35, 42 (1966).

448

liquor in a national park over which it had ceded jurisdiction to the United States;[5] nor does it disable Congress from regulating the importation of liquors from abroad;[6] nor does it permit a State to tax imported Scotch whiskey still in the original package in the hands of the original importer;[7] nor does it prevent the enforcement of the Sherman Anti-Trust Act against a conspiracy to raise prices;[8] and when a State seeks to control the passage *through* it of liquor coming from another State and destined for a third State, it is no longer exercising any power granted it by the amendment, but its customary police power. Its regulations, therefore, must be "reasonable" in the judgment of the Court, and may be set aside by Congress under the Commerce Clause.[9]

Early in the current term, the Supreme Court rendered its sure-to-be widely talked about "bottomless" dancers decision. Justice Rehnquist, speaking for the Court said: ". . . we conceive the State's authority in the area to be somewhat broader than did the District Court. This is not to say that all such conduct and performance is without the protection of the First and Fourteenth Amendments. But we would poorly serve both the interests for which the State may validly seek vindication and the interests protected by the First and Fourteenth Amendments were we to insist that the sort of Bacchanalian revelries which the Department sought to prevent by these liquor regulations were the constitutional equivalent of a performance by a scantily clad ballet troupe in a theater.

"The Department's conclusion, embodied in these regulations, that certain sexual performances and the dispensation of liquor by the drink ought not to occur simultaneously at premises which have licenses was not an irrational one. Given the added presumption in favor of the validity of the state regulation in this area which the Twenty-first Amendment requires, we cannot hold that the regulations on their face violate the Federal Constitution."[10]

[5] Collins *v.* Yosemite Park and Curry Co., 304 U.S. 518 (1938).
[6] Jameson & Co. *v.* Morgenthau, 307 U.S. 171 (1939); Hostetter *v.* Idlewild Bon Voyage Liquor Corp., 377 U.S. 324 (1964).
[7] Department of Revenue *v.* James Beam Co., 377 U.S. 341 (1964); "The tax here in question is clearly the kind prohibited by the Export-Import Clause [Art. I § 10, ch. 2]," *ibid.*, 343.
[8] Joseph E. Seagram & Sons, Inc. *v.* Hostetter, 384 U.S. 35, 45 (1966).
[9] Duckworth *v.* Ark., 314 U.S. 390 (1941); Carter *v.* Va., 321 U.S. 131 (1944).
[10] California *v.* LaRue, 41 *LW* 4039, 4042 (1972).

# AMENDMENT XXII

No person shall be elected to the office of President more than twice, and no person who has held the office of President, or acted as President, for more than two years of a term to which some other person was elected President shall be elected to the office of President more than once. But this article shall not apply to any person holding the office of President when this article was proposed by the Congress, and shall not prevent any person who may be holding the office of President, or acting as President, during the term within which this article becomes operative from holding the office of President or acting as President during the remainder of such term.

This amendment was proposed by Congress on March 24, 1947; and ratification of it by the required three-fourths of the States was completed on February 27, 1951. On March 1st Jess Larson, Administrator of General Services, certified its adoption.[1] Formerly this service was performed by the Secretary of State.

The Twenty-second Amendment was a response to President Franklin D. Roosevelt's successful defiance of the no third-term tradition. It is difficult to resist the temptation to observe that much of the impetus for the amendment came from Republicans who wanted to punish Roosevelt posthumously.[2] But the debate in Congress which was a prelude to the proposal seems to have been on the merits.[3] There were fears that the amendment would make the President a lame-duck President in the last two years of his second term and less effective. Such does not seem to have happened. As Malcolm Moos, an aide to President Eisenhower, observed, ". . . it may be that the President is using the Twenty-second amendment as a political weapon aimed at Congress. In other words, the President can gain support for his policies because he can convince the people he has nothing to gain personally. The amendment eliminates self-interest."[4] President Lyndon B.

[1] 16 *Fed. Reg.* 2019.
[2] Edward S. Corwin, *The President*, 38; Henry S. Commager, "Only Two Terms for a President?" *New York Times Magazine*, April 27, 1947, p. 73.
[3] Everett S. Brown, "Terms of Office of the President," 41 *American Political Science Review*, 447 (1947).
[4] Malcolm Moos, "The President and the Constitution," 48 *Kentucky Law Journal*, 103, 120 (1959).

Johnson's announcement that he would not run again speaks to the same point.

During the Eisenhower years, there was some effort to repeal the amendment.[5] Such efforts now have abated.

[5] Edward S. Corwin, *The President*, p. 37-38 and 338.

# AMENDMENT XXIII

## SECTION I

The District constituting the seat of Government of the United States shall appoint in such manner as the Congress may direct:

A number of electors of President and Vice President equal to the whole number of Senators and Representatives in Congress to which the District would be entitled if it were a State, but in no event more than the least populous State; they shall be in addition to those appointed by the States, but they shall be considered, for the purposes of the election of President and Vice President, to be electors appointed by a State; and they shall meet in the District and perform such duties as provided by the twelfth article of amendment.

## SECTION II

The Congress shall have power to enforce this article by appropriate legislation.

This Amendment was proposed by Congress in 1960 and was declared by the Administrator of General Services on April 3, 1961, to have been ratified.[1] The clear purpose of the amendment was "to provide the citizens of the District of Columbia with appropriate rights of voting in national elections for President and Vice President of the United States"[2] and was in keeping with the developing ideas of "one man-one vote" of the period. (*See* pp. 419-424.)

[1] U.S.C. Amend. 22.
[2] 1 *U.S. Cong. & Adm. News*, 1459, 1460 (1960).

# AMENDMENT XXIV

## SECTION I

The right of citizens of the United States to vote in any primary or other election for President or Vice President, for electors for President or Vice President, or for Senator or Representative in Congress, shall not be denied or abridged by the United States or any State by reason of failure to pay any poll tax or other tax.

## SECTION II

The Congress shall have power to enforce this article by appropriate legislation.

This amendment was proposed by Congress in 1962 and declared ratified on February 4, 1964.[1]

As the House Report accompanying the proposal indicated: "Federal legislation to eliminate poll taxes, either by constitutional amendment or statute, has been introduced in every Congress since 1939."[2] Yet five States still required the payment of a poll tax by voters. In a test case in 1965, the Supreme Court held that "For federal elections, the poll tax is abolished absolutely as a prerequisite to voting, and no milder substitute may be imposed."[3] When Virginia sought to retain the poll tax for those who vote in State elections, a sharply-divided Court, struck it down in 1966 as a violation of the Equal Protection Clause: "In a recent searching reexamination of the Equal Protection Clause, we held, . . . that 'the opportunity for equal participation by all voters in the election of state legislators' is required. . . . We decline to qualify that principle by sustaining this poll tax."[4]

[1] U.S.C. Amend. 24.
[2] 1962 *U.S. Cong. & Adm. News*, 4033, 4034. *See also* Congressional Quarterly Service, *Congress and the Nation* (Washington, 1969), II, 360 and 353.
[3] Harman *v.* Forssensius, 380 U.S. 528, 542 (1965).
[4] Harper *v.* Virginia Bd. of Elections, 383 U.S. 663 (1966).

# AMENDMENT XXV

## SECTION I

In case of the removal of the President from office or of his death or resignation, the Vice President shall become President.

## SECTION II

Whenever there is a vacancy in the office of the Vice President, the President shall nominate a Vice President who shall take office upon confirmation by a majority vote of both Houses of Congress.

## SECTION III

Whenever the President transmits to the President pro tempore of the Senate and the Speaker of the House of Representatives his written declaration that he is unable to discharge the powers and duties of his office, and until he transmits to them a written declaration to the contrary, such powers and duties shall be discharged by the Vice President as Acting President.

## SECTION IV

Whenever the Vice President and a majority of either the principal officers of the executive departments or of such other body as Congress may by law provide, transmit to the President pro tempore of the Senate and the Speaker of the House of Representatives their written declaration that the President is unable to discharge the powers and duties of his office, the Vice President shall immediately assume the powers and duties of the office as Acting President.

Thereafter, when the President transmits to the President pro tempore of the Senate and the Speaker of the House of Representatives his written declaration that no inability exists, he shall resume the powers and duties of his office unless the Vice President and a majority of either the principal officers of the executive department or of such other body as Congress may by law provide, transmit within four days to the President pro tempore of the Senate and the Speaker of the House of Representatives their written declaration that the President is unable to discharge the powers and duties of his office.

Thereupon Congress shall decide the issue, assembling within forty-eight hours for that purpose if not in session. If the Congress, within twenty-one days after receipt of the latter written declaration, or, if Congress is not in session, within twenty-one days after Congress is required to assemble, determines by two-thirds vote of both Houses that the President is unable to discharge the powers and duties of his office, the Vice President shall continue to discharge the same as Acting President; otherwise, the President shall resume the powers and duties of his office.

This amendment was proposed in 1965 and ratified in 1967.[1] It was an attempt to resolve one of the thorniest problems of the American political system—what to do when a President is disabled.[2] How important that problem is can be measured by the fact that in the twentieth century, two Presidents, Wilson and Eisenhower, lay gravely ill while in office. Another, Franklin D. Roosevelt, was apparently very ill in his last days, and John F. Kennedy lay mortally wounded for a short time.

For several presidencies prior to enactment of the amendment, Presidents and Vice Presidents exchanged letters specifying how and under what terms the President would relinquish the reins of office if disabled.[3] This arrangement begged some of the basic issues in the disability problem. For one thing, it made it appear that only the President and Vice President had an interest in what was done. Certainly, the people of the United States have a big concern in a President's fitness to hold office. Also, those agreements were vague as to what

---

[1] U.S.C. Amend. 24.

[2] Edward S. Corwin, *The President*, 53-59, 345-346; Ruth C. Silva, "Presidential Succession and Disability," 21 *Law and Contemporary Problems*, 646 (1956); U.S. 88th Congress, 2nd Sess., Senate, Report No. 1382 (1964).

[3] Congressional Quarterly Service, *Congress and the Nation* (Washington, 1965), 1436, II, p. 647. The following was the agreement made by Eisenhower-Nixon, Kennedy-Johnson, and Johnson-Humphrey: " (1) In the event of inability the President would—if possible—so inform the Vice President, and the Vice President would serve as Acting President, exercising the powers and duties of the office until the inability had ended. (2) In the event of an inability which would prevent the President from so communicating with the Vice President, the Vice President, after such consultation as seems to him appropriate under the circumstances, would decide upon the devolution of the powers and duties of the office and would serve as Acting President until the inability had ended. (3) The President, in either event, would determine when the inability had ended and at that time would resume the full exercise of the powers and duties of the office."

was to be done if a President were not in a condition to determine his own fitness. Suppose a President became mentally ill? The amendment supposedly takes care of those issues by not relying on the President's judgment alone. But this does not resolve the practical political dynamics which will be involved every time a President is gravely ill. Typically, the Vice President is from another wing of the party chosen to give the ticket "balance." The President's advisors are more generally picked on the basis of political views similar to the President's. It would be in their interest at least on some occasions to shield the office from a Vice President of differing political views. It may not be impossible to "protect" a disabled President and profess to be doing his bidding. We are told that Mrs. Wilson did so rather successfully.[4] In brief, whenever a President is stricken, we can still anticipate the kind of power struggle which took place at the bedside of President Eisenhower between Presidential aide Sherman Adams and Vice President Richard Nixon.[5] Nor is this to suggest ill will on the part of those participating in the struggle. The stakes are high in terms of ability to do well by the nation, and it is natural for political rivals to view themselves as the salvation of the nation and their rivals as menaces.

4 Ruth C. Silva, "Presidential Succession," p. 652.
5 Jack Bell, *The Splendid Misery* (New York, 1960), 384ff.

# AMENDMENT XXVI

## SECTION I

The right of citizens of the United States, who are eighteen years of age or older, to vote shall not be denied or abridged by the United States or by any State on account of age.

## SECTION II

The Congress shall have power to enforce this article by appropriate legislation.

This amendment was proposed and ratified in 1971.[1] The impetus for the amendment was explained in the Senate report accompanying the proposal this way: "Thus the Committee is convinced that the time has come to extend the vote to 18-year-olds in all elections: because they are mature enough in every way to exercise the franchise; they have earned the right to vote by bearing responsibilities of citizenship; and because our society has so much to gain by bringing the force of their idealism and concern and energy into the constructive mechanism of elective government."[2]

It is significant that prior to enactment of the Twenty-sixth Amendment, Congress in the Voting Rights Act of 1970[3] had already lowered the minimum age of voters from 21 to 18 in both State and Federal elections. But the Supreme Court decided in 1970 that "the 18-year-old vote provisions of the Act are constitutional and enforceable insofar as they pertain to federal elections and unconstitutional and unenforceable insofar as they pertain to state and local elections."[4] For a short time, this created administrative confusion in the States and undoubtedly explains why the Twenty-sixth Amendment was ratified so swiftly.

The passage of the amendment set in force strong efforts to register young voters.[5] One of the sticky problems in registering young voters, at the outset, was to determine whether students should be required to vote where they went to school

1 U.S.C. Amend. 26.
2 3 U.S. Cong. News, 367 (1971). The whole report is worthy of attention. See also 1971 Cong. Quart. Weekly Report, 1436-1439 and 2296-2300.
3 84 Stat. 314.
4 Oregon v. Mitchell, 400 U.S. 112, 118 (1970).
5 Jules Witcover, "The Youth Vote: A Question Mark—25 Million Potential," Washington Post, Sept. 8, 1971.

or where their parents lived. In 1972, the Supreme Court upheld a lower Federal court ruling that students unable to register in their school communities would have to take their cases to court as individuals and not seek redress in a class action.[6] The lower court had held that "This is not a class action [within the Federal Rules]. The facts and circumstances controlling the right of applicants to register may vary in respect to each of them, especially in such matters as residence and domicile, as well as in regard to the nature and content of the questions propounded to them by their respective registrars at the time they first sought registration. Therefore, the plaintiffs here cannot be said to be representative of other students desiring registration."[7] Prior to the election of 1972, we were assured by the *New York Times* that most States do in fact aid student voters.[8]

Several important State court decisions have held that requiring a minimum age over 18 for holding office or for serving on juries did not violate the Twenty-sixth Amendment.[9] However, the Colorado Supreme Court held that qualified electors between the ages of eighteen and twenty could not be precluded by law from signing and circulating initiative petitions.[10]

[6] Manard *v.* Miller, 405 U.S. 982 (1972).
[7] Manard *v.* Miller, 53 F.R.D. 610 (1971).
[8] "Most States Aid Student Voters," *New York Times,* June 4, 1972.
[9] Opatz *v.* St. Cloud, 196 N.W. 2d. 298 (1972); State *v.* Silva, 259 So. 2d. 153 (1972); Johnson *v.* State, 260 So. 2d. 436 (1972); Shelby *v.* State, 479 S.W. 2d. 31 (1972).
[10] Colorado Project-Common Cause *v.* Anderson, 495 P. 2d. 220 (1972).

# PROPOSED
## CONSTITUTIONAL AMENDMENT

The following resolution was passed by Congress on March 22, 1972, submitting the proposed Equal Rights Amendment to the States for ratification:

> Resolved by the Senate and House of Representatives of the United States of America in Congress assembled (two-thirds of each House concurring therein), That

The following article is proposed as an amendment to the Constitution of the United States, which shall be valid to all intents and purposes as part of the Constitution when ratified by the legislature of three-fourths of the several States within seven years from the date of its submission by the Congress:

"Article —

"Section 1. Equality of rights under the law shall not be denied or abridged by the United States or by any State on account of sex.

"Section 2. The Congress shall have the power to enforce, by appropriate legislation, the provisions of this article.

"Section 3. This amendment shall take effect two years after the date of ratification."

The House Report which accompanied the resolution explained the purpose of the proposed amendment in these words:

"In recommending the proposed amendment to the Constitution, your Committee recognizes that our legal system currently contains the vestiges of a variety of ancient common law principles which discriminate unfairly against women. Some of these discriminatory principles are based on the old common law doctrine of 'coverture' which treated the husband and wife as a single legal entity, but which regarded the husband alone as 'the one.' Other discriminatory principles still discernible in our legal system are based on an invidious and outmoded double-standard which affords men a greater freedom than women to depart from conventional moral standards. Still other forms of discriminatory laws have their

459

origins in obsolete and often irrational notions of chivalry which in a modern context regard women in a patronizing or condescending light. Regardless of the historical antecedents of these varieties of sex discrimination, they are in many cases without rational justification and are no longer relevant to our modern democratic institutions. Their persistence even in vestigial form creates disharmony between the sexes. Therefore, we strongly recommend that all irrational discrimination on the basis of sex be eliminated."[1]

Significantly, the report conceded that "These discriminatory features of our legal system could be eliminated without amending the Constitution if the Supreme Court were eventually to accord women the full benefit of the equal protecttion clause." But the report went on to include the observation that "to date the case law in this area has not been thoroughly developed. As a result, it is your Committee's view that the proposed Constitutional amendment would be a means of articulating a National policy against sex discrimination which is needed and has not yet been fully articulated by the judicial system."[2] In the report and, indeed, in the long and interesting debate in the Senate, fears were expressed that the amendment would require *identical* legal treatment for men and women. If such would be the case, it was suggested that "Such a per se rule would be undesirably rigid because it would leave no room to retain statutes which may reasonably reflect differences between the sexes. . . . For example, not only would women, including mothers be subject to the draft but the military would be compelled to place them in combat units alongside of men. The same rigid interpretation could also require that work protective laws reasonably designed to protect the health and safety of women be invalidated. . . ."[3]

As of this writing, it is not prudent to predict whether or not the amendment will be ratified. But it is safe to predict that, if it is ratified, the courts are going to be very busy determining its meaning in the years to come. For example, what of a State statute which makes it a more serious offense for a male

1 U.S. 92d Congress, *House Report* 92-359 (1971).
2 *Ibid.*
3 *Ibid.* See also the fascinating debate in the Senate in 188 *Cong. Rec.* No. 42, pp. S4247-S4273 and No. 44, S4531-S4537. *See* particularly statement of Paul Freund, Dean Pound and other lawyers and legal scholars. *Ibid.* S4263-S4264. *Also see Cong. Quart. Weekly Report*, 692ff.

to assault a female than for a female to do so? Recently, a Texas court found that this was not a denial of equal protection.[4] Would the proposed amendment require a different result?

[4] Buchanan *v.* State, 480 S.W. 2d. 207 (1972). For another suggestion of the kinds of issues which will undoubtedly be litigated, *see* Jones Metal Products Co. *v.* Walker, 281 N.E. 2d. 1 (1972).

# EPILOGUE

One cannot parse the meaning of the Constitution without coming away from it with great admiration and respect for the document and its authors. Yet, as one canvasses the problems of the 1970's, one cannot help but wonder if a restructuring of our governmental system is not in order. This is said as no disrespect to the Framers. For, as Professor James M. Burns pointed out (*see* quote, p. 158), the Constitution has, indeed, served us well for nearly two hundred years. But that fact in itself does not mean that it will continue to serve us well as our problems change. For example, are the separation of powers principle and the inordinate series of checks and balances as viable for our maturity as a nation with all the responsibility maturity brings, as they were in our birth and youth? We do not pass judgment on that question; we respectfully suggest that we should be thinking about it. We make no claim to novelty in offering our suggestion. Professor Corwin as early as 1948 and James M. Burns as late as 1972 were suggesting the same thing.[1] Nor do we make the suggestion light-heartedly. We find ourselves much in accord with the ambivalent feelings expressed by McGeorge Bundy a few years ago: ". . . it is not unthinkable (I want to be careful how I say this)—it is something to be thought about—that this country may need a new or radically amended Constitution. If I had to vote on this question today, I would vote No, because I believe that we very likely could not do better, even now, than our forefathers. One can easily conceive of constitutions very much worse than the one we have, and it is at least possible that some of the parts of the Constitution, that all of us here prize most, might fail in a truly democratic test today. Would we pass the Bill of Rights? But as I express doubt and register this tentative negative, I worry about my own worries. If mistrust of our government is part of our problem, it is at least possible that mistrust of our capacity to change our government is a deeper error still. Our universities and colleges are surely in a time of constitutional reform. Is there no parallel need for the nation? This question is already being asked, and I think rightly, on the issue of the direct election of Presidents. But what

[1] Edward S. Corwin, "Our Constitutional Revolution and How To Round It Out," 19 *Penn. Bar Assoc. Quarterly*, 261 (1948), and James M. Burns *Uncommon Sense* (New York, 1972).

about the powers of states and the needs of the growing number of great cities that cross state boundaries in all of our real economic and social life? And at another level, what about the need to prepare for a time when certain basic powers of government should be exercises above the level of the nation-state?

"I say these things are not unthinkable. I do not say that a new constitution is right. It may well turn out, even on issues as large as these, that precisely because it is a *constitution* with which we are living, a *constitution* which the Justices are expounding, precisely because a *constitution* can fit itself to new times, new duties, that even these issues can be met within the four corners of the document of 1787. But it is not certain, and it does need thought."[2]

[2] Mt. Holyoke College, *The Inauguration Issue* (South Hadley, Mass., 1969), pp. 54-55.

# THE CONSTITUTION

## PREAMBLE

W E, the people of the United States, in order to form a more perfect union, establish justice, insure domestic tranquillity, provide for the common defense, promote the general welfare, and secure the blessings of liberty to ourselves and our posterity, do ordain and establish this Constitution for the United States of America.

## ARTICLE I

### SECTION I

All legislative powers herein granted shall be vested in a Congress of the United States, which shall consist of a Senate and House of Representatives.

### SECTION II

[1] The House of Representatives shall be composed of members chosen every second year by the people of the several States, and the electors in each State shall have the qualifications requisite for electors of the most numerous branch of the State legislature.

[2] No person shall be a Representative who shall not have attained to the age of twenty-five years, and been seven years a citizen of the United States, and who shall not, when elected, be an inhabitant of that State in which he shall be chosen.

[3] Representatives and direct taxes shall be apportioned among the several States which may be included within this Union, according to their respective numbers, which shall be determined by adding to the whole number of free persons, including those bound to service for a term of years, and excluding Indians not taxed, three-fifths of all other persons. The actual enumeration shall be made within three years after the first meeting of the Congress of the United States, and within every subsequent term of ten years, in such manner as they shall by law direct. The number of Representatives shall not exceed one for every thirty thousand, but each State shall have at least one Representative; and until such enumeration shall be made, the State of New Hampshire shall be entitled to choose three; Massachusetts, eight; Rhode Island and Provi-

dence Plantations, one; Connecticut, five; New York, six; New Jersey, four; Pennsylvania, eight; Delaware, one; Maryland, six; Virginia, ten; North Carolina, five; South Carolina, five; and Georgia, three.

[4] When vacancies happen in the representation from any State, the executive authority thereof shall issue writs of election to fill such vacancies.

[5] The House of Representatives shall choose their Speaker and other officers, and shall have the sole power of impeachment.

### SECTION III

[1] The Senate of the United States shall be composed of two Senators from each State, chosen by the legislature thereof for six years; and each Senator shall have one vote.

[2] Immediately after they shall be assembled in consequence of the first election, they shall be divided as equally as may be into three classes. The seats of the Senators of the first class shall be vacated at the expiration of the second year, of the second class at the expiration of the fourth year, and of the third class at the expiration of the sixth year, so that one-third may be chosen every second year; and if vacancies happen by resignation or otherwise during the recess of the legislature of any State, the executive thereof may make temporary appointments until the next meeting of the legislature, which shall then fill such vacancies.

[3] No person shall be a Senator who shall not have attained to the age of thirty years, and been nine years a citizen of the United States, and who shall not, when elected, be an inhabitant of that State for which he shall be chosen.

[4] The Vice-President of the United States shall be President of the Senate, but shall have no vote, unless they be equally divided.

[5] The Senate shall choose their other officers and also a President *pro tempore* in the absence of the Vice-President, or when he shall exercise the office of President of the United States.

[6] The Senate shall have the sole power to try all impeachments. When sitting for that purpose, they shall be on oath or affirmation. When the President of the United States is tried,

the Chief Justice shall preside; and no person shall be convicted without the concurrence of two-thirds of the members present.

[7] Judgment in cases of impeachment shall not extend further than to removal from office, and disqualification to hold and enjoy any office of honor, trust, or profit under the United States; but the party convicted shall, nevertheless, be liable and subject to indictment, trial, judgment, and punishment, according to law.

SECTION IV

[1] The times, places, and manner of holding elections for Senators and Representatives shall be prescribed in each State by the legislature thereof; but the Congress may at any time by law make or alter such regulations, except as to the places of choosing Senators.

[2] The Congress shall assemble at least once in every year, and such meeting shall be on the first Monday in December, unless they shall by law appoint a different day.

SECTION V

[1] Each House shall be the judge of the elections, returns, and qualifications of its own members, and a majority of each shall constitute a quorum to do business; but a smaller numer may adjourn from day to day, and may be authorized to compel the attendance of absent members, in such manner, and under such penalties, as each House may provide.

[2] Each House may determine the rules of its proceedings, punish its members for disorderly behavior, and with the concurrence of two-thirds, expel a member.

[3] Each House shall keep a journal of its proceedings, and from time to time publish the same, excepting such parts as may in their judgment require secrecy, and the yeas and nays of the members of either House on any question shall, at the desire of one-fifth of those present, be entered on the journal.

[4] Neither House, during the session of Congress, shall, without the consent of the other, adjourn for more than three days, nor to any other place than that in which the two Houses shall be sitting.

## SECTION VI

[1] The Senators and Representatives shall receive a compensation for their services, to be ascertained by law and paid out of the Treasury of the United States. They shall, in all cases except treason, felony, and breach of the peace, be privileged from arrest during their attendance at the session of their respective Houses, and in going to and returning from the same; and for any speech or debate in either House they shall not be questioned in any other place.

[2] No Senator or Representative shall, during the time for which he was elected, be appointed to any civil office under the authority of the United States, which shall have been created, or the emoluments whereof shall have been increased during such time; and no person holding any office under the United States shall be a member of either House during his continuance in office.

### SECTION VII

[1] All bills for raising revenue shall originate in the House of Representatives; but the Senate may propose or concur with amendments as on other bills.

[2] Every bill which shall have passed the House of Representatives and the Senate shall, before it become a law, be presented to the President of the United States; if he approve he shall sign it, but if not he shall return it, with his objections, to that House in which it shall have originated, who shall enter the objections at large on their journal and proceed to reconsider it. If after such reconsideration two-thirds of that House shall agree to pass the bill, it shall be sent, together with the objections, to the other House, by which it shall likewise be reconsidered, and if approved by two-thirds of that House it shall become a law. But in all such cases the vote of both Houses shall be determined by yeas and nays, and the names of the persons voting for and against the bill shall be entered on the journal of each House respectively. If any bill shall not be returned by the President within ten days (Sundays excepted) after it shall have been presented to him, the same shall be a law, in like manner as if he had signed it, unless the Congress by their adjournment prevent its return, in which case it shall not be a law.

[3] Every order, resolution or vote to which the concurrence

of the Senate and House of Representatives may be necessary (except on a question of adjournment) shall be presented to the President of the United States; and before the same shall take effect shall be approved by him, or being disapproved by him, shall be repassed by two-thirds of the Senate and House of Representatives, according to the rules and limitations prescribed in the case of a bill.

## SECTION VIII

[1] The Congress shall have power to lay and collect taxes, duties, imposts and excises, to pay the debts and provide for the common defense and general welfare of the United States; but all duties, imposts and excises shall be uniform throughout the United States;

[2] To borrow money on the credit of the United States;

[3] To regulate commerce with foreign nations, and among the several States, and with the Indian tribes;

[4] To establish an uniform rule of naturalization, and uniform laws on the subject of bankruptcies throughout the United States;

[5] To coin money, regulate the value thereof, and of foreign coin, and fix the standard of weights and measures;

[6] To provide for the punishment of counterfeiting the securities and current coin of the United States;

[7] To establish post offices and post roads;

[8] To promote the progress of science and useful arts by securing for limited times to authors and inventors the exclusive right to their respective writings and discoveries;

[9] To constitute tribunals inferior to the Supreme Court;

[10] To define and punish piracies and felonies committed on the high seas and offenses against the law of nations;

[11] To declare war, grant letters of marque and reprisal, and make rules concerning captures on land and water;

[12] To raise and support armies, but no appropriation of money to that use shall be for a longer term than two years;

[13] To provide and maintain a navy;

[14] To make rules for the government and regulation of the land and naval forces;

[15] To provide for calling forth the militia to execute the laws of the Union, suppress insurrections, and repel invasions;

[16] To provide for organizing, arming and disciplining the militia, and for governing such part of them as may be em-

ployed in the service of the United States, reserving to the States respectively the appointment of the officers, and the authority of training the militia according to the discipline prescribed by Congress;

[17] To exercise exclusive legislation in all cases whatsoever over such district (not exceeding ten miles square) as may, by cession of particular States and the acceptance of Congress, become the seat of the Government of the United States, and to exercise like authority over all places purchased by the consent of the legislature of the State in which the same shall be, for the erection of forts, magazines, arsenals, dockyards, and other needful buildings;

[18] To make all laws which shall be necessary and proper for carrying into execution the foregoing powers, and all other powers vested by this Constitution in the Government of the United States, or in any department or officer thereof.

SECTION IX

[1] The migration or importation of such persons as any of the States now existing shall think proper to admit shall not be prohibited by the Congress prior to the year one thousand eight hundred and eight, but a tax or duty may be imposed on such importation, not exceeding ten dollars for each person.

[2] The privilege of the writ of habeas corpus shall not be suspended, unless when in cases of rebellion or invasion the public safety may require it.

[3] No bill of attainder or ex post facto law shall be passed.

[4] No capitation or other direct tax shall be laid, unless in proportion to the census or enumeration hereinbefore directed to be taken.

[5] No tax or duty shall be laid on articles exported from any State.

[6] No preference shall be given by any regulation of commerce or revenue to the ports of one State over those of another; nor shall vessels bound to or from one State be obliged to enter, clear or pay duties in another.

[7] No money shall be drawn from the Treasury but in consequence of appropriations made by law; and a regular statement and account of the receipts and expenditures of all public money shall be published from time to time.

[8] No title of nobility shall be granted by the United States; and no person holding any office of profit or trust under them

shall, without the consent of the Congress, accept of any present, emolument, office, or title of any kind whatever from any king, prince, or foreign state.

## SECTION X

[1] No State shall enter into any treaty, alliance, or confederation; grant letters of marque and reprisal; coin money, emit bills of credit; make anything but gold and silver coin a tender in payment of debts; pass any bill of attainder, ex post facto law or law impairing the obligation of contracts, or grant any title of nobility.

[2] No State shall, without the consent of the Congress, lay any imposts or duties on imports or exports, except what may be absolutely necessary for executing its inspection laws; and the net produce of all duties and imposts, laid by any State on imports or exports, shall be for the use of the Treasury of the United States; and all such laws shall be subject to the revision and control of the Congress.

[3] No State shall, without the consent of Congress, lay any duty of tonnage, keep troops and ships of war in time of peace, enter into any agreement or compact with another State or with a foreign power, or engage in war, unless actually invaded or in such imminent danger as will not admit of delay.

## ARTICLE II

### SECTION I

[1] The executive power shall be vested in a President of the United States of America. He shall hold his office during the term of four years, and together with the Vice-President, chosen for the same term, be elected as follows:

[2] Each State shall appoint, in such manner as the legislature thereof may direct, a number of Electors, equal to the whole number of Senators and Representatives to which the State may be entitled in the Congress; but no Senator or Representative, or person holding an office of trust or profit under the United States, shall be appointed an Elector.

[3] The Electors shall meet in their respective States and vote by ballot for two persons, of whom one at least shall not be an inhabitant of the same State with themselves. And they shall make a list of all the persons voted for, and of the number of votes for each; which list they shall sign and certify, and

471

transmit sealed to the seat of government of the United States, directed to the President of the Senate. The President of the Senate shall, in the presence of the Senate and House of Representatives, open all the certificates, and the votes shall then be counted. The person having the greatest number of votes shall be the President, if such number be a majority of the whole number of Electors appointed; and if there be more than one who have such majority, and have an equal number of votes, then the House of Representatives shall immediately choose by ballot one of them for President; and if no person have a majority, then from the five highest on the list the said House shall in like manner choose the President. But in choosing the President the votes shall be taken by States, the representation from each State having one vote; a quorum for this purpose shall consist of a member or members from two-thirds of the States, and a majority of all the States shall be necessary to a choice. In every case, after the choice of the President, the person having the greatest number of votes of the Electors shall be the Vice-President. But if there should remain two or more who have equal votes, the Senate shall choose from them by ballot the Vice-President.

[4] The Congress may determine the time of choosing the Electors and the day on which they shall give their votes, which day shall be the same throughout the United States.

[5] No person except a natural-born citizen, or citizen of the United States at the time of the adoption of this Constitution, shall be eligible to the office of President; neither shall any person be eligible to that office who shall not have attained to the age of thirty-five years, and been fourteen years a resident within the United States.

[6] In case of the removal of the President from office, or of his death, resignation, or inability to discharge the powers and duties of the said office, the same shall devolve on the Vice-President, and the Congress may by law provide for the case of removal, death, resignation, or inability, both of the President and Vice-President, declaring what officer shall then act as President, and such officer shall act accordingly until the disability be removed or a President shall be elected.

[7] The President shall, at stated times, receive for his services a compensation, which shall neither be increased nor diminished during the period for which he shall have been

elected, and he shall not receive within that period any other emolument from the United States or any of them.

[8] Before he enter on the execution of his office he shall take the following oath or affirmation:

"I do solemnly swear (or affirm) that I will faithfully execute the office of President of the United States, and will to the best of my ability preserve, protect, and defend the Constitution of the United States."

### SECTION II

[1] The President shall be Commander-in-Chief of the Army and Navy of the United States, and of the militia of the several States when called into the actual service of the United States; he may require the opinion, in writing, of the principal officer in each of the executive departments, upon any subject relating to the duties of their respective offices, and he shall have power to grant reprieves and pardons for offenses against the United States, except in cases of impeachment.

[2] He shall have power, by and with the advice and consent of the Senate, to make treaties, provided two-thirds of the Senators present concur; and he shall nominate, and, by and with the advice and consent of the Senate, shall appoint ambassadors, other public ministers and consuls, judges of the Supreme Court, and all other officers of the United States whose appointments are not herein otherwise provided for, and which shall be established by law; but the Congress may by law vest the appointment of such inferior officers, as they think proper, in the President alone, in the courts of law, or in the heads of departments.

[3] The President shall have power to fill up all vacancies that may happen during the recess of the Senate, by granting commissions which shall expire at the end of their next session.

### SECTION III

He shall from time to time give to the Congress information of the state of the Union, and recommend to their consideration such measures as he shall judge necessary and expedient; he may, on extraordinary occasions, convene both Houses, or either of them, and in case of disagreement between them with respect to the time of adjournment, he may adjourn them to such time as he shall think proper; he shall receive ambassadors and other public ministers; he shall take care that the laws be faithfully executed, and shall commission all the officers of the United States.

The President, Vice-President and all civil officers of the United States shall be removed from office on impeachment for and conviction of treason, bribery, or other high crimes and misdemeanors.

## ARTICLE III

The judicial power of the United States shall be vested in one Supreme Court, and in such inferior courts as the Congress may from time to time ordain and establish. The judges, both of the Supreme and inferior courts, shall hold their offices during good behavior, and shall, at stated times, receive for their services a compensation which shall not be diminished during their continuance in office.

[1] The judicial power shall extend to all cases, in law and equity, arising under this Constitution, the laws of the United States, and treaties made, or which shall be made, under their authority; to all cases affecting ambassadors, other public ministers, and consuls; to all cases of admiralty and maritime jurisdiction; to controversies to which the United States shall be a party; to controversies between two or more States; between a State and citizens of another State; between citizens of different States; between citizens of the same State claiming lands under grants of different States, and between a State, or the citizens thereof, and foreign states, citizens, or subjects.

[2] In all cases affecting ambassadors, other public ministers and consuls, and those in which a State shall be party, the Supreme Court shall have original jurisdiction. In all the other cases before mentioned the Supreme Court shall have appellate jurisdiction, both as to law and fact, with such exceptions and under such regulations as the Congress shall make.

[3] The trial of all crimes, except in cases of impeachment, shall be by jury; and such trial shall be held in the State where the said crimes shall have been committed; but when not com-

mitted within any State, the trial shall be at such place or places as the Congress may by law have directed.

### SECTION III

[1] Treason against the United States shall consist only in levying war against them, or in adhering to their enemies, giving them aid and comfort. No person shall be convicted of treason unless on the testimony of two witnesses to the same overt act, or on confession in open court.

[2] The Congress shall have power to declare the punishment of treason, but no attainder of treason shall work corruption of blood or forfeiture except during the life of the person attainted.

## ARTICLE IV

### SECTION I

Full faith and credit shall be given in each State to the public acts, records, and judicial proceedings of every other State. And the Congress may by general laws prescribe the manner in which such acts, records, and proceedings shall be proved, and the effect thereof.

### SECTION II

[1] The citizens of each State shall be entitled to all privileges and immunities of citizens in the several States.

[2] A person charged in any State with treason, felony, or other crime, who shall flee from justice, and be found in another State, shall, on demand of the executive authority of the State from which he fled, be delivered up, to be removed to the State having jurisdiction of the crime.

[3] No person held to service or labor in one State, under the laws thereof, escaping into another, shall, in consequence of any law or regulation therein, be discharged from such service or labor, but shall be delivered up on claim to the party to whom such service or labor may be due.

### SECTION III

[1] New States may be admitted by the Congress into this Union; but no new State shall be formed or erected within the jurisdiction of any other State; nor any State be formed by the junction of two or more States or parts of States, without

the consent of the legislatures of the States concerned as well as of the Congress.

[2] The Congress shall have power to dispose of and make all needful rules and regulations respecting the territory or other property belonging to the United States; and nothing in this Constitution shall be so construed as to prejudice any claims of the United States or of any particular State.

### SECTION IV

The United States shall guarantee to every State in this Union a republican form of government, and shall protect each of them against invasion, and on application of the legislature, or of the executive (when the legislature cannot be convened), against domestic violence.

## ARTICLE V

The Congress, whenever two-thirds of both Houses shall deem it necessary, shall propose amendments to this Constitution, or, on the application of the legislatures of two-thirds of the several States, shall call a convention for proposing amendments, which in either case shall be valid to all intents and purposes as part of this Constitution, when ratified by the legislatures of three-fourths of the several States, or by conventions in three-fourths thereof, as the one or the other mode of ratification may be proposed by the Congress; provided that no amendment which may be made prior to the year one thousand eight hundred and eight shall in any manner affect the first and fourth clauses in the Ninth Section of the First Article; and that no State, without its consent shall be deprived of its equal suffrage in the Senate.

## ARTICLE VI

[1] All debts contracted and engagements entered into, before the adoption of this Constitution, shall be as valid against the United States under this Constitution as under the Confederation.

[2] This Constitution, and the laws of the United States which shall be made in pursuance thereof, and all treaties made, or which shall be made, under the authority of the United States, shall be the supreme law of the land; and the judges in every State shall be bound thereby, anything in the

Constitution or laws of any State to the contrary notwithstanding.

[3] The Senators and Representatives before mentioned and the members of the several State legislatures, and all executive and judicial officers both of the United States and of the several States, shall be bound by oath or affirmation to support this Constitution; but no religious test shall ever be required as a qualification to any office or public trust under the United States.

## ARTICLE VII

The ratification of the conventions of nine States shall be sufficient for the establishment of this Constitution between the States so ratifying the same.

---

## AMENDMENT I

Congress shall make no law respecting an establishment of religion, or prohibiting the free exercise thereof; or abridging the freedom of speech or of the press; or the right of the people peaceably to assemble, and to petition the government for a redress of grievances.

## AMENDMENT II

A well-regulated militia being necessary to the security of a free State, the right of the people to keep and bear arms shall not be infringed.

## AMENDMENT III

No soldier shall, in time of peace, be quartered in any house without the consent of the owner, nor in time of war, but in a manner to be prescribed by law.

## AMENDMENT IV

The right of the people to be secure in their persons, houses, papers, and effects, against unreasonable searches and seizures, shall not be violated, and no warrants shall issue but upon probable cause, supported by oath or affirmation, and particularly describing the place to be searched, and the persons or things to be seized.

## AMENDMENT V

No person shall be held to answer for a capital, or otherwise infamous crime, unless on a presentment or indictment of a grand jury, except in cases arising in the land or naval forces, or in the militia, when in actual service in time of war or public danger; nor shall any person be subject for the same offense to be twice put in jeopardy of life or limb; nor shall be compelled in any criminal case to be a witness against himself, nor be deprived of life, liberty or property, without due process of law; nor shall private property be taken for public use without just compensation.

## AMENDMENT VI

In all criminal prosecutions, the accused shall enjoy the right to a speedy and public trial, by an impartial jury of the State and district wherein the crime shall have been committed, which district shall have been previously ascertained by law, and to be informed of the nature and cause of the accusation; to be confronted with the witnesses against him; to have compulsory process for obtaining witnesses in his favor, and to have the assistance of counsel for his defense.

## AMENDMENT VII

In suits at common law, where the value in controversy shall exceed twenty dollars, the right of trial by jury shall be preserved, and no fact tried by a jury shall be otherwise re-examined in any court of the United States, than according to the rules of the common law.

## AMENDMENT VIII

Excessive bail shall not be required, nor excessive fines imposed, nor cruel and unusual punishments inflicted.

## AMENDMENT IX

The enumeration in the Constitution of certain rights shall not be construed to deny or disparage others retained by the people.

## AMENDMENT X

The powers not delegated to the United States by the Constitution, nor prohibited by it to the States, are reserved to the States respectively, or to the people.

## AMENDMENT XI

The judicial power of the United States shall not be construed to extend to any suit in law or equity, commenced or prosecuted against one of the United States by citizens of another State, or by citizens or subjects of any foreign state.

## AMENDMENT XII

[1] The Electors shall meet in their respective States and vote by ballot for President and Vice-President, one of whom, at least, shall not be an inhabitant of the same State with themselves; they shall name in their ballots the person voted for as President, and in distinct ballots the person voted for as Vice-President, and they shall make distinct lists of all persons voted for as President and of all persons voted for as Vice-President, and of the number of votes for each; which lists they shall sign and certify, and transmit sealed to the seat of the government of the United States, directed to the President of the Senate. The President of the Senate shall, in the presence of the Senate and House of Representatives, open all the certificates and the votes shall then be counted. The person having the greatest number of votes for President shall be the President, if such number be a majority of the whole number of Electors appointed; and if no person have such majority, then from the persons having the highest numbers not exceeding three on the list of those voted for as President, the House of Representatives shall choose immediately, by ballot, the President. But in choosing the President the votes shall be taken by States, the representation from each State having one vote; a quorum for this purpose shall consist of a member or members from two-thirds of the States, and a majority of all the States shall be necessary to a choice. And if the House of Representatives shall not choose a President whenever the right of choice shall devolve upon them, before the fourth day of March next following, then the Vice-President shall act as President, as in the case of the death or other constitutional disability of the President.

[2] The person having the greatest number of votes as Vice-President shall be the Vice-President, if such number be a majority of the whole number of Electors appointed; and if no person have a majority, then from the two highest numbers on the list the Senate shall choose the Vice-President; a quorum

for the purpose shall consist of two-thirds of the whole number of Senators, and a majority of the whole number shall be necessary to a choice. But no person constitutionally ineligible to the office of President shall be eligible to that of Vice-President of the United States.

## AMENDMENT XIII

### SECTION I

Neither slavery nor involuntary servitude, except as a punishment for crime whereof the party shall have been duly convicted, shall exist within the United States, or any place subject to their jurisdiction.

### SECTION II

Congress shall have power to enforce this article by appropriate legislation.

## AMENDMENT XIV

### SECTION I

All persons born or naturalized in the United States, and subject to the jurisdiction thereof, are citizens of the United States and of the State wherein they reside. No State shall make or enforce any law which shall abridge the privileges or immunities of citizens of the United States; nor shall any State deprive any person of life, liberty or property, without due process of law; nor deny to any person within its jurisdiction the equal protection of the laws.

### SECTION II

Representatives shall be apportioned among the several States according to their respective numbers, counting the whole number of persons in each State, excluding Indians not taxed. But when the right to vote at any election for the choice of Electors for President and Vice-President of the United States, Representatives in Congress, the executive and judicial officers of a State, or the members of the legislature thereof, is denied to any of the male inhabitants of such State, being twenty-one years of age, and citizens of the United States, or in any way abridged except for participation in rebellion or other crime, the basis of representation therein shall be reduced in the proportion which the number of such male citizens shall bear to the whole number of male citizens twenty-one years of age in such State.

### SECTION III

No person shall be a Senator or Representative in Congress, or elector of President and Vice-President, or hold any office, civil or military, under the United States or under any State, who, having previously taken an oath as a member of Congress, or as an officer of the United States, or as a member of any State legislature, or as an executive or judicial officer of any State, to support the Constitution of the United States, shall have engaged in insurrection or rebellion against the same, or given aid or comfort to the enemies thereof. But Congress may, by a vote of two-thirds of each House, remove such disability.

### SECTION IV

The validity of the public debt of the United States, authorized by law, including debts incurred for payment of pensions and bounties for services in suppressing insurrection or rebellion, shall not be questioned. But neither the United States nor any State shall assume or pay any debt or obligation incurred in aid of insurrection or rebellion against the United States, or any claim for the loss or emancipation of any slave; but all such debts, obligations, and claims shall be held illegal and void.

### SECTION V

The Congress shall have power to enforce, by appropriate legislation, the provisions of this article.

## AMENDMENT XV

### SECTION I

The right of citizens of the United States to vote shall not be denied or abridged by the United States or by any State on account of race, color, or previous condition of servitude.

### SECTION II

The Congress shall have power to enforce this article by appropriate legislation.

## AMENDMENT XVI

The Congress shall have power to lay and collect taxes on incomes, from whatever source derived, without apportionment among the several States, and without regard to any census or enumeration.

## AMENDMENT XVII

### SECTION I

The Senate of the United States shall be composed of two Senators from each State, elected by the people thereof, for six years; and each Senator shall have one vote. The electors in each State shall have the qualifications requisite for electors of the most numerous branch of the State legislatures.

### SECTION II

When vacancies happen in the representation of any State in the Senate, the executive authority of such State shall issue writs of election to fill such vacancies: Provided, that the legislature of any State may empower the executive thereof to make temporary appointments until the people fill the vacancies by election as the legislature may direct.

### SECTION III

This amendment shall not be so construed as to affect the election or term of any Senator chosen before it becomes valid as part of the Constitution.

## AMENDMENT XVIII

### SECTION I

After one year from the ratification of this article the manufacture, sale or transportation of intoxicating liquors within, the importation thereof into, or the exportation thereof from the United States and all territory subject to the jurisdiction thereof, for beverage purposes, is hereby prohibited.

### SECTION II

The Congress and the several States shall have concurrent power to enforce this article by appropriate legislation.

## SECTION III

This article shall be inoperative unless it shall have been ratified as an amendment to the Constitution by the legislatures of the several States, as provided in the Constitution, within seven years from the date of the submission hereof to the States by the Congress.

# AMENDMENT XIX

## SECTION I

The right of citizens of the United States to vote shall not be denied or abridged by the United States or by any State on account of sex.

## SECTION II

Congress shall have power to enforce this article by appropriate legislation.

# AMENDMENT XX

## SECTION I

The terms of the President and Vice-President shall end at noon on the 20th day of January, and the terms of Senators and Representatives at noon on the 3d day of January, of the years in which such terms would have ended if this article had not been ratified; and the terms of their successors shall then begin.

## SECTION II

The Congress shall assemble at least once in every year, and such meeting shall begin at noon on the 3d day of January, unless they shall by law appoint a different day.

## SECTION III

If, at the time fixed for the beginning of the term of the President, the President-elect shall have died, the Vice-President-elect shall become President. If a President shall not have been chosen before the time fixed for the beginning of his term or if the President-elect shall have failed to qualify, then the Vice-President-elect shall act as President until a President shall have qualified; and the Congress may by law provide for the case wherein neither a President-elect nor a Vice-President-elect shall have qualified, declaring who shall then act as President, or the manner in which one who is to act shall be selected, and such person shall act accordingly until a President or Vice-President shall have qualified.

### SECTION IV

The Congress may by law provide for the case of the death of any of the persons from whom the House of Representatives may choose a President whenever the right of choice shall have devolved upon them, and for the case of death of any of the persons from whom the Senate may choose a Vice-President whenever the right of choice shall have devolved upon them.

### SECTION V

Sections I and II shall take effect on the 15th day of October following the ratification of this article.

### SECTION VI

This article shall be inoperative unless it shall have been ratified as an amendment to the Constitution by the legislatures of three-fourths of the several States within seven years from the date of its submission.

## AMENDMENT XXI

### SECTION I

The eighteenth article of amendment to the Constitution of the United States is hereby repealed.

### SECTION II

The transportation or importation into any State, territory, or possession of the United States for delivery or use therein of intoxicating liquors, in violation of the laws thereof, is hereby prohibited.

### SECTION III

This article shall be inoperative unless it shall have been ratified as an amendment to the Constitution by conventions in the several States, as provided in the Constitution, within seven years from the date of the submission hereof to the States by the Congress.

## AMENDMENT XXII

No person shall be elected to the office of President more than twice, and no person who has held the office of President, or acted as President, for more than two years of a term to which some other person was elected President shall be elected to the office of President more than once. But this Article shall not apply to any person holding the office of President when this Article was proposed by the Congress, and shall not prevent any person who may be holding the office of President, or acting as President, during the term within which this Article becomes operative from holding the office of President or acting as President during the remainder of such term.

## AMENDMENT XXIII

### SECTION I

The District constituting the seat of Government of the United States shall appoint in such manner as the Congress may direct:

A number of electors of President and Vice-President equal to the whole number of Senators and Representatives in Congress to which the District would be entitled if it were a State, but in no event more than the least populous State; they shall be in addition to those appointed by the States, but they shall be considered, for the purposes of the election of President and Vice-President, to be electors appointed by a State; and they shall meet in the District and perform such duties as provided by the twelfth article of amendment.

### SECTION II

The Congress shall have power to enforce this article by appropriate legislation.

## AMENDMENT XXIV

### SECTION I

The right of citizens of the United States to vote in any primary or other election for President or Vice-President, for electors for President or Vice-President, or for Senator or Representative in Congress, shall not be denied or abridged by the United States or any State by reason of failure to pay any poll tax or other tax.

## SECTION II

The Congress shall have power to enforce this article by appropriate legislation.

# AMENDMENT XXV

## SECTION I

In case of the removal of the President from office or of his death or resignation, the Vice-President shall become President.

## SECTION II

Whenever there is a vacancy in the office of the Vice-President, the President shall nominate a Vice-President who shall take office upon confirmation by a majority vote of both Houses of Congress.

## SECTION III

Whenever the President transmits to the President pro tempore of the Senate and the Speaker of the House of Representatives his written declaration that he is unable to discharge the powers and duties of his office, and until he transmits to them a written declaration to the contrary, such powers and duties shall be discharged by the Vice-President as Acting President.

## SECTION IV

Whenever the Vice-President and a majority of either the principal officers of the executive departments or of such other body as Congress may by law provide, transmit to the President pro tempore of the Senate and the Speaker of the House of Representatives their written declaration that the President is unable to discharge the powers and duties of his office, the Vice-President shall immediately assume the powers and duties of the office as Acting President.

Thereafter, when the President transmits to the President pro tempore of the Senate and the Speaker of the House of Representatives his written declaration that no inability exists, he shall resume the powers and duties of his office unless the Vice-President and a majority of either the principal officers of the executive department or of such other body as Congress may by law provide, transmit within four days to the President pro tempore of the Senate and the Speaker of the House of Representatives their written declaration that the President is unable to discharge the powers and duties of his office. Thereupon Congress shall decide the issue, assembling within forty-eight hours for that purpose if not in session. If the Congress, within twenty-one days after receipt of the latter written declaration, or, if Congress is not in session, within twenty-one days after Congress is required to assemble, determines by two-thirds vote of both Houses that the President is unable to discharge the powers and duties of his office, the Vice-President shall continue to discharge the same as Acting President; otherwise, the President shall resume the powers and duties of his office.

## AMENDMENT XXVI

### SECTION I

The right of citizens of the United States, who are eighteen years of age or older, to vote shall not be denied or abridged by the United States or by any State on account of age.

### SECTION II

The Congress shall have power to enforce this article by appropriate legislation.

# TABLE OF CASES

489

497

513

# INDEX

impeachment *(cont.)*
President, 13-14, 159-60; provisions for, 11, 13-14, 159; of Vice President, 159-60
Implied Consent Laws, 322-23
imposts, 35, 99, 105, 437
impounding of funds, by President, 101-102
"incidents of ownership," 436
"income," definition of, 437
income tax, 401-402, 436-40
Income Tax Act of 1894, 390
Income Tax cases of 1895, 35
incompetent criminal defendants, 404
Indiana, 404
Indians, 9, 272-73, 424: as citizens of United States, 66-67
indictments, 352-53, 393
"indirect sanctions," 122-23
"infamous crime," defined, 313
"inferior courts," 166
"inferior officers": appointment of, 139, 145-46; liability of, 159-60
Ingersoll, Jared, 235
inherent powers: of Congress, 6, 8, 21-22, 33, 67-72, 82, 92-93; of National government, 6
inheritance tax, 35, 436
*in personam* judgments: and Due Process Clause, 400; and "full faith and credit" clause, 201-202
*in rem* proceedings, 180-81, 400: and "full faith and credit" clause, 201-202
Insular Cases of 1901, 2n
insurance, as commerce, 48
Inter-American Conference for Peace at Buenos Aires in December 1936, 134
International Labor Organization, 139
International Law, 99, 123, 175n, 181: relation of President to, 124, 153; relation of States to, 103, 374; relation of United States to, 76-77, 85, 135
Interstate Agreement on Detainers Act of 1970, 341
Interstate Commerce Act, 54n
Interstate Commerce Commission,

5, 7, 42, 44n, 63, 148, 159, 162: and due process, 334-35
invidious discrimination, 412-14, 429
involuntary servitude: Court's interpretation of, 382-84; abolition of, 382-84
Iowa Supreme Court, ruling of, 204n

Jackson, Andrew, 30, 120n: and Departmental Construction, 178
Jackson, Robert H., xvii, 32n, 144n, 157, 197n, 243, 252, 272n, 329n: on Electors, 380; on "Flag Salute" case, 277n; on incorporation of Bill of Rights, 397; on substantive due process, 279n
Jackson, William, 235
Jackson, Mississippi, 412
Jacksonville, Florida, Ordinance Code, 352
James II, 128
Japan, agreements with, 137
Japanese: in America during World War II, 79-81, 328; limitation on immigration of, 137
Jay Treaty, 132, 156
Jefferson, Thomas, 113, 120n, 147, 153, 175n, 379: and doctrine of Departmental Construction, 178; on freedom of press, 281-82; on freedom of religion, 270; on impeachment process, 159; on President's role, 148
Jencks case, 183
Jenifer, Daniel, of St. Thomas, 235
Jews, 257-58, 276-77, 278n
Jim Crow law, 62
Johnson, Andrew, 14
Johnson, Lyndon Baines, 101-102, 450-51: agreement in case of disability of President, 455n; and Fortas nomination, 258n; on governing District of Columbia, 91; on limited war, 84-85; takes oath of office for Presidency, 119
Johnson, Thomas, F., 24-25
Johnson, William, 55: on Constitution, xv; on due process, 326
Johnson, William Samuel, 235
joint resolution, use of, 139, 212

# 1973 SUPPLEMENT

These addenda to the Text take into account events and court decisions from the time the Text was completed through June 30, 1973. This Supplement must be read in conjunction with the Text. The page number preceding each item indicates the Text page with which the addendum should be read.

*Page 3*          PREAMBLE

Congressional restiveness gave way to something akin to rebellion by the middle of 1973. Following a smashing electoral victory in 1972, President Nixon impounded in wholesale fashion funds appropriated by Congress, made extraordinary claims for executive privilege, unilaterally reorganized the executive branch, and dealt cavalierly with Congressional reaction to his foreign and military policies. At the height of his assertions of executive power, the revelations constituting the "Watergate Affair" blossomed into full flower. At this writing, a beleaguered President is now finding it difficult to hold his own in the contest with Congress which he in large part initiated. Regretfully, the profound issues over which the contest rages are more likely to be settled for a time on the basis of this President's declining political power rather than on their merits. The specific issues are dealt with in this Supplement in discussions of the pertinent constitutional provisions. (See pp. 565, 570, 569, 567 and 564.)

*Page 6*          ARTICLE I, SECTION I, ¶ 1

For further discussion of Congress's power to legislate with respect to Indians, see Supplement, p. 562.

*Page 9*          ARTICLE I, SECTION II, ¶ 1

In 1973, Justice Rehnquist, speaking for the Court, indicated that the cases following in the wake of Wesberry v. Sanders interpreted the "command" that one man's vote be worth as much as another to mean that it "permits only the limited population variances which are unavoidable despite a good faith effort to achieve absolute equality, or for which justification is shown."[1] Significantly, the opinion explicitly distinguished between the requirements of Article I, Section II, and the Fourteenth Amendment in regard to apportionment stating that "in the implementation of the basic constitutional principle—equality of population among the districts—more flexibility was constitutionally permissible with respect to state legislative reapportionment than in congressional redistricting." (See Supplement p. 599.)

[1] Mahan v. Howell, 93 S. Ct. 979, 983 (1973).

*Page 26*                    ARTICLE I, SECTION VI, ¶ 1

In its latest decision on the Speech and Debate Clause, the Supreme Court reaffirmed the broad protections afforded Congressmen-committee members, committee staff, consultant and investigator "for introducing material at committee hearings that identified particular individuals, for referring the Report that included the material to the Speaker of the House, and for voting publication of the report."[2] Justice White, speaking for a divided Court, explained that "Doubtless, also, a published report may, without losing Speech or Debate Clause protection, be distributed to and used for legislative purposes by Members of Congress, congressional committees, and institutional or individual legislative functionaries. . . ." But he then went on to add these significant words: "However, the question remains whether the act . . . [of informing the public], simply because authorized by Congress must always be considered 'an integral part of the deliberative and communicative processes by which Members participate in committee and House proceedings' with respect to legislative or other matters before the House. . . . A Member of Congress may not with impunity publish a libel from the speaker's stand in his home district, and clearly the Speech and Debate Clause would not protect such an act even though the libel was read from an official committee report." Consequently, "By the same token, others, such as the Superintendent of Documents or the Public Printer or legislative personnel, who participate in distributions of actionable material beyond the reasonable bounds of the legislative task, enjoy no Speech or Debate Clause immunity." In this case the Court also dealt with the doctrine of "official immunity." See page 573 of the Supplement for discussion of that issue.

*Page 28*                    ARTICLE I, SECTION VI, ¶ 2

On April 23, 1973, the Supreme Court granted *certiorari* in the case involving the effort to expel Senators and Representatives from commissioned status as Reserve and National Guard officers.[3]

The argument about General Alexander M. Haig's holding his post as Vice Chief of Staff of the Army while serving as President Nixon's White House Chief of Staff did not turn, however, on this constitutional provision. Senator Symington objected on the grounds that the *U.S. Code* provides that no military officer "may hold a civil office by election or appointment" and that "the acceptance of such a civil office or the exercise of its function by such an officer terminates his military appointment." The Defense Department's legal officer contended that this provision did not apply since General Haig was performing his duties under the Presi-

---

2 Doe *v.* McMillan, 93 S. Ct. 2018, 2024-2025 (1973). The controversy over which the case arose is itself noteworthy for the emotions it stirred up. Parents of children in the District of Columbia schools were incensed by the dissemination of a congressional report on the D.C. school system which identified students in derogatory contexts.

3 Richardson *v.* Reservists Committee to Stop the War, 93 S. Ct. 1927 (1973).

dent's role as Commander in Chief.[4] The argument was cut short when it was announced that General Haig will retire from the Army on August 1, 1973 and be appointed an assistant to the President.[5]

*Page 37*                    ARTICLE I, SECTION VIII, ¶ 1

The Federal Government's practice of providing matching funds for public assistance programs was attacked in a case decided in the United States Court of Appeals, Second Circuit, in early 1973. The City of New York, Mayor Lindsay, and several other city officials contended that the Social Security Act *mandates* the State (and, under the New York State plan, the city) to share in responsibility for public assistance. They argued that the public assistance problem is national in scope and that only Congress has the power to provide for the general welfare under the Constitution. Further, to require States and cities to provide funds for public assistance deprived them of funds to pay the cost of purely local concerns like police and educational services. Since these functions are reserved to the states by the Tenth Amendment, it was argued that to make it impossible to perform them is unconstitutional. The court was patently unimpressed by that line of argument.[6]

*Page 41*                    ARTICLE I, SECTION VIII, ¶ 3

The test case involving the Chicago Seven did at length make its way to the Supreme Court in 1973 on the issue of the constitutionality of the law. The Court denied *certiorari*, thus permitting the appeals court decision to stand.[7]

Attention is invited to the highly publicized 4-4 Supreme Court affirmation of a lower court decision forbidding any substantial degradation of clean air. Worth noting here is that the lower court's decision was based on construction of the Clean Air Act of 1970 and did not deal with constitutional issues.[8]

*Page 61*                    ARTICLE I, SECTION VIII, ¶ 3

That the Supreme Court will continue to be plagued in its arbitral role by difficult tax cases was manifested by a pair of cases it decided in late 1972. One of the cases dealt with South Carolina's assessing a tax on an out-of-state liquor-producing corporation for the income derived from the sale of its goods in South Carolina.[9] Basically, the corporation's transactions in South Carolina appeared to be precisely those covered in a

---

[4] *New York Times*, May 27, 1973.

[5] 1973 *Cong. Quart. Weekly Report*, 1445.

[6] City of New York *v.* Richardson, 473 F. 2d. 923, 928 (1973).

[7] Dellinger *v.* United States, 93 S. Ct. 1443 (1973). The citation for the appeals court decision is 472 F. 2d. 340 (1972).

[8] Sierra Club *v.* Ruckelshaus, 344 F. Supp. 253 (1972); *affirmed,* U.S. Court of Appeals, D.C. Circuit, 41 *LW* 2255 (1972). Supreme Court citation is styled Fri *v.* Sierra Club, 41 *LW* 4825 (1973).

[9] Heublein, Inc. *v.* South Carolina Tax Com'n, 93 S. Ct. 483 (1972).

statute enacted by Congress in 1959 which provided that no state can impose "a net income tax on the income derived within such State by any person from interstate commerce," if the business activities within the State constituted only the solicitation of orders which "are sent outside the State for approval or rejection, and, if approved are filled by shipment or delivery from a point outside the State."[10] However, South Carolina law requires that, to do business in the State, liquor producers must have a resident representative to whom the shipments of liquor into the State must go before being passed on to licensed wholesalers. Consequently, South Carolina could and did contend that Heublein, Inc., the liquor producer, was, by virtue of its required representative's performing his required functions, doing more than just soliciting business in the State. Heublein, understandably, argued that a State should not be able to evade the purpose of the Federal law by *requiring* "a firm to do more than solicit business within the State and then taxing the firm for engaging in this compelled additional activity." The Court held "the requirement that, before engaging in the liquor business in South Carolina, a manufacturer do more than merely solicit sales there, is an appropriate element in the State's system of regulating the sale of liquor. The regulation in question here is therefore valid, and . . . [the federal statute] does not apply." In so holding, the Court stressed that, under the Twenty-first Amendment, the State is "unconfined by traditional Commerce Clause limitations when it restricts the importation of intoxicants destined for use, distribution, or consumption within its borders."

The other case dealt with New Mexico's emergency school and gross receipts tax on a New Mexico corporation which creates and designs instructional programs. This generally involves developing products such as camera-ready copies of programmed textbooks or audio tapes which are delivered to out-of-state customers who reproduce them. The issue in the case boiled down to whether the tax on the proceeds from selling the reproducible originals was a tax on *services performed within the State* or a tax on *tangible property in another State*. The Supreme Court pointed out that, by its previous decisions, States were permitted to tax services performed within the State, but that "a tax levied on the gross receipts from the sales of tangible personal property in another State is an impermissible burden on commerce."[11] Since the New Mexico Court of Appeals had "found in effect that the reproducible originals were the *sine qua non* of the contract and that it was a sale of that tangible property in another State that New Mexico had taxed," the Supreme Court held that the tax was not constitutionally permissible.

*Page 64*          ARTICLE I, SECTION VIII, ¶ 3

Back in 1886, the Supreme Court took a limited view of the meaning of commerce with the Indian tribes. For the power to regulate Indian matters other than commerce, the Court relied on the concept of sov-

---

[10] 15 U.S.C. 381.          [11] Evco *v.* Jones, 409 U.S. 91, 93 (1972).

ereignty: "The power of the federal government over these remnants of a race once powerful, now weak and diminished in numbers, is necessary to their protection, as well as to the safety of those among whom they dwell. *It must exist in that government,* because it never existed anywhere else. . . ."[12] (Emphasis supplied.)

Over the years there has been substantial slippage from this position. In 1973, in a highly significant footnote to a case involving Indians, Justice Marshall speaking for the Court observed: "The source of federal authority over Indian matters has been the subject of some confusion, but it is now generally recognized that the power derives from federal responsibility for regulating commerce with Indian tribes and for treaty making."[13]

*Page 72*          ARTICLE I, SECTION VIII, ¶ 4

By a 5-4 decision, the Supreme Court held in 1973 that a filing-fee requirement for bankruptcy did not deny an indigent equal protection of the laws. In so holding, the majority speaking through Justice Blackmun made these important observations: (1) "There is no constitutional right to obtain a discharge of one's debts in bankruptcy"; (2) "the rational basis for the fee requirement is readily apparent"; (3) "congressional power over bankruptcy, of course, is plenary and exclusive."[14]

*Page 75*          ARTICLE I, SECTION VIII, ¶ 8

The Supreme Court, in upholding by a 5-4 vote a California law which made it a misdemeanor to "pirate" recordings and tapes, reasoned that "the Constitution neither explicitly precludes the States from granting copyrights nor grants such authority exclusively to the Federal government. The subject matter to which the copyright clause is addressed may at times be of purely local concern. No conflict will necessarily arise from a lack of uniform state regulation, nor will the interest of one State be significantly prejudiced by the actions of another. No reason exists why Congress must take affirmative action either to authorize protection of all categories of writings or to free them from all restraint. We therefore conclude that, under the Constitution, the States have not relinquished all power to grant authors 'the exclusive Right to their respective Writings.' "[15] The Court went on to hold that California "has exercised a power which it retained under the Constitution, and that the challenged statute, as applied in this case, does not intrude into an area which Congress has up to now pre-empted." (Significantly, Congress had, in 1971, passed legislation providing protection of sound recordings from "piracy" after February 15, 1972. The acts of "piracy" involved in this case, however, took place before the Congressional action.)

[12] United States *v.* Kagama, 118 U.S. 375, 384 (1886).
[13] McClanahan *v.* Arizona Tax Com'n, 93 S. Ct. 1257 (1973). *But see* Robinson *v.* Wolff, 349 F. Supp. 514, 521 (1972).
[14] United States *v.* Kras, 93 S. Ct. 631, 638-639 (1973).
[15] Goldstein *v.* State of California, 41 *LW* 4829, 4833 (1973).

*Page 84*                    ARTICLE I, SECTION VIII, ¶ 11

The frustration and unhappiness with the war in Indochina continued through the year and so did congressional efforts to reassert what they regarded as their constitutional duty with respect to war-making. The Senate Foreign Relations Committee on May 17 reintroduced the bill described in the Text (p. 84). The House Foreign Affairs Committee on June 7 approved legislation setting a 120-day limit to the President's power to commit troops to combat without Congressional consent and providing that Congress could stop military action earlier than 120 days by concurrent resolution.[16]

More dramatic than efforts to curb the President's war powers generally was the struggle to force the President to end the bombing in Cambodia. After a monumental effort, including a foray into the courts,[17] Congress passed a rider to an appropriations bill cutting off all funds for the bombing. President Nixon promptly vetoed the bill, and the House, 35 votes short, failed to override.[18] A substantial number of Congressmen continued to press on, however, and the President agreed to a compromise to end the bombing by August 15, 1973, saying that he would seek congressional help if further action became necessary "to win the peace."[19]

*Page 90*                    ARTICLE I, SECTION VIII, ¶ 16

In a case growing out of the tragedy at Kent State University in 1970, the Supreme Court in 1973 decided that "The relief sought . . . requiring initial judicial review and continuing surveillance by a federal court over the training, weaponing and orders of the Guard would . . . embrace critical areas of responsibility vested by the Constitution in the Legislative and Executive branches of the Government."[20] It went on to state, however, that "it should be clear that we neither hold nor imply that the conduct of the National Guard is always beyond judicial review or that there may not be accountability in a judicial forum for violations of law or for specific unlawful conduct by military personnel."

*Page 94*                    ARTICLE I, SECTION IX, ¶ 2

The Supreme Court held in 1973 that "when a state prisoner is challenging the very fact or duration of his physical imprisonment, and the relief he seeks is a determination that he is entitled to immediate or more

---

[16] 1973 *Cong. Quart. Weekly Report*, 1454.

[17] Mitchell *v.* Laird, 476 F. 2d. 533 (1973). 13 members of Congress filed suit to enjoin the President and the Secretaries of State, Defense, Army, Navy and Air Force from prosecuting the war in Indochina unless, within 60 days from that date, Congress explicitly authorized continuation. The court declined to adjudicate the question. *Cf.* Holtzman *v.* Richardson, 42 *LW* 2015 (1973).

[18] *New York Times*, June 28, 1973. (Contains text of the veto message.)

[19] *New York Times*, July 2, 1973. The President signed the Social Security bill, which contained a rider cutting off funds for United States combat activities in Indochina.

[20] Gilligan *v.* Morgan, 41 *LW* 4966, 4968 (1973).

speedy release from that imprisonment, his sole federal remedy is a writ of habeas corpus."[21] This holding came out of a case where several New York State prisoners challenged the cancellation of their good-behavior-time credits (toward reduction of maximum sentence), invoking the Civil Rights Act as well as making a *habeas corpus* claim. As the Supreme Court saw it: "The question before us is whether state prisoners seeking such redress may obtain equitable relief under the Civil Rights Act, even though the federal habeas corpus statute . . . clearly provides a specific federal remedy." Further, the Court said that the case presented "an unresolved and important problem in the administration of federal justice," a problem involving the interrelationship of two important federal laws. In short, if the Civil Rights Act prevailed, the prisoners could bring their suits to a Federal court "so as to avoid the necessity of first seeking relief in a state forum." If the *habeas corpus* laws prevailed, then the exhaustion of adequate State remedies was required before the invocation of Federal judicial relief. The Court reasoned that "Congress has determined that habeas corpus is the appropriate remedy for state prisoners attacking the validity of the fact or length of their confinement, and that specific determination must override the general terms of . . . [the Civil Rights Act]."

*Page 98*        Article I, Section IX, ¶ 3

Attention is invited to a group of lower court decisions involving the *Ex Post Facto* Clause.[22]

*Page 101*        Article I, Section IX, ¶ 7

Presidential impoundment of funds appropriated by Congress provoked a bitter battle in 1973. President Nixon, euphoric over the 1972 election results and before developments in the Watergate Affair, cut a great swathe through Congressional appropriations. The White House put the total of impoundments at $8.7 billion for Fiscal 1973, but critics suggested that the figure was much higher. Representative Joe L. Evins, chairman of the Appropriations public works sub-committee suggested that the proper figure was at least $12.2 billion.[23]

Incensed Congressmen fought back in both the legislative and judicial arenas. Two bills limiting impoundments are presently making their way through the legislative mill.[24] The Senate bill would require specific Congressional consent (by resolution) to the impoundment of funds for

[21] Preiser *v.* Rodriguez, 93 S. Ct. 1827 (1973).

[22] United States *v.* Williams, 475 F. 2d. 355, 356 (1973); State *v.* Bullock, 269 So. 2d. 824, 826 (1972); State *v.* Dickerson, 298 A. 2d. 761 (1973); People *v.* Sobiek, 106 Cal. Rptr. 519, 529 (1973); State *v.* Waddell, 194 S.E. 2d. 19 (1973); People *v.* Wilkins, 104 Cal. Rptr. 89, 96 (1972).

[23] 1973 *Cong. Quart. Weekly Report*, 270.

[24] *Ibid.*, 788. *See also* U.S. Cong., 1st Sess., *Senate Hearings*, "Impoundment of Appropriated Funds" (1973).

more than two months. The House bill would allow funds to remain impounded unless Congress passed legislation releasing them.

Surprisingly, at least to us, in view of what we wrote in the Text just a few months ago, when the State Highway Commission of Missouri sued for the release to it of impounded highway funds, 14 of the Senate's 17 committee chairmen intervened as friends of the court. Speaking for the chairmen, an angry Senator Sam J. Ervin, Jr. said, "This practice of impoundment is contemptuous of the role of Congress in our tripartite system. The power of the purse belongs exclusively to Congress under the Constitution."[25] Surprising to us, too, was the decision of the United States Court of Appeals for the Eighth Circuit. To the argument of the Secretary of Transportation (the defendant in the case) that the executive power to control the rate of expenditure was a political question, the court answered: "We disagree. The only issue before the district court and this court is the question of statutory construction, i.e., whether the Secretary of Transportation, pursuant to his delegated duties under the Federal Highway Act, can withhold from the State of Missouri, for the reasons he stated, the authority to obligate funds duly apportioned to the State under the Act. Surely such a determination is within the competence of the courts."[26] On the merits, the court held that the act did not authorize the Secretary to withhold the funds.

In defense of the position we took in the Text, it is important to note what the court said it was *not* doing: "Resolution of the issue before us does not involve analysis of the Executive's constitutional powers. Nothing in this present record demonstrates that the Secretary of Transportation will continue to exercise controls beyond that which judicial construction finds permissible within the *statute*." (Emphasis supplied.)

*Page 105*          Article I, Section X, ¶ 1

A flurry of interesting State court decisions involved the Contract Clause. With a few exceptions these decisions upheld the exercise of State police power against the claims that the exercise unconstitutionally impaired the obligation of contracts.[27] In addition, there were State court

25 *Ibid.*, 3.
26 The State Highway Com'n of Missouri *v.* Volpe, U.S. Court of Appeals, Eighth Circuit, No. 72-1572, p. 7. More recently a United States District Court signed a restraining order barring the return of impounded Federal library and education funds to the U.S. Treasury at the beginning of the new fiscal year on the grounds that the States stood a good chance of winning a suit to get them. Also, another district court ordered the release of funds for Neighborhood Youth Corps summer programs. *New York Times*, June 29, 1973.
27 Meegan *v.* Village of Tinley Park, 288 N.E. 2d. 423 (1972); Michigan Transportation Co. *v.* Secretary of State, 201 N.W. 2d. 83 (1972); Moses Lake School District *v.* Big Bend Com. Col., 503 P. 2d. 86 (1972); D'Addario *v.* McNab, 342 N.Y.S. 2d. 342 (1973). Police Ben. Ass'n. of N.Y. St. Police, Inc. *v.* Osterman, 340 N.Y.S. 2d. 291 (1973); Tower Plaza Investments, Limited *v.* DeWitt, 508 P. 2d. 324 (1973). *But see* exceptions, Ruano *v.* Spellman, 505 P. 2d. 447, 452 (1973); Haught *v.* City of Dayton, 288 N.E. 2d. 846 (1972); Ketcham *v.* King County Medical Service Corp., 502 P. 2d. 1197 (1973).

decisions holding that pension[28] and marital rights[29] were not contractual rights within the meaning of Article I, Section X.

*Page 106*                    ARTICLE I, SECTION X, ¶ 2

State courts have been endeavoring to determine precisely *when* imported goods are actually being put to the "use for which they were imported" and can be legitimately taxed by the States. The trouble comes in deciding what part of an inventory can be said to have been put to use. For that purpose a phrase and a formula has found favor with State jurists. The phrase is "current operational needs" and the formula is: "current operational needs" of a company equals the number of days the company needs to replenish its stock, multiplied by the daily average of the amount of stock used.[30]

*Page 116*                    ARTICLE II, SECTION I, ¶ 2

A Federal district court recently reaffirmed the States' power to pass laws regulating the selection of electors, stressing, however, that in doing so they could not impose burdens on the right to vote, "where such burdens are expressly prohibited in other Constitutional provisions."[31]

*Page 124*                    ARTICLE II, SECTION II, ¶ 1

When President Nixon's directive ordering the mining of the ports and harbors of North Vietnam and the continuation of air and naval strikes against North Vietnamese military targets was challenged, the U.S. Court of Appeals, Second Circuit, handled the issues with all the care attributed to porcupines making love. The court narrowed the contention in the case, saying: "We do not understand appellant to argue that every tactical decision made by the President is subject to challenge under the theory advanced in this case. Any such contention would necessarily be unpersuasive in light of the Constitution's specific textual commitment of decision-making responsibility in the area of military operations in a theatre of war to the President, in his capacity as Commander in Chief. What is unique about the President's action, according to . . . [the appellant] is the 'unilateral escalation' involved in the decision. With this characterization in hand, the appellant draws on language . . . [from one of our previous decisions] where we said, 'if the Executive were now escalating the prolonged struggle instead of decreasing it, additional supporting action by the Legislative Branch over what is presently afforded, might well be required' . . . and argues that the 'escalation' represented by the order to mine North Vietnam's harbors is illegal because unsupported by additional

---

[28] Jones *v.* Cheney, 489 S.W. 2d. 785, 788 (1973).
[29] *In re* Marriage of Walton, 104 Cal. Rptr. 472 (1972).
[30] Production Steel Strip Corp. *v.* City of Detroit, 202 N.W. 2d. 719 (1972) and cases cited therein.
[31] Raza Unida Party *v.* Bullock, 349 F. Supp. 1272 (1972).

congressional authorization."[32] The court then held: "Thus it is our judgment that this Court is without power to resolve the issue narrowly presented in this case. Having previously determined, in accordance with our duty, that the Vietnamese war has been constitutionally authorized by the mutual participation of Congress and the President, we must recognize that those two coordinate branches of government—the Executive by military action and the Congress, by not cutting off appropriations that are the wherewithal for such action—have taken a position that is not within our power, even if it were our wish, to alter by judicial decree."

*Page 127*                ARTICLE II, SECTION II, ¶ 1

President Nixon in early 1973 designated three department heads "to serve simultaneously as Counsellors to the President with coordinating responsibilities in these three broad areas of concern.

"Earl L. Butz, Secretary of Agriculture will take on the additional post of Counsellor for Natural Resources. Caspar Weinberger, Secretary-designate of Health, Education and Welfare, will become Counsellor for Human Resources. James Lynn, Secretary-designate of Housing and Urban Development, will become Counsellor for Community Development."[33]

Two aspects of the President's action are particularly noteworthy. The President explicitly stated that "The individual department heads and the Counsellors will routinely report to me via the appropriate Assistant to the President, but will continue to work directly with me on important matters." On the face of it, such a practice would seem to diminish the importance of department heads as Presidential advisers at least vis-à-vis the "appropriate Assistant." Second, the President took the action after Congress had not acted upon his request in 1971 for legislation to accomplish the same objective. The President explained: "Though the actual integration of fragmented departmental operations must wait on Congressional action, the broadening of policy perspectives on the part of top managers and advisers can be achieved at once. . . . I am therefore taking the first of a series of steps aimed at increasing the management effectiveness of both the Cabinet and White House staff, by reordering the time-worn and in many cases obsolete relationships among top staff and line officials to the full extent of my legal authority to do so."

*Page 131*                ARTICLE II, SECTION II, ¶ 2

For contention that Federal authority over Indian matters extends, at least in part, from the treaty-making power see p. 562 of Supplement.

*Page 141*                ARTICLE II, SECTION II, ¶ 2

In part, as a tactical maneuver in the controversy over the impoundment of funds (see p. 565 of Supplement), Congress passed a bill requiring

---

[32] Da Costa *v.* Laird, 471 F. 2d. 1146, 1154-1155 (1973).
[33] 1973 *Cong. Quart. Weekly Report*, 35-39.

Senate confirmation of the director and deputy director of the Office of Management and Budget.[34] When Congress had created the old Bureau of the Budget in 1921 (predecessor of OMB) the prevailing theory was that these offices were personal to the President and should not require Senate confirmation. The Senate Committee reporting the bill stated that OMB now "has developed into a major governmental agency with enormous policy-making and operational functions, responsibilities and authority" and as such requires that Congress play a role in the appointment of its chief officers. Ultimately, the President vetoed the bill and the House failed to override the veto. Undaunted, the Senate in June 1973 passed a bill which would require confirmation of *future* nominees for those high offices as well as several others.[35]

The situation would be different were this the case of Congress setting up new offices providing for Senate confirmation. Then the President would have had to worry that a veto would have the effect of preventing the offices from being established. But here legislation already permitted the President to appoint without confirmation, and his veto had the effect of maintaining the status quo.

*Page 142*          ARTICLE II, SECTION II, ¶ 2

In his statement explaining the government reorganization he initiated in early 1973 (see p. 568 of the Supplement), President Nixon said that "Through a combination of Presidential directives, reorganization plans, and budgetary changes, I shall assign or propose reassignment of most of the activities currently carried on by a number of organizations within the Executive Office of the President, to appropriate line departments and agencies." Although present law requires that executive reorganization plans be submitted to the Congress and that Congress have the opportunity to scuttle them by a resolution of either house,[36] the President apparently holds that he has the legal power to make changes unilaterally within the Executive Office but needs the approval of Congress for changes in the rest of the executive branch. The concluding words of his statement support such an observation: "I hope the Congress will accept this practical proof and join me in adopting throughout the executive branch the same concepts on which I am now patterning my own staff and Executive Office."[37]

The Supreme Court reversed the lower court in the Hatch Act case. See p. 577 of the Supplement for discussion.

---

[34] *1973 Cong. Quart. Weekly Report*, 250, 313, 1330-1331.

[35] *New York Times*, June 26, 1973. In June a Federal judge ruled that Howard J. Phillips was acting as the head of OEO illegally because his name had not been submitted to the Senate for approval. President Nixon directly nominated a new director. *New York Times*, June 27, 1973. The case is reported in Williams *v.* Phillips, 41 *LW* 2677 (1973).

[36] 5 U.S.C. 901-913.

[37] *1973 Cong. Quart. Weekly Report*, 39.

As the mire of the Watergate Affair increasingly threatened to suck in high administration officials, indeed eventually the President himself, the meaning of the executive privilege was debated with a ferocity which made previous contests seem desultory.[38] To forestall the Senate inquiry, the Administration at first made some extraordinary claims for the privilege. For example, to Senator Muskie's question "Does . . . [the executive privilege] apply to every one of the employees of the executive branch of the federal government of the United States?" the then-Attorney General, Richard G. Kleindienst, answered: "Boy, if a President directed him not to, I think logically I'd have to say that's correct."[39] Later, some backtracking put the Administration more in line with previous claims. The White House issued a statement in May 1973 that "The President desires that the invocation of Executive Privilege be held to a minimum." His guidance was that "Past and present members of the President's staff questioned by the FBI, the Ervin Committee, or a Grand Jury should invoke the privilege only in connection with conversations with the President, conversations among themselves (involving communications with the President) and as to Presidential papers. Presidential papers are all documents produced or received by the President or any member of the White House Staff in connection with his official duties."[40] But, as unfolding events and Presidential counsel Leonard Garment attested, there is no way a President can force an aide to invoke the privilege, if the aide does not want to.[41]

As he warmed up to the task of investigating the Watergate Affair, Senator Ervin intimated that his committee might well consider the possibility of issuing a subpoena to the President himself! Contrary to conventional wisdom on the subject, Senator Ervin felt that there was some precedent to support him.[42] President Nixon responded through his press secretary that for him to provide oral or written testimony to the Senate committee would be "constitutionally inappropriate" and a violation of the separation of powers.[43] In assessing Senator Ervin's claim for support, one should reflect on the latest situation reminiscent of the present one. As an *ex*-President, Harry S Truman in 1953 declined to answer a subpoena served on him by the House Un-American Activities Committee, which was inquiring into the charge that Harry Dexter White (who had been promoted from Assistant Secretary of the Treasury to Executive Director of the International Monetary Fund) "was known to be a Communist spy by the very people who appointed him to the most sensitive and important position he ever held in government service." In a detailed letter to the committee citing sixteen precedents, Mr. Truman explained that "I feel constrained by my duty to the people of the United States to

38 *Ibid.*, 181, 184-185, 294-295, 518, 557, 729, 862, 895, 1120, 1203.
39 *Ibid.*, 862.
40 *Ibid.*, 1120.                          41 *Ibid.*, 1203.
42 *Ibid.*, 1353.                          43 *Ibid.*

decline to comply with the subpoena."[44] President Eisenhower, who had been very critical of his predecessor's general performance in office, nonetheless publicly lent his support to Mr. Truman in this matter.[45]

*Page 161*                    ARTICLE III, SECTION I

During the last Term, the Supreme Court decided a brace of cases dealing with judicial review of the actions of administrative agencies.[46] Although these cases do not raise constitutional questions, they are exceptionally interesting for the substantive issues they raise as well as for what the Court had to say about judicial review, i.e., degradation of the environment, railroad rates, and pre-marketing of new drugs.

*Page 164*                    ARTICLE III, SECTION I

The U.S. Court of Appeals, Seventh Circuit, added to the meaning of the 1968 and 1971 Supreme Court decisions on criminal contempts, cited in the Text, when it reviewed the contempt convictions emanating from the trial of the Chicago Seven. Judge Hoffman, who presided over the original trial, had sentenced most of the Chicago Seven to several months for *each* act of misbehavior, making the aggregate sentence for them more than six months. The circuit court held that "each appellant whose sentences aggregated more than 6 months was entitled to a jury trial."[47] Further, the circuit court held that the decision in *Mayberry* applies to lawyers as well as others. The court evidently felt compelled to address that issue because the opinion (as distinguished from the judgment) in *Mayberry* suggested that a trial judge *must* disqualify himself *only* if he waits until the conclusion of a trial to act against a contemnor[48] but at the same time indicated that contempts involving lawyers might be another matter. Justice Douglas had written: "Generalizations are difficult. Instant treatment of contempt where lawyers are involved *may* greatly prejudice their clients but it *may* be the only wise course where others are involved. . . . Where, however, he does not act the instant the contempt is committed, but waits until the end of the trial, on balance, *it is generally wise* where the marks of the unseemly conduct have left personal stings to ask a fellow judge to take his place."[49] (Emphasis sup-

---

[44] *New York Times*, Nov. 13, 1953.
[45] *New York Times*, Nov. 12, 1953.
[46] Atchinson, T. & S.F. R. Co. *v.* Wichita Bd. of Trade, 41 *LW* 4905 (1973); United States *v.* SCRAP, 41 *LW* 4866 (1973); Weinberger *v.* Hynson, Westcott & Dunning, 41 *LW* 4848 (1973); USV Pharmaceutical Corp. *v.* Weinberger, 41 *LW* 4861 (1973); Weinberger *v.* Bentex Pharmaceuticals, Inc., 41 *LW* 4858 (1973).
[47] *In re* Dellinger, 461 F. 2d. 389, 397 (1972). See also United States *v.* Seale, 461 F. 2d. 345 (1972).
[48] *See* Justice Black's cryptic concurring opinion. Mayberry *v.* Pennsylvania, 400 U.S. 466 (1971).
[49] *Ibid.*, pp. 463-464. Compare this language with Justice Douglas's description of the Court's actual judgment as quoted in the Text (p. 164).

plied.) Whatever the true meaning of the *Mayberry* decision, the circuit court decided that "while the possible prejudice to the lawyer's clients may counterbalance the need to preserve order in the court through immediate action, this consideration simply has no bearing on whether the trial judge may himself proceed summarily or must call in another judge to take his place when he has already decided to wait."[50]

*Page 166*                    ARTICLE III, SECTION I

Faced with the proposition "that an Article III judge [lifetime tenure] preside over every proceeding in which charge, claim, or defense is based on an Act of Congress or a law made under its authority," the Supreme Court found that "There is no support for this view in either constitutional text or in constitutional history and practice."[51] Congress could constitutionally, therefore, set up Article I courts to hear and decide criminal cases in the District of Columbia.

*Page 168*                    ARTICLE III, SECTION II, ¶ 1

Whatever impression the Court might have conveyed in *Flast* that it might become very loose in its application of the doctrine of standing, it dispelled this past term. Although the Court held that tenants had standing to file a complaint against a landlord who discriminated against non-whites on the grounds that they lost the "important benefits from interracial associations," three justices per Justice White agreed in a concurring opinion that they "would have great difficulty in concluding that petitioners complaint in this case presented a case or controversy within the jurisdiction of the District Court under Article III of the Constitution. But with . . . [the Civil Rights Act of 1968] purporting to give all those who are authorized to complain to . . . [the Secretary of Housing and Urban Development] the right also to sue in court, I would sustain the statute insofar as it extends standing to those in the position of petitioners in this case."[52] In one of the latest cases, the Supreme Court held that the Texas mother of an illegitimate child did not have standing to challenge the constitutionality of a Texas statute which makes it a misdemeanor to fail to support a child and which has been interpreted by Texas courts to apply only to parents of legitimate children.[53] But, later, apparently relying on the Administrative Procedure Act, which gives standing to those who are "adversely affected" or "aggrieved" by an agency action, the Court decided that a group of students had standing to challenge an ICC action not to suspend a raise in railroad rates. The students contended that the rate increase would result in "the nonuse of recyclable

50 *In re* Dellinger, 461 F. 2d. 389, 395 (1972).
51 Palmore *v.* United States, 93 S. Ct. 1670 (1973).
52 Trafficante *v.* Metropolitan Life Ins. Co., 93 S. Ct. 364 (1972).
53 S. *v.* D., 93 S. Ct. 1146, 1148 (1973).

goods" and that this in turn would result in harming forests, streams, mountains and other natural resources which they used.[54]

In a noteworthy lower court decision, a court of appeals reversed a district court which had found that any member of the military, indeed *any citizen*, has standing "to challenge the validity of action by which large scale international combat, or a new departure in belligerency is initiated."[55] By way of contrast, another court of appeals held that associations of railroad passengers had standing to seek an injunction to prevent AMTRAK from discontinuing service.[56] That court relied on the "zone of interest" concept which Justice Douglas had enunciated for the Supreme Court in 1970.[57]

A more startling development threatening to limit access to the Federal courts was a recent decision rendered by a three-judge Federal court on which Judge Harold R. Medina sat. The decision, unavailable at this writing, was reported in the press as requiring, in certain class action suits, that the class on behalf of whom a suit was filed be personally notified by the symbolic plaintiffs.[58]

*Page 172*          ARTICLE III, SECTION II, ¶ 1

In judging that it was without power to decide the issue of whether or not the President had exceeded his constitutional powers in ordering the mining of North Vietnamese harbors and stepping up the bombing, the U.S. Court of Appeals, Second Circuit, reviewed succinctly the political question doctrine. Summing up, it observed "Clearly, some of the principles enumerated call for discretionary judgments that will not always require a court to refrain from action. Nevertheless, we are at a loss to understand how a court may decide a question when there are no judicially discoverable or manageable standards for resolving it."[59]

*Page 183*          ARTICLE III, SECTION II, ¶ 1

In a case discussed earlier under the Speech and Debate Clause (see p. 560 of Supplement), the Supreme Court also dealt with the question of the "official immunity doctrine." The Court concluded that "for the pur-

[54] United States *v.* SCRAP (Students Challenging Regulatory Agency Procedures), 41 *LW* 4866 (1973).

[55] Da Costa *v.* Laird, 471 F. 2d. 1146 (1973).

[56] Potomac Passengers Ass'n *v.* Chesapeake & Ohio R. Co., 475 F. 2d. 325 (1973).

[57] According to Justice Douglas, the question of standing "concerns, apart from the 'case' or 'controversy' test, the question whether the interest sought to be protected by the complainant is arguably within the zone of interests to be protected or regulated by the statute or constitutional guarantee in question." Association of Data Processing Service Org., & TVC. *v.* Camp, 397 U.S. 150, 153 (1970).

[58] *New York Times*, May 6, 1973.

[59] Da Costa *v.* Laird, 471 F. 2d. 1146, 1153 (1973).

poses of the judicially fashioned doctrine of immunity, the Printer and the Superintendent of Documents are no more free from suit in the case before us than would be a legislative aide who made copies of the materials at issue and distributed them to the public at the direction of his superiors. . . . The scope of inquiry becomes equivalent to the inquiry in the context of the Speech and Debate Clause, and the answer is the same. The business of Congress is to legislate; congressmen and aides are absolutely immune when they are legislating. But when they act outside the 'sphere of legitimate legislative activity,' . . . they enjoy no special immunity from local laws protecting the good name or the reputation of the ordinary citizen."[60]

*Page 210*        ARTICLE IV, SECTION II, ¶ 1

In one of the Abortion Decisions of 1973, the Supreme Court held unconstitutional a Georgia statute limiting abortions performed in the state to Georgia residents: "Just as the Privileges and Immunities Clause . . . protects persons who enter other States to ply their trade . . . so it must protect persons who enter Georgia seeking the medical services that are available there."[61]

*Page 212*        ARTICLE IV, SECTION II, ¶ 3

The U.S. Attorney's letter alluded to in footnote 18 follows in part:
"The conclusions reached in our discussion were admittedly simplistic; however, I am tempted to believe they are sound. It was pointed out that the defendant could not be taken into the custody of either state B or state A officers until dissolution of the federal custody status. Once the defendant posts bond and is released from federal custody, the defendant physically enters the jurisdiction of state B. The defendant's presence in state B is no longer a mere geographical incident; the defendant is subject to the sovereignty of state B. If state B takes the defendant into custody, the federal government can proceed personally against the defendant only by procuring his presence in federal court through a writ of habeas corpus directed against defendant's state B custodian."

*Page 225*        ARTICLE VI, ¶ 2

Three important Supremacy Clause cases were decided by the Supreme Court in 1973. In the first, the Court affirmed 5-4 the lower court decision in the *Lockheed* case mentioned in footnote 7 of the Text. Justice Douglas writing for the majority acknowledged that "there is to be sure no express provision of pre-emption in the 1972 [Federal Noise Control] Act. That, however, is not decisive. . . . It is the pervasive nature of the scheme of federal regulation of aircraft noise that leads us to conclude that there is pre-emption."[62]

60 Doe *v.* McMillan, 93 S. Ct. 2018 (1973).
61 Doe *v.* Bolton, 93 S. Ct. 739, 751 (1973).
62 City of Burbank *v.* Lockheed Air Terminal, Inc., 93 S. Ct. 1854 (1973).

In one of the other cases, the Court demonstrated that it would not be cavalier with State claims in matters arising under the Supremacy Clause. The majority, again speaking through Justice Douglas, held that it was not to be presumed that Congress in extending the Fair Labor Standards Act to certain State employees intended to take away the constitutional immunity of States from suits in Federal courts involving their own citizens. (The act provides for suits by employees against their employer for damages as well as unpaid minimum wages and overtime.) Justice Douglas concluded: "We are reluctant to believe that Congress in pursuit of a harmonious federalism desired to treat the States so harshly. The policy of the Act so far as the States are concerned is wholly served by allowing the delicate federal-state relationship to be managed through the Secretary of Labor."[63]

The third case involved New York's controversial Work Rules Law, which was designed to get welfare recipients off welfare rolls and into jobs. The Supreme Court reversed a lower court ruling that the Federal work incentive program pre-empts the New York law.[64]

*Page 268*      THE BURGER COURT AND THE FUTURE

While it remains true that the Nixon Court has not yet become a reality, the decisions of the October 1972 term have made it increasingly clear that the Court's drift is to the political Right, a phenomenon attributable in fair measure to Justice White's new-found affinity with the four Nixon appointees. Apart from the Court's tightening polarization, a tendency which is only somewhat abated on issues such as environmental regulation, what is most significant is that the conservative undertow has begun to reach beyond the area of criminal procedure and into cases involving First Amendment rights (notably on obscenity, see p. 578 of Supplement) and equal protection (particularly reapportionment, see p. 599 of Supplement, and school desegregation, p. 597). With its constant emphasis on the methodology of interest balancing, its avowed concern for the limitations of the judicial institution in solving society's major problems, and its increasing reverence for the Federal system, the emerging conservative majority is coming more and more to pattern the Court after its patron saint, the late Justice Harlan.

*Page 274*      AMENDMENT I

Following the Supreme Court's 1971 decision in *Lemon*, the Pennsylvania General Assembly passed a new law which provided funds to reimburse parents for a portion of the tuition paid to send their children to private schools. The law was drawn up to avoid the "entanglement problem" on which the law in *Lemon* had run afoul by precluding the administrative authority from involvement in the administration of non-public

---

[63] Employees of Dept. of Public Health & Welf. *v.* Missouri, 93 S. Ct. 1614 (1973).

[64] New York State Dept. of Social Services *v.* Dublino, 41 *LW* 5047 (1973).

schools. The Court, however, held that "Pennsylvania's tuition grant scheme violates the constitutional mandate against the 'sponsorship' or 'financial support' of religion or religious institutions."[65] It also struck down provisions of a New York State statute which provided for (1) tuition reimbursements to parents of children in non-public schools; (2) money grants to non-public schools for maintenance and repair of facilities "to ensure the health, welfare and safety of enrolled pupils"; (3) income tax relief to parents who did not qualify for tuition reimbursement. The Court concluded that "Our examination . . . in light of all relevant considerations, compels the judgment that each, as written, has a 'primary effect that advances religion' and offends the constitutional prohibition against laws 'respecting the establishment of religion.' "[66]

On the same day it handed down the aforementioned decisions, the Court upheld a South Carolina act which assists institutions of higher education, primarily through the use of revenue bonds, in constructing facilities except those which might be used for sectarian or religious purposes. The Court concluded that the act and the transactions under it which had come under challenge in the case "confine the scope of assistance to the secular aspects of this liberal arts college and do not foreshadow excessive entanglement between State and religion."[67]

Illustrative of many cases involving the Establishment Clause which have surfaced in the State and lower Federal courts in the past decade was a case decided by the United States Court of Appeals, Tenth Circuit. In that case, the court held that the erection and maintenance on government property of a granite monolith inscribed with the Ten Commandments was "primarily secular, and not religious in character; that neither its purpose or effect tends to establish religious belief."[68] The court had explained prior to the holding that "we cannot say that the monument, as it stands, is more than a depiction of a historically important monument with both secular and sectarian effects."

*Page 276* AMENDMENT I

In three terse decisions involving conscientious objectors' claims on religious grounds, U.S. courts of appeals held (1) that compelling a conscientious objector to perform civilian work does not violate the First and Thirteenth Amendments;[69] (2) that refusal to stand in court at the

---

[65] Sloan v. Lemon, 41 *LW* 5181 (1973). Earlier in the Term, the Court had to deal with another problem stemming from the *Lemon* case. A U.S. District Court had permitted the State to reimburse non-public schools for services provided under the State law before the Supreme Court's decision in *Lemon* declared the law invalid. The Supreme Court affirmed the district court's decision. The several opinions in the case include a significant wide-ranging discussion of the issue of retroactivity. Lemon v. Kurtzman (*Lemon II*), 93 S. Ct. 1463 (1973).

[66] Committee for Public Education v. Nyquist, 41 *LW* 5153 (1973).

[67] Hunt v. McNair, 41 *LW* 5174 (1973).

[68] Anderson v. Salt Lake City Corp., 475 F. 2d. 29 (1973). The decision contains citations and descriptions of a number of like cases.

[69] United States v. Anderson, 467 F. 2d. 210 (1972).

insistence of the court on the grounds of religious scruple was punishable under a contempt statute;[70] (3) that a member of an Amish sect who had been classified as a conscientious objector was "entitled to fulfill his obligation of citizenship by performing alternative service," and failure to report for such service was a violation of law.[71]

*Page 287*                          AMENDMENT I

Although Justice Douglas and two other dissenters saw the Hatch Act (see Text, p. 142) as a limitation on government employees' "right to speak, to propose, to publish, to petition government, to assemble," a majority had no difficulty finding that "neither the First Amendment nor any other provision of the Constitution invalidates a law barring . . . partisan political conduct by federal employees."[72]

In two other recent cases, the Supreme Court made notable observations with regard to free speech. In a case involving an expulsion at a *State* university for matter published in a campus newspaper the Court said: "We think *Healy* makes it clear that mere dissemination of ideas—no matter how offensive to good taste—on a state university campus may not be shut off in the name alone of 'conventions of decency.' "[73] The highly controversial case involving school financing and property taxes (see p. 598 of Supplement) confronted the Supreme Court with the argument that "education is itself a fundamental personal right because it is essential to the effective exercise of First Amendment freedoms" because "The right to speak is meaningless unless the speaker is capable of articulating his thoughts intelligently and persuasively."[74] The Court did not agree.

A canvass of State and lower Federal court decisions supports the following observations: (1) though there may still be occasional differences of opinion, governmental interests in promulgating hair and dress codes[75] and in prohibiting flag desecration[76] have been repeatedly upheld; (2) use of the most offensive language has been clearly sustained as expression as long as it is not aimed directly at someone so as to become "fighting words" and thus incite;[77] (3) residential as well as labor picketing is a protected form of expression,[78] though picketing which verges on be-

---

[70] *In re* Chase, 468 F. 2d. 128 (1972).
[71] Slabaugh *v.* United States, 474 F. 2d. 592 (1973).
[72] CSC *v.* Letter Carriers, 41 *LW* 5122 (1973).
[73] Papish *v.* Board of Curators of University of Missouri, 93 S. Ct. 1197 (1973).
[74] San Antonio Independent School District *v.* Rodriguez, 93 S. Ct. 1278, 1298 (1973). This was not the leading argument in the case.
[75] For a complete discussion and compendium of cases, *see* Breeze *v.* Smith, 501 P. 2d. 159 (1972); *and* Greenwald *v.* Frank, 337 N.Y.S. 2d. 225 (1972); *but cf.* Copeland *v.* Hawkins, 352 F. Supp. 1022 (1973).
[76] *See* State *v.* Spence, 506 P. 2d. 293 (1973); *and* Delorme *v.* State, 488 S.W. 2d. 808 (1973); *but cf.* State *v.* Zimmelman, 301 A. 2d. 129 (1973).
[77] *See* Reese *v.* State, 299 A. 2d. 848 (1973); *and* State *v.* Rosenfeld, 303 A. 2d. 889 (1973).
[78] People Acting Through Community Effort *v.* Doorley, 468 F. 2d. 1143 (1972).

coming a secondary boycott is in for rough-sledding;[79] and (4) while public institutions may operate on a "first come-first served" approach to organizations seeking use of the facilities, they may not discriminate against such organizations because of their membership or views but only where there is serious threat to destruction of the property.[80]

Regarding expression on the campus, a Federal district court has struck down a college regulation which prohibited political canvassing in dormitories unless two-thirds of the residents had given their approval.[81] Other courts have ruled against the First Amendment claims of some students that a university-imposed activity fee (to defray expenses of a speakers program and school newspaper) resulted in supporting the expression of views opposed to those of the students bringing suit.[82] Finally, a lower Federal court invalidated a provision of the Higher Education Act which terminated funds to any student committing a "serious" crime or found contributing to any "serious disruption" on the campus.[83]

*Page 291*  AMENDMENT I

The decisions of the Supreme Court regarding obscenity promise to be the most widely hailed and criticized decisions of the year. Chief Justice Burger, speaking for the majority in a 5-4 decision, reviewed the "somewhat tortured history" of the Court's obscenity decisions and stated: "This much has been categorically settled by the Court, that obscene material is unprotected by the First Amendment. . . . We acknowledge, however, the inherent dangers of undertaking to regulate any form of expression. State statutes designed to regulate obscene materials must be carefully limited." The Chief Justice then went on to explain what the States could do by way of regulation: "We now confine the permissible scope of such regulation to works which depict or describe *sexual conduct.* That conduct must be specifically defined by the applicable state law as written or authoritatively construed. A state offense must also be limited to works which, taken as a whole, appeal to the prurient interest in sex, which portray sexual conduct in a patently offensive way, and which, *taken as a whole,* do not have serious literary, artistic, political, or scientific value."[84] (Emphasis supplied.) The majority explicitly rejected the

79 *See* C. Comella, Inc. *v.* United Farm Workers Organizing Comm., 292 N.E. 2d. 647 (1972).

80 *See* National Socialist White People's Party *v.* Ringers, 473 F. 2d. 1010 (1973); *and* Wood *v.* Davison, 351 F. Supp. 543 (1972). The latter case involved a homosexual group, the Committee on Gay Education.

81 James *v.* Nelson, 349 F. Supp. 1061 (1972).

82 Lace *v.* University of Vermont, 303 A. 2d. 475 (1973); *and* Veed *v.* Schwartzkopf, 353 F. Supp. 149 (1973). *Cf.* Justice Black's and Justice Douglas's dissents in International Ass'n of Machinists *v.* Street, 367 U.S. 740 (1961).

83 Rasche *v.* Board of Trustees, 353 F. Supp. 973 (1972).

84 Miller *v.* California, 41 *LW* 4925, 4927 (1973). *See also* Paris Adult Theatre I *v.* Slaton, 41 *LW* 4935 (1973); Kaplan *v.* California, 41 *LW* 4958 (1973).

*"utterly* without redeeming social value" of Memoirs *v.* Massachusetts, pointing out that "that concept has never commanded the adherence of more than three Justices at one time." As to the guidelines for the triers of fact in obscenity cases, the Court held "that obscenity is to be determined by applying 'contemporary community standards' . . . not national standards.' "[85] In a powerful dissent in one of the cases, Justice Brennan wrote: "In short, while I cannot say the interest of the State—apart from the question of juveniles and unconsenting adults—are trivial or nonexistent, I am compelled to conclude that these interests cannot justify the substantial damage to constitutional rights and to this Nation's judicial machinery that inevitably results from state efforts to bar the distribution even of unprotected material to consenting adults. . . . I would hold, therefore, that at least in the absence of distribution to juveniles or obtrusive exposure to unconsenting adults, the First and Fourteenth Amendments prohibit the state and federal governments from attempting wholly to suppress sexually oriented materials on the basis of their allegedly 'obscene' contents. Nothing in this approach precludes those governments from taking action to serve what may be strong and legitimate interests through regulation of the *manner of distribution* of sexually oriented material."[86] (Emphasis supplied.)

The Court also held that carrying obscene materials in interstate commerce for personal use was not the same as possessing such materials in one's own home and was, consequently, subject to congressional regulations.[87] On the other side of the ledger, the Court held that an allegedly obscene movie could not be seized at a commercial movie house without "a constitutionally sufficient warrant," even where the law officer viewed the film himself. The Court held that such a seizure was unreasonable "because prior restraint of the right of expression, whether by books or films, calls for a higher hurdle in the evaluation of reasonableness."[88]

Some State and lower Federal courts continued to tighten the application of libel law consistent with the Supreme Court's holdings in *Rosenbloom* and *New York Times.* Among those who found themselves in the category of a "public figure" or who found malice tough to prove were: (1) a convict whose release was imminent after 27 years in prison and who was identified together with the crime he had committed (murder) in an article which focused on the admission of a new inmate who just happened to cross paths with the plaintiff and afforded a contrast;[89] (2) a lawyer representing the family of a victim killed by a police officer, who, in an article appearing in a right-wing magazine, was called "Red" and a

85 *Ibid.,* 4931.
86 Paris Adult Theatre I *v.* Slaton, 41 *LW* 4935, 4955 (1973).
87 U.S. *v.* Orito, 41 *LW* 4956 (1973) *and* U.S. *v.* 12,200 Ft. Reels, 41 *LW* 4961 (1973).
88 Roaden *v.* Kentucky, 41 *LW* 5070 (1973). *Cf.* Heller *v.* New York, 41 *LW* 5067 (1973).
89 Kent *v.* Pittsburgh Press Co., 349 F. Supp. 622 (1972).

"Communist-fronter";[90] (3) a woman about whose divorce a national magazine had published an article.[91] On the other hand, recovery was allowed by non-union mailmen who were characterized as "scabs" and vilified in a postal union newpaper,[92] and by the operators of a public opinion poll for a running attack made upon it as "corrupt, dishonest, and rigged" by a California multi-millionaire after it had shown him favored by only one per cent of the State's Republicans as their preference for the 1966 gubernatorial nomination.[93] Finally, in a case that went considerably beyond the merely verbal attacks on privacy at issue in the cases above, Jackie Onassis won a law suit involving serious physical intrusion.[94] In a lengthy opinion settling an action filed against her by photographer Richard Galella for false arrest and malicious prosecution, a Federal district court found the photographer's over-zealous behavior not only to be unprotected by the First Amendment but, in fact, actionable assault, battery, and harassment.

*Page 291*                              AMENDMENT I

The Supreme Court decided in 1973 that the application to a newspaper of the Human Relations Ordinance of the City of Pittsburgh aimed at ending discrimination was constitutional. Emphasizing that they were deciding the case on very narrow grounds, a majority held "that the Commission's [on Human Relations] modified order, narrowly drawn to prohibit placement in sex-designated columns of advertisements for non-exempt job opportunities, does not infringe the First Amendment rights of the Pittsburgh Press."[95] The lineup of the Court in this decision is intriguing. Powell, Brennan, White, Marshall, and Rehnquist constituted the majority; the dissenters were Burger, Douglas, Stewart, and Blackmun. Justice Douglas saw the issue in these terms: "there can be no valid law censoring the press or punishing it for publishing its views or the views of subscribers or customers who express their ideas in letters to the editor or in want ads or other commercial spaces"[96] unless it in someway was "closely brigaded" with illegal action.

Two cases cited above which speak of impermissible curbs on freedom of the press should be noted in this context.[97] In addition, a number of interesting issues surfaced in State and lower Federal courts over the last year. Among them were rulings: (1) that the broadcasting industry's union

90 Gertz *v.* Robert Welch, Inc., 471 F. 2d. 801 (1972).
91 Firestone *v.* Time, Inc., 271 So. 2d. 745 (1972).
92 Old Dominion Branch No. 496, Nat'l Ass'n of Letter Carriers *v.* Austin, 192 S.E. 2d. 737 (1972).
93 Field Research Corp. *v.* Patrick, 106 Cal. Rptr. 473 (1973).
94 Galella *v.* Onassis, 353 F. Supp. 196 (1972).
95 Pittsburgh Press Co. *v.* The Pittsburgh Com'n on Human Relations, 41 *LW* 5055, 5060 (1973).
96 *Ibid.,* 5062.
97 Papish *v.* Board of Curators of University of Missouri, cited on p. 577 of Supplement, *and* Roaden *v.* Kentucky, cited on p. 579 of Supplement.

shop requirement does and does not violate a commentator's freedom of speech;[98] (2) that, while academic institutions are entitled to take steps to prevent disruption of the educational process, they may not impose overly broad regulations indulging in prior restraint of student publications or prohibit dissemination of material simply because of taste or to protect the school's image;[99] (3) that upheld a FCC decision which denied reissuance of a broadcasting license to a station (dominated by followers of Dr. Carl McIntyre, a right-wing minister), which had ignored the Fairness and Personal Attack Doctrines and misrepresented its programming;[100] (4) that the Smothers Brothers had no grounds for recovering damages under the Federal Communications Act against a television network for censoring their program material and finally taking them off the air;[101] and (5) that trial judges could not restrict newspapermen to report information only divulged on testimony in court[102] or prohibit them from describing or taking pictures of the scene of the crime or of witnesses,[103] or suppress a bill of particulars in a case absent any showing of adverse pre-trial publicity.[104]

In a complicated case involving complaints of the Democratic National Committee and the Business Executives' Move for Vietnam Peace that radio station WTOP of Washington, D.C., would not sell advertising time to them to speak out on issues, the Supreme Court once more spoke on the Fairness Doctrine. The Court reiterated its position that "under the Fairness Doctrine broadcasters are responsible for providing the listening and viewing public with access to a balanced presentation of information on issues of public importance.[105] But the Court held that the Doctrine need not be applied to editorial advertising and that the question of a broadcaster's fairness was to be determined, when appropriate to do so, by his overall performance.

*Page 297*                              AMENDMENT I

The Supreme Court, 5-4, held that a New York law requiring voters to enroll in the party of their choice before the general election in order to be eligible to vote in the following primary (a period of months) did not

[98] Evans *v.* American Federation of Television and Radio Artists, 354 F. Supp. 823 (1973) (does not); *and* Lewis III *v.* American Federation of Television and Radio Artists, 336 N.Y.S. 2d. 56 (1972), *affirmed on appeal*, 341 N.Y.S. 2d. 625 (1973) (does).

[99] Jacobs *v.* Board of School Commissioners, 349 F. Supp. 605 (1972); Bazaar *v.* Fortune, 476 F. 2d. 570 (1973).

[100] Brandywine-Main Line Radio, Inc. *v.* FCC, 473 F. 2d. 16 (1972).

[101] Smothers *v.* Columbia Broadcasting Sys., 351 F. Supp. 622 (1972).

[102] State *ex rel.* Miami Herald Publishing Co. *v.* Rose, 271 So. 2d. 483 (1972).

[103] Sun Company of San Bernardino *v.* Superior Court, 105 Cal. Rptr. 873 (1973).

[104] United States *v.* General Motors Corp., 352 F. Supp. 1071 (1973).

[105] Columbia Broadcasting Sys., Inc. *v.* Democratic Nat. Comm., 93 S. Ct. 2080, 2097 (1973).

violate the right to freely associate.[106] The dissenters made explicit their view that a "less drastic enrollment deadline than the eight or 11 months now imposed" would be more in accord with the Constitution and would be adequate to protect against political party raiding.

Another intriguing claim for the right of association was made by Justice Douglas in a concurring opinion in a case dealing with the Food Stamp Act's provision that excludes from participation any household containing an individual who is unrelated to other members. He wrote: "I suppose poor people holding a meeting or convention would be under the same constitutional umbrella as others. The dimensions of the 'related' person problem under the Food Stamp Act are in that category. As the facts of this case show, the poor are congregating in households where they can better meet the adversities of poverty. This banding together is an expression of the right of freedom of association that is very deep in our traditions."[107]

*Page 305*                     AMENDMENT IV

Voices have been raised protesting the use of grand jury proceedings as a means of denying rather than protecting individual liberty.[108] Two examples of the kind of grand jury actions which have caused concern became the bases of cases which ultimately reached the Supreme Court. One case dealt with a grand jury subpoena to about twenty persons to give voice exemplars for identification purposes. In the view of the Federal court of appeals which reviewed the case first, the grand jury was "seeking to obtain the voice exemplars of the witnesses by the use of its subpoena powers because probable cause did not exist for their arrest or for some other, less unusual, method of compelling production of the exemplars"[109] and that court held that this would not be done without a demonstration of the reasonableness of the seizure because the Fourth Amendment applied to the grand jury process. The Supreme Court held otherwise, saying that "a subpoena to appear before a grand jury is not a 'seizure' in the Fourth Amendment sense, even though that summons may be inconvenient or burdensome."[110] But the Court did go on to caution that "This is not to say that a grand jury subpoena is some talisman that dissolves all constitutional protections. The grand jury cannot require a witness to testify against himself. It cannot require the production by a person of private books and records that would incriminate him." (The self-incrimination question raised in the case is noted on p. 587 of the Supplement.) The Court also rejected the argument "that the grand jury's subsequent directive to make the voice recording was itself an

---

[106] Rosario v. Rockefeller, 93 S. Ct. 1245 (1973).

[107] U.S. Dept. of Agriculture v. Moreno, 41 *LW* 5105 (1973).

[108] P. Cowan, "Kind of Immunity That Leads to Jail: The New Grand Jury," *N.Y. Times Magazine*, April 29, 1973, p. 18.

[109] U.S. v. Dionisio, 93 S. Ct. 764, 767 (1973).

[110] *Ibid.*, 769.

infringement of . . . rights under the Fourth Amendment." The other case, much like the first, dealt with a *narrowly drawn* grand jury subpoena for handwriting samples to determine whether or not the recipient of the subpoena was the author of certain writings. The Supreme Court, tying the two cases together, held that the "government was under no obligation here, any more than in *Dionisio* to make a preliminary showing of 'reasonableness.' "[111]

Two men were convicted for transporting and conspiring to transport stolen goods in interstate commerce. A co-conspirator, who was in possession of the goods, successfully challenged the introduction of the stolen goods as evidence on the grounds that they were obtained from his store on a faulty warrant and his case was tried separately. When the aforementioned duo sought to do the same, their *standing* to do so was challenged. The Supreme Court held that, under the facts of the case, they did not have standing to do so because "Fourth Amendment rights are personal rights which, like some other constitutional rights, cannot be vicariously asserted."[112] But the Court explicitly refrained from clearing up some of the confusion remaining over the question of whether or not there is "automatic" standing "where possession at the time of the contested search and seizure is 'an essential element of the offense charged.' " (Here, the convicted had been tried for transporting and conspiring to transport—possession was not an element.)

A sharply divided Supreme Court held that *roving patrols* of the Border Patrol cannot stop and search cars 20 miles from the border in an effort to detect the illegal importation of aliens without probable cause or a warrant. The Court distinguished these searches from routine inspections and searches at the border or "its functional equivalent" (airports' receiving non-stop passengers from foreign countries), which the Court indicated are legal. Apparently, the matter is not closed, however, for one of the five-man majority, Justice Powell, indicated that he would approve a warrant for an "area search," i.e., "to obtain advance judicial approval of the decision to conduct roving searches on a particular road or roads for a reasonable period of time."[113]

In a case decided the same day, the Supreme Court reviewed extensively its previous decisions with respect to warrantless searches of automobiles. The review caused Justice Rehnquist, speaking for the majority, to observe that "this branch of the law is something less than a seamless web."[114] He pointed out that "Although vehicles are 'effects' within the meaning of the Fourth Amendment, 'for purposes of the Fourth Amendment there is a constitutional difference between houses and cars' " and that "warrantless searches by state officers have been sustained in cases in which the possibilities of the vehicle being removed or evidence in it being destroyed

---

111 United States *v.* Mara, 93 S. Ct. 774, 776 (1973).
112 Brown *v.* United States, 93 S. Ct. 1565 (1973).
113 Almeida-Sanchez *v.* United States, 41 *LW* 4970, 4975 (1973).
114 Cady *v.* Dombrowski, 41 *LW* 4995, 4997 (1973).

were remote, if not non-existent." He went on to assert that, with respect to warrantless searches and seizures of automobiles, the general standard was "unreasonableness" and that previous decisions as well as this one "can usefully refine the language of the Amendment itself in order to evolve some detailed formula for judging cases such as this."[115]

In short, according to the majority, courts must look to the fact situation in each particular case to determine whether or not the warrantless search of an automobile is reasonable. The dissenters speaking through Justice Brennan argued that there were only three exceptions to the proposition that a warrantless search is per se unreasonable: (1) where an automobile may be quickly moved; (2) where the search is incident to a valid arrest; (3) where the evidence is in "plain view."

*Page 307*                          AMENDMENT IV

The Court seemed to retreat substantially from its previous position on searches without warrants where there is no arrest (see Text, p. 307). The Court decided, after a careful weighing of the facts in this case, that the police did not violate the Constitution by taking a sample of fingernail scrapings from an unwilling person who had voluntarily come to the station house to answer questions about the murder of his estranged wife. The Court held that "considering the existence of probable cause, the very limited intrusion undertaken incident to the station house detention, and the ready destructibility of the evidence, we cannot say that this search violated the Fourth and Fourteenth Amendments."[116] (See Text, p. 305.)

When it was argued that the seizure without warrant of an allegedly obscene film by a sheriff, who had viewed the film, was a seizure incident to a lawful arrest, the Supreme Court suggested that guns and knives should be distinguished from books and movies in appraising the reasonableness of a seizure. The Court concluded that "The seizure is unreasonable, not simply because it would have been easy to secure a warrant, but rather because prior restraint of the right of expression . . . calls for a higher hurdle in the evaluation of reasonableness."[117]

After an erudite canvass of the meaning of "waiver," "consent," and "voluntariness" in the context of other constitutional rights, Justice Stewart, speaking for a majority of the Court, held with respect to consent to a search that: "Our decision today is a narrow one. We hold only that when the subject of a search is not in custody and the State attempts to justify a search on the basis of his consent, the Fourth and Fifteenth Amendments require that it demonstrate that the consent was in fact voluntarily given, and not the result of duress or coercion, express or implied. Voluntariness is a question of fact to be determined from all the circumstances, and *while the subject's knowledge of a right to refuse is a*

---

115 *Ibid.*, 4999.
116 Cupp *v.* Murphy, 93 S. Ct. 2000, 2004 (1973).
117 Roaden *v.* Kentucky, 41 *LW* 5070 (1973).

*factor to be taken into account, the prosecution is not required to demonstrate such knowledge as a prerequisite to establishing a voluntary consent.*[118] (Emphasis supplied.)

## Page 307        AMENDMENT IV

In the year that has elapsed since we noted the initiation of airport searches, a substantial body of law has grown up surrounding them. Numerous rulings since that of the *Bell* case,[119] and others cited in the Text, have affirmed the constitutional validity of that exercise in principle and have sustained the admissibility of evidence gained from such searches.[120] However, several cases in which the fruits of airport searches were held inadmissible, or were otherwise distinguished, suggest limitations on the practice:[121] (1) Searches may be initiated only on reasonable suspicion (i.e., fitting the "hijacker profile," tripping the magnetometer, failing to properly identify oneself); (2) searches may extend only to areas continuing to justify suspicion (e.g., containers or enclosures large enough to conceal weapons or explosives); (3) searches yield admissible evidence when the articles are in plain sight; (4) searches must afford warning to passengers that they have the right to avoid the search by not boarding the plane, so that consent is entirely voluntary; and (5) searches not executed as a condition of passenger boarding are justified only under customary "stop and frisk" circumstances.

Searches incident to entry to a military base and to the grounds of a correctional facility were also sustained in general, though the courts split on the scope of the search justified.[122]

By way of contrast to these areas in which protection of an obvious interest justified significant governmental surveillance, lower Federal and State courts continued to assess what circumstances furnished a reasonable expectation of privacy as to warrant the most stringent prohibition from intrusion. Among those were: a wastebasket in a private office even after the occupant had left for the day,[123] a detective's office when a husband and wife had been left alone to talk,[124] a public washroom,[125] and the

---

118 Schneckloth *v.* Bustamonte, 93 S. Ct. 2041, 2059 (1973).

119 United States *v.* Bell, 335 F. Supp. 797 (1971), *affirmed on appeal* 464 F. 2d. 667 (1972).

120 *See* United States *v.* Mitchell, 352 F. Supp. 38 (1972); People *v.* Botos, 104 Cal. Rptr. 193 (1972); State *v.* Damon, 502 P. 2d. 1360 (1972); United States *v.* Moreno, 475 F. 2d. 44 (1973); United States *v.* Riggs, 474 F. 2d. 699 (1973); People *v.* Boyles, 341 N.Y.S. 2d. 967 (1973); People *v.* Lopez, 342 N.Y.S. 2d. 420 (1973).

121 *See* United States *v.* Allen, 349 F. Supp. 749 (1942); United States *v.* Kroll 351 F. Supp. 148 (1972); United States *v.* Meulener, 351 F. Supp. 1284 (1972).

122 *Cf.* United States *v.* Vaughan, 475 F. 2d. 1262 (1973); *with* Mathis *v.* Appellate Dept. of Sup. Ct. of Sacramento Cty., 105 Cal. Rptr. 126 (1972).

123 United States *v.* Kahan, 350 F. Supp. 784 (1972); *See also* Ball *v.* State, 205 N.W. 2d. 353 (1973). *But cf.* United States *v.* Mustone, 469 F. 2d. 970 (1972).

124 North *v.* Sup. Ct. of Riverside Cty., 502 P. 2d. 1305 (1972).

125 People *v.* Triggs, 506 P. 2d. 232 (1973), *and also* cases cited therein.

view through one's windows when standing on private grounds.[126] On the other hand, the courts found prison cells[127] and school lockers[128] to be areas affording substantially less protection than the Constitution guaranteed generally.

*Page 314*                          AMENDMENT V

For two recent cases dealing with the power of grand juries see page 582 of Supplement.

*Page 315*                          AMENDMENT V

As to the question of whether or not *O'Callahan* was to be applied retroactively, the Supreme Court held that "the purpose to be served by O'Callahan, the reliance on the law as it stood before that decision, and the effect of a holding of retroactivity, all require that *O'Callahan* be accorded prospective application alone."[129] The Court, however, did not speak as one as to the reasons for its judgment.

*Page 317*                          AMENDMENT V

In a case where an acquittal on a smuggling charge was followed by a civil suit to forfeit goods allegedly smuggled, the Supreme Court upheld the proposition that "Congress may impose both a criminal and civil sanction in respect to the same act or omission; for the double jeopardy clause prohibits merely punishing twice, or attempting a second time to punish criminally for the same offense."[130] Nor did the Court find "That the measure of recovery fixed by Congress . . . is so unreasonable or excessive that it transforms what was clearly intended as a civil remedy into a criminal penalty."

In other double jeopardy cases, the Supreme Court: (1) reaffirmed its earlier decision in North Carolina *v.* Pearce (see Text, p. 318) with some additional caveats;[131] (2) held that its previous decision in *Waller* re two prosecutions within one *system* of government (municipal and state prosecutions in this case) was to be accorded full retroactivity;[132] (3) held, 5-4, that a declaration of a mistrial after the jury was impaneled but before any evidence was taken did not bar another trial under a valid indictment.[133]

126 According to a very recent decision rendered by the California Supreme Court, *see Los Angeles Times,* June 21, 1973, p. 3.

127 United States *v.* Hitchcock, 467 F. 2d. 1107 (1972).

128 *In re* W, 105 Cal. Rptr. 775 (1973); *but cf.* People *v.* Bowers, 339 N.Y.S. 2d. 783 (1973).

129 Gosa *v.* Mayden, 41 *LW* 5075 (1973).

130 One Lot Emerald Cut Stones *v.* United States, 93 S. Ct. 489, 492 (1972).

131 Chaffin *v.* Stynchcombe, 93 S. Ct. 1977 (1973).

132 Robinson *v.* Neil, 93 S. Ct. 876 (1973).

133 State of Illinois *v.* Somerville, 93 S. Ct. 1066 (1973).

*Page 323*                    AMENDMENT V

The Supreme Court saw no violation of the Self-Incrimination Clause in grand juries' requiring voice exemplars and handwriting samples.[134] Nor did the Court find it a violation of the privilege against self-incrimination for a district court to compel an accountant to turn over a client's tax records. As the Court saw it, the client was not the one being coerced.[135]

*Page 331*                    AMENDMENT V

We saw again the application of substantive due process in a case challenging the constitutionality of the Food Stamp Act of 1964. The law provided that "any household which includes a member who has reached his eighteenth birthday and who is claimed as a dependent child for Federal income tax purposes by a taxpayer who is not a member of an eligible household, shall be ineligible to participate in any food stamp program."[136] Patently, this provision was aimed at college students and children of wealthy parents. Justice Douglas, writing for the majority, held that "The deduction taken for the benefit of the parent in the prior year is not a rational measure of the need of a different household with whom the child of the tax deducting parent lives and rests on an irrebuttable presumption often contrary to fact. It therefore lacks critical ingredients of due process. . . ."[137] But a majority of the Court did not find the Four Installment Rule of the Truth in Lending Act, which requires the seller to make disclosures to those whom he extends consumer credit without a finance charge if the sum owed is payable in more than four installments, presumptive or violative of due process.[138]

Unable to apply the Fourteenth Amendment's Equal Protection Clause per se to the Federal government (see p. 331 of Text), the Supreme Court in two cases again dealt with unequal treatment by the Federal government as violations of the Due Process Clause of the Fifth. One was a case involving the denial of food stamps to any household containing an individual unrelated to any other member of the household.[139] The other was the case of a woman Air Force officer who sought to claim her husband as a dependent in order to receive the benefits that male officers receive for their wives.[140]

A survey of discrimination claims litigated under the Fifth Amendment in the lower Federal courts over the last year yields some contradictory

[134] United States *v.* Dionisio, 93 S. Ct. 764 (1973), *and* United States *v.* Mara, 93 S. Ct. 774 (1973).
[135] Couch *v.* United States, 93 S. Ct. 611 (1973).
[136] 7 U.S.C. 2011 *et seq.*
[137] U.S. Department of Agriculture *v.* Murry, 41 *LW* 5099 (1973).
[138] Mourning *v.* Family Publications Service, Inc., 93 S. Ct. 1652 (1973).
[139] U.S. Department of Agriculture *v.* Moreno, 41 *LW* 5105 (1973).
[140] Frontiero *v.* Richardson, 93 S. Ct. 1764 (1973).

but not entirely surprising findings. While a Federal district court rejected outright a class action suit naming the United States government as defendant and challenging the unrepresentative composition of the civil service, as an affront to the sovereign immunity doctrine, that tribunal heartily sanctioned affirmative action efforts to seek relief against specific governmental officeholders.[141] The Federal courts also continued to legitimate efforts at making the construction trades more representative by approving governmentally imposed quota hiring practices,[142] and upheld the decision of at least one Federal agency which let a contract to a minority-controlled company without first opening the project to competitive bidding.[143] On the other hand, Federal district courts dismissed a suit by an unwed mother to prevent her discharge from the Navy, which she said evidenced double moral standards as applied between men and women,[144] and refused to enjoin the VFW's "men only" membership policy even though the organization bore a charter from Congress.[145] However, the U.S. District Court for the District of Massachusetts held that the same educational assistance benefits offered to "eligible veterans" of "active duty" with the military must also be extended to conscientious objectors who have completed their social service work.[146] And finally, a three-judge U.S. District Court, held part of the Dependents' Medical Care Act[147] unconstitutional insofar as it denied benefits to, and thereby invidiously discriminated against, the illegitimate children of servicemen.[148] (For cases dealing with State discrimination, see p. 595 of Supplement.)

*Page 332*                     AMENDMENT V

One of the most hotly debated cases of the past Term will surely be the so-called entrapment case.[149] A Federal narcotics agent supplied some manufacturers of "speed" with an essential ingredient on the condition that he be shown a sample of the drug they were making and the laboratory in which it was produced. Justice Rehnquist, speaking for the majority of five (the Nixon appointees plus Justice White), held that "The law enforcement conduct here stops far short of violating that 'fundamental fairness, shocking to the universal sense of justice,' mandated by the Due Process Clause of the Fifth Amendment."[150] As he saw it, the "Narc's" contribution to the "criminal enterprise already in process was scarcely objectionable." The measure of the dissenter's disdain for the majority opinion are these words from Justice Douglas: "Federal agents play a debased role when they become the instigators of the crime, or partners in

141 Penn v. United States, 350 F. Supp. 752 (1972).
142 Southern Illinois Builders' Ass'n v. Ogilvie, 471 F. 2d. 680 (1972).
143 Fortec Constructors v. Kleppe, 350 F. Supp. 171 (1972).
144 Flores v. Secretary of Defense, 355 F. Supp. 93 (1973).
145 Stearns v. Veterans of Foreign Wars, 353 F. Supp. 473 (1972).
146 Robison v. Johnson, 352 F. Supp. 848 (1973).
147 10 U.S.C. 1072 (2) E.
148 Miller v. Laird, 349 F. Supp. 1034 (1972).
149 United States v. Russell, 93 S. Ct. 1637 (1973).
150 Ibid., 1643.

its commission, or the creative brain behind the illegal scheme." And that was precisely what the case was about according to Justice Douglas.[151]

In a case involving a district court's instruction to a jury that "possession of recently stolen property, if not satisfactorily explained, is ordinarily a circumstance from which you may reasonably draw the inference and find, in the light of the surrounding circumstances shown by the evidence in the case, that the person in possession knew the property had been stolen," the Supreme Court traced "four recent decisions which have considered the validity under the Due Process Clause of criminal law presumptions and inferences." The Court concluded that "What has been established by the cases . . . is at least this: that if a statutory inference submitted to the jury as sufficient to support conviction satisfies the reasonable doubt standard (that is, the evidence necessary to invoke the inference is sufficient for a rational juror to find the inferred fact beyond a reasonable doubt) as well as the more-likely-than-not standard, then it clearly accords with due process."[152]

When an Oregon court "prevented a criminal defendant from introducing any evidence to support his alibi defense as a sanction for his failure to comply with a notice of alibi rule which, on its face, made no provision for reciprocal discovery," the Supreme Court held that due process "forbids enforcement of alibi rules unless reciprocal discovery rights are given to criminal defendants."[153]

*Page 336*        AMENDMENT V

The Supreme Court held in two cases this past Term that property was *not* taken when: (1) Congress mandated that a certain percentage of royalties accruing from tribal mineral leases on an Indian reservation go for certain benefits to the Indians even though that action enlarged the number of beneficiaries;[154] (2) a person is detained as a material witness and paid only $1 a day plus subsistence ("The detention of a material witness, in short, is simply not a 'taking' under the Fifth Amendment and the level of his compensation, therefore, does not as such, present a constitutional question").[155]

In two cases elucidating the meaning of just compensation, the Supreme Court held: (1) that in taking property where there is a lease involved, government must consider the additional value "based on the expectation that the lease might be renewed" (its actual market value, had there been

---

[151] *Ibid.*, 1646. In a notable dissent, Justice Stewart endeavored to fashion a general rule to cover entrapment cases: "Government agents may engage in conduct that is likely, when objectively considered, to afford a person ready and willing to commit the crime an opportunity to do so." In this case he felt that the agent had gone beyond "the mere offering of such an opportunity." *Ibid.*, 1649.

[152] Barnes *v.* United States, 41 *LW* 4917 (1973).

[153] Wardius *v.* Oregon, 41 *LW* 4804 (1973).

[154] United States *v.* Jim, 93 S. Ct. 261 (1972).

[155] Hurtado *v.* United States, 93 S. Ct. 1157 (1973).

no taking);[156] (2) that, where the Federal Grazing Act issues permits allowing livestock owners to graze their stock on Federal government lands with the stipulation that it will not create any property rights, the value which the permits added to other property required no compensation.[157] (Significantly, this was a 5-4 decision.)

*Page 340*            AMENDMENT VI

Contrary to precedent, a court of appeals fashioned a remedy short of dismissal of the indictment in a case where it was decided that the defendant had not been accorded a speedy trial. The Supreme Court reversed, saying "In light of the policies which underlie the right to a speedy trial, dismissal must remain . . . 'the only possible remedy.' "[158]

*Page 348*            AMENDMENT VI

The differing stances of Justices on criminal law issues was recently highlighted in a case where a majority *seemed* to be holding that nothing in a judge's instruction to the jury should have "the effect of substantially reducing the government's burden of proof."[159] Justice Rehnquist, speaking for three dissenters, let loose this blast: "The Court's reversal on the ground that one of the instructions contained a 'negative pregnant' smacks more of the scholastic jurisprudence . . . than it does of the common sense approach to appellate review. . . ."

*Page 356*            AMENDMENT VI

Justice Blackmun spoke for the majority of the Supreme Court when it was called upon to answer this question: Does the accused have the right to have counsel present when witnesses are shown a post-indictment photographic display containing his picture, for the purpose of having the witness attempt to identify the perpetrator of the crime for which the accused has been indicted? The answer was "No."[160] But the majority explained the difference it saw between this situation and post-indictment police lineups (see p. 356 of Text). Blackmun wrote "Since the accused himself is not present at the time of the photographic display . . . no possibility arises that the accused might be misled by his lack of familiarity with the law or overpowered by his professional adversary."

Prison censorship practices as they effect communications between inmates and lawyers or courts, the representativeness of jury panels, and the dispensing of summary military justice were three areas of Sixth Amendment concern to receive notable attention recently from lower Federal and

[156] Almota Farmers Elevator & Whse. Co. *v.* United States, 93 S. Ct. 791 (1973).
[157] United States *v.* Fuller, 93 S. Ct. 801 (1973).
[158] Strunk *v.* United States, 41 *LW* 4794 (1973).
[159] Cool *v.* United States, 41 *LW* 3310 (1973).
[160] United States *v.* Ash, 41 *LW* 4981 (1973). The various opinions in the case provide a rich discussion of the meaning of right to counsel.

State courts. Several rulings suggest that arbitrary censorship and suppression of prisoners' mail are at an end especially where such sweeping and overly broad practices infringe the right to counsel.[161] These new decisions indicate that regulation may be justified, but that it must be carefully and narrowly applied. Second, while ratification of the Twenty-Sixth Amendment does not overturn State laws requiring jurors to be at least 21 years old,[162] recent decisions do hold that states using voter registration lists for the purpose of choosing jury panels must not systematically preclude young voters from the possibility of selection,[163] though reasonable administrative delay in keeping selection lists up to date is constitutionally tolerable.[164] Finally, in a decision that effected the release of approximately 1500 convicted enlisted men from Navy and Marine Corps brigs around the world, a Federal judge has ruled that summary courts-martial deny defendants the constitutionally guaranteed right to representation by counsel.[165]

*Page 358*                        AMENDMENT VII

As the Supreme Court majority (5-4) explained, in 1970 it had upheld a State statute providing for six-member juries in certain criminal cases (see p. 343 of Text) but it had left open whether "additional references to the 'common law' that occur in the Seventh Amendment might support a different interpretation" in civil cases. The majority in 1973 concluded that they do not.[166]

*Page 366*                        AMENDMENT VIII

Courts have generally conceded the government substantial latitude in its handling of convicted offenders because, as one Federal court acknowledged, the Eighth Amendment does not "give constitutional dimension to the theories of penologists."[167] Nevertheless, lower Federal and State tribunals have been alert to check the more extraordinary and well-substantiated deprivations. These courts have recently used the amendment with increasing frequency to attack conditions in correctional facilities

---

[161] *See* e.g., Lamar *v.* Kern, 349 F. Supp. 222 (1972); *and* Simmons *v.* Russell, 352 F. Supp. 572 (1972). This increasing concern over prisoners' general right to communicate was evidenced recently by the ruling of a U.S. Court of Appeals reversing six of the seven convictions against Rev. Daniel Berrigan and his wife, the former Sister Elizabeth McAlister, for smuggling letters into and out of a Federal prison. *See, New York Times,* June 28, 1973.

[162] United States *v.* Olson, 473 F. 2d. 686 (1973).

[163] *See* United States *v.* Guzman, 468 F. 2d. 1245 (1972); United States *v.* Blair, 470 F. 2d. 331 (1972); State *v.* Willis, 293 N.E. 2d. 895 (1972); Brown *v.* State, 205 N.W. 2d. 566 (1973).

[164] *See* United States *v.* Blair, 470 F. 2d. 331 (1972); State *v.* Taylor, 508 P. 2d. 731 (1973); Brown *v.* State, 205 N.W. 2d. 566 (1973).

[165] Henry *v.* Warner, 41 *LW* 2598 (1973).

[166] Colegrove *v.* Battin, 41 *LW* 5025 (1973). Although Justice Marshall complained that "my Brethren have not given this curtailment of the jury right the careful scrutiny which the problem demands," the various opinions do an extensive canvass of the appropriate history and Rules of Civil Procedure.

[167] LaReau *v.* MacDougall, 473 F. 2d. 974, 977-978 (1972).

such as severe overcrowding,[168] excessive use of tranquilizing drugs,[169] the commission of brutal indignities by guards[170] and among inmates,[171] wanton use of corporal punishment,[172] intentional refusal to provide proper medical care,[173] and the debasing and unhygienic conditions of some solitary confinements.[174] The courts have also continued to uphold the use of corporal punishment in schools[175] and the rights of teachers to use reasonable force to eject disruptive students from the classroom.[176]

*Page 368*                     AMENDMENT IX

The Abortion Cases afforded the Supreme Court another opportunity to caress the Ninth Amendment without embracing it. Speaking for the majority, Justice Blackmun said "This right of privacy, whether it be founded in the Fourteenth Amendment's concept of personal liberty and restrictions upon state action, as we feel it is, or, as the District Court determined, in the Ninth . . . is broad enough to encompass a woman's decision whether or not to terminate her pregnancy."[177] But a more ardent admirer of the Ninth Amendment, Justice Douglas, in his concurring opinion, issued a catalogue of what he regards as Ninth Amendment rights.[178]

Despite the alleged libertarian bent of *Griswold* (see p. 368 of Text) and its progeny, the conception of the penumbras of privacy envisioned by Justice Douglas has yet to be realized, namely, the protection of personal tastes in lifestyle and individual autonomy in matters of sexual relations.[179] Just this term, the Supreme Court dismissed an appeal taken from the Minnesota Supreme Court which denied two individuals of the same sex the legal right to marry.[180] Earlier it vacated the judgment of a three-judge district court invalidating the Texas sodomy statute.[181]

168 Gates *v.* Collier, 349 F. Supp. 881 (1972).
169 Nelson *v.* Heyne, 355 F. Supp. 451 (1972).
170 Gates *v.* Collier, 349 F. Supp. 881 (1972); United States *ex rel.* Bracey *v.* Grenoble, 356 F. Supp. 673 (1973).
171 Gates *v.* Collier, 349 F. Supp. 881 (1972); Penn *v.* Oliver, 351 F. Supp. 1293 (1972).
172 Gates *v.* Collier, 349 F. Supp. 881 (1972); Nelson *v.* Heyne, 355 F. Supp. 451 (1972).
173 Newman *v.* Ala., 349 F. Supp. 278 (1972); United States *v.* Pardue, 354 F. Supp. 1377 (1972).
174 LaReau *v.* MacDougall, 473 F. 2d. 974 (1972).
175 Glaser *v.* Marietta, 351 F. Supp. 555 (1972).
176 Simms *v.* School Dist. No. 1, Multnomah Cty., 508 P. 2d. 236 (1973).
177 Roe *v.* Wade, 93 S. Ct. 705, 727 (1973).
178 *Ibid.*, 757-760.
179 *See especially* his concurring opinion in the 1973 Abortion Cases, 93 S. Ct. at 756 *et seq.* For his views about the necessity of an activist role for the courts in guaranteeing protections contained in the penumbras of constitutional provisions, *see* Younger *v.* Harris, 401 U.S. 37, 58 (1970) (dissenting opinion).
180 Baker *v.* Nelson, 191 N.W. 2d. 185 (1971); *appeal dismissed*, 93 S. Ct. 37 (1972).
181 Buchanan *v.* Batchelor, 308 F. Supp. 729 (1970); *judgment vacated*, 91 S. Ct. 1221, 1222 (1971).

Worth noting, however, is a decision rendered recently by a Federal district court to the effect that a school board's policy against hiring homosexuals as teachers infringes upon the individual's right of privacy. As that court said, "The time has now come for private, consenting, adult homosexuality to enter the sphere of constitutionally protected interests."[182]

*Page 375*                    AMENDMENT XI

In a case involving a suit against Missouri by State employees for overtime compensation under the Fair Labor Standards Act, the Supreme Court was unprepared to find that Congress had intended to take away the constitutional immunity of States.[183] The Court did make clear, however, that Congress could do so in the exercise of its power under the Commerce Clause. To understand the Court's reasoning in this case, one must recall that two propositions had been established by earlier decisions: (1) that, contrary to the language of the amendment, an unconsenting State is immune from suits in Federal courts brought by its own citizens as well as citizens of another State;[184] and (2) that when a State engages in enterprises normally subject to control by congressional enactment, it is consenting to that control.[185]

Among those suits against States which were spurned by the lower Federal judiciary this past year as violative of the Eleventh Amendment were two worth noting. In one instance, present and former patients in Georgia's mental hospitals sought to litigate claims for inadequate diagnosis, care, and treatment. A Federal district court dismissed the case on grounds that the plaintiffs failed to show "a denial of a *constitutionally* protected right or a *federally* guaranteed statutory right," which would distinguish this suit from those falling within the amendment's prohibition.[186] In the other instance, survivors of the students who were killed in the Kent State riots of a few years ago sought damages in an action filed against the governor, the adjutant general of the Ohio National Guard, and the president of the university, among others. A U.S. Circuit Court of Appeals affirmed dismissal of the suits because these State officials, acting in their official capacities, were also clothed with the State's immunity.[187] (This case should not be confused with Gilligan v. Morgan; see p. 564 of Supplement.)

---

[182] 41 *LW* 2691 (1973).

[183] Employees of Dept. of Public Health & Welf. *v.* Missouri, 93 S. Ct. 1614 (1973).

[184] Hans *v.* Louisiana, 134 U.S. 1 (1890).

[185] Parden *v.* Terminal R. of Ala., 377 U.S. 190, 196 (1964).

[186] Burnham *v.* Dept. of Public Health of State of Georgia, 349 F. Supp. 1335 (1972).

[187] Krause *v.* Rhodes, 471 F. 2d. 430 (1972). Also covered by the State's mantle of immunity under the amendment are subdivisions of the State, *see* Washington *v.* Brantley, 352 F. Supp. 559 (1972); Harris *v.* Tooele Cty. School Dist., 471 F. 2d. 218 (1973); and a state university construction fund, *see* Charles Simkin & Sons, Inc. *v.* State University Construction Fund, 352 F. Supp. 177 (1973).

*Page 384*                    AMENDMENT XIII

The Supreme Court found "no substance" to the argument that paying
people, held as material witnesses, $1 per day was imposing involuntary
servitude on them.[188] But two lower Federal court decisions, premised on
the Thirteenth Amendment, significantly strengthened governmental efforts to ward off the phenomenon of panic selling by white home-owners
which stems from the circulation of racial rumors by unscrupulous realtors
who subsequently turn handsome profits when neighborhood properties
are sold to incoming Blacks. The U.S. Court of Appeals, Fifth Circuit,
unanimously sustained the constitutionality of that provision of the Fair
Housing Act of 1968[189] which prohibited this practice of "blockbusting."[190]
In a second decision, a Federal district court upheld a Gary, Indiana,
ordinance which prohibited display of "For Sale" or "Sold" signs on property located in residential sections of the city.[191]

*Page 387*                    AMENDMENT XIV

Within the meaning of the Fourteenth Amendment, the District of
Columbia is not a "state," consequently "neither the District nor its officers
are subject to its restrictions," the Supreme Court reaffirmed in 1973.[192]

*Page 387*                    AMENDMENT XIV

After surveying at some length the question of whether or not "a fetus is
a person within the meaning of the Fourteenth Amendment," Justice
Blackmun speaking for the Supreme Court concluded "In short, the un-
born have never been recognized in the law as persons in the whole
sense."[193] For discussion of other points of the Abortion Cases, see p. 595
of Supplement.

*Page 388*                    AMENDMENT XIV

There were three important applications of substantive due process by
the Supreme Court this past term. The Court held that, "since Connecticut
purports to be concerned with residency in allocating the rates for tuition
and fees at its university system, it is forbidden by the Due Process Clause
to deny an individual the resident rates on the basis of a permanent and
irrebuttable presumption of nonresidence, when that presumption is not
necessarily or universally true in fact, and when the state has reasonable
alternative means of making the crucial determination."[194] Also, recall

188 Hurtado v. United States, 93 S. Ct. 1157 (1973).
189 42 U.S.C. 3604 (e).
190 United States v. Bob Lawrence Realty, Inc., 474 F. 2d. 115 (1973).
191 Barrick Realty, Inc. v. City of Gary, Ind., 354 F. Supp. 126 (1973).
192 District of Columbia v. Carter, 93 S. Ct. 602 (1973). *But see* p. 331 of Text.
193 Roe v. Wade, 93 S. Ct. 705 (1973). *See also* The California Welfare Rights
Organization v. Brian, 107 Cal. Rptr. 324 (1973).
194 Vlandis v. Kline, 41 *LW* 4796 (1973). In an interesting concurring opinion,
Justice Marshall wrote: "I recognize that in Starnes v. Malkerson, 401 U.S. 985
(1971), we summarily affirmed a district court decision sustaining a one-year

that one of the Abortion Cases decisions was bottomed at least in part on "the Fourteenth Amendment's concept of personal liberty" (see p. 592 of Supplement),[195] while another brought forth a holding that the "accredited hospital provision and the requirements as to approval by the hospital abortion committee, as to confirmation by two independent physicians, and as to residence in Georgia are all violative of the Fourteenth Amendment."[196]

In connection with the constitutionally protected liberty of a person to decide matters involving reproduction, a U.S. Court of Appeals has recently held that a city hospital could not bar use of its facilities for consensual sterilization.[197]

*Page 402*                    AMENDMENT XIV

Among the host of cases in which the Supreme Court held actions within State law enforcement systems violative of the requirements of procedural due process were the following: (1) sending a forfeiture notice to the home of a man who was in jail when State officials should have known he could not receive it;[198] (2) trying a person for a traffic offense before a judge who was also the mayor and thus had an interest in the collection of fines which provided a substantial portion of village funds;[199] (3) depriving a man at trial of his only witness when the judge admonished the witness, who was serving a jail term, that he had better tell the truth or he would probably have to serve more time thus frightening him into a refusal to testify;[200] (4) failing to inquire of jurors as to race bias after a petitioner's timely request and where petitioner was a "bearded Negro" (but failing to ask about beard bias was not constitutional error in view of the fact that the court had made inquiries about bias in general);[201] (5) denying an accused a fair trial by not letting him cross-examine his own witness nor introduce the witness's hearsay statements where that was the only way to establish the truth under the complicated facts in the case;[202] (6) revoking a probation on the grounds that failure to report a traffic citation was tantamount to failure to report an "arrest."[203]

*Page 405*                    AMENDMENT XIV

The Supreme Court continued to be flooded with contentions of the denial of equal protection. This Term the Supreme Court held that the

residency requirement for receipt of in-state tuition benefits. But I now have serious question as to the validity of that summary decision."

195 Roe v. Wade, 93 S. Ct. 705, 727 (1973).
196 Doe v. Bolton, 93 S. Ct. 739, 752 (1973).
197 Hathaway v. Worcester City Hospital, 475 F. 2d. 701 (1973).
198 Robinson v. Hanrahan, 93 S. Ct. 30 (1972).
199 Ward v. Village of Monroeville, Ohio, 93 S. Ct. 80 (1972).
200 Webb v. Texas, 93 S. Ct. 351 (1972).
201 Ham v. South Carolina, 93 S. Ct. 848 (1973).
202 Chambers v. State of Mississippi, 93 S. Ct. 1038 (1973).
203 Douglas v. Buder, 93 S. Ct. 2199 (1973).

following contravened the requirement of equal protection: (1) application of Texas laws which "grant legitimate children a judicially enforceable right to support from their natural fathers and at the same time deny that right to illegitimate children";[204] (2) application of the New Jersey "Assistance to Families of the Working Poor" program to limit benefits to "qualified families" so as to deny illegitimate children benefits granted to legitimate ones;[205] (3) a rule promulgated by the Superior Court of Connecticut that allows only citizens to take the State bar examinations;[206] (4) a New York Civil Service Law provision which allows only citizens to hold permanent positions in the competitive class of the State civil service.[207] But the Court did not find the following to be denials of equal protection: (1) An Oregon appellate filing fee as applied to indigents who seek to appeal an adverse welfare decision;[208] (2) an Illinois constitutional provision which authorizes *ad valorem* taxes on personal property of corporations but not of individuals.[209]

In a potpourri of cases bearing upon public employment and electoral rights, the recent trend of lower Federal and State court rulings could best be described as ambiguous. On the one hand, Seattle's practice of giving city residents a clear preference in hiring for certain city jobs was found to be unconstitutional,[210] but on the other hand, Pennsylvania's practice of giving veterans an automatic bonus on the State's civil service examinations was acceptable.[211] A Federal appellate court has found that a non-policy-making public employee cannot be removed for patronage reasons,[212] but a State court upheld dismissal of a 60-year-old State police officer under a mandatory retirement law.[213] Finally, in two cases involving the electoral process, the individual's interest has more clearly been vindicated. The Colorado Supreme Court struck down a five-year residency requirement imposed by one municipality as a prerequisite to run for public office,[214] and the California Supreme Court recently ruled that the State may not deny the franchise to ex-felons.[215]

A few cases pertaining to the rights of welfare recipients also reveal a split trend. In a case stemming from the refusal of rental agents to consider welfare recipients as applicants for vacant apartments, a U.S. Court of Appeals ruled that such discrimination is arbitrary and unjustified where

204 Gomez v. Perez, 93 S. Ct. 872 (1973).

205 New Jersey Welfare Rights Organization v. Cahill, 93 S. Ct. 1700 (1973).

206 *In re* Griffiths, 41 *LW* 5143 (1973).

207 Sugarman v. Dougall, 41 *LW* 5138 (1973).

208 Ortwein v. Schwab, 93 S. Ct. 1172 (1973).

209 Lehnhausen v. Lake Shore Auto Parts Co., 93 S. Ct. 1001 (1973).

210 Eggert v. City of Seattle, 505 P. 2d. 801 (1973).

211 *See* Koelfgen v. Jackson, 355 F. Supp. 243 (1972); Feinerman v. Jones, 356 F. Supp. 252 (1973); Williams v. State Civil Service Com'n, 300 A. 2d. 799 (1973).

212 Illinois State Employers Union, Council 34, Etc. v. Lewis, 473 F. 2d. 561 (1972).

213 McIlvanie v. Pennsylvania State Police, 296 A. 2d. 630 (1972).

214 Bird v. City of Colorado Springs, 507 P. 2d. 1099 (1973).

215 Ramirez v. Brown, 507 P. 2d. 1345 (1973).

those on welfare are generally furnished with supplementary housing allowances.[216] And, in what appear to be two rather contradictory decisions, a Federal appellate court upheld Maine's termination of AFDC payments to families with fathers who were unemployed while continuing payments to those families with fathers who were absent, deceased, or incapacitated;[217] but a district court has struck down Pennsylvania's attempt to cut off aid (in the instant case, a general assistance grant of $68 every two weeks) to full-time college students.[218]

The lower Federal courts have given clear approval to affirmative action aimed at ending racial discrimination by both labor and management.[219] The courts have not only upheld the imposition of quota hiring in the construction trades,[220] but they have, by their own actions, ordered unions and businesses to participate in minority recruitment, training, and placement programs,[221] to publicize fully the expectation of equal treatment,[222] and, in at least one instance, to follow a complete set of rigid guidelines closely regulating an entire circuit of training, certification, and hiring practices.[223] And, if a decision by the Washington Supreme Court, involving a qualified white student who was rejected by the law school using a quota admissions system,[224] is any reflection of a trend, we can say that the courts are not likely to be sympathetic to claims of reverse discrimination by those non-minority applicants who find themselves excluded.

*Page 412*                    AMENDMENT XIV

Several Supreme Court decisions were critical in the continuing struggle over school desegregation. First, the Supreme Court by a 4-4 decision[225] (Justice Powell did not participate) affirmed the judgment of the United States Court of Appeals, Fourth Circuit, with respect to the issue of whether or not (in a case of *de facto* segregation) a district judge could order the consolidation of separate school districts to effect desegregation.[226]

---

216 Male *v.* Crossroads Associates, 469 F. 2d. 616 (1972).

217 United Low Income, Inc. *v.* Fisher, 470 F. 2d. 1074 (1972).

218 Stewart *v.* Wohlgemuth, 355 F. Supp. 1212 (1972).

219 *See* Sims *v.* Sheet Metal Workers Int'l Ass'n, Local Union No. 65, 353 F. Supp. 22 (1972). *But see* report of a decision by New York State's highest court that a New York City program allowing Blacks and Hispanic persons to bypass civil service procedures for certain jobs was unconstitutional. *New York Times,* July 4, 1973.

220 Southern Illinois Builders Ass'n *v.* Ogilvie, 471 F. 2d. 680 (1972).

221 *See* United States *v.* Local Union No. 212, Etc., 472 F. 2d. 634 (1973); *and also see* NLRB *v.* Mansion House Center Management Corp., 473 F. 2d. 471 (1972).

222 *See* Sims *v.* Sheet Metal Workers Int'l Ass'n, Local Union No. 65, 353 F. Supp. 22 (1972).

223 *Ibid.*; *see also* United States *v.* Wood, Wire & Metal Lathers Int'l Union, Local No. 46, 471 F. 2d. 408 (1973).

224 DeFunis *v.* Odegaard, 507 P. 2d. 1169 (1973).

225 School Board of City of Richmond *v.* Bradley, 93 S. Ct. 1952 (1973).

226 Bradley *v.* School Board of City of Richmond, 462 F. 2d. 1058, 1069 (1973).

Then, in June 1973, the Court decided the Denver case which, as Justice Powell pointed out in his separate opinion, was "the first school desegregation case to reach this Court which involves a major city outside the South."[227] The Supreme Court, speaking through Justice Brennan, held "that a finding of intentionally segregative school board actions in a meaningful portion of a school system, as in this case, creates a presumption that other segregated schooling within the system is not adventitious. It establishes, in other words, a *prima facie* case of unlawful segregative design on the part of school authorities, and shifts to those authorities the burden of proving that other segregated schools within the system are not also the result of intentionally segregative actions. . . . We emphasize that the differentiating factor between *de jure* segregation and so-called *de facto* segregation to which we referred in Swann is *purpose* or *intent* to segregate."[228] The case was remanded to the district court to afford the school board an opportunity to prove it was not deliberately segregating students. But, the Court said, if it is determined, that the Denver school system is a dual school system then the "School Board has the affirmative duty to desegregate the entire system 'root and branch.' "

It is important to note that, in this case, the Court also held that the district court had been wrong in "separating Negroes and Hispanos for purposes of defining a 'segregated' school," suggesting that a school with "a combined predominance of Negroes and Hispanos" might very well be considered a segregated school.

The Supreme Court also decided that Mississippi could not provide free textbooks to students in private as well as public schools when the private schools practice racial discrimination. To do so, the Court reasoned, was to support discrimination. Since on its face, such a decision does not seem to square with parallel decisions with respect to parochial schools, Chief Justice Burger, speaking for the Court, felt compelled to distinguish between the two situations: "But the transcendent value of free religious exercise in our constitutional scheme leaves room for 'play in the joints' to the extent of cautiously delineated secular governmental assistance to religious schools, despite the conflicting values of the Establishment Clause."[229]

The Supreme Court *did* decide in 1973 the eagerly awaited "property tax" case mentioned in the Text, reversing by a 5-4 vote the district court in the Texas case. In a long and elaborate opinion, the Court, speaking through Justice Powell, concluded that "The constitutional standard under the Equal Protection Clause is whether the challenged state action rationally furthers a legitimate state purpose or interest. . . . We hold that the Texas plan abundantly satisfies this standard."[230]

227 Keyes *v.* School District No. 1, Denver, Colo., 41 *LW* 5002, 5009 (1973).
228 *Ibid.*, 5007.
229 Norwood *v.* Harrison, 41 *LW* 5094, 5098 (1973). The religion cases referred to are *Nyquist* and *Levitt* (see p. 576 of Supplement).
230 San Antonio Independent School District *v.* Rodriguez, 93 S. Ct. 1278, 1308 (1973). The Court specifically rejected (it said after careful consideration) the

*Page 414* AMENDMENT XIV

Although it was not decided on Fourteenth Amendment grounds, the case in which the Court upheld a city commission's order forbidding newspapers to carry sex-designated want ads against a First Amendment claim is worthy of mention in this context.[231]

Federal and State tribunals have also demonstrated increasing sensitivity to restrictions imposed unequally as between men and women. While the courts have continued to sanction the health and safety justifications offered by public schools in enforcing maternity leaves for women teachers[232] and by colleges in imposing different curfew regulations on female students,[233] on other issues their decisions have leaned in the opposite direction: The courts have held that (1) girls may not be barred from competing with boys in high school non-contact sports;[234] (2) a State legislative body may not discriminate against employing girls as pages;[235] and (3) facilities open to the public, such as restaurants, may not reserve admittance during certain times of the day to "men only."[236]

*Page 424* AMENDMENT XIV

The statement of three dissenting Supreme Court Justices speaking through Justice Brennan indicates that at least one of the recent reapportionment cases "reflects a substantial and very unfortunate retreat from the principles established in our earlier cases."[237] In four cases the Supreme Court held *among other things* (1) that "neither we nor the district courts have a constitutional warrant to invalidate a state plan, otherwise within tolerable limits, because it undertakes, not to minimize or eliminate the political strength of any group or party, but to recognize it and, through districting, provide a rough sort of proportional representation in the legislative halls of the State";[238] (2) that State reapportionment statutes were not subject to the stricter standards of congressional reapportionment under Article I, Section II;[239] (3) that setting district boundaries

---

district court's finding that education is a fundamental right or liberty acquiring strict judicial scrutiny of State action which infringes on it. *Ibid.*, 1299.

[231] Pittsburgh Press Co. *v.* Pittsburgh Com'n on Human Relations, 41 *LW* 5055 (1973).

[232] Cohen *v.* Chesterfield Cty. School Bd., 474 F. 2d. 395 (1973); Green *v.* Waterford Bd. of Educ., 349 F. Supp. 687 (1972).

[233] Robinson *v.* Bd. of Regents of East. Kentucky Univ., 475 F. 2d. 707 (1973).

[234] *See* Morris *v.* Michigan State Bd. of Educ., 472 F. 2d. 1207 (1973); *and* Haas *v.* South Bend Community School Corp., 289 N.E. 2d. 495 (1972); *but cf.* Bucha *v.* Illinois High School Ass'n, 351 F. Supp. 69 (1972).

[235] Eslinger *v.* Thomas, 476 F. 2d. 225 (1973).

[236] Bennett *v.* Dyer's Chop House, Inc., 350 F. Supp. 153 (1972).

[237] Gaffney *v.* Cummings, 41 *LW* 4891, 4897 (1973).

[238] *Ibid.*, 4897.

[239] White *v.* Register, 41 *LW* 4885 (1973) *and* Mahan *v.* Howell, 93 S. Ct. 979 (1973).

to protect present incumbents is not per se invidious;[240] (4) that "respecting the boundaries of political subdivisions" is constitutional provided the population disparities are within "tolerable" limits (in this case a 16.4 per cent variation from the ideal was considered to be approaching but not exceeding tolerable limits).[241] Interestingly enough, Justice Rehnquist, speaking for the majority, contended that there was no retreat; they were only reaffirming the holding of Reynolds v. Sims (see p. 419 of Text). Perhaps one measure of whether or not there has been a retreat is that in several of the cases the Supreme Court was reversing lower Federal courts which thought they were following previous Supreme Court decisions.

The Supreme Court held that the California voter qualification laws for water storage district elections, limiting voting to landholders in proportion to the value of their lands, were rationally based and therefore not in violation of the Equal Protection Clause.[242] Similarly, the Court upheld a Wyoming statute limiting voting in a watershed improvement district to landowners in proportion to the acreage they held.[243]

*Page 434*          AMENDMENT XV, SECTION II

In a significant case dealing with the Voting Rights Act of 1965 (see p. 433, Text), the Supreme Court held that the district court did not abuse its discretion by denying as untimely the NAACP's motion to intervene under the 1965 Act in a case involving a New York law which required among other things the ability to read and write English and a literacy test for voting. That more than procedural technicalities were at stake was suggested by the bitter dissent of Justice Douglas: "Here it is plainly evident that the United States is an eager and willing partner with its allies in New York to foreclose inquiry into the barriers to minority voting. What the facts may produce, no one knows. All that is requested is a hearing on the merits."[244]

*Page 449*          AMENDMENT XXI

In addition to the *LaRue* case (see p. 449, Text), the Supreme Court decided three other Twenty-First Amendment cases. One, it held that *incident to a valid scheme of regulating the sale of liquor,* a State could require that a liquor manufacturer, as a condition of doing business in the State, do more than merely solicit sales"[245] (see p. 561 of Supplement). Two, it held that a district court had erred "in ruling that the Twenty-first Amendment empowered the State Tax Commission . . . [to take a]

[240] White v. Weiser, 41 *LW* 4900 (1973).
[241] Mahan v. Howell, 93 S. Ct. 979 (1973).
[242] Salyer Land Company v. Tulare Lake Basin Water Storage District, 93 S. Ct. 1224 (1973).
[243] Associated Enterprises, Inc. v. Toltec Watershed Improvement District, 93 S. Ct. 1237 (1973).
[244] NAACP v. State of New York, 41 *LW* 5037, 5046 (1973).
[245] Heublein v. South Carolina Tax Com'n, 93 S. Ct. 483 (1972).

markup . . . [on] transactions between out-of-state distillers and nonappropriated fund activities [military officers' clubs] located on the two exclusively federal enclaves."[246] Three, the Court let stand a Maine law barring State liquor and food licenses to "whites only" private clubs.[247]

A Federal district court has recently held that Oklahoma may not impose discriminatory prosecution on AMTRAK employees for dispensing liquor on interstate trains since such burdensome regulation bears no reasonable or substantial relation to the welfare of the State's citizenry.[248]

*Page 458*          AMENDMENT XXVI

A Federal district court has recently ruled that voting age students cannot be made to meet a more stringent residency test than other persons in an attempt to freeze them out of participation in local elections.[249] With regard to young voters and discrimination in jury selection, see p. 591 of Supplement.

*Page 461*          PROPOSED CONSTITUTIONAL AMENDMENT

The campaign to ratify the proposed Equal Rights Amendment has "bogged down in the trenches of Southern and rural state legislatures with only nine more states to go to attain the necessary 38 ratifications."[250]

*Page 463*          EPILOGUE

The current Watergate Affair disclosures suggest further reasons for wondering if a restructuring of our governmental system is not in order. One question is certainly worth pondering: should the system contain an efficacious way to remove a President if and when he loses the confidence of the people by way of something like a vote of confidence in the Congress?

[246] United States *v.* State Tax Com'n of Mississippi, 41 *LW* 4774, 4780 (1973).
[247] B.P.O.E. Lodge No. 2043 *v.* Ingraham, 41 *LW* 3549.
[248] National Railroad Passenger Corp. *v.* Harris, 354 F. Supp. 887 (1972).
[249] Sloane *v.* Smith, 351 F. Supp. 1299 (1972).
[250] Nick Thimmesch, "The Sexual Equality Amendment," *N.Y. Times Magazine,* June 24, 1973, p. 8. Some formidable arguments pro and con are contained in the article and other articles mentioned therein.